[redacted]

SMALL-BUSINESS MANAGEMENT

SIXTH EDITION

H. N. Broom, Ph.D.
Emeritus Professor/Chairman
Management/Statistics
Baylor University

Justin G. Longenecker, Ph.D.
Chavanne Professor of Christian Ethics in Business
Baylor University

Carlos W. Moore, Ph.D.
Associate Professor of Marketing
Baylor University

Published by

G25 **SOUTH-WESTERN PUBLISHING CO.**

CINCINNATI WEST CHICAGO, ILL. DALLAS PELHAM MANOR, N.Y. PALO ALTO, CALIF.

ISBN: 0-538-07250-4

Library of Congress Catalog Card Number: 81-51803

1 2 3 4 5 6 **K** 7 6 5 4 3 2

Printed in the United States of America

CONTENTS

PART D MANAGING SMALL-BUSINESS OPERATIONS

PREFACE

This Sixth Edition of *Small-Business Management* presents a thoroughly rewritten and reorganized treatment of the creation and management of small firms. We have increased the emphasis on entrepreneurial opportunities and new-venture processes and continued the thorough coverage of managerial activities needed for the successful operation of small firms.

A number of new features which contribute to the attractiveness and usefulness of this Sixth Edition include:

1. "Looking Ahead" and "Looking Back" sections for each chapter to give the student a preview and a review of basic chapter topics.
2. "Action Reports" that dramatize the text material with the experiences of real-world entrepreneurship, thus demonstrating the practical significance of specific chapter topics.
3. Annotated "References to Small Business in Action" at the end of each chapter that identify published articles about practical applications of chapter topics.
4. An outline (in Chapter 3) that can be used by students in preparing *new-venture plans.*
5. A *diagnostic checklist* (in Chapter 12) that can be used by students in evaluating small-business firms.
6. Numerous photographs, graphs, tables, and illustrations that communicate key materials more clearly to meet students' needs.
7. A franchise investigation checklist in Appendix A, an actual franchise contract in Appendix B, and a list of free small-business publications in Appendix C—all of which are *new*.

Four *new* chapters have been written for this edition. *Chapter 1* (Entrepreneurs: The Energizers of Small Business) highlights the unlimited opportunities in entrepreneurship and the growing emphasis on new ventures. *Chapter 5* (Analyzing the Market) explains market segmentation and the marketing analyses needed to launch a new business. *Chapter 9* (Consumer Behavior and Product Strategies) examines the impact of consumer behavior on the marketing strategies of the small business. *Chapter 20* (Computerizing the Small Business) probes the rapidly increasing use of computers in the modern world of small business.

The cases found at the end of each Part of the text present *real* problems faced by *real* firms in the *real* world of small business, thus constituting a laboratory for practical learning. Of the 25 end-of-Part cases, 19 are *new*. The comprehensive case at the end of the text, Cornerstone Lumber Company, is also *new*.

The Sixth Edition is supplemented by an extensively revised *Student Learning Guide*, an enhanced *Instructor's Manual*, and achievement tests. Each chapter in the *Student Learning Guide* presents specific learning opportunities, key points and brief definitions to remember in understanding the chapter, comprehensive "programmed" self-reviews, and creative exercises for the application of learning. It also contains a continuous learning incident, based on a small family-owned dairy business, which gives the student an opportunity to act as a special management consultant on various phases of the operations of this business. In addition, a series of "Pretests," based on each Part of the text, simulates an actual testing situation and helps students evaluate themselves prior to course examinations. The *Instructor's Manual* contains suggested options for creative teaching by way of experiential exercises, chapter outlines, answers to end-of-chapter discussion questions, and discussions of text cases.

In preparing the Sixth Edition, the authors have been aided by colleagues, students, business owners, and others in providing case materials and in other ways. In addition to those identified elsewhere, we especially acknowledge the contributions of Helen Ligon, William K. Ghee, Terry S. Maness, John and Loretta Ambrose, and Zella H. Stone. We are grateful for the special contribution of Kris K. Moore in the writing of Chapter 20. We also appreciate the generous support of Mr. and Mrs. Harry J. Chavanne and our dean, Richard C. Scott. We thank Suzanne Granger and Sandy Tighe for their secretarial assistance. Finally, we gratefully acknowledge the understanding and cooperation of our wives, Norma, Frances, and Gwen, to the completion of this book.

January, 1983
Waco, Texas

H. N. Broom
Justin G. Longenecker
Carlos W. Moore

Part A

BENEFITS OF SMALL BUSINESS

Chapter 1

Entrepreneurs: The Energizers of Small Business

LOOKING AHEAD

Watch for the following important topics:

1. Examples of highly successful entrepreneurs.
2. Rewards of entrepreneurship.
3. Personal characteristics of entrepreneurs.
4. Personal readiness for the various types of entrepreneurial roles and ventures.
5. Families and entrepreneurial teams as special types of entrepreneurs.

Each year millions of Americans, from teenagers to retirees, respond to the call of **entrepreneurship**, or the opportunity to pursue independent business careers. These enterprising persons, who choose to own and manage their own firms, are called **entrepreneurs**—the people who provide the spark and the dynamic leadership for our economic system by taking risks and being innovative. Although some writers restrict the term "entrepreneur" to founders of business firms, in this text we use a broadened definition that includes all active owner-managers. Obviously this definition includes second-generation members of family-owned firms and owner-managers who buy out the founders of existing firms. Our definition, however, excludes salaried managers of large corporations, even those who are described as "entrepreneurial" because of their flair for innovation and their willingness to assume risk.[1]

Have you ever wondered what sorts of opportunities knock on the doors of would-be entrepreneurs? How attractive can the rewards of entrepreneurship be? Are there any special characteristics or personalities that entrepreneurs must possess in order to succeed? Is there a "right" time to plunge into entrepreneurship or must some special events take place to trigger this plunge? In what types of roles, ventures, or styles can entrepreneurs be involved? This chapter will discuss all these questions and include a brief introduction to family businesses and entrepreneurial teams as distinct types of entrepreneurship.

UNLIMITED OPPORTUNITIES

The reality of entrepreneurial opportunities can be communicated most vividly by giving examples of a few entrepreneurs who have succeeded. Reading these brief accounts of successful ventures should give you, the reader, a "feel" for the potential that you can achieve if you dream of having your own business. Even though the examples described below are few, they can help you to visualize the broad spectrum of opportunities that may arise at any point in time. Of course, there are thousands of variations and alternatives for independent business careers. In fact, you may achieve great success in business endeavors that are far different from those described here.

T-Shirts Plus (Waco, TX)

In the early 1970s, Ken Johnson, Sr., detected the growing popularity of T-shirts that displayed various decorations and slogans.[2] Without wasting much time, in 1975 he opened a small T-shirt specialty shop in Waco, TX. He started with the idea of making his store, T-Shirts Plus, a family-oriented store that contrasted with what he called "flaky" shops which were operating at that time. By "flaky" he meant stores which practiced poor merchandising and marketing or which provided pornographic transfers and operated in conjunction with "head shops."

T-Shirts Plus was successful, and within a short period of time Johnson quickly established franchised outlets in other areas. Sales grew from $8.5

---

1. For an extended discussion of the nature of entrepreneurship, see Justin G. Longenecker and John E. Schoen, "The Essence of Entrepreneurship," *Journal of Small Business Management*, Vol. 13, No. 3 (July, 1975), pp. 26-32.

2. This account of T-Shirts Plus is written with the permission of Kenneth E. Johnson, Sr., of Waco, TX.

Figure 1-1 Kenneth E. Johnson, Sr., and T-Shirts Plus

million in 1978 to $14.5 million in 1979 and topped $45 million in 1981. By 1981, T-Shirts Plus had 275 stores in 46 states, Canada, and Europe. (Each of these stores also represented opportunities for franchisees to enter business for themselves.) Johnson's firm grew to the point that its Waco offices employed 220 persons, including 14 full-time artists!

The story of T-Shirts Plus—starting as a small business and rapidly expanding—demonstrates the fantastic success possible for well-conceived entrepreneurial ventures. By creating a T-shirt specialty shop and using the franchise method of expansion, Ken Johnson was able to ride the crest of this fashion trend and become an international marketer of T-shirts.

Shelton's Marketbasket (Washington, DC)

In December, 1976, George L. Shelton opened Shelton's Marketbasket, an inner-city supermarket, just a few blocks from the Capitol in Washington, DC.[3]

---

3. This account of Shelton's Marketbasket is written with the permission of George L. Shelton of Washington, DC.

The Great Atlantic and Pacific Tea Company (A&P) had operated this store earlier but closed it as a "loser." Shelton, who had worked almost 12 years for a major supermarket chain, started operations with the help of a $160,000 bank loan guaranteed by the Small Business Administration. Although sales in the first week totaled only $8,000, average weekly sales rose to $55,000 per week by 1978. And net profit, in addition to Shelton's salary of $38,000, was $50,000 in 1977.

Shelton's Marketbasket carried Spanish, Italian, Jewish, and Chinese foods to attract various segments of the local cosmopolitan community. Shelton also created a safe and friendly atmosphere within the store. For example, when asked about the location of some item, Shelton's employees were expected to lead customers to the products they were seeking. As another gesture of friendliness, Shelton sent Christmas cards to customers thanking them for their patronage. In addition, he ran a bus to and from a local senior citizens' housing area.

Shelton's success provides a dramatic example of an independent entrepreneur's ability to succeed where big business fails. He took a marginal situation and turned it into a thriving business that produced personal rewards and also helped strengthen the local community.

Courtesy, NATION'S BUSINESS magazine

Figure 1-2 George L. Shelton and Shelton's Marketbasket

Hudson Oil Company (Kansas City, KS)

With annual sales in excess of $230 million, the Hudson Oil Company is no longer a *small* business! It was started as a *very small* business, however. Its founder, Mary Hudson, still serves as president and active manager of the company.[4]

Figure 1-3 Mary Hudson, Founder of Hudson Oil

After an accident claimed the life of her husband in 1933, Miss Hudson, a 21-year-old widow and mother of an infant daughter, borrowed $200 from her father to buy a closed-down service station in Kansas City. Within

4. This account of the Hudson Oil Company is written with the permission of Mary Hudson of Kansas City, KS.

six years, she owned forty Hudson Oil stations in Kansas, Missouri, and Nebraska. Over the years, the company prospered as it emphasized price competition and undersold the major oil companies by one to two cents per gallon. It is now one of the largest independent gasoline-marketing companies in the United States, with its own refinery and 270 service stations in 35 states. Even though the company has grown, Miss Hudson is still an active entrepreneur.

As one writer noted:

> Miss Hudson remains firmly in control. Any capital expenditure at the stations involving more than $1,000 must get her approval. When she is on vacation, her daughter takes over. "Mother tries to delegate, but then she's right there on top again," says Joyce. An outside admirer adds: "Miss Hudson is independent, entrepreneurial, and aggressive. Her biggest problem is ego. She knows she's good and she likes to be told she's good."[5]

By starting a business on borrowed funds during the depths of the Great Depression, Miss Hudson demonstrated what an aggressive female entrepreneur could do in a "man's world." Furthermore, the combination of her humble beginnings and stunning success provides another dramatic example of the unlimited opportunities in this country's free enterprise system.

REWARDS OF ENTREPRENEURSHIP

Individuals are *pulled* toward entrepreneurship by various powerful incentives, or rewards. These rewards may be grouped, for the sake of simplicity, into three basic categories: profit, independence, and a satisfying life-style.

Profit

The financial return of any business must compensate its owner for investing his or her personal time (a salary equivalent) and personal savings (an interest and/or dividend equivalent) in the business before any "true" profits are realized. All entrepreneurs expect a return that will not only compensate them for the time and money they invest, but also reward them *well* for the risks and initiative they take in operating their own businesses. Not surprisingly, however, the profit incentive is a more powerful motivator for some entrepreneurs than for others. For example, people like Billy J. (Red) McCombs of San Antonio, TX have a rather simple objective of making as much money as they can. Even as a boy, Red McCombs possessed an obvious entrepreneurial instinct, as noted by one writer's account:

---

5. Susie Gharib Nazem, "A Penny-Pinching Strategy Pays Off at the Gas Pumps," *Fortune*, Vol. 97, No.11 (June 5, 1978), p. 141.

> This single-mindedness baffled and sometimes distressed his gentle, middle-class parents. "When I was 11, I'd wash dishes in a cafe downtown from 4 p.m. until midnight and deliver newspapers at 5 a.m.," he recalls. "My mother would get tears in her eyes. 'You don't need to do this,' she'd say, and of course she was right. My father was an auto mechanic and we never wanted for anything. But I wanted to make money."[6]

Red McCombs's desire to make money led him into many entrepreneurial ventures. He has ownership interests in a chain of 100 Mr. M convenience stores, 7 radio stations, oil exploration in 2 states, a contract drilling company, real estate, a Rolls-Royce dealership, and San Antonio's NBA (National Basketball Association) franchise—the Spurs.

This drive for profit continues to motivate entrepreneurs even after they achieve their original profit goals. For example, when Petros Kogiones came to the United States from Greece in 1961, he opened a restaurant in Chicago, hoping to make $40,000 in 2 or 3 years and then to go back to Greece. But after achieving his goal, he found that he wanted more. "I wanted to live in a better neighborhood, then I wanted a bigger car, and more." (Kogiones lives in the swank Lake Point Tower, drives a Stutz-Bearcat replica for pleasure, and is chauffered around the city for business appointments in a white Lincoln limousine!)[7]

The preceding examples portray entrepreneurs who possess an extremely strong interest in financial rewards. However, there are also those for whom profits are primarily a way of "keeping score." Such entrepreneurs may spend their profit on themselves or give it away, although most of them are not satisfied unless they make a "reasonable" profit. Indeed, some profit is necessary for survival because a firm which continues to lose money eventually becomes insolvent.

Independence

Freedom to operate independently is another basic reward of entrepreneurship. We know that the United States has long been known as a nation of rugged individualists. Many of us have a strong, even fierce, desire to make our own decisions, take risks, and reap the rewards for ourselves. Being one's own boss seems an attractive ideal. And those who are in business for themselves have, to a considerable extent, realized this ideal.

One example of an individual who was drawn to entrepreneurship more by the reward of independence than any other incentive is Richard Blasco. He left corporate employment in 1980 at the age of 33 to become an independent consultant in the electronics industry.[8] Blasco held a master's degree in elec-

---

6. "Red McCombs: Making Money's Fun," *Forbes*, Vol. 126 (September 15, 1980), p. 124.

7. "Breathing New Life into Small Business," *Forbes*, Vol. 124 (September 17, 1979), p. 197.

8. "Free-Lance Engineers," *Venture*, Vol. 2, No. 12 (December, 1980), p. 46.

trical engineering from Columbia University and had worked in corporate laboratories for a number of years. Although he expected to earn less money—at least initially—than he would earn as a salaried employee, he valued the independence of entrepreneurship when he stated:

> Being independent is what I have always wanted, and I am prepared to tighten my belt for a while in order to make it. If I'm still in business a year from now, I'll consider myself a success. And after that, I intend to see things get better and better.[9]

Of course, independence does not guarantee an easy life. Most entrepreneurs work very hard for long hours. But they do have the satisfaction of making their own decisions within the constraints imposed by economic and other environmental factors.

A Satisfying Way of Life

Entrepreneurs frequently speak of the personal satisfaction they experience in their own businesses. Some even refer to business as "fun." Part of this enjoyment may derive from the independence described above, but some of it also apparently comes from the peculiar nature of the business, the entrepreneur's role in the business, and the entrepreneur's opportunities to be of service.

In some types of small business, for example, owner-managers find that they can devote more attention to home and family obligations. Occasionally couples are able to share business responsibilities and to enjoy spending time together at work as well as at home. Although such arrangements may also involve family conflict, many successful family endeavors—such as the joint operation of a country inn and the family management of a women's clothing store—have been reported.[10]

Some people, such as hobbyists, go into a business which involves a product or service that has a special interest for them. One example is Harry J. Shay, the founder, president, and sole proprietor of a small firm described as the "sixth largest U. S. auto manufacturer." An old-car buff himself, Shay operates the Model A and Model T Motor Car Reproduction Corporation. At the end of the corporation's first model year, it had produced 10,000 new model A's. Noting his own interest in such cars, Shay observed, "It's kind of like an alcoholic wanting to own a bar."[11]

---

9. *Ibid*.

10. Michelle Bekey, "Living Together, Working Together," *Venture*, Vol. 3, No. 1 (January, 1981), pp. 34-39.

11. "Sixth Is Sweeter," *Forbes*, Vol. 126 (October 13, 1980), p. 224.

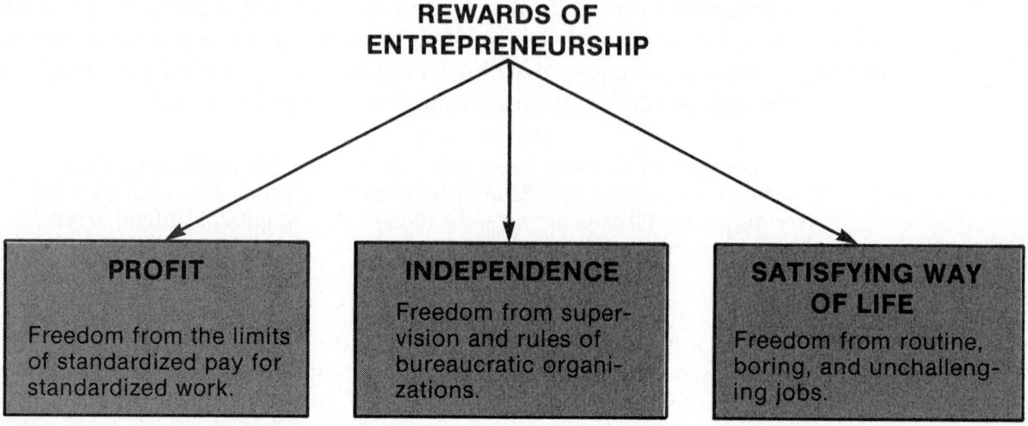
REWARDS OF ENTREPRENEURSHIP
PROFIT
Freedom from the limits of standardized pay for standardized work.
INDEPENDENCE
Freedom from supervision and rules of bureaucratic organizations.
SATISFYING WAY OF LIFE
Freedom from routine, boring, and unchallenging jobs.

Figure 1-4 Entrepreneurial Incentives

CHARACTERISTICS OF ENTREPRENEURS

Entrepreneurs seem to have some qualities that distinguish them from the general population and even from professional managers. Researchers have emphasized such qualities as their need for achievement, willingness to take risks, self-confidence, and need to seek refuge from any of various environmental factors. However, since research on this topic is far from definitive, any statements that identify entrepreneurial characteristics should be taken somewhat tentatively. Furthermore, since there are exceptions to every rule, many "unlikely" prospects may turn out to be highly successful entrepreneurs.

High Need for Achievement

Psychologists recognize that people differ in their need for achievement. Individuals with a low need for achievement are those who seem to be contented with their present status. On the other hand, individuals with a high need for achievement like to compete with some standard of excellence and prefer to be personally responsible for their own assigned tasks.

A leader in the study of achievement motivation is David C. McClelland, a Harvard psychologist.[12] He discovered a positive correlation between the need for achievement and entrepreneurial activity. In other words, those who

12. David C. McClelland, *The Achieving Society* (New York: The Free Press, 1961); David C. McClelland and David G. Winter, *Motivating Economic Achievement* (New York: The Free Press, 1969).

become entrepreneurs have, on the average, a higher need for achievement than do members of the general population. McClelland also experimented in raising the achievement motivation of entrepreneurs in India. It appeared that his experiment was successful in raising the level of entrepreneurial activity in that country.[13]

This drive for achievement is reflected in the ambitious individuals who start new firms and then guide them in their growth. In some families such entrepreneurial drive is evident at a very early stage. For example, sometimes a child takes a paper route, subcontracts it to a younger brother or sister, and then tries another venture. Also, some college students take over or start various types of student-related businesses or businesses that can be operated while pursuing an academic program.

Willingness to Take Risks

The risks that entrepreneurs take in starting and/or operating their own businesses are varied. Patrick R. Liles, a former Harvard professor, has identified four critical risk areas. These are:

1. *Financial risk*. Entrepreneurs invest their savings and guarantee their bank loans.
2. *Career risk*. Entrepreneurs who fail may find it difficult to find employment afterward.
3. *Family risk.* The entrepreneur's spouse and children may suffer from inattention and the emotional stress of coping with a business failure.
4. *Psychic risk*. The entrepreneur may be identified so closely with a venture that he or she takes business failure as a personal failure.[14]

David C. McClelland discovered in his studies that individuals with a high need for achievement also have moderate risk-taking propensities.[15] This means that they prefer risky situations in which they can exert some control on the outcome in contrast to gambling situations in which the outcome depends on pure luck. This preference for moderate risk reflects self-confidence, the next entrepreneurial characteristic that will be discussed.

---

13. David C. McClelland, "Achievement Motivation Can Be Developed," *Harvard Business Review*, Vol. 43, No. 6 (November-December, 1965), pp. 6-24ff.

14. Patrick R. Liles, "Who Are the Entrepreneurs?" *MSU Business Topics*, Vol. 22 (Winter, 1974), pp. 13-14.

15. McClelland, *The Achieving Society*, *op. cit.*, Chapter 6. See also Robert H. Brockhaus, Sr., "Risk Taking Propensity of Entrepreneurs," *Academy of Management Journal*, Vol. 23 (September, 1980), pp. 509-520. He questions the extent to which entrepreneurial risk-taking propensities differ from those of managers and the general population.

Self-Confidence

Individuals who possess self-confidence feel that they can meet the challenges which confront them. They have a sense of mastery over the types of problems that they might encounter. Studies show that successful entrepreneurs tend to be self-reliant individuals who see the problems in launching a new venture but believe in their own ability to overcome these problems.

Some studies of entrepreneurs have measured the extent to which they are confident of their own abilities. According to J. B. Rotter, a psychologist, those who believe that their success depends upon their own efforts have an **internal locus of control**. In contrast, those who feel that their lives are controlled to a greater extent by luck or chance or fate have an **external locus of control**.[16] On the basis of research to date, it appears that entrepreneurs have a higher internal locus of control than is true of the population in general.

A Need to Seek Refuge

Although most people go into business to obtain the rewards of entrepreneurship discussed earlier, there are some who become entrepreneurs to escape from some environmental factor. Professor Russell M. Knight of the University of Western Ontario has identified a number of environmental factors that "push" people to found new firms and has labeled such entrepreneurs as "refugees."[17]

In thinking about these kinds of "refugees," we should recognize that many entrepreneurs are motivated as much or more by entrepreneurial rewards than by an "escapist" mind set. Indeed, there is often a mixture of positive and negative considerations in this regard. Nevertheless, this typology of "refugees" is suggestive, if not exhaustive, in clarifying some important considerations involved in much entrepreneurial activity.

The "Foreign Refugee." There are many individuals who escape the political, religious, or economic constraints of their homelands by crossing national boundaries. Frequently such individuals face discrimination or handicaps in seeking salaried employment in the new country. As a result, many of them go into business for themselves. For example, two sisters who were refugees from Castro's Cuba, Angela Pedraza and Elena Gomez, opened a discount

---

16. See J. B. Rotter, "Generalized Expectancies for Internal Versus External Control of Reinforcement," *Psychological Monographs*, 1966a. A recent review is given in Robert H. Brockhaus, Sr., "The Psychology of the Entrepreneur," in Calvin A. Kent, Donald L. Sexton, and Karl H. Vesper (eds.), *Encyclopedia of Entrepreneurship* (Englewood Cliffs, NJ: Prentice-Hall, Inc., 1982), pp. 39-57.

17. Russell M. Knight, "Entrepreneurship in Canada," a paper presented at the Annual Conference of the International Council for Small Business, Asilomar, CA, June 22-25, 1980.

store in Miami, FL in 1977. It was one of more than 12,000 Cuban-owned businesses in that city.[18]

The "Corporate Refugee." Individuals who flee the bureaucratic environment of big business (or even medium-size business) by going into business for themselves are identified by Professor Knight as **corporate refugees**. Some corporations spawn so many entrepreneurial offspring that they are described as "incubator organizations." For example, take the Silicon Valley, a section south of San Francisco, CA, which is populated by small electronic firms that have been "spun off" from large companies or otherwise started by corporate refugees.

Other "Refugees." Other types of "refugees" mentioned by Professor Knight are the following:

1. The *parental (paternal) refugee* who leaves a family business to show the parent that "I can do it alone."
2. The *feminist refugee* who experiences discrimination and elects to start a firm in which she can operate independently of male chauvinists.
3. The *housewife refugee* who starts her own business after her family is grown or at some other point when she can free herself from household responsibilities.
4. The *society refugee* who senses some alienation from the prevailing culture and expresses it by indulging in entrepreneurial activity—selling paintings to tourists, operating an energy-saving business, or starting some other type of firm.
5. The *educational refugee* who tires of an academic program and decides to enter the "real world" by going into business.

READINESS FOR ENTREPRENEURSHIP

Many people think about getting into business for themselves but are waiting for the right opportunity to come along. Others become so well-established in careers that they tend to get "locked into" salaried employment. They acquire interests in retirement programs and achieve promotion to positions of greater responsibility and higher salaries. And some look back over their careers as salaried personnel, thinking of "what might have been" if only they had gone into business for themselves, but recognize that it is now too late.

---

18. "Breathing New Life into Small Business," *op. cit.*, p. 200.

The Free-Choice Period

There is no question that education and experience are a part of the necessary preparation for most entrepreneurs. Although requirements vary with the nature and demands of a particular business, some type of "knowhow" is required. In addition, prospective entrepreneurs must build their financial resources in order to make initial investments. Nevertheless, there is a "right" time to get into business. As Figure 1-5 shows, the "free-choice period" occurs between a person's mid-twenties and mid-thirties. During this period, there tends to be a balance between preparatory experiences on the one hand and family obligations on the other.

Obviously there are exceptions to this generalization. Some teenagers start their own firms. And other persons, even at 50 or 60 years of age, walk away from successful careers in big business when they become excited by the prospects of entrepreneurship.

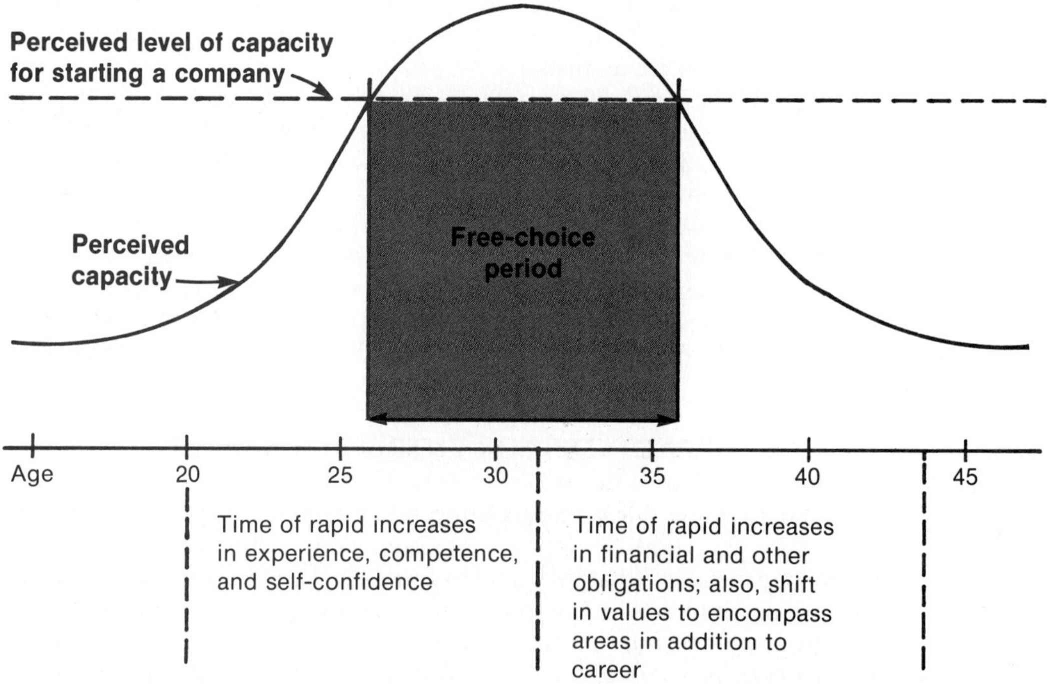

Source: Patrick R. Liles, "Who Are the Entrepreneurs?" *MSU Business Topics*, Vol. 22 (Winter, 1974), p. 11. Reproduced with permission.

Figure 1-5 The Free-Choice Period for Would-be Entrepreneurs

Precipitating Events

As suggested earlier, many potential entrepreneurs never take the fateful step of launching their own business ventures. Some of those who actually make the move are stimulated by precipitating events such as job termination, job dissatisfaction, or unexpected opportunities.

For example, after being educated at Andover, Yale, and Harvard Business School, Louis F. Polk, Jr., became chief financial officer at General Mills and later chief executive officer at MGM. At MGM he was a "young star among big-business executives." When he was fired by MGM, he took the $1 million he received for his employment contract and started Leisure Dynamics, a toy company. Finding it more satisfying to be an entrepreneur, Polk says, "You spend less time administering and more time executing. . . . It's a lot of fun."[19]

Getting fired is only one of many types of experiences which may serve as a catalyst in "taking the plunge" as an entrepreneur. Some individuals become so disenchanted with formal academic programs that they simply walk away from the classroom and start new lives as entrepreneurs. Others become exasperated with the rebuffs or perceived injustices at the hands of superiors in large organizations and leave in disgust to start their own businesses.

In a more positive vein, prospective entrepreneurs may unexpectedly stumble across business opportunities. A friend may offer, for example, to sponsor an individual as an Amway distributor. Or a relative may suggest that the individual leave a salaried position and take over a family business or other small firm.

Many prospective entrepreneurs, of course, simply plan for and seek out independent business opportunities. There is little in the way of a "precipitating event" involved in their decision to become entrepreneurs. We cannot say what proportion of new entrepreneurs make their move because of some particular event. However, many who launch new firms or otherwise go into business for themselves are obviously helped along by precipitating events.[20]

Self-Evaluation for Entrepreneurship

A number of questionnaires have been developed over the years to permit individuals to assess their aptitude for entrepreneurship. These questionnaires may be useful in that they encourage individuals to reflect on their personal values and to evaluate their strengths and weaknesses. And such

---

19. "Fun and Games," *Fortune*, Vol. 101 (March 24, 1980), p. 19.

20. For a study of job dissatisfaction as a precipitating event, see Robert H. Brockhaus, Sr., "The Effect of Job Dissatisfaction on the Decision to Start a Business," *Journal of Small Business Management*, Vol. 18, No. 1 (January, 1980), pp. 37-43.

questionnaires can be interesting, perhaps even fun, to complete. Unfortunately they do not yet provide a reliable guide for individual decision making.

The questionnaire shown in Figure 1-6 was developed on the basis of a study of 500 entrepreneurs by Dr. Alan Jacobowitz, a psychology professor at Trenton State College, Trenton, NJ. The entrepreneurial image conveyed by the Jacobowitz questionnaire is that of a restless, independent individual who tends to be a loner and somewhat arrogant. Intuitively we can think of some entrepreneurs who match that stereotype very well. Furthermore, some research seems to support such a picture of the entrepreneurial personality.[21] Research evidence is mixed, however. The truth is that no one yet knows how to predict prospects for entrepreneurial success very accurately. Consequently, you may find some confirmation of your entrepreneurial inclinations in a questionnaire, but you should not allow a negative evaluation to deter you. Although there is much that is unknown about entrepreneurs, we do know that they are a very diverse lot!

ENTREPRENEURIAL ROLES, VENTURES, AND STYLES

The field of small business encompasses a great variety of entrepreneurial roles, ventures, and styles. Entrepreneurial roles refer to the type of activity in which entrepreneurs are involved. Entrepreneurial ventures refer to types of businesses in terms of their potential for growth and profits. Different entrepreneurial styles usually result from the varied personal backgrounds of entrepreneurs.

Types of Entrepreneurial Roles

Although categories tend to overlap, entrepreneurial roles may be classified into three types: founders, general managers, and franchisees.

Founding Entrepreneurs. Generally considered to be the "pure" entrepreneurs, **founders** may be inventors who initiate businesses on the basis of new or improved products or services. They may also be craftsmen who develop skills and then start their own firms. Or they may be enterprising individuals, often with marketing backgrounds, who draw upon the ideas of others in starting new firms. Whether acting as individuals or in groups, these people bring firms into existence by surveying the market, raising funds, and arranging for the necessary facilities. After the firm is launched, the founding entrepreneur may preside over the subsequent growth of the business.

---

21. See, for example, Orvis Collins and David G. Moore, *The Organization Makers: A Behavioral Study of Independent Entrepreneurs* (New York: Appleton-Century-Crofts, 1970). Conflicting evidence is presented in Arnold C. Cooper and William C. Dunkelberg, "Influences upon Entrepreneurship—A Large-Scale Study," a paper presented to the Academy of Management, San Diego, CA, August 4, 1981.

Are you tough enough to be an entrepreneur? Do you have what it takes to start up your own business? We've put together a list of questions, based on Alan Jacobowitz's theory of entrepreneurial personality, that you can try to measure up against.

1. Were your parents, close relatives, or close friends entrepreneurs?
2. Did any of that business carry over into your home when you were growing up?
3. Did you have a lemonade stand or a paper route as a kid?
4. Was your academic record in school less than outstanding?
5. Did you feel like an outsider among peers at school?
6. Were you often reprimanded for your school behavior?
7. Do you have difficulty attaining satisfaction from any job with a large firm?
8. Do you often feel that you could do a better job than your boss?
9. Would you rather play sports than watch them on television?
10. Do you prefer nonfiction to fiction?
11. Have you ever been fired from a job or left one under pressure?
12. Do you never lose sleep at night over your work or personal business?
13. Would you rather jump into a project than plan one?
14. Would you consider yourself decisive, a good thinker on your feet?
15. Are you active in community affairs?

If you answered yes to 12 or more of these questions and you are not an entrepreneur already, you may be missing your big chance. If you answered yes to fewer than 12 and you already are an entrepreneur . . . well, good luck!

Source: Neil Cohen, "The Five Ages of the Entrepreneur," *Venture*, Vol. 2, No. 7 (July, 1980), p. 40. Reproduced with permission.

Figure 1-6 Entrepreneurial Personality Quiz

General Managers. As new firms become well-established, founders become less innovators and more administrators. Thus, we recognize another class of entrepreneurs called **general managers**. General managers preside over the operation of successful ongoing business firms. They manage the week-to-week and month-to-month production, marketing, and financial functions of small firms. The distinction between founders and general managers is often hazy. In some cases, small firms grow rapidly, and their orientation is more akin to the founding than to the management process. Nevertheless, it is helpful to distinguish those entrepreneurs who found and substantially change firms (the "movers" and "shakers") from those who direct the continuing operations of established firms.

Franchisees. It is also helpful to recognize a third category of entrepreneurial role—that of the franchisee. Franchisees differ from general managers in the degree of their independence. Because of the constraints and guidance provided by contractual relationships with franchising organizations, franchisees function as limited entrepreneurs.

Types of Entrepreneurial Ventures

Small-business ventures differ greatly in terms of their potential for growth and profits. To account for such variation, Patrick R. Liles has suggested the following categories: marginal firms, attractive small companies, and high-potential ventures.[22] In thinking about small business, however, one can easily fall into the trap of considering only one end of the spectrum. Some writers treat only the tiny, marginal firms whose owners barely survive, while others focus entirely on high-growth, high-technology firms. A balanced view must recognize the entire range of ventures with the varied problems and rewards presented by each point on the spectrum.

Marginal Firms. The very small dry cleaners, independent garages, beauty shops, service stations, appliance repair shops, and other small firms which provide a very modest return to their owners are the **marginal firms**. We do not call them "marginal" because they are in danger of bankruptcy. Some marginal firms, it is true, are on "thin ice" financially, but their distinguishing feature is their limited ability to generate significant profits. Entrepreneurs devote personal effort to such ventures and receive a profit return that does little more than compensate them for their time. Part-time businesses typically fall into this category of marginal firms.

Attractive Small Companies. In contrast to marginal firms, numerous **attractive small firms** offer substantial rewards to their owners. Entrepreneurial income from these ventures may easily range from $50,000 to $150,000 annually. These are the strong segment of small business—the "good" firms which can provide rewarding careers even to well-educated young people. One example of such a business is a restaurant established in the late 1970s with a waterfront atmosphere and motif. This business has thrived with customers waiting in line at peak periods, and its owners' net income easily exceeds $100,000 per year.

High-Potential Ventures. A few firms have such great prospects for growth that they may be called **high-potential ventures**. Frequently these are also high-technology ventures. At the time of the firm's founding, the owners

---

22. Patrick R. Liles, "Who Is the Entrepreneur?" *Wharton Quarterly*, Vol. 7 (Spring, 1974), pp. 14-31.

ACTION REPORT: Polly Reilly's Part-Time Business — One Type of Marginal Firm

Polly Reilly of Westfield, NJ discovered a business opportunity in a personal hobby. A wife and mother, she enrolled in an evening art class and was soon making tissue-paper collages, pressed-flower pictures, and pine-cone candle holders. When friends bought them, she began selling them in local specialty shops. In November, 1968, she invited three fellow crafts enthusiasts to join her in a Christmas boutique in her home. The sale lasted three days and was highly successful.

A few years later, Mrs. Reilly employed a sales representative, and her ornaments were sold in fine stores throughout the country, including Bloomingdale's and Lord & Taylor's in New York. In 1979, she began to market her designs at craft shows on the Eastern seaboard, and she had plans to initiate a mail-order business.

In spite of success and growth, Mrs. Reilly continues to operate the business from her home. She described her home work area as follows:

> Even though I like my privacy, I am a gregarious soul at heart. I had an extension phone installed by my side, so I could talk to friends while I painted. A television set was placed on a nearby table so I could keep abreast of news and entertainment programs. Talk shows became my favorites, but I had to concentrate on the fact that only one of the glasses on my desk contained coffee. When one is absorbed in her work *and* Stanley Siegel, it's easy to gulp down a container of red paint.

Source: Polly Reilly, "How My Hobby Became a Business," *McCall's*, Vol. 107 (September, 1980), p. 106. Reprinted by permission of the McCall Publishing Company.

often anticipate rapid growth, a possible merger, or "going public" within a few years. Some of the more spectacular examples within recent years include Digital Equipment Corporation, Polaroid, Amway Corporation, Wendy's, and Word, Inc. In addition to such widely-recognized successes, there are at any time thousands of less-well-known ventures being launched and experiencing rapid growth. Extrepreneurial ventures of this type appeal to many engineers, professional managers, and venture capitalists who see the potential rewards and exciting prospects.

Types of Entrepreneurial Styles

Perhaps because of their varied backgrounds, entrepreneurs display great variation in their styles of doing business. They analyze problems and approach decision making in drastically different ways. Norman R. Smith has suggested two basic entrepreneurial patterns: craftsman entrepreneurs and opportunistic entrepreneurs.[23]

The Craftsman Entrepreneur. According to Smith, the education of the **craftsman entrepreneur** is limited to technical training. Such entrepreneurs have technical job experience, but they lack good communications skills. Their approach to business decision making is characterized by the following features:

1. They are paternalistic. (This means they direct their businesses much as they might direct their own families.)
2. They are reluctant to delegate authority.
3. They use few (one or two) capital sources to create their firms.
4. They define marketing strategy in terms of the traditional price, quality, and company reputation.
5. Their sales efforts are primarily personal.
6. Their time orientation is short, with little planning for future growth or change.

The typical mechanic who starts an independent garage and the beautician who operates a beauty shop illustrate the craftsman entrepreneur.

The Opportunistic Entrepreneur. Smith's definition of the **opportunistic entrepreneur** is one who has supplemented technical education by studying such nontechnical subjects as economics, law, or English. Opportunistic entrepreneurs avoid paternalism, delegate authority as necessary for growth, employ various marketing strategies and types of sales efforts, obtain original capitalization from more than two sources, and plan for future growth. An example of the opportunistic entrepreneur is the small building contractor and developer who uses a relatively sophisticated approach to management. Because of the complexity of the industry, successful contractors use careful record keeping, proper budgeting, precise bidding, and systematic marketing research.

In Smith's model of entrepreneurial styles, we see two extremes of managerial approach. At the one end, we find a craftsman in an entre-

---

23. For a recent treatment, see Gary McCain and Norman R. Smith, "A Contemporary Model of Entrepreneurial Style," a paper presented at the Annual Conference of the International Council for Small Business, Asilomar, CA, June 22-25, 1980. A similar model was earlier presented in Norman R. Smith, *The Entrepreneur and His Firm: The Relationship Between Type of Man and Type of Company*, Occasional Paper (East Lansing: Division of Research, Graduate School of Business Administration, Michigan State University, 1967).

preneurial position. At the other end, we find a well-educated and experienced manager. The former flies "by the seat of his pants," and the latter uses systematic management procedures and something resembling a scientific management approach. In practice, of course, the distribution of entrepreneurial styles is less polarized than suggested by the model, with entrepreneurs scattered along a continuum in terms of their managerial sophistication. This book is intended to help the student move toward the opportunistic end and away from the craftsman end of the continuum.

THE FAMILY BUSINESS

One category of small business that merits specific recognition is the family business. Family firms and their owner-managers fall into each of the categories noted earlier—founders, general managers, and franchisees; marginal firms, attractive small companies, and high-potential ventures; and craftsman entrepreneurs and opportunistic entrepreneurs. They are distinguished as **family firms** in each of these various categories by the family relationships that are significant in the business.

Firms become clearly recognizable as family businesses when second-generation managers become influential in business operations. Other features which often identify the firms as family businesses include the following:

1. Grooming of an heir to enter or to move into the management of the firm.
2. Appointment of relatives of the owner-manager to the board of directors.
3. Adherence of the business to important values espoused by the founding family.

The fact of family relationships affects small-firm management in various ways which can be noted only briefly at this point. Management succession, for example, becomes a crucial matter which requires the adequate preparation of family successors and the limiting of succession opportunities for nonfamily members. Operating management may also be affected in various ways. For example, the rate of expansion may be limited in order to preserve family control or inefficient performance of a family member may be tolerated.

As we examine various areas of small-business management, it is necessary to think specifically of the implications for family firms. In the discussion of management succession in Chapter 15, for example, we will look expressly at the unique feature of succession in the family business.

ENTREPRENEURIAL TEAMS

In the discussion thus far, we have assumed that entrepreneurs are individuals. And, of course, this is usually the case. However, the entrepreneurial team is another possibility that is becoming popular, particularly in ventures of substantial size. An **entrepreneurial team** is formed by bringing together two or more individuals to function in the capacity of entrepreneurs.

One of the fabulous success stories in recent years involved the development and marketing of the Apple computer. Steven P. Jobs and Stephen G. Wozniak, the inventors of this computer model, were both in their twenties, graduates of the same high school, and college dropouts. Described as "self-taught computer whizzes," they designed their first machine in Jobs's bedroom, built it in his parents' garage, and showed it to a local computer-store owner, who ordered 25 units. The young inventors sought help and found it in A. C. (Mike) Markkula, who had been marketing manager at Intel, and Michael Scott, who left a job as director of manufacturing at National Semiconductor. Markkula became chairman of Apple in May, 1977, and Scott became president a month later. When the firm's stock was made available to the public in 1980, each of the 4 participants owned shares ranging between $62 million and $165 million in market value![24] This entrepreneurial team successfully combined the inventive and business talents necessary for developing, producing, marketing, and financing the venture.

The Apple story is clearly unique. Rarely can an inventor take a garage prototype and become a multimillionaire in less than five years! However, the entrepreneurial team principle is also applicable on a more modest scale. In many less spectacular cases, entrepreneurial teams are now being formed to bring together the necessary diverse talents for launching a new venture. Although the entrepreneur is still typically an individual, entrepreneurial teams are rapidly gaining in popularity and offer great potential for further development.

LOOKING BACK

1. Entrepreneurial opportunities are unlimited, as evidenced by various dramatic success stories of successful entrepreneurs.
2. Entrepreneurial rewards include profits, independence, and a satisfying way of life.
3. Individuals who become entrepreneurs have a high need for achievement, a willingness to take moderate risks, and a high degree of self-confidence.

24. Susie Gharib Nazem, "The Folks Who Brought You Apple," *Fortune*, Vol. 103 (January 12, 1981), p. 68.

4. The period between a person's mid-twenties and mid-thirties is described as the "free-choice period" in which entry into entrepreneurial careers tends to be easiest. The specific step into many entrepreneurs' businesses is often triggered by a "precipitating event" such as losing a job. Entrepreneurship includes a variety of entrepreneurial roles (founding versus managing, for example); types of ventures (marginal firms versus high-potential ventures, for example); and management style (craftsman versus opportunistic entrepreneurs, for example).
5. One special type of entrepreneurial venture is the family firm, in which family considerations affect management in various ways. Another distinctive type of entrepreneurship is the entrepreneurial team, in contrast to the individual entrepreneur, which provides leadership for the firm.

DISCUSSION QUESTIONS

1. What is meant by the term entrepreneur?
2. When we read the outstanding success stories at the beginning of the chapter, we realize they are exceptions to the rule. What, then, is their significance in illustrating entrepreneurial opportunity? Are these stories misleading?
3. Some corporate executives receive annual compensation in excess of $3 million. Profits of most small businesses are much less. How, then, can profits constitute a meaningful incentive for entrepreneurs?
4. What is the most significant reason for following an independent business career by the entrepreneur whom you know best?
5. In view of the fact that entrepreneurs must satisfy customers, employees, bankers, and others, are they really independent? Explain the nature of their independence as a reward for self-employment.
6. What is shown by the studies of David C. McClelland regarding an entrepreneur's need for achievement?
7. What types of risks are faced by entrepreneurs, and what degree of risks do they prefer?
8. Explain the internal locus of control and its significance for entrepreneurship.
9. On the basis of your own knowledge, can you identify a "foreign refugee" who is an entrepreneur?
10. Why is the period from the mid-twenties to the mid-thirties in a person's life considered to be the "free-choice period" for becoming an entrepreneur?
11. What is a precipitating event? Give some examples.
12. What is the difference between a marginal firm and a high-potential venture?

13. Distinguish between a craftsman entrepreneur and an opportunistic entrepreneur.

14. What is the advantage of using an entrepreneurial team?

REFERENCES TO SMALL BUSINESS IN ACTION

"The Boss' Son." *Forbes*, Vol. 126, No. 11 (November 24, 1980), pp. 93-96.

This business, Vertipile, Inc., was founded in 1939 by the father of the present entrepreneur. Even though it is a relatively small family business in the textile industry, it has shown impressive profit returns.

Merwin, John. "Have You Got What It Takes?" *Forbes*, Vol. 128, No. 3 (August 3, 1981), pp. 60-64.

This article profiles a number of prosperous entrepreneurs and outlines the qualities that made them successful.

Parker, Robert. "Making It: Heeding His Own Advice." *Nation's Business*, Vol. 68, No. 8 (August, 1980), p. 14.

Leonard L. Schley has an enviable record of starting and nurturing a number of successful small businesses. His entrepreneurial motivations and experiences are described in this article.

"Rules Is Made When Brains Has Run Out." *Forbes*, Vol. 116, No. 1 (July 1, 1975), pp. 34-38.

The entrepreneurial qualities of Jim Walter are evident in the operation of the business which bears his name.

"Women in Charge: Eight Who Made It." *U. S. News & World Report*, Vol. 88, No. 11 (March 24, 1980), pp. 64-66.

Women often show great success as entrepreneurs. This article describes eight "winners" in such varied fields as asphalt paving, wire-rope sales, and construction.

Chapter **2**

Small Business: Vital Component of the Economy

LOOKING AHEAD

Watch for the following important topics:

1. The definition of small business used in this book.
2. Size standards proposed by the Small Business Administration.
3. The types of industry in which small businesses operate.
4. The proportion of all business activity which can be classified as small business.
5. Unique contributions of small businesses.

Many people tend to overestimate the importance of big business because of its greater visibility over small business. We see small businesses dwarfed by such corporate giants as General Motors (850,000 employees), Bank of America ($85 billion deposits), Prudential Life Insurance Company ($354 billion worth of insurance in force), and American Telephone and Telegraph Company (over $5 billion annual profits).[1] Yet small firms, even though less conspicuous, are a vital component of our economy. In this chapter we will not only examine the extent and trends of small-business activity, but also evaluate the unique contributions of small businesses that help preserve the economic well-being of our country. But first, we need to look at the different criteria used to define small business.

DEFINITION OF SMALL BUSINESS

Specifying any size standard to define small business is necessarily arbitrary, for people adopt different standards for different purposes. Legislators, for example, may exclude small firms from certain governmental regulations and may specify ten employees as the cutoff point. Moreover, a business may be described as "small" when compared to larger firms, but "large" when compared to smaller ones. Most people, for example, would classify independently owned gasoline stations, neighborhood restaurants, and locally owned retail stores as small businesses. Similarly, most would agree that the major automobile manufacturers are big businesses.[2] And the firms of in-between sizes would be classified by many people as large or small on the basis of their individual viewpoints.

Even the criteria used to measure the size of businesses vary. Some criteria are applicable to all industrial areas, while others are relevant only to certain types of business. Examples of criteria used to measure size are:

1. Number of employees.
2. Sales volume.
3. Asset size.
4. Insurance in force.
5. Volume of deposits.

Although the first criterion listed above — number of employees — is the most widely used yardstick, the best criterion in any given case depends upon the user's purpose.

Another complicating factor in deciding what is small is the variation among industries. In some industries that are capital-intensive, such as steel making, the typical business is very large. In some types of service businesses, such as beauty shops, the typical firm is quite small.

---

1. *Moody's Manuals* for Industrials, Banking and Finance, and Public Utilities (New York: Moody's Investors Service, Inc., 1980).

2. In 1966, the Small Business Administration classified American Motors, the nation's 63d largest company with more than 28,000 employees, as a small business. This decision permitted American Motors to enjoy special advantages in bidding on government contracts. It also illustrated the arbitrary nature of such definitions and the unusual classifications that are possible.

SBA Standards

The Small Business Administration (SBA) establishes size standards which determine eligibility for SBA loans and for special consideration in bidding on government contracts. As of 1981, the SBA proposed standards based on the number of employees, which varied widely from 15 to 2,500 employees. Some of these proposed standards, which covered 750 industries, are shown in Table 2-1.

Table 2-1 Examples of Proposed SBA Standards

	Number of Employees
Copper ores mining	2,500
Pulp mills	2,500
Metal can manufacturing	2,500
Newspaper publishing and printing	250
Poultry dressing plants	250
Radio broadcasting	50
Employment agencies	25
General contractors — single-family houses	25
Furniture stores	20
Radio and television repair shops	15

Source: *Federal Register*, Vol. 45, No. 48 (March 10, 1980), pp. 15441-15453.

Size Standards Used in This Book

To provide a clearer image of the small firm discussed in this book, we suggest the following general criteria for defining a small business:

1. Financing of the business is supplied by one individual or a small group. Only in a rare case would the business have more than 15 or 20 owners.
2. Except for its marketing function, the firm's operations are geographically localized. Typically it operates in only one city or community.
3. Compared to the biggest firms in the industry, the business is small.
4. The number of employees in the business is usually fewer than 100.

Obviously there will be some small firms that fail to meet *all* of the above standards. For example, a small executive search firm—a firm that helps corporate clients recruit managers from other organizations—may operate in many sections of the country and thereby fail to meet the second criterion. Nevertheless, the discussion of management concepts in this book is aimed primarily at the type of firm that fits the general pattern described above.

SMALL BUSINESS IN THE MAJOR INDUSTRIES

Small firms operate in all industries, but they differ greatly in their nature and importance from industry to industry. In thinking about their economic contribution, therefore, we need first to identify the eight major industries and to note the types of small firms that function in these industries. These eight major industries are: wholesale trade; contract construction; retail trade; services; finance, insurance, and real estate; mining; transportation and other public utilities; and manufacturing.

Wholesale Trade

The wholesaler's primary function is to act as an intermediary between manufacturers and retailers or industrial users by assembling, storing, and distributing products. Small firms are dominant in the area of wholesaling. They sell a wide range of products such as drugs, groceries, hardware, fruits and vegetables, grain and farm produce, farm implements and supplies, machinery, industrial supplies, and electrical appliances. Petroleum bulk stations are also considered wholesale businesses, as are agents and brokers who buy or sell raw materials or manufactured products for the account of others.

Contract Construction

General contractors who erect skyscrapers and mammoth factory buildings are big-business firms. But there are also thousands of small firms serving as general contractors on a more modest scale. In addition to general contracting, small firms play an important role in contracting for work in such specialized fields as electrical, plumbing, and painting jobs. Even public-construction contractors, such as those who build streets, bridges, and sewers, many times are small businesses.

Retail Trade

Examples of small businesses abound in the field of retailing. Among these are drugstores, independent grocery and meat markets, clothing stores, shoe stores, variety stores, auto accessories dealers, appliance dealers,

Figure 2-1 Small Firms in Diverse Industries

bookstores, music stores, service stations, and restaurants. Other examples include jewelry stores, hardware stores, record shops, sporting goods stores, toy stores, furniture stores, and vending machine businesses. While most small retailers operate as single-unit firms, others function successfully as small chains.

Service Industries

Any attempt to catalog service firms immediately reveals their diversity. For example, there are business services such as accounting firms, advertising agencies, private employment agencies, blueprint services, and managerial consultants. Personal services include barber and beauty shops, dry cleaners, photographic studios, funeral homes, travel agencies, and so on. Then there are automobile repair services, entertainment and recreational services, hotels, and motels.

Finance, Insurance, and Real Estate

Small banks, loan companies, pawnbrokers, real estate brokerage firms, and insurance agencies illustrate the types of small firms which operate in the industrial category of finance, insurance, and real estate. The insurance agency, for example, is an independent business which sells insurance policies for large insurance companies. Insurance and real estate brokerage services are often combined in the same organization.

Mining

Small-scale mining involves many types of minerals. There are thousands of small bituminous coal mines, for example. Some of them are strip mines operated with only a few employees. Similarly, wildcatters who operate on a shoestring have brought in many an oil well. Some small quarries and sand and gravel companies also belong to the mining industry.

Transportation and Other Public Utilities

The required investment is so great in the industry of transportation and other public utilities that big business is dominant in this field. Even so, some small firms find a niche in which to operate. Examples of such firms include taxicab companies, local bus lines, privately owned water systems, chartered flight services, local radio and television stations, and community newspaper publishers.

ACTION REPORT: Small Business in a Big-Business Industry

Although railroading is big business, some small lines are operated as individual or family businesses. An example is the Willamina and Grande Ronde Railroad Company. One of 16 short-line operations in Oregon alone, W&GR uses a 35-year-old diesel locomotive to transport lumber to the Southern Pacific Railroad at Willamina—a 17-mile round trip. The railroad was acquired in 1980 by the Root family, with the help of relatives and friends. Michael Root is general manager, vice-president, engineer, and owner of one eighth of the stock. In addition to Root, W&GR employs an engineer, a section foreman, a section man, and a part-time freight agent and office manager.

Source: "Little Engines That Could—And Will Again," *Venture*, Vol. 3, No. 2 (February, 1981), pp. 70-72.

Manufacturing

Although big business overshadows small business in the manufacturing industry, there are nonetheless hundreds of thousands of small firms in this field. They include bakeries, sawmills, toy factories, job printing shops, shoe factories, bookbinding plants, ice cream plants, and soft-drink bottling works. Small machine shops, ironworks, ready-mixed concrete plants, cabinet shops, furniture manufacturing plants, and clothing manufacturing plants also fit this category.

SMALL-BUSINESS STRENGTH IN NUMBERS

A number of measures can be used to evaluate the relative numerical strength of small business. One of these classifies business firms in terms of the number of employees on their payroll.[3] Figure 2-2 shows the percentage of paid employees working in small business—that is, in firms with fewer than 100 employees. Using this criterion, we can see that small-business firms employ almost 40 percent of all employees in all industries. Of course, in some fields small business is much stronger. Figure 2-2 shows that small firms account for 73 percent of all employees in wholesale trade, 71.8 percent of all employees in contract construction, 54.4 percent of all employees in retail trade, and 50.3 percent of all employees in the services industry.

---

3. One weakness of this payroll criterion is that it overlooks the contributions of proprietors, partners, and unpaid family help who are not on the payroll.

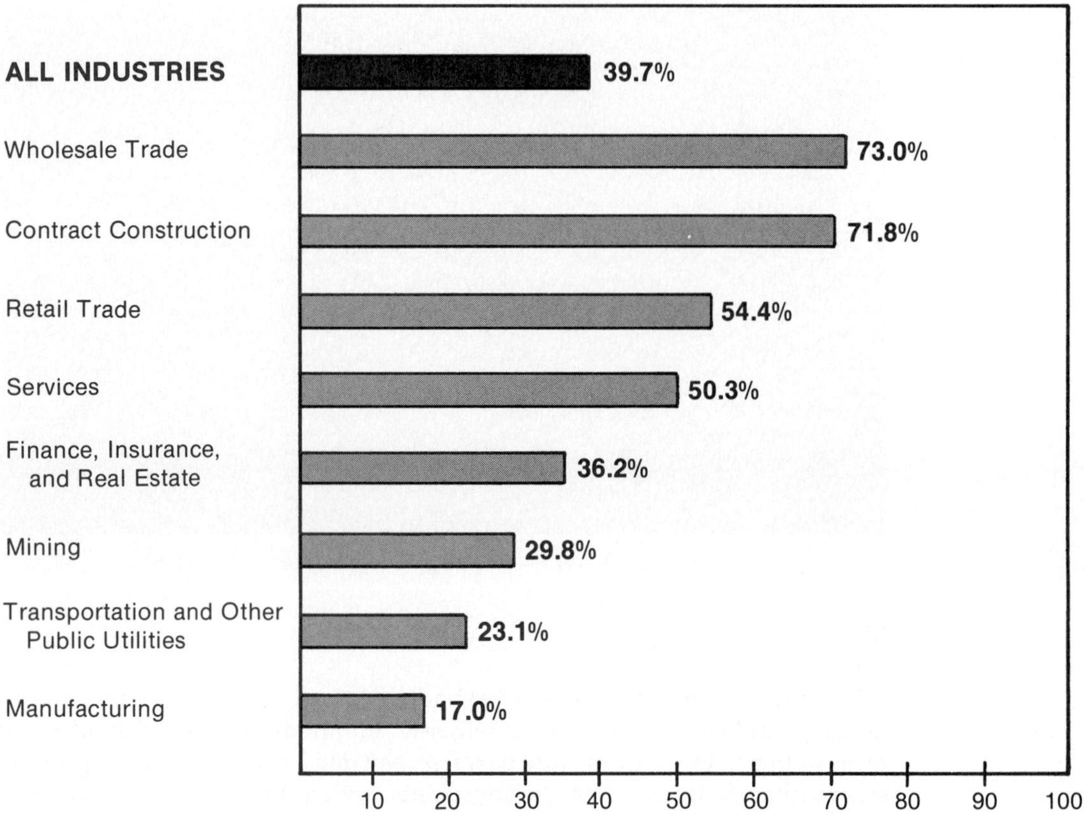

Source: U. S. Department of Commerce, Bureau of the Census, *County Business Patterns, 1977: Enterprise Statistics* (Washington: U. S. Government Printing Office, 1979), Table 2.

Figure 2-2 Percentage of Employees in Small Firms (Firms with fewer than 100 employees)

Again, using 100 employees as the criterion for being small is obviously arbitrary. Many firms that have 200 or 300 employees are regarded as small by their owners. These firms operate in one locality, obtain their capital from one or a few individuals, and are much smaller than other firms in their industries. Thus, if we used a larger-size criterion, we would find that a larger percentage of business is classified as small. Regardless of the exact point at which one draws the line, it is apparent that much—roughly 40 to 50 percent—of American business may be classed as small.

SPECIAL CONTRIBUTIONS OF SMALL BUSINESS

As part of the business community, small firms unquestionably contribute to our nation's economic welfare. They produce a substantial portion of our total goods and services. Thus, their general economic contribution is similar to that of big business. Small firms, however, possess some qualities which make them more than miniature versions of big business corporations. They provide new jobs, introduce innovations, stimulate competition, aid big business, and produce goods and services efficiently.

Providing New Jobs

As the population and the economy grow, small businesses must provide many of the new job opportunities. Some persons feel, indeed, that small business must produce the "lion's share" of the new jobs. For example, in hearings before the U. S. House Subcommittee on Antitrust, Consumers, and Employment, Carter Henderson, co-director of the Princeton Center for Alternate Futures, testified as follows on the role of small business in providing jobs:

> In my opinion, the future of small business in our country is going to have a great deal to do with helping the U. S. economy remain strong as we come down after 25 years of absolutely cornucopian growth to a rather slower-growing economy.[4]

Henderson's statement is one of hope concerning the future economic role of small business. Fortunately recent research indicates that this hope is not unfounded. In 1978 congressional hearings, MIT economist David Birch reported results of his research on the special contribution of new and small firms to the growth of employment:

> Young firms account for a large percentage (about 80 percent) of all new jobs created. After the age of four (years), job growth slows down considerably. Firms with 50 or fewer employees generate about half of all new jobs. Firms 250 and under create almost 80 percent. Large firms (those over 250) are responsible for only one out of five new jobs.[5]

New jobs, therefore, come from the birth of new firms and their subsequent expansion. Some new firms, of course, expand to the point that they are no longer small. Also, obviously large corporations expand and create additional jobs. The statistics reported above, however, reveal the unique, disproportionate contribution of small business to the creation of new jobs.

---

4. Statement of Carter Henderson included in U. S. Congress, House, Committee on Small Business, *Future of Small Business in America*, Report No. H95-1810, 95th Congress, 2d Session, 1978, p. 4.

5. Testimony of David Birch, U. S. Congress, House, Hearings before the Committee on Small Business, *Small Business and Job Creation*, 95th Congress, 2d Session, 1978, p. 37.

Introducing Innovation

New products which originate in the research laboratories of big business make a valuable contribution to our standard of living. There is a question, however, as to the relative importance of big business in achieving the truly significant innovations. The record shows that many scientific breakthroughs originated with independent inventors and small organizations. Below are some twentieth-century examples of new products created by small firms:

1. Xerography.
2. Insulin.
3. Vacuum tube.
4. Penicillin.
5. Cottonpicker.
6. Zipper.
7. Automatic transmission.
8. Jet engine.
9. Helicopter.
10. Power steering.
11. Kodachrome.
12. Ball-point pen.

An interesting current example of an innovative product which originated outside the laboratories of big business is the 35-mm camera which produces prints and transparencies that exhibit a realistic three-dimensional effect.[6] This camera was developed by Jerry C. Nims and Allen Lo and their obscure Atlanta company, Nimslo Technology, Inc. It will be produced by Timex Corporation, which had prior experience as a producer of Polaroid cameras from 1952 to 1979.

It is interesting to note that research departments of big business tend to emphasize the improvement of existing products. In fact, it is quite likely that some ideas generated by personnel in big business are sidetracked because they are not related to existing products or because of their unusual nature. Unfortunately preoccupation with an existing product can sometimes blind one to the value of a *new* idea. The jet engine, for example, had difficulty securing consideration by those who had been accustomed to internal combustion engines.

The greater effectiveness of small firms in research and development was cited in a National Science Foundation study:

---

6. "The Sudden Exposure of a New 3-D Camera," *Business Week*, No. 2629 (March 24, 1980), pp. 53-54.

> On the basis of a sample of major innovations introduced to the market between 1953 and 1973, small firms (up to 1,000 employees) were found to produce about four (4) times as many innovations per research and development dollar as medium-size firms (1,000 to 10,000 employees) and about twenty-four (24) times as many as large firms (over 10,000 employees).[7]

Innovation contributes to productivity by providing better products and better methods of production. A slowing of innovation has been blamed for our nation's recent sluggish rate of growth in productivity.[8] The millions of small firms that provide the centers of initiative and sources of innovation are thus in a position to help improve American productivity.

Stimulating Economic Competition

Many economists, beginning with Adam Smith, have expounded the values inherent in economic competition. In a competitive situation, the individual businessperson driven by self-interest is motivated to act in a socially desirable manner. It is competition that acts as the regulator to transform selfishness into service.

When producers consist of only a few big businesses, the customer is at their mercy. They may set exorbitant prices, withhold technological development, exclude new competitors, or otherwise abuse their position of power. If competition is to have a "cutting edge," there is need for small firms. One contributor to congressional hearings on the future of small business has stressed the peculiar importance of small firms in creating a healthy, competitive economy:

> A free enterprise economy simply cannot function as such without an active and effective small-business component. Just as soon as competition becomes sufficiently "imperfect" because of the disappearance of competitors, we then evolve into a "managed" economy.[9]

Not every competitive effort of small firms is successful, but big business may be kept on its toes by small business. Some entrepreneurs have no qualms about competing with giant corporations. For example, in Winchester, KY a small soft-drink producer is marketing a ginger-ale-like product that outsells Coke, Pepsi, RC, and Dr Pepper in its home territory. And the younger member of the firm's family management team, Frank "Buddy"

---

7. U. S. Congress, Senate, Joint Hearings before the Select Committee on Small Business and other committees, *Small Business and Innovation*, August 9-10, 1978, p. 7.

8. See "The Sad State of Innovation," *Time* (October 22, 1979), pp. 70-71; and "A Diminished Thrust from Innovation," *Business Week*, No. 2643 (June 30, 1980), pp. 60-61.

9. U. S. Congress, House, Committee on Small Business, *Future of Small Business in America* (Washington: U. S. Government Printing Office, 1979), p. 6.

Rogers III, is quoted as saying, "My goal is to make Coca-Cola the No. 2 soft-drink company in this country."[10]

ACTION REPORT: An Innovative, Competitive Small Firm

When Minnetonka, Inc., a tiny company in Chaska, MN, introduced a liquid soap named Softsoap in 1980, the majors tended to dismiss it as a fad. However, the product's sales rose to $35 million in its introductory year. Large companies are reportedly watching the product and considering entries of their own.

Minnetonka had been founded in 1964 to make packaged specialty soap and gift products. About 1978, its founder, Robert Taylor, heard how well a new item, the Incredible Soap Machine, was selling. He decided to use the pump concept to break into volume sales in supermarkets. "He reasoned that consumers would find the pump easier to use than bar soap, which gets slippery and dirty, fouls soap dishes, and shrinks to a barely usable sliver."

An analyst commented favorably on Minnetonka's prospects in the light of expected big-business competition, as follows: "It's little companies that are on the offensive. The big companies with their committees of MBAs afraid of failing in their own organization are not entrepreneurially oriented."

Source: Reprinted from the January 12, 1981 issue of *Business Week* by special permission,

However, there is no guarantee of competition in numbers alone. Many tiny firms may be no match for one large firm or even for several firms that dominate an industry. Nevertheless, the existence of many healthy small businesses in an industry may be viewed as a desirable bulwark of the American capitalistic system.

Aiding Big Business

The fact that some functions are more expertly performed by small business enables small firms to contribute to the success of larger ones. If small businesses were suddenly removed from the contemporary scene, big businesses would find themselves saddled with a myriad of activities that they could only inefficiently perform. Two functions which small business can perform more efficiently than big business are the distribution function and the supply function.

10. "Going After Coke," *Fortune*, Vol. 101, No. 8 (April 21, 1980), p. 19.

Distribution Function. Few large manufacturers of inexpensive consumer products find it desirable to own wholesale and retail outlets. Take, for example, the successful small-business operation of Genesco retail cast-offs.[11] Genesco, Inc., a $1 billion manufacturer of footwear and clothing, sold off a number of its lackluster retail divisions to entrepreneurs who changed them into thriving businesses. One of its retail divisions—Gidding Jenny, a fashionable women's store in Cincinnati, OH—was sold in July, 1978, to Barry Miller, a former executive with Federated Department Stores. Genesco's main problem, according to Miller, was that "they couldn't adjust to stores that were atypical, that served a select trade." It looks as if he will double the sales volume in only three years after taking over from Genesco.

Supply Function. Small businesses act as suppliers and subcontractors for large firms. General Motors, for example, purchases goods and services from more than 37,000 small businesses. Over three fourths of these small firms employ fewer than 100 persons.[12]

ACTION REPORT: Small Business as Supplier

An interesting example of a highly successful small supplier is provided by Zero Corporation of Burbank, CA. In 1951, Jack Gilbert bought the business, which had about ten employees, from Herman Zierold. (After receiving so many letters addressed to the Zero Corporation, Gilbert finally changed the name.) The business is devoted to the production of aluminum boxes, which are used for such purposes as covering electronic gadgets. The firm simply produces aluminum boxes in standard sizes. If an order is received for a fairly standard box, Gilbert absorbs the cost of building a die. Although he merely breaks even on the original order, he then owns the die and can profit from additional orders for boxes of that size. To illustrate Zero's type of relationship with big business, consider Digital Equipment Corporation, which produces thousands of computer printers each year. "But Digital Equipment can't be bothered building the stands the printers rest on. Enter Zero, which produces the simple stand for about $40. Digital Equipment writes the book, so to speak, Zero the cover."

Source: "Getting Rich on Little Nothings," *Forbes*, Vol. 126 (November 1, 1980), pp. 104-109.

---

11. "Revamping Genesco's Cast-Offs," *Venture*, Vol. 2, No. 11 (November, 1980), pp. 14-16.

12. James M. Roche, "Understanding: The Key to Business-Government Cooperation," *Michigan Business Review*, Vol. 21, No. 2 (March, 1969), p. 9.

Table 2-2 Earnings, Including Compensation of Officers, per Dollar of Assets for Corporations With and Without Net Income, by Asset Class, 1972

Asset Class (Thousands of dollars)	Earnings per Dollar of Assets				
	Manufacturing	Services	Construction	Transportation	Wholesale and Retail Trade
Under $25	$0.49	$2.42	$0.85	$0.42	$0.49
$25-$50	.39	1.03	.53	.26	.34
$50-$100	.35	.53	.40	.26	.29
$100-$250	.28	.29	.30	.23	.24
$250-$500	.24	.19	.23	.18	.21
$500-$1,000	.22	.13	.19	.15	.20
$1,000-$2,500	.18	.11	.16	.13	.17
$2,500-$10,000	.16	.09	.13	.11	.15
$10,000-$25,000	.14	.09	.09	.10	.12
$25,000-$100,000	.12	.09	.08	.08	.12
Over $100,000	.10	.07	.05	.05	.09

Note: Income = Total receipts − (Total deductions + Officers' compensation + Charitable contributions).

Source: U.S. Congress, Senate, Joint Hearing before the Select Committee on Small Business and the Joint Economic Committee, *The Role of Small Business in the Economy: Tax and Financial Problems*, 94th Congress, 1st Session, November 21, 1975, p. 39. (Primary source: Office of Tax Analysis, Office of the Secretary of the Treasury.)

In addition to supplying services directly to large corporations, small firms provide services to customers of big business. For example, they service automobiles, repair appliances, and clean carpets produced by large manufacturers.

Producing Goods and Services Efficiently

In considering the contributions of small business, we are concerned with an underlying question of small-business efficiency. Common sense tells us that the efficient size of business varies with the industry. We can easily recognize, for example, that big business is better in manufacturing automobiles but that small business is better in repairing them.

The continued existence of small business in a competitive economic system is in itself evidence of efficient small-business operation. If small firms were hopelessly inefficient and making no useful contribution, they would be forced out of business quickly by stronger competitors.

Additional evidence for the operating efficiency of small business is found in some studies of profitability. These studies compare small firms and large firms according to profits earned per dollar of assets. We expect highly efficient companies to earn higher profits than less efficient companies from dollars invested in plant, equipment, and inventory. And according to Table 2-2, small firms have significantly better earnings than larger firms.[13] In manufacturing, for example, the smallest firms earned 49 cents per dollar of assets, whereas the largest firms earned only 10 cents per dollar of assets. In fact, smaller companies have higher earnings in every industry group. Contrary to a common misconception, therefore, earnings per dollar of assets are inversely related to size of firm. This supports the conclusion that small business contributes in a special way to the economic welfare of our society.

LOOKING BACK

1. Many definitions of small business are necessarily arbitrary and differ according to purpose. Although there are exceptions, we generally think of a business as small when it has one or a small group of investors, operates in a geographically restricted area, is small compared to the biggest firms in the industry, and has fewer than 100 employees.
2. Size standards proposed by the Small Business Administration relate to eligibility for SBA loans and to considerations in bidding for government contracts.
3. Small firms operate in all industrial areas but are particularly dominant—in terms of number of employees on their payroll—in the fields of wholesale trade, contract construction, retail trade, and personal services.
4. The proportion of total business activity accounted for by small business ranges from 40% to 50%.
5. Small businesses make several unique contributions to our economy. They provide employment for millions of employees and play a special role in generating an unusually large share of new jobs needed for a growing labor force. They are responsible for introducing many innovations and originating such scientific breakthroughs as xerography and insulin. Small firms act as vigorous economic competitors to help our economy maintain a healthy state. The fact that small firms perform some business functions, such as distribution and supply, more expertly than large firms enables them to aid

---

13. For a discussion of small-firm profitability, including the rationale for including officer compensation in earnings, see Stahrl W. Edmunds, "Performance Measures for Small Businesses," *Harvard Business Review,* Vol. 57, No. 1 (January-February, 1979), pp. 172-176.

large firms in many ways. Small firms can also produce goods and services efficiently as evidenced by a study that shows how small firms compare to large firms when measured in terms of earnings per dollar of assets.

DISCUSSION QUESTIONS

1. In view of the numerous definitions of small business, how can you decide which definition is correct?
2. Of the businesses with which you are acquainted, which is the largest that you consider to be in the small-business category? Does it conform to the size standards used in this book?
3. On the basis of your acquaintance with small-business firms, give an example of a specific small firm in the field of transportation and other public utilities.
4. What generalizations can you make about the relative importance of large and small business in the United States?
5. In which sectors of the economy is small business most important? What accounts for its strength in these areas?
6. What special contribution is made by small business in providing jobs?
7. How can you explain the unique contributions of small business to product innovation?
8. In what way does small business serve as a bulwark of the capitalistic system?
9. If all small businesses could be merged into large firms in some way, what would be the impact on industrial efficiency and on our standard of living? Why?
10. What is shown by Table 2-2 about the apparent relative efficiency of large and small firms? What might account for the relatively large amount of earnings reported for the smallest firms in services?

REFERENCES TO SMALL BUSINESS IN ACTION

"DeLorean's Fantasy Can Be Your Reality (For a Dreamy Price)." *The Wall Street Journal*, May 22, 1981, p. 1.

A former GM executive, John Z. DeLorean, left GM to start his own company. He established a manufacturing plant in Northern Ireland, where the $25,000 DeLorean sports car is being produced.

"Enterprise Zones: Elixir for Blight?" *Nation's Business*, Vol. 69, No. 2 (February, 1981), pp. 56-58.

A proposed solution for urban blight and unemployment is the creation of urban enterprise zones. These zones would encourage the formation of small-business firms and the creation of jobs in depressed urban areas.

"Just a Different Glue." *Forbes*, Vol. 126, No. 11 (November 24, 1980), pp. 101-104.

Large corporations rejected a new invention—a lighter, cheaper support beam used in building construction. Then the inventor and a partner founded a business to produce it. The firm now has annual sales exceeding $100 million and earnings exceeding $7 million.

"New Issues: A New Gold and Silver Rush." *Venture*, Vol. 2, No. 12 (December, 1980), pp. 16-18.

Although big business is dominant in the mining industry, small firms are still thriving. This article describes a number of small gold and silver mining entrepreneurs who are using the public financial market to finance their ventures.

Smith, Lee. "The Cadillac Dealership That Became an El Dorado." *Fortune*, Vol. 99, No. 3 (February 12, 1979), pp. 124-130.

The Cadillac Division owned and operated two agencies in Manhattan in order to "maintain a presence" there. They performed poorly and showed huge losses. Then a veteran General Motors dealer took over the two dealerships and turned them into spectacular performers. The entrepreneur succeeded where the big corporation had failed.

CASE A-1

Construction Equipment Dealership*

Weighing a career with IBM against running the family business

As Professor Alan Stone talked on the telephone one day in the early 1980s, he watched his graduate assistant, Jerry Weston, shifting nervously in his chair. When Stone had completed his call, the following conversation with Jerry took place.

Professor: Sorry we were interrupted, Jerry! You said you have a problem. How can I help you?
Jerry: Dr. Stone, I'll be finishing my M. B. A. next month, and I still haven't been able to decide which job offer to accept. Two of the companies want answers next week, so I simply have to make some decisions.
Professor: Well, Jerry, you will have to make the final determination yourself, but we can certainly discuss the various alternatives. As a matter of curiosity, did any of the consulting work we did for IBM ever result in a job offer?
Jerry: Yes, sir! IBM has offered me a really intriguing project-planning job in their National Marketing Division in Atlanta at $27,800. I would have a lot of responsibility from the start, and I would be coordinating the efforts of personnel from several functional departments. If all went well, they have indicated I'd probably have a good chance to be the head of product development for the entire division. Of course, they would pay all moving expenses, and they really have a package of fringe benefits.
Professor: That sounds awfully good! What else do you have?
Jerry: Samsonite, Shell Development, and Boise Cascade. If my wife has her way, we'll go to San Francisco with Boise Cascade. My only question is, can two people live in San Francisco on $24,000 a year, particularly if one of them is my wife?
Professor: Say, what about the family business? Have you given up the idea of being the biggest construction equipment dealer in Billings, Montana?
Jerry: No, sir, not really! As a matter of fact, that is one of the complicating factors. I've been getting some pressure to go back to Billings.
Professor: How do you mean, Jerry?
Jerry: Well, I never really noticed how subtle Dad has been until I started thinking about it. As far as I can recall, he has never specifically said that he thought I should come into the business. But he always said that the opportunity was there if I wanted to take it. His classic statement is how good the business and Billings have been to the family, and I think it is fair to say he

*This case was prepared by John E. Schoen, Richards Equipment Company, Waco, TX.

influenced me to go to Iowa State, his alma mater, and even to major in accounting. My uncle, who is the accountant in our company, is retiring this year, and I see now that I was probably being prepared all along for that position.

Professor: Does your mother voice an opinion?

Jerry: Yes, sir! She voices more than an opinion! To give you an idea, the last time I talked to her about some of the job offers, she burst into tears and said that it would break my father's heart if I didn't join the business. She said they built the business for me and that they hadn't worked all those years to turn it over to some stranger. Since my uncle has to retire because of his health, she accused me of turning my back on Dad just when he needs me the most. By the time she finished, she had me feeling confused, miserable, and mad!

Professor: Mad?

Jerry: Yeah! Mom made some statements about Carol, my wife. Mom thinks Carol is trying to persuade me not to go back to Billings because it's too small and I'd be too close to the family. I suppose I wouldn't have been so angry if it hadn't been partially the truth!

Professor: You mean your wife doesn't want to go to Billings?

Jerry: Oh, I'm sure she'll go if that's what I decide to do, but I think she'd greatly prefer San Francisco. She is from Seattle and likes all the bright lights and activity in big cities. In addition, she has a degree in interior design and the opportunities for employment and learning would be greater in San Francisco than any of the other places, particularly Billings. She has worked to help put me through school the last two years, so I may owe this to her. She also believes it would be better for me to stand on my own two feet and asks why I went for an M. B. A. if all I was going to do was join the family business. She made me mad, too, last week when she said the worst thing she can imagine is being barefoot and pregnant and eating at my folks' house three times a week.

Professor: What about the Shell and the Samsonite offers?

Jerry: Oh, they're really just offers I've had. It is basically San Francisco, IBM, or home!

Professor: Well, Jerry, you do seem to have a problem. Can you compare the nature of the work in each job?

Jerry: Yes, sir! The IBM job looks very interesting, and the possibilities for advancement are good. Boise Cascade, on the other hand, has a typical cost accounting position. I suppose it would be all right for a couple of years while Carol does her thing and we see if we like San Francisco, but something else would have to come along eventually!

Professor: What about your work in the family business?

Jerry: That's the funny part of it! Everything about the IBM offer — the salary, fringes, authority, prestige, promotion possibilities, and so forth — appeals to me, but I like the family business, too. I mean I've grown up in the business; I know and like the employees, customers, and suppliers; and I really like

Billings. Of course, I'd be working as an accountant for awhile; but I would eventually succeed my father, and I've always thought I'd like to run the business someday.

Professor: What about salary in the family business?

Jerry: That's a part I've forgotten to tell you! Last week, my uncle was in town, and even he was dropping broad hints about the family looking forward to our return to Billings and how he will give me a short orientation and then "get the heck outa Dodge." His parting comment was that he was certain Dad would match anything the big companies could do on starting salary.

Professor: Even $27,800?

Jerry: Apparently! Well, there it is, Dr. Stone! What do you think? I've got to let IBM know by the end of the month.

Professor: I don't know, Jerry. Could you go with IBM or Boise Cascade for a couple of years and then go back to the family business?

Jerry: I thought of that possibility, but I think that if I'm going to go with the family business, this is the right time. Uncle Phil is retiring, so there is a position; and I know Dad was a little hesitant about the M. B. A. versus getting experience in the family business. Dad is approaching 60, and the business is hitting all-time highs, so I believe he will try to sell it if I go somewhere else. No, I think it's now or never!

Professor: Well, you were right about one thing, Jerry. You do have a dilemma! This reminds me of the cases in management textbooks—no easy solution! Good luck, and let me know your decision.

Jerry: Thanks, Prof!

Questions

1. Does Jerry Weston have an obligation to the family to provide leadership for the family business?
2. What obligation does Jerry have to his wife in view of her background, education, and career interests?
3. Should Jerry simply do what he wants to do? Does he know what he wants to do?
4. In view of the conflict between Jerry's own interests and those of his wife, what should his career choice be?

CASE A-2

Frost Jewelry Store

Can the smallest jewelry store in a large shopping mall survive?

The Monday morning coffee break during football season is a popular time for college professors to gather in faculty lounges for "Monday morning quarterbacking." On one particular occasion, Professor Charles Morris, a long-time marketing professor, was visiting with Professor Mike Agee who was recently employed to teach accounting. After Saturday's game had been replayed, Charles learned that Mike and his wife Jean operated a business. Charles was interested in the small-business area and began to inquire into their business experiences. The ensuing conversation ran as follows:

Mike: My wife Jean and I operate a very small jewelry store in Fort Collins, Colorado. It's located in the city's biggest mall. It occupies a very small space—only about 450 square feet.
Charles: How did you get into that particular business?
Mike: I saw a little ad in the newspaper one day. I was teaching accounting in Fort Collins at the time. I had been looking for something—kind of wanted to see if I could make a profit. The ad didn't name the business. After answering the ad, I learned where it was and recognized the store name—Frost Jewelry Store.
Charles: I don't believe I've heard of that name.
Mike: It started out as a franchise. It seems the franchisor owners lost interest and got into some other things, but they still have the lease on the mall space. I have a sublease with them. However, I am not operating as a franchise, and my contract with them gives me control over renewing the lease.
Charles: How did you finally decide to make the purchase?
Mike: Let me give you a little more background. The previous owner who ran the ad wanted to leave Fort Collins and go back home to Louisiana. Also, his wife was not in very good health. He was the sole owner. I knew his accountant and, with the owner's permission of course, got three years' sales figures on the business. Sales in the past year (1979) had dipped considerably from the previous years. The accountant was sure that the owner had been skimming (not reporting cash income). In fact, the owner had actually told us he was skimming. We figured about $15,000 in cash had been taken in the last part of the year. When we compared the last-quarter figures of 1979 with those for 1977 and 1978, it was pretty obvious.
Charles: Did this almost scare you away from the deal?
Mike: No, not really. We certainly planned to operate the business honestly, and other factors made the deal look good. David Jones, a friend of mine, and

his wife decided to join Jean and me in buying the business as a partnership. The financing was no problem. We went to the bank which had the loan with the previous owner. We took over during the last week of March, 1980.

Charles: Tell me more about the store.
Mike: My wife's first impression of the store was that it had junk. She never went in there. It was just sort of a cheapie earring-type place. She was a little bit surprised when we did go in and look at it and saw the amount of 14-karat gold stuff they had. We, of course, bought his inventory. We have changed the inventory mix and gotten much more costume jewelry and much lower-priced merchandise. Currently costume jewelry accounts for about 50 percent of our sales. We also sell gift items such as belt buckles, plastic trays, combs, hairbrushes, and mirrors. Most of these items can be personalized, which we send out to have done. Gift items probably account for 30 percent of our business. Most of our jewelry and gift items are relatively inexpensive. We do have some 14-karat gold items that run up to $60. These sell to customers who go to May D&F, a department store, and stop and shop with us. However, most of our customers tend to be of the lower middle class. Also, we still do ear piercing. In fact, it accounts for almost 20 percent of our business. It's the number-one place in the county for ear piercing. We have days where we've done as high as 40 on a Saturday. You get all kinds—we've had a few guys, too.

Charles: Does your store have a good location in the mall?
Mike: The ad said this was the best location in the mall. And that's probably true. You go in the main entrance, then you go straight back; there's a fountain and a May D&F store, which is a fine department store. We are next to May D&F on the corner, with an entrance open from two sides. On the other corner is Flowerama, a shop which sells live plants.

Charles: How is the partnership working out?
Mike: I forgot to mention it's no longer a partnership. A partnership is just not like owning your own business. We were leaving Fort Collins to come here, and so we all decided to sell. Toward the end of 1980, we put the store up for sale. We had a number of people talk to us about it. One party seemed to be pretty serious about it and asked us to try to clarify the lease arrangement. This person wanted to be sure she wouldn't have any problem renewing the lease in three years when it expires. My partner sent a letter asking the property managers, located in Boston, to give us some encouragement. The reply was a little upsetting to us.

Charles: What was in the letter?
Mike: It referred to a decrease in sales from 1979 to 1980 but overlooked the fact that we generated $80,000 in the 9 months and 1 week of 1980 that we were owners. If the previous owner had been up to par for the first 2 months and 3 weeks, we probably would have had an increase over 1979. Also, we have spent a considerable amount of money on the appearance of the store with new paint, carpet, and display cases. We have had some new signs and

different things made, and we got a lot of favorable comments from people, including the manager of the mall. I don't believe the property managers looked at anything but the computer printout showing sales and the square footage of the store. I've heard some of the mall people say they would like to see a franchise store selling nuts in my location. A store like that would probably make more revenue per square foot. I suspect that, at the end of the lease, people will be after that space. I'll show you a copy of the letter sometime.
(*Editor's note*: See Figure A-1 for a copy of this letter.)

March 4, 1981

Dear Mr. Agee

We received your letter of February 23 asking for an extension of your lease for the purpose of making a sale of the business. This is a most unusual request at this time, but we do understand your concern.

We have, therefore, reviewed the sales performance of this store so that we can make some kind of sensible decision. In doing so, we have discovered that, for the calendar year 1980, the store produced approximately $90,000 in volume, which was a decrease of 1.6% from the previous year. You should be aware that there was a general overall increase in the mall during that calendar year. Further, in the category of jewelry, you have the smallest store which has the lowest sales per square foot of all the stores in the category. Normally the smallest store would have the highest sales per square foot.

The general appearance of the store does not seem to fit the standard of better costume jewelry stores that we have seen in various parts of the country. Based on these assessments, there does not seem to be any reason for us to extend the lease as per your request. It seems to us that both Landlord and Tenant should seriously consider whether this is the proper use for this space.

Very truly yours

Property Managers
Fort Collins Mall

Figure A-1 Letter Received from the Mall's Property Managers

Charles: How are lease payments arranged?
Mike: There is a minimum monthly rent paid to the mall, and I cannot remember exactly what it is. It's either the minimum or 8 percent of sales. Now, this means that we have to sell about $96,000 a year, or close to that, before we have to pay more than the minimum. There are some additional bills, such as utilities and taxes, which are prorated to tenants based on their square footage. Anyway, to make a long story short, Jean and I decided to keep the store. So, we made an offer to our partners and they accepted.
Charles: What are you going to do about the lease when the time comes for renewal?
Mike: A very good question!

Questions

1. Assess the bargaining position of Professor Mike Agee in dealing with the property management firm. How does the smallness of the store affect its bargaining power?
2. How would you respond to the property managers' criticisms regarding decreased sales volume and low sales per square foot? Is it too early for Professor Agee to worry about the lease?
3. What alternatives are available to Professor Agee if he cannot obtain a lease extension? Evaluate the alternatives you have suggested.
4. Of what significance is the jewelry store's location next to the May D&F department store?
5. What is the nature of "skimming" as described by Professor Agee? What are its implications in assessing the health of this business and its prospects for the future?

Part B

STARTING THE SMALL BUSINESS

Chapter 3 Creating a New Venture or Buying an Existing Business

Chapter 4 Franchising

Chapter 5 Analyzing the Market

Chapter 6 Selecting a Location and Physical Facilities

Chapter 7 Initial Financial Planning

Chapter 8 Choosing the Legal Form of Organization

Chapter 3

Creating a New Venture or Buying an Existing Business

LOOKING AHEAD

Watch for the following important topics:

1. Sources of ideas for creating new ventures.
2. Benefits of preparing a written new-venture plan.
3. Reasons for buying an existing business.
4. Investigation and evaluation of a business being considered for purchase.
5. Calculation of the value of a business based on its net income.

People become entrepreneurs by launching entirely new businesses, by purchasing existing firms, or by acquiring franchised outlets. In this chapter we will emphasize the analysis and the planning that are needed when creating a new venture or when buying an existing business. Since we will treat franchising as a special route to entrepreneurship, Chapter 4 is devoted to that topic. However, the planning process in creating a new venture is comparable to that required in opening a new franchised outlet. If the entrepreneur is taking over an existing franchise, the planning process is comparable to that required in buying an existing business.

CREATING A NEW VENTURE

For various reasons, some entrepreneurs prefer to start new ventures rather than to buy existing firms. These reasons include the following:

1. The entrepreneur has developed a new product or service that necessitates a new type of business.
2. The entrepreneur can select what he or she considers to be the ideal location, equipment, products or services, employees, suppliers, and bankers.
3. The entrepreneur can avoid undesirable precedents, policies, procedures, and legal commitments of existing firms.

Regardless of the reason involved, the would-be entrepreneur should ask the following questions before deciding to implement the venture concept: Have I found a genuine business opportunity? What sources of new-venture ideas are available? Have I refined the idea? Do I have the necessary education and experience for this type of venture?

Find a Genuine Business Opportunity

The various types of opportunities portrayed in Figure 3-1 may be visualized as alternative routes to successful new-business ventures. Note that the opportunity may involve an entirely new product or service. More frequently, however, the opportunity involves a market not adequately served by existing businesses.

Whatever type of business opportunity is involved, it must be genuine. This means that the new business must have some type of advantage that will provide a competitive edge. This special edge is necessary because the marketplace generally does not welcome a new competitor. As Karl Vesper has pointed out, the newcomer needs an "entry wedge."[1] The prospective entrepreneur must visualize some new product or service or location or "angle" that will not only "get the foot in the door" but keep it there.

Some apparent opportunities are insufficient for the long-term success of a new venture. For example, an influx of population during the construction of a large power plant or dam may provide a sizable market now but an inadequate market later, because of the population decline when construction is completed. Of course, in this situation one could purposely go into business—for instance, a mobile food service that provides hot meals on site—with plans for temporary operation, large profits, and closure or relocation when the "boom" is over.

---

1. Karl H. Vesper, *New Venture Strategies* (Englewood Cliffs, NJ: Prentice-Hall, Inc., 1980), p. 176.

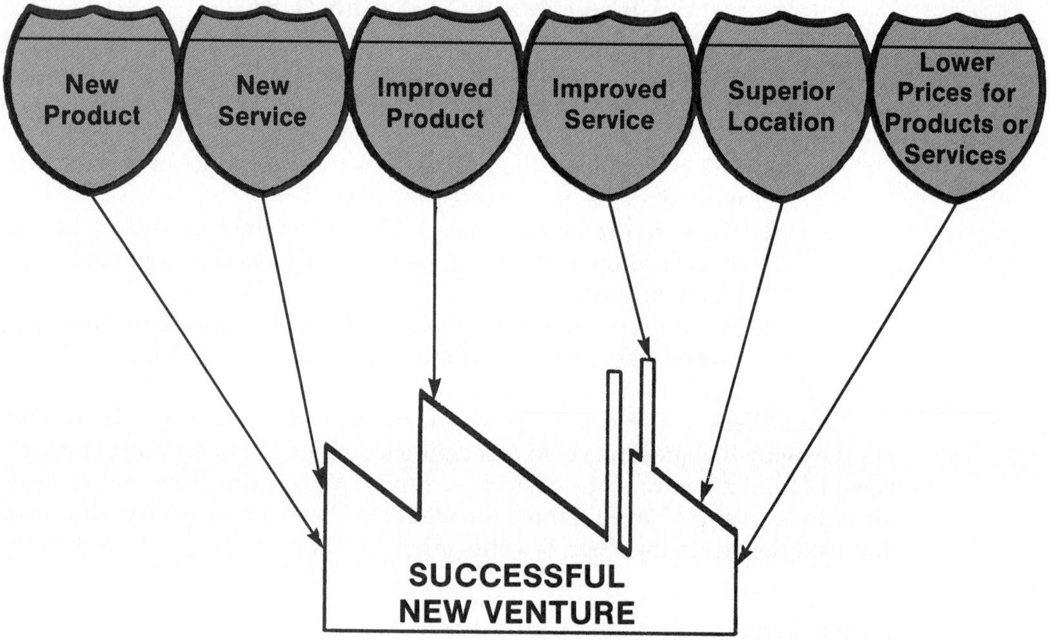

Figure 3-1 Routes to New-Business Ventures

Identify Sources of New-Venture Ideas

Since the new venture starts with an idea, let's consider the circumstances which tend to spawn such new ideas. Some of the numerous possibilities discussed below are: work experience, invention of a new product, hobbies, accidental discovery, and deliberate search.

Work Experience. A basis for new-venture ideas to many entrepreneurs is their work experience. From the knowledge of their present or recent jobs, they see possibilities in modifying an existing product, improving a service, or duplicating a business concept in a different location. For example, a furniture salesperson may see the possibility of opening a new furniture store in a different area of the city. The new store may follow the business strategy of the existing store, or it may feature different or restricted or expanded lines of merchandise. It may also adopt credit or delivery policies which are more appealing to customers in that area.

Work experience may well be the most productive of all venture-idea sources. After studying the histories of approximately 100 highly successful entrepreneurs, Karl Vesper summarized his findings as follows:

> The pattern of close connection between prior work and new-venture ideas was common to a large majority of the successful start-ups—between 60% and 90%, depending on the industry—the correlation being highest in advanced technology areas like computers and medical instruments and lowest in enterprises of a relatively unspecialized nature such as nursing homes, fast-food franchises, and other consumer-oriented businesses.[2]

Invention of a New Product. Another idea which can grow into a business involves the invention of a new product. The entrepreneur may invent a product or acquire an invention from the original inventor. An invention may be acquired, for example, by consulting General Electric Company's publication called *New Product/New Business Digest*. This publication describes over 500 products and processes that are available for acquisition or licensing.[3] One advertisement in this publication tells the reader, "You may find the *one* product you need to start your own business."

ACTION REPORT: New Business Idea from the College Classroom

The idea for one of the biggest and most successful start-ups in recent years, Federal Express Corporation, originated in a college classroom. Frederick Wallace Smith wrote a paper for an economics class at Yale, advocating a new system for handling airfreight. His idea ran contrary to conventional theory, which considered airfreight to be a sideline of passenger service, and Smith's paper received a low grade. After a tour of military service in Vietnam, Smith raised the necessary venture capital and started the all-freight airline. Beginning in 1973, the new company flew primarily at night, bringing all freight to a central point (Memphis) and then dispersing it to its ultimate destination. By 1980, revenues hit $415 million; operating profits, $90 million.

Source: "Breathing Under Water," *Forbes,* Vol. 119 (March 1, 1977), pp. 36-38; and *Standard & Poor's Register of Corporations, Directors, and Executives* (New York: Standard & Poor's Corporation, 1981), I.

Hobbies. Sometimes hobbies grow beyond their stature as hobbies to become businesses. For example, a coin collector who buys and sells coins to build a personal collection may easily become a coin dealer. Recall the story of Polly Reilly, related in Chapter 1, whose artwork evolved into a successful business venture.

---

2. Karl H. Vesper, "New-Venture Ideas: Do Not Overlook the Experience Factor," *Harvard Business Review*, Vol. 57, No. 4 (July-August, 1979), p. 165.
3. See, for example, *Venture*, Vol. 3, No. 2 (February, 1981), p. 76.

Accidental Discovery. As a source of new-venture ideas, accidental discovery involves something we call **serendipity**—the faculty for making desirable discoveries by accident. Any person may stumble across a useful idea in the ordinary course of day-to-day living. This was true of Jim and Betty Smulian whose search for lighting fixtures, recounted below, led to the creation of their own business, Trimble House, in Atlanta, GA.

> When Betty Smulian was redecorating her home in Atlanta, she began shopping around for a candle chandelier. None of the stores had exactly what she wanted. Neither did the catalogs featuring specialty lighting items.
>
> Most homeowners would have given up at that point and settled for a conventional chandelier. But Betty, a design engineer, created her own fixture. And her husband, Jim, a mechanical engineer, fabricated the fixture in their basement, using Betty's precise design drawing.
>
> When friends and neighbors saw the chandelier, they oohed and aahed. They each wanted one of their own. And so a multimillion-dollar lighting fixture business was born about 20 years ago.[4]

Deliberate Search. A new business may also emerge from a prospective entrepreneur's **deliberate search**—a purposeful exploration to find a new-venture idea. M. L. Gimpl suggests two approaches to this search: an inside-out approach and an outside-in approach. When an **inside-out approach** is used, entrepreneurs first survey their own capabilities and then look at the new products or services they are capable of producing. When entrepreneurs follow an **outside-in approach**, they first look for needs in the marketplace and then relate those needs to their own existing or potential capabilities.[5]

The outside-in (or market first) thinking has apparently produced more successful ventures, especially in the field of consumer goods and services. To explore the marketplace, prospective entrepreneurs can reflect upon the changing life-styles and markets in the world around them and then talk to consumers, salespersons, attorneys, engineers, business owners, and so on, who may provide ideas. One entrepreneur's deliberate search for ideas is described as follows:

> A different view about whom best to contact was adopted by another entrepreneur who decided to make the rounds of purchasing agents, whom he asked about what things they found hard to obtain. This way he identified a particular product, the electronic delay line, and was able to form a company that produced it and made him wealthy.[6]

---

4. "The Entrepreneurs: For Want of a Lamp . . . a Flourishing Firm," *Nation's Business*, Vol. 69, No. 3 (March, 1981), p. 18.

5. M. L. Gimpl, "Obtaining Ideas for New Products and Ventures," *Journal of Small Business Management*, Vol. 16, No. 4 (October, 1978), pp. 21-26.

6. Vesper, *New Venture Strategies*, *op. cit.*, p. 138.

ACTION REPORT: Students Launch New Ventures

Students frequently develop ideas for new ventures and implement them while they are still pursuing their degrees. Three such student ventures are described below.

Scott Burns, a business student, noticed that many parking lots in front of Waco stores needed cleaning. So, he bought a mechanical sweeping machine and contracted with store owners to provide such a service. "Wherever there is a parking lot, there's a potential market," he says. His business prospered, and he acquired customers not only in Waco but also in other nearby cities.

Another business student, Karen Adams, founded Baylor Balloons with a friend, using the slogan "Flowers are nice, but balloons are fun." They delivered bouquets of balloons to customers in the university area. Karen later became sole owner of the business and eventually sold it as a flourishing concern.

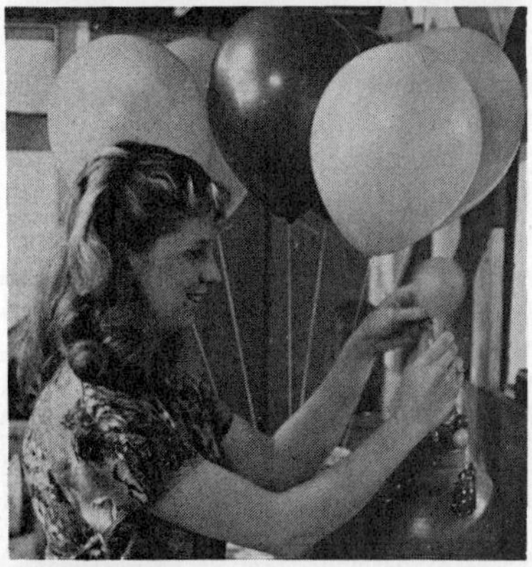

Brent Pennington designed a safety switch which automatically cuts off a home cooling and heating system in the event of a fire. A fusible link in the device melts when the house temperature reaches a certain level. Brent assembled the switches in his apartment and was hard-pressed to meet the demand from builders and electrical contractors!

Source: Adapted from Alan Hunt, "Practicing Private Enterprise . . . Baylor Style," *Baylor University Report,* Vol. 1, No. 32 (April 17, 1981), pp. 2-3.

A deliberate search also helps in a general way by stimulating a readiness of mind. If a prospective entrepreneur thinks seriously about new-business ideas, he or she will be more receptive to new ideas from any source.

Since a truly creative person may find useful ideas in many different ways, the sources of new-venture ideas mentioned above are suggestive, not exhaustive. We encourage you to seek and reflect upon new-venture ideas in whatever circumstance you find yourself.

Refine a New-Venture Idea

A new-venture idea often requires an extended period of time for refinement and testing. This is particularly true for original inventions which necessitate developmental work to make them operational. Consider, for example, the three-dimensional camera (mentioned in Chapter 2) which the Timex Corporation agreed to produce for Nimslo Technology in 1980. Actually, almost ten years had elapsed since Jerry C. Nims and Allen Lo had started laboratory work on this three-dimensional camera, as evidenced by the following account:

> In late 1970, the partners leased a bankrupt factory in Hong Kong, buying the equipment to help speed up their R&D phase and to begin making prototypes from their blueprints.
>
> Nims and Lo recruited and trained a team of 10 Chinese researchers (all of whom moved with Nimslo to Atlanta in 1972 to continue research). The next eight years were spent in what Nims calls "the perspiration school of invention rather than the inspiration school."
>
> The entrepreneur concedes that although he expected a long haul, "We thought we could accomplish our goals much sooner." The technology proved much more complex than anticipated. "Remember the Manichean devil in philosophy? You can't beat him in chess because he changes the rules every time you sit down to play. I thought we were in that situation sometimes. And we finally had to decide if we should go on. Our decision was to bang away until they carried us out feet first."
>
> In 1978, a viable product had passed from the drawing board to the prototype stage, and Nimslo was ready to line up backers to produce the camera.[7]

Even low-technology business ideas may require extended study and modification. Indeed, entrepreneurs must refine their venture ideas to some extent as they prepare the venture plans discussed later in this chapter.

Evaluate Your Education and Experience

A successful start-up calls not only for a sound business idea, but also for some minimum amount of entrepreneurial education and experience. Even

7. "3-D Camera Odyssey in the Home Stretch," *Venture*, Vol. 2, No. 10 (October, 1980), p. 78.

so, it is impossible to prescribe exacting requirements. Fabulously successful exceptions will always exist.

It is a matter of record, however, that many business failures are the result of *avoidable* inadequacies on the part of the entrepreneur. In a study of manufacturing failures, William Hoad and Peter Rosko discovered that deficiencies in education and experience were associated with those failures. Of 36 entrepreneurs who failed, 11 were deficient in education, 11 in experience, and 11 in both. Only three of the failing entrepreneurs possessed the appropriate combination of training and experience.[8]

Incompetence, a cause of many failures, frequently reflects inadequate educational preparation. Today a high school education is a virtual necessity for business ownership. A college education with graduate study in business might be recommended as the ideal academic preparation.

Academic education is no substitute for experience, however. Lack of experience in the industry, lack of managerial experience, and lack of general experience in production, marketing, and finance are all common causes of failure. Naturally the length of desirable experience varies from one type of enterprise and/or person to another. Individuals contemplating a business of their own typically do well to consider several years of employment in a similar business. Preferably this experience should be such as to bring them into contact with the full range of activities and problems associated with the given type of business.

We must temper our remarks about entrepreneurial qualifications by recognizing that the necessary blend of education and experience varies with the nature of the business. This is apparent in the Vesper study cited in Footnote 2 on page 53. Vesper found that nearly all entrepreneurs involved in starting successful high-technology companies had earned one or more college degrees, while most entrepreneurs who started successful machining businesses had worked in machine shops but not attended college.[9]

Implement the Venture Concept

Much work is required—some of it tedious, much of it exciting—to go from the idea stage to the operation stage. The effort expended during this preoperating period is extremely important in laying the foundation for a successful start-up. In spite of its importance, however, for various reasons beginning entrepreneurs tend to neglect the preliminary investigation and related work. Some of the most common reasons are:

---

8. William M. Hoad and Peter Rosko, *Management Factors Contribute to the Success or Failure of New Small Manufacturers*, Michigan Business Report No. 44 (Ann Arbor: Bureau of Business Research, Graduate School of Business Administration, University of Michigan, 1964), Table 47. An entrepreneur with more than five years' experience as owner-manager or manager of the same or a similar kind of business was classified as "experienced." An entrepreneur with formal education of one or more years beyond high school was classified as "educated."

9. Vesper, "New-Venture Ideas," *loc. cit.*

1. An impatience to get started.
2. Insufficient funds to carry on expensive market studies or even much personal observation.
3. Lack of training and skill to conduct an adequate feasibility study.

To improve prospects for a successful start-up, a prospective entrepreneur should personally undertake a series of steps to analyze and plan the venture. These steps deserve extensive explanation, and the next five chapters are devoted to that purpose. The steps and the related chapters are:

1. Evaluate the franchise opportunity if the new venture entails a franchise arrangement. (Chapter 4)
2. Analyze the market for the new product or service. (Chapter 5)
3. Select a suitable location and physical facilities. (Chapter 6)
4. Determine financial needs and locate sources of financing. (Chapter 7)
5. Select the most appropriate legal form of organization. (Chapter 8)

Careful attention to these steps will help the prospective entrepreneur avoid a downhill path which leads from wild enthusiasm to disillusionment to failure. All of this preliminary work and investigation should be incorporated into the new-venture plan.

PREPARING A NEW-VENTURE PLAN

As part of the preparation for launching a new venture, the prospective entrepreneur should prepare a written business plan. This plan describes the new-venture idea and projects the marketing, operational, and financial aspects of the proposed business for the first three to five years. Although we will explain the new-venture planning process and present an outline for a business plan in this chapter, we wish to make it clear that you should use the ideas in Chapters 4 through 8 when preparing such a plan.

Benefits of Preparing a Written Plan

Any activity that is initiated without adequate preparation tends to be haphazard and unsuccessful. This is particularly true of such a complex process as initiating a new business. Although planning is a mental process, it must go beyond the realm of thought. Thinking about a proposed business becomes more rigorous as rough ideas must be crystallized and quantified on paper. The written plan is essential to assure the systematic coverage of all important features of the new business.

One benefit derived from preparing a formal written plan is the discipline provided for the prospective entrepreneur. For example, in order to prepare a written statement about marketing strategy, the prospective entrepreneur must perform some market research. Likewise, a study of financing requirements is necessary. In commenting on a venture which never quite succeeded, Ted Harwood stressed the crucial importance of the written business plan as follows:

> It [the business plan] forces a useful discipline in thinking about how each stage of the venture will proceed and especially about how to anticipate expenditures and revenues month by month. Even with a good product, unanticipated negative cash balances can kill a venture despite the fact that orders are coming in and sales growing.[10]

Thus, preparing a written plan forces the prospective entrepreneur to exercise the discipline that good managers must possess.

Another benefit of the written plan is that it may be used by the new entrepreneur as an initial operating plan. The written new-venture plan provides direction for the early decisions to be made, and it establishes standards for evaluating business performance during the early months of operation.

Perhaps an even more important benefit of the written new-venture plan lies in its use by outside parties. Practically every new entrepreneur faces the

ACTION REPORT: Venture Capitalist Comments on New-Venture Plan

Citicorp Venture Capital, Ltd., is an investment company which invests risk capital in new ventures. Its president, Rick Roesch (a University of California MBA), was asked what might improve the chances of an applicant for new-business financing. His answer stressed the importance of a well-thought-out, persuasive, *written* business plan:

> The most successful entrepreneurs have thought through their business plans. They know their strengths and weaknesses. They know what the competition is offering. . . . The entrepreneur is doing himself a disservice to think he can go in eye-to-eye with a prospective investor and simply sell his company. It's safe to say that if it is not on paper, it is not well enough thought out for a venture capitalist to consider it.

Source: Sam Adams, "What a Venture Capitalist Looks For," *MBA*, Vol. 7 (June-July, 1973), p. 9.

---

10. Ted Harwood, "A Venture Is Not a Game," *In Business*, Vol. 2 (November-December, 1980), p. 45.

task of raising financial resources to supplement personal savings. Unless the entrepreneur has relatives who will supply funds, he or she must appeal to prospective investors, bankers, the Small Business Administration, or other outsiders. Such parties will typically want to review the new-business plan before participating in the new venture. Chapter 7 discusses the financial aspects of new-venture planning in some detail.

Tendency to Neglect Initial Planning

Some prospective entrepreneurs tend to neglect the planning stage of a new venture. They are eager to get started, and they do not always realize the importance of a written plan. Of course, sometimes they are forced to engage in a minimum of planning in order to gain a hearing from venture capitalists—the potential investors in their business.

The neglect of initial planning is evident from a study by G. M. Naidu of business start-ups in Wisconsin.[11] For example, Naidu found that:

1. 63 percent of the new entrepreneurs did not evaluate the location of the business.
2. 72 percent did not conduct a trade-area analysis.
3. 52 percent did not evaluate their competition.
4. Almost 25 percent did not even estimate revenues and expenses.

Failure to prepare an initial written plan for a new venture undoubtedly contributes to the early failure of some firms.

Content of the New-Venture Plan

A prospective entrepreneur needs a guide for the preparation of a new-venture plan. Figure 3-2 presents such a guide. It outlines the type of information that should be included in a business plan and suggests a pattern for organizing the material.[12]

---

11. G. M. Naidu, "Problems and Perceptions of Emerging Businesses in Wisconsin: Some Implications," a paper presented at the International Council for Small Business Conference, Western Carolina University, Cullowhee, NC, June, 1978.

12. For other examples of planning outlines, see Jeffry A. Timmons, "A Business Plan Is More Than a Financing Device," *Harvard Business Review*, Vol. 58, No. 2 (March-April, 1980), p. 34; William L. Brockhaus, "How to Develop a Plan for Securing Venture Capital," *Business Horizons*, Vol. 19 (June, 1976), pp. 285-286; Bank of America, "Financing Small Business," *Small Business Reporter,* Vol. 14 (1980), p. 19; Gordon B. Baty, *Entrepreneurship for the Eighties* (Reston, VA: Reston Publishing Company, Inc., 1981), Chapter 11; and Donald M. Dible (ed.), *Winning the Money Game* (Santa Clara, CA: Entrepreneur Press, 1975), Chapter 5.

I. INTRODUCTION
   A. General statement of purpose and objectives
   B. Overview of the industry

II. PRODUCTS/SERVICES
   A. Description
   B. Proprietary features
   C. Patent or copyright protection
   D. Quality level
   E. Breadth of product line

III. MARKET RESEARCH
   A. Description of market to be served
   B. Market size and segments
   C. Market trends
   D. Customers – type and locations
   E. Competition – strengths and weaknesses
   F. Sales forecast

IV. MARKETING PLAN
   A. Overall marketing strategy
   B. Channels of distribution
   C. Personal selling
   D. Advertising and promotion
   E. Pricing
   F. Service and warranty policies

V. OPERATIONS
   A. Location
   B. Facilities
   C. Raw materials
   D. Inventory control
   E. Quality control
   F. Production control
   G. Staffing
   H. Research and development

VI. ORGANIZATION AND MANAGEMENT
   A. Legal form of organization
   B. Managerial organization – roles and relationships
   C. Key management personnel
   D. Management compensation and ownership
   E. Board of directors
   F. Outside professional services

VII. FINANCIAL PLAN
   A. Initial financial requirements
   B. Profit-and-loss forecast
   C. Cash-flow forecast
   D. Break-even analysis
   E. Projected source of funds
   F. Projected balance sheet
   G. Ownership interests
   H. Risks and contingency plans

Figure 3-2 Outline for Preparing a Business Plan

BUYING AN EXISTING BUSINESS

For logical reasons some would-be entrepreneurs choose to buy an existing business rather than create a new venture. We will first discuss the nature of such reasons and then explain the various activities that should be undertaken before closing the deal on an existing business.

Reasons for Buying an Existing Business

One reason for buying an existing business is that it reduces the uncertainties involved in launching an entirely new venture. A successful going concern has demonstrated an ability to attract customers, to control costs, and to make a profit. Although future operations may be different, the firm's past record shows what it can do under actual market conditions. For example, the satisfactory location of a going concern eliminates one major uncertainty. Although traffic counts are useful in assessing the potential value of a location, the acid test comes when a business opens its doors at that location. And this test has already been met in the case of an existing firm, with the results available in the form of sales and profit data.

Another reason is that the buyer of an existing business typically acquires its personnel, inventories, physical facilities, established banking connections, and ongoing relationships with trade suppliers. Consider the time and effort otherwise required in acquiring them "from scratch." Of course, this situation is an advantage only under certain conditions. For example, the firm's skilled, experienced employees constitute a valuable asset only if they will continue to work for the new owner. The physical facilities must not be obsolete, and the relationships with banks and suppliers must be healthy.

Still another reason is that a going business may become available at what seems to be a low price. Whether it is actually a "good buy" must be determined by the prospective new owner. The price may appear low, but several factors could make the "bargain price" anything but a bargain. For example, the business may be losing money; the location may be deteriorating; or the seller may intend to reopen another business as a competitor. However, the business may indeed be a bargain and turn out to be a wise investment.

Find a Business to Buy

Frequently in the course of day-to-day living and business contacts, a would-be buyer comes across an opportunity to buy an existing business. For example, a sales representative for a manufacturer or a wholesaler may be offered an opportunity to buy a customer's retail business. In other cases, the would-be buyer may need to search for a business to buy. Advertisements in local newspapers and *The Wall Street Journal* provide some leads. Figure 3-3 shows an example of business opportunity ads in *The Wall Street Journal*.

Other sources of business leads include suppliers, distributors, trade associations, and even bankers, who may know of business firms available for purchase. In addition, realtors—particularly those who specialize in the sale of business firms and business properties—can also provide leads. Moreover, these realtors, or brokers, can assist in closing the transaction. Naturally the buyer would wish to deal with a reputable broker and be aware of a broker's motivations in making the sale.

BUSINESS OPPORTUNITIES

INVESTOR(S) MERGER-ACQUISITION

Milwaukee Area Distributor and Manufacturer seeks Executive Investor(s) with manufacturing and/or marketing background to purchase interest in company. We have two new capital equipment products (Patents Applied For) developed and ready for marketing worldwide to Governmental Units and Contractors for maintenance of Highways, Streets and Parking Lots. $350,000.00 required. Anticipated growth will required additional capital in near future or sale of business. Non active investors should inquire. Merger with or acquisition by qualified company will be considered now.

Box ME-838, Wall Street Journal

FOR SALE

Roseville, Michigan; Mr. Bo Jingles Restaurant and Lounge. Lots of leaded stained glass. Casa Blanca fanlites and tiffany lamps enhance the decor of this Restaurant/Lounge. Gazebo style booths surround a fireplace with stained glass above. Seating for 200, parking for 100 cars. Two bars. Heavy traffic area. Near Lake St. Clair, easily accessible to major freeways. 4 yr old building built by energy conscious owner. Building, business, equipment, $500,000 with $150,000 down. **Call Paul Buscemi Mon-Fri 9-5 (313) 296-5560.**

RETIRE FROM THE RATRACE

$160,000. will buy you a resort in Ark. Ozark Mts. It's interesting work, and as easy or involved as YOU want to make it. Spring, summer, fall tourists, fishermen keep you busy, but in winter you have time to relax, plan, build, or travel. Write

PO Box 140, Mt. Home, AR 72653, or call 1-501-467-5277.

TAX SHELTER

$3,987 down payment now provides $24K write-off for '81 & '82 in proven medical equipment leasing program.

CALL: **BAY AREA (415) 836-4700**
CALIF. (800) 772-2672
U.S. (800) 227-2276

NURSING HOMES

If you are interested in selling your facility, contact me at once. Confidentiality assured. **TERRY SULLIVAN, RESOURCE DEVELOPMENT DIVISION, YAMPOL & ASSOCIATES (312) 743-6400**

FOR SALE

Recently completed retail store in prestigious North Chicago Suburban Shopping Center now available. A turnkey operation for high quality line of soaps, toiletries and comestibles. $100 M + range.

Box ME-870, The Wall Street Journal

ACQUISITION WANTED

(1) Sewn product manufacturer
(2) Cut and sew operator
(3) Outer wear manufacturer
(4) Jacket manufacturer – large or small

If you fit any of the above descriptions, and are for sale, reply to:
Box ME-724, The Wall Street Journal

INVESTORS FOR CASINOS AND PROPERTY IN ATLANTIC CITY

Currently operating. Principals only.

(412) 344-4751

KRON franchises are available in select areas. If interested, contact **KRON CHOCOLATIER INC, 419 Park Avenue South, NYC 10016 (212) 686-2001.** This offering is by prospectus only.

Maintain your Capitol Hill, Washington, DC business/personal address for as little as $6.50 per month. Also desk space available. **Capitol Hill Mail & Telephone Message Center (202) 546-2326.**

Hundreds of businesses for sale by owners and agents listed each issue. 1 issue-$4.50 (2 month trial-$12.) Satis. guaranteed. **National Business Opportunities Journal, 5037 Newport Ave. Dept. 485, San Diego, CA 92107. 800-854-6570 (800-532-3928 in CA).**

MAIL ORDER CO. FOR SALE

Sells wood kit furniture and clocks. Sales 1.5 Mill. 300k name list. Buy assets only 400k required.

312/346-5265 weekdays.

TO BUY OR SELL

a business, property, home or investment for tax shelter in Florida, call **(305) 968-8300 or eves, Bob Eaton Assoc. 793-5027. Abbington International Realty**

Retail Photofinishing Stores located in downtown East Coast major market. 1982 gross sales est. at $4.2 million. Price $4 million. $2 million cash req. Prin. only.

Box ME-799, The Wall Street Journal

CLEAN CORPORATE SHELLS FOR SALE

T. Lowe 3267 Wolfson Drive
Baldwin Harbor, NY 11510

OFF SHORE BANK
For Sale—$31,500
TPIA (806) 358-3443

NEW BUSINESS OFFERINGS

JOINT VENTURE

250 Billion Dollar Industry

Become a Business & Financial Consultant

As part of the #1 COMPUTERIZED NATIONWIDE NETWORK listing buyers and sellers of businesses throughout the U.S. Clients come to your office and by pushing a button, will have instant access to available business opportunities.

We require that you have a solid business background and be ready to make this big move.

$27,000 CASH REQ.
Xlnt Financing Available
Call Mr. Lewis
(213) 463-4841

INTERNATIONAL BUSINESS OPPORTUNITIES

6922 Hollywood Blvd.
Los Angeles, CA 90028

CAN YOU SELL AIR?

Become a dealer for one of the fastest growing products in the service station/convenience store market. AIR-serv coin-op tire inflators have proven sales potential. No royalties or fees. Small inventory req. Call Mr. Hamil PERSON-TO-PERSON COLLECT: 612/944-3604. **AIR-vend, Inc.** 9809 Valley View Rd., Eden Prairie, MN 55344.

Source: *The Wall Street Journal*, October 26, 1981.

Figure 3-3 Business Opportunity Ads

Investigate and Evaluate the Existing Business

Regardless of the source of business leads, each opportunity requires a background investigation and careful evaluation. As a preliminary step, the would-be buyer needs to acquire information about the business. Some of this information can be obtained through personal observation or discussion with the seller. Also important is the need to talk with other parties such as suppliers, bankers, and possibly customers of the business. Although some of this investigation requires personal checking, the would-be buyer can also seek the help of outside experts. The two most valuable sources of assistance in this regard are accountants and lawyers.

The seller's real reasons for selling a going business may or may not be disclosed. The buyer must be wary, therefore, of taking the seller's explanations at face value. Here, for example, are some of the reasons why owners offer their businesses for sale:

1. Old age or illness.
2. Desire to relocate in a different section of the country.
3. Decision to accept a position with another company.
4. Unprofitability of the business.
5. Discontinuance of an exclusive sales franchise.

The buyer will also be interested generally in the history of the business and the direction in which it is moving. To form a clear idea of the firm's value, however, the buyer must eventually examine the financial data pertaining to its operation. This calls for an independent audit of the firm offered for sale.

The Independent Audit. The major purpose of an independent audit is to reveal the accuracy and completeness of the financial statements of the business. It also determines whether the seller has used acceptable accounting procedures in depreciating equipment and in valuing inventory. To accept statements prepared by the seller's bookkeeper without an independent audit would be dangerous. Therefore, the would-be buyer should contact a competent, independent auditor for this purpose.

Of course, the would-be buyer may refer to an audit report prepared by an independent certified public accountant if this report is available and can be obtained directly from the auditor. If audit reports are available for the past five or ten years, or even longer, the would-be buyer can obtain some idea of trends for the business.

Adjustment of Audited Statements. Even audited statements may be misleading and require adjustment to obtain a realistic picture of the business. For example, business owners sometimes understate business income by concealing receipts from the tax collector. This illegal practice consists in receiving cash payments from customers without recording them on the books or including them in the firm's income tax returns. Adjustment may also be required if the pricing of goods and/or services is abnormally low—lower than necessary to attract a satisfactory volume of business.

Other items in audited income statements that may also need adjustment include personal or family expenses and wage or salary payments. For example, costs related to the family use of business vehicles frequently appears as a business expense. And in some situations, family members receive excessive compensation or none at all. All these items must be examined carefully to be sure that they relate to the business and are realistic. Figure 3-4 shows an income statement which has been adjusted by a prospective buyer.

	Original Income Statement		Required Adjustments	Adjusted Income Statement	
Estimated sales		$172,000			$172,000
Cost of goods sold		84,240			84,240
Gross profit		$ 87,760			$ 87,760
Operating expenses:					
Rent	$20,000		Rental agreement will expire in six months; Rent is expected to increase 20 percent.	$24,000	
Salaries	19,860			19,860	
Telephone	990			990	
Advertising	11,285			11,285	
Utilities	2,580			2,580	
Insurance	1,200		Property is underinsured; adequate coverage will double present cost.	2,400	
Professional services	1,200			1,200	
Credit-card expense	1,860		Amount of credit-card expense appears unreasonably large; buyer assumes that approximately $1,400 of this amount may be better classified as personal expense.	460	
Miscellaneous	1,250	60,225		1,250	64,025
Net income		$27,535			$23,735

Figure 3-4 Income Statement as Adjusted by Prospective Buyer

The buyer should also scrutinize the seller's balance sheet to see whether asset book values are realistic. Property often appreciates in value after it is recorded on the books.[13] In other cases, physical facilities or inventory or receivables decline in value so that their actual worth is less than their inflated book value.

Valuation of the Business. Prior to negotiating with the seller of a business, the buyer needs to estimate the worth, or value, of the business. The basis for the buyer's estimate is the adjusted financial statements described above. Two simple approaches to calculating the value of a business are explained below.

Value Based on the Balance Sheet. The balance sheet of a firm shows its total assets and total liabilities, or obligations. The difference between the total assets and the total liabilities is the **net worth**, or **book value**, of the business.

Difficulties arise, however, when one estimates the value of a business based on its balance sheet. First, asset values shown on the balance sheet often differ from their current value. As stated earlier, the historical costs of assets shown on the books may bear little resemblance to the current value of the assets. Second, the real value of individual assets is often different from their combined value as part of a going concern. The total is more than the sum of its parts. This situation can be compared, for example, to a hungry person who enjoys eating a piece of cake much more than eating the individual ingredients. In a similar manner, many individual assets are combined in a productive pattern to form a more valuable going concern.

Value Based on the Income Statement. Because of the difficulties associated with valuing a business on the basis of its balance sheet, we wish to emphasize another simple method of valuation, which is based on net income, or profit, as reported in the income statement. In most cases this method provides a reasonably accurate value for negotiating purposes.[14] Valu-

---

13. Standard accounting practice requires land, for example, to be recorded at cost. No adjustments are subsequently made to recognize its increasing or decreasing value. When real estate values are changing substantially, therefore, the amounts shown on the books do not correspond with reality.

14. The method described here is reasonably accurate if anticipated cash flows are fairly consistent from year to year. However, the more complex *discounted cash flow* method, described in Chapter 19, is theoretically superior and may be considered as an alternative to the simple method explained here. Use of the *discounted cash flow* method in purchasing a business is discussed in John H. Hand and William P. Lloyd, "Determining the Value of a Small Business," *MSU Business Topics*, Vol. 28 (Summer, 1980), pp. 5-10; and in James W. Carland, Jr., and Larry R. White, "Valuing the Small Business," *Journal of Small Business Management*, Vol. 18, No. 4 (October, 1980), pp. 40-48.

ation based on net income requires the use of a process known as **capitalization of profit**. Using this process, the buyer first estimates the dollars of profit that may be expected and then determines the dollar amount of investment which should logically earn the estimated dollars of profit. The dollar amount of investment constitutes the value of the business.

To illustrate, suppose that the adjusted income statement of a business shows that its annual net income is $60,000. What should a buyer be willing to pay for such a business? To answer this question, the buyer should follow four steps:

> *Step 1*: Estimate the probable *future* profit on the basis of *past* profit data. In doing this, the buyer must adjust past profit figures to eliminate nonrecurring gains or losses — for example, a loss from a fire. The buyer must ask what profit the business can be expected to earn in the future.
>
> *Step 2*: Allow for personal time invested in the business. In the case of a sole proprietorship, see whether the expenses shown on the income statement include a proper salary for the owner-manager. If no allowance has been made for the owner-manager's salary, a reasonable amount should be deducted before capitalizing the profit. Of course, this assumes that the buyer intends to devote personal time to the business — time that might otherwise be spent productively elsewhere. In the case of a partnership, the "salary" for a partner is not identified as an expense but is included as part of the firm's net profit.
>
> *Step 3*: Estimate the degree of risk involved in the business. One might expect a 30 to 40 percent return in businesses that entail considerable risk; in a less hazardous venture, 20 or 25 percent might be quite satisfactory.
>
> *Step 4*: Determine the existence and amount of goodwill, if any. Goodwill derives from the loyalty of customers or other advantages that cause earnings to be exceptionally high in view of the physical resources involved. Goodwill tends to be less durable than other assets and thus is worth proportionately less to the buyer.

Example of Calculating the Value Based on Net Income. Following the four steps noted above, let us now calculate the value of a business whose annual net income is estimated to be $60,000.

According to Step 1, we must decide whether the $60,000 can be expected to continue in the future. An examination of the income statement may show no unusual expense or income items. A general review of business prospects, moreover, may suggest no drastic changes in the foreseeable future. We might assume, therefore, that the $60,000 constitutes a reasonable prediction of future profit.

Following Step 2, we may find that no salary expense has been shown for the owner-manager in arriving at the $60,000 profit. If the buyer places a value of $25,000 on personal time and effort, this amount should be deducted from the $60,000, leaving $35,000 to be capitalized. This $35,000 is the profit which will compensate the buyer for the dollars invested in the business.

When estimating the degree of risk involved in the business as prescribed in Step 3, we assume that the buyer considers the business to be moderately safe and feels that a 20 percent profit would be a good return on investment (ROI) in comparison with alternative investment opportunities. We can then calculate the value of the business as follows, assuming that no goodwill exists:

$$\text{Value of business} \times \text{Desired rate of return} = \text{Net profit}$$
$$\text{Value of business} \times 20\% = \$35{,}000$$
$$\text{Value of business} = \$35{,}000/.20$$
$$\text{Value of business} = \$175{,}000$$

Thus, the $175,000 provides a benchmark for use in negotiating the purchase price of the business.

In following Step 4, the buyer inquires about the existence of goodwill. If the profit is unreasonably high in view of the physical resources of the business, the buyer will be purchasing goodwill along with the physical assets of the business. And if a substantial amount of the firm's profit is attributable to goodwill, the buyer should value the firm more conservatively due to the intangible and somewhat fragile nature of goodwill. Under these circumstances the buyer needs to use a higher rate for capitalizing the profit. Assuming that the higher rate, adjusted for goodwill, is 30 percent rather than 20 percent, the value of the business can then be calculated as follows:

$$\text{Value of business} \times \text{Desired rate of return} = \text{Net profit}$$
$$\text{Value of business} \times 30\% = \$35{,}000$$
$$\text{Value of business} = \$35{,}000/.30$$
$$\text{Value of business} = \$116{,}667$$

Clearly, the estimated value of the business is lower when we assume that we are paying for goodwill, which may soon disappear.

Other Factors to Evaluate. A number of other factors remain to be explored when evaluating an existing business. Some of these are:

1. *Competition* —The prospective buyer should look into the extent, intensity, and location of competing businesses. In particular, the buyer should check to see whether the business in question is gaining or losing in the race with competitors.

2. *Market* —The adequacy of the market to maintain all competing business units, including the one to be purchased, should be determined. This entails market research, study of census data, and personal, on-the-spot observation at each competitor's place of business.
3. *Future community developments* —Examples of community developments planned for the future include:
   a. Changes in zoning ordinances already enacted but not yet in effect.
   b. Land condemnation suits for construction of a public building, a municipally operated parking lot, or a public park.
   c. Change from two-way traffic flow to one-way traffic.
   d. Discontinuance of bus routes that will eliminate public transportation for customers and employees.
4. *Legal commitments* —These may include contingent liabilities, unsettled lawsuits, delinquent tax payments, missed payrolls, overdue rent or installment payments, and mortgages of record against any of the real property acquired.
5. *Union contracts* —The prospective buyer should determine what type of labor agreement, if any, is in force, as well as the quality of the firm's employee relations.
6. *Buildings* —The quality of the buildings housing the business, particularly the fire hazard involved, should be checked. In addition, the buyer should determine if there are restrictions on access to the building. For example, is there access to the building without crossing the property of another? If necessary, a right of way should be negotiated before the purchase contract is closed.
7. *Future national emergencies* —The buyer should determine the potential impact of possible future national emergencies such as price and wage controls, energy shortages, human-resources shortages, raw-material shortages, and the like.
8. *Product prices* —The prospective owner should compare the prices of the seller's products with manufacturers' or wholesalers' catalogs or prices of competing products in the locality. This is necessary to assure full and fair pricing of goods whose sales are reported on the seller's financial statements.

Negotiate the Purchase Price and Terms

The purchase price of the business is determined by negotiation between buyer and seller. Although the calculated value is not the price of the business, it gives the buyer an estimated value to use in negotiating price.

Typically the buyer tries to purchase the firm for something less than the full estimated value. Likewise, the seller tries to get more than the estimated value.

An important part of this negotiation is the terms of purchase because, in many cases, the buyer is unable to pay the full price in cash and must seek extended terms. Generous terms have a great deal to do with the overall attractiveness of the business opportunity. As one writer put it:

> A buyer should be willing to pay any price that a seller asks if the buyer can set the terms of the purchase. This appears to be an irrational statement until an extreme example of terms is given—$1 down and $1 per month until the price is paid. Obviously no buyer or seller is going to accept extreme terms or extreme selling prices. However, there is room for negotiation and agreement in the trade-off between selling price and terms. The amount of trade-off will depend on the goals of both the buyer and seller.[15]

Terms become more attractive to the buyer as the amount of the down payment is reduced or the length of the repayment period is extended.

Close the Deal

As in the purchase of real estate, the purchase of a business is closed at a specific time. The closing may be handled, for example, by a title company or an attorney. Preferably the closing should occur under the direction of an independent third party. If the seller's attorney is suggested as the closing agent, the buyer should exercise caution. Regardless of the closing arrangements, the buyer should never go through a closing without extensive consultation with a qualified attorney.

A number of important documents are completed during the closing. These include a bill of sale, certifications as to taxing and other governmental authorities, and agreements pertaining to future payments and related guarantees to the seller.

LOOKING BACK

1. Ideas for new ventures come from many different sources, including work experience, inventions, hobbies, accidental discovery, and deliberate search. Such ideas require study and refinement before the business is launched.

15. Richard C. Scott, "Pricing the Going Concern," *Journal of Small Business Management*, Vol. 15, No. 3 (July, 1977), p. 40.

2. Preparing a written new-venture plan is beneficial in that it stimulates a careful study of the new venture, provides an initial operating plan, and explains the venture to bankers and other outside parties.
3. A number of reasons exist for buying a business. Fewer uncertainties are involved than in launching an entirely new firm. Also, the facilities, personnel, and other elements of a going business are already assembled. The business may also be available at a bargain price.
4. In purchasing a going concern, the buyer should conduct a thorough investigation, including an analysis of audited and corrected financial statements of the business. After correct statements are available, a buyer can estimate the value of the business by capitalizing the expected net profit for the business.
5. The value of a business based on its net income can be calculated by taking the following steps: (a) estimating the probable future profit based on past profit data, (b) allowing a proper salary for the owner-manager's personal time invested in the business, (c) estimating the degree of risk involved in the business, and (d) determining the existence and amount of goodwill.

DISCUSSION QUESTIONS

1. Why should an entrepreneur prefer to launch an entirely new venture rather than buy an existing firm?
2. Can you identify a business that grew out of the entrepreneur's hobby and one that resulted from the entrepreneur's work experience?
3. Can you suggest a product or a service not currently available that might lead to a new small business? How safe would it be to launch a new small business depending solely on that one new product or service? Why?
4. What is the difference between an "inside-out" approach and an "outside-in" approach in seeking new-venture ideas? Explain.
5. What benefits are associated with the preparation of a written new-venture plan? Who uses it?
6. What reasons for buying an existing business, in contrast to starting from scratch, appear most important?
7. Is uncertainty eliminated or merely minimized when an existing business is purchased? Explain.
8. What is the significance of the seller's real reasons for selling? How might you discover them?
9. How should a buyer determine the estimated profit and rate of return to use in capitalizing business profits?
10. Suppose that a business firm available for purchase has shown an average net profit of $40,000 for the past 5 years. During these years, the amount of profit fluctuated between $20,000 and $60,000. State your assumptions and then calculate the value that you might use in negotiating the purchase price.

REFERENCES TO SMALL BUSINESS IN ACTION

"How to Start a Sideline Business." *Business Week*, No. 2597 (August 6, 1979), pp. 94-97.

Many small firms begin as sidelines of entrepreneurs whose principal livelihood comes from other sources. A number of sideline ventures are described, and some of their special problems are explained.

"Phoenix." *Forbes*, Vol. 125, No. 8 (April 14, 1980), pp. 122-124.

A small business called Shopsmith started a few years ago in a suburb of Dayton, OH. The entrepreneur built the business by taking over a line of workshop tools abandoned by a major corporation.

Silver, A. David. "Venture Financing: A Pre-Buyout Audit." *Venture*, Vol. 1, No. 11 (November, 1979), pp. 18-21.

In this article, which advocates a thorough evaluation prior to the purchase of a business, the author describes the type of investigation carried out by the buyer of a firm in an energy-related field. The seller's offering price was reduced because of information developed during the course of an audit by a CPA firm and a review by a management consulting firm.

"What's Brewing at Celestial." *Business Week*, No. 2679 (March 16, 1981), p. 138.

J. Siegel, at the age of 21, revolutionized the stodgy tea industry by introducing teas made from herbs. His product was first sold in health-food stores but later moved into supermarkets. The company, Celestial Seasonings, Inc., is planning the introduction of a caffeine-free hot drink to compete with coffee.

Chapter 4

Franchising

LOOKING AHEAD

Watch for the following important topics:

1. Types of franchising systems.
2. Advantages of franchising.
3. Limitations of franchising.
4. Locating and investigating franchise opportunities.
5. Considerations in selling a franchise.

"Mister Softee, Dr. Personnel, Mr. Chipper, Mr. Maintenance"

Are these nicknames of famous sports figures like "Dr. J" of professional basketball fame? Are they names for those special teachers you had last semester? They could be good "labels" in both situations, but they are not. These are creative names for some real franchised businesses. Franchising itself is a creative form of business which helps thousands of entrepreneurs realize their business-ownership dreams. The franchising concept is an attractive option for operating a small business.

SCOPE AND DEVELOPMENT OF FRANCHISING

The term *franchising* is defined in many ways. In this text we use a broad definition to encompass its wide scope. **Franchising** is a marketing system that revolves around a two-party legal agreement whereby one party is granted the privilege to conduct business as an individual owner but is required to operate according to certain methods and terms specified by the other party. The legal agreement is known as the **franchise contract**, and the privileges it contains are called the **franchise**. The sponsor of the privileges is the **franchisor**. The party receiving the privileges is called the **franchisee**.

The potential value of any franchising arrangement is determined by the rights contained in the franchise contract, and the extent and importance of these rights are quite varied. For example, a potential franchisee may desire the right to use a name. Alternatively, the potential franchisee may need an entire marketing system, often with a new retail store and a standardized method of operation. Regardless of the specific need, a franchise is the mechanism which gives birth to an independently owned business, with the franchisee hiring the employees and assuming the operating responsibilities.

ACTION REPORT: The Value of a Name

Tom Gatto had been operating a haircutting salon in Illinois for 12 years. Gatto wanted his business to grow from the existing one-salon operation. To achieve this growth, he decided to purchase a franchise as a tool to penetrate a bigger market. He joined the franchisor, Hair Performers, Inc., by paying a $15,000 fee. In return, he received training for beauticians, franchisor advertising, and, of course, use of the Hair Performers name. The name gave Gatto's salon an identity which prospective customers found appealing. Gatto realized the benefits of franchising because one year later profits were 30 percent higher. Gatto then began making plans to open additional salons.

Source: Susan Sherman, "Franchise Opportunities for the Entrepreneur," *Venture*, Vol. 2, No. 11 (November, 1980), p. 54.

Types of Franchising Systems

Three types, or levels, of franchising systems offer opportunities for entrepreneurs. Figure 4-1 depicts each of these systems and provides examples. In *System A*, the producer/creator (the franchisor) grants a franchise to a

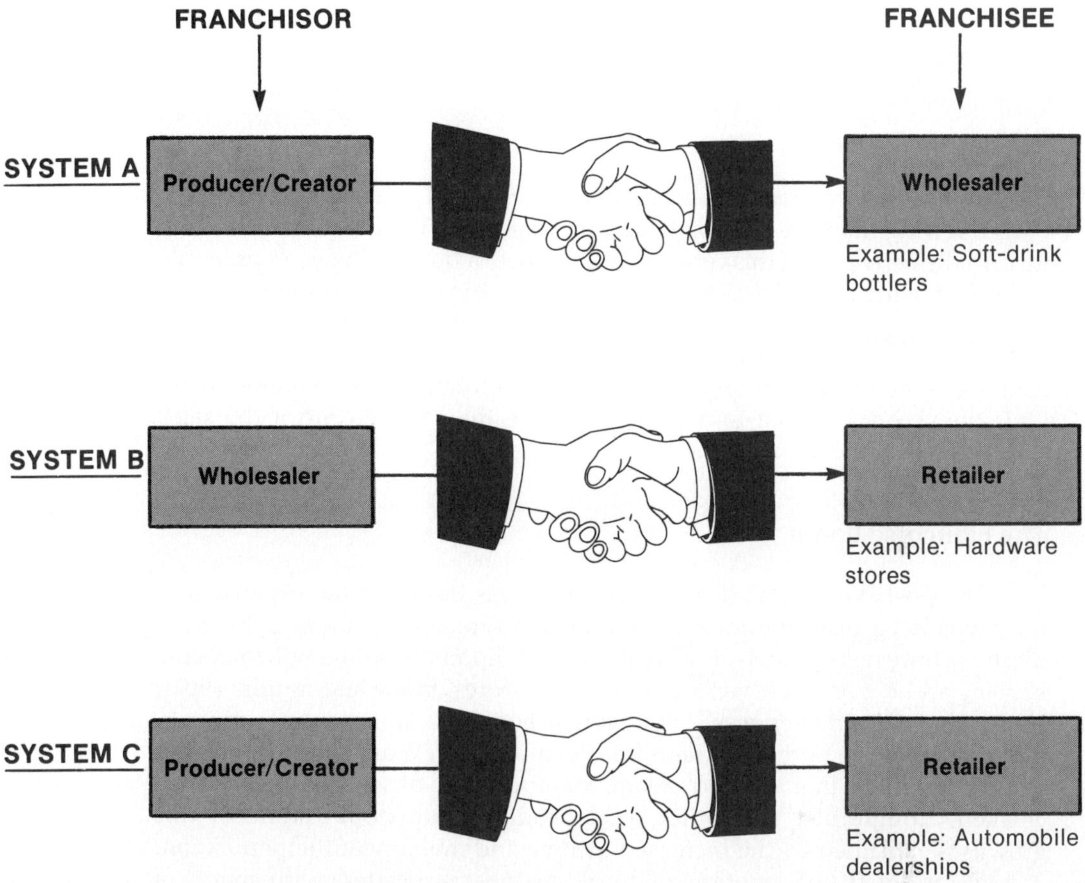

Figure 4-1 Alternative Franchising Systems

wholesaler (the franchisee). This system is often used in the soft-drink industry. Dr Pepper and Coca-Cola are examples of System A franchisors.

In the second level, designated as *System B,* the wholesaler is the franchisor. This system prevails among supermarkets and general merchandising stores. Ben Franklin, Gamble-Skogmo, and Ace Hardware are examples of System B franchisors.

The third type, *System C*, is the most widely used. This system finds the producer/creator as franchisor and the retailer as franchisee. Automobile dealerships and gasoline service stations are prototypes of this system. In recent years this system also has been used successfully by many fast-food outlets and printing services. Notable examples of System C franchisors are Burger Chef and Kwik-Kopy. The Kwik-Kopy Corporation has enjoyed tremendous growth and success as shown by the increase in the cost of its franchise. To illustrate, in the middle 1970s a franchise for this fast-printing service cost about $15,000. Five years later, a potential franchisee needed to invest $54,500![1]

Early Franchising

One of the first franchise arrangements involved a relationship between Singer Sewing Machine Company and its dealers during the nineteenth century. In the early part of this century, other types of franchising were primarily associated with the sale of automobiles, soft drinks, and gasoline. Today almost every type of product and service is marketed through franchised outlets. Nevertheless, automobile dealerships and gasoline service stations continue to be the most important franchises in terms of sales volume. As of 1981, they were believed to account for more than 80 percent of the sales volume of all franchised businesses.

The Franchise Boom

The post-World War II franchise boom was based on the expansion of the franchising principle into many different types of businesses. Some of these are franchised motels, beauty parlors, equipment-renting outlets, bookkeeping and tax services, variety stores, drugstores, brake and muffler repair shops, dry cleaning services, employment agencies, laundromats, and car-rental services. In addition, there has been a great expansion of franchised fast-food outlets that sell ice cream, hamburgers, pizza, root beer, fried chicken, doughnuts, and other food products. No doubt some of this growth is explained by the increased income and mobility of the population, as well as by the promotion of brand names associated with many of these products.

The franchise boom may be illustrated by the growth of McDonald's, one of the sensationally successful fast-food franchisors. The first two units of McDonald's chain opened in 1955 and grossed $235,000. This hamburger chain expanded so rapidly that it grossed more than $2 billion in 1980.[2] The individual who acquires a McDonald's franchise today must make an initial investment of approximately $300,000. As of 1980, the company had 3,340 franchised outlets.[3]

---

1. Sharon Reier, "Will the Next Ray Kroc Please Stand Up?" *Forbes*, Vol. 124, No. 6 (September 17, 1979), p. 178.

2. "McDonald's: The Original Recipe Helps It Defy a Downturn," *Business Week*, No. 2686 (May 4, 1981), pp. 161-162.

3. "Seasoned Franchisors Can Offer Stability," *Venture*, Vol. 2, No. 11 (November, 1980), p. 60.

Franchising During the Seventies

The expansion of franchised business continued rapidly through the 1970s. Total franchised sales increased from $116.5 billion in 1970 to approximately $312 billion in 1979.[4] The rate of expansion has varied, however, among the various business areas. Table 4-1 provides a comparison of the sales growth rates for the biggest kinds of franchised business. The two traditional lines of franchising—automobiles and gasoline—are still by far the most important. Nonfood retailing is the only major class showing a decline in franchising during the seventies.[5]

Franchising in the Eighties

All indicators point to a continuation of growth for franchising in the 1980s. One writer has isolated the following seven most promising new franchise areas:

Table 4-1 Franchising Growth over the Seventies for Selected Kinds of Business

Kind of Business	Sales (In 1,000s) 1970	Sales (In 1,000s) 1979	Percent Increase
Automobile and truck dealers	$55,622,000	$155,738,000	179.9%
Gasoline service stations	29,340,000	71,894,000	145.0
Restaurants (all types)	4,602,111	24,765,916	438.1
Soft-drink bottlers	4,102,000	12,194,000	197.3
Retailing (nonfood)	13,133,434	8,901,928	(32.2)
Automotive products and services	1,936,412	7,226,822	273.2
Hotels and motels	3,539,914	6,625,437	87.2
Business aids and services	723,031	6,280,412	768.6
Convenience stores	1,727,116	6,131,885	255.0

Note: Remember that increases caused by inflation make the real growth less than what the percentage indicates.

Source: U. S. Department of Commerce, *Franchising in the Economy: 1979-1981* (Washington: U. S. Government Printing Office, 1981), Tables 4 and 6.

4. U. S. Department of Commerce, *Franchising in the Economy: 1979-1981* (Washington: U. S. Government Printing Office, 1981), Tables 4 and 6.

5. A more detailed history of franchising for the period preceding 1970 can be found in Donald W. Hackett, *Franchising: The State of the Art* (Chicago: American Marketing Association, 1977).

1. Personal-computer stores.
2. Real estate.
3. Sporting-goods stores.
4. Hair salons.
5. Video-related sales and services.
6. Energy-related stores or products.
7. Health-food snacks.[6]

An even greater influx of foreign franchisors is anticipated in the 1980s. These franchisors are expected to concentrate on restaurants, clothing, automotive products and services, and furniture.

BUYING A FRANCHISE

"Look before you leap" is an old adage which should be heeded by potential franchisees. Entrepreneurial enthusiasm should not cloud the eyes to the realities, both good and bad, of franchising. We shall first look at the advantages of buying a franchise and then examine the weaknesses of this decision. Read these topics carefully, and remember them when you are evaluating a franchise.

Franchising *vs.* Starting an Independent Business

One way to compare the advantages of franchising with the alternative of launching an independent business is to look at a side-by-side comparison. Figure 4-2 isolates eight major differences between buying a franchise and starting an independent business. Neither approach is a winner in all cases. However, in their particular circumstances many people find the franchise form of business to be better.

Advantages of Franchising

A franchise is attractive for many good reasons. Three advantages in particular warrant further analysis. A franchise can offer (1) managerial guidance and formal training, (2) financial assistance, and (3) marketing benefits. Naturally all franchises may not be equally strong on all these points. But it is these advantages which cause many persons to consider the franchise arrangement.

Formal Training and Managerial Guidance. The importance of formal training and managerial guidance received from the franchisor is underlined by the

6. "The Newest Franchises Promise Growth," *Venture*, Vol. 2, No. 11 (November, 1980), pp. 56, 60.

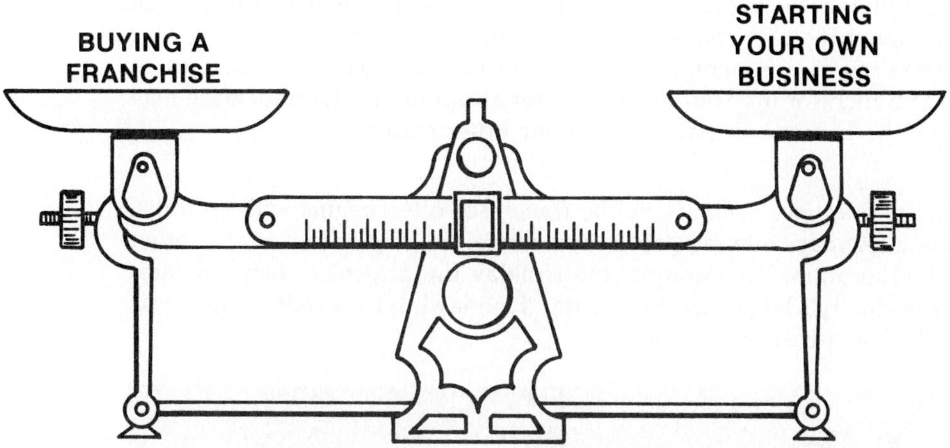

1. Right to use a known trademark or brand with established public acceptance.
2. Availability of operational training usually provided by franchisor.
3. Possibility that sales territory is restricted by franchisor.
4. Benefits from the franchisor's advertising program.
5. More accurate forecasts of financial needs and greater ease in obtaining initial capital.
6. Franchisor often the sole source of supplies.
7. Fixtures, equipment, and other premise-related assets often specified by franchisor.
8. Possible restrictions in contract on franchisee's decisions to sell or to expand.

1. Requires time, effort, and cost to establish a new name in the market.
2. Managerial ability based on entrepreneur's expertise.
3. Sales territory as large as entrepreneur can serve.
4. Advertising load carried by entrepreneur but permits freedom in advertising.
5. More difficult to plan and obtain financing needs.
6. May obtain supplies anywhere at the best available prices.
7. Freedom to develop the store image that entrepreneur feels is most appropriate.
8. Total freedom to operate as entrepreneur sees fit.

Source: Adapted with permission from *Buying a Franchise* (Montreal, Quebec: Federal Business Development Bank, 1979), p. 3.

Figure 4-2 Major Considerations in Deciding Between a Franchise and Starting an Independent Business

generally glaring weakness in managerial ability of small entrepreneurs. To the extent that this weakness can be overcome, therefore, the training program offered by the franchisor constitutes a major benefit.

The value and the effectiveness of training are evident from the records of business failures, a large majority of which is caused by deficiencies in management. For example, franchisors such as McDonald's and Kentucky Fried Chicken have reputedly never experienced a failure. There appears to be little question that the failure rate for independent small businesses in general is much higher than for franchised businesses in particular.

Operating as a franchisee, however, in no way guarantees success. A particular franchisor may offer unsatisfactory training, or the franchisee may not apply the training or may fail for some other reason.

Initial Training. Training by the franchisor often begins with an initial period of a few days or a few weeks at a central training school or at another established location. For example, the Holiday Inn franchise chain operates the hotel industry's largest training center, Holiday Inn University, which was built in 1972 at a cost of $5 million.

ACTION REPORT: Hamburger Homework

Applications for Burger King franchises run about 1,000 a year. About 10 percent of the applicants become franchisees. Burger King is not looking for someone who knows food but rather for someone who knows how to follow instructions. Applicants who can provide the liquid assets required by Burger King spend over eight weeks in training. The first week is spent in an existing restaurant, followed by six weeks of basic training at a regional center. The final nine days of training are conducted at Burger King University, the company's training center in Miami, FL.

Source: Lee Smith, "Burger King Puts Down Its Dukes," *Fortune*, Vol. 101, No. 12 (June 16, 1980), p. 96.

Figure 4-3 shows the training provided by selected franchising systems as reported to the U. S. Department of Commerce. Figure 4-4 is a photograph of a training session for franchisees conducted by T-Shirts Plus (described in Chapter 1). Initial training programs typically cover not only the specific operating procedures to be used by the business, but also broader topics such as record keeping, inventory control, insurance, and human relations. The Mister Donut franchise requires an initial training course of four weeks, including such topics as doughnut making, accounting and controls, advertising and merchandising, scheduling of labor and production, purchasing, and so on. Naturally the nature of the product and the type of business affect the amount and type of training required in the franchised business. In most cases, training constitutes a potent advantage of the franchising system and permits individuals who are deficient in training and education to start and succeed in businesses of their own.

FRANCHISOR	TRAINING DESCRIPTION
AAMCO TRANSMISSIONS, INC.	You receive two weeks operational training in Ft. Lauderdale, Florida. At that time you will learn every aspect of our business. When it is time for your Grand Opening, two of our Area Developers will spend two weeks at your location to assist you in all operational procedures, including the developing of Fleet accounts in your territory. Developmental Services will continue to provide you with weekly assistance on paperwork and accounting procedures.
H & R BLOCK, INC.	Each year a training program is held in November for all new managers. Prior to tax season each year, a training program for all employees is conducted in major centers. Each summer a meeting is held for all managers for three days to discuss all phases of the operation and new developments and ideas.
JUST PANTS	Just Pants will furnish a training program consisting of two weeks or more of "on-the-job training" in two or more actual operating Just Pants stores plus much additional instruction for the manager with respect to other aspects of the business. The Licensee will be responsible for the travel and living expenses and the compensation of the manager while enrolled in the training program.
DUNKIN' DONUTS OF AMERICA, INC.	Five-week training course for franchisees at Dunkin' Donuts University in North Quincy, Massachusetts, consisting of production and shop management training. Initial training of donutmen and managers, and retraining, is carried out at Dunkin' Donuts University without charge.
RODEWAY INNS OF AMERICA	Seminars in the various operational areas of concern. Training facility being established.
PRINTMASTERS, INC.	Technical, managerial, and promotional training provided. Minimum of one week at the franchise training center. Minimum of one week at the franchisee's location. Managerial and promotional input, as well as technical assistance, continue through quality control visits and direct contact with franchisee. All aspects of owning and operating an instant printing center are covered in detail.
RED CARPET CORPORATION OF AMERICA	Franchisee receives a six-day seminar on office management and continued sales personnel training. Training tapes are also available to franchisee.
UNITED AIR SPECIALISTS, INC.	Comprehensive three-day factory training program, field training, and regional meetings.

Source: U. S. Department of Commerce, *Franchise Opportunities Handbook* (Washington: U. S. Government Printing Office, 1979).

Figure 4-3 Training Programs in Selected Franchising Systems

Figure 4-4 Training Session at T-Shirts Plus

Continuing Guidance. Initial training is ordinarily supplemented with subsequent continued training and guidance. This may involve refresher courses and/or training by a traveling representative who visits the franchisee's business from time to time. The franchisee may also receive manuals and other printed materials that provide guidance for the business. However, guidance shades into control so that in particular cases it may be difficult to distinguish the two. The franchisor normally places a considerable emphasis upon observing strict controls. Still, much of the continued training goes far beyond the application of controls.

While some franchising systems have developed excellent training programs, this is by no means universal. Some unscrupulous promoters falsely promise satisfactory training. The following account illustrates the unfortunate consequences of a franchise arrangement which lacked a properly organized training program:

> John Smith worked nearly 10 years with the same company before a magazine advertisement caught his eye. The ad read: "Be your own boss. Earn a living in the profitable carpeting business. No previous experience is necessary. We'll teach you all the ropes."
>
> John talked it over with his wife and decided to take the big step into self-employment.

John sent in the clipping and in turn was invited for an interview by the company. After a red carpet tour of the city, franchisor-paid, and an elaborate slide presentation at the franchisor's "Executive Offices," John could hardly wait to get home and start selling carpets. He signed the franchise agreement, which did not mention training, assured by the soothing tone of the company vice-president's words. "Don't worry about a thing," he said. "We'll teach and train you in every aspect of carpet merchandising at one of our best outlets." John returned home after investing the required $8,000 and revamped his personal affairs—and waited for the franchisor's call to report for training. Finally, the call came in the form of a "Do-It-Yourself" book on carpet installation and merchandising. Having signed leases, ordered merchandise, and invested $8,000, he could do little but try it on his own. Even with the help of a fairly experienced "carpeting man" he was in deep trouble within 3 months. After a few more weeks, John was approached by a company representative. "Look Mr. Smith, let's face it. The carpet business is not for you. Our company is prepared to make you an offer of $4,700 for your franchise." John, bewildered and frightened at the prospects of bankruptcy, accepted the offer—a considerable loss from his original $8,000 investment.[7]

Financial Assistance. The costs of starting a new business are often high and the prospective entrepreneur's sources of capital quite limited. The entrepreneur's standing as a prospective borrower is weakest at this point. But by teaming up with a national franchising organization, the aspiring franchisee will enhance the likelihood of obtaining financial assistance.

If the franchising organization considers the applicant to be a suitable prospect with a high probability of success, it frequently extends a helping hand financially. For example, the franchisee seldom is required to pay the complete cost of establishing the business. In addition, the beginning franchisee is normally given a payment schedule that can be met through successful operation. Also, the franchisor may permit delay in payments for products or supplies obtained from the parent organization, thus increasing the franchisee's working capital.

Association with a well-established franchisor may also improve the new franchisee's credit standing with a bank. The reputation of the national franchising organization and the managerial and financial controls that it provides serve to recommend the new franchisee to a banker. Also, the franchisor frequently will cosign notes with a local bank, thus guaranteeing the franchisee's loan.

Marketing Benefits. Most franchised products and services are widely known and accepted. For example, customers will readily buy McDonald's ham-

7. Robert M. Dias and Stanley I. Gurnick, *Franchising: The Investor's Complete Handbook* (New York: Hastings House, 1969), pp. 73-74.

burgers or Baskin-Robbins ice cream because they know the reputation of these products. Or travellers who recognize a restaurant or a motel because of its name, type of roof, or some other feature may turn into a Denny's Restaurant or a Holiday Inn motel because of their previous experience and the knowledge that they can depend upon the food and service that these outlets provide. Thus, franchising offers both a proven successful line of business and product identification.

The entrepreneur who enters a franchising agreement acquires the right to use the franchisor's nationally advertised trademark or brand name. This serves to identify the local enterprise with the widely recognized product or service. Of course, the value of product identification differs with the type of product or service and the extent to which it has received widespread promotion. In any case, the franchisor maintains the value of its name by continued advertising and promotion.

In addition to offering a proven successful line of business and readily identifiable products or services, franchisors have developed and tested their methods of operation. The standard operating manuals and procedures they supply have permitted other entrepreneurs to operate successfully. This is one reason why franchisors insist upon the observance of standardized methods of operation and performance. If some franchisees were allowed to operate at substandard levels, they could easily destroy the customer's confidence in the entire system.

Without well-standardized operating methods, an independent business owner is often inclined to do what comes naturally and throw effective management to the wind. Recall that many small-business owners tend to disregard financial planning, records, and control. Observing operating methods that have proven successful elsewhere, therefore, should strengthen the new franchisee and offer some assurance of success.

The existence of proven products and methods, however, does not guarantee that a franchised business will succeed. For example, what appeared to be a satisfactory location as a result of the franchisor's marketing research techniques may turn out to be inferior. Or the franchisee may lack ambition or perseverance. Yet the fact that a franchisor can show a record of successful operation proves that the system can work and has worked elsewhere.

Limitations of Franchising

Franchising is like a coin — it has two sides. Given the positive side of the coin, the negative side should not be flipped over hurriedly, but rather examined with the same detail. A few limitations to franchising keep it from being a business panacea. In particular, three shortcomings permeate the franchise form of business. These are: the cost of a franchise, the restrictions on growth which can accompany a franchise contract, and the inherent loss of absolute independence on the part of the franchisee.

Cost of a Franchise. Fees of various types must be paid to the franchisor. Generally speaking, the higher fees will be asked by the more successful and well-known franchisors. For example, Tidy Car in Buffalo, NY asks for a franchise fee of only $1,500 and a royalty of $2 for each car serviced. On the other hand, the Sheraton Corporation charges a $15,000 franchise fee plus a royalty of 4 percent of gross room sales. If entrepreneurs could earn the same income independently, they would save the amount of these fees and royalties. However, this is not a valid objection if the franchisor provides the benefits previously described. In that case, franchisees are merely paying for the advantages of their relationship with the franchisor. And this may be a good investment, indeed.

Restrictions on Growth. A basic principle of business growth is to expand the existing sales territory. Obviously this is easier said than done. Competition is always a compelling force that works against this objective. Or a firm's own resource limitations can also be restrictive. Additionally, many franchise contracts restrict the franchisee to a defined sales territory, thereby eliminating this form of growth. However, the franchisor usually will agree not to grant another franchise to operate within the same territory. The potential franchisee, therefore, should weigh this limitation against the advantages.

Loss of Absolute Independence. Frequently individuals leave salaried employment for entrepreneurship because they dislike working under the direct supervision and control of others. By entering into a franchise relationship, such individuals may simply find that a different pattern of close control over personal endeavors has taken over. The franchisee does surrender a considerable amount of independence upon signing a franchise agreement.

Even though the franchisor's regulation of business operations may be helpful in assuring success, it may be unpleasant to an entrepreneur who cherishes independence. In addition, some franchise contracts may go to extremes by covering unimportant details or specifying practices that are more helpful to others in the chain than to the local operation. Thus, as an operator of a franchised business, the entrepreneur occupies the position of a semi-independent businessperson.

EVALUATING FRANCHISE OPPORTUNITIES

Once an interest in becoming a franchisee emerges, much remains to be done before the dream materializes. The prospective franchisee must locate the right opportunity, investigate a franchise offer for possible fraud, and examine the franchise contract carefully.

Locate the Right Franchise Opportunity

With the proliferation of franchising over the years, the task of locating the most suitable opportunities has become difficult. Sources of franchise opportunities are not always obvious. Yet one source that is readily available to anyone is the advertisements in newspapers and trade publications. For example, in any issue of *The Wall Street Journal* numerous franchise opportunities are advertised. *Franchising Today* and *Venture* magazines also include information on many franchise opportunities. In following up these advertisements, the prospective franchisee needs to beware of advertising claims that are misleading or that promise more than is warranted.

Other helpful guides in locating franchise opportunities are the following:

1. *Franchise Opportunities Handbook* published by the U.S. Department of Commerce. This handbook contains a comprehensive listing of franchisors with a brief statement about the nature and requirements of each franchise. It also cites many other sources of franchising information and assistance and is updated frequently. The handbook may be purchased from the Government Printing Office, Washington, DC 20402.
2. Pilot Books, 347 Fifth Avenue, New York, NY 10016, publishes several franchising guides. One of its publications is *The 1981 Directory of Franchising Organizations*, which lists over 700 leading franchise firms.
3. International Franchise Association, 7315 Wisconsin Avenue, Suite 600W, Washington, DC 20014, is a trade association which compiles and distributes information on various aspects of franchising.

Information concerning franchise opportunities may also be obtained from the franchisors themselves. They are usually very helpful in explaining the necessary steps to opening a franchise business. For example, the Jack 'N' Jill franchisor provides the information sheet shown in Figure 4-5.

In recent years, franchise consultants have appeared and now offer their services to individuals in seeking and evaluating franchise opportunities. As in choosing any type of consultant, the prospective franchisee needs to select a reputable, rather than a fly-by-night, consultant. This is not always easy in view of the newness of this consulting field.

Investigate the Franchise Offer

The nature of the commitment required in franchising justifies a careful investigation inasmuch as a franchised business typically involves a sub-

Jack 'N' Jill

10 STEPS TO OPENING YOUR

JACK 'N' JILL DONUT SHOP

1) YOU'VE TAKEN THE FIRST STEP by requesting our information package. After reviewing the material, you should have an idea of what is involved.

2) FILL OUT THE PERSONAL INFORMATION AND FINANCIAL STATEMENTS and return to us. This will indicate your willingness to explore the possibilities further. Your information will be held in strict confidence and will not obligate you in any manner.

3) IT'S TIME FOR A MEETING. After we have reviewed your personal and financial data, an appointment will be made between you and a JACK 'N' JILL representative. If a mutual interest exists at that time, a franchise offering will be made. All necessary documents and cost figures will be made at that time.

4) YOUR DEPOSIT DEMONSTRATES FURTHER INTEREST. If you have finally decided you want a JACK 'N' JILL shop, you will remit a deposit to JACK 'N' JILL. JACK 'N' JILL will then help you select a site for your business. Upon signing of the final franchise, your deposit will be applied to your franchise fee.

5) SEARCH FOR LOCATION. An intensive search will begin for the best possible location for your business. JACK 'N' JILL will utilize its experience and knowledge to provide you the best site available.

6) FINANCING. JACK 'N' JILL will help you gather and complete all the data necessary for you to obtain financing. Upon obtaining satisfactory financing, you will present JACK 'N' JILL a letter of confirmation from the lending institution.

7) SIGNING OF THE FRANCHISE. After the site has been selected and financing has been obtained, you will sign the franchise agreement and remit the franchise fee to JACK 'N' JILL.

8) BUILDING PERIOD. Construction of your building will begin if necessary and JACK 'N' JILL will supply all assistance necessary to see the project brought to a successful conclusion.

9) TRAINING. Two to four weeks before your store opens, you will receive two weeks training in all phases of operation in JACK 'N' JILL's training facility.

10) OPENING. This is the time you've waited for. JACK 'N' JILL representatives will help you with all phases including advertising.

Source: Jack 'N' Jill Donut Flour Company, Waco, TX. Reproduced with permission.

Figure 4-5 Steps to Opening Your Jack 'N' Jill Donut Shop

stantial investment, possibly many thousands of dollars. Furthermore, the business relationship is one that may be expected to continue over a period of years.

Ordinarily the investigation process is a two-way effort. The franchisor wishes to investigate the franchisee, and the franchisee obviously wishes to evaluate the franchisor and the type of opportunity offered. Time is required for this kind of investigation. One should be skeptical of a franchisor who is overly hurried or who pressures a franchisee to sign at once without allowing for proper investigation.

Beware of Franchising Frauds

Every industry has its share of shady operations, and franchising is no exception. Unscrupulous fast-buck artists offer a wide variety of fraudulent schemes to attract the investment of unsuspecting individuals. The franchisor in such cases is merely interested in obtaining the capital investment of the franchisee and not in a continuing relationship. The growth of the franchising industry and the substantial opportunities in legitimate franchising create an opportunity for illegitimate operators who attempt to fleece the public.

As one example of the fraudulent operator, a national marketing firm in Tulsa, OK took more than $400,000 from some 400 investors. The president and officers of this firm received up to ten years in prison, but this did not restore the investments of their victims.[8] The possibility of such fraudulent schemes requires alertness on the part of prospective franchisees. Only careful investigation of the company and the product can distinguish between fraudulent operators and legitimate franchising opportunities. Certainly visits to, and discussion with, other franchisees operating in the same field are mandatory. Finally, a formal checklist, such as that provided in Appendix A at the end of this text, can be an extremely helpful tool.

Examine the Franchise Contract

The basic features of the relationship between the franchisor and the franchisee are embodied in the franchise contract. The contract is typically a complex document, often running to several pages. Because of its extreme importance in furnishing the legal basis for the franchised business, no franchise contract should ever be signed by the franchisee without legal counsel. As a matter of fact, many reputable franchisors insist that the franchisee have legal counsel before signing the agreement. An attorney would be useful in anticipating trouble and in noting objectionable features of the franchise contract.

---

8. *Ibid.*, pp. 99-100.

In addition to consulting an attorney, you as a prospective franchisee should use as many other sources of help as possible. In particular, you should discuss the franchise proposal with a banker, going over it in as much detail as possible. You should also obtain the services of a professional accounting firm in examining the franchisor's statements of projected sales, operating expenses, and net income. The accountant can be of invaluable help in evaluating the quality of these estimates and in discovering projections which may be unlikely to occur.

Termination, Transfer, and Renewal Provisions. One of the most important features of the contract is the provision relating to termination and transfer of the franchise. Some franchisors have been accused of devising agreements that permit arbitrary cancellation. Of course, it is reasonable for the franchisor to have legal protection in the event that a franchisee fails to obtain a satisfactory level of operation or to maintain satisfactory quality standards. However, the prospective franchisee should avoid contract provisions that contain overly-strict cancellation policies. Similarly, the rights of the franchisee to sell the business to a third party should be clearly stipulated. Any franchisor who can restrict the sale of the business to a third party can assume ownership of the business at an unreasonable price. The right of the franchisee to renew the contract after the business has been built up to a successful operating level should also be clearly stated in the contract.

Other Provisions. Among the many other items to be examined in any franchise contract are the following (an actual contract is shown in Appendix B at the end of this text):

1. Fees that are involved.
2. Territorial limits of the franchise.
3. Training provisions.
4. Restrictions upon the purchase of materials.
5. Control of operations and performance standards.
6. Quota clauses.
7. Prohibitions against the sale of competing lines.
8. Price requirements.
9. Record-keeping requirements.
10. Necessary hours and days of operation.
11. Advertising provisions.
12. Grants of franchise.

SELLING A FRANCHISE

Franchising contains opportunities on both sides of the fence. We have already presented the franchising story from the viewpoint of the potential franchisee. Now we shall look through the eyes of the potential franchisor.

Why would a businessperson wish to become a franchisor? At least three general benefits may be identified. An American Marketing Association study sees these advantages as follows:

1. *Source of capital*. The firm involved in franchising, in effect, through fee and royalty arrangements, borrows capital from the franchisee for channel development and thus has lower capital requirements than does the wholly owned chain.
2. *Increased motivation through franchising*. The franchisee as an independent businessman is probably more highly motivated than salaried employees because of profit incentives and growth opportunities.
3. *Less susceptibility to labor organization*. Since franchising is decentralized, the franchisor is less susceptible to labor organizing efforts than centralized organizations.[9]

Amid the older and highly successful large franchisors, such as McDonald's, are many small businesses which are finding success as franchisors. In fact, some of them begin as franchisors rather than evolve into franchisors by adding franchised outlets to an already established operation (see box). Regardless of when the franchise program is developed, it should be planned well. The many decisions to be made when developing a franchise program have been conveniently condensed into the following areas:

1. Deciding on the prospective franchisee.
2. Structuring the franchise package.
3. Marketing the franchise package.
4. Building a sales, cost, or profit forecast.
5. Setting market criteria.
6. Developing the franchise agreement.[10]

FRANCHISING — THE LAST FRONTIER

During the rapid expansion of the franchising industry, many small-business franchisees were hurt. Some of the ventures simply lacked a sound economic base. They were not opportunities in the strict sense of the word. In other cases, franchisees were victimized by fraudulent operators. Also, many franchisees felt that they were treated unfairly by franchising companies. Automobile dealers, for example, expressed various complaints against

---

9. Hackett, *op. cit.*, p. 14.

10. Adapted from Charles L. Vaughn, *Franchising* (Lexington, MA: Lexington Books, 1974), p. 47.

ACTION REPORT: Lighting the Franchise Candle

The idea of Wicks 'N' Sticks was born as Harold R. Otto was strolling around in a shopping center. At that time, Otto was a salesperson for an electrical equipment company. His plans were to begin operation with one store, and the initial financing was achieved routinely. About two months before the grand opening, Otto was asked to "share ideas" about a candle shop with a couple who wanted to get into business. The mall developer, who had contacted Otto on behalf of the couple, was amazed when Otto said, "I'll tell you what I'll do. We'll sell them a franchise." And that's what happened. For a fee of $2,500 and a 5 percent royalty, Wicks 'N' Sticks sold its first franchise. Otto has since opened several corporate-owned stores along with franchised outlets.

Cash problems beseiged the business in the early 1970s. Analysis of unit profits showed that the franchising stores were doing better than the corporate-owned stores. By emphasizing franchising outlets, Wicks 'N' Sticks began to recover. Otto is now a strong supporter of what actually marked the beginning of Wicks 'N' Sticks—franchising. He says, "It took several years to understand, but now I'm a 100 percent believer in franchising."

Source: "The House of Wax," *Forbes* (November 10, 1980), pp. 100-105.

the major automobile producers. Famous celebrities also allowed their names to be used in franchised businesses, sometimes with little attention to the business itself. The whole arrangement conveyed the impression of a scheme to take the small investor's money.[11]

Because of these facts and developments, many questions have been raised concerning the franchising industry. As might be expected, Congress has entered into these investigations. For example, the Select Committee on Small Business of the United States Senate has conducted hearings concerning the impact of franchising on small business.[12] Although the abuses in franchising clearly justify some measure of skepticism and public scrutiny, the undesirable aspects should not be allowed to obscure the positive values of franchising.

Franchising has been called the last frontier for American business. This statement is based upon the many thousands of business opportunities that have become available to independent business owners in the years of the

11. For further information, see H. Nicholas Windeshausen and Mary L. Joyce, "Franchising: An Overview," *American Journal of Small Business*, Vol. 1 (January, 1977), pp. 10-16.

12. See U. S. Congress, Senate, Hearings before the Subcommittee on Urban and Rural Economic Development of the Select Committee on Small Business, *The Impact of Franchising on Small Business*, 91st Congress, 2d Session, 1970.

franchising boom. Franchising has undoubtedly enabled many individuals to enter business who otherwise would never have escaped the necessity of salaried employment. Thus, franchising has contributed to the development of many successful small businesses.

In order for franchising to have a continuing, positive impact upon the small-business segment of the economy, it is important that abuses in franchising be eliminated. In any new and growing field, there are practices that deserve examination. And some type of control—either self-control or legislative control—becomes desirable. Legitimate franchising has contributed to the strength of small business in past years and should, assuming proper restraint, continue to provide thousands of small-business opportunities.

LOOKING BACK

1. Three basic types of franchising systems are: System A, where the producer is the franchisor and the wholesaler is the franchisee; System B, where the wholesaler is the franchisor and the retailer is the franchisee; and System C, where the producer is the franchisor and the retailer is the franchisee. The most widely used is System C.
2. Franchising provides three main advantages to the franchisee. These are: formal training and managerial guidance, financial assistance, and marketing expertise—all provided by the franchisor.
3. Three shortcomings permeate the franchise form of business. These are: the cost of a franchise, the restrictions on growth which can accompany a franchise contract, and the inherent loss of absolute independence on the part of the franchisee.
4. The task of locating the right franchise opportunity has become difficult. Helpful guides in locating franchise opportunities are *Franchise Opportunities Handbook*, *The 1981 Directory of Franchising Organizations*, and various publications of the International Franchise Association. A potential franchisee should examine a franchise opportunity to be sure that it is a legitimate franchise. An attorney should be consulted for aid in examining the franchise contract.
5. Selling a franchise can be advantageous to a franchisor because it provides a source of capital, increases motivation, and reduces susceptibility to labor problems.

DISCUSSION QUESTIONS

1. What makes franchising different from other forms of business? Be specific.
2. Explain the three types of franchising systems. Which is most widely used?
3. Briefly recount franchising changes from a historical perspective.
4. Evaluate the marketing benefits derived from a franchise.
5. Evaluate "loss of control" as a disadvantage of franchising.
6. How would you go about locating a franchise which you could be interested in buying? Be specific.
7. Do you think franchise contracts should be simpler? Why or why not?
8. What do you think the major weaknesses in a franchise contract might be?
9. Why would a business consider selling a franchise?
10. What, in your opinion, does the future hold for franchising?

REFERENCES TO SMALL BUSINESS IN ACTION

Carson, Linda G. "T-Shirts Plus Cashing in on the T-Shirt Craze." *Franchising Today*, Vol. 1, No. 6 (March-April, 1981), pp. 39-46.

Referred to as the "McDonald's of the T-shirt industry," this company's experiences with training, pricing, site location, promotion, and people are each discussed in an exciting fashion.

Merwin, John. "Postal Instant Success." *Forbes*, Vol. 127 (February 2, 1981), p. 56.

The article begins with an account of Bill Levine, founder and president of Postal Instant Press. In 1965, LeVine visited an old high school buddy who showed him an Itek commercial camera used in his dress business. LeVine's career in commercial printing helped him recognize the potential of this Itek camera, and he used it to begin business as a franchisor.

Rosene, Marcella. "Franchise Entrepreneurs of the 1980's." *Venture*, Vol. 2, No. 7 (July, 1980), pp. 27-30.

The theory behind the strength of franchising is brought to life with numerous quotes from operating franchisors. Their experiences are used to demonstrate problems and successes of franchise entrepreneurs.

Wrege, Rachael. "Subway: Success on Both Sides of the Franchising Coin." *Franchising Today* (February, 1981), pp. 54-56.

Subway is a fast-food franchise which began as a nonfranchised business in 1965. The franchise's aggressive marketing program is discussed in detail. The chain claims to be the second largest franchisor of its kind.

Chapter 5

Analyzing the Market

LOOKING AHEAD

Watch for the following important topics:

1. Types of marketing management philosophies.
2. Definition and types of market segmentation.
3. Steps in the marketing research procedure.
4. Purpose of marketing-information systems.
5. Considerations in forecasting sales.

A small business can be successful only if a market exists for its product or service. Therefore, one would expect every entrepreneur to be knowledgeable about his or her market. To find out if this is true, simply ask the manager of a small firm to describe that firm's market. Be prepared for vague generalities! Surprisingly enough, you will find how little thought small-business managers give to understanding their markets.

Analyzing a market is particularly important prior to starting a business. Without it, the entrepreneur enters the marketplace much like a high diver who leaves the board without checking the depth of the water. Many types of information from numerous sources are required for a market analysis. Proper techniques for gathering market information must be understood. Therefore, marketing research methods and forecasting techniques are explained in this chapter also.

DEFINITIONS OF A MARKET

The term *market* means different things to different people. Sometimes it simply refers to a location where buying and selling take place, as when we hear, "She went to the market." On other occasions the term is used to describe selling efforts, as when business managers say, "We must market this product aggressively." Still another meaning is the one we use in this chapter. We define a **market** as a group of *customers* or potential customers who have *purchasing power* and *unsatisfied needs*.

Notice carefully the three components of our definition of a market. First, a market must have a buying unit, or customers. These units may be individuals or business entities. For example, consumer products are sold to individuals and industrial products are bought for use by businesses. Thus, a market is more than a geographic area. It must contain potential customers.

Second, customers in a market must have purchasing power. Assessing the level of purchasing power in a potential market is very important. Customers who have unsatisfied needs but who lack the money and/or credit are poor markets because they have nothing to offer in exchange for a product or service. In such a situation, no transactions can occur.

Third, a market must contain buying units with unsatisfied needs. Final consumers, for instance, will not buy unless they are motivated to do so. Motivation can occur only when an individual has unsatisfied needs. It would be difficult, for example, to sell tent dehumidifiers to desert nomads!

In light of our definition of a market, therefore, analyzing a market is the process of locating and investigating buying units that have purchasing power and needs that can be satisfied with the product or service that the entrepreneur has to offer.

THE PROCESS OF MARKET ANALYSIS

A good market analysis is predicated on certain key concepts. Three of these concepts are: marketing management philosophies, market segmentation strategies, and consumer behavior. Since consumer behavior affects all marketing efforts—including pricing, promotion, and distribution—the discussion of this concept in this book is reserved for Chapter 9.

Understanding Marketing Management Philosophies

A person's philosophy will naturally influence the tactics used to achieve a particular goal. For example, consider the football coach who believes in "three yards and a cloud of dust." This coach overlooks neither passing nor the role of the defense. But success begins with the ground game, so the running attack is used as the major tool. Similarly, the small-business manager can subscribe to a particular philosophy. The type of market analysis performed depends on the marketing management philosophy selected.

Types of Marketing Management Philosophies. Three distinct philosophies are evident among small firms. These are commonly referred to as production-oriented, sales-oriented, and consumer-oriented philosophies. A consumer-oriented philosophy is the essence of what is called the **marketing concept**.

Over a period of time from the late nineteenth century to the present, big business has shifted its marketing emphasis from production to sales to consumer satisfaction.[1] The production-oriented philosophy associated with the Industrial Revolution created a period of very limited "marketing." Later, emphasis was placed on sales, so marketing managers concentrated on personal selling and advertising as the major marketing activities. Finally, businesses turned to the marketing concept, which required marketing activities to discover customer needs and preferences before making and trying to sell products.[2]

What can the small-business manager learn from this brief history lesson? Is this evolution limited to large businesses? The answer is no. It need not be. Indeed, it should not be. Is one philosophy more consistent with success? The answer is yes. In the long run nothing is better than consumer orientation.[3]

Factors That Influence a Marketing Management Philosophy. Why have some firms failed to adopt the marketing concept? The answer lies in three crucial factors which strongly influence a firm's marketing orientation. First, *the state of competition for providing a bundle of satisfaction largely determines a firm's orientation*. If there is little or no competition and if demand exceeds supply, a firm's emphasis naturally turns to production efficiency. On the other hand, an increase in competition forces the firm to emphasize consumer-based marketing activities for the potential edge that these can provide in the marketplace.

Second, *small-business managers show an enormous range of interest and ability in gathering market-related information and interpreting consumer characteristics*. For example, some small-business managers are strongest in production and weakest in sales. Therefore, production considerations receive the major-

---

1. Some people argue otherwise. See, for example, Martin L. Bell and C. William Emory, "The Faltering Marketing Concept," *Journal of Marketing*, Vol. 35 (October, 1971), pp. 37-42.

2. For a more complete discussion of these different eras, see William M. Pride and O. C. Ferrell, *Marketing: Basic Concepts and Decisions* (2d ed.; Boston: Houghton Mifflin Co., 1980), p. 15.

3. This is naturally a generalization. Ultimately it is the firm's individual circumstances which dictate its philosophy.

ity of their attention. Surely it is difficult to be aggressive in areas of weaker personal expertise.

Third, *a specific orientation may exist because of the manager's shortsightedness*. A sales-oriented philosophy, for example, is a shortsighted approach to marketing. Emphasis on "moving" merchandise can often create customer dissatisfaction if high-pressure selling is used with little regard for customers' needs. On the other hand, the marketing concept contributes to a long-range survival by emphasizing customer satisfaction.

If these three factors are inconsistent with the marketing concept, a production-oriented or sales-oriented philosophy will likely emerge.[4] Such philosophies may permit success. However, the marketing concept is preferable because it not only recognizes production-efficiency goals and professional selling, but also adds concern for the consumer's satisfaction. In effect, a firm that adopts the marketing concept considers the consumer as the beginning and the end for its exchange transactions.

Understanding Market Segmentation Strategies

Even though all people are similar, market segmentation is built on the premise that differences exist among them. Formally defined, **market segmentation** is the process of analyzing one market to find out if it should be viewed as more than one market. A small business may view its market in either general or specific terms. It may consider its market as all women or as only the 24-to-35-year-old single women living in the eastern United States. In the latter case, the firm is segmenting its market.

The Need for Market Segmentation. If a business had control of the only water supply in the world, its sales volume would be huge. This business would not be concerned about differences in personal preferences for taste, color, or temperature. It would consider its customers to be *one* market. As long as the water product was "wet," it would satisfy everyone. However, if someone else discovered a second water supply, the view of the market would change. The first business might discover that sales were drying up and turn to a modified strategy. The new approach could well emerge from an understanding of consumer behavior.

In the real world, a number of preferences for liquid drinks exist. What may seem to be a homogeneous market is actually heterogeneous. The different preferences may take a number of forms. Some preferences may relate to the way consumers react to the taste or to the container. Other preferences may relate to the price of the liquid drink or to the availability of "specials."

---

4. An interesting case for production emphasis when orders compete for limited manufacturing resources is made in William E. Sandman and Sam Pakenham-Walsh, "Don't Let Customers Ruin Your Profits," *Journal of Applied Management*, Vol. 4, No. 2 (March-April, 1979), pp. 14-21. Most small firms, however, do not have a demand which exceeds their resources.

Preferences might also be uncovered with respect to different distribution strategies or to certain promotional tones and techniques. In other words, markets may actually be composed of several submarkets.

Types of Market Segmentation Strategies. The three types of market segmentation strategies discussed in this text can best be illustrated by using an example of a hypothetical firm—the Worldwide Writing Company. These strategies are the unsegmented approach, the multisegmentation approach, and the single-segmentation approach.

The Unsegmented Strategy. When a business defines the total market as its target market, it is following an **unsegmented strategy**. This strategy can be successful occasionally, but it assumes that all buying units desire the same general benefit from the product or service. This may hold true for water but probably not for shoes, which satisfy numerous needs through many styles, prices, colors, and sizes. With an unsegmented strategy, the firm

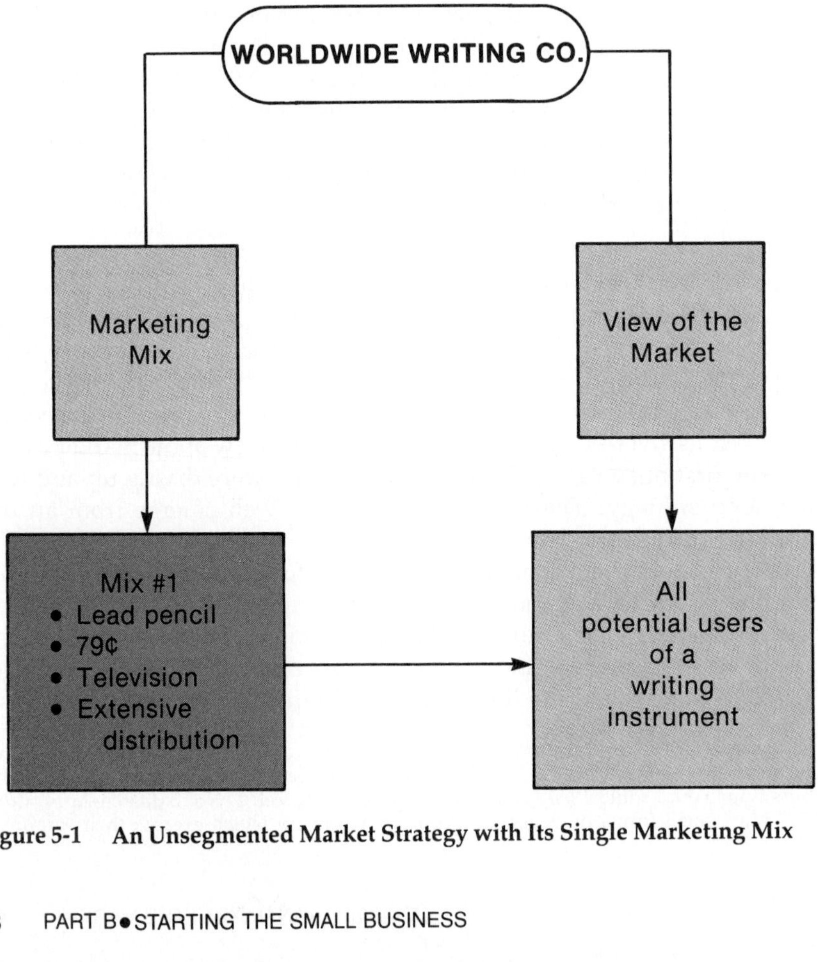

Figure 5-1 An Unsegmented Market Strategy with Its Single Marketing Mix

would develop a **single marketing mix**, which means one combination of the product, price, promotion, and distribution plan. For the unsegmented strategy of Worldwide Writing Company, see Figure 5-1. Worldwide Writing Company's product is a lead pencil which is sold at the one price of 79¢ and is communicated with a single promotional and distribution plan. Notice how the marketing mix is aimed at everybody. With this strategy only one sales forecast is required.

The Multisegmentation Strategy. With a view of the market which recognizes individual segments that have different preferences, a firm is in a position to tailor-make different strategies. For example, if a firm feels that two or more homogeneous market segments can be profitable, it will follow a **multisegmentation strategy** by developing a unique marketing mix for each segment.

Let us now assume that Worldwide Writing Company has discovered three separate market segments: students, professors, and executives. Following the multisegmentation approach, the company develops three mixes, which might be based on differences in pricing, promotion, distribution, or the product itself, as shown in Figure 5-2. Mix #1 consists of selling felt-tip pens to students through vending machines at the slightly higher-than-normal price of $1.00 and supporting this effort with a promotional campaign in campus newspapers. With Mix #2 the company might market the same pen to universities for use by professors. Personal selling is the only promotion used in this mix, distribution is direct from the factory, and the product price of 49¢ is extremely low. Finally, with Mix #3, which is aimed at executives of companies of the *Fortune 500* type, the product is a solid gold ink-writing instrument sold only in exclusive department stores. It is promoted in prestigious magazines and carries the extremely high price of $50. Although students might conceivably buy the solid gold pens for classroom writing, they are not viewed as members of this target market.

Notice the dramatic differences in the three marketing mixes. Small businesses, however, tend to postpone the use of multisegmentation strategies because of the risk of spreading resources too thinly among several marketing efforts.

The Single-Segmentation Strategy. When a firm recognizes that several distinct market segments exist but chooses to concentrate on reaching only one segment, it is following a **single-segmentation strategy**. The segment selected will be one which the business feels will be most profitable. One real-life example is "The Limited" in Chicago, IL, a women's clothing store that aims at a relatively small but very profitable market. Its typical customer is a young woman, probably an executive secretary who is very fashion-oriented. Worldwide Writing Company, our hypothetical example, selects the

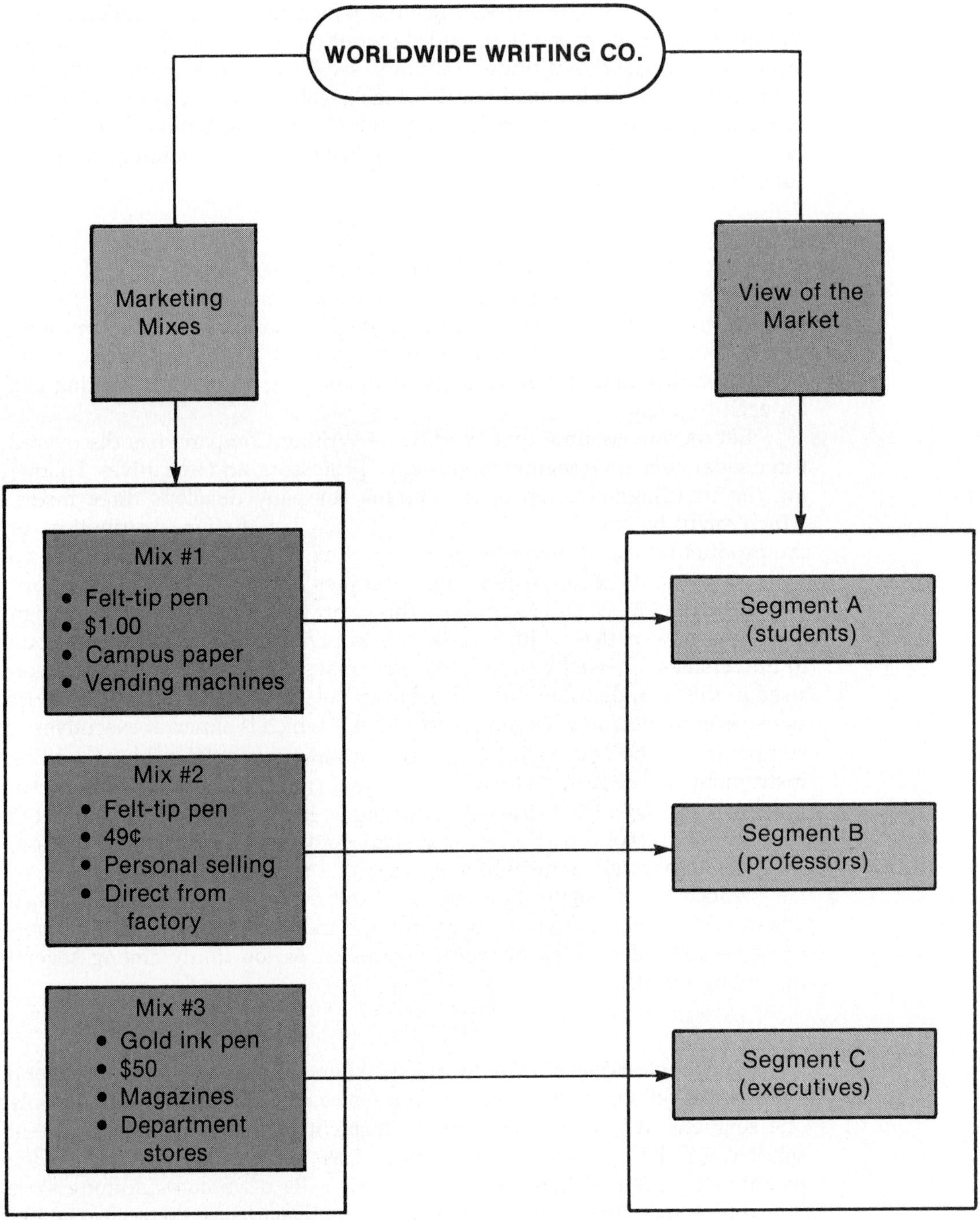

Figure 5-2 **A Segmented Market Strategy with Multiple Marketing Mixes**

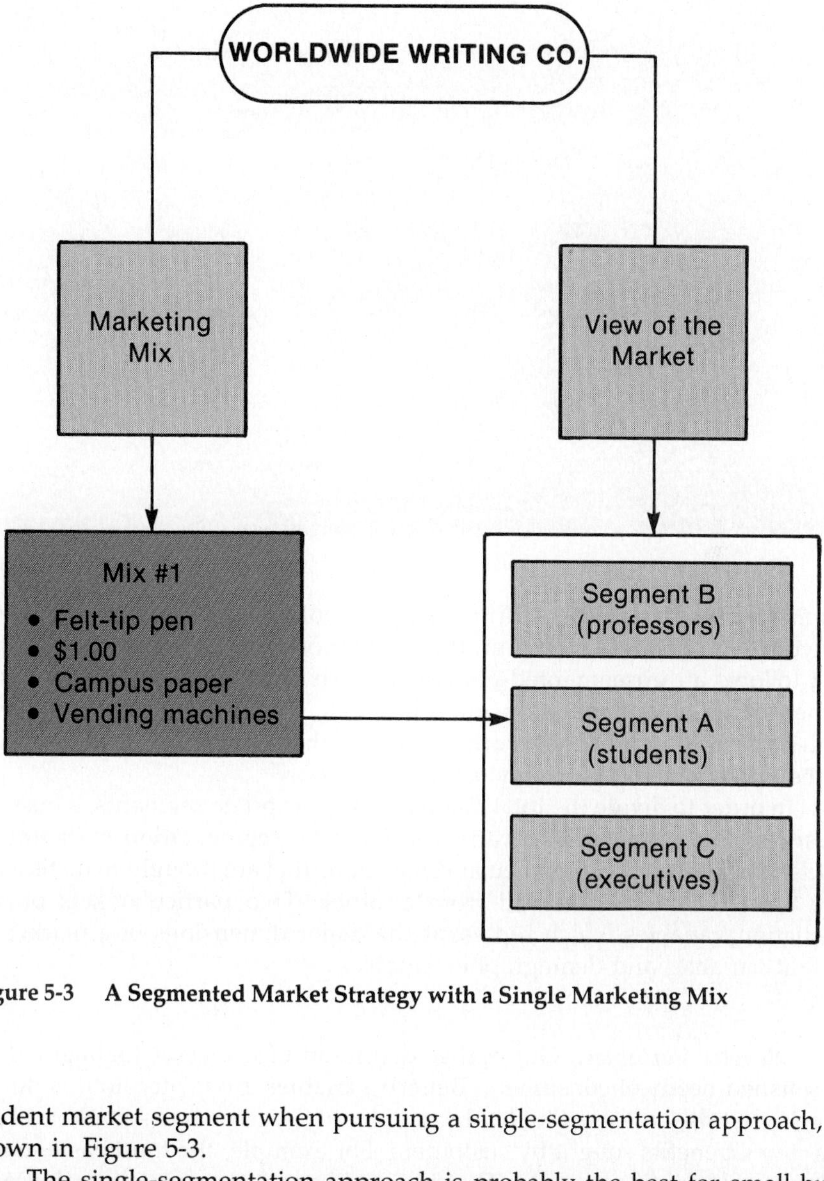

Figure 5-3 A Segmented Market Strategy with a Single Marketing Mix

student market segment when pursuing a single-segmentation approach, as shown in Figure 5-3.

The single-segmentation approach is probably the best for small businesses during their initial stages of growth. This approach allows them to specialize and make better use of their more limited resources. Then, when a reputation has been built, it is easier for them to enter new markets.[5]

5. See, for example, Susie Gharib Nazem, "Mamma Marcella Takes to the Air with Pasta Power," *Fortune*, Vol. 100, No. 4 (August 27, 1979), pp. 118-119.

ACTION REPORT: Zeroing in on a Market

Hurco Manufacturing Co., Inc., is a manufacturer of high-technology machine tools which was started by Jerry Roch in 1968 with little more than an idea. The idea, named Autobend, was an electronic control for a machine tool used to bend sheet metal. His idea cut costs by 50 percent. By the end of 1980, Hurco's sales had topped $28 million.

But Autobend was not merely thrown into the marketplace. It was targeted to a significant niche in the market. Hurco's vice-president of sales says, "Jerry's forte has been his ability to define our market and hold us to it. We've identified this concept of zeroing in now, but initially Jerry did it intuitively." Jerry has continued to isolate additional market segments by introducing microprocessors in machine-tool controls in 1975.

Source: John Halbrooks, "Making Money Isn't the Religion at Hurco," *Inc.*, Vol. 3, No. 4 (April, 1981), pp. 104-110.

Segmentation Variables. A firm's market could be defined very simply as "anyone who is alive"! However, this is too broad to be useful even for a firm that follows an unsegmented approach. With any type of market analysis, some degree of segmentation must be made. Notice in Figure 5-1, which represents an unsegmented market strategy, that the market is *not* everyone in the universe but rather only *potential* users.

In order to divide the total market into appropriate segments, a business must consider segmentation variables. Basically **segmentation variables** are labels which identify the particular dimensions that are thought to distinguish one form of market demand from another. Two particular sets of segmentation variables which represent the major dimensions of a market are benefit variables and demographic variables.

Benefit Variables. Our earlier definition of a market highlighted the unsatisfied needs of consumers. **Benefit variables** are related to this dimension in that they are used to divide and identify segments of a market according to the benefits sought by customers. For example, the toothpaste market has several benefit segments. The principal benefit to parents may be cavity prevention for their young children. On the other hand, the principal benefit to a teenager might be freshness. In both cases toothpaste is the product, but it has two different markets.

Demographic Variables. Benefit variables alone are insufficient for market analysis. It is impossible to implement forecasting and marketing strategy without defining the market further. Therefore, small businesses commonly use demographics as part of market segmentation. Typical demographics are age, marital status, sex, occupation, and income. Remember again our definition of a market—customers with purchasing power and unsatisfied needs. Thus, **demographic variables** refer to certain characteristics which describe customers and their purchasing power.

The market scenario for Segment A in Figure 5-2 can easily be divided into additional segments with benefit variables and demographic variables.

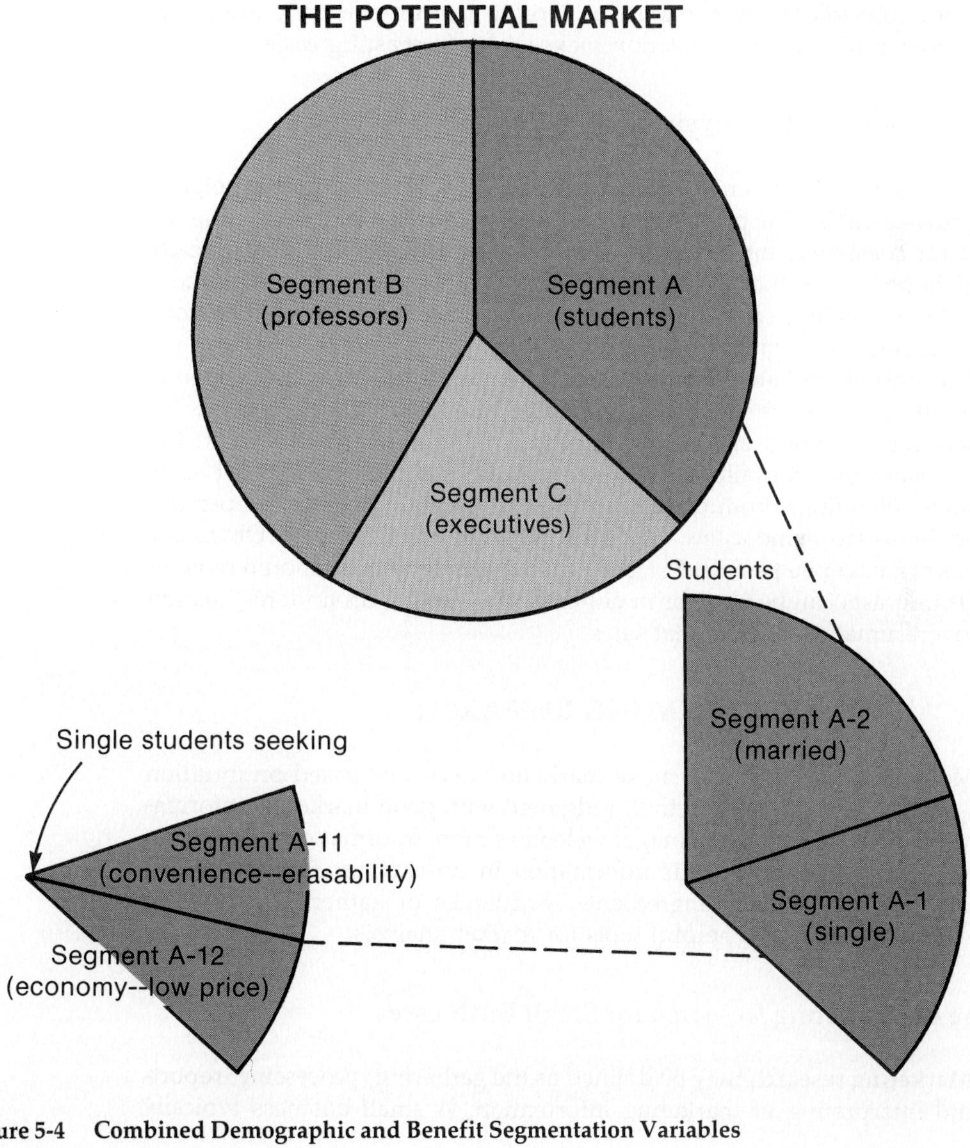

Figure 5-4 Combined Demographic and Benefit Segmentation Variables

(Occupation as a demographic variable was used in Figure 5-2.) This possibility is illustrated in Figure 5-4. Notice that the Segment A market, consisting of students, can be subdivided into Segments A-1 and A-2 according to the demographic variable of marital status. In addition, Segment A-1 can be subdivided into Segments A-11 and A-12 according to the benefit variables of convenience and economy.

Based on this hypothetical case, a sales forecast for a single-segmentation approach could be structured. The single-segmentation strategy could aim at the number of people in a geographic market who are single students looking mainly for convenience features in the writing instruments they purchase. Such precision in market delineation makes sales forecasting easier.

Benefits of a Market Analysis

A market analysis benefits the entrepreneur in several ways. It helps to conceptualize further the product idea or the service idea. After examining the market for cosmetics, for example, one business decided that it was really selling "hope" rather than cosmetic ingredients! This gave an added dimension to the marketing effect. A market analysis also aids in other decisions such as pricing, packaging, and store location.

The most immediate benefit of a market analysis, however, is the prediction of sales. The sales forecast is probably the most critical measure for assessing the feasibility of a new venture. If the market is insufficient, the business is destined for failure. The sales forecast is also useful in other areas of business planning. Production schedules, inventory policies, and personnel decisions—to name a few—all start with the sales forecast. Obviously forecasts can never be perfect. Furthermore, the entrepreneur should remember that forecasts can be in error in either of two ways—an underestimation or an overestimation of potential sales.

MARKETING RESEARCH

Marketing managers can make marketing decisions based on intuition alone, or they can supplement their judgment with good marketing information. More often than not, a manager welcomes more information for decision making. The availability of this information in no way guarantees a good decision, but it is a major ingredient. Techniques of gathering marketing information are therefore helpful tools for market analysis.

Nature of Marketing Research for Small Businesses

Marketing research may be defined as the gathering, processing, reporting, and interpreting of marketing information. A small business typically conducts less marketing research than a big business. The small firm's marketing research activity is usually informally organized and relies largely on outside assistance.[6] Part of the reason for this situation is cost. Another factor is a lack of understanding of the marketing research process. Our coverage of marketing research will emphasize the more widely used practical techniques that small-business firms can use as they analyze their market and make other operating decisions.

Evaluating the cost of research against the expected benefits is another step that the small-business manager should consider. Although this is a difficult task, increasingly sophisticated methods are available.[7]

Steps in the Marketing Research Procedure

A knowledge of good research procedures benefits the small-business manager. It helps in evaluating the validity of research done by others and in guiding the manager's own efforts. The various steps in the marketing research procedure include: identifying the problem, searching for secondary data and primary data, and interpreting and reporting the information gathered.

Identify the Problem. The first step in the marketing research procedure is to define precisely the informational requirements of the decision to be made. Although this may seem too obvious to mention, the fact is that needs are too often identified without sufficient probing. If the problem is not defined clearly, the information gathered will be useless. For example, a sales decline may be only a symptom of the true problem, which is the sudden resignation of key salespeople.

Search for Secondary Data. Information that has already been compiled is known as **secondary data.** Generally speaking, secondary data are less expensive to gather than new, or primary, data. The small business should exhaust all the available sources of secondary data before going further into the research process. Marketing decisions often can be made entirely with secondary data.

Secondary data may be internal or external. **Internal secondary data** consist of information which exists within the small business. The records of the business, for example, may contain useful information for the decision to be made. **External secondary data** abound in numerous periodicals, trade

---

6. Daniel S. Juhn and Kenneth J. Lacho, "Getting Information: Where Do Small Businessmen Go?" *Louisiana Business Survey*, Vol. 6, No. 3 (July, 1975), pp. 11-13.

7. One approach utilizes decision theory and Bayesian analysis. See Thomas C. Kinnear and James R. Taylor, *Marketing Research: An Applied Approach* (New York: McGraw-Hill Book Company, 1979), pp. 604-618.

associations, private informational services, and government publications. A particularly excellent source for the small business is the Small Business Administration. This agency publishes extensive bibliographies relating to many decision areas, including market analysis.

Unfortunately several problems accompany the use of secondary data. One problem is that such data may be outdated and, therefore, less useful. Another problem is that the units of measure in the secondary data may not fit the current problem. For example, a firm's market might consist of individuals with incomes between $20,000 and $25,000, while the secondary data show the number of individuals with incomes between $15,000 and $25,000. Finally, the question of trust is always present. Some sources of secondary data are less trustworthy than others. Publication of the data does not in itself make the data valid and reliable.[8]

Search for Primary Data. If the secondary data are insufficient, a search for new information, or **primary data**, is the next step. Several techniques can be used in accumulating primary data. These techniques are often classified as observational methods and questioning methods. Observational methods avoid contact with respondents, while questioning methods involve respondents in varying degrees.

Observational Methods. Observation is probably the oldest form of research in existence. Indeed, learning by observing is quite a common occurrence. Thus, it is hardly surprising that observation can provide useful information for small businesses, too. Observational methods can be used very economically. Further, they avoid a potential bias that results from a respondent's awareness of his or her participation under questioning methods.

Observation can be conducted by a human or a mechanical observer. The small-firm manager can easily use the less sophisticated personal observation method. For example, a restaurant manager can observe the preferences of customers as they order items from the menu. The major kinds of mechanical observation devices include cameras, recorders, and counting machines. Other mechanical devices, which are usually beyond the budget of most small businesses, are eye-camera equipment, pupilometers, and the Audimeter used by A. C. Nielsen Co. A major disadvantage of observational methods, however, is that they are limited to descriptive studies.

Questioning Methods. Both surveys and experimentation are questioning methods that involve contact with respondents. Surveys include contact by mail, telephone, and personal interviews. Mail surveys are

8. Michael F. d'Amico, "Marketing Research for Small Business," *Journal of Small Business Management*, Vol. 16, No. 1 (January, 1978), pp. 41-49.

ACTION REPORT: Look and Observe

Wanda Myers is a successful businesswoman who founded her own consulting business in 1977. Her firm offers supervisory training programs which emphasize principles of behavior modification. She started the business with $400 worth of second-hand furniture, a small office, and a volunteer secretary.

Myers has a master's degree in educational psychology, but she didn't start the full-time business until she had done her own informal market analysis. She says, "I became concerned when I looked around and observed that employers . . . were constantly creating dependency with the little tricks." She further analyzed the market, as she notes, "When I examined the existing supervisory programs, I noticed they all were either technical or motivational in nature. Mine is neither."

Her observation led her to the unsatisfied market niche which now provides revenues in the six-figure category.

Source: "Making 'b-mod' Pay," *Texas Business* (April, 1981), pp. 30-31.

often used when respondents are widely dispersed; however, these are characterized by low response rates. Telephone surveys and personal interview surveys involve verbal communication with respondents and provide higher response rates. Personal interview surveys, however, are more expensive

ACTION REPORT: Consumer Surveys Can Help

In October, 1968, Ed Hagerty was Market Research Director of *Popular Science* when he presented a 200-plus page report of a consumer survey to the magazine's board of directors. The report, which cost over $100,000, showed a strong reader interest in articles which dealt with "new products or discoveries." As a result of the study, the magazine added a highly successful pictorial digest of new products.

Regular editorial surveys by *Popular Science* allow the staff to "clearly identify those elements of the magazine's editorial format or mix which sparked reader interest," Mr. Hagerty states. "The need for customer surveys is just as great for a magazine with 10,000 circulation . . . as for the million-plus magazine."

Mr. Hagerty now publishes his own magazine, *Rugby*.

Source: Ed Hagerty, "Customer Surveys Can Steer You Right," *In Business*, Vol. 3, No. 2 (March-April, 1981), p. 27.

than mail and telephone surveys. Moreover, individuals often are reluctant to grant personal interviews because they feel that a sales pitch is forthcoming.

Experimentation is a form of research that concentrates on investigating cause-and-effect relationships. The goal of experimentation is to establish the effect which an experimental variable has on a dependent variable. For example, the problem might be defined as: What effect will a price change have on sales? Here the price is the experimental variable, and sales volume is the dependent variable. Measuring the relationship between these two variables would not be difficult if it were not for the many other variables which confound the true relationship. Rain,a new display, and different packaging all could distort an experiment attempting to measure the effect of a lower price on sales of umbrellas. A properly designed experiment will control those confounding variables so that the actual effect of the experimentation can be measured.

Developing a Questionnaire. A questionnaire is the basic instrument for guiding the researcher and the respondent when surveys are being taken. The questionnaire should be developed carefully and pretested before it is used in the market. Several major considerations in designing a questionnaire are listed below:

1. Ask questions that relate to the decision under consideration. An "interesting" question may not be relevant. Assume an answer to each question, and then ask yourself how you would use that information. This provides a good test of relevance.
2. Select a form of question that is appropriate for the subject and the conditions of the survey. Open-ended and multiple-choice questions are two popular styles.
3. Carefully consider the order of the questions. The wrong sequence can cause biases in answers to later questions.
4. Ask the more sensitive questions near the end of the questionnaire. Age and income, for example, are usually sensitive subjects.
5. Carefully select the words of each question. They should be as simple and clear as possible.

Figure 5-5 shows a one-page questionnaire developed for a small business by one of the authors of this text. The firm's research problem was to assess the market potential for its new product—wooden pallets. Potential users of wooden pallets were identified and mailed the one-page questionnaire. Notice the use of both multiple-choice and open-ended questions in this questionnaire. Responses to Item 6 provided some extremely useful information for this firm.

QUESTIONNAIRE

Special Note. If you would like to receive information on our wooden pallets once production is started, please check the square below and write in your current mailing address.

I would like to receive this information ☐
Address: ______________________
____
____

1. Does your business currently use wooden pallets? (If *No*, skip to Question 7.)

Yes	______	(1.1)
No	______	(1.2)

2. What percentage of your wooden pallet needs require *Expendable Pallets* (pallets used only one time)?

0-25%	______	(2.1)
26-50%	______	(2.2)
51-75%	______	(2.3)
76-100%	______	(2.4)

3. For each of the following types of wooden pallets, please indicate the approximate quantity you require each year.

Type	*Quantity*	
Pallet Bins (All Sizes)	______________	(5-10)
Pallet Bases (All Sizes)	______________	(15-20)
Other (Please Specify)	______________	(25-30)
______________	______________	(35-40)
______________	______________	(45-50)
______________	______________	

4. Please indicate which one of the following statements best describes your firm's buying patterns for wooden pallets. (Please check only one.)

Purchase each month	______	(60.1)
Purchase about twice a year	______	(61.1)
Purchase only once a year	______	(62.1)

5. Approximately how close to your business site is your major supplier of wooden pallets?

Less than 20 miles	______	(63.1)
20 to 50 miles	______	(63.2)
51 to 80 miles	______	(63.3)
81 to 120 miles	______	(63.4)
121 to 150 miles	______	(63.5)
Over 150 miles	______	(63.6)

6. What suggestions would you make to help us provide wooden pallets to better meet your needs?

____
____
____

7. Please indicate the major products of your firm.

____
____

Please mail the questionnaire in the enclosed self-addressed envelope.

THANK YOU FOR YOUR COOPERATION ! ! !

Figure 5-5 Questionnaire for a Mail Survey

Interpret and Report the Information. After the necessary data have been accumulated, they should be transformed into usable information. Large quantities of data are only facts without a home. They must be organized and molded into meaningful information. Numerous methods of summarizing and simplifying information for users are available including tables, charts, and other graphic methods. Descriptive statistics, such as the mean, mode, and median, are most helpful during this step in the research procedure.

Marketing-Information Systems

Marketing-information systems refer to an organized way of gathering information for the purpose of providing useful information on a regular basis. These systems emerge when managers realize the repetitive nature of their informational needs. A formal marketing-information system helps them stay in contact with the firm's changing market profile.

The marketing-information system should be tailored to reflect a consumer orientation. This may require extension beyond the traditional sources of information for marketing-information systems. For example, a small business might conceivably use a consumer advisory board consisting of representative customers in order to keep in touch with market needs and problems. Also, the small business can structure a consumer communication system for hearing consumer complaints and questions. Some businesses have referred to this system as a "cool-line." Much of the information received through this approach can be used for decision making.[9]

Most people associate marketing-information systems with computerized systems. However, a marketing-information system does not necessarily require computers. In a very small business, the needed information flow may not justify the cost of computers. Furthermore, collecting marketing information is not as magical as some small-business people believe. Once they have done it, or seen it done, many of their reservations about it are removed.[10]

SALES FORECASTING

It is difficult enough to document the past, much less forecast the future. Nevertheless, businesses indulge in forecasting to reap the benefits of "knowing" what lies ahead. A knowledge of possible future sales levels is particularly valuable to the new business.

---

9. Priscilla A. La Barbera and Larry J. Rosenberg, "How Marketers Can Better Understand Consumers," *MSU Business Topics*, Vol. 28, No. 1 (Winter, 1980), pp. 29-36.

10. A very precise and helpful example of a primary research effort is given in Robert T. Justis and Bill Jackson, "Marketing Research for Dynamic Small Businesses," *Journal of Small Business Management*, Vol. 16, No. 4 (October, 1978), pp. 10-20.

The Sales Forecast

Formally defined, a **sales forecast** is the prediction of how much of a product or service will be purchased by a market for a defined time period. The sales forecast can be stated in terms of dollars and/or units.

Notice that a sales forecast revolves around a *specific market*. This means that the market should be defined as precisely as possible. The market description forms the forecasting boundary. For example, consider the sales forecast for a manual shaving device. If the market for this product is described simply as "men," the potential sales forecast would be extremely large. Alternatively, a more precise definition, such as "men between the ages of 15 and 25 who are dissatisfied with electric shavers," will result in a smaller but more useful forecast.

Also note that the sales forecast implies a *defined time period*. One sales forecast may cover a year or less, while another extends over several years. Both the short-term and the long-term forecasts are needed in the entrepreneur's business plan.

Limitations to Forecasting

For a number of practical reasons, forecasting is used more successfully by large firms than by small companies. First, the typical small-business manager is unable to use or to appreciate the methods of quantitative analysis.[11] This is not to say that all forecasting must be quantitatively oriented. Qualitative forecasting is helpful and may be sufficient. However, quantitative methods have proven their value in forecasting over and over again.

Second, the small-business entrepreneur is not familiar with the forecasting process, and it is unlikely that the small firm employs a forecaster. To overcome these deficiencies, some small firms attempt to keep in touch with industry trends through contacts with their trade association. From the standpoint of its professional staff members, the trade association is frequently better qualified to engage in business forecasting. Also, small-business entrepreneurs provide themselves with current information about business trends by regularly reading trade publications and economic newsletters such as the *Kiplinger Washington Letter*, *Business Week*, and *The Wall Street Journal*. Figure 5-6 shows a typical forecast from one of these sources. This information would be useful in developing the sales forecast for the business plan of an entrepreneur entering the videodisc market.

---

11. Students who have a special interest in forecasting should review the methods described in Steven C. Wheelwright and Darral G. Clarke, "Corporate Forecasting: Promise and Reality," *Harvard Business Review*, Vol. 54, No. 6 (November-December, 1976). Specific statistical techniques involved in forecasting cannot be explored in detail in a textbook of this type. Standard textbooks on business statistics should be consulted.

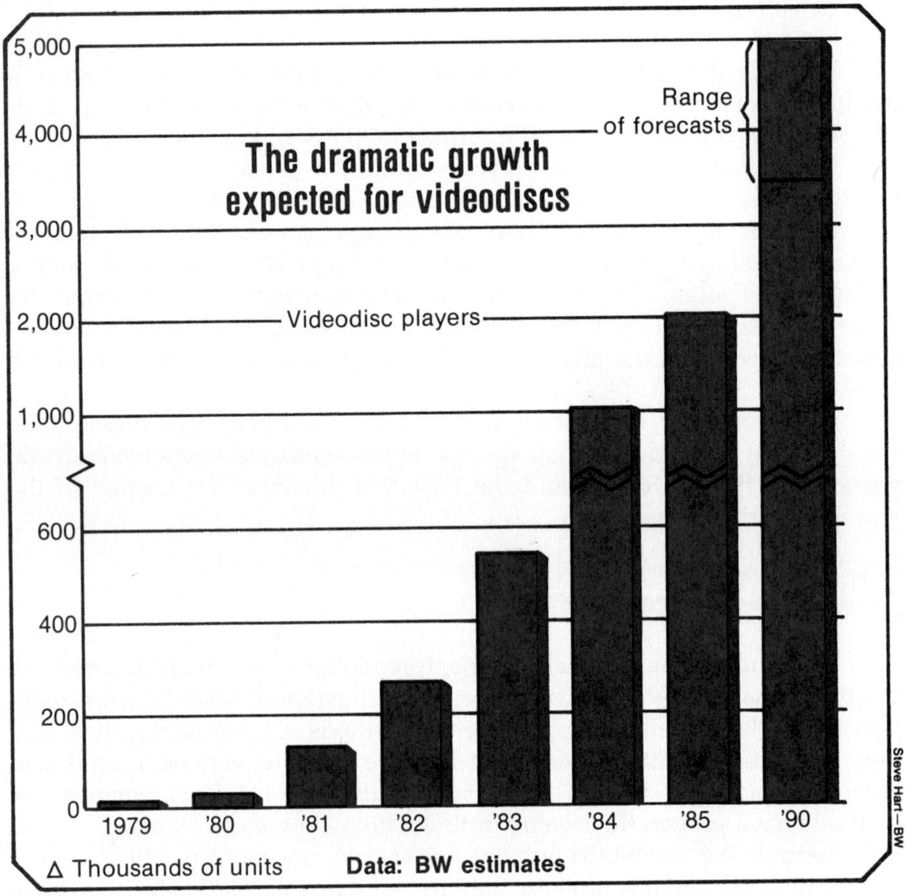

Source: Reprinted from the July 7, 1980 issue of *Business Week* by special permission, © 1980 by McGraw-Hill, Inc., New York, NY 10020. All rights reserved.

Figure 5-6 Forecast of Sales for Videodisc Players

Government publications, such as *Survey of Current Business*, *Federal Reserve Bulletin*, and *Monthly Labor Review*, are also of interest in a general way. Then there is the possibility of subscribing to professional forecasting services, which provide forecasts of general business conditions or specific forecasts for given industries.

Third, the entrepreneur's forecasting circumstances are unique. Inexperience coupled with a new idea represents the most difficult forecasting situation, as depicted in Figure 5-7. An ongoing business which needs only an updated forecast for its existing product is in the most favorable forecasting position.

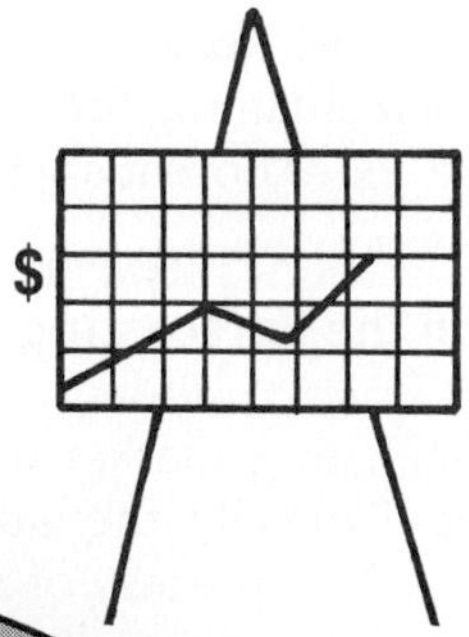

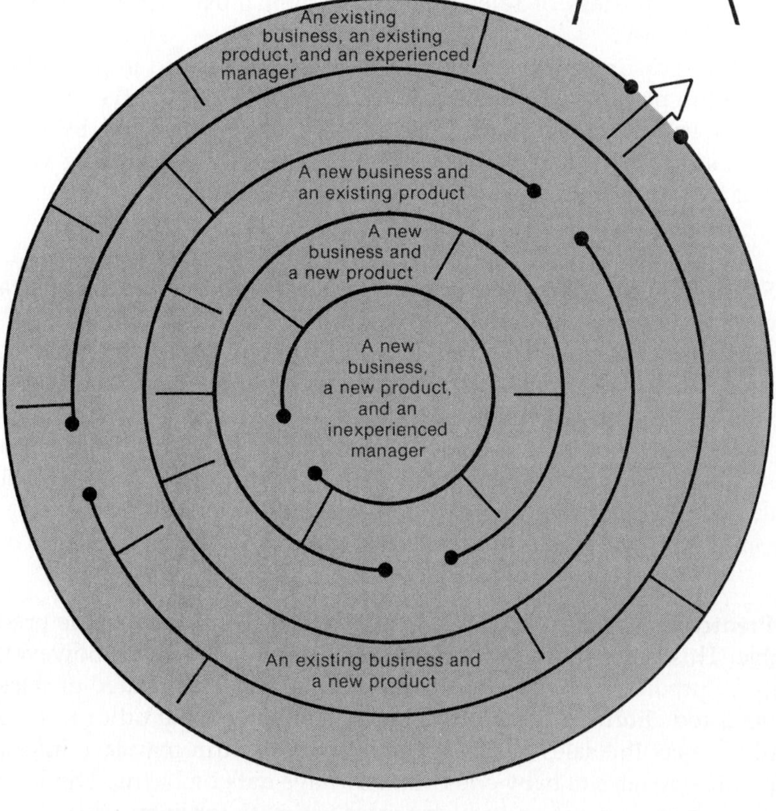

MOST COMPLEX TO LEAST COMPLEX

1. A new business with a new product, operated by an inexperienced manager.
2. A new business with a new product.
3. A new business with an existing product.
4. An existing business with a new product.
5. An existing business with an existing product, operated by an experienced manager.

Figure 5-7 Selected Situations Ranked by General Difficulty to Forecast

Yet the small business should not slight the forecasting task because of its limitations. Remember how important the sales outlook is to the business plan when obtaining financing! The statement "We can sell as many as we can produce" does not satisfy the information requirements of potential investors.

Steps in the Forecasting Process

Estimating market demand with a sales forecast involves a multistep process. Typically the sales forecast is a composite of several individual forecasts. The process of sales forecasting then must merge the individual forecasts properly.

The forecasting process can be characterized by two important dimensions: (1) the point at which the process is started, and (2) the nature of the predicting variable. The starting point is usually designated by the terms *buildup process* or *breakdown process*. The nature of the predicting variable is denoted by either *direct forecasting* or *indirect forecasting*.

The Starting Point. A **breakdown process** starts with the forecast of a variable at the macro level and systematically reduces the value of that variable to the appropriate micro level. For example, if a firm has access to a relevant industry forecast (macro level), it can use this forecast and break it down to the firm's sales forecast (micro level).

A **buildup process** is used as the starting point for forecasting when no industry figures are available. In this case a firm might conduct a limited survey of individual customers to determine their buying intentions. Using the results, the firm could build its sales forecast for its entire target market.

The Predicting Variable. In **direct forecasting**, sales is used as the predicting variable. This is the simplest form of forecasting. Many times, however, sales cannot be predicted directly. In this case other variables related to sales must be forecasted. **Indirect forecasting** takes place when the other forecasts are used to project the sales forecast. For example, a firm may lack information about industry sales of baby cribs but may have data on births. The figures for births can help forecast an industry sales estimate for baby cribs.

Forecasting Techniques

Many forecasting techniques can be used in a small business. Some techniques are simple, while others are extremely complex. But do not assume that the most complex are necessarily the best! A simple method can be just as accurate as a complex method. If you want to know the number of new homes which will be constructed on the north side of town, for example, a drive in the area may give you the correct figure. Conversely, you might consider a complex model incorporating a statistical forecast of several key factors such as interest rates and building-material costs.

Forecasting techniques are classified in many ways. Most classifications make distinctions based on the complexity of quantitative methods, the amount of available information, and the source of the information. The time series techniques, for example, rely on historical data and on quantitative tools. For a new venture, a time series technique could be used with an indirect forecasting process even though no historical sales data for the specific firm exist. On the other hand, the Delphi method is a qualitative technique that requires no objective historical data since the source of the Delphi forecast is a panel of experts.

Generally it is preferable to state the sales forecast as a range of possible sales levels. For example, a forecast of $50,000 to $65,000 in sales is better than a forecast of $57,500. In the final analysis, however, the entrepreneur must judge the validity of the sales forecast.

LOOKING BACK

1. The three major marketing management philosophies are production-oriented, sales-oriented, and consumer-oriented. The consumer-oriented philosophy is the essence of the marketing concept.
2. Market segmentation is the process of analyzing a market to decide if it should be considered as more than one market. There are three types of market segmentation strategies: the unsegmented strategy, the multi-segmentation strategy, and the single-segmentation strategy.
3. The first step in the marketing research procedure is to identify accurately the problem to be solved. The second step is to search for secondary and primary data, which are two forms of marketing information. Data are collected by observational and questioning methods. Finally, the data are interpreted and reported to the appropriate people.
4. Marketing-information systems refer to an organized way of gathering marketing information so as to obtain the needed data on a regular basis.
5. Estimating market demand with a sales forecast involves a multistep process. The starting point of the sales forecast can be designated as a buildup process or a breakdown process. Direct forecasting and indirect forecasting are two basic forms of forecasting sales. Forecasting techniques are usually classified in two ways: qualitative techniques and quantitative techniques.

DISCUSSION QUESTIONS

1. Explain why the three components in our definition of a market must be viewed as having a multiplicative relationship rather than an additive relationship.

2. Why is it so important to understand the target market? What difference would it make if the entrepreneur simply ignored the characteristics of market customers?

3. How do the three marketing management philosophies differ? Select a consumer product and discuss your marketing tactics for *each* philosophy.

4. How does a multisegmentation view of the market differ from a single-segmentation approach? Be specific.

5. Assume your instructor desired to design this course using benefit variables. What various types of benefits do you believe exist for your classmates (consumers)? How would this influence your instructor's course requirements?

6. Assume you are contemplating to market a new facial tissue product. Write a detailed market profile of your target customers. Use benefit and demographic variables in your profile. Redefine one or more of these variables. How would this change the marketing mix?

7. What research methods would you use to measure the number of blonde males at your school?

8. What research method would you use to determine if a warranty helped product sales? Be specific.

9. What is the basic difference between marketing research and marketing-information systems?

10. Distinguish between direct sales forecasting and indirect sales forecasting. Give examples.

REFERENCES TO SMALL BUSINESS IN ACTION

Bartos, Rena. "Over 49: The Invisible Consumer Market." *Harvard Business Review*, Vol. 58, No. 1 (January-February, 1980), pp. 140-148.

This article provides an excellent quantitative and qualitative analysis of a market which can be segmented into a number of groupings, and it demonstrates the untapped opportunities which many other markets hold.

Benner, Susan. "Next Stop Wall Street." *Inc.*, Vol. 3, No. 3 (March, 1981), pp. 36-41.

The experiences of Lore Harp and her computer business demonstrate that companies with the same market data select different target markets. Her firm identified a small-business market in 1976 from a market with no clearly defined market segments at that time.

Kinkead, Gwen. "A 'Me Too' Strategy That Paid Off." *Fortune*, Vol. 100, No. 4 (August 27, 1979), pp. 86-88.

Uniqueness is not the only road to success. Copycatting tactics of Helene Curtis Industries in the high-priced shampoo market are discussed in this article.

Chapter 6

Selecting a Location and Physical Facilities

LOOKING AHEAD

Watch for the following important topics:

1. Considerations in choosing a location.
2. Sources of information about locations.
3. Spatial, functional, and structural requirements for the business's building.
4. Efficient layouts for small factories and retail stores.
5. Equipment and tooling needs of small factories and retail stores.

Every business needs a base of operations, be it a million-dollar plant or just a suitcase. The emergence of a business facility should be more than a chance happening. Locating and designing the physical facility deserve careful analysis. Although individual venture circumstances will determine the eventual business location and facility design, most entrepreneurs can benefit from evaluating certain factors that commonly influence decisions about these matters. These factors are discussed in this chapter.

IMPORTANCE OF A WELL-CHOSEN LOCATION

For most small businesses, a location decision is made only when the business is first established or purchased. Occasionally, however, a business considers relocation to reduce operating costs, get closer to its customers, or gain other advantages. Also, as a business expands, it sometimes becomes desirable to begin additional operations at other locations. The owner of a custom drapery shop, for example, may decide to open a second unit in another section of the same city or even in another city.

It is not the frequency but the lasting effects of location decisions that make them so important. Once the business is established, it is costly and often impractical, if not impossible, to "pull up stakes" and move. If the business depends upon a heavy flow of customer traffic, a shrewdly selected site that produces maximum sales will increase profits throughout its existence at that location. In contrast, a site with light traffic will reduce the sales figure on every income statement throughout the life of the business. If the choice is particularly poor, the business may never be able to "get off the ground," even with adequate financing and superior ability in purchasing and selling merchandise. This enduring effect is so clearly recognized by national chain-store organizations that they spend thousands of dollars investigating sites before establishing new stores.

The choice of a location is much more vital to some businesses than to others. For example, the site chosen for a dress shop can make or break it. In contrast, the exact location of a painting contractor is of relatively minor importance. Even painting contractors, however, may suffer from certain locational disadvantages. All cities have buildings that need painting, but property is kept in better repair and painted more frequently in some communities than in others.

CONSIDERATIONS IN SELECTING A LOCATION

It is possible that more than one location is satisfactory. An automobile garage may do an equal amount of business at either of two corner buildings. On the other hand, many undesirable locations appear satisfactory on the surface. Only careful investigation will reveal the good and bad features of any particular location.

General Considerations

Large business firms have professionally qualified personnel whose analysis and advice are invaluable in evaluating prospective locations. In contrast, the small-business entrepreneur must personally do the major part of the investigational work. Four general factors are important in this investigation. These factors are: personal preference, environmental conditions, resource availability, and customer accessibility. In a particular situation one factor may have a stronger pull than the others, but each always has an influence. These factors and their impact on location decisions are depicted in Figure 6-1. Notice that the compass needle is influenced by all four factors, moving restlessly and unable to point to the best location until specific venture circumstances are provided.

Personal Preference. All too often, a prospective entrepreneur considers only the home community for locating the business. Frequently the possibility of locating elsewhere never enters one's mind. Home community preference, of course, is not the only personal factor influencing location. The owner may, for example, wish to locate in an area of the country that offers warm weather, fishing opportunities, or a desired religious or social atmosphere.

Choosing one's hometown for personal reasons is not necessarily an illogical decision. In fact, there are certain advantages. For one thing, the individual generally accepts and appreciates the atmosphere of the home

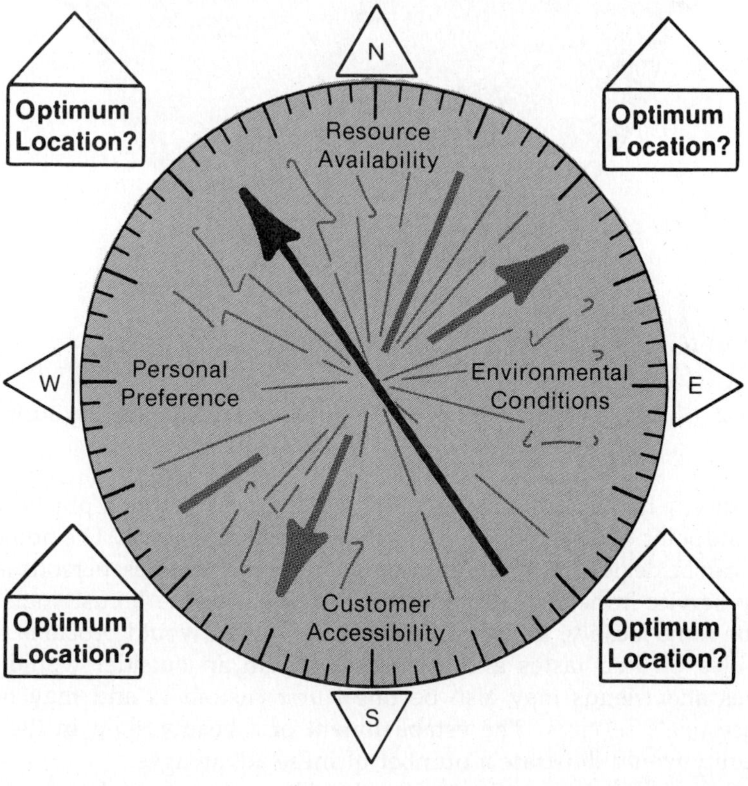

Figure 6-1 Location Compass for a Small Business

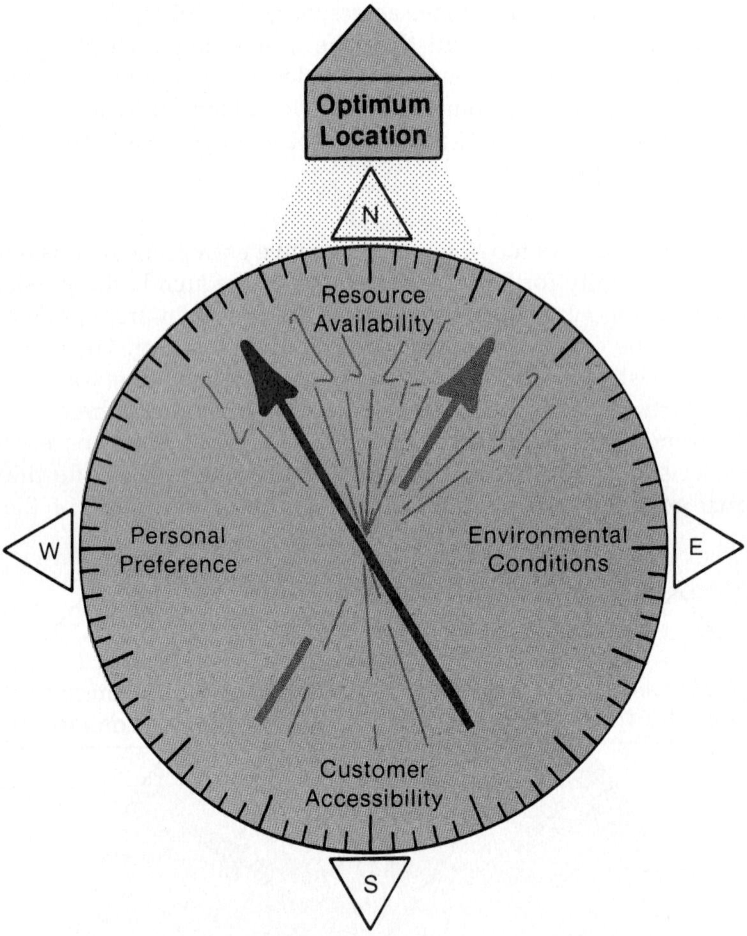

Figure 6-2 Location Compass for a Small Manufacturing/Wholesaling Business

community, whether it is a small town or a large city. From a practical business standpoint, the beginner can more easily establish credit. The hometown banker can be dealt with more confidently, and other businesspersons may be of great service in helping evaluate a given opportunity. If customers come from the same locality, the prospective entrepreneur would probably have a better idea of their tastes and peculiarities than an outsider would have. Relatives and friends may also be one's first customers and may help to advertise one's services. The establishment of a beauty shop in the home community would illustrate a number of these advantages.

Personal preferences, however, should not be allowed to cancel out location weaknesses even though such preferences may logically be a primary factor. Just because an individual has always lived in a given town does not automatically make it a satisfactory business location.

Environmental Conditions. A small business must operate within the environmental conditions of its location. These conditions can hinder or promote success. For example, weather is an environmental consideration which has traditionally influenced location decisions. In recent years the harsh winters of the northern United States have moved businesses further south. Other environmental conditions, such as competition, laws, and citizens' attitudes, to name a few, are all part of the business environment. The time to evaluate all these environmental conditions is prior to making a location decision.

Resource Availability. Resources associated with the location site and the ongoing operation of a business are an important factor to consider when selecting a location. Land, water supply, labor supply, and waste disposal are just a few of the many site-related resources that have a bearing on site costs.

Raw materials and labor supply are particularly critical considerations to the location of a manufacturing business. A wholesale business is also dependent on a convenient location to receive the goods for redistribution to its customers. The location compass in Figure 6-2 symbolizes the prominent role of resource availability to manufacturers and wholesalers. The compass needle has settled considerably and now points in one general direction—a location that favors resource availability. However, personal preference or environmental conditions may exert a stronger influence on the final location decision and thus sacrifice some resource advantage.

Customer Accessibility. Sometimes the foremost consideration in selecting a location is customer accessibility. Retail outlets and service firms are typical examples of businesses that must be located conveniently to customers. Figure 6-3 shows the compass needle settling in the general direction of the customer-accessibility variable, reflecting its importance in locating service/retail businesses. Once again, the precise location may be influenced more strongly by the variables of personal preference or environmental conditions.

Specific Considerations in Evaluating Geographical Locations

For some businesses—a barbershop or drugstore, for example—the choice of a geographical area is simple. These businesses can operate successfully in most areas of the country. Personal preference is their major consideration. Other types of small businesses, however, need to analyze the problem of geographical location with extreme care. Their location decision need not be played like the Monopoly game in Figure 6-4. A logical step-by-step process in evaluating the region, city, or actual site for the business can aid the entrepreneur in making this decision.

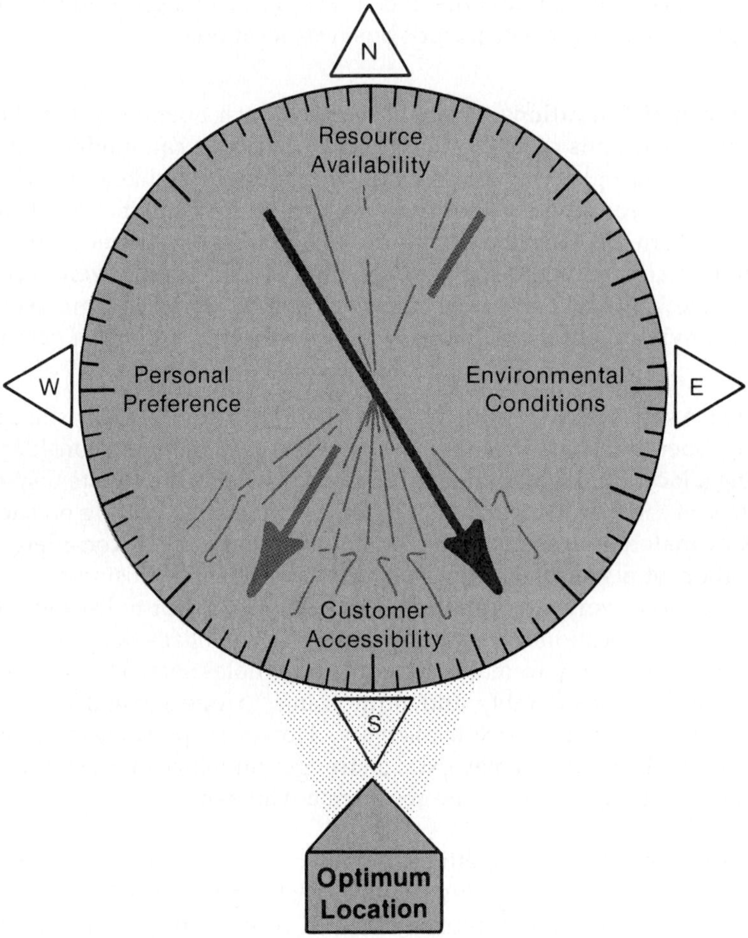

Figure 6-3 Location Compass for a Small Service/Retail Business

Choice of Region. Some markets for goods and services are restricted to certain regions. The following examples will make this point clear:

1. A ski lodge is practical only in an area with slopes and snow.
2. A boat repair service must locate near the water.
3. Stores selling home air conditioners have a larger market potential in the southern states than in the northern states.
4. Subcontractors to aircraft manufacturers produce parts for use in nearby production plants.

"I'm putting two hotels on Park Place, a house on Boardwalk and a McDonald's on Marvin Gardens."

Source: *The Saturday Evening Post*, Vol. 253, No. 3 (April, 1981), p. 38. Reprinted with permission from The Saturday Evening Post Company, © 1981.

Figure 6-4 Location Decisions Based on Chance

Several basic considerations that enter into evaluations concerning a regional choice, particularly for manufacturing businesses, are: nearness to the market, availability of raw materials, and adequacy of labor supply.

Nearness to the Market. Locating near the center of the market is clearly desirable if other factors are approximately equal. This is especially true of industries in which the cost of shipping the finished product is high relative to its value. For example, bricks and soft drinks require production facilities that are close to the consuming markets. And even though toy manufacturers are able to serve both national and international markets, they must think in terms of their heaviest concentration of customer orders.

Availability of Raw Materials. If the raw materials required by the business are not abundantly available throughout the country, then the region in which these materials abound would offer locational advantages. Bulky or heavy raw materials that lose much of their bulk or weight in the manu-

ACTION REPORT: The Fair's Location Works Well

Locating near the market is less critical for a specialty retail store than for a convenience store. Personal preferences and environmental factors can overshadow market considerations.

The Fair in Lott, TX is an excellent example of this location circumstance. The Fair is a specialty western store emphasizing quality boots and jeans at low prices. Its current owner, Mrs. R. W. Hailey, says, "Our customers are not from Lott. . . . Of course, we still sell to people here, but we sell mostly to out-of-towners." The population of Lott is around 800, and it's not unusual to see The Fair quadruple Lott's population in a single afternoon. Over 2 days after Thanksgiving in 1980, the store had 6,222 customers.

Customers from as far away as Canada make regular shopping trips to The Fair. But Mrs. Hailey plans to stay in Lott. "I have never wanted to move," she says. "My husband thought about building another business to expand, but I told him it would only take away from the business we have here." The owner's grandson, Bert Hailey, manages the store, which grossed around $6 million in 1980.

Source: Carolyn Ladendorf, "Crowds Crave The Fair's Fare," *Waco Tribune-Herald*, December 10, 1980, pp. 1A-2A.

facturing process are powerful forces that affect location. The sawmill is an example of a plant which must stay close to its raw materials in order to operate economically.

Adequacy of Labor Supply. A manufacturer's labor requirements depend upon the nature of its production process. In some cases the need is for semiskilled or unskilled labor, and the problem is to locate in a surplus labor area. Other firms find it desirable to seek a pool of highly skilled labor — the highly skilled machine trade of New England is a well-known example of such a labor supply. In addition, wage rates, labor productivity, and a history of peaceful industrial relations are particularly important considerations for labor-intensive firms.

Choice of City. For several decades many cities have tried to attract new industry. Much of this effort has been directed toward obtaining new manufacturing plants, but other types of business are welcomed also. In the last few years, however, the drive for environmental protection and the growing shortage of energy sources have led some cities to reduce or abandon their attempts. This seems especially true where suburban, rather than central-city, locations are contemplated.

ACTION REPORT: Going to the Labor

In certain manufacturing industries, labor is the most critical factor. This is particularly true where raw materials and the finished product can be transported easily. Pencils and pens, for example, are transported with little difficulty. Therefore, a pencil and pen factory can be located with labor as the prominent consideration.

The Blackfeet Indian Writing Company in Browning, MT provides 300,000 pencils and 100,000 ballpoint pens each day to office-supply dealers in all 50 states. This business is located on a 1.5 million-acre reservation adjoining Canada.

The entrepreneurial force behind the business is Chief Earl Old Person. He says, "The tribe has oil and gas resources, but unemployment is chronic. . . . We are trying to market their skills." The pencil factory is a business where "the work is labor intensive . . . and a labor force was available."

Source: "We Want Your Business, Not Help," *Nation's Business*, Vol. 69, No. 1 (January, 1981), p. 16.

Growth or Decline of a City. Some cities are on the upgrade. They are growing in both population and business activity, and the income levels of their citizens are advancing. In contrast, other cities are expanding slowly or are even declining in population. Economic factors, such as shifts in markets, technological changes, and transportation advantages, apparently favor some cities at the expense of others. Table 6-1, for example, shows the varying percentages of expansion and decline in population between 1970 and 1980 for eight cities.

Extent of Local Competition. Most small businesses are concerned about the nature and the amount of local competition. Manufacturers who serve a national market are an exception to this rule, and there are perhaps others. But overcrowding can occur in the majority of small-business fields. The quality of competition also affects the desirability of a location. If existing businesses are not aggressive and do not offer the type of service reasonably expected by the customer, there is likely to be room for a newcomer.

Published data can sometimes be used to shed light upon this particular problem. The average population required to support a given type of business can frequently be determined on a national or a regional basis. By comparing the situation in the given city with these averages, it is possible to get a better picture of the intensity of local competition.

Unfortunately objective data of this type seldom produce unequivocal answers. The population's income level and nearness to other shopping centers

Table 6-1 Population Growth and Decline Between 1970 and 1980

City	Percent of Growth
Fort Myers, FL	34.0
Anaheim, CA	33.3
Houston, TX	29.2
Columbus, GA	9.3
Salt Lake City, UT	− 7.3
Jersey City, NJ	−14.1
Dayton, OH	−16.2
Rochester, NY	−18.1

Source: U. S. Department of Commerce, Bureau of the Census, *1980 Census of Population and Housing* (Washington: U. S. Government Printing Office, March, 1981).

might account for certain discrepancies. There is no substitute for personal observation. In addition, the entrepreneur will do well to seek the opinion of those well acquainted with local business conditions. Wholesalers frequently have an excellent notion of the potential for additional retail establishments in a given line of business.

Other Factors. As in the choice of region, the supply of skilled labor may be a significant factor in the choice of city. The city of Portsmouth, OH has an adequate supply of skilled shoe workers, while Detroit and Flint in Michigan have a large pool of auto workers. The prevailing wage scale is particularly important for manufacturers competing with other firms who have lower wage costs.

The amount and the character of industry in a given city are likewise significant. A one-industry town is often subject to severe seasonal and cyclical business fluctuations in contrast to a city of diversified industries. In addition, the necessary customers and suppliers of essential services should be available.

Local government can help or hinder a new business. In choosing a city, the prospective entrepreneur should be assured of satisfactory police and fire protection, streets, water and other utilities, street drainage, and public transportation. Unreasonably high local taxes or severely restrictive local ordinances are to be avoided.

Finally, the city might also qualify with respect to civic, cultural, religious, and recreational affairs that make it a better place in which to live and do business.

Choice of Actual Site. After the entrepreneur chooses a region and a city in which to locate, the next step is to select a specific site for the business. Some critical factors to consider at this stage include costs, customer accessibility, amount of customer traffic, neighborhood conditions, and the trend toward suburban development.

Costs. Some firms stress the operating costs and purchasing costs associated with a specific business site. Examples of these firms are most manufacturers, wholesalers, bookkeeping services, plumbing contractors, and painting contractors. It would be foolish for these firms to pay high rent for locations in central business districts.

Customer Accessibility. Earlier we recognized customer accessibility as a general consideration in selecting a location. This factor becomes more critical when evaluating a specific site for certain retail stores. For example, a shoe store or a drugstore may fail simply because it is on the wrong side of the street. On the other hand, a store that sells a specialty good—such as pianos—has greater freedom in selecting a site. Furthermore, some restaurants have achieved such distinction that customers drive for miles to patronize them in spite of their relatively inaccessible locations.

Unless one has a product or a service sufficiently powerful to attract the customer, however, one must locate where the customer wants to buy. In the case of motels and service stations, this means a location convenient to many motorists. For clothing stores and variety stores, it means a downtown or suburban shopping center location. For some drugstores and food stores, it means a location in or close to the residential areas.

Amount of Customer Traffic. Customer traffic is recognized and discussed more frequently than it is measured. To make a count of pedestrian traffic, the investigator is stationed in front of the potential site and records the number of passersby. This may be done at alternate half-hour intervals during the day for enough different days to get a representative sample of the traffic. The results should be compared with the amount of traffic at other available sites and at sites known to be successful. Naturally the traffic must also be evaluated carefully to tell whether it provides prospective customers for the particular business. A ladies' shoe store, for example, will profit little from a high flow of pedestrian traffic that is primarily male.

Of course, other factors in addition to amount of traffic must be taken into consideration. The general location must be in keeping with the prestige of the product or service. Business neighbors may likewise contribute to making a given site either desirable or undesirable. To illustrate, a high-class restaurant generally could not successfully locate in a low-income neighborhood. Neither would it locate next to a laundry.

Neighborhood Conditions. We pointed out earlier that certain cities are on the decline while others are growing more or less rapidly. What is true of cities is also true of sections within cities. City growth occurs in a given direction, and that section thrives as a result of the development. Older sections of the city are blighted and display the picture of a past more prosperous than their present. Small retail firms and, to some extent, small service businesses must consider this factor in the selection of a business site. However, since blight can be eliminated, the small retailer should also consider the impact of urban renewal programs on site values in or close to renewal areas.

Suburban Development. The trend toward suburban shopping centers has been an impressive development of recent decades. Increasing suburban population, greater use of the family car, traffic congestion and lack of parking space downtown, and other factors have contributed to the relative decline of central business district activity in many cities. Suburbanites who find it difficult or unpleasant to shop downtown turn to shopping centers located nearer the residential areas.

This shift in business has created problems in the downtown area, as well as offered opportunities in the suburbs. For the small retail business, an opportunity is often presented by the shopping center or other suburban location that has a greater future and that can be handled with limited capital more easily than a downtown spot.

Significant Considerations for Special Types of Small Businesses

Small wholesalers, retailers, service firms, and manufacturers face the same sequence of location choices as to region, city, and actual site. For each of these types of businesses, however, certain factors are more significant than others.

The Small Wholesaler. Perhaps the most significant geographical consideration for the small wholesaler and the industrial distributor is the selection of a city. The wholesaler of consumer goods is particularly interested in the volume of retail sales, both for the separate lines of goods that will be sold and for the total. Certain cities serve as wholesaling centers, and the wholesaler's market includes not only the central city but also the surrounding towns. The small wholesaler must discover which city is the wholesaling center and measure the intensity of local competition in considering any given city.

In addition, specialized types of wholesalers perform functions that dictate particular locations. For example, a resident buyer of clothing must locate in a major market city, but an assembler of farm products must locate in a rural area.

Small wholesalers considering specific sites for their warehouses often must choose between locations within and outside the central wholesale district. The warehouses should be near the center of the trading area to be served, while remaining accessible to highways and railways. Locations within the central wholesale district command higher rent or provide less space for a given amount of rent. Locations outside the district, but still accessible to railways and highways and having suitable loading and unloading facilities, will often mean lower rent, more space, lower operating expenses, and faster deliveries — and possibly newer and more attractive quarters and parking facilities.

The Small Retailer. The suburban areas of cities provide excellent opportunities for many small retailers. In contrast, the older areas of a city are generally less preferable than the new, expanding areas. The retailer's specific site must attract the customers who patronize it, and parking facilities must be adequate.

Restaurants and other eating establishments are typically classified as retail businesses. The chief executive of a major corporation engaged in the fast-food business stressed the importance of restaurant location in these words:

> Good management and site are essential. You don't have to know simply which intersection is best, you have to know which corner of the intersection. Restaurants across the road from one another can experience entirely different results.[1]

A summary of the special location problems that are pertinent to restaurants and retail businesses in general is shown in Figure 6-5.

The Small Service Firm. The location problem of most small service firms is much like that of small retailers. A convenient location is imperative, except in the case of those firms that can build reputations for such high-quality or unique service that customers will seek them out. For example, barbershops, beauty shops, and photographic studios are visited by their customers and must be located conveniently for them. On the other hand, plumbers or television repairers are seldom visited by customers. Calls for their services are typically received by telephone. Consequently, such firms can be located in their owners' homes or in some low-rent area. Their location problem is thus cost-oriented rather than customer-oriented.

---

1. "Shaking up a Company for Solid Growth," *Nation's Business*, Vol. 65, No. 10 (October, 1977), p. 39.

Picking a Location

It has been said that being at the right place at the right time is essential to success. That certainly applies to the selection of a restaurant site. However, finding the right place requires considerable study. Much time should be devoted to the search since, in the final analysis, the restaurant isn't likely to prove any better than its location.

A wise person doesn't open a restaurant in the first vacant building discovered. All the factors affecting restaurant location must be weighed and analyzed. First, the prospective restaurant owner usually decides the kind of eating establishment he or she prefers to operate. Attention should be turned to the neighborhood desired. What is its character? Is it a business locality? Industrial? Residential? Is it on the way up?

Study the Neighborhood

Many conditions that might appear comparatively unimportant can have a great influence on successful restaurant operation. For instance:

- Neighborhoods should be avoided if they harbor loafers, have an unpleasant odor, or are noisy. Restaurants seldom are popular when located in or near undertaking homes, hospitals, or cemeteries. In addition, churches and schools do not make good restaurant neighbors. They may alter conditions on liquor licenses and quite often cause congestion on the sidewalks, noise, or other disturbing factors.
- Parking facilities are a factor, too. A water hydrant at the front of a restaurant prevents parking, slows down food deliveries, and is very often responsible for puddles of water and congestion near the entrance. On the other hand, value may be increased immeasurably by such a simple thing as an abutting alley. The alley will provide delivery facilities not always available on the thoroughfare.
- Competition must be studied. Is there ample opportunity for the business in the area, or is it already overcrowded with eating places? Are the other restaurants making a profit? What is their history? To determine whether the area can use another eating place, it is necessary to ascertain the success of existing places and the types of patronage they are receiving. And it is wise to know whether or not the community is growing.
- It will be important to know the population in surrounding businesses, hotels, apartments, and the like. Changing conditions in the area will have a bearing on the value of the location. Just as construction work in the neighborhood causes traffic congestion that often temporarily drives away business, so new buildings on the opposite side of the street may deprive a restaurant of customers. It is a fact that the general public favors the side of the street having new buildings.
- Being on a busy thoroughfare often enhances the value of a restaurant, but value of the traffic cannot always be determined by counting the people as they pass. It is necessary to know where the traffic is going and the type of persons riding. Many people may pass the restaurant, but the type of eating place planned may not necessarily appeal to sufficient numbers of them.
- The new restaurant must be planned to suit the pocketbooks and the likes and dislikes of its potential customers, for the people who live and work around it are the ones who will eventually decide whether it is to succeed. The new restaurant owner will want to know where the customers come from, the kind of transportation they will use, what they will want to eat, how much they will be willing to spend, group potential, whether they will want quality or quantity, and types of service to be offered.

Figure 6-5 A Summary of Special Location Problems for a Restaurant (Page 1)

- If the location is in a residential section, the prospective restaurant owner must realize that luncheon trade will be light and should consider evening trade. The very nature of the neighborhood will determine whether customers will come in singly, in couples, or in family groups. Such information may be obtained through talks with other persons operating small-business houses in the area or with some of the older and representative residents of the neighborhood.
- A restaurant located in an industrial area presents a special problem. Since much of its business will stem from the surrounding plants, it will be necessary to know whether the plants operate their own lunchrooms, how many persons they employ, the hours they work, and the percentage of persons who bring their own lunch. The type of work the employees do and the wages they receive will have much to do with the kind of food they want and the amount of money they will be willing to spend on their meals. Here, of course, a convenient location is vital as workers will not travel far for the noon meal. Also, in an industrial neighborhood the problem is to serve large portions at a reasonable figure. The best source of information will be the workers themselves. Why not ask them?
- Regardless of the type of eating place, good transportation facilities are of prime importance. A corner location at intersecting public transportation lines may attract many persons leaving buses or waiting to board them.
- A roadside restaurant or cafe has still other problems. It should be on a main highway, preferably just on the outskirts of a city. Plenty of parking space should be provided, and the place should have an attractive exterior if it is to catch the eye.
- It is important to keep in mind that the restaurant should be in a neighborhood adequately supplied with gas, electricity, or other forms of fuel and water.

Source: Adapted from the National Cash Register Company, Merchants Service Department, *Success in the Restaurant Business*, undated pamphlet, pp. 16-17.

Figure 6-5 A Summary of Special Location Problems for a Restaurant (Page 2)

The Small Manufacturer. While costs are an important location factor even for the small retail business, they are the very crux of the problem for the cost-oriented small manufacturer. This means that the small manufacturer should analyze the major cost factors on a comparative basis. Figure 6-6 shows the major cost factors to be analyzed. For any one business, however, other significant costs may require serious study.[2] The small manufacturer must recognize that the process of cost comparison and analysis can become extremely involved and difficult. Some location problems are sufficiently complex as to justify the use of professional help.

2. See Gerald J. Karaska and David F. Bramhall, *Locational Analysis for Manufacturing* (Cambridge, MA: The M. I. T. Press, 1969); James H. Thompson, *Methods of Plant Site Selection Available to Small Manufacturing Firms* (Morgantown: West Virginia University, 1961); and Leonard C. Yaseen, *Plant Location* (Roslyn, NY: Business Reports, Inc., 1952). The latter manual provides useful data on the making of cost comparisons and other evaluative studies of different available business locations.

MANUFACTURER'S COMPARATIVE COST ANALYSIS FORM			
Cost Element	Location A	Location B	Location C
MATERIALS Raw Materials Fuels			
OPERATING COSTS Labor Rent (or Depreciation) Power and Heat Other Utilities Insurance			
TAXES Property Income Payroll Other			
TRANSPORTATION Raw Materials Finished Goods			

Figure 6-6 Manufacturer's Comparative Cost Analysis Form

Sources of Information About Locations

A knowledge of local business conditions and the history of given sites makes certain sources especially valuable in the choice of a business location. Some of these sources are:

1. *Bankers* —The contribution of bankers would be rather limited in the case of a business whose choice must be based on differences in costs and who has technical operating requirements. Many banks do have real estate departments that provide advice on proper locations.
2. *Chambers of commerce* —Although chambers of commerce may tend to oversell locations in the hope of attracting business, they can be of substantial aid in recommending desirable sites.
3. *Wholesalers and manufacturers* —With their experience and knowledge of the way products are currently marketed in a given location, wholesalers and manufacturers often know whether there is room for another aggressive business in a given line.

4. *Trade associations* —In a specific line of business, trade associations can often furnish valuable advice because of their close contact with and study of its peculiar problems.
5. *Government agencies* —The field offices of the Department of Commerce and the Small Business Administration can suggest an optimum location or provide leads that the prospective entrepreneur may follow up.
6. *Industrial parks* —The industrial park is a different type of source from those listed above. It is somewhat similar to an apartment building, with facilities and equipment already installed. A small manufacturing-type business may be able to occupy a unit of the industrial park without incurring excessive costs for street paving, sewage systems, building design and construction, railroad sidings, and the like.
7. *Professional area development groups* —More than 7,000 of these groups now operate in the United States. They provide information on wage and tax rates and help contact the "right people" for location information.[3]
8. *Railroads and power companies* —The typical data obtainable from these sources include (a) the cost and availability of raw materials; (b) available transportation and communication facilities in the area; (c) type, condition, and cost of buildings on given sites; (d) land costs; (e) adequacy of water, power, and fuel supplies; (f) size and skill level of the labor force; (g) existing tax rates, labor laws, and laws and ordinances regulating business activity; and (h) market possibilities.

THE BUILDING AND ITS LAYOUT

Starting a new business usually involves the purchase or lease of an existing building. Only in rare cases would a new building need to be designed and constructed for a beginning business. Although buying an existing building has its advantages, it is often desirable for the new business to rent building space. Assuming suitable rented space is available, the entrepreneur would gain the following advantages by leasing:

1. A large cash outlay is avoided. This is extremely important for the new small firm, which typically lacks adequate financial resources.
2. Risk is reduced by avoiding substantial investment and by postponing commitments for building space until the success of the business is assured and the nature of building requirements is better known.

---

3. For further discussion, see Ted M. Levine, "Outsiders Can Ease the Site Selection Process," *Harvard Business Review*, Vol. 59, No. 3 (May-June, 1981), pp. 12–16.

The suitability of the building would depend upon the spatial, functional, and structural requirements of the business being contemplated. Similarly, an efficient layout of the physical facilities would depend to a considerable extent upon the type of business.

Spatial Requirements

When planning initial building requirements, the entrepreneur must avoid commitments for a building space that is too large or too luxurious. At the same time, the space should not be too small or too austere for efficient operation. Buildings do not produce profits directly. They merely house the operations and personnel which produce the profits. Therefore, the ideal building is practical but not pretentious.

The amount of space required varies with both the type and size of business. The number of employees is one index of business size. Obviously a business employing 50 people will need more space than one employing 5 or 10. As to type of business, a drugstore requires less space than a furniture store because the latter must display heavy, bulky items. Similarly, a jewelry store requires less space than a supermarket.

ACTION REPORT: Beginning in the Basement

A new business must locate in an affordable building. Initial facilities are often makeshift and barely adequate. But with growth, building space can be improved.

Micro-Term, Inc., is a firm which was started in 1976 in the basement of a rented house. The founders—Robert Morley, David Scharon, and Thomas Monsees—were Washington University students who designed and built a homemade computer terminal to assist them in their class work. Instructors and fellow students were impressed with the terminal, so Morley, Scharon, and Monsees began producing and selling terminals.

By the end of the summer of 1976, the entrepreneurs had produced and delivered 50 computer terminals from the basement factory. This location soon proved too small, however, and the company eventually moved to a 33,000-square-foot production facility. By 1981, these quarters housed 95 full-time employees producing 1,000 terminals a month.

Source: Del Marth, "A Terminal Was the Beginning," *Nation's Business*, Vol. 69, No. 6 (June, 1981), p. 86.

Functional Requirements

The general suitability of a building for a given type of business operation relates to its functional character. For example, the floor space of a restaurant should normally be on one level. Other important factors to consider are the shape, age, and condition of the building; fire hazards; heating and air conditioning; lighting and restroom facilities; and entrances and exits. Obviously these factors carry different weights for a factory operation as compared with a wholesale or retail operation. In any case, the comfort, convenience, and safety of employees and customers of the business must not be overlooked.

A desirable building should also have adequate aisles, traffic lanes, elevators, and stairs (or escalators) for moving customers and merchandise in the store or raw materials and goods-in-process in the factory. The internal transportation of merchandise or raw materials requires platforms and ramps for the loading and unloading of trucks. Chutes or conveyors may also be required to transport materials to the receiving room. Other internal transportation facilities include hand trucks, dollies, pipelines, conveyors, hoists, cranes, and forklift trucks.

General-purpose buildings are preferable to buildings that have features which limit their resale value. Although some types of business require spe-

Courtesy of Interlake, Inc.

Figure 6-7 Materials Handling Equipment

cialized buildings, most can operate efficiently in less specialized structures. A standard prefabricated building typically is better than a custom-designed building for a new firm.

Expansion possibilities should also be considered when making the original building plan. For example, a building might provide excellent expansion opportunities by having a temporary wall on the side where there is vacant land.

Structural Requirements

A structurally sound building with a traditional appearance could imply stability and conservatism. However, its architecture may identify it with a bygone era — a matter that is more or less serious depending upon the type of business. Customers and others may identify old-fashioned architecture with outmoded, inefficient management. Other things being equal, most businesses find that modernization is highly desirable.

Factory floors should be capable of supporting heavy equipment. Concrete floors are often used, but they are hard on the feet. Store floors may require appropriate special finishes or carpeting.

Interior load-bearing walls and supporting columns must be adequate to carry the necessary load. Attention to this feature is particularly important for factories and other firms using heavy machinery in the production process. However, freestanding walls are extensively used today — and their use facilitates changes in plant layout.

Layouts

Layout refers to the logical arrangement of physical facilities in order to provide efficiency of business operations. To provide a concise treatment of layouts, we will limit our discussion to two very different layout problems — layout for manufacturers (whose primary concern is production operations) and layout for retailers (whose primary concern is customer traffic).

Factory Layout. The factory layout presents a three-dimensional space problem. Overhead space may be utilized for power conduits, pipelines for exhaust systems, and the like. A proper design of storage areas and handling systems makes use of space near the ceiling. Space must be allowed also for the unobstructed movement of machine parts from one location to another.

The ideal manufacturing process would have a straight-line, forward movement of materials from receiving room to shipping room. If this ideal cannot be realized for a given process, backtracking, sidetracking, and long hauls of materials can at least be minimized. This will reduce production delays.

Two contrasting types of layout are used in industrial firms. One of these is called **process layout** and has similar machines grouped together. Drill presses, for example, are separated from lathes in a machine shop layout. The alternative to such a process layout is called a **product layout**. This is used for continuous-flow, mass production — usually conveyorized, with all machines needed for balanced production located beside the conveyor. Thus, similar machines are used at the same points on the different conveyor lines set up to process a given product.

In smaller plants which operate on a job-lot basis, a product layout cannot be used because it demands too high a degree of standardization of both product and process. Thus, small machine shops are generally arranged on a process layout basis. Small firms with highly standardized products, such as dairies, bakeries, and car wash firms, can use a product layout.

Retail Store Layout. The objectives for a retail store layout differ from those for a factory layout. Among the goals of the small retailer is the proper display of merchandise to maximize sales. A second objective is customer convenience and service. Normally the convenience and attractiveness of the surroundings contribute to a customer's continued patronage. An efficient layout also contributes to operating economy. A final objective is the protection of the store's equipment and merchandise. In achieving all these objectives, the flow of customer traffic must be anticipated and planned.

Many retailers use a self-service layout which permits customers direct access to the merchandise. Not only does self-service reduce the selling expense, but it also permits shoppers to examine the goods before buying. Today practically all grocery merchandising follows this principle.

Some types of merchandise — for example, ladies' hosiery, cigarettes, magazines, and candy — are often purchased on an impulse basis. Impulse goods should be placed at points where customers can see them easily. Products which the customers will buy anyway and for which they come in specifically may be placed in less conspicuous spots.

Various areas of a retail store differ markedly in sales value. Customers typically turn to the right upon entering a store, and so the right front space is the most valuable. The second most valuable are the center front and right middle spaces. One department store places high-margin gift wares, cosmetics, and jewelry in these areas. The third most valuable are the left front and center middle spaces. And the left middle space is fourth in importance. Since the back areas are the least important so far as space value is concerned, most service facilities and the general office typically are found in the rear of a store. Certainly the best space should be given to departments or merchandise producing the greatest sales and profits. Finally, the first floor has greater space value than a second or higher floor in a multistory building. Generally the higher the floor, the lower its selling value.

EQUIPMENT AND TOOLING

The final step in arranging for physical facilities involves the purchase or lease of equipment and tooling. Here again, the types of equipment and tooling required obviously depend upon the nature of the business. We will also limit our discussion of equipment needs to the two diverse fields of manufacturing and retailing. Of course, even within these two areas there is great variation in the needed tools and equipment.

Factory Equipment

Machines in the factory may be either general-purpose or special-purpose in character. **General-purpose equipment** for metalworking includes lathes, drill presses, and milling machines. In a woodworking plant, general-purpose machines include ripsaws, planing mills, and lathes. In each case, jigs, fixtures, and other tooling items set up on the basic machine tools can be changed so that two or more shop operations can be accomplished. Bottling machines and automobile assembly-line equipment are examples of **special-purpose equipment**.

Advantages of General-Purpose Equipment. General-purpose equipment requires a minimum investment and is well-adapted to a varied type of operation. Small machine shops and cabinet shops, for example, utilize this type of equipment. General-purpose equipment also contributes the necessary flexibility in industries where the product is so new that the technology has not yet been well-determined or where there are frequent design changes in the product.

Advantages of Special-Purpose Equipment. Special-purpose equipment permits cost reduction where the technology is fully established and where a capacity operation is more or less assured by high sales volume. The large-volume production of automobiles, for example, justifies special-purpose equipment costing hundreds of thousands of dollars. Not all special-purpose equipment is that expensive, however. Even though it is used most in large-scale industry, the same principle can be applied on a more modest scale in many small manufacturing plants. A milking machine in a dairy illustrates specialized equipment used by small firms. Nevertheless, a small firm cannot ordinarily and economically use special-purpose equipment unless it makes a highly standardized product on a fairly large scale.

The use of a specialized machine using permanently set up special-purpose tooling results in greater output per machine-hour operated. Hence, the labor cost per unit of product is lower. However, the initial cost of such equipment and tooling is much higher, and its scrap value is little or nothing due to its highly specialized function.

Retail Store Equipment

Small retailers must have merchandise display counters, storage racks, shelving, mirrors, seats for customers, customer push carts, cash registers, and various items necessary to facilitate selling. Such equipment may be costly but is usually less expensive than equipment for a factory operation.

If the store attempts to serve a high-income market, its fixtures typically should display the elegance and beauty expected by such customers. Polished mahogany and bronze fittings on showcases will lend a richness of atmosphere. Indirect lighting, thick rugs on the floor, and big easy chairs will also make a contribution to the air of luxury. In contrast, a store that caters to lower-income brackets would find luxurious fixtures a handicap in building an atmosphere of low prices. Therefore, such a store should concentrate on simplicity.

Figure 6-8 Modern Check-Out Equipment

Automated Equipment

Automation has come into use to a limited extent in small-business operations. It is quite well-developed in some general-office operations. However, some persons say that it is too expensive for the small business. Others disagree, saying that automation can be used on a small scale as well as on a large scale.

In a small plant the major barrier to automation is found in short production runs which do not require the automated process to be in action most of the time. But if a small plant produces a given product in large volume, with infrequent changes in design, the owner should seriously consider the many benefits derived from automation. Among these are:

1. Operator errors are minimized.
2. Processing costs are lowered by speed of operation and machine efficiency.
3. Human resources are conserved while personnel skill requirements are upgraded.
4. Safety of manufacturing and handling operations is promoted.
5. Inventory requirements tend to be reduced because of faster processing.
6. Maintenance and inspection are improved by incorporating lubrication systems and devices in the automatic transfer machines.

LOOKING BACK

1. In a given business, one of the four general considerations in selecting a location may have the greatest influence. Personal preferences should not be allowed to cancel out a location's weaknesses. Environmental conditions should be evaluated prior to making a location decision. The availability of raw materials, labor supply, and other resources affects the ongoing operation of a business. Customer accessibility can be the foremost consideration in some situations.

   Evaluating a geographical location is a step-by-step process. First, the region must be examined, then the city, and finally the actual site.

   For small wholesalers/industrial distributors, perhaps the most significant geographical consideration is the selection of a city. Small retailers and service firms, as a general rule, must locate in a convenient and attractive site. Location problems for small manufacturers are cost-oriented.

2. Information about various locations is available through such sources as bankers, local chambers of commerce, wholesalers and manufacturers, trade associations, government agencies, industrial parks, professional area development groups, railroads, and power companies.
3. Building requirements depend upon the nature of the business. In most cases a new business should plan to lease rather than to buy building space.
4. Proper layout of building space also depends upon the type of business. Manufacturing firms use layout patterns that facilitate production operations and provide for the efficient flow of materials. Retailers lay out building space in terms of customer needs and the flow of customer traffic.
5. Most small manufacturing firms use general-purpose equipment, although some have sufficient volume and a standardized operation which permit the use of special-purpose equipment. The type of equipment and tooling in retail firms should be related to the general level and type of the business.

DISCUSSION QUESTIONS

1. Is the hometown of the business owner likely to be a good location? Why? Is it logical for an owner to allow personal preference to influence the decision on a business location? Why?
2. For the five small businesses which you know best, would you say that their locations were based upon the evaluation of location factors, chance, or something else?
3. In the selection of a region, what types of businesses should place greatest emphasis upon (a) markets, (b) raw materials, and (c) labor? Explain.
4. How may one measure the extent of existing competition in a given city? How is the quality of pedestrian traffic measured?
5. In the choice of specific sites, what types of businesses must show the greatest concern with customer accessibility? Why?
6. How do site factors differ for a wholesaler and a retailer?
7. What are "backtracking" and "sidetracking" as they apply to factory layout and materials movement? Do they affect operating costs? If so, how?
8. When should the small manufacturer utilize process layout, and when product layout? Explain.
9. Discuss the conditions under which a new small manufacturer should buy general-purpose and special-purpose equipment.
10. Describe the unique problems concerning store layout and merchandise display that confront a new small jeweler.

REFERENCES TO SMALL BUSINESS IN ACTION

Knight, James H. "Moving: People Were the Best Reason—and the Biggest Problem." *Inc.*, Vol. 3, No. 3 (March, 1981), pp. 116–120.

Various labor-related considerations are discussed by the president of a company which relocated.

Lappen, Alyssa A. "'The Mechanic Will See You Now.'" *Forbes*, Vol. 127, No. 9 (April 27, 1981), pp. 90–93.

The equipment requirements and high costs involved in properly equipping automobile repair shops are described.

Moreno, Dan. "Successful Sites." *American Demographics*, Vol. 1, No. 9 (October, 1979), pp. 19–23.

The importance of demographic changes to site selection is discussed, using fast-food retail businesses as principal examples.

Nazem, Susie Gharib. "Mamma Marcella Takes to the Air with Pasta Power." *Fortune*, Vol. 100, No. 4 (August 27, 1979), pp. 118–119.

Marcella Aitken, who came to the United States from Italy to study business administration at Boston College, opened a pizzeria in 1952 with $600 and 2 small ovens. The expansion of the business and its changes in building and equipment are described.

Schwab, Priscilla. "Why They Froze the Bagel." *Nation's Business*, Vol. 68, No. 10 (October, 1980), pp. 72–76.

The founding and growth of a business which produces bagels are described. The production process originally involved much handwork but has since become automated.

Chapter 7

Initial Financial Planning

LOOKING AHEAD

Watch for the following important topics:

1. Analyzing the nature of capital requirements of a new business.
2. Estimating the dollar amounts of initial capital requirements.
3. Individual investors and business suppliers as sources of funds.
4. Financial institutions as sources of funds.
5. Government-sponsored agencies as sources of funds.

Starting a business is similar to preparing an automobile for a family vacation. How? Consider the following scenario:

> Mr. Ready has washed the car, checked the air in the tires, and obtained a current inspection sticker. Hurriedly, he fills the gas tank from a can in the garage. His family piles into the car and off they go on the family vacation. Two hours later the car engine begins to knock and soon stops. In his rush to start the vacation, Mr. Ready had gassed up with kerosene!

Mr. Ready's eagerness to start the vacation caused him to hurry through the fueling process. Don't let a similar scenario describe the "start-up" of your business. An entrepreneur must fuel the new business venture, also. Of course, the "gas" of the new venture isn't kerosene but money—money to fund the capital needs of the new business.

A new business must have funds mixed in the proper quantities to meet its different needs. Four basic questions must be answered during initial financial planning:

1. What types of capital do I need in my new business?
2. How can I estimate the amounts needed?
3. Where can I obtain the required funds?
4. What should my financing proposal include?

NATURE OF CAPITAL REQUIREMENTS

The specific needs of a proposed business venture govern the nature of its initial financial requirements. If the firm is a food store, financial planning must provide for the store building, cash registers, shopping carts, inventory, office equipment, and other items required in this type of operation. An analysis of capital requirements for this or any other type of business must consider its needs for current-asset capital, fixed-asset capital, promotion-expense capital, and funds for personal expenses.

Current-Asset Capital

Current assets are the plus side of the working-capital equation.[1] Three current-asset items are cash, inventories, and accounts receivable. The term **circulating capital** is sometimes applied to these three items, emphasizing the constant cycle from cash to inventory to receivables to cash, and so on. Careful planning is needed to provide adequate current-asset capital for the new business.

Cash. Every firm must have the cash essential for current business operations. A reservoir of cash is needed because of the uneven flows of funds into the business (as income) and out of the business (as expense). The size of this reservoir is determined not only by the volume of sales, but also by the regularity of cash receipts and cash payments. Uncertainties exist because of unpredictable decisions by customers as to when they will pay their bills and because of emergencies that require substantial cash outlays. If an adequate cash balance is maintained, the firm can take such unexpected developments and irregularities in stride.

1. Current liabilities—debts which must be paid within the near future—represent the minus side of the working-capital equation. Accountants technically define working capital as the difference between current assets and current liabilities.

Inventories. Although the relative importance of inventories differs considerably from one type of business to another, they often constitute a major part of the working capital. Seasonality of sales and production affects the size of the minimum inventory. Retail stores, for example, may find it desirable to carry a larger-than-normal inventory during the Christmas season.

Accounts Receivable. The firm's accounts receivable consist of payments due from its customers. If the firm expects to sell on a credit basis—and in many lines of business this is virtually imperative—provision must be made for financing receivables. The firm cannot afford to wait until its customers pay their bills before restocking its shelves.

Factoring is an option which makes cash available to the business *before* accounts receivable payments are received from customers. Under this option another firm, known as a **factor**, purchases the accounts receivable for their full value. The factor charges a servicing fee, usually 1 percent of the value of the receivables, and an interest charge on the money advanced. The interest charge may range from 2 percent to 3 percent above the **prime rate**, which is the interest rate that commercial banks charge their most creditworthy customers.

Assume, for example, that a retailer sells products valued at $10,000 to a customer on 30-day credit terms. The $10,000 is listed as an account receivable on the books of the retailer. Normally the retailer would receive the $10,000 from the customer within 30 days. However, by selling the receivable to a factor, the retailer can receive approximately $9,750 immediately. The $250 factoring cost includes the 1 percent servicing fee (1 percent of $10,000 = $100) and the interest charge (18 percent of $9,900 prorated for 30 days = $150). The 18 percent interest charge assumes a 15 percent prime rate plus a 3 percent factoring premium.

Of course, the proportion of cash sales to credit sales significantly affects the size of receivables, as do the terms of sale offered to credit customers. The size of the receivables is likewise affected by seasonality of sales and changes in business conditions, which influence promptness of payment by many customers.

Fixed-Asset Capital

Fixed assets are the relatively permanent assets that are intended for use in the business rather than for sale. For example, a delivery truck used by a grocer to deliver merchandise to customers is a fixed asset. In the case of an automobile dealer, however, a delivery truck to be sold would be part of the inventory and thus a current asset.

The types of fixed assets needed in a new business may include the following:

1. Tangible fixed assets—such as buildings, machinery, equipment, and land (including mineral rights, timber, and the like).
2. Intangible fixed assets—such as patents, copyrights, and goodwill. Many new firms have no intangible fixed assets.
3. Fixed security investments—such as stocks of subsidiaries, pension funds, and contingency funds. In most cases a new business has no fixed security investments.

The nature and size of the fixed-asset investment are determined by the type of business operation. A modern beauty shop, for example, might be equipped for around $80,000, whereas a motel sometimes requires 50 or more times that amount. In any given kind of business, moreover, there is a minimum quantity or assortment of facilities needed for efficient operation. It would seldom be profitable, for example, to operate a motel with only one or two units. It is this principle, of course, that excludes small business from automobile manufacturing and other types of heavy industry.

A firm's flexibility is inversely related to its investment in fixed assets. Investments in land, buildings, and equipment involve long-term commitments. Equipment typically is specialized, and substantial losses and delays often occur in liquidation. The inflexibility inherent in fixed-asset investment underscores the importance of a realistic evaluation of fixed-asset needs.

Promoter-Expense Capital

Persons who expend time and money establishing or promoting a business expect repayment of their personal funds and payment for their services. Payment to these promoters may take the form of a cash fee or an ownership interest in the business. Of course, many new businesses come into being as sole proprietorships, with the entrepreneur acting as the promoter. In this case the proprietor must have sufficient funds to pay all necessary out-of-pocket promotional costs.

Funds for Personal Expenses

In the truly small business, financial provision must also be made for the personal living expenses of the owner during an initial period of operation. Technically this is not part of the business capitalization, but it should be considered in the business financial plan. Inadequate provision for personal expenses will inevitably lead to a diversion of business assets and a departure from the financial plan.

ESTIMATING CAPITAL REQUIREMENTS

When estimating the magnitude of capital requirements for a small business, the entrepreneur quickly feels the need for a "crystal ball." The uncertainties surrounding an entirely new venture make estimation difficult.[2] But even for established businesses, forecasting is never exact. Nevertheless, when seeking initial capital, the entrepreneur must be ready to answer the question "How much?"

The amount of capital needed by various types of new businesses varies considerably. High-technology companies, such as computer manufacturers, designers of semiconductor chips, and gene-splicing companies, often require several million dollars in initial financing. One firm of this type, Applied Molecular Genetics, Inc., was financed in the amount of $19.4 million![3]

Most service businesses, on the other hand, require smaller amounts of initial capital. For example, Elsie Kelly started her temporary employment service with $70,000. Her initial facility consisted of a room with a card table and three telephones. Approximately 1 year after start-up, however, her company had 350 employees and expected sales of $300,000.[4]

The explanations that follow will show how a prospective entrepreneur may use a "double-barreled" approach to estimating capital requirements by (1) applying industry standard ratios to estimate dollar amounts, and (2) cross-checking the dollar amounts by empirical investigation. Dun & Bradstreet, Inc., banks, trade associations, and other organizations compile industry standard ratios for numerous types of businesses. If no standard data can be located, then estimating capital requirements inevitably involves educated guesswork.

Estimate the Sales Volume

As a first step in estimating capital needs, the volume of sales should be estimated. One approach to estimating sales is to select a desired profit figure and to work backward from that figure to sales. For example, assume that the proposed business is a job printing shop and that its prospective owner hopes to earn annual profits of $40,000. If the industry standard ratio shows that job printers typically earn 5 percent on sales, the prospective owner must then achieve sales of $40,000/.05 = $800,000, or 20 times the expected profit.

The $800,000 sales figure now constitutes the minimum sales one must secure to make the venture sufficiently attractive. It does not prove, however, that the proposed business will guarantee this amount of sales. In fact, this figure should be cross-checked in as many ways as possible. In an existing business, past sales records should be compared with the estimated sales figure. In a new business, the sales records of other, somewhat similar firms may provide a benchmark for checking.

2. The subject of forecasting is discussed in Chapter 5 as a part of market analysis and sales estimation. Most sales forecasting techniques apply to forecasting in general.

3. *The Wall Street Journal*, March 18, 1981, p. 27.

4. Nancy J. White, "Supplying Temporary Help," *Venture*, Vol. 3, No. 2 (February, 1981), p. 28.

Calculate the Asset Requirements

Having arrived at a sales estimate as objectively as possible, the entrepreneur next must compute the dollar value of all assets consistent with the particular sales volume.

Cash Requirements. Anticipated payments for labor, utilities, rent, supplies, and other expenses following the initiation of the firm must be studied in estimating cash requirements. A generous amount of cash must be set aside for those items, as well as for any unexpected expenses. For a new business, the standard amount of cash that is specified for the industry may be too small. Some additional cash may be needed for a margin of safety.

In many types of businesses, a cash balance adequate to pay one or two months' expenses is desirable. This is a good rule of thumb. But the prospective entrepreneur should realize that much subjective judgment is needed in estimating the desired cash balance for a particular business.

Inventory Requirements. Adequate levels of inventory must be maintained. Industry ratios help estimate these levels. Suppose a retailer's estimated sales is $600,000 and the standard sales-to-inventory ratio is 6. This means that the retailer would need $600,000/6 = $100,000 worth of inventory to keep up with the industry ratio of 6.

In cross-checking inventory requirements through empirical investigation, the entrepreneur must consider the specific types and quantities of items to be kept in inventory. In the case of a clothing retailer, for example, the entrepreneur must make a distribution by sizes and styles of items to be sold to customers. The costs in stocking this merchandise can then be computed by reference to prices quoted by suppliers. Likewise, a prospective manufacturer would need to identify the types and quantities of raw materials to be kept on hand, considering the rate of usage, the location of suppliers, and the time required to replenish supplies.

Level of Accounts Receivable. Since accounts receivable, in effect, are loans to customers, these assets tie up capital. It is important to know how much capital will be involved in these assets. To estimate the amount of capital tied up in accounts receivable, we must first calculate the **average collection period**. This period is the average length of time that a firm must wait before it receives cash from a credit sale. It measures the turnover of accounts receivable and is computed in two steps:

1. Divide annual credit sales by 360 to get the average daily credit sales.
2. Divide accounts receivable by daily credit sales to find the number of days' credit sales tied up in receivables.

Suppose that the average collection period for a particular type of retailing (that is, the average for the entire industry) is 36 days. Suppose, further, that a beginning retailer in this industry anticipates annual credit sales of $600,000. The level of accounts receivable that this retailer must maintain to conform to the industry standard may be calculated as follows:

Step 1. $\frac{\$600{,}000 \text{ (annual credit sales)}}{360 \text{ (days)}} = \$1{,}666 \text{ (average daily sales)}$

Step 2. $\frac{\text{Accounts receivable}}{\$1{,}666 \text{ (average daily sales)}} = 36 \text{ days (average collection period)}$

Step 3. Accounts receivable $= 36 \times \$1{,}666 = \$60{,}000$

Fixed-Asset Requirements. The **fixed-asset turnover**, defined as the ratio of sales to fixed assets, can be used to calculate fixed-asset requirements. It measures the extent to which plant and equipment are being utilized productively. Suppose that the industry fixed-asset turnover is 4 in the case of the retailer with an estimated sales of $600,000. This means that the retailer would require $600,000/4 = $150,000 in fixed assets.

Cross-Check Estimates by Empirical Investigation

Although ratio analysis is useful in estimating asset requirements, it is hazardous to rely exclusively on this approach. Either prior to, concurrently, or subsequent to ratio analysis of capital requirements, the prospective entrepreneur should make an independent, empirical investigation of capital needs.

For example, inventory requirements of a business should be checked with those who have experience in the same line of business. Similarly, land, building, and equipment cost estimates may be compared with prices asked by sellers. If there are substantial discrepancies in estimates provided by the two different approaches, rechecking is necessary to decide which is more likely to be accurate.

Minimize Investment in Fixed Assets

The need for adequate working capital deserves special emphasis. A common weakness in small-business financing is the disproportionately small investment in current assets relative to fixed assets. In such weakly financed firms, too much of the money is tied up in assets that are difficult to convert to cash. Danger arises from the fact that the business depends upon daily receipts to meet obligations coming due from day to day. If there is a slump in sales or if there are unexpected expenses, creditors may force the firm into bankruptcy.

The lack of flexibility associated with the purchase of fixed assets suggests the desirability of minimizing this type of investment. Often, for example, there is a choice between renting or buying property. For perhaps the majority of new small firms, renting provides the better alternative. A rental arrangement not only reduces the capital requirement, but also provides the flexibility that is helpful if the business is more successful or less successful than anticipated. It also provides a tax-deductible operating expense.

LOCATING SOURCES OF FUNDS

We have examined the nature of capital needs and ways to estimate these requirements. Now we turn our attention to locating the sources of these funds and establishing the necessary financial arrangements to obtain them.

The initial financing of a small business is quite often patterned after the typical personal financing plan, as the following indicates:

> A prospective entrepreneur, inspired by a vision of success and profit, canvasses first his own means, then those of his immediate family, and finally more remote relatives. If he is a man well regarded by friends and neighbors, he may be able to secure supporting financing from them. His aspiration is to do well, repay family and friends with a generous garnish of profits, and then to live well. If the entrepreneur approaches the more formal channels of finance—banks and the like—his application for funds is likely to be treated in much the same terms as any personal loan.[5]

Every lender wants a feeling of confidence in the borrower and the borrower's idea. A well-prepared assessment of capital needs and sources of funds can help to win that confidence.

Types of Initial Capital

Initial capital consists of **owner capital** and **creditor capital**. Sometimes the terms *ownership equity* and *debt capital* are used, respectively. Traditionally owner capital in a new firm should be at least two thirds of the total initial capital. This two-thirds dictum is quite conservative, and many small businesses are started with ownership equities that are smaller. Sometimes initial ownership equity is even nonexistent! However, many small firms fail every year due to inadequate ownership equity. The conservative approach thus provides the prospective entrepreneur with a margin of safety that the shoestring operator lacks.

5. Roland I. Robinson, "The Franchising of Small Business in the United States," in *Small Business in American Life*, edited by Stuart W. Bruchey (New York: Columbia University Press, 1980), p. 280.

> **ACTION REPORT: Success Without Equity Financing**
>
> There are exceptions to most patterns. This is true of the initial financial structure of a business. On rare occasions, successful operation can begin with no equity financing. Some well-known examples are the following:
>
> David H. McConnell started Avon with a $500 loan and no equity. Sales last year were $1.1 billion.
>
> Ray Kroc, with no capital, was able to leverage, with a $2 million insurance company loan, the exclusive McDonald's franchise into a $2 billion business.
>
> Frank Sieberling began operations at Goodyear Tire with a $13,500 debt and no equity. Current sales: $8.3 billion.
>
> Joseph Campbell started Campbell Soup with absolutely no equity. Sales in 1979 were $2.2 billion.
>
> **Source:** "Debt and Taxes, Part 2," by Richard Greene, *Forbes* (September 15, 1980), p. 88.

The sources of funds discussed in this chapter are particularly important in establishing the original financial structure of the new firm. Of course, the use of these and other sources of funds is not limited to initial financing. They can also be tapped to finance growing day-to-day operating requirements and business expansion. Figure 7-1 gives a visual overview of the funding sources discussed in this chapter.

Individual Investors as Sources of Funds

A popular avenue for funding begins close to home. The entrepreneur invests his or her own funds and often persuades parents, relatives, and other acquaintances to supply capital. These investors typically make loans (debt capital) to the entrepreneur rather than provide equity capital.

If the entrepreneur so desires, he or she can also appeal to individual investors beyond the circle of close friends and relatives by offering to sell capital stock. By using this financing option, the entrepreneur can share ownership of the new company with many individuals.

Personal Savings. A financial plan which includes the entrepreneur's personal funds helps build confidence among potential investors. It is important, therefore, that the entrepreneur have some personal assets in the business. Indeed, the ownership equity for a beginning business typically comes from personal savings.

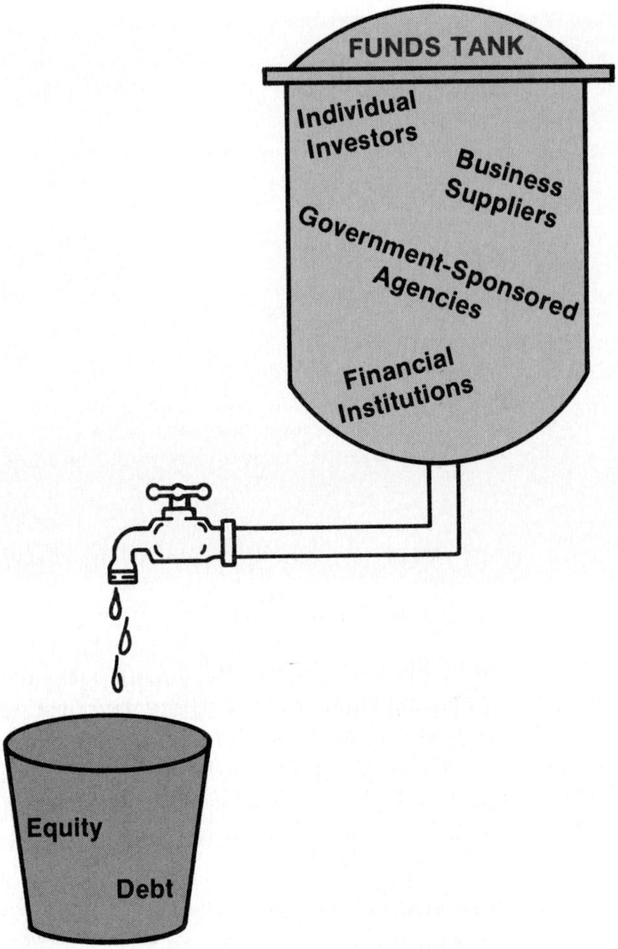

Figure 7-1 Sources of Initial Financing for Small Business

Personal savings invested in the business eliminate the requirement of fixed interest charges and a definite repayment date. If profits fail to materialize exactly as expected, the business is not strapped with an immediate drain on capital.

Funds from Friends, Relatives, and Local Investors. At times, loans from friends or relatives may be the only available source of new small-business financing. Friends and relatives can often be a shortcut to borrowing.

Mr. Wells, a Dallas banker, says, "If Momma's got the money, get it from her. She loves you. She knows you're great, and her interest rate is low."[6] However, friends and relatives who provide capital loans feel that they have the right to interfere in the management of the business. Hard business times may also strain the bonds of friendship. If relatives and friends are indeed the only available source, the entrepreneur has no alternative. However, the financial plan should provide, if possible, for repayment within the first six months of operation.

Local capitalists—for example, lawyers, physicians, or others who wish to invest funds—are good sources of financing. But the small firm must compete with other investment opportunities for the resources of such financial "backers." Local capitalists are not inclined to invest money in a risky small-business venture unless it bears the prospect of a significantly better rate of return than is available elsewhere.

ACTION REPORT: Friend or Foe?

Obtaining funds from friends and relatives has certain disadvantages. Sometimes these investors are too close to the business, disagreeing with decisions in the business and causing a strain on friendships.

Derek F. du Toit started an investment group in 1965. Friends and business associates made contributions to the business. At one point, 35 investors had supplied money to join as equal shareholders.

Investment risk was reduced by du Toit, who personally guaranteed each shareholder that he would be a "buyer of last resort" and pay the balance-sheet value of the shares if the shareholder wished to sell his or her interest in the business. This guaranteed friends against complete loss of investments. Many shareholders later decided to convert their investments into cash in order to make down payments on houses or cars. By July, 1969, the number of shareholders had dropped to approximately 13.

Differences in investment ideas between du Toit and the remaining shareholders resulted in a buy-out by du Toit. After the deal was consummated, du Toit commented, "The bonds of friendship from our previous relationships were irreparably broken. The shareholders discounted the financial reward they received because they felt I had virtually placed a shotgun at their heads to achieve my ambitions."

Source: Reprinted by permission of the *Harvard Business Review.* Excerpt from "Confessions of a Successful Entrepreneur" by Derek F. du Toit (November/December 1980).

6. Sanford L. Jacobs, "Aspiring Entrepreneurs Learn Intricacies of Going It Alone," *The Wall Street Journal*, March 23, 1981, p. 23.

Sale of Capital Stock. A third way to obtain capital is through the sale of stock to individual investors beyond the scope of one's immediate acquaintances. Periods of high interest rates turn entrepreneurs to this equity market. This involves, of necessity, a dilution of ownership, and many owners are reluctant to take this step for that reason. Whether the owner is wise in declining to use outside equity financing depends upon the firm's long-range prospects. If there is an opportunity for substantial expansion on a continuing basis and if other sources are inadequate, the owner may decide logically to bring in other owners. Owning part of a larger business may be more profitable than owning all of a smaller business.

Private Placement. One way to sell capital stock is through **private placement**. This means that the firm's capital stock is sold to selected individuals, who are most likely to be the firm's employees, the owner's acquaintances, local residents, customers, and suppliers. Private sale of stock is difficult because the new firm is not known and has no ready market for its securities. However, the entrepreneur avoids many requirements of the securities law when a stock sale is restricted to a private placement.

Public Sale. Some small firms "go public" by making their stock available to the general public. These are typically the larger small-business firms. The reason often cited for a public sale is the need for additional working capital or, less frequently, for other capital needs. The personal financial objectives of owners may also enter into the reasoning behind the public sale of stock.

In undertaking the public sale of stock, the small firm subjects itself to greater public regulation. There are state regulations pertaining to the public sale of securities, and the Securities and Exchange Commission (SEC) also exercises surveillance over such offerings.[7] The SEC is quite tolerant of small offerings, however, by permitting "Regulation A" offerings to be sold with minimum requirements for financial data and information.[8]

Common stock may also be sold to underwriters, who guarantee the sale of securities. The compensation and fees paid to underwriters typically make the sale of securities in this manner expensive. The fees themselves may range from 10 percent to 30 percent, with 18 percent to 25 percent being typical. In addition, there are options and other fees that may run the actual costs higher. The reason for the high expense is, of course, the element of uncertainty and risk associated with public offerings of stock of small, relatively unknown firms.

Studies of public sale of stock by small firms reveal the fact that small companies frequently make financial arrangements that are not sound.

---

7. An excellent discussion of these security laws can be found in Raymond D. Watts, "Selling Stock to Finance a New Business," *In Business* (November-December, 1980), p. 17.

8. As of 1981, the maximum amount of stock that could be issued under Regulation A in any 12-month period was $1.5 million.

Indeed, the lack of knowledge on the part of small-firm owners often leads to arrangements with brokers or securities dealers that are not in the best interest of the small firms.

The condition of the financial markets at any given time has a direct bearing on the prospects for the sale of capital stock. Entrepreneurs found the early years of the 1980s to be strong for new-venture stock sales. For example, George Ryan, founder and chairman of CADO Systems Corp., a microprocessor-computer manufacturer, said that going public with a stock sale was easy because "today's venture market is so hot that if you had a corner hot dog stand, you could take it public. There is a push to take companies public."[9] Market conditions do change, however, and therefore must be studied carefully.

Business Suppliers as Sources of Funds

Companies with which a new firm has business dealings also represent a source of funds for the firm's merchandise inventory and equipment. Thus, both wholesalers and equipment manufacturers/suppliers can be used to provide trade credit or equipment loans and leases.

Trade Credit. Credit extended by suppliers is of unusual importance to the beginning entrepreneur. In fact, trade (or mercantile) credit is the small firm's most widely used source of short-term funds. Trade credit is of short duration—30 days being the customary credit period. Most commonly, this type of credit involves an unsecured, open-book account. The supplier (seller) sends merchandise to the purchasing firm and sets up an *account receivable*. The buying firm sets up an *account payable* for the amount of the purchase.

The amount of trade credit available to a new firm depends upon the type of business and the suppliers' confidence in the firm. For example, shoe manufacturers provide business capital to retailers by granting extended payment dates on sales made at the start of a production season. The retailers, in turn, sell to their customers during the season and make the bulk of their payments to the manufacturers at or near the end of the season. If the retailer's rate of stock turnover is greater than the scheduled payment for the goods, cash from sales may be obtained even before paying for the shoes.

Suppliers are inclined to place greater confidence in a new firm and to extend credit more freely than bankers because of the former's interest in developing new customers. A bank might require financial statements and possibly a cash-flow budget. A supplier, on the other hand, may simply check the general credit standing of the purchaser and extend credit without requiring detailed financial statements. The supplier also tends to be

9. Loretta Kuklinsky Huerta, "The Ups and Downs of Going Public," *Venture*, Vol. 2, No. 11 (November, 1980), p. 22.

less exacting than a banker or other lender in requiring strict observance of credit terms.

Costs of Failing to Use Trade Credit Properly. When considering the use of trade credit, one should give attention to the pertinent costs for failing to use it properly. For example, there is a cost involved if the buying firm makes payment before the permissible date. By paying unnecessarily early, the buying firm commits funds that might have been used for other purposes. The more critical cost, however, involves the failure to take an offered cash discount. Stated in terms of equivalent annual interest, the real cost of failing to take an offered cash discount is much higher than the nominal discount rate—a concept developed in Chapter 19.

Careful Selection of Trade Suppliers. Suppliers of merchandise or raw materials on credit should be selected carefully. A supplier should have a reputation for maintaining scheduled deliveries of materials or merchandise so that the buyer will neither lose sales nor experience operating delays because of late deliveries. The trade supplier who is willing to participate in the small firm's advertising is a boon to the small entrepreneur. Moreover, in times of unavoidable emergency, it is desirable for a firm to have a supplier who is willing to wait for payment and, in some cases, to extend direct financial assistance.

Equipment Loans and Leases. Some small businesses—for example, restaurants—utilize equipment that may be purchased on an installment basis. A down payment of 25 to 35 percent is ordinarily required, and the contract period normally runs from 3 to 5 years. The equipment manufacturer or supplier typically extends credit on the basis of a **conditional sales contract** (or mortgage) on the equipment. During the loan period, the equipment cannot serve as collateral for a bank loan.

The small-business firm should be aware of the danger in contracting for so much equipment that it becomes impossible to meet installment payments. It is a mark of real management ability to recognize the desirable limits in this type of borrowing.

Equipment leasing, a practice that has grown rapidly in recent years, provides an occasionally attractive alternative to equipment purchase. Cars, trucks, business equipment, and machinery used in manufacturing are examples of assets that may be leased. Possible advantages of equipment leasing include greater investment flexibility and smaller capital requirements. Offsetting these advantages is the typically higher total cost of leasing compared to the cost of purchasing. However, leasing may be desirable in cases where continuing specialized maintenance and protection against obsolescence are necessary—as with electronic computers, for example.

ACTION REPORT: Lease and Grow

In the early life of a business, it is difficult to show potential creditors how solid and profitable the new firm can be. This difficulty can slow efforts to grow through the use of borrowed capital. Leasing of equipment is an alternative to waiting for profits and creditors to provide financing. Dick Moen, president of Moen Foam Corporation in Carson, CA, explains how his company used leasing to grow.

> "A major reason for our annual sales volume growth," said Moen, "is that we lease instead of purchase or finance much of our production equipment." The company, founded in 1977, had sales of about $4 million in its first year, increasing to approximately $8 million the second year.
>
> What makes this growth "astounding," according to Moen, is that his fledgling company was almost stymied in its first efforts to expand. "We tried umpteen different sources and got nowhere," he recalls.
>
> The big break came one day when Moen's stockbroker, an account executive with Bateman, Eichler, Hill, Richards, Inc., called to suggest an investment for him. The first lease arrangement with BEHR Leasing, in August, 1977, provided Moen with a $75,000 polyurethane laminating machine and platform, complete with a conveyor and slitter. Just four months later Moen leased a second piece of equipment worth $95,000. With the new equipment, Moen Foam was able to enter still another market, one which was booming.
>
> In May, 1978, came two more leases through BEHR Leasing. One brought Moen $67,000 worth of equipment which further automated the production. That was followed by a lease with BEHR Leasing for $100,000 worth of saws and transportation and fabrication equipment to expand production capacity.
>
> "That will bring the total value of the leased equipment to more than half a million dollars," Moen said.
>
> What would have happened if he hadn't been able to lease the equipment?
>
> "We would have had to wait until we generated enough profits to buy the equipment we needed," Dick said. "Our growth would have been delayed for years."

Source: Ray Corob, "Equipment Leasing—An Idea Whose Time Has Come," *Franchising Today* (February, 1981), p. 47.

Financial Institutions as Sources of Funds

Two major financial institutions which supply beginning capital for new firms are banks and venture-capital companies. Historically, banks have provided a steady, though limited, source of start-up funds. On the other hand, venture-capital companies are in and out of start-up investments. Expansion financing typically accounts for most of the venture-capital investment portfolios. Their start-up investments were low in the mid-1970s but appeared strong in the early 1980s.[10]

Commercial Banks. Although commercial banks tend to limit their lending to working-capital needs of going concerns, some initial capital does come from this source. If the small firm is adequately financed in terms of equity capital and if the entrepreneur is of good character, the commercial bank may lend on the basis of signature only. Of course, this is less likely for the beginning firm than for the established one. In any event, collateral and/or personal guarantees are often required.

Collateral Arrangements. On some notes, the name of the cosigner provides adequate security to satisfy the bank. If the borrowing firm is a corporation, such an arrangement is often used to hold the principals personally liable. Assets such as life insurance policies, equipment, and real estate may also be pledged. Chattel mortgages and real estate mortgages are particularly useful in supporting longer-term loan requests.

Line of Credit. The entrepreneur should arrange for a line of credit in advance of actual need because banks extend credit only in situations about which they are well-informed. Obtaining a loan on a spur-of-the-moment basis, therefore, is virtually impossible. If the entrepreneur attempts this and fails, the business usually becomes a bankruptcy failure. When the line of credit is arranged prior to the beginning of operations, the entrepreneur should ask for the maximum amount likely to be needed as shown by projected business plans. And, when subsequently requesting a loan, he or she should be ready to demonstrate that the firm's current financial condition still provides an adequate basis for borrowing.

Long-Term Loans. Permanent working capital and fixed assets should be financed by ownership equity or long-term loans. It is often disastrous to finance a substantial portion of the fixed investment by short-term loans. This is because the debt matures before the fixed investment can be amortized from the income it yields.

Long-term borrowing actually is divided into intermediate-term and long-term. Intermediate-term loans mature in two to five years. Long-term loans mature after 5 years, and they are likely to be 10- to 25-year loans.

---

10. Ann M. Morrison, "The Venture Capitalist Who Tries to Win Them All," *Fortune*, Vol. 101, No. 2 (January 28, 1980), p. 97.

Unused Debt Capacity. Initial financing should be carried out with an eye to the future. This means that initial commitments should not preclude financial moves that will become desirable or necessary later. If emergencies arise, the new firm may need additional capital to weather the storm. As the business becomes successful, it will also need additional capital to finance expansion. For these reasons, the firm should not totally exhaust its borrowing capacity at first.

Selection of a Bank. The varied services provided by a bank make the choice of a bank important. For the typical small firm, the provision of checking-account facilities and the extension of short-term (and possibly long-term) loans are the two most important services of a bank. Normally loans are negotiated with the same bank in which the firm maintains its checking account. In addition, the firm may use the bank's safety deposit vault or its

ACTION REPORT: Educating Your Banker

An effective banking relationship requires a banker who understands the nature of a small-business customer. In 1975, Charles Pierce founded Numanco, Inc., a firm which "rents out" crews of radiation technicians to nuclear utilities. Dana Bishop was Pierce's banker until the time he left the bank in Attleboro, MA for another job. Pierce described Bishop as "an adviser, a father confessor, someone I could worry with." This relationship grew over time.

Pierce's first loan application for $6,000 from the Attleboro bank was turned down by Bishop. Pierce recounts the problem as follows:

> I guess I'd always assumed bankers were experts on any business. . . That isn't true. If you want them to deal with your needs intelligently, you've got to spend time going over every last nut and bolt. If there's anything you forget to explain, they're sure not going to pick it up out of thin air.

After Pierce explained company operations, the market, and his own background, Bishop began to see the potential for the business. With a personal guarantee from Pierce on the loan, the bank finally provided $1,500.

Pierce became a frequent customer of the bank, and he and Bishop spent more and more time together discussing Numanco's growth opportunities. Bishop became Numanco's advocate. Eventually, the $1,500 loan grew to a $200,000 line of credit.

Source: Jeffrey Tarter, "What Do Bankers Know About a Service Business?" *Inc.*, Vol. 2, No. 10 (October, 1980), pp. 87-90.

services in collecting notes or securing credit information. An experienced banker can also provide management counsel, particularly in financial matters, to the beginning entrepreneur.

The factor of location limits the range of choices possible for the small firm. For reasons of convenience in making deposits and in conferring with the banker concerning loans and other matters, it is essential that the bank be located in the same vicinity. Any bank is also interested in its home community and therefore tends to be sympathetic to the needs of business firms in the area. Except in very small communities, however, two or more local banks are available, thus permitting some freedom of choice.

Lending policies of banks are not uniform. Some bankers are extremely conservative, while others are more venturesome in the risks they will accept. If a small firm's loan application is neither obviously strong nor obviously weak, its prospects for approval depend as much upon the bank as upon the borrowing firm. Such differences in willingness to lend have been clearly established by research studies, as well as by the practical experience of many business borrowers. In addition to variations in their conservative or venturesome orientation, banks also differ in length of loans, interest rates, types of security required, and other such features. The bank's reputation for sticking with a firm in times of adversity is also pertinent. Some banks are more flexible than others in assisting a firm that is experiencing temporary difficulty. The beginning small business certainly needs a banker who is willing to make reasonable concessions in times of stress.[11]

Venture-Capital Companies. Technically speaking, anyone investing in a new-business venture is a venture capitalist. However, the term **venture capitalist** is usually associated with those corporations or partnerships which operate as investment groups. Each year more venture-capital groups are being organized.[12] The investment philosophy of many venture-capital companies is shown by the following quote:

> Technology Venture Investors (TVI) is a privately held venture-capital partnership organized in 1980 to make equity investments in businesses having the potential for extraordinary increases in value over the long term. We are patient, capital-gains-oriented investors; i.e., we have the same overall objectives as the entrepreneurs in whom we invest.
>
> Our interests run the gamut from start-ups to secondary stock purchases in mature venture companies. Indeed, our initial TVI investments have ranged from "two guys and an idea" to profitable growth companies

---

11. For a more detailed discussion on choosing a bank, see James McNeill Stancill, "Getting the Most from Your Banking Relationship," *Harvard Business Review*, Vol. 58, No. 2 (March-April, 1980), pp. 20-28.

12. For an excellent discussion of the revived venture-capital industry, see David E. Gumpert, "Venture Capital Becoming More Widely Available," *Harvard Business Review*, Vol. 57, No. 1 (January-February, 1979), pp. 178-192.

who are seeking their first significant outside capital as a means to obtain help and counsel in guiding further rapid growth.[13]

Some venture-capital companies provide management assistance to the young business. They also can assist in later financing needs.

Special resource directories are available for the entrepreneur seeking venture capital. One such book, compiled by Stanley Pratt, lists over 500 venture-capital sources plus several informative articles written by venture capitalists.[14]

Government-Sponsored Agencies as Sources of Funds

The federal government has a long-standing reputation for helping new businesses get started. Statistics gathered from the federal agencies show that some $1.3 billion was put into small-business start-ups in 1979.[15]

Small Business Administration Loans. To qualify for an SBA loan, the prospective borrower must have been unable to obtain financing from private sources on reasonable terms. At the same time, the loan must be of such sound value or so secured that repayment is reasonably assured. These loans are normally secured by real estate mortgages or chattel mortgages, or by assignment of accounts receivable, life insurance policies, franchises, securities, and so forth. In addition, the Small Business Administration guarantees bank loans up to $350,000.

Different types of loans are provided by the Small Business Administration. **Direct loans** are made for a maximum amount of $150,000.[16] These generally provide for monthly payments with maturities up to 10 years, or 15 years on loans for new construction. The SBA also grants **participation loans**, which are made in cooperation with private banks and in which the degree of participation by the SBA ranges up to 90 percent. **Disaster relief loans**, examples of which are the loans extended to small businesses after devastating tornadoes, are one important phase of the SBA lending program. Finally, the SBA provides **economic opportunity loans** to minority and other disadvantaged groups. Management assistance is given as part of the economic opportunity loan program, and an effort is made to seek out deserving applicants in ghetto and other depressed areas.

---

13. From a draft of a brochure for Technology Venture Investors provided by Burton J. McMurtry through personal correspondence.

14. Stanley Pratt (ed.), *Guide to Venture Capital Sources* (5th ed.; Wellesley Hills, MA: Capital Publishing Company, 1981).

15. "Sam Wants to Put You into Business," *Venture*, Vol. 2, No. 11 (November, 1980), p. 31.

16. The agency can raise the ceiling to $350,000 for direct loans and $500,000 for guarantees for special "social policy purposes."

Small Business Investment Companies (SBICs). In 1958, Congress passed the Small Business Investment Act, which provides for the establishment of privately owned capital banks whose purpose is to provide long-term loans and/or equity capital to small businesses. SBICs are licensed and regulated by the Small Business Administration. They may obtain a substantial part of their capital from the SBA at attractive rates of interest. In 1979, approximately 40 percent of all SBIC investments were in start-ups.[17]

Although SBICs may either lend funds or supply equity funds, the act was intended to place a strong emphasis upon equity financing. The SBIC that provides equity financing may do so either by directly purchasing the small firm's stock or, quite commonly, by purchasing the small firm's convertible debentures (bonds), which may be converted into stock at the option of the SBIC.

The typical SBIC wishes to invest in companies that have rapid growth prospects. In addition, the cost of investigating investment opportunities makes it more profitable for the SBIC to concentrate its attention upon the bigger investments required by the larger small businesses. These considerations and the reluctance of many small-business owners to accept a dilution of equity have limited the use of SBICs by small-business firms that need long-term capital.

Many SBICs have provided not only funds but also counsel and advice to the small firms they have served. It is not uncommon for an SBIC to have a representative on the board of directors of the borrowing firm. The SBIC does not normally wish to assume operating control of a business, but it is often able to provide constructive advice, particularly of a financial nature. Some SBICs provide management counsel and advice on a fee basis, in addition to the unofficial counsel that accompanies the original investment or loan.

Miscellaneous Sources of Funds

Commercial finance companies lend money to small-business firms on a secured basis. Their loans may be backed by inventories, accounts receivable, equipment, or other items. They participate in floor planning arrangements and also purchase installment paper from small firms. The interest rates charged by commercial finance companies tend to be higher than those charged by commercial banks.

Insurance companies have also made term loans available to small business.[18] Although their major financing efforts have been directed toward big business, some insurance companies have established small-business loan departments. These companies place considerable emphasis on the submission of financial statements and projections by the borrowing company.

---

17. "Sam Wants to Put You into Business," *op. cit.*, p. 34.

18. For an example, see "Equitable Courts Small Business," *Business Week*, No. 2488 (June 20, 1977), p. 114.

Consequently, small businesses are often reluctant to subject themselves to such effort and evaluation.

Other financial institutions and groups that make financing available to small-business firms from time to time include: savings and loan associations, credit unions, mutual savings banks, factors, personal finance companies, universities, and investment bankers.

POINTS TO CONSIDER IN THE FINANCING PROPOSAL

Once the entrepreneur has determined what capital is needed, how much is needed, and the most likely sources of these funds, he or she must structure the financing proposal. A potential investor in the business wants something concrete to substantiate the entrepreneur's claims of profit and success! This "something concrete" is a document known as the financing proposal.

A financing proposal is constructed from the business plan outlined on page 61 in Chapter 3. The detailed financial section of that plan can be used to show the capital needs and the plans for funding these needs. Potential investors will also be interested in an abbreviated version of the other parts of the plan. The complete financial proposal should be as brief as possible, while still including the necessary information.

It is also desirable to discuss in the financing proposal some of the problems facing the proposed business. Most investors realize that business prospects are not all rosy. For example, venture capitalist Fred Adler says:

> The ideal [financing] proposal has a business plan and a market analysis, with a full explanation of how and why the plan will work. It discusses the problems—every company has problems—and tells how they will be overcome.... In short, we want proposals that give us precise information and are concise and candid about the company's problems as well as its successes.[19]

In order to prepare your financing proposal properly, you should analyze the informational needs of your potential investors. If you are seeking funds from government-sponsored sources, banks, or venture-capital companies, you can easily learn their exact informational needs by telephoning or writing them.

A concluding word of advice for the new entrepreneur who is seeking start-up capital is expressed by one businessman who put together $3 million for a new venture. He says, "Don't be bashful. Tell your venture-capital guy your dream. He wants to believe you're the next Apple Computer or Xerox."[20]

---

19. Burton W. Teague, "Venture Capital—Who Gets It, and Why?" *Inc.*, Vol. 2, No. 6 (June, 1980), p. 72.

20. Jacobs, *loc. cit.*

Remember, the potential investor is most interested in who you are, what your idea is, what you will do with the money, how much you want, and how it will be repaid.

LOOKING BACK

1. Current-asset capital, fixed-asset capital, promoter-expense capital, and funds for personal expenses constitute the capital requirements in starting a new business.
2. The dollar amounts of initial capital requirements can be estimated by using industry ratios and cross-checking with empirical investigation. A small business should be careful to avoid a disproportionately small investment in current assets relative to fixed assets.
3. Individual investors as sources of funds include the owner(s) of the business, friends, relatives, and local people. The capital stock of the business may be sold by private placement or by a public sale. The condition of the financial markets at any particular time has a direct bearing on the feasibility of a public sale of capital stock. Business suppliers as sources of funds include suppliers who provide trade credit and manufacturers/wholesalers who provide equipment loans and leases.
4. Commercial banks as sources of funds grant both short-term and long-term loans. The selection of a bank is of prime importance to the beginning entrepreneur. Venture-capital companies as sources of funds are usually corporations or partnerships which operate as investment groups. They provide both debt and equity capital and assist in later financing needs. They also provide management assistance to the young business.
5. Government-sponsored agencies as sources of funds include the Small Business Administration and Small Business Investment Companies (SBICs). The federal government is a major supplier of funds for small business.

DISCUSSION QUESTIONS

1. Define working capital. What three items make up circulating capital? What is the typical cycle involving the three components of circulating capital?
2. Why should personal expenses be included in the initial financial planning?

3. Suppose that a retailer's estimated sales are $900,000 and the standard sales-to-inventory ratio is 6. What dollar amount of inventory would be estimated for the new business?

4. If the industry average collection period for accounts receivable is 72 days, what level of accounts receivable must be maintained with estimated sales of $900,000?

5. Distinguish between owner capital and creditor capital.

6. What are the major problems involved in obtaining loans from friends and relatives? How should they be repaid?

7. What are some of the major advantages and disadvantages of "going public"?

8. Explain how trade credit and equipment loans provide initial capital funding.

9. Discuss banks as a source of funds.

10. How does the federal government help with initial financing for a small business?

REFERENCES TO SMALL BUSINESS IN ACTION

Halbrooks, John. "They Never Quit." *Inc.*, Vol. 3, No. 3 (March, 1981), pp. 58–62.

This article tells the story of a husband-and-wife team who, prior to marriage, pooled $2,000 in savings to start a new business venture. It describes how they went public, later were "capital-poor," and made personal sacrifices to reach their current $22 million sales level.

Linderff, Dave. "Investment Bankers Take the Venture Plunge." *Venture*, Vol. 3, No. 1 (January, 1981), pp. 42–47.

Numerous examples of small-business financing problems are provided in this article as it profiles the participation of investment bankers in the venture-capital market.

"Making It with the Ladies." *International Entrepreneurs*, Vol. 5, No. 8 (October, 1977), pp. 6–13.

This is an account of a retail business venture which started with 1 store financed by $20,000 of borrowed capital and grew into 5 stores 7 years later. A typical profit-and-loss statement showing working-capital needs is included in the article.

"One Day, at an Earthquake Party . . ." *Forbes*, Vol. 126, No. 8 (October 13, 1980), pp. 197–200.

The rise of a business initially financed by friends and relatives is the subject of this story. Later funding was raised from equipment manufacturers and bank loans.

Chapter 8

Choosing the Legal Form of Organization

LOOKING AHEAD

Watch for the following important topics:

1. Characteristics of the proprietorship.
2. Characteristics of the general partnership, the partnership agreement, and the limited partnership.
3. Characteristics of the corporation and the limited liability of stockholders.
4. Relevance of contracts, agency relationships, negotiable instruments, real property, trademarks, patents, copyright, and libelous acts to the small business.
5. How to choose an attorney for a small firm.

Should a new firm be organized as a proprietorship, a partnership, or a corporation? Anyone who buys or starts a business faces this question at once. Moreover, the problem reappears as a business grows. Firms begun as proprietorships later may find it desirable to become partnerships or corporations.

In this chapter we will examine the three major forms of business organization and also the areas of law relevant to small business. In view of the need for legal counsel both in forming the organization and in dealing with various legal issues, we will conclude the chapter by discussing the choice of an attorney for the small firm.

RELATIVE IMPORTANCE OF FORMS OF BUSINESS ORGANIZATION

The proprietorship is the simplest and most popular form of business organization. As shown in Figure 8-1, the large majority (71.5 percent) of our enterprises function as proprietorships. The corporate form is the next most popular in industry as a whole (19.3 percent), with partnerships in third place (9.2 percent). Although the percentages of corporations and partnerships appear small, we should note that there are more than one million partnerships and two million corporations in the United States.

The proprietorship form is dominant in each industry, although the proportion varies somewhat from industry to industry. In the services, for example, the proprietorship form is used by 81.7 percent of the firms, whereas it is used by only 46.5 percent of the firms in manufacturing. In all industries, corporations outnumber partnerships although there are more partnerships than corporations in mining and in finance, insurance, and real estate.

The relatively large percentage of proprietorships, however, gives an incorrect impression of their relative importance. The reason for this is that many small firms function as proprietorships, whereas most very large firms organize as corporations. As a result, the corporate form actually accounts for the largest share of business receipts. There are valid reasons for this, of course, as will become evident in the latter part of this chapter.

Figure 8-2 shows the percentage of total business receipts accounted for by each type of business organization. A glance at this illustration reveals the overwhelming importance of corporations. In all industries, corporations account for almost 90 percent of total business receipts. Proprietorships account for a higher proportion of the receipts than do partnerships, but their relative importance varies from industry to industry.

The pattern of organization that emerges, therefore, is this: Each of the three major forms of organization is important both in numbers and in total receipts. The proprietorship is by far the most popular form, a reflection of small businesses which operate with a simple form of legal organization. More significantly, however, the corporation is by far the most important form of organization when we look beyond the number of business units to the volume of business activity.

CHARACTERISTICS OF THE PROPRIETORSHIP

The most popular form of organization is the **proprietorship** — a business owned and operated by one person. The individual proprietor has title to all business assets, subject to the claims of creditors. He or she receives all

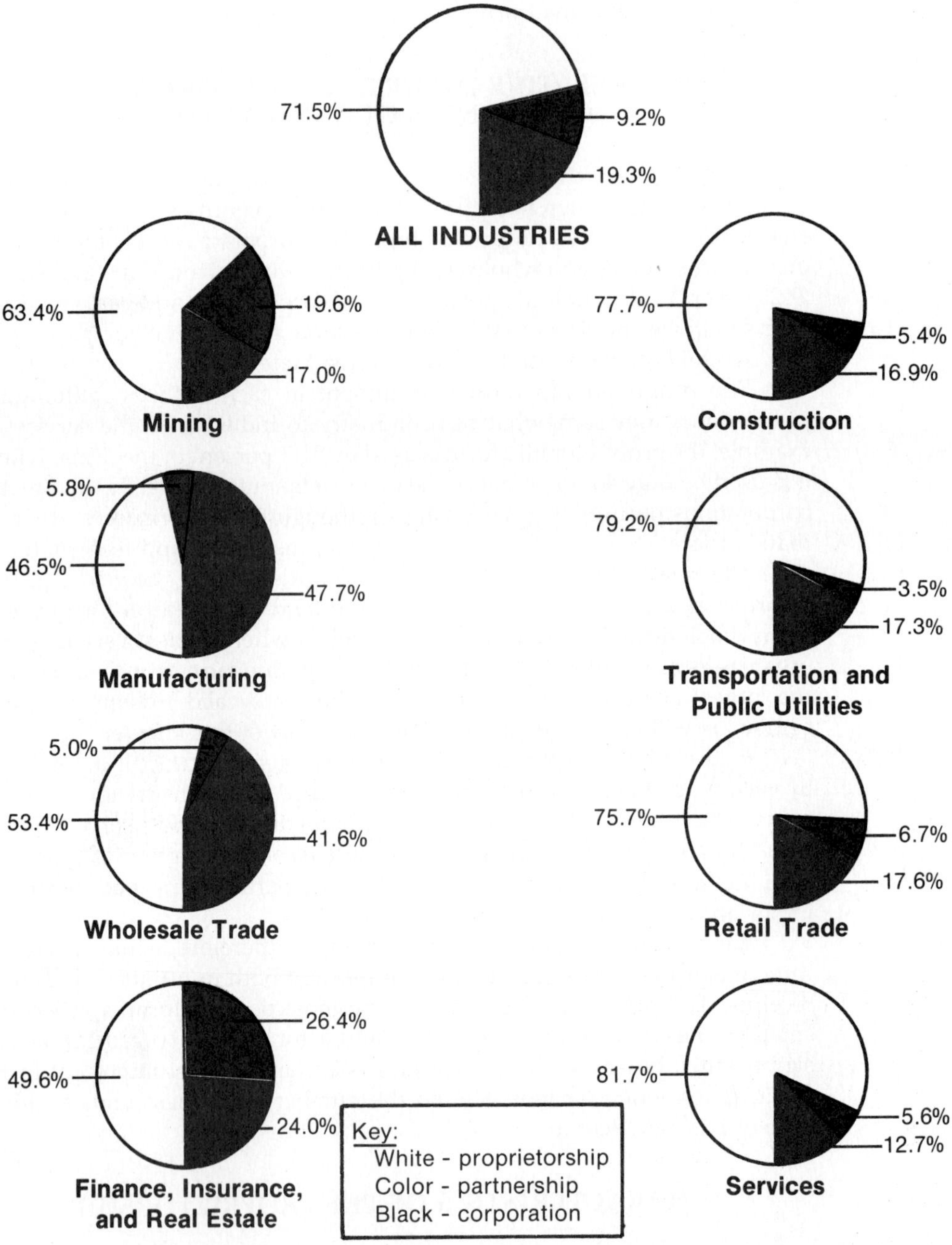

Source: *Statistical Abstract of the United States: 1980* (101st edition), Washington, D. C., 1980, Table 929, p. 557.

Figure 8-1 Mix of Legal Organizational Forms in Industry

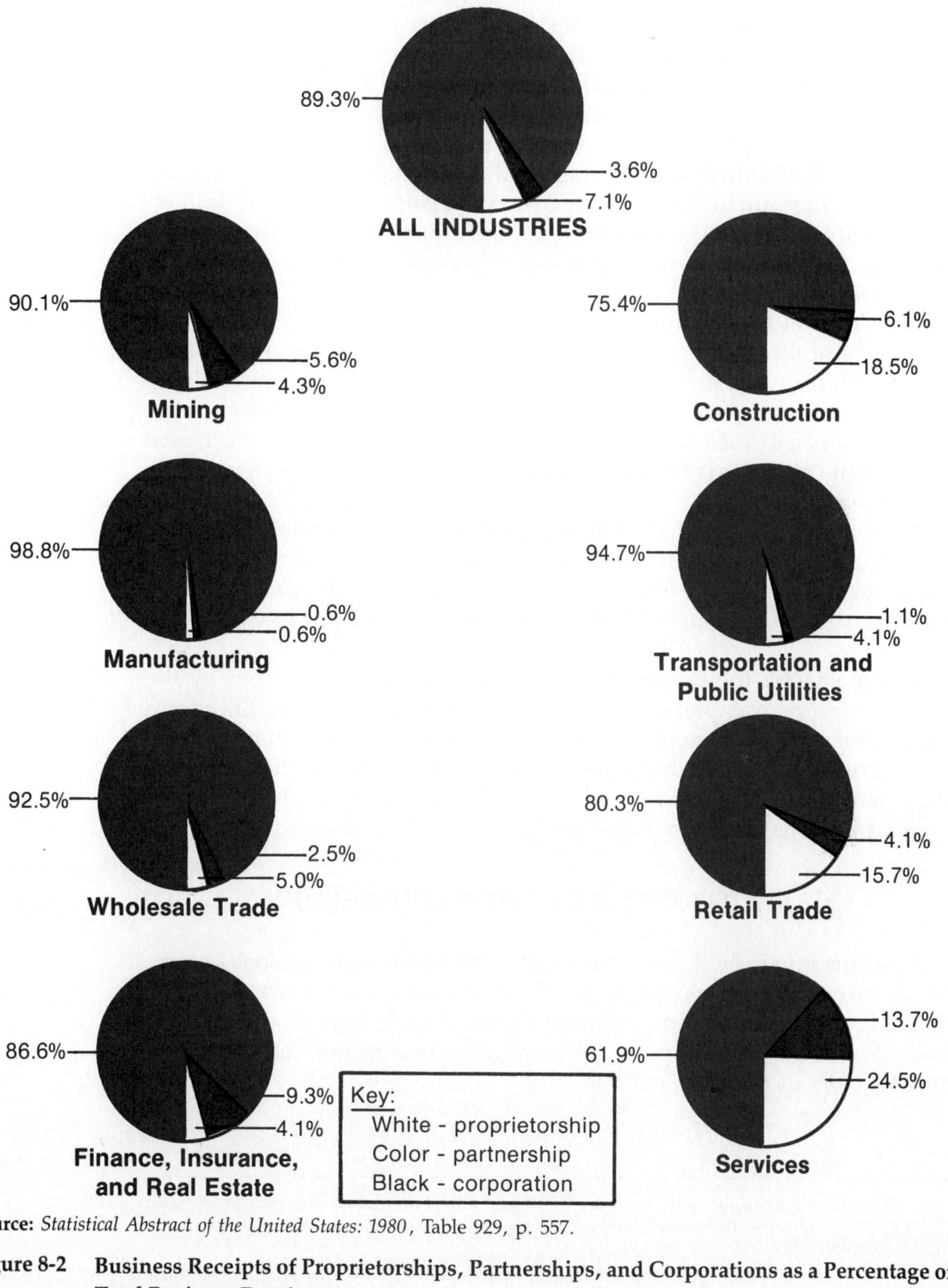

Source: *Statistical Abstract of the United States: 1980*, Table 929, p. 557.

Figure 8-2 Business Receipts of Proprietorships, Partnerships, and Corporations as a Percentage of Total Business Receipts

profits but must also assume all losses, bear all risks, and pay all debts of the business. Such a business can be established merely by starting operation and requires no legal documentation.[1] In view of this fact, the proprietorship is the simplest and cheapest way to start operation and is frequently the most appropriate form for a new business. In the proprietorship the owner is free from interference by partners, shareholders, directors, and officers.

The proprietorship form lacks some of the advantages of other forms. As noted above, there are no limits on the owner's personal liability. In addition, proprietors are not employees and cannot receive some of the tax-free benefits customarily provided by corporations—for example, insurance and hospitalization plans.

The death of the proprietor terminates the business since the proprietorship is basically nothing more than the proprietor. The possibility of the owner's death may cloud relationships between the business and its creditors and employees. The need for a will is suggested because the assets of the business less its liabilities belong to the heirs. In the will the owner can give an executor the power to run the business for the heirs until they can take over or until it can be sold.

Another contingency that must be provided for is the possible incapacity of the proprietor. If he or she were badly hurt in an automobile accident, and unconscious for weeks, the business could be ruined. But the proprietor can guard against this by giving a legally competent person a power of attorney to carry on.

In some cases, the proprietorship option is virtually ruled out by the circumstances. For example, a high exposure to legal risks may require a form that provides greater protection against personal liability, as in the case of a manufacturer of potentially hazardous consumer products. At the beginning stage, however, most small businesses can make a choice on the basis of legal, tax, and operational features of the various forms of organization.

CHARACTERISTICS OF THE PARTNERSHIP

A **partnership** is a voluntary "association of two or more persons to carry on as co-owners a business for profit."[2] Because of its voluntary nature, a partnership is quickly set up—without the legal requirements of corporate organization. A partnership pools the managerial talents and capital of those joining together as business partners.

---

1. This does not imply that there are no legal obligations, such as compliance with zoning and licensing laws, but merely states that no legal documents are necessary to create a proprietorship.

2. This is the definition given in the Uniform Partnership Act—now adopted by most states.

Qualifications of Partners

Any person capable of contracting may legally become a business partner. Individuals may become partners without contributing to capital or sharing in the assets at the time of dissolution. Such persons are partners only as to management and profits.

Aside from legal aspects, however, partnership formation deserves serious study. A strong partnership requires partners who are honest, healthy, capable, and compatible.

Rights and Duties of Partners

Partners' rights and duties should be stated explicitly in the **articles of partnership**. These articles are drawn up during the preoperating period and should cover the following items as a minimum:

1. Date of formation of the partnership.
2. Names and addresses of all partners.
3. Statement of fact of partnership.
4. Statement of business purpose(s).
5. Duration of the business.
6. Name and location of the business.
7. Amount invested by each partner.
8. Sharing ratio for profits and losses.
9. Partners' rights, if any, for withdrawals of funds for personal use.
10. Provision for accounting records and their accessibility to partners.
11. Specific duties of each partner.
12. Provision for dissolution and for sharing the net assets.
13. Restraint on partners' assumption of special obligations, such as endorsing the note of another.
14. Provision for protection of surviving partners, decedent's estate, etc.

Unless specified otherwise in the articles, a partner is generally recognized as having certain implicit rights. For example, partners share profits or losses equally if they have not agreed on a profit-and-loss-sharing ratio.

In a partnership each partner has **agency power**, which means that a partner can bind all members of the firm. Good faith, together with reasonable care in the exercise of management duties, is required of all partners in a business. Since their relationship is fiduciary in character, a partner cannot compete in business and remain a partner. Nor can a partner use business information solely for personal gain.

Termination of Partnership

Death, incapacity, or withdrawal of a partner terminates a partnership and necessitates liquidation or reorganization of the business. Liquidation often results in substantial losses to all partners. It may be legally necessary, however, because a partnership is a close personal relationship of the parties that cannot be maintained against the will of any one of them.

This disadvantage may be partially overcome at the time a partnership is formed by stipulating in the articles of partnership that surviving partners can continue the business after buying the decedent's interest. This can be facilitated by having the partners carry mutual life insurance. Or the executor might act as a partner until the heirs become of age. In the latter case, the agreement should also provide for liquidation in the event of unprofitability or in the event of major disagreements with the executor as partner.

The Limited Partnership

A small business sometimes finds it desirable to use a special form of the partnership called the **limited partnership**.[3] This form consists of at least one

ACTION REPORT: Limited Partnerships in Oil Exploration

Oil exploration ventures have led to the extensive use of the limited partnership. One of many possible examples of such ventures is provided by Robert Charlebois of Cazenovia, NY. An adventuresome individual, Charlebois has hunted polar bears in the Arctic and man-eating tigers in India and has invested in real estate, commodities, and silver, as well as exploring for oil.

Charlebois concentrates his oil exploration activity in the East. In 1979, he moved into drilling by participating in several limited partnerships. Some producing wells in New York have been developed by a limited partnership of which he owns more than 50 percent. These wells were expected to provide him with an income of $100,000 to $150,000 in 1980 and substantially higher revenues in 1981. At that time, Charlebois was attempting to raise $1 million to $5 million in a limited partnership to do further exploratory drilling in the vicinity of his home base in Cazenovia, NY.

Source: Len Albin, "The New Search for Energy in the East," *Venture*, Vol. 3, No. 2 (February, 1981), pp. 62-63.

---

3. For an excellent discussion of the limited partnership, see W. K. Daugherty, "The Limited Partnership—A Financing Vehicle," *Journal of Small Business Management*, Vol. 18, No. 2 (April, 1980), pp. 55-60.

ACTION REPORT: Compatibility Among "Partners"

As in marriage, a major factor in the survival and success of business firms is the quality of relationships among partners. This is true both in partnerships and in closely held corporations in which two or more owners are actively involved. Partners need not be identical, but they should be compatible. An example of a successful blend of talents and temperaments of two unlike partners is found in the "partnership" of Keith Blakely, the 24-year-old president of Advanced Refractory Technologies, Inc., and Peter Shaffer, 51, the company's vice-president and chief scientist. Notes one writer:

> Yet the people who meet them think that Blakely and Shaffer are a perfect match. "Pete likes to be the chief scientist and I like the business. It's a good synergism," explains Blakely. Adds Shaffer: "Keith is interested in numbers. I'm not. I can blow up a lab and go right back to work, but I just can't make a decision that will influence somebody's life."
>
> To guarantee that their partnership will work, Blakely and Shaffer have outlined their areas of responsibility and authority to make sure that each one does his job without stepping on the other's toes. With care, the partners will build a business capable of reaching its stated goal of $2 million in sales and $500,000 in profits in 1982 as a producer of heat-resistant products for the nuclear industry.

Source: Susan Alai, "How to Make Partnerships Work," *Venture*, Vol. 3, No. 6 (June, 1981), pp. 52-54.

general partner and one or more limited partners. The **general partner** remains personally liable for the debts of the business, but all **limited partners** have limited personal liability as long as they do not take an active role in the management of the partnership. In other words, limited partners risk only the capital which they invest in the business. Because of this feature, an individual with substantial personal assets can invest money in a limited partnership without exposing his or her total personal estate to liability claims that might arise through activities of the business.

The limited partnership form is frequently used to provide real estate tax shelters to the limited partners. For example, the limited partnership may acquire a piece of undeveloped real estate, apartment houses, or commercial buildings. Most of the interest and other costs of the partnership are prorated to the limited partners, who report them as tax-deductible expenditures on their personal income tax returns. (Of course, income from the property must likewise be reported on the partners' tax returns, but the costs frequently exceed revenue in the early going.) When the property is finally sold, it may produce a capital gain, which is taxed at a lower rate than ordinary income.

CHARACTERISTICS OF THE CORPORATION

In the Dartmouth College Case of 1819, Chief Justice John Marshall of the United States Supreme Court defined a **corporation** as "an artificial being, invisible, intangible, and existing only in contemplation of the law." By these words the court recognized the corporation as a legal entity. This means that a corporation can sue and be sued, hold and sell property, and engage in business operations stipulated in the corporate charter.

The corporation is the creature of a state, being chartered under its laws. Its length of life is independent of owners' lives. It is the corporation, and not its owners, that is liable for debts contracted by it. Its directors and officers serve as agents to bind the corporation.

Rights and Status of Stockholders

Ownership in a corporation is evidenced by stock certificates, each of which stipulates the number of shares held by the given stockholder. An ownership interest does not confer a legal right to act for the firm or to share in its management. It does evidence the right to receive dividends in proportion to stockholdings—but only when they are properly declared by the board of directors. And it typically carries the right to buy new shares, in proportion to stock already owned, before the new stock is offered for public sale.

In the initial organization of a corporation, the owner does well to consider a type of stock known as **Section 1244 stock**. By issuing stock pursuant to Section 1244 of the Internal Revenue Code, the stockholder is somewhat protected in case of failure. If the stock becomes worthless, the loss (up to $50,000 on a joint return) may be treated as an ordinary tax-deductible loss. This applies only to corporations whose total equity capital does not exceed $1 million.

A stockholder casts one vote per share in stockholders' meetings. Thus, the stockholder indirectly participates in management by helping elect the directors. The board of directors is the governing body for corporate activity. It elects the firm's officers, who manage the enterprise with the help of management specialists. The directors also set or approve management policies, receive and consider reports on operating results from the officers, and declare dividends (if any).

The legal status of stockholders and managers is fundamental, of course, but it may be overemphasized. In the case of many small corporations, the owners may also be directors and managing officers. The person who owns most of the stock can control the business as effectively as if it were a proprietorship. In such a case, this person can name his or her spouse and an outsider as fellow directors. The directors can meet only when legally required to do so, and they can elect the principal owner as president and general manager of the firm. This is not to imply that it is good business practice to ignore a board of directors, but simply to point out that direction and control may be exercised as forcefully by a majority owner in a small corporation as by an individual proprietor. The corporate form is thus applicable to individual and family-owned businesses.

Major stockholders must be concerned with their working relationships, as well as their legal relationships, with other owners, particularly with those who are active in the business. Cooperation among the entire owner-manager team of a new corporation is necessary for its survival. Legal technicalities are important, but they provide an inadequate basis for successful collaboration by those who are in reality "partners" in the enterprise.

Limited Liability of Stockholders

One of the advantages of the corporate form of organization is the limited liability of its owners. However, new small-business corporations often are in somewhat shaky financial circumstances during the early years of operation. As a result, the stockholders, few in number and active in management, frequently assume personal liability for the firm's debts by endorsing its notes.

Death or Withdrawal of Stockholders

Unlike the partnership, ownership in a corporation is readily transferable. Exchange of shares of stock is all that is required to convey an ownership interest to a different individual.

In a large corporation, stock is being exchanged constantly without noticeable effect upon the operations of the business. In a small firm, however, the change of owners, though legally just as simple, may produce numerous complications. To illustrate, suppose that two of the three equal shareholders in a business for one reason or another sold their stock to an outsider. The remaining stockholder would then be at the mercy of the outsider, who might decide to remove the former from any managerial post he or she happened to hold. In fact, a minority stockholder may be legally ousted from the board of directors and have no voice whatsoever in the management of the business.

The death of the majority stockholder could be equally unfortunate. An heir, executor, or purchaser of the stock might well insist upon direct control, with possible adverse effects for the other stockholders. To prevent problems of this nature from arising, legal arrangements should be made at the time of incorporation to provide for management continuity by surviving stockholders, as well as for fair treatment of heirs of a decedent stockholder. As in the case of the partnership, mutual insurance may be carried to assure ability to buy out the decedent. This arrangement would require an option for the corporation or surviving stockholders to: (1) purchase the decedent's stock ahead of outsiders, and (2) specify the method for determining the stock's price per share. A similar arrangement might be included to protect remaining stockholders if a given stockholder wished to retire from the business at any time.

Corporate Charter

In most states three or more persons are required to apply to the secretary of state for permission to incorporate. After preliminary steps, including required publicity and payment of the incorporation fee and initial franchise tax, the written application is approved by the secretary of state and becomes the corporation's charter. A corporation charter typically provides for the following:

1. Name of the company.
2. Formal statement of its formation.
3. Purposes and powers—that is, type of business.
4. Location of principal office in the state of incorporation.
5. Duration (perpetual existence, 50-year life and renewable charter, etc.).
6. Classes and preferences of classes of stock.
7. Number and par or stated value of shares of each class of stock authorized.
8. Voting privileges of each class of stock.
9. Names and addresses of incorporators and first year's directors.
10. Names and addresses of, and amounts subscribed by, each subscriber to capital stock.
11. Statement of limited liability of stockholders (required specifically by state law in many states).
12. Statement of alterations of directors' powers, if any, from the general corporation law of the state.

A corporation's charter should be brief, in accord with the law, and broad in the statement of the firm's powers. Details should be left to the bylaws. The charter application should be prepared by an attorney.

The Subchapter S Corporation

For many small firms the corporate income tax is a disadvantage of the corporate form of organization.[4] One solution in such cases is to organize as a **Subchapter S corporation**, an arrangement which allows stockholders to be

---

4. The corporate income tax is not a disadvantage in *all* cases—for example, in a new firm which is not yet profitable.

taxed as partners and thus avoid the corporate income tax. The name of this type of corporation comes from Subchapter S of the Internal Revenue Code, which permits corporations to retain the limited-liability feature while being taxed as partnerships. During the early years of corporate life, the Subchapter S arrangement also permits corporate losses to flow through to stockholders, who can use them to offset other types of income on their tax returns.

A number of restrictions exist in the creation of Subchapter S corporations. For example, the number of stockholders is limited to 10 initially and 15 after 5 years. Various other restrictive features should be checked with an attorney at the time of organization, but the potential advantages of the Subchapter S corporate form are such as to justify its serious consideration.

AREAS OF BUSINESS LAW RELEVANT TO THE SMALL BUSINESS

Some of the legal issues that affect small businesses are evident in the discussion of the various topics in this book. For example, in buying a business, reviewing a franchise contract, or incorporating, the need for legal counsel is clear. In addition, some broad areas of business law are relevant to small-business operation.

Contracts

Managers of small firms frequently make agreements with employees, customers, suppliers, and others. In some of these agreements, called **contracts**, the parties intend to create mutual legal obligations. For a valid contract to exist, the following requirements must be met:

1. *Voluntary agreement.* A genuine offer must be accepted unconditionally by the buyer.
2. *Competent contracting parties.* Contracts with parties who are under legal age, insane, seriously intoxicated, or otherwise unable to understand the nature of the transaction are typically unenforceable.
3. *Legal act.* The subject of the agreement must not be in conflict with public policy, such as a contract to sell an illegal product.
4. *Consideration*. Something of value, or consideration, must be received by the seller.
5. *Form of contract*. Contracts may be written or oral. Some contracts must be in written form to be enforceable. Under the **statute of frauds**, sales transactions of $500 or more, sales of real estate, and contracts extending for more than 1 year must be in writing. The existence of an oral contract must be demonstrated in some way; otherwise it may prove difficult to establish.

If one party to a contract fails to perform in accordance with the contract, the injured party may have recourse to certain remedies. Occasionally a court will require specific performance of a contract when money damages are not adequate. However, courts are generally reluctant to rule in this manner. In other cases the injured party has the right to rescind, or cancel, the contract. The most frequently used remedy takes the form of money damages, which are intended to put the injured party in the same condition that he or she would have been in had the contract been performed. In many cases a creditor-seller arranges for certain security devices so that he or she need not rely exclusively on the credit standing or ability of the debtor to pay.

Another claim against property that is quite important to some types of small businesses is the **mechanic's lien**. For example, materials suppliers or contractors who perform repair or construction would have a lien against the property if the property owner or tenant defaulted in payments for either materials or labor.

State laws that require creditors to be reasonably prompt in filing their claims are known as **statutes of limitations**. These laws are intended to protect debtors from claims in which the evidence is so old that the facts have become difficult to establish. Although time periods under the statute of limitations vary depending on the type of contract, an action for breach of contract on a sale of goods must be started within four or other state-specified number of years. For small creditors this means that legal action should not be postponed indefinitely if there is any expectation of forcing payment.

Various states have enacted **bulk sales laws**, which effectively preclude a debtor from making a secret sale of an entire business before a creditor can take the necessary legal action to collect. In general, bulk sales laws provide that any debtor's sale of a business inventory down to the bare walls must be preceded by written notification to the creditors of the business. Otherwise, such bulk sales are fraudulent and void with respect to the creditors.

Agency Relationships

An **agency** is a relationship whereby one party, the **agent**, represents another party, the **principal**, in dealing with a third person. Examples of agents are: the manager of a branch office who acts as the agent of the firm, a partner who acts as an agent for the partnership, and real estate agents who represent buyers or sellers.

Agents, however, differ in the scope of their authority. The manager of a branch office is a *general agent*, whereas a real estate agent is a *special agent* with authority to act only in a particular transaction.

The principal is liable to a third party for the performance of contracts made by the agent acting within the scope of the agent's authority. A principal is also liable for fraudulent, negligent, and other wrongful acts of an agent executed within the scope of the agency.

An agent has certain obligations to the principal. In general, the agent must accept the orders and instructions of the principal, act in good faith, and use prudence and care in the discharge of agency duties. Moreover, the agent is liable if he or she exceeds stipulated authority and causes damage to the third party as a result—unless the principal ratifies the act, whereupon the principal becomes liable.

It is apparent that the powers of agents can make the agency relationship a potentially dangerous one for small firms. For this reason, small firms should exercise care in selecting agents and clearly stipulate their authority and responsibility.

Negotiable Instruments

Credit instruments that can be transferred from one party to another in place of money are known as **negotiable instruments**. Examples of negotiable instruments are promissory notes, drafts, trade acceptances, and ordinary checks. When a negotiable instrument is in the possession of an individual known as a **holder in due course**, it is not subject to many of the defenses possible in the case of ordinary contracts. For this reason, the small-business firm should secure instruments that are prepared in such a way as to make them negotiable. In general, the requirements for negotiable instruments are:

1. There must be a written, signed, unconditional promise or order to pay.
2. The amount to be paid must be specified.
3. The instrument must provide for payment on demand, at a definite time, or at a determinable time.
4. The instrument must be payable to the bearer or to the order of some person.

Real Property

As distinguished from **personal property**, which refers to things that are movable in nature, **real property** consists of land and buildings and other installations permanently attached to land. Real property is also commonly called real estate.

When the ownership in real property is absolute, that property in a legal sense is known as an **estate in fee simple**. Absolute ownership implies that owners can do what they wish with the property except for any government restrictions imposed. For example, an owner can sell, rent, lease, or even give away the real property. A conveyance of real property must be in written form to be valid. Legal counsel is desirable to assure that transactions are legally correct and truly represent the desires of the contracting parties. The transfer of ownership is accomplished by the transfer of a deed, which should be recorded in the office of the county recorder.

A **lease** is an agreement whereby a property owner (the landlord) confers upon a tenant the right of possession and use of real property for which the tenant pays rent. Leases may be either oral or written. According to the laws of most states, leases for periods longer than one year must be written.

Tenancies may be either definite or indefinite with regard to the time period of a lease. Under a **tenancy at will**, the lease may be terminated at any time upon the request of either party. A few states require the party terminating such a lease to provide some notice of the impending termination.

Registration of Trademarks

A **trademark** is a word, figure, or other symbol used to distinguish a product sold by one manufacturer or merchant. Small manufacturers, in particular, often find it desirable to adopt a particular trademark and to feature it in advertising.

Common law recognizes a property right in the ownership of a trademark. In addition, registration of trademarks is permitted under federal law, a step that generally makes protection easier if infringement is attempted. A trademark registration lasts for 20 years and may be renewed for additional 20-year periods. The different states also have trademark registration laws although it is still the common law that provides the basic protection for the owner of the trademark. Full registration is recommended because the growth of a business firm may eventually make its trademark an extremely valuable asset. Even with proper registration, the trademark owner may be considered to have abandoned the trademark if extensive disregard of it is allowed.

Application for Patents

A **patent** is the registered right of an inventor to make, use, and sell an invention. Items that may be patented include machines and products, improvements on machines and products, and new and original designs. Some small manufacturers have patented items which constitute the major part of their product line. Indeed, some businesses can trace their origin to a patented invention.

A patent attorney is often retained to act for a small-business applicant in preparing an application. In addition to an attorney's fees, a modest filing fee is required. When obtained, a patent is good for a period of 17 years. Since improvements may be patented, even a small-business firm obtaining an original patent may perpetuate control of the device through timely improvements or design changes. The new patent extends the original period of protection for another 17 years.

ACTION REPORT: Protection for a Student Invention

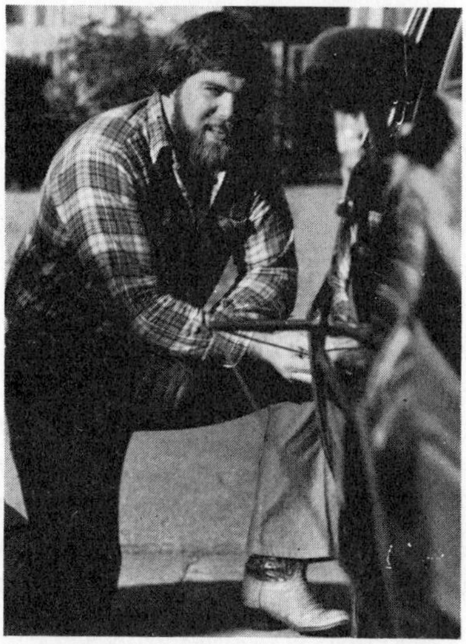

The process of obtaining legal protection for original work can be both time-consuming and costly. Joe Bays, a defensive lineman for Southern Methodist University, grew tired of parking-lot dents inflicted on his blue Mercury Cougar. So, he devised a door protector which was invisible when not in use but which could be deployed in 30 seconds. Prior to marketing the invention, Bays decided to obtain both trademark and patent protection.

At a cost of $150, the trademark search identified 18 other firms already using in their names his tentative product name, "Bodyguard." He then came up with the name "SUPA" (an acronym for "Security Unit Protecting Automobiles"). This time, at the cost of another $150, the trademark cleared, and Bays filed the trademark for another $250.

Bays also submitted a patent application in May, 1978. The first application was returned after ten months by the U. S. Patent Office with a notation that a patent had been awarded earlier for a device to protect whitewall tires from curb abrasions. Bays realized his application may have been misunderstood, so he filed a second application in May, 1979. After later making a substantial improvement in the door protector, he invested in still another patent application. The new application, together with the trademark applications and already-pending patent application, ran his legal fees into the $4,000 to $5,000 range.

Source: Dave Clark, "Cockeyed Inventive Optimist," *Texas Business* (April, 1981), pp. 102-103.

Suits for patent infringements may be brought, but they are costly and should be avoided if possible. Finding the money and legal talent with which to enforce one's legal rights is one of the major problems of patent protection in small business. Monetary damages and injunctions are available, however, if an infringement can be proved.

Copyright Protection

A **copyright** is the registered right of a creator (author, composer, designer, or artist) to reproduce, publish, and sell the work which is the product of the intelligence and skill of that person. According to the Copyright Act of 1976, the creator of an original work that has been copyrighted receives protection for the duration of the creator's life plus 50 years. The law provides that copyrighted, creative work cannot be reproduced by another person or persons without authorization. Even photocopying of such work is prohibited, although an individual may copy a limited amount of material for research purposes. A copyright holder can sue a copyright violator for damages.

Libelous Acts

Libel may be defined as printed defamation of one's reputation. Unless proper precautions are taken, there is a danger of including materials in credit correspondence that may be held by the court to be libelous. Even ordinary collection letters to a debtor have in some cases been held to be libelous by virtue of being dictated by a creditor to a stenographer. This was held to constitute "publication" of the statement.

Under the Fair Debt Collection Act of 1977, it is a federal offense for debt collectors to do the following, among other things:

1. Threaten consumers with violence.
2. Use obscene language.
3. Publish "shame" lists.

Violators are liable for any actual damages as well as additional civil damages determined by the court up to $1,000.

CHOOSING AN ATTORNEY

A review of legal organizational forms and areas of business law makes evident the need for proper legal counsel. Unless the entrepreneur is trained in law, he or she cannot be expected to know the law sufficiently well to avoid the use of professionals. Nor should the small business wait to establish a working relationship with a competent attorney until an emergency arises. The small firm's team of professional counselors should include an attorney, a CPA, a banker, and other specialists.

The small firm needs an attorney experienced in legal practice related to small business. Lawyers might be selected by using the Yellow Pages of a telephone directory, but an informed choice requires a recommendation based on some acquaintanceship with the legal profession. Suggestions of possible attorneys may be obtained from the firm's banker, CPA, or even from other business owners. Lawyers who practice in other areas of law or law school professors, for example, may also be in a position to make recommendations.

What factors should be considered in selecting an attorney to represent the business? Following is one set of recommended criteria:

1. *Size of practice*. Even though a small firm can offer personalized attention, a large firm may have a broader range of expertise. Either way, satisfy yourself that the lawyer is not too busy to be accessible, and not so available that you can't help wondering why.
2. *Client base*. Find out if representing other small-business owners is a major part of the lawyer's practice.
3. *Experience and specialty*. The lawyer's background should qualify him or her to advise you on routine matters, as well as on major decisions.
4. *Sounding board*. A cautious lawyer will consult other lawyers, both generalists and specialists, for your benefit. Find out whom the lawyer consults, and when.
5. *Philosophy*. You won't learn everything in one interview, but try to assess the lawyer's basic attitudes toward the law and the conduct of business. It is important that the lawyer's views be compatible with yours so that you can feel comfortable in relying on his or her judgment.
6. *Style*. You will want a lawyer who can clearly, objectively, and logically present both sides of an issue. Avoid the highly opinionated, the pedantic, the overly glib, and the paternalistic.
7. *Fee structure*. Minimum fee schedules have been jettisoned, so you are left to informal comparisons and your own judgment of what is reasonable. Fees are a big source of attorney-client conflict, so discuss them openly at your first meeting.[5]

The firm's relationship with its attorney is most effective when courtroom battles are unnecessary. Much of an attorney's contribution is made by providing information when specific questions arise, when contracts or other documents are reviewed, and when counseling is needed. The relationship should preferably be a continuing one. Once an attorney-client relationship is established, the client should utilize the attorney's services promptly whenever the need arises.

LOOKING BACK

1. In a proprietorship the owner receives all profits and bears all losses. The principal limitation of this form is the owner's unlimited liability.
2. A general partnership should be established on the basis of a partner-

---

5. Reprinted, by permission of the publisher, from LEGAL HANDBOOK FOR SMALL BUSINESS, by Marc J. Lane, ©1977 by AMACOM, a division of American Management Associations, p. 101. All rights reserved.

ship agreement. Partners can individually commit the partnership to binding contracts. In a limited partnership, general partners are personally liable for the debts of the business, while limited partners have limited personal liability as long as they do not take an active role in managing the business.

3. Corporations are particularly attractive because of their limited-liability feature. The fact that ownership is easily transferable makes them well-suited for combining the capital of numerous owners. Corporations whose total equity capital does not exceed $1 million may issue stock pursuant to Section 1244 of the Internal Revenue Code. If the stock becomes worthless, the loss (up to $50,000 on a joint return) may be treated as an ordinary tax-deductible loss.
4. Contracts are binding agreements for legal acts made by competent contracting parties and involve something of value for both parties. A small firm should exercise care in selecting its agents and clearly stipulate their authority and responsibility. Negotiable instruments permit the transfer of credit from one party to another. Real property—or real estate—consists of land, buildings, and other installations. Small firms may seek protection of their names and original work by registering their trademarks and applying for patents or copyrights. Libel refers to the printed defamation of one's reputation, so precautions should be taken to avoid libelous statements about others.
5. The small firm needs an attorney experienced in legal practice related to small business. The most important contributions of the attorney are typically made by providing counsel and reviewing legal documents rather than appearing in court for the firm, although the latter may be required occasionally.

DISCUSSION QUESTIONS

1. Discuss the relative importance of the three major legal forms of organization.
2. Suppose a partnership is set up and operated without formal articles of partnership. What problems might arise? Explain.
3. Explain why the agency status of business partners is of great importance.
4. What is a limited partnership, and how does it differ from a general partnership?
5. What is the advantage of Section 1244 stock in a small corporation?
6. What is a Subchapter S corporation, and what is its advantage?
7. Evaluate the three major forms of organization from the standpoints

of management control by the owner and the sharing of the firm's profits.

8. Is degree of liability for debt ordinarily a significant factor in choosing the legal form of organization? Why? Is it ever possibly a factor of negligible concern in selecting the form of organization? Why?

9. Give the legal requirements that must be fulfilled to make a contract valid and binding.

10. Define the following: (a) statute of frauds, (b) mechanic's lien, and (c) statute of limitations.

REFERENCES TO SMALL BUSINESS IN ACTION

Camenzind, Hans R. "The Agony and Ecstasy of a Start-Up." *MBA*, Vol. 8, No. 9 (October, 1974), pp. 12-14.

The author describes the experience of starting a new business and seeing it through its first three years. He devotes specific attention to the legal aspects and to what he has learned as a result of experiences in dealing with legal issues.

"Holiday Inns: Legal Setback for Franchisers." *Business Week*, No. 2299 (September 29, 1973), pp. 108-110.

Holiday Inn's franchise contract was taken to court. The court ruled on two provisions that violated the Sherman Act.

Kolbenschlag, Michael. "Is Monopoly a Monopoly?" *Forbes*, Vol. 125, No. 4 (February 18, 1980), p. 46

A professor of economics at San Francisco State University created and marketed a game which he called "Anti-Monopoly." This led to extensive litigation because of alleged trademark infringement charged by Parker Brothers, maker of the "Monopoly" game. The legal problems of a new small firm are detailed in this article.

"Nurturing New Business with R&D Tax Shelters." *Venture*, Vol. 3, No. 4 (April, 1981), pp. 60-62.

The limited partnership has been used to finance research-based new businesses and new-product development in young firms. A number of such applications are described in this article.

Sommer, Elyse. "Friends and Relatives as Partners." *In Business*, Vol. 3, No. 1 (January-February, 1981), pp. 37-39.

Partnerships place strains on friendships and family relationships. A number of partnerships involving troublesome relationships are described, and suggestions are offered for the successful operation of such businesses.

CASE B-1

Asphera Lens Company

Launching a new venture with a new product

The Asphera Lens Company was organized on the basis of an invention related to aspheric optical lenses.

Nature of the Invention

The invention that formed the basis for this venture was a method and/or machine for manufacturing aspheric lenses. The concept of an aspheric lens is not new. Scientists in the field of optics have long known of its potential superiority. A conventional spheric spectacle lens, for example, produces accurate vision at its center but involves some distortion of vision in peripheral areas. A person who threads a needle while wearing such glasses must position the needle at just the right place relative to the center of the lenses. An aspheric lens, in contrast, can give visual acuity even in peripheral areas.

The problem in the past has been the lack of a method for accurately and economically producing an aspheric lens surface. The inventor, with a Ph.D. in physics, had learned of the problem while temporarily employed by a lens manufacturer several years earlier. After leaving that company, this person continued to work on the problem and eventually devised a solution.

Market Assessment Problems

In considering market prospects, the first question was concerned with the industrial area to be studied. The possibilities were numerous. Production of ophthalmic lenses (prescription spectacle and contact lenses) was one possibility. Photographic lenses, rifle sights, and instrument lenses were also investigated. In addition, the invention's concept had possible applications in solar energy, military research, and even nonlens areas. It was difficult to specify the application in which an aspheric lens might have the greatest advantage or face the least intensive competition.

Somewhat arbitrarily, but partially because of market size, the inventor selected the field of ophthalmic lens production for further study. The inventor knew, for example, that more than 50 percent of the United States population wore prescription lenses. However, there was no certainty as to the segment of this market in which the aspheric lens would be applicable. While it seemed clear that the aspheric lens would have value for cataract patients and others using extremely strong lenses, its potential value for the average person wearing glasses was unknown. Doctors of ophthalmology explained that individuals could adapt themselves to various types of lenses. It was possible, however, that the average wearer might experience less discomfort and tiredness by using aspheric lenses. In fact, even individuals wearing nonprescription sunglasses might find aspheric lenses more comfortable.

More detailed data on the production and sale of ophthalmic lenses were unavailable. Several apparently related trade associations disclaimed knowledge, many of them responding to inquiries by referring the inventor to someone else. After completing this circle to no avail, the inventor decided that a substantial market did exist, provided the manufacturing process and the resultant lenses lived up to expectations. Admittedly, the range of potential volume was great, but the business could break even on only a tiny percentage (less than 1 percent) of the total potential market.

Financing Problems

The search for capital sources began with the preparation of a crude prospectus. In addition, discussions were held with technically oriented people—ophthalmologists, optometrists, opticians, operators of optical laboratories, and optical engineers—and with other individuals who might be interested as investors. However, the difficulty in understanding the concept of the aspheric lens and in appreciating its potential represented one impediment in these discussions. Some who apparently grasped the idea in an abstract way evidenced little excitement about its possibilities. Ophthalmologists were cautious and seemed to perceive themselves as medical scientists whose major concern was the proper functioning of the human eye. They regarded lenses as "hardware" items to be produced by subprofessional tradespeople and sold by hucksters. The reaction from optometrists was typically more encouraging. Their interest was evident as they began to discuss the usefulness of aspheric ophthalmic lenses.

Understanding the aspheric lens principle, however, did not guarantee recognition of the value of this specific invention. Believing in its merits called for a considerable measure of faith, if not credulity. There was no patent, and no formal patent application had yet been filed. The inventor was reluctant to divulge any secrets to strangers, and most potential investors were unqualified to assess the quality of the invention even if they read its technical description.

Two entrepreneurially oriented optometrists eventually agreed to invest in the business. They recognized the tremendous potential of the invention and were not so exclusively professional that they were afraid to act like businesspeople. The total amount of approximately $50,000, including additional smaller sums invested by others, was quite limited relative to anticipated needs. However, it would finance the building of the first machine, thereby demonstrating the practicality of the invention. It was hoped that additional investors would become interested as progress became evident.

The volume of equity capital was not sufficient for rapid development of the machine. This was clear at the beginning, but it became even more obvious as time went on and original cost estimates proved to be unrealistic. At the time, the principals had seemingly faced a choice of either starting "on a shoestring" or not starting at all, and so had chosen the former.

As additional cash was required, the principals sought help from friendly local bankers. The principals' efforts in obtaining bank assistance were less fruitful than one would have anticipated from the bank's advertising jingles. However, the bank eventually agreed to a modest loan as long as the note was properly authorized by the corporation and further guaranteed by the personal signature of each of the principals—any one of whom could have repaid the loan many times. As a further reflection of their willingness to go the second mile with a new venture, the bank specified an interest rate substantially above the prime rate.

The problem of inadequate financing continued. Although there appeared to be attractive opportunities and genuine interest on the part of potential investors, the next step was difficult. The new firm's bank account approached zero at a time when cash was needed for market studies, preparation of a prospectus, further development of the machine, payment of patent attorneys, conferences with prospective investors, and living expenses of the inventor. The investors were unwilling to accept a major dilution of ownership for anything less than a substantial infusion of capital. In the meantime, they hung on, confident that a big breakthrough was just around the corner.

Incorporation of the Business

Incorporation of the business was necessary for a number of reasons, including limitation of liability for investors. This process of incorporation was complicated by the nature of the invention. Legal documents were drawn to transfer ownership of the invention to the corporation with provision for reversion of ownership to the inventor in case of corporate failure. Provisions also covered the amount of royalty to be paid to the inventor, the extent of the inventor's stock ownership, and the extent of the inventor's services during further development of the invention.

Another agreement was formulated to protect minority stockholders. This voting agreement, in effect, required general agreement of most minority stockholders on corporate decisions during an initial period or until the ownership base was broadened.

Invention Protection Problems

Having little prior knowledge of patent law, the inventor experienced some uncertainties regarding the extent of protection. The first step taken by the patent attorney was a patent search, which showed no prior conflicting patents, and a patent disclosure statement to the U. S. Patent Office. The latter document apparently gave official notice of this idea, without divulging details, and guaranteed a period of two years to file a formal application. Delaying the formal application as long as possible seemed desirable because competitors could not pick up key ideas of the invention until they obtained the information contained in the formal application.

The inventor was aware that a patent would yield incomplete protection at best. If someone were to steal the idea, the inventor would be hard pressed to find enough money for adequate legal defense. Furthermore, one novel idea may, in turn, generate another which is not covered by the original patent. The inventor spent many days and weeks developing background materials and working with the legal and technical staff of the attorney. The amount of time could have been reduced if additional technical support had been available. Lack of money precluded any search for a qualified engineer or designer who could have provided such assistance.

Production/Operations Problems

The beginning step of production was to build a prototype model of a surfacing machine. Most of the problems in doing this were related to the financial limitations described earlier. As an economy measure, the inventor turned over the machine design process to a designer employed by a major manufacturer who did the necessary design work on a "moonlighting" basis. Some delays occurred as a result of preparing the drawings on a part-time basis. A more serious problem involved design errors that became evident. It seemed likely that design deficiencies might have been reduced if better engineering and design consulting services had been used.

The decision was made to use a relatively new local shop that promised superior quality of workmanship. Relationships with the machine shop vacillated between "cooperative" and "strained." In production scheduling, the machine shop tended to give higher priority to other orders, thereby delaying work on the new machine far beyond the anticipated completion date. To some extent, these delays were occasioned by design changes that were necessary during the machine-shop work.

Another irritant was related to financing of the machine-shop work. The contract called for payment as invoices were provided from time to time, covering both purchased component parts and work by the shop. Money was short and payments were sometimes delayed. The result was a strain in the relationship as well as a delay in building the machine.

Original cost estimates, as no doubt might have been predicted by an experienced analyst, were grossly out of line. Cost estimates had been prepared in cooperation with the machine-shop owner, using a full set of working drawings. As the actual cost almost doubled, the thin financing and the good nature of both parties stretched almost to the breaking point. Eventually the machine was completed and the bill paid, with the process being twice as long, twice as expensive, and twice as hectic as planned.

Future Plans

The lack of additional funds meant that further development must proceed very slowly. It appeared to the inventor that the future availability of funds would determine the time period within which this concept would get its market test.

Questions

1. Evaluate the market assessment carried out by the inventor. Was it adequate for starting the business?
2. Evaluate the financing plan developed by the inventor, including both stockholder investment and bank borrowing.
3. How could the inventor have improved the invention protection process?
4. What mistakes, if any, were made in the beginning production stage of building the machine?
5. What course of action should be followed by the owners in view of the present lull in the new business?

CASE B-2

Al's Car-Care

Evaluating a franchise opportunity

During most of his college career, Al Mendez had taken a full academic load. However, during the current semester he had reduced his class schedule to a part-time level in order to work as the manager of a local car-care business operating as a Tidy Car franchise. The prospects for this business seemed so attractive that Al was giving some thought to obtaining his own franchise for another area of the city.

Al's Background and Personal Ambitions

Al was an enterprising young man who had earned most of his way through college. Some of his experience was entrepreneurial in nature. For example, he and his brother had contracted with the owner of an apartment house to perform all of the maintenance work for the apartment. By taking projects on a contract basis, he had been able to work efficiently and to earn a much higher hourly income than would have been possible in salaried employment.

Al was also an industrious student — earning mostly A's. In some classes, he had performed so well that, even as an undergraduate, he had been made a student assistant. In fact, he had been given responsibility for conducting some classes on his own for brief periods of time.

Another part of Al's experience was centered in leadership of youth activities in religious and camp settings. During two summers, for example, he worked in a youth camp, carrying responsibility for directing a major segment of the camp's activities.

Although Al expressed general confidence in entering business, he did admit to some concerns. He said:

> The concerns are a lack of experience with paperwork and not being able to afford an accountant right off. Also, I worry about the business involving a greater commitment than I want. That would mean becoming a workaholic, and I am trying to stay away from that. I easily fall into that trap.

Although Al had taken a number of college courses in business, he had not majored in business. Some of his business education had been acquired through personal study outside formal classes. Al explained his informal pattern of study as follows:

> I've always studied textbooks on the side. I didn't want to waste time getting a degree in business when I was going to end up being in my own business where I wouldn't have to impress anyone with a degree. As long as I could acquire the knowledge, I didn't care about the grades. Generally, when I got as much as I wanted to learn, I'd end up with an A. But I didn't learn as much as I wanted to. It's been mainly just learning on my own.

During his college years, Al had given considerable thought to the possibility of getting into business for himself. As he expressed it, "I wanted to be my own boss." Working for others had been generally harmonious, but he had at times experienced dissatisfaction. Speaking of certain people he had worked for, he said: "I get frustrated a little bit at their incompetence. Sometimes it relates to things I have already learned. If they haven't learned it yet and they are supposed to be teaching me, I figure this just isn't the place I'm supposed to be."

Al's Problem of Priorities

Al had completed most of his bachelor's degree program at a nearby liberal arts college and could finish his program by taking one additional semester on a full-time basis. If he continued to manage the present franchise, he could finish in two semesters. If he were to take his own franchise, he would need to drop out of school until he could get the business established.

Part of the problem involved in combining a new franchise of his own with a continuation of his education lay in the location of the available franchise. It was located approximately 50 to 75 miles from his college. The distance involved would make it difficult to be at his best in both endeavors. Even after he started his own franchise, he would need to limit his further study to a part-time basis.

How a Tidy Car Franchise Operated

The Tidy Car franchise provided a protective finish to the exterior of automobiles. The finish was a silicone rather than an ordinary wax, and it was guaranteed to last for as long as the owner kept the car. It was applied by an orbital applicator developed by the same company. The applicator had two rotating heads that vibrated at the same time. An ordinary buffer would spin and could burn the paint. However, the orbital applicator would stop if too much pressure was applied. It heated sufficiently to establish the bond between the paint and the preservative finish, but not so much that it damaged the paint. Al planned to charge $114 for the exterior finish, and he would be charged a franchise fee of $2 for each such job.

The franchisor had also developed a product for preserving the interior finish of the car's upholstery. The upholstery was first cleaned with a dry cleaning process, and then a protective coating was applied. After the coating was applied, liquids which were spilled would not stain the fabric but could be easily removed. This coating, like the exterior finish, was designed to last as long as the owner kept the automobile.

Franchises were issued on the basis of one franchise for each area with a population of 20,000. The available franchise that Al was considering was located in an affluent area of the city. It seemed to Al that people living there, especially those who owned such cars as Porsches and Audis, would be willing to pay for proper car care.

In contrast to a franchised operation, Al had also given some thought to operating a "detail" shop which would give various types of car care—reupholstering, reshining rims, cleaning engines, or other treatments related to the surface of automobiles. He would simply try to operate as an "appearance specialist." However, he assumed that the franchise would offer credibility and an advertising program that he could use. Also, Al was impressed with the quality of the products that had been developed by the Tidy Car organization.

How Al Could Become a Franchisee

The cost of starting as a Tidy Car franchisee would run as much as $5,000. This amount included $1,400 for the orbital applicator, a vacuum cleaner, and an inventory of supplies. Al thought that he could obtain the necessary capital.

Two ways of conducting the business were possible: to operate as a mobile unit or to establish a central business shop. Al would need to own a van, small truck, or other vehicle if he were to operate as a mobile unit. The equipment could be carried in the trunk of a car, so there were no necessary large investment costs involved for transportation. Al already owned a car that could be used for this purpose or be traded for one slightly more suitable. Establishing a central business shop, on the other hand, would entail much more operating expense. In the long run, however, a suitable location would give the business a measure of credibility.

In the short run, Al thought he could begin by keeping his investment at a minimum if he operated a mobile unit. He felt that such a venture would involve very little overhead and had the possibility of producing many thousands of dollars in profits. Prospects were attractive for getting contracts with auto rental organizations and other businesses having many autos to maintain. Al thought he might be able to earn as much as $6,000 per month by employing 3 persons. Obviously this was an optimistic estimate. Much of the business would be generated by recommendations of satisfied customers, and Al planned to stress quality to the point that his work produced many referrals.

Questions

1. Evaluate Al Mendez's potential for successful entrepreneurship. What are his greatest strengths? What are his most crucial weaknesses?
2. Evaluate the prospects for Al as a Tidy Car franchisee.
3. In this case, what are the relative merits of acquiring a franchise in contrast to going into business on his own? Which alternative would you recommend?
4. What additional steps do you recommend that Al should take before he commits himself to this franchise?
5. How should Al resolve the conflict between the exciting prospects for a successful business venture and his own educational program?

CASE B-3

The Cannery

Conducting a survey to analyze a market

Andy Harvey, age 25, grew up on a tobacco farm in central Virginia. He enjoyed farm life and, at one time, planned to be a farmer. But his parents encouraged him to get a college degree and do something besides farming.

After finishing his master's degree, Andy returned to the rural setting and took a teaching job at a small school near his childhood home. Married and with two small children, he still enjoyed working with his hands and was a large-scale home gardener. He cultivated over a half acre of vegetables. His love for growing things sometimes overburdened his wife, especially during the canning season when she would rush to process vegetables before they spoiled. His two children were still too young to be of much assistance.

The Idea for a Cannery Business

One day in 1978, Andy read in the magazine *Organic Gardening and Farming* an article about the nearly 4,000 community canning centers which existed in the United States during the war years of the 1940s. The article posed the question: Would a canning center be a good business venture for an individual? An initial investment of around $15,000 was indicated. This seemed reasonable to Andy, particularly because a high-school friend of his was working at the local bank.

Andy became very excited about the idea of opening a cannery which, for a fee, would can the homegrown produce of individual customers. Andy did not teach school during the summer and felt this would allow him to concentrate on the cannery operations during one of its busiest times. His wife also was enthusiastic with the thought that she could use the cannery, which would release her from her canning chores.

After investigating the equipment requirements of a canning facility, Andy learned that two major suppliers—the Ball Corporation and the Dixie Canner Equipment Company—produced the majority of canning equipment. The biggest investment was a prefabricated food processor unit. Ball's unit had 4 pressure cookers with a capacity of 16 quarts, a steam-jacketed 10-gallon kettle, an atmospheric cooker, a blancher/sterilizer, a pulper-juicer, 4 table carts, a boiler, a hot water heater, and miscellaneous hardware. Some units even had meat-cutting saws and sausage stuffers to expand their capabilities. The standard Ball jar "unit" could operate at 300- to 500-quart capacity per 8-hour day. Andy also learned that a cannery could operate in a very limited area—only 250 to 350 square feet of space. It seemed that using jars was much less expensive than cans. Therefore, Andy decided to use jars only.

The Need for Market Information

After Andy's initial fact-finding efforts, he soon realized that he was only analyzing the supply-side considerations such as machinery and labor costs.

The "rest of the story" lay with demand. He was an avid gardener, but were there enough people like him who could make his venture a profitable one? Thus, he decided to research the demand side more closely.

Andy's master's degree was from a local university which offered a BBA degree. Andy remembered that his college roommate was a marketing major who, during one semester, had worked on a survey project. So, Andy called the university's marketing department, explained his situation, and arranged a conference with one of the professors the next week. The professor asked Andy to list three or four objectives of the survey he was contemplating and bring this list to their meeting. Andy came up with the following objectives:

1. I want to know the number of potential users of the proposed cannery.
2. I would like to have an idea of the potential quantity of food that would be brought to the cannery for processing.
3. It would be helpful to know people's attitudes toward a business of this type.
4. I also would like some ideas on site locations.

During the meeting, the professor agreed to use Andy's survey needs as a class project. He told Andy that the students would randomly select enough households in the tri-county area to provide at least 300 usable interviews. Large cities would be excluded, but small communities (under 10,000) and rural households would be included. The professor indicated that about half of the interviews would be personal interviews and half would be telephone interviews. The professor said that he would begin immediately to construct the questionnaire for the survey.

Questions

1. What general demand-side factors do you think are favorable to the success of Andy Harvey's cannery? What factors may be unfavorable?
2. List the reasons, in order of importance, you anticipate people would give for not using a cannery. (Assume that these reasons are from people who have already indicated a lack of interest in the cannery facility.)
3. Assuming that Andy would prefer the cannery to be located as close to home as possible, how could the survey be used to estimate cannery potential in units of quarts per year? Be specific.
4. Draft a questionnaire you would propose that the professor's students use in their telephone interview.
5. If Andy opens the cannery, what additional services would you advise he consider adding at some later date?

CASE B-4

HOT Magazine*

Evaluating the location for a new venture

Kate Johnson, director of public information for a social-service organization in Waco, TX, was scanning the newspaper at lunch with her friend Susan Baldwin, an advertising account representative for the *Waco Tribune Herald*.

"Did you see this story about the city magazine the Waco Chamber of Commerce may start?" asked Kate.

"Yeah, sounds interesting. They'd probably have to hire an editor. Would you be interested? You've had a lot of experience with publications."

"I just don't know, Sue. I think Waco is ripe for a city magazine, but I just can't get excited about a chamber of commerce publication. They're all so boring."

"You're right about that. But what do you expect? The editors don't have much freedom, having to answer to the business establishment," Susan added.

"I really think Waco needs a city magazine. We've got a lot going on here, and we're virtually ignored by *Texas Monthly* and the special-interest magazines. They've all written us off as a small town," Kate said. "What we really need is a high-quality, independent city magazine like *D, the Magazine of Dallas* or *Philadelphia*."

"Do you really think a magazine like that would go in Waco?"

"I know it would, and I think we're the ones who could pull it off, Sue," Kate replied.

"There would be quite a bit of risk involved, and we'd have to quit our jobs," Susan commented.

"Well, I don't want to be an employee and a public servant all my life. I'm ready for something new and challenging, something on my own," said Kate.

"A city magazine would certainly be a challenge, Kate."

Background of the Would-Be Entrepreneurs

Kate, who was 35 years old, had worked in public affairs positions for local, regional, and state organizations during the past 13 years, editing a variety of organizational newsletters, magazines, and brochures. In addition, she had been editor of both a small-town newspaper and a special-interest publication about music. Kate's longest tenure in any of the jobs was less than

*This case was prepared by Minette E. Drumwright, Lecturer in Marketing at Baylor University.

three years. As soon as she mastered a job, she would begin looking around for a new challenge. Kate had lived in Waco a total of 11 years, including the time she spent studying journalism at Baylor University.

Although the Waco Chamber of Commerce eventually abandoned the idea of sponsoring a city magazine, Kate held tenaciously to her aspirations for an independent city magazine. She persuaded her 30-year-old sister, Debra Lunsford, and Susan Baldwin, who was 23 years old, to join her in the venture. Although Susan had been out of college for only 2 years, she had worked for the newspaper in her hometown since she was 16 years old. Debra was the vice-president and business manager of a shipping company in Houston. The three women would form the full-time staff of the publication with Kate serving as editor. Susan would be the advertising sales director, and Debra would be the business manager. All the stories, photography, and graphics would be contracted on a free-lance basis, providing local artists a showcase for their work.

The *HOT* Idea

Kate proposed to call the publication *HOT*, which was a commonly used abbreviation for "Heart of Texas." *HOT* would include an entertainment guide, features on local personalities, and a variety of stories focusing on social, economic, and political trends of the locality. The target audience would be central Texans between the ages of 25 and 55 years with annual incomes ranging from $18,000 to $50,000.

The percentage of advertising in each issue is a key variable for any publication, representing the primary source of revenue. Susan projected that the initial advertising-to-editorial contents ratio would be 60:40 and that eventually a 70:30 ratio would be attained.

Debra determined that an initial investment of $400,000 would need to be contributed by local investors to launch the magazine. The $400,000 would be used to sustain the magazine through the initial periods of loss, providing for salaries, free-lance work, promotion, and production.

Together, the 3 entrepreneurs interested James Jenkins, a 32-year-old accountant, in the magazine idea. James, who was from an established Waco family, was president of Downtown Waco, Inc., a group of retail merchants with a vested interest in reviving the downtown area. His family owned and operated one of the city's highly successful specialty retail businesses.

Before approaching potential investors about the city magazine, James insisted that the entrepreneurs substantiate their feelings that the magazine would be a success. In an effort to get the necessary information, Kate called a professor specializing in marketing research at Baylor University's Hankamer School of Business. The professor referred the entrepreneurs to two graduate students in his seminar in marketing research.

The Research

The graduate students set out to develop a profile of independent city magazines to determine the feasibility of initiating a successful venture in Waco. Using a structured, undisguised questionnaire, they surveyed city-magazine publishers throughout the nation. The sample included the publishers of all the city magazines with complete listings in Standard Rate and Data Service. Participants were asked to enclose a recent issue of their magazine along with the completed questionnaires. A $2 incentive was enclosed to defray the cost of the magazine and the mailing expense. The following were among the survey questions:

General Information

1. How many employees do you have?

   In editorial ___________

   In advertising ___________

   Other ___________

2. On the average, what percentage of the stories are written by free-lance writers? ___________

3. What is your production cost per issue?

   _______ less than $25,000 _______ $40,001-$50,000

   _______ $25,000-$30,000 _______ more than $50,000

   _______ $30,001-$40,000

Advertising

4. What was the approximate ratio of advertising to editorial contents . . .

	Advertising		Editorial
in the first issue	_______	to	_______
after a year of issues	_______	to	_______
currently	_______	to	_______

5. What was the advertising revenue during the magazine's first year?

_______ less than $100,000 _______ $500,001-$1,000,000

_______ $100,000-$500,000 _______ more than $1,000,000

6. What was the advertising revenue last year? (Please omit this question if last year was your first year of publication.)

_______ less than $100,000 _______ $500,001-$1,000,000

_______ $100,000-$500,000 _______ more than $1,000,000

7. What businesses are your major advertisers in?

____

____

Subscriptions

8. At the time of the first issue, what was the total circulation of the magazine?

_____ less than 5,000 _____ 10,001-15,000 _____ 25,001-40,000

_____ 5,000-10,000 _____ 15,001-25,000 _____ more than 40,000

9. When the first issue was published, how many paid subscriptions did the magazine have?

_____ less than 5,000 _____ 10,001-15,000 _____ 25,001-40,000

_____ 5,000-10,000 _____ 15,001-25,000 _____ more than 40,000

10. What is the average income bracket of your readership?

_____ less than $15,000 _____ $30,001-$50,000 _____ more than $75,000

_____ $15,000-$30,000 _____ $50,001-$75,000 _____ don't know

11. What is the average age of your readership?

_____ less than 25 years _____ 36 to 45 years _____ 56 to 65 years

_____ 25 to 35 years _____ 46 to 55 years _____ more than 65 years

12. Please rank in priority order the subject matter your readers prefer. Let a "1" represent the most preferred topic and a "5" represent the least preferred topic.

_____ local politics _____ local news analysis _____ business news

_____ entertainment _____ local personalities

13. What adjectives would you use to describe your readership?

____

14. What advice would you give to someone interested in starting a city magazine?

____

____

Analysis of the Questionnaire

The response rate to the survey was 63 percent. As the questionnaires were returned, the data were analyzed with a computer using a variety of procedures. The means for some of the quantitative variables are listed below:

Percentage of stories written by free-lance writers	59.4%
Percentage of advertising in the first issue	40.3%
Percentage of advertising after one year of issues	45.5%
Percentage of advertising currently	49.5%
Promotion expenditure before publication	$29,000
Promotion expenditure during the first year	$39,958
SMSA population*	671,924
Circulation**	59,178
Newsstand price***	$1.80

Readership Profile

Ninety percent of the participants responded to the open-ended question asking them to describe their readerships with the word "affluent." Ninety-six percent of the readership had an annual income greater than $30,000, and more

*The populations of the Standard Metropolitan Statistical Areas (SMSA) in which the magazines were located were taken from the *1980 Census of Population and Housing: United States Summary*.

**The circulations were listed in consumer magazines and farm publications published by Standard Rate and Data Service, Inc.

***The issue prices were taken from the covers of the sample issues submitted by participants.

than 80 percent ranged from 36 to 45 years of age. Participants ranked the subjects their readers preferred in the following order: (1) feature stories on local personalities, (2) entertainment, (3) local news analysis, (4) local politics, and (5) business news.

Major Sources of Advertising

Participants were asked to list the businesses of their major advertisers to enable an analysis of the primary sources of advertising in city magazines. Eighty-eight percent of the respondents listed retail businesses, while 38 percent included restaurants and banks in their lists. Nineteen percent mentioned real estate companies.

National advertising appeared in the lists of only two respondents, and one of the two specified that the national ads were "occasional." The respondent who indicated that national advertising was a frequent source of revenue was the publisher of a magazine in an SMSA with a population exceeding 3,000,000.

Profile of Waco SMSA (McLennan County)*

Population	172,800
Population ranking in the United States	194
Number of households	63,000
Total effective buying income (in thousands of dollars)	$1,189,402
Retail sales	$840,358,000
Retail sales per household	$13,381
Age groups:	
18-24	24,000
25-34	23,000
35-49	27,000
50-64	28,000
65 or older	23,000
Undetermined	1,000
Median age	44
Income Distribution of Adult Population:	
Under $10,000	37,000
$10,000-$19,999	38,000
$20,000 or more	51,000
Median income	$16,800

Questions

1. Do you see any flaws in the sample selection that would create a bias toward larger, metropolitan areas?
2. What other questions should have been included in the questionnaire?
3. Do the survey data support the entrepreneur's plans for the advertising-to-editorial ratio?
4. What additional information about the Waco market is needed by the entrepreneurs?
5. Given the research findings, do you recommend that a city-magazine venture be initiated in Waco? Why or why not?

*This abbreviated profile was obtained from federal government Census publications.

CASE B-5

Walker Machine Works*

Financing arrangements for a new venture

Jim Walker was a management consultant on a continuing but indefinite assignment with a medium-sized plastics company. He was also an M.B.A. candidate at a nearby university. He had thought that the consultant's position would be challenging and would add a dimension of practical experience to his academic background. But after several months Jim had become very disenchanted with his job. Although he seemed to have much freedom in his duties, he began to discover that his reports and suggestions could not be translated into meaningful results and solutions. He realized that the management was interested only in maintaining the status quo and that he was hired as a more or less token consultant. His efforts to help the company were largely ignored and overlooked. It seemed as if his job was quickly becoming nothing more than an exercise in futility.

Jim discussed the situation with a few friends, most of whom urged him to seek a more fulfilling position with another company. But he had another idea—why not start a small company of his own? He had toyed with this idea for the last couple of years, and there was no better time than the present to give it a try. At least it would be a real test of his management abilities.

After a few days and considerable thought, Jim had several potential ventures in mind. The most promising idea involved the establishment of a machine shop. Before entering college, he had worked two years as a general machinist and acquired diversified experience operating a variety of lathes, milling machines, presses, drills, grinders, and more. And he really enjoyed this sort of work. He guessed that making things on machines satisfied some sort of creative urge he felt.

After a very comprehensive and systematic research of the local market, it appeared that there was a definite need for a quality machine-shop operation. Thus, Jim's mind was made up. He was sure that he had an adequate knowledge of machining processes (and enough ambition to find out what he didn't know), and his general business education was also a valuable asset. The problem was money. The necessary machinery for a small shop would cost about $12,000, yet he had only about $3,000 in savings. Surely he could borrow the money or find someone willing to invest in his venture.

A visit to one of the local banks was something less than productive. The vice-president in charge of business investments was quite clear. "You don't have a proven track record. It would be a big risk for us to lend so much money to someone with so little actual experience," the vice-president said. Jim was

*This case was prepared by Richard L. Garman.

greatly disappointed but unwilling to give up yet. After all, there were six other banks in town, and one of them might be willing to lend him the money.

Financing Proposal #1

One possibility lay in a suggestion the banker had given Jim. He was told to contact Russ Williams, the president of a local hydraulics company. The banker felt that Russ might be interested in investing a little money in Jim's venture. It was certainly worth a try, so Jim called Russ and made an appointment to see him.

Russ had been involved in manufacturing for over 40 years. As a young man, he had begun his career as Jim had—in the machine shop. After several years of experience as a journeyman machinist, Russ was promoted to shop supervisor. Rising steadily through the ranks, Russ, now in his early sixties, had been promoted to president of the hydraulics company only two years ago.

Jim had never met Russ before and knew little about the man or his background. Nevertheless, Jim soon found Russ to be pleasant in nature and very easy to talk to. Jim spent about an hour presenting his business plan to Russ, who seemed impressed with the idea. Although Russ's time and energies were currently committed to an expansion project for the hydraulics company, he indicated that he might be interested in contributing both money and management. As Jim rose to leave, Russ proposed a 50-50 deal and asked Jim to think it over for a few days.

Financing Proposal #2

A few days later, Stan Thomas came by to see Jim. They had been good friends for about a year and had even roomed together as undergraduates. Stan had talked with his father about Jim's idea and perhaps had even glorified the possibilities a little. Stan's father was intrigued with the plan and offered to meet with Jim to discuss the possibility of a partnership.

Phil Thomas, Stan's father, was a real estate investor who owned his own agency. Although he had been in business only a few years, he was very successful and constantly looking for new investment prospects. He drove the 250 miles from his home to meet with Jim one Saturday. After looking over the business plan and some pro forma financial statements that Jim had prepared, he agreed that it might be a worthwhile venture. "I'll contribute all of the capital you need and give you a fair amount of freedom in running the business. I know that most investors would start out by giving you only 10 or 15 percent of the equity and then gradually increase your share, but I'll make you a better deal. I'll give you 40 percent right off the bat, and we'll let this be a sort of permanent arrangement," he said. Jim was a little unsure about that, so he said he'd think it over for a few days and then let him know.

Jim didn't know quite what to do. He had several options to choose from, and he wasn't sure which would be best. The sensible thing would be to talk to someone who could offer some good advice. So, he went to the business school to talk to a professor he knew fairly well.

Financing Proposal #3

Jim found Professor Wesley Davis in his office and described the situation to him. The professor was an associate dean and a marketing specialist. Although he had no actual manufacturing experience, he had edited some semitechnical publications for the Society of Manufacturing Engineers. Thus, he had at least a general knowledge of the machining processes involved in Jim's proposed business.

The professor had been aware of Jim's interests in starting a business and frequently inquired about the progress Jim was making. At the end of this discussion, Jim was surprised to hear the professor offer to help by investing some of his own money. "It sounds like you have an excellent idea, and I'd like to see you give it a try. Besides, a little 'real-world' experience might be good for an old academic type like me," said the professor. "And I would suggest bringing in Joe Winsett from the accounting department. I know neither one of us relishes keeping the books. Besides, Joe is a C.P.A. who could provide some valuable assistance. I'll talk to him if you like." The professor suggested that the equity be split into equal thirds, giving Jim the first option to increase his share of the equity.

Questions

1. Evaluate the backgrounds of the possible "partners" in terms of the business and management needs of the proposed firm.
2. Evaluate the three financing proposals from the standpoint of Jim Walker's control of the firm and the support or interference he may experience.
3. Compare Jim's equity position under each of the three proposals.
4. What are some important characteristics to look for in a prospective business partner?
5. Which option should Jim choose? What reasons can you give to defend your answer?

CASE B-6

"No Strain" Testers

An inventor seeks to obtain a patent on his own

Harvey Strain was an employee of a highly successful lithographic printing equipment manufacturer in Dallas, TX. He had worked more than 15 years as a "trouble-shooter" for the company, solving customers' problems with purchased printing presses. Harvey had always been interested in mechanical devices. During his teenage days, he was constantly working in the family garage modifying automobiles for drag racing. His creative skills had remained active. For example, only last year, at age 44, he finished building a custom-designed car from new and used parts.

The Invention

Recently Harvey turned his creative talents and mechanical skills toward an idea which had the potential to be a marketable product. His invention would be used with lithographic printing presses such as those produced by his employer. His invention was an automatic testing reservoir used in connection with dampening systems on those lithographic printing presses. Figure B-1 shows promotional material designed by Harvey for his invention. The device maintained a constant alcohol solution level, continuously sampling the circulating solution to give an accurate, specific gravity reading. This product overcame the existing problems, time, and expense involved in maintaining the proper alcohol percentage with existing battery-type testers.

Harvey realized the potential value of a patent but was uncertain if he could handle the patenting process or whether he should turn it over to a lawyer. In a recent article of a trade magazine, *Machine Design,* he read some hints on how to market an invention. The article encouraged Harvey to "try it on his own." The article stated further that a patent could be obtained at a cost in the neighborhood of $1,000.

The Patenting Process

On December 22, 1975, Harvey wrote a privately owned Washington-based patent search company. Its response was cordial, requesting that he fill out the enclosed patent Protection Forms ". . . giving us as detailed a sketch of your invention as possible . . ." and offering to conduct a patentability search for $50. "In the meantime," the letter continued, ". . . no attempt should be made to sell your invention since under our present laws you have nothing to

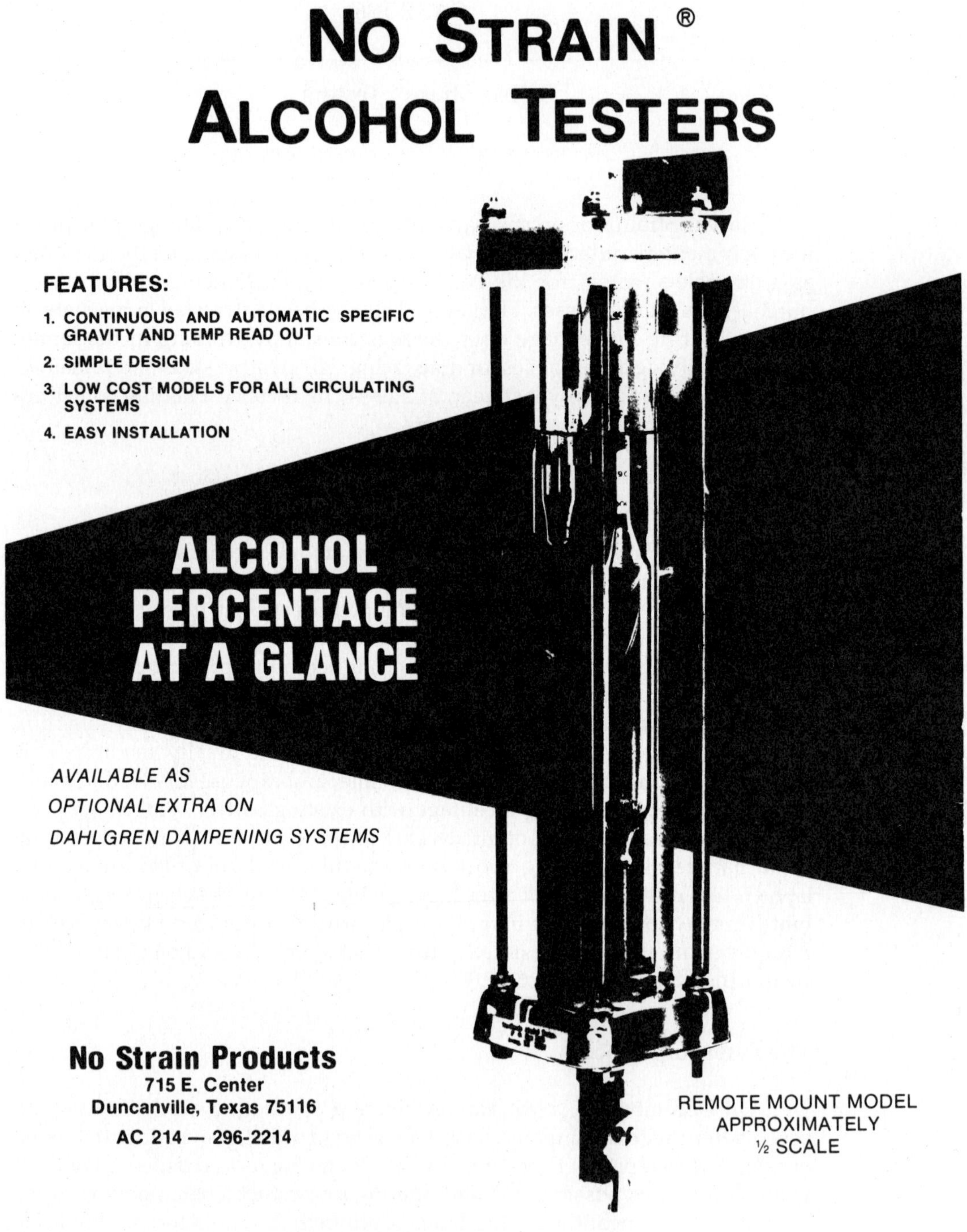
NO STRAIN ®
ALCOHOL TESTERS
FEATURES:
1. CONTINUOUS AND AUTOMATIC SPECIFIC GRAVITY AND TEMP READ OUT
2. SIMPLE DESIGN
3. LOW COST MODELS FOR ALL CIRCULATING SYSTEMS
4. EASY INSTALLATION
ALCOHOL PERCENTAGE AT A GLANCE
AVAILABLE AS OPTIONAL EXTRA ON DAHLGREN DAMPENING SYSTEMS
No Strain Products
715 E. Center
Duncanville, Texas 75116
AC 214 — 296-2214
REMOTE MOUNT MODEL
APPROXIMATELY
½ SCALE

Figure B-1 Promotional Material for Alcohol Testers

sell (no legal property), until an application for patent has actually been filed in the Patent Office and you have *PATENT PENDING.*"

On January 19, 1976, Harvey authorized the patent search, enclosing the completed Record of Disclosure and the $50 fee. On February 4, 1976, A. Mercedes, Managing Director for the Washington Patent Office Search Bureau, wrote Harvey saying, "We are pleased to report that your invention appears to be patentable." A. Mercedes urged Harvey to proceed with the preparation and filing of a patent application. He also offered his company's services in helping Harvey prepare the specifications, claims, and the Official United States Patent Office Drawing. The fee for this assistance would be $500 plus the $65 Official United States Government Filing Fee.

Harvey decided to "continue on his own." He prepared his own drawings and specifications. On February 16, 1976, he filed his Petition for Patent and other required documents. His letter of transmittal is shown in Figure B-2.

P.O. Box 3185
Irving, Texas 75061
February 16, 1976

Commissioner of Patents
United States Patent Office
Washington, D.C. 20231

To the Commissioner of Patents

Enclosed are my Petition for Patent, Oath to Accompany my Petition, Abstract, Specifications, Claim, and a check in the amount of $65.00, which I understand is the initial filing fee.

The preliminary patentability search was completed by the Washington Patent Office Search Bureau, P.O. Box 7167, Washington, D.C. 20044, who reported that my invention appeared to be patentable.

I am unable to utilize their additional services or the services of a patent attorney and will appreciate your indulgence in considering the attached drawings and specifications which I have prepared.

Yours sincerely

(Sgd.) Harvey A. Strain

HAS:pss

Figure B-2 Letter of Transmittal

Six long months later, Harvey received a letter from the Commissioner of Patents and Trademarks. Harvey quickly opened the letter. His application had been rejected. Although this was bad news, Harvey did not want to give up.

The rejection decision was based on three reasons, two of which were minor and one serious. One minor problem concerned the oath (or declaration) provided by Harvey in his letter of February 16, 1976. The form required to correct this problem was enclosed in the letter from the Commissioner of Patents and Trademarks. The other minor problem involved errors in the drawings, which could be corrected by the Patent Office for $24. The serious problem was that the Patent Office claimed that Harvey's idea fell under the requirement that "A patent may not be obtained. . .if the differences between the subject matter sought to be patented and the prior art are such that the subject matter as a whole would have been obvious at the time the invention was made to a person having ordinary skill in the art to which said subject matter pertains." This pronouncement sounded very "final."

Questions

1. Would you have believed the magazine article about a patent for less than $1,000, or would you have gone to a lawyer? What difficulties are involved in being one's own attorney?
2. What do you think Harvey Strain should do now to get his patent? Be specific.
3. Do you believe Harvey should forget the patent and market his product without patent protection? Why or why not?

Part C

SMALL-BUSINESS MARKETING

Chapter 9

Consumer Behavior and Product Strategies

LOOKING AHEAD

Watch for the following important topics:

1. Activities which are encompassed by small-business marketing.
2. Economic, psychological, and sociological concepts of consumer behavior.
3. Decision-making stages of consumer behavior.
4. Product strategy, product development, and the product life cycle.
5. How a firm can build a total product using branding, packaging, labeling, and warranties.

Ultimately the success of every business requires an acceptable level of sales. Those activities that have the most direct impact on achieving success in sales are marketing activities. It is vital, therefore, that small-business managers recognize the importance of marketing and understand how to develop good marketing strategies. A business cannot rely on a strong financial strategy, a tight accounting system, or a sound organizational plan as a substitute for good marketing.

In Chapter 5 we analyzed market segmentation, marketing research, and sales forecasting because of the close relationship of these marketing activities to starting the small business. Many additional activities are also necessary for ongoing, successful small-business marketing. Consumer behavior analysis and product strategies are examined in this chapter. Distribution, pricing, and credit policies are analyzed in Chapter 10. Personal selling, advertising, and sales promotion are discussed in Chapter 11.

Before discussing consumer behavior, we need to examine the scope of small-business marketing more closely. This will provide an overall perspective for the treatment of various marketing topics.

SCOPE OF MARKETING ACTIVITIES FOR SMALL BUSINESSES

Marketing has been defined as "the performance of business activities that affect the flow of goods and services from producer to consumer or user."[1] Notice that this definition emphasizes distribution. Many people view marketing in this manner. Actually marketing is much more. Many marketing activities occur even *before* a product is produced! In an effort to portray the complete scope of marketing and to make our discussion useful for small business, we will propose a definition for small-business marketing which focuses on marketing activities. *Marketing consists of those business activities which relate directly to determining target markets and preparing, communicating, and delivering a bundle of satisfaction to these markets*. Every small business should initially engage in marketing to determine its target markets. Then, and only then, can final preparation of the "product" be achieved. Communication and delivery of the "product" are the remaining purposes of marketing.

From the definition of marketing given above, we can identify the marketing activities which are essential to every small business. These activities, called *core marketing activities*, are depicted in Figure 9-1. Notice that the core marketing activities have been appropriately matched with the key terms in our definition of marketing. The activities numbered 1 through 3 constitute the process of market analysis. The activities numbered 4 through 7 comprise a firm's marketing mix and are the focal points in Part C of this text.

Obviously the sophistication of the marketing effort in a small business will vary from situation to situation. Financial conditions often restrict the resources devoted to these activities. However, these realities in no way lessen the importance of understanding the benefits of executed marketing activities.

CONCEPTS OF CONSUMER BEHAVIOR

Having adopted both the marketing concept and a market segmentation strategy, the small-business manager is started on the road to successful sales.

---

1. Committee on Definitions, *Marketing Definitions: A Glossary of Marketing Terms* (Chicago: American Marketing Association, 1960), p. 15.

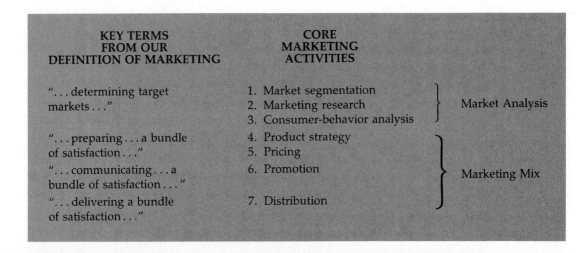

KEY TERMS FROM OUR DEFINITION OF MARKETING	CORE MARKETING ACTIVITIES	
". . . determining target markets . . ."	1. Market segmentation 2. Marketing research 3. Consumer-behavior analysis	Market Analysis
". . . preparing . . . a bundle of satisfaction . . ."	4. Product strategy 5. Pricing	Marketing Mix
". . . communicating . . . a bundle of satisfaction . . ."	6. Promotion	
". . . delivering a bundle of satisfaction . . ."	7. Distribution	

Figure 9-1 Core Marketing Activities for Small Business

Before proceeding to develop a marketing program, however, one must first understand the realities of consumer behavior. We will begin this analysis by touching on the economic, psychological, and sociological aspects of consumer behavior.

Traditional Economic Concepts

Traditional economic theories visualize the consumer as a rational buyer who possesses perfect information. "Rational" means that emotional buying factors are not considered. Maximization of value is an assumed goal for the consumer. Price, therefore, becomes the sole mediator between supply and demand.

The entrepreneur should not totally ignore these economic theories because they can help explain types of behavior. For example, if a consumer sees a half-price special on a nationally branded grocery product, she or he may buy more at the lower price. This buying decision follows the classic economic theory of consumer behavior.

Another assumption of classic economic theory is the existence of a homogeneous market where consumers behave in a fairly similar manner. Recall the total-market approach in our earlier discussion on market segmentation in Chapter 5. The total-market view has roots in the economic concept of consumer behavior.

While recognizing the contribution of economic theories, the entrepreneur should bear in mind that they are overly restrictive and lacking in scope. There is much consumer behavior that cannot be captured by the traditional image of the "economic man." A fuller explanation is needed.

A Modern Consumer-Behavior Roadmap

The complexity of consumer behavior is staggering. Exploration of this world of behavior requires a model, or "roadmap." Many models exist in the literature of consumer behavior, but our version is intended for the small-business situation. The roadmap in Figure 9-2 has a psychological, a sociological, and a decision-making phase. Study it carefully. When the totality of the trip is seen first, each leg of the journey should then become clearer. We will examine each "roadsign" and show its relevance to consumer behavior.

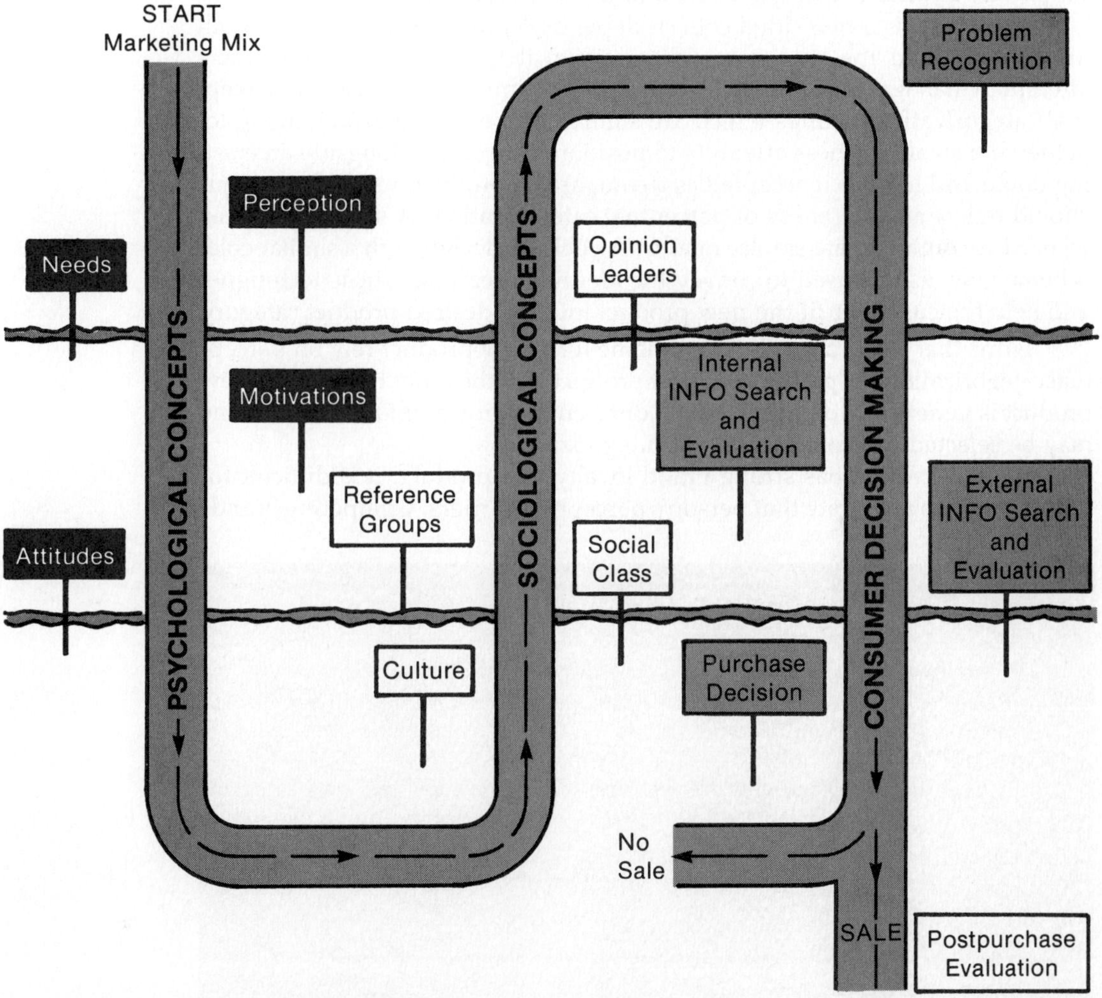

Figure 9-2 Roadmap to Understanding Consumer Behavior

Psychological Concepts. Psychological factors may be labeled as hypothetical because they cannot be seen or touched. By process of inference, however, several factors have been "identified." The four factors that have the greatest relevance to small business are perception, needs, motivations, and attitudes.

Perception. Our initial psychological roadsign in Figure 9-2 is perception. **Perception** describes those individual processes which ultimately give meaning to the stimuli that confront consumers. The "meaning" is not easily transferred, however. It may be severely distorted or entirely blocked. Perception can screen a firm's marketing effort and make it ineffective.

Perception is a two-sided coin. It depends on the characteristics of both the stimulus and the perceiver. For example, it is known that consumers attempt to manage huge quantities of incoming stimuli by a process of **perceptual categorization**. Things which are similar are perceived as belonging together. If a small business attempts to position its product alongside an existing brand and to have it accepted as a comparable product, its marketing mix should reflect an awareness of perceptual categorization. A similar price can be used to communicate similar quality. A package design with a similar color scheme may also be used to convey the identical meaning. These techniques will help the customer fit the new product into the desired product category.

Firms that select a family brand name for a new product rely on perceptual categorization to "presell" the new product. On the other hand, if the new product is generically different or of a different quality, a unique brand name may be selected to avoid perceptual categorization.

If an individual has strong brand loyalty to a product, it is difficult for other brands to penetrate that person's perceptual barriers. Competing brands

ACTION REPORT: Product "Look-Alikes"

A small business can use perceptual categorization to position its own brands against the brands of big business. Leon Levine uses this strategy with his Family Dollar brands in his variety discount stores in Charlotte, NC.

Levine uses packaging as one means of implementing the positioning strategy, as evidenced by the following comments:

> He points to a bottle of Family Dollar window cleaner that is next to bottles of Bristol-Myers' Windex. "Look familiar?" he asks. They do. The Family Dollar bottle looks like the Windex bottle. Is that on purpose? "I take the Fifth," he says, smiling.

Source: "The Leon and Al Show," *Forbes*, Vol. 126, No. 7 (September 29, 1980), pp. 52-56.

will likely experience distorted images because of the individual's attitude. The perceptual mood presents a unique communication challenge.

Needs. We will define **needs** as the basic seeds of (and the starting point for) all behavior. Without needs, there would be no behavior. There are many lists of consumer needs, but the major points we wish to convey do not require an extensive listing.[2] Needs are either *physiological*, *social*, *psychological*, or *spiritual*.

Needs are never completely satisfied. This favorable characteristic of needs assures the continued existence of business. An unfavorable characteristic of needs is the way they function together in generating behavior. In other words, various "seeds" (remember the definition) can blossom together. This makes it more difficult to understand which need has been satisfied by a specific product or service. Nevertheless, a careful assessment of the need-behavior connection can be very helpful in developing marketing strategy. For example, many food products in supermarkets are purchased by consumers to satisfy physiological needs. But food is also selected in status restaurants to satisfy social and/or psychological needs. A need-based strategy would add a different flavor to the marketing strategy in each of these two situations.

Motivations. Unsatisfied needs create tension within an individual. When this tension reaches a certain level, a person becomes uncomfortable and attempts to reduce the tension.

We are all familiar with "hunger pains." These are manifestations of tension created by an unsatisfied physiological need. What is it that directs a person to seek food so the "hunger pains" can be relieved? The answer is motivation. **Motivations** are goal-directed forces within humans which organize and give direction to tension caused by unsatisfied needs. Marketers cannot create needs, but they can create and offer unique motivations to consumers. If an acceptable reason for purchasing is provided, it will probably be internalized as a motivating force. The key for the marketer is to determine which motivation the consumer will perceive as an acceptable solution for the "hunger pains." The answer is found in analyzing the other consumer behavior variables.

Each of the other three classes of needs is similarly connected to behavior via motivations. For example, when a person's social needs create tension due to incomplete satisfaction, a firm may show how its product can fulfill that need by providing acceptable social motivations to that person.

Understanding motivations is not easy. Several motives may be present in each situation. Many times the motivations are subconscious, but they

2. Several more complete listings can be found in Kenneth E. Runyon, *Consumer Behavior and the Practice of Marketing* (2d ed.; Columbus: Charles E. Merrill Publishing Co., 1980), pp. 207-211.

must be determined if the marketing effort is to have an improved chance for success.

Attitudes. Like the other psychological variables, attitudes cannot be observed, but all persons know that they have attitudes even before these are defined. Do attitudes imply knowledge? Do they imply a feeling of good/bad or favorable/unfavorable? Does an attitude have a direct impact on behavior? Probably you answered "yes" to all these questions. An **attitude** is a feeling toward an object organized around knowledge which regulates behavioral tendencies.

An attitude can be an obstacle or a catalyst in bringing a customer to your product. Armed with an understanding of the structure of an attitude, the marketer can approach the consumer more intelligently. One of the more popular structural views of an attitude is based on the original work of Martin Fishbein.[3] As adapted to a marketing situation, Fishbein's idea is that a person's attitude toward a brand results from the belief that the brand has certain attributes that are weighted by the importance of these attributes to that person. A more precise formulation is:

$$A_0 = \sum_{i=1}^{j} B_i I_i$$

where: A_0 = attitude toward an object (brand)

B = belief that the brand has a certain attribute

I = importance of the attribute to the individual

i = the particular attribute of concern

j = number of relevant attributes

Table 9-1 shows that two hypothetical market segments for a ballpoint pen have equal attitude scores but relatively different unfavorable attitudes. The strategies to improve these individual attitudes would be totally different. To improve the attitudes of consumers in Segment A, the seller needs to persuade them that the pen is attractive because attractiveness is important to them (importance rating of 7). Currently they do not believe the pen is attractive (belief rating of 2). They recognize that the pen is inexpensive to buy, but this is obviously not very important to them. If the seller feels that price is a distinct marketing advantage, consumers need to place more importance on low price.

3. *Ibid.*, pp. 293-294.

Table 9-1 Attitude Structures of Two Market Segments

Object = Worldwide Ballpoint Pen®

SEGMENT A		SEGMENT B	
Attribute	B_i* I_i*	**Attribute**	B_i* I_i*
Attractive–	2 × 7 = 14	Attractive–	6 × 1 = 6
High quality–	3 × 4 = 12	High quality–	5 × 6 = 30
Writes well–	5 × 6 = 30	Writes well–	3 × 7 = 21
Inexpensive–	7 × 1 = 7	Inexpensive–	2 × 3 = 6
**A_0	= 63	**A_0	= 63

*The scale ranges from 1 to 7, with a higher value meaning greater importance of the attribute to the individual or a greater belief that the attribute is present in the product.
**The most favorable attitude score would be 196.

The company has a different problem with consumers in Segment B. How well the pen writes is very important to them. They see the pen as being attractive, but this attribute isn't important to them. Mathematically, you can see various possibilities for increasing their attitude score.

Sociological Concepts. Up to this point in our "trip," our roadmap has presented only psychological roadsigns. As we turn the corner in Figure 9-2, we are confronted with several social considerations. We cannot ignore the people around us and their influence on our actions. Among these social influences are culture, social class, reference groups, and opinion leaders. Notice that each of the sociological concepts represents different degrees of people aggregation. Starting with culture, we see large masses of people. Then we see smaller groups—social classes and reference groups—until we find a single individual who exerts influence—the opinion leader.

Culture. Mankind's social heritage is called culture. This heritage has a tremendous impact on the purchase and use of products. Marketing managers will often overlook the cultural variable because its influences are so neatly concealed within the society. Cultural influence is somewhat like the presence of air. You really do not notice air or think about its function until you are in water over your head! Then you realize the role that air has played in your existence. On the other hand, international marketers who have experienced more than one culture can readily attest to the reality of cultural influence.

It is the prescriptive nature of culture which most concerns the marketing manager. Cultural norms create a range of product-related acceptable behavior which tells consumers what they should buy or at least what they ought to buy. Culture does change, however. It adapts slowly to new situations. Therefore, what works today as a marketing strategy may not work next year.

An investigation of culture with a narrower definitional boundary, such as age, religious preference, ethnic orientation, or geographical location, is called **subcultural analysis**. Here, too, the unique patterns of behavior and social relationships concern the marketing manager. For example, the needs and motivations of the youth subculture are far different from those of the senior-citizen subculture. Certain food preferences are unique to Jewish culture. Cigarettes do not sell well among Mormons. If small-business managers familiarize themselves with cultures and subcultures, they will prepare better marketing mixes.

Social Class. Another sociological concept in consumer behavior is social class. **Social class** describes divisions in a society with different levels of social prestige. There are important implications for marketing in a social-class system. Different life-styles correlate with the different levels of social prestige, and products are often symbols of life-styles.

Unlike a caste system, a social-class system provides for upward mobility. It is not the status position of parents which permanently fixes the social class of their child. Occupation is probably the single most important determinant of social class. Other determinants that are used in social-class research include possessions, source of income, and education.

For some products, like consumer packaged goods, social-class analysis will probably not be very useful. For others, like home furnishings, it may help to explain variations in shopping and communication patterns.

Reference Groups. Although social class could, by definition, be considered to be a reference group, we are more generally concerned with smaller groups such as the family, the work group, a neighborhood group, or a recreational group. Not every group is a reference group. **Reference groups** are only those groups from which an individual allows influence to be exerted upon his or her behavior.

The existence of group influence is well-established.[4] The challenge to the marketer is to understand why this influence occurs and how the influence can be used to promote the sale of a product. Individuals tend to accept group influence for the benefits perceived. These perceived benefits allow the influencers to use various kinds of power. Bertram Raven and John French have

---

4. For a good discussion of social group influence, see Chapter 10 in David L. Loudon and Albert J. Della Bitta, *Consumer Behavior: Concepts and Applications* (New York: McGraw-Hill Book Company, 1979).

classified these forms of power as reward, coercive, expert, referent, and legitimate. Each of these power forms is available to the marketer.

Reward power and **coercive power** relate to a group's ability to give and to withhold rewards. Rewards can be material or psychological. Recognition and praise are typical psychological rewards. A Tupperware party is a good example of a marketing technique which takes advantage of reward power and coercive power. The ever-present threat of displeasure from the hostess-friend tends to encourage the guest to buy.

Referent power and **expert power** involve neither rewards nor punishments. These types of power exist because an individual attaches a unique importance to being like the group or perceives the group as being in a more knowledgeable position than the individual. Referent power causes consumers to conform to the group's behavior and to choose products selected by the group's members. Young children will often be influenced by referent power. Marketers can create a desire for products similar to those used by adults whom children seek to emulate. For example, young cowboys and young baseball players are now using a chewing gum product cleverly designed and packaged to look like chewing tobacco in packs. Figure 9-3 shows the wrapper of one of these products.

Source: Amurol Products Co., Naperville, IL. Reproduced with permission.

Figure 9-3 Package Using Reference Group Appeal

Legitimate power involves the sanction of what one ought to do. We saw legitimate power at the cultural level when we talked about the prescriptive nature of culture. This type of power can also be used at a smaller group level.

Opinion Leaders. The concept of opinion leaders is largely a communication idea. According to this concept, consumers receive a significant amount of information through individuals called opinion leaders. Thus, an **opinion leader** is a group member playing a key communications role.

Generally speaking, opinion leaders are knowledgeable, visible, and exposed to the mass media. Small-business firms can enhance their own product and image by identifying with such leaders. For example, a farm-supply dealer may promote agricultural products in a community by arranging demonstrations on the farms of outstanding farmers. These farmers are the community's opinion leaders. Also, department stores may use attractive students as models in showing campus fashions.

Consumer Decision Making. Having passed the psychological and sociological roadsigns of consumer behavior, we will now examine those of consumer decision making. One theory about human-information processing holds that humans are problem-solvers. We will adopt this view for our discussion. Under this theory the stages of consumer decision making are:

1. Problem recognition.
2. Internal information search and evaluation.
3. External information search and evaluation.
4. Purchase decision.
5. Post-purchase evaluation.

The first roadsign of the consumer-decision phase of our roadmap tells us that the consumer must recognize a problem before making a purchase. This first stage cannot be circumvented. It is a mistake to concentrate on helping the consumer at later stages when, in reality, the consumer has not recognized a problem.

The time required for the second and third stages—internal and external information search and evaluation—varies with the product and the consumer. The scheduling of various communication strategies should reflect such time-dimension differences. The decision to buy a new product—the fourth stage—will naturally take longer than a decision involving a known product. For example, an industrial-equipment dealer may find it necessary to call on a prospective new customer over a period of months before making the first sale. Some decisions become routine and programmed; others do not.

The decision process does not terminate with a purchase. A small firm which desires repeat purchases from its customers should follow them into the post-purchase stage. A helpful concept for understanding the post-purchase process is **cognitive dissonance**, which takes the form of an uncomfortable psychological tension or a feeling of inequity. Cognitive dissonance tends to occur when a consumer has purchased one brand from among several which had attractive features. Second thoughts or doubts about the decision are bound to occur. The firm whose product was purchased should attempt to reduce the consumer's tension by communicating with that customer after the sale.

Consumers are complex creatures and will never be completely understood. However, the concepts we have presented are relevant to strategy development. Even a simple recognition of their existence, without a thorough understanding, can save a small business from serious mistakes. Too often these concepts are considered to be "big-business tools."

The ultimate benefit from what has been said so far in this chapter can be found by turning Figure 9-2 so that "START" is in the top right-hand corner and "SALE" is in the lower left-hand corner. Do you see the big dollar sign? The most successful small-business manager will likely be the best student of consumer behavior.

DEFINITIONS OF PRODUCT TERMINOLOGY

In this book, **product strategy** describes the manner in which the product component of the marketing mix is used to achieve the objectives of a firm. A **product** is the total "bundle of satisfaction" which is offered to customers in an exchange transaction. The product can be tangible, like a watch, or intangible, like a tax service.

A product includes not only the main element of the "bundle," which is the physical product itself, but also complementary components such as packaging. Of course, the physical product is usually the most important component. But sometimes the main element of a product is perceived by customers to be like that of all other products. The complementary components can then become the most important features of the product.

A **product mix** is the collection of product lines within a firm's ownership and control. A **product line** is the sum of the individual product items that are related. The relationship is usually defined generically. Two brands of bar soap would be two product items in one product line. A **product item** is the lowest common denominator in a product mix. It is the individual item.

The more items in a product line, the more *depth* it has. The more product lines in a product mix, the greater the *width* of the product mix. Finally, **product mix consistency** refers to the closeness of the product lines. Closeness signifies the similarity of the product lines.

PRODUCT STRATEGIES FOR SMALL BUSINESS

Small-business managers are often weak in their understanding of product strategy. This creates ineffectiveness and conflict in the marketing effort. In order to provide a better understanding of product strategy in small business, we will now examine product strategy in greater detail.

Product Strategy Alternatives

The overall product strategy alternatives of a small business can be presented in eight categories. We identify these strategy alternatives as follows:

1. Current product/current market.
2. Current product/new market.
3. Modified product/current market.
4. Modified product/new market.
5. New similar product/current market.
6. New similar product/new market.
7. New unrelated product/current market.
8. New unrelated product/new market.

Each alternative represents a different approach to product strategy. Some strategies can be pursued concurrently. Usually, however, the small firm will find that it will adopt the alternatives in basically the order listed. Keep this premise in mind as you read about each one.

Current Product/Current Market. In the earliest stage of a new venture, the current product/current market product strategy is followed. Most entrepreneurs start with one product. Growth can be achieved under this strategy in three ways. First, current customers can be encouraged to use *more* of the product. Second, potential customers within the same market can be sold on the product. Third, current customers can be educated to use the existing product for additional purposes, thereby increasing demand. An example is Minnetonka's Softsoap, which was originally positioned as a replacement for bar soap. More recently, it has been promoted as a gift item and a skin-care product.

Current Product/New Market. An extension of the first alternative is the current product/new market product strategy. With a small commitment in resources, a current product can often be targeted to a new market. Taking a floor-cleaning compound from the commercial market into the home market would be an example of this strategy.

ACTION REPORT: Same Product, New Market

One growth strategy involves taking the current product and fitting it into a new market. A friend of Wyoming entrepreneur James Lind asked Lind to design a belt buckle for his company. Lind had never produced business buckles before, even though he had been making buckles for 15 years. But his friend's idea sounded good, and now the Wyoming Studio's business specialty buckles bring in around $500,000 in sales a year.

Lind charges businesses $250 for designing the buckle and preparing the mold. He receives $2.75 for each buckle cast in pewter and plated in brass, copper, or nickel.

Some of Lind's larger accounts include Coca-Cola Co., General Motors, and Ralston Purina Co. His buckles are creatively designed. Dial Soap's buckle, for example, looks like a bar of soap, and the Oscar Mayer buckle is shaped like a pack of weiners.

Mr. Lind "heads a little company in a little warehouse in this little Wyoming town" (Jackson, WY) and "supplies . . . of course, a little product."

Source: Reprinted by permission of *The Wall Street Journal* (May 21, 1981),

Modified Product/Current Market. Customers seemingly anticipate the emergence of "new, improved" products. With the modified product/current market strategy, the existing product can be either replaced, gradually phased out, or left in the product mix. If the existing product is to be retained, the impact on sales of the modified product must be carefully assessed. It doesn't do much good to make an existing product obsolete unless the modified product has a larger profit margin. The product modification can involve a very minor change. For example, adding colored specks to a detergent can give the business a "new" and extremely sales-attractive product.

Modified Product/New Market. A modified product can also be used to reach a new market. The only difference in the modified product/new market strategy from the previous one is its appeal to a new market segment. For example, a furniture manufacturer currently selling finished furniture to customers might market unfinished furniture to the "do-it-yourself" market.

New Similar Product/Current Market. Current, satisfied customers make good markets for new additions to the product assortment of a small business. Many products can be added which are more than product modifications but are still similar to the existing products. These new products are considered to be similar when they have a generic relationship. For example, Celestial Seasonings, Inc., of Boulder, CO has moved into a caffeine-free hot drink called Breakaway, which is a recent addition to its herb teas.[5] The new product is generically similar to the tea products. It is aimed at the same health-care market.

New Similar Product/New Market. Going after a different market with a new but similar product is still another product strategy. This approach is particularly appropriate when there is concern that the new product may reduce sales of the existing product in a current market.

New Unrelated Product/Current Market. A product strategy which includes a new product generically different from existing products can be very risky. However, the new unrelated product/current market strategy is sometimes used by small businesses especially when the new product fits existing distribution and sales systems. For example, a local dealer selling Italian sewing machines may add a line of microwave ovens.

New Unrelated Product/New Market. The final product strategy occurs when a new unrelated product is added to the product mix to serve a new market. This strategy has the most risk among all the alternatives since the business is attempting to market an unfamiliar product to an unfamiliar market. For example, one electrical equipment service business added a private employment agency.

With this product strategy, however, a hedge can be built against volatile shifts in market demand. If the business is selling snowshoes and suntan lotion, it hopes that demand will be high in one market at all times.

Managing the Product Mix

The management of the firm's product mix is guided by many considerations. Competition, market demand, pricing flexibility—to name just a few—are important influences in this regard.

Two marketing concepts are extremely useful to the small-business manager in any efforts to control and develop the firm's product mix. These are the product development curve and the product life cycle. Both of these concepts provide concise summaries of activities or circumstances relating to the management of the product mix.

---

5. "What's Brewing at Celestial," *Business Week*, No. 2679 (March 16, 1981), p. 138.

The Product Development Curve. A major responsibility of the entrepreneur is to recognize, prepare, and implement any of the product strategy alternatives discussed earlier. Many of these strategies require a structured mechanism for new-product development. In big business, committees or even entire departments are created for that purpose. In a small business this responsibility will usually rest with the entrepreneur.

The product development curve can help the entrepreneur organize development ideas. As shown in Figure 9-4, the product development curve can be remembered as having the shape of one end of a classic suspension bridge. The curve, simulated by the bridge cable, represents the number of new-product ideas under consideration.

The first phase of the product development curve, labeled Idea Accumulation, shows the need to increase the number of ideas under consideration. New products start with new-product ideas, and these ideas have varied origins. Some of the many possible sources of ideas are:

1. Sales, engineering, or other personnel within the firm.
2. Government-owned patents, which are generally available on a royalty-free basis.
3. Privately owned patents listed in the *Official Gazette* of the U. S. Patent Office.
4. Other small companies which may be available for acquisition or merger.
5. Competitors' products and advertising.
6. Requests and suggestions from customers.

Business Analysis is the next stage in the process. Every new-product idea must be carefully analyzed in relation to several considerations.

Relationship to Existing Product Line. Any products to be added should be consistent with, or properly related to, the existing product line. For example, a new product may be designed to fill a gap in the company's product line or in the price range of the products it currently manufactures. If the product is completely new, it should normally have at least a family relationship to existing products. Otherwise, the new products may call for drastic and costly changes in manufacturing methods, distribution channels, type of advertising, or manner of personal selling.

Cost of Development and Introduction. One problem in adding new products is the cost of development and introduction. The capital outlays may be considerable. These include expenditures for design and development, market research to establish sales potential and company volume potential, advertising and sales promotion, patents, and the equipment and tooling that

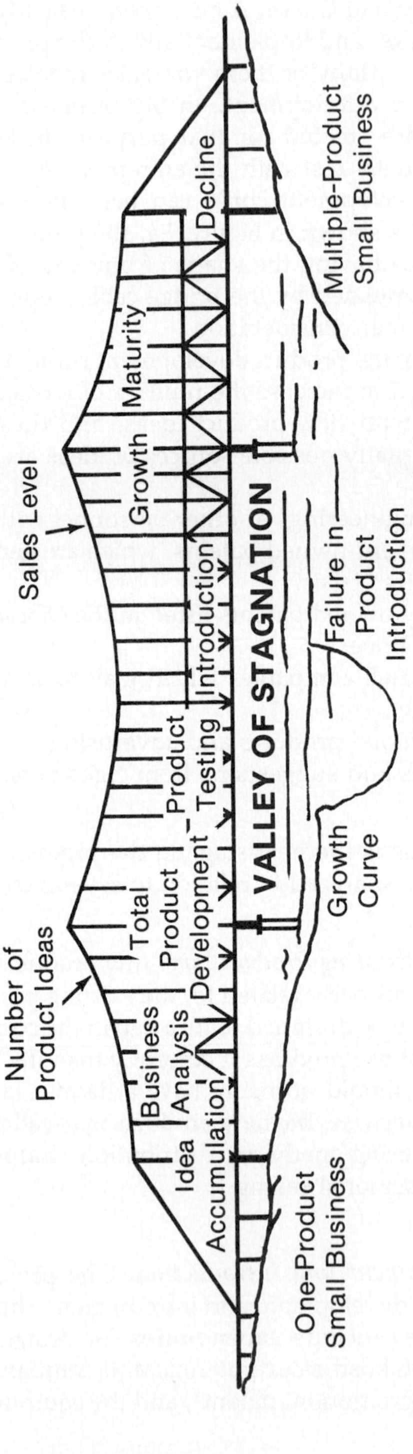

Figure 9-4 Suspension Bridge of Product Mix Development

must be added. It may be from one to three years before profits may be realized on the sale of the contemplated new or altered product.

Personnel and Facilities. Obviously, having adequate skilled personnel, managers, and production equipment is better than having to add personnel and buy equipment. Hence, introducing new products is typically more logical if the personnel and the required equipment are already available.

Competition and Market Acceptance. Still another factor to be considered is the character of the market and the potential competition facing the proposed product. Competition must not be too severe. Some authorities, for example, think that new products can be introduced successfully only if a 5 percent share of the total market can be secured. The ideal solution, of course, is to offer a sufficiently different product or one in a cost and price bracket that avoids direct competition.

The next stage, Total Product Development, entails the planning for suitable branding, packaging, and other supporting efforts such as pricing and promotion. After these components are considered, many new-product ideas may be discarded.

The last step in the product development curve is Product Testing. This means that the physical product should be proven to perform correctly. While the product can be evaluated in a laboratory setting, a test of market reaction to the total product should also be conducted. This test can be performed only in the marketplace.

The Product Life Cycle. Another valuable concept for managing the product mix is the product life cycle. The life cycle of a product is depicted by the remaining end of the suspension bridge in Figure 9-4. The cable symbolizes the sales curve. Initial sales are low at introduction, peak later, and then fall. The suspension bridge cable follows this general pattern.

The product life cycle gives the small-business manager a planning tool. Promotional, pricing, and distribution policies are a reflection of the curve. This gives the entrepreneur valuable insights into marketing mix modifications.[6]

When a small business is committed to the product development concept, it can look forward to expanding its product mix successfully and to staying above the nemeses of the "Valley of Stagnation" pictured in Figure 9-4.

---

6. A detailed discussion of these changes is beyond the scope of this book. For more details, see Charles D. Schewe and Reuben M. Smith, *Marketing: Concepts and Applications* (New York: McGraw-Hill Book Company, 1979), Chapter 10.

Building the Total Product

A major responsibility of marketing is to transform a basic product into a total product. An idea for a unique new writing pen which has already been developed into a physical reality is still not ready for the marketplace. The total product, in this example, would incorporate more than the materials molded into the shape of the new pen.[7] To be marketable, the basic product must be named, have a package, perhaps have a warranty, and be supported by many other product components. We will now examine a few of these components.

Branding. An identification for a product is termed a **brand**. A brand includes both the identification which can be verbalized and that which cannot. The name Xerox is a brand, as are the "golden arches" of a famous hamburger chain. A name and a trademark are important to the image of the business and its products. Therefore, considerable attention should be given to every decision in a branding strategy.

In general, there are five rules to follow in naming a product:

1. Select a name which is easy to pronounce. You want customers to remember your product. Help them with a name that can be spoken easily. An entrepreneur's own name should be carefully evaluated to be sure it is acceptable. The founder of a major fast-food chain used his daughter's name for the company. Her name? Wendy. The name of the business? Wendy's.
2. Choose a descriptive name. A name which is suggestive of the major benefit of the product can be extremely helpful. The name Rocky Road would be a poor selection for a mattress! However, consider the gasoline brand named El Cheapo.
3. Use a name which can have legal protection. Be careful that you select a name that can be defended successfully. This is sometimes difficult, but do not risk litigation by intentionally copying someone else's brand name. A new soft drink named Prof. Pepper would likely be contested by the Dr Pepper company.
4. Consider names that have promotional possibilities. Exceedingly long names are not, for example, compatible for good copy design on billboards, where space is at such a premium. A competitor of the McDonald's hamburger chain is called Wuv's. This name will easily fit on any billboard.
5. Select a name which can be used on several product lines of a similar nature. Many times customer goodwill is lost when a name doesn't fit a new line. A company producing a furniture

7. An intangible service is also a basic product that requires additional product development.

polish called Slick-Surface could not easily use the same name for its new sidewalk surfacing compound, which purports to increase traction.

A small business also should carefully select its trademark. The mark should be unique, easy to remember, and related to the product.[8]

Trademark registration for products in interstate commerce is handled through the U. S. Patent and Trademark Office under the authority of the Lanham Trademark Act. This act also covers the registration of service marks, certification marks, and collective marks.

Once a trademark is selected by a small business, it is important to protect its use. Two rules can help. One is to be sure the name is not carelessly used in place of the generic name. For example, the Xerox company never wants a person to say that he or she is "xeroxing" something. Second, the business should inform the public that the brand is a brand by labeling it with the symbol ®. If the trademark is unusual or written in a special form, it is easier to protect.

Packaging. Packaging is another important part of the total product. In addition to protecting the basic product, packaging is also a significant tool for increasing the value of the total product. Consider for a moment some of the products you purchase. Are any bought primarily because of preference for the package design and/or color?

ACTION REPORT: Molding a Product with Cartoon Characters

Certain entertainment efforts can sometimes be interlaced with the physical product to make a more competitive product. Cartoon characters have been used in this manner through a license arrangement.

A spokeswoman at Binney & Smith, Inc., the maker of Crayola Crayons and Silly Putty, states, "Kids don't really care about our putty; they care about their favorite characters." Silly Putty has lost market share to competitors who use cartoon characters for product identity. Recent competitors have been Bugs Bunny Putty, Spiderman Putty, and Hulk Putty.

St. Regis Paper Co. is using the cartoon concept with the Strawberry Shortcake character on its line of school and home products. Plans are to add Ziggy, Holly Hobbie, and Dungeons and Dragons licenses.

Source: Reprinted by permission of *The Wall Street Journal* (June 1, 1981), © Dow Jones & Company, Inc. (1981). All rights reserved.

8. For more extensive treatment of trademarks, see Section 7 of William A. Hancock, *Executive's Guide to Business Law* (New York: McGraw-Hill Book Company, 1979).

Packaging is also used for promotional purposes. It is important for some food products, for example, to be visible through the package. The manager of Dryden & Palmer Co. in Norwalk, CT, which employs 30 people and produces rock candy, talks about the package for his product this way: "Basically you've got a round product that's put in a square box. Rock candy needs to be seen. It's really quite attractive."[9]

Packaging can also open the door to new markets. Sam Gallo, president of a small Baton Rouge company, has introduced coffee in coffee bags. Coffee bags have been tried before but failed due to packaging, which allowed the coffee to become stale. Mr. Gallo guarantees a nine-month shelf life for his product and calls it "Morning Treat."[10]

Labeling. Another part of the total product is its label. Labeling is particularly important to manufacturers who apply most labels. A label serves several purposes. It often shows the brand, particularly when branding the basic product would be undesirable. For example, a furniture brand is typically shown on a label and not on the basic product. On some products, visibility of the brand label is highly desirable. Calvin Klein jeans would probably not sell well with the name labeled only inside the jeans.

A label is also an important informative tool for the small business. It can contain information on product care. It can inform consumers how to use the product correctly. It can even include information on how to dispose of the product.

Laws on labeling requirements should be consulted carefully.[11] Be innovative in your labeling information. Include information that goes beyond the specified minimum legal requirements.

Warranties. A **warranty** is simply a promise that a product will do certain things. It may be express (written) or implied. An implied warranty refers to the seller's clear title to the product and to its quality.

An express warranty on a product is not necessary. As a matter of fact, many firms operate without written warranties. They are concerned that a written warranty will only serve to confuse customers and make them suspicious. Figure 9-5 may be somewhat representative of this attitude among small businesses.

The Magnuson-Moss Warranty Act of 1974 has had an impact on warranty practices. This law covers several warranty areas, including warranty

---

9. Doron P. Levin, "Rock-Candy Maker Takes Its Licks: An Ailing Vestige of Simpler Times," *The Wall Street Journal*, June 17, 1981, p. 25.

10. "Morning Treat Tilts with Giants," *Sales and Marketing Management*, Vol. 122, No. 7 (May 14, 1979), p. 13.

11. Laws that affect packaging and labeling are treated in Joe L. Welch, *Marketing Law* (Tulsa, OK: The Petroleum Publishing Company, 1980), pp. 127-133.

"But we are completely satisfied with your money."

Source: *The Saturday Evening Post*, Vol. 253, No. 1 (January-February, 1981), p. 28. Reprinted with permission from The Saturday Evening Post Company, ©1981.

Figure 9-5 Satisfaction Guaranteed

terminology. The most notable change in terminology is the use of the terms "Full" and "Limited" on an express warranty for a product that costs over $15.

Warranties are important for products which are innovative, relatively expensive, purchased infrequently, relatively complex to repair, and positioned as high-quality goods. The major considerations which help decide the merits of a warranty policy are:

1. Costs.
2. Service capability.
3. Competitive practices.
4. Customer perceptions.
5. Legal implications.

LOOKING BACK

1. Marketing consists of those business activities which relate directly to determining target markets and preparing, communicating, and delivering

a bundle of satisfaction to these markets. The core marketing activities are: market segmentation, marketing research, consumer-behavior analysis, product strategy, pricing, promotion, and distribution.

2. Traditional economic concepts of consumer behavior visualize the consumer as a rational buyer who possesses perfect information, and they assume the existence of a homogeneous market where consumers behave in a fairly similar way. Psychological concepts include perception, needs, motivations, and attitudes. Sociological concepts include culture, social class, reference groups, and opinion leaders.
3. The stages of consumer decision making include problem recognition, internal information search and evaluation, external information search and evaluation, the decision to purchase, and the post-purchase evaluation.
4. The eight product strategy alternatives are: current product/current market, current product/new market, modified product/current market, modified product/new market, new similar product/current market, new similar product/new market, new unrelated product/current market, and new unrelated product/new market.

   Two concepts useful to the management of the product mix are the product development curve and the product life cycle. The product development curve consists of four phases: idea accumulation, business analysis, total product development, and product testing. The product life cycle consists of four stages: introduction, growth, maturity, and decline.
5. When choosing a good brand name, the entrepreneur should follow five basic rules. Packaging can be used for protection, promotion, and opening new markets. Labels are informative tools for the marketer. A warranty is simply a promise that a product will do certain things.

DISCUSSION QUESTIONS

1. Select a magazine advertisement and analyze it for the use of reference-group influence and cultural uniqueness.
2. Give some examples of the way in which legitimate power is used in marketing.
3. What kinds of consumer behavior occur in the post-purchase stage? Be specific.
4. What are the three ways to grow when using a current product/current market strategy?
5. How does the new similar product/new market strategy differ from the new unrelated product/new market strategy? Give examples.
6. A manufacturer of power lawn mowers is considering the addition

of a line of home barbecue equipment. What factors would be important in a decision of this type?

7. List some of the major activities in the business analysis stage of the product development curve.
8. Select two product names and evaluate each with the five rules for naming a product listed in this chapter.
9. Would a small business desire to have its name considered to be the generic name for the product area? Defend your position.
10. For what type of firm is the packaging of products most important? For what firms is it unimportant?

REFERENCES TO SMALL BUSINESS IN ACTION

Berman, Phyllis. "Close to the Vest." *Forbes*, Vol. 127, No. 9 (April 27, 1981), pp. 102-104.

The product-line expansion experiences of Aztec Manufacturing are related by the company's president.

"Is the Bar of Soap Washed Up?" *Business Week*, No. 2670 (January 12, 1981), pp. 109-116.

Several aspects of the product development curve and the product life cycle concepts are detectable in this discussion of Minnetonka's Softsoap product.

Kilich, Betty. "When Two Ventures Are Better than One." *Venture*, Vol. 2, No. 2 (February, 1980), pp. 42-45.

The diversification experiences of four separate businesses are discussed in this article.

Marion, Larry. "The Survival Instinct." *Forbes*, Vol. 127, No. 2 (January 19, 1981), pp. 57-58.

This article shows the advantages of adding new products that can be produced on existing facilities.

Chapter 10

Distribution, Pricing, and Credit Policies

LOOKING AHEAD

Watch for the following important topics:

1. Functions of intermediaries in a channel of distribution.
2. Considerations in choosing a distribution system.
3. Considerations for the small-business exporter.
4. Cost and demand considerations in pricing.
5. Managing credit in a small business.

A product is finally prepared for exchange with a customer when it is readied for delivery and priced; and, increasingly, pricing must be augmented by credit. Thus, distribution, pricing, and credit policies are critical activities to a complete small-business marketing program and are examined in this chapter.

DISTRIBUTION ACTIVITIES

The term **distribution** in marketing includes both the physical movement of products and the establishment of intermediary (middleman) relationships to guide and support the movement of the product. The physical movement activities form a special field called **physical distribution** or **logistics**. The intermediary system is called a **channel of distribution**.

Distribution is critical for both tangible and intangible goods. Since distribution activities are more visible for tangible goods, our discussion will concentrate on them. Most intangible goods (services) are delivered directly to the user. An income tax preparer, for example, serves a client directly. But even a person's labor can involve channel intermediaries as when, for example, an employment agency is used to find an employer.[1]

Channels of Distribution

A channel of distribution can be either direct or indirect. If it is a *direct* channel, there are no intermediaries. The product goes directly from producer to user. If the channel is *indirect,* one or more intermediaries may exist between the producer and the user.

Figure 10-1 depicts the basic ABCs of options available for structuring a channel of distribution. Channel A has no intermediaries. Door-to-door retailing is a familiar form of this channel system for consumer goods.

Channel B incorporates one intermediary. The B-type channels are used for both consumer and industrial goods. As final consumers, we are all familiar with retailers. Industrial purchasers are equally familiar with industrial distributors. Channel C shows two levels of intermediaries. This is probably the most typical channel for small businesses that have a large geographic

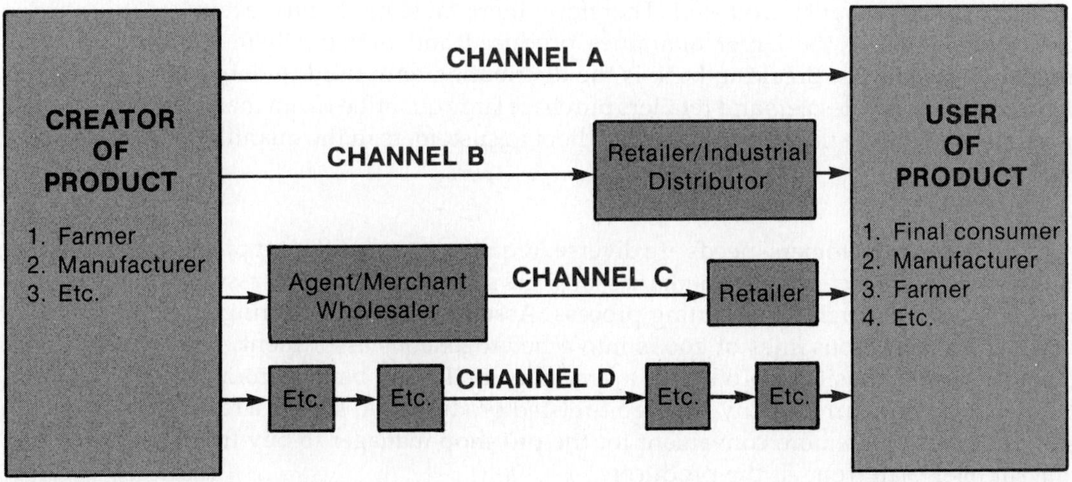

Figure 10-1 Alternative Channels of Distribution

1. Some additional examples of service distribution are found in James H. Donnelly, Jr., "Marketing Intermediaries in Channels of Distribution for Services," *Journal of Marketing,* Vol. 40, No. 1 (January, 1976), pp. 55-57.

market. The last channel in Figure 10-1 is labeled D. This represents the many other extensions of Channel C. For example, there may be three or more separate intermediaries in the channel.

Justifying Channels of Distribution. The small-business manager is often puzzled over the use of intermediaries in a channel of distribution. Are they really necessary? What kinds of small businesses really need them? The answer to the first question is "yes," and to the second, "maybe yours."

Intermediaries exist to carry out marketing functions which must be performed and which they can perform better than the producer or the user of a product. Small businesses cannot always perform these necessary functions as well as the intermediaries. This is why intermediaries are necessary. Four main functions of channel intermediaries are: breaking-bulk, assorting, providing information, and shifting risks.

As an example of the need for intermediaries, consider the small producers. The small producer can perform the four functions mentioned above if the geographic market is extremely small, if customers' needs are highly specialized, and if risk levels are low. Otherwise, the producer may find intermediaries to be a more efficient means of performing distribution activities. Of course, many types of small firms also function as intermediaries—for example, retail stores.

Breaking-Bulk. Very few individual customers demand quantities which are equal to the amounts produced. Therefore, there must be channel activities which will take the larger quantities produced and prepare them for individual customers. **Breaking-bulk** is the distribution term used to denote these activities. Wholesalers and retailers purchase large quantities from manufacturers, store these inventories, and sell them to customers in the quantities they desire.

Assorting. Customers' needs are diverse, requiring many different products to obtain satisfaction. Intermediaries facilitate shopping for a wide assortment of goods through the assorting process. **Assorting** consists of bringing together homogeneous lines of goods into a heterogeneous assortment. For example, a small business producing a special golf club can benefit from an intermediary who carries many other golf-related products and sells to a retail pro shop. It is much more convenient for the pro shop manager to buy from one supplier than from all the producers.

Providing Information. One of the major benefits of using an intermediary is information. Intermediaries can provide the producer with extremely helpful data on market size and pricing considerations.

Shifting Risks. By using intermediaries, the small-business manager can often share or totally shift business risks. This is possible by using **merchant middlemen**, who take title to the goods they distribute. Other intermediaries, such as **agents** and **brokers**, do not take title to the goods.

Choosing a Distribution System. One alternative for the small-business producer, as it decides on a distribution system, is to look at the competition. Some useful ideas about distribution are obtained from observing what others do. In all likelihood the competition will have made their decisions on the basis of practical considerations. At least their distribution system model can be used as a starting point.

ACTION REPORT: Doing What the Competition Does

Patterning a distribution system after that of the competition doesn't always work. Sometimes an independent analysis will suggest a different and better channel.

This was the experience of B. H. Thomas, president of Preway Company of Wisconsin Rapids, WI. In the early 1970s, Preway produced an energy-efficient fireplace. The initial distribution was attempted through manufacturers' representatives who carried space heaters.

> "We tried to copy the marketing strategy of other fireplace makers, selling direct to retailers," says Thomas. "We tried for 18 months, but it didn't work. They were not going down the same street as fireplace buyers."

Having recognized the distribution problem, Thomas sought an alternative. He recalls:

> While mulling over the problem at a meeting, a bell rang in my head. Based on my past experience, I suggested that we go to a two-step distribution system. Like appliance manufacturers, Preway would sell to local distributors, who would then supply area retailers. It gave us more manpower—almost double the field representatives.

The "new" distribution system was a major factor in the doubling of sales between 1973 and 1974. Today Thomas concedes, "Oh, there's nothing secret or unusual about our market strategy. We just got a head start, recruiting most of the good distributors."

Source: "The Survival Instinct," by Larry Marion, *Forbes,* Vol. 127, No. 2 (January 19, 1981), pp. 57-58.

Basically there are three main considerations in structuring a channel of distribution. We will call these the "three C's" of channel choice: costs, coverage, and control.

Costs. The small business must consider the cost of a channel carefully. A good beginning is to forget the idea that a direct channel is less expensive than an indirect channel. This idea is not inherently true. A small business may well be in a situation in which the less expensive channel is indirect. We should look at distribution costs as an investment. You have to spend money in order to make money. Ask yourself whether the money you would invest in intermediaries would get the job done if you used direct distribution.[2] And don't forget to cost your time fairly.

Coverage. Small businesses use indirect channels of distribution to increase market coverage. To illustrate this point, consider a small-business manufacturer whose sales force can make ten contacts a week. This direct channel provides ten contacts a week with the final users of the product. Now consider an indirect channel involving ten industrial distributors who (for convenience in illustration) each make ten contacts a week with the final users of the product. With this indirect channel, and no increase in the sales force, the small-business manufacturer is now able to expose the product to how many final users a week? If you said 100, you are correct!

Control. A third consideration in choosing a distribution channel is control. Obviously there is more control in a direct channel of distribution. With indirect channels, products may not be marketed as intended. The small business must select channels which provide the desired support from intermediaries.

The Scope of Physical Distribution

The main component of physical distribution is transportation. Additional components are storage, materials handling, delivery terms, and inventory management. In the following sections we will briefly examine all of these topics except inventory management, which is discussed in Chapter 17.

Transportation. The major decision area regarding transportation concerns the mode to use. Alternative modes are traditionally classified as airplanes,

---

2. The reduction in product price given an intermediary is the investment cost to which we refer.

trucks, railroads, pipelines, and waterways. Each mode has its unique advantages and disadvantages.[3]

Transportation intermediaries are of three types: common carriers, contract carriers, and private carriers. These are legal classifications which subject the first two types to regulations by federal and/or state agencies. **Common carriers** are available for hire to the general public, while **contract carriers** engage in individual contracts with shippers. Shippers who own their means of transport are called **private carriers**.

Storage. Space is a common problem for a small business because there is never enough. When the channel system uses merchant wholesalers, for example, title to the goods is transferred, as is the storage function. On other occasions, the small business must plan for its own warehousing. If a small business is too small to own a private warehouse, it can rent space in public warehouses. If storage requirements are simple and involve little special handling equipment, a public warehouse can provide an economical storage function.

Materials Handling. A product is worth little if it is in the right place at the right time but is damaged. Therefore, a physical distribution plan must consider materials-handling activities. Forklifts and special containers and packages are part of a materials-handling system. Tremendous improvements have been made through the years in materials-handling methods.

Delivery Terms. A small but important part of a physical distribution plan is the terms of delivery. Delivery terms specify the following:

1. Who pays the freight costs?
2. Who selects carriers?
3. Who bears the risk of damage in transit?
4. Who selects the modes of transport?

The simplest delivery term and the one most advantageous to a small-business seller is F.O.B. origin, freight collect. These terms shift all the responsibility to the buyer.[4]

---

3. A good basic discussion of each of these modes of transportation is found in Chapter 14 of Charles D. Schewe and Reuben M. Smith, *Marketing: Concepts and Applications* (New York: McGraw-Hill Book Company, 1979).

4. For a more detailed discussion of various delivery terms, see Lynn Edward Gill, "Delivery Terms—Important Element of Physical Distribution," *Journal of Business Logistics*, Vol. 1, No. 2 (Spring, 1979), pp. 60-82.

Distribution Abroad

In the past, small business failed to take advantage of opportunities in foreign markets. But this is changing rapidly.[5] One author sees the reasons as follows:

1. Some foreign markets have higher growth rates with less competition.
2. Some foreign governments are encouraging imports.
3. Associating with foreign businessmen can help spark new-business ideas for use at home.
4. Small business can react more quickly to prevailing market forces.[6]

Understanding the Foreign Market. There are basically three ways to learn about a foreign market: read publications which deal with the market, go to the market, or talk with people who have been to the market.

Available Publications. The United States government encourages exporting and offers an array of publications on methods of reaching foreign markets. Universities and other private organizations also provide information on exporting opportunities. Figure 10-2 shows some of these sources.

Personal Visits. Learning about a foreign market through personal visits is expensive but can be worth the cost. The United States government sponsors foreign trade missions which provide economical alternatives to private travel.

Talks with Others. Someone who is a native of a foreign market or who has visited the foreign country can be a valuable source of information about that market. Contacts with international students and with faculty who teach international courses at a local university can often help locate these individuals.

Channels to Foreign Markets. Channel options for foreign distribution are numerous. The channels can be direct or can involve intermediaries who work for commissions or who take title and assume all risks. Figure 10-3 shows the channels to foreign markets that are available to the small business.

---

5. Some of the challenges and rewards of international marketing by small business are discussed in Grant C. Moon, "International Enterprise: A Small Business Challenge," *Journal of Small Business Management,* Vol. 19, No. 2 (April, 1981), pp. 1-6.

6. Changiz Pezeshkpur, "Systematic Approach to Finding Export Opportunities," *Harvard Business Review,* Vol. 57, No. 5 (September-October, 1979), p. 182.

ACTION REPORT: Foreign Markets Are Different

The entrepreneur needs to understand the unique cultural features of the export market. Today the People's Republic of China provides the most current and exciting example of a foreign market challenge.

Erik Bogh is China trade division manager for the East Asiatic Company. Concerning the China market, he notes:

> You cannot go directly to the customer, the person who will ultimately use the product you aim to sell. The foreign firm attempting to sell will rarely meet with end-user personnel during business trips to the Canton Trade Fair, or to Peking at the invitation of one of the corporations.

Other potential exporters to China have found patience to be essential. However, once the Chinese like what you've presented, "they can do business faster than anybody."

John T. Kamm, author of *China Trade Quarterly* and who has visited China frequently, has learned the Chinese sense of commercial law. He puts it this way: "It is wise to bear in mind that the Chinese sense of commercial law is very different from the usual Western nation. A man's word at the negotiating table is as valid as a signed piece of paper, basically."

Many veterans of business negotiations in China also point out that you should "be prepared to drink many cups of Chinese tea." Exporting to foreign markets can be difficult but profitable.

Source: Reprinted with special permission from the June, 1978 issue of INTERNATIONAL MANAGEMENT.

PRICING ACTIVITIES

The **price** of a product is the seller's measure of what he or she is willing to receive from a buyer in exchange for ownership or use of that product. **Pricing** is the systematic determination of the "right" price for a product. While setting a price is easy, pricing is complex and difficult. Before we examine the process of product pricing for the small business, let us first consider why this process is important.

Importance of Pricing

The revenue of a small business is a direct reflection of two components: sales quantity and product price. In a real sense, then, the product price is half

U. S. FOREIGN TRADE SOURCES

Agencies

Director
Bureau of Export Development
U. S. Department of Commerce
Washington, D. C. 20230
202-377-5261

Export-Import Bank of the United States
811 Vermont Avenue NW
Washington, D. C. 20571
Toll-free number: 800-424-5201
(Larry Luther, small business specialist)

Director
Export Trade Services Division
Foreign Agricultural Service
U. S. Department of Agriculture
Washington, D. C. 20250
202-447-6343

Federal Trade Commission
Public Reference Branch
6th Street and Pennsylvania Avenue NW
Room 130
Washington, D. C. 20580
202-523-3830

Department of the Treasury
U. S. Customs Service
1301 Constitution Avenue NW
Washington, D. C. 20229
202-566-8195

Office of Commercial Affairs
Bureau of Economic and Business Affairs
Room 33-34
U. S. State Department
Washington, D. C. 20520
202-632-8097

Publications

Government and Business: A Joint Venture in International Trade
(free booklet published by the U. S. State Department's Office of Commercial Affairs)
To order, write to:
Office of Public Communication
Bureau of Public Affairs
U. S. State Department
Room 48-27A
Washington, D. C. 20520
202-632-6575

Guide to United Nations' Conference of Trade and Development (UNCTAD) Publications
(free catalog published by UNCTAD)
To order, write to:
United Nations Sales Section
Editorial and Documents Section
Palais des Nations 1211
Geneva 10, Switzerland

Lorna M. Daniells, *Business Information Sources* (Berkeley, California: University of California Press, 1976) p. 258, list of reference data sources for exporters.

Quarterly Economic Review (London, England: Economist Intelligence Unit), reviews 45 countries quarterly.

Foreign Economic Trends and Their Implications for the United States. (Washington, D. C.: U. S. Bureau of International Commerce), semiannual.

OECD Economic Surveys (Paris, France: Organization for Economic Cooperation and Development), individual annual reviews listed by country.

Investing, Licensing, and Trading Conditions Abroad (New York, New York: Business International), two volumes.

Source: Reprinted by permission of the *Harvard Business Review*. Exhibit from "Systematic Approach to Finding Export Opportunities" by Changiz Pezeshkpur (September/October 1979).

Figure 10-2 Foreign Trade Information Sources

Sales Representatives or Agents—A sales representative is the equivalent of a manufacturer's representative here in the United States. Product literature and samples are used to present the product to the potential buyer. He usually works on a commission basis, assumes no risk or responsibility, and is under contract for a definite period of time (renewable by mutual agreement). This contract defines territory, terms of sale, method of compensation, and other details. The sales representative may operate on either an exclusive or non-exclusive basis.

Distributor—The foreign distributor is a merchant who purchases merchandise from a U. S. manufacturer at the greatest possible discount and resells it for his profit. This would be the preferred arrangement if the product being sold requires periodic servicing. The prospective distributor should be willing to carry a sufficient supply of spare parts and maintain adequate facilities and personnel to perform all normal servicing operations. Since the distributor buys in his name, it is easier for the U. S. manufacturer to establish a credit pattern so that more flexible or convenient payment terms can be offered. As with a sales representative, the length of association is established by contract, which is renewable if the arrangement proves satisfactory.

Foreign Retailer—Generally limited to the consumer line, this method relies mainly on direct contact by traveling sales representatives but, depending on the product, can also be accomplished by the mailing of catalogs, brochures, or other literature. However, even though it would eliminate commissions and traveling expenses, the U. S. manufacturer who uses the direct mail approach could suffer because his proposal may not receive proper consideration.

Selling Direct to the End-User—This is quite limited and again depends on the product. Opportunities often arise from advertisements in magazines receiving overseas distribution. Many times this can create difficulties because casual inquirers may not be fully cognizant of their country's foreign trade regulations. For several reasons they may not be able to receive the merchandise upon arrival, thus causing it to be impounded and possibly sold at public auction, or returned on a freight-collect basis that could prove costly.

State Controlled Trading Companies—This term applies to countries that have state trading monopolies, where business is conducted by a few government-sanctioned and controlled trading entities. Because of worldwide changes in foreign policy and their effect on trade between countries, these areas can become important future markets. For the time being, however, most opportunities will be limited to such items as raw materials, agricultural machinery, manufacturing equipment, and technical instruments, rather than consumer or household goods. This is due to the shortage of foreign exchange and the emphasis on self-sufficiency.

New Product Information Service (NPIS)—This special service, offered

Source: U. S. Department of Commerce, *A Basic Guide to Exporting* (Washington: U. S. Government Printing Office, 1979), pp. 3-4.

Figure 10-3 Foreign Market Channels of Distribution (Page 1)

by the Department of Commerce, can facilitate your direct selling effort to potential overseas customers. It enables U. S. companies interested in selling a new product overseas to submit appropriate data through Commerce Department District Offices for placement in the Department's publication, *Commercial News USA*, which is distributed exclusively abroad through 240 U. S. Foreign Service posts. The new product data is extracted and reprinted in individual post newsletters that are tailored to local markets. Selected product information also is broadcast abroad by the International Communication Agency's (formerly the U. S. Information Agency) Voice of America.

Commission Agents—Commission or buying agents are "finders" for foreign firms wanting to purchase U. S. products. These purchasing agents obtain the desired equipment at the lowest possible price. A commission is paid to them by their foreign clients.

Country Controlled Buying Agents—These are foreign government agencies or quasi-governmental firms empowered to locate and purchase desired goods.

Export Management Companies—EMCs, as they are called, act as the export department for several manufacturers of noncompetitive products. They solicit and transact business in the name of the manufacturers they represent for a commission, salary, or retainer plus commission. Many EMCs also will carry the financing for export sales, assuring immediate payment for the manufacturer's products.

This can be an exceptionally fine arrangement for smaller firms that do not have the time, personnel, or money to develop foreign markets, but wish to establish a corporate and product identity internationally.

Export Merchants—The export merchant purchases products direct from the manufacturer and has them packed and marked to his specifications. He then sells overseas through his contacts, in his own name, and assumes all risks for his account.

Export Agents—The export agent operates in the same manner as a manufacturer's representative, but the risk of loss remains with the manufacturer.

In transactions with export merchants and export agents the seller is faced with the possible disadvantage of giving up control over the marketing and promotion of the product, which could have an adverse effect on future success.

Figure 10-3 Foreign Market Channels of Distribution (Page 2)

of the revenue figure. Yet a small change in price can drastically influence total revenue. For emphasis, consider the following situations.[7]

Situation 1

Quantity sold	×	Price per unit	=	Revenue
500,000	×	$10	=	$5,000,000

Situation 2

Quantity sold	×	Price per unit	=	Revenue
500,000	×	$9.90	=	$4,950,000

The price per unit in Situation 2 is only ten cents lower than in Situation 1. However, the total reduction in revenue is $50,000! Thus, a small business can lose revenue unnecessarily if a price is too low.

Another reason why pricing is important is that a price has an indirect impact on sales quantity. In the examples above, quantity sold was assumed to be independent of price—which it may well be for a change in price from $10 to $9.90. However, a larger change, up or down, from $10 might change the quantity sold.

Pricing, therefore, has a double impact on total sales. It is important *directly* as one part of the revenue equation and *indirectly* through its impact on quantity demanded.

Cost Considerations in Pricing

In a successful business, price must be adequate to cover total cost plus some margin of profit. **Total cost** includes three elements. The first is the cost of goods (or services) offered for sale. An appliance dealer, for example, must include in the price the cost of the appliance and freight charges. The second element is the selling cost. This includes the direct cost of the salesperson's time as well as the cost of advertising and sales promotion. The third element is the general overhead cost applicable to the given product. Included in this cost are such items as office supplies, utilities, taxes, office salaries, and management salaries. This is the necessary payment for entrepreneurial services and the risk of doing business.

Another cost consideration concerns the way costs behave as the quantity marketed increases or decreases. **Total variable costs** are those costs that increase as the quantity marketed increases. The sales commission costs and material costs for production are typical variable costs. These are incurred as a product is made and sold. **Total fixed costs** are those costs that remain

7. Perfect inelastic demand is assumed to emphasize the point. Other demand situations are analyzed in a later section of the chapter.

constant at different levels of quantity sold. An advertising campaign expenditure and factory equipment cost would be fixed costs. These are incurred even without production or sales.

By understanding these different kinds of costs, a small-business manager can keep from pricing too low to meet costs. If all costs are considered to behave in the same way, pricing can be inappropriate. Small businesses will often disregard fixed and variable costs and treat them identically for pricing. An approach called average pricing is an example of this disregard. **Average pricing** occurs when the total cost over a previous period is divided by the quantity sold in that period. The resulting **average cost** is then used to set the current price. Such a procedure overlooks the reality of a higher average cost at a lower sales level. This is, of course, due to a constant fixed cost spread over fewer units.

Demand Considerations in Pricing

Cost considerations provide a floor below which a price would not be set for normal pricing purposes. Cost analysis does not tell the small-business manager how far the "right" price should exceed that minimum figure. Only after considering the nature of demand can this be determined.

Demand Factors. Several factors make up the demand consideration. One is the appeal of the product itself. If consumers perceive the product as an important solution to their unsatisfied needs, there will be demand.

Only in rare cases are identical "packages" of products and services offered by competing firms. In many cases the products are dissimilar in some way. Even when products are similar, the accompanying services typically differ. Speed of service, credit terms, delivery arrangements, personal attention by a top executive, and willingness to stand behind the product or service are but a few of the areas that distinguish one business from another. The pricing implications depend on whether the small firm is inferior or superior in these respects to its competitors. Certainly, there is no absolute imperative for the small business to conform slavishly to the prices of others. Its unique combination of goods and services may well justify a premium price.

Another factor that affects demand for a product is the marketing effort. Good promotion and distribution, for example, build demand. Currently several entrepreneurs are entering the water business by selling bottled water. "Demand for water has exploded in today's market," says water lawyer Raphael J. Moses, whose firm deals with water rights. Others in the business characterize the product demand as a *created* demand. "Water today is pure marketing."[8]

---

8. Phil Fitzell, "The Emerging Water Industry," *Venture*, Vol. 3, No. 8 (August, 1981), pp. 72-76.

ACTION REPORT: Status Pricing

Status is a visible motivator for many consumers. These consumers will pay high prices to purchase status symbols.

S. T. Dupont Co. relies on these kinds of motivations to sell its products, which are priced accordingly. It markets $65 million of luxury goods a year to the rich. The company's newest addition is "the most luxurious fountain pen ever manufactured." It will retail for around $400!

The Dupont fountain pen is carved from a solid block of brass and is covered with five coats of lacquer from the sap of the rhus tree, which grows in China. The new pen is priced well above the typical $1 to $2 pens but is actually below a German firm's $9,000 platinum pen.

Dupont is appealing to the same motivations which sell its $150 to $400 cigarette lighters. The Dupont lighter "makes a recognizably different ringing sound that labels it to the discerning" when a smoker snaps open the lighter.

Source: Reprinted by permission of *The Wall Street Journal* (June 12, 1981),

The third factor which has a major influence on demand is the product price itself, as mentioned earlier. This influence varies from market to market. Higher-income-level markets are less sensitive to prices than lower-income groups. For example, Gary Klein of Chehalis, WA manufactures bicycles which sell for up to $6,600.[9] Therefore, each market must be examined individually.

Elasticity of Demand. The effect that a change in price has on the quantity demanded is called **elasticity of demand.**[10] If a change in price produces a significant change in the quantity demanded, the product is said to have an **elastic demand**. On the other hand, if a price change does not bring about a significant difference in the quantity demanded, the product is considered to have **inelastic demand**.

Consider the simplest hand-held calculator, which retailed for about $45 in the early 1970s. When its price was reduced by about 50 percent, consumers responded with substantially higher orders. Salt, however, is a product with inelastic demand. Regardless of its price, the demand will not change significantly because consumers generally use a fixed amount of salt.

---

9. Sanford L. Jacobs, "$6,600 May Seem High for a Bicycle, but at Least the Frame Won't Bend," *The Wall Street Journal*, June 25, 1981, p. 25.

10. Methods of estimating price elasticity for products of small firms are suggested in William J. Kehoe, "Demand Curve Estimation and the Small Business Manager," *Journal of Small Business Management*, Vol. 10, No. 3 (July, 1972), pp. 29-31.

Break-Even Analysis in Pricing

Break-even analysis entails a formal comparison of cost and demand for the purposes of determining the acceptability of alternative prices. There are two stages of a complete break-even analysis: cost break-even and cost-adjusted break-even. Break-even analysis can be explained via formulas or graphs. We will use the graphic presentation.

Cost Break-Even Stage. The objective of the cost break-even stage is to determine the quantity at which the product, with an assumed price, will generate enough revenue to start earning a profit. Figure 10-4(a) presents a simple cost break-even chart. The fixed costs are portrayed as a horizontal section in view of the fact that they do not change with the volume of production. The variable-cost section slants upward, however, because of the direct fluctuation of variable costs with output. The area between the slanting total cost line and the horizontal base line thus represents the combination of fixed and variable costs. The area between the sales and total cost lines reveals the profit or loss position of the company at any level of production. The intersection of these two lines is called the **break-even point** because sales revenue covers total cost at this point.

Additional sales lines at other prices can be charted on the break-even graph to evaluate new break-even points. This gives a flexible break-even chart as shown in Figure 10-4(b). The assumed higher price of $18 in Figure 10-4(b) plots a more steeply sloped sales line, resulting in an earlier break-even point. Similarly, the lower price of $7 produces a "flatter" sales line, increasing the break-even point. Additional prices could be plotted to evaluate several proposed prices.

The cost break-even chart implies that quantity sold can increase continually (as shown by the larger and larger profit area to the right). This is misleading and can be corrected by adjusting the cost break-even analysis with demand data.

Cost-Adjusted Break-Even Stage. The indirect impact of price on quantity sold is a confounding problem for pricing decisions. Occasionally more of a product is demanded as its price increases. This was the situation with a small poodle-grooming service. Business was slow with the original pricing. A friend suggested an increase in price. The owner heeded the advice and business grew immediately. Usually, however, a smaller quantity is demanded at higher prices.

Break-even analysis can incorporate the estimated demand and greatly increase its usefulness. A cost-adjusted break-even chart is built by using the cost break-even data and adding a demand schedule. A demand schedule showing the estimated number of units demanded and total revenue at various prices is listed below at the bottom of page 249.

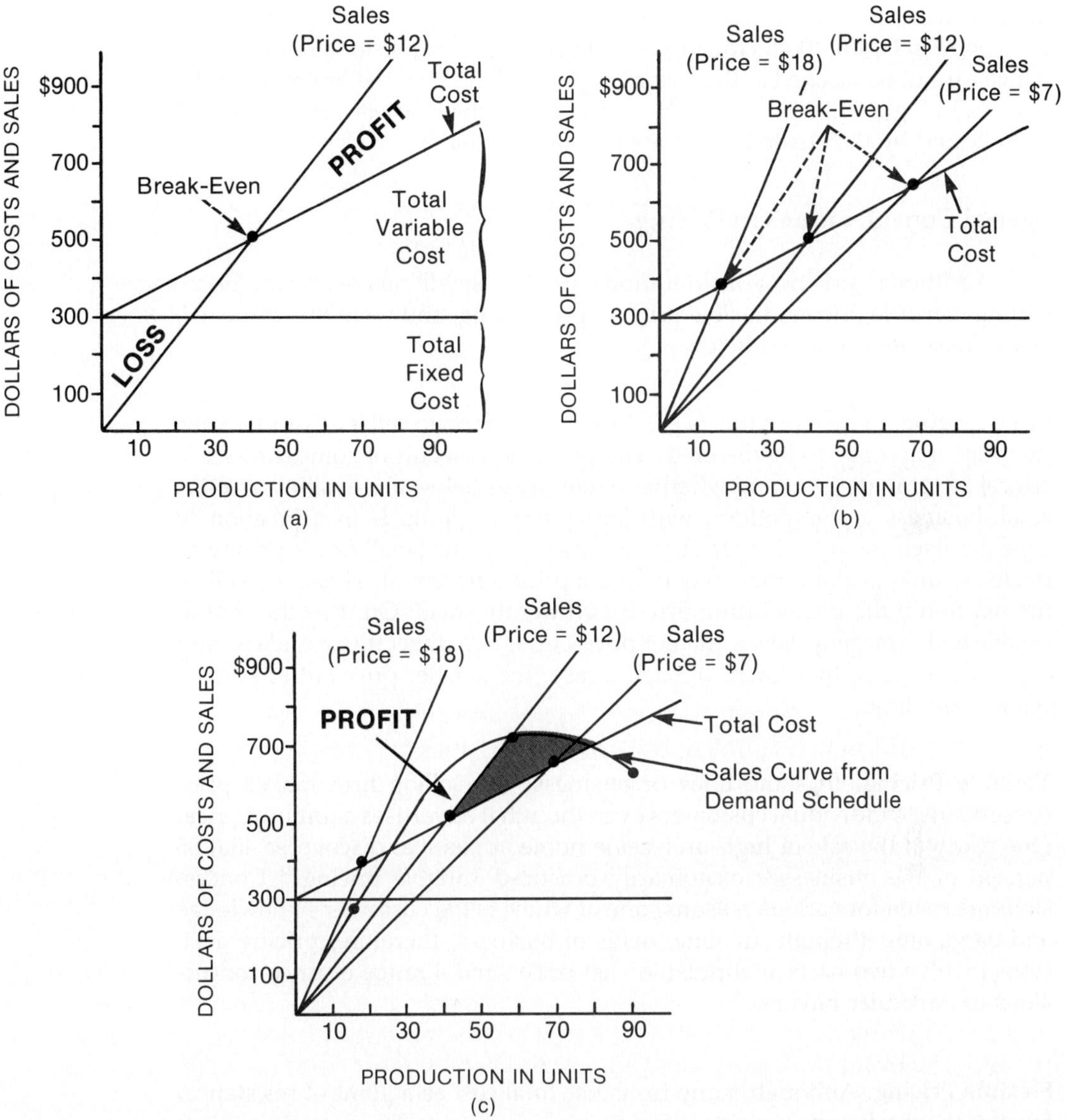

Figure 10-4 Break-Even Charts for Pricing

Price	Demand (Units)	Revenue ($)
$ 7	90	$630
12	60	720
18	15	270

When this demand schedule is plotted on a flexible break-even chart, a more realistic profit area is identified, as shown in Figure 10-4(c). The break-even point in Figure 10-4(c) for an $18 unit price corresponds to sales quantities which cannot be reached at the assumed price. Therefore, the optimum of the 3 prices in Figure 10-4(c) is $12. This price shows the greatest profit potential as indicated by the shaded profit area in Figure 10-4(c).

Special Considerations in Pricing

Additional pricing considerations for the small business are: price-cutting, variable pricing, flexible pricing, price lining, and what the traffic will bear. These are discussed below.

Price-Cutting. Once a product is produced and efforts to sell it are under way, the price may have to be lowered. The probable reaction of competitors is a critical factor in determining whether to cut prices below a prevailing level. A small business in competition with larger firms seldom is in a position to consider itself the price leader. If competitors view the small firm's pricing as relatively unimportant, they may permit a price differential. This may well be the reaction if the price-cutting firm is sufficiently small. On the other hand, established firms may view a smaller price-cutter as a direct threat and counter with reductions of their own. In such a case, the smaller price-cutter accomplishes very little.

Variable Pricing. In some lines of business, the selling firm makes price concessions to individual customers even though it advertises a uniform price. One study of the sale of high-unit-value home appliances discovered that 86 percent of the businesses customarily practiced variable pricing.[11] Concessions are made for various reasons, one of which is the customer's knowledge and bargaining strength. In some fields of business, therefore, pricing decisions involve two parts: a stipulated "list price" and a range of price concessions to particular buyers.

Flexible Pricing. Although many firms use total cost as a point of resistance, most of them take into consideration special market conditions and practices of competitors in arriving at their prices. The following cases illustrate this point:

---

11. W. Warren Haynes, *Pricing Decisions in Small Business*, Small Business Management Research Report. Prepared by the University of Kentucky under a grant by the Small Business Administration, Washington, DC (Lexington: University of Kentucky Press, 1962), pp. 27-29. Used by permission of the publisher.

1. *Contractor A* estimates the full cost of building a house, but he modifies the price to meet market conditions. Even his concept of cost reflects variable estimates of the opportunity costs of his time. His time is less valuable in the winter, when business is slack, than at other seasons; he adjusts his estimates of cost accordingly. He also shades price on a cash sale of a house, recognizing the avoidance of a risk as compared with sales involving complicated financing. Thus, the stress on full cost does not mean inattention to demand.
2. *Printing Company B* also pays considerable attention to full-cost estimates. While the management insists that prices should be kept on a full-cost basis, actual practice is more flexible. The managers are critical of "rate cutters," who, they claim, are responsible for the low industry profits, but they themselves show some willingness to adjust to market conditions when the necessity arises.
3. *Furniture Company C* starts with a cost estimate, including an allocation of indirect labor and factory overhead. But the management modifies the target return to meet market conditions.

On certain occasions it may be logical to price at less than total cost. For example, if the facilities of a business are idle, their cost may be continuing whether they are used or not. In any case, the price should cover all marginal or incremental costs—that is, those costs specifically incurred to get the added business. In the long run, however, all overhead costs must be covered as well.

Price Lining. A **price line** is a range of several distinct prices at which merchandise is offered for sale. For example, men's suits might be sold at $150, $200, or $250. The general level of the different lines would depend on the income level and buying desires of a store's customers. Price lining has the advantage of simplifying choice for the customer and reducing the necessary minimum inventory.

What the Traffic Will Bear. The policy of pricing on the basis of what the traffic will bear can be used only when the seller has little or no competition. Obviously this policy will work only for unstandardized products. For example, a food store might offer egg roll wrappers which the competitors do not carry. Busy consumers who want to fix egg rolls but who have neither the time nor the knowledge to prepare the wrappers will buy them at the price offered.

Calculating the Selling Price

In calculating the selling price for a particular item, retailers, wholesalers, and even manufacturers must add a markup percentage to cover the following:

1. Operating expenses.
2. Profit.
3. Subsequent price reductions—for example, markdowns and employee discounts.

Markups may be expressed as a percentage of either the *selling price* or the *cost*. For example, if an item costs $6 and is selling at $10, the markup of $4 would be 40 percent of the selling price or 66⅔ percent of the cost. Although either method is correct, consistency demands that the same method be used in considering the components entering into the markup. If operating expenses amount to 35 percent of sales and a profit of 5 percent of sales is desired, the markup (assuming no markdown) must be 40 percent of selling price. This is clearly different from 40 percent markup based on cost. In fact, an incorrect application of the 40 percent figure to cost would produce a markup amounting to less than 29 percent of sales, which is not enough to cover operating expenses. Table 10-1 presents simple formulas for markup calculations.

Table 10-1 Formulas for Markup Calculations

$$\text{Cost} + \text{Markup} = \text{Selling price}$$

$$\text{Cost} = \text{Selling price} - \text{Markup}$$

$$\text{Markup} = \text{Selling price} - \text{Cost}$$

$$\frac{\text{Markup}}{\text{Selling price}} \times 100 = \text{Markup expressed as a percent of selling price}$$

$$\frac{\text{Markup}}{\text{Cost}} \times 100 = \text{Markup expressed as a percent of cost}$$

If a seller wishes to translate markup as a percent of selling price into a percent of cost, or vice versa, the two formulas below are useful:

$$\frac{\text{Markup as a percent of selling price}}{100\% - \text{Markup as a percent of selling price}} \times 100 = \text{Markup as a percent of cost}$$

$$\frac{\text{Markup as a percent of cost}}{100\% + \text{Markup as a percent of cost}} \times 100 = \text{Markup as a percent of selling price}$$

CREDIT IN SMALL BUSINESS

Credit involves a sale on the basis of trust. In a credit sale, the seller conveys goods or services to the buyer in return for the buyer's promise to pay. The major objective in granting credit is an expansion of sales by attracting new customers and an increase in volume and regularity of purchases by existing customers. Some retail firms—furniture stores, for example—cater to newcomers in the city, newly married couples, and others by inviting the credit business of individuals with established credit ratings. In addition, credit records may be used for purposes of sales promotion by direct mail appeals to credit customers. Adjustments and exchanges of goods are also facilitated through credit operations.

Benefits of Credit to Sellers and Buyers

If credit buying and selling did not benefit both parties to the transaction, its use would cease. Firms extend credit to customers because they can obtain increased sales volume in this way. They expect the increased revenue to more than offset credit costs so that profits will increase.

Buyers also benefit from the use of credit. Their most obvious advantage is the deferred-payment privilege. Small firms, in particular, benefit from the judicious extension of credit by suppliers. Credit supplies the small firm with working capital and also permits continuation of marginal businesses that would otherwise expire. Buyers also find credit to be a convenience in many cases. Ultimate consumers need not carry large amounts of cash, and business buyers need not become involved in the cumbersome process of delivering cash prior to shipment of purchased goods.

Kinds of Credit

There are two broad classes of credit: consumer credit and trade credit. **Consumer credit** is granted by retailers to final consumers who purchase for personal or family use. **Trade credit** is extended by nonfinancial firms, such as manufacturers or wholesalers, to customers which are other business firms.

Consumer credit and trade credit differ as to types of credit instruments used and sources for financing receivables. Another important distinction is the availability of credit insurance for trade credit only. They also differ markedly as to terms of sale.

Consumer Credit. The four major kinds of consumer-credit accounts are: ordinary charge accounts, installment accounts, budget accounts, and revolving credit accounts. Many variations of these are also used.

Charge Accounts. Under the **ordinary charge account**, the customer obtains possession of goods (or services) when purchased, with payment due when billed. Stated terms typically call for payment at the end of the month, but customary practice allows a longer period for payment than that stated. The charge account is best used for recurring family expenses. Small accounts at department stores are a good example of such use.

Three types of credit cards are issued today by business organizations. One type is issued by major department stores and oil companies to customers with proved credit standings. Another type is issued by businesses engaged in the area of travel and entertainment such as American Express Company. Other popular credit cards are VISA and MASTER CARD, which are issued by a network of franchise-holding banks and can be used for virtually any good or service. In the case of VISA and MASTER CARD, the bank collects from the card-holding consumer and remits the amount to the participating retailer, less commission. Participating retailers also pay certain fees for joining, cash accommodation, merchant membership advertising, and rental for imprinting machines. The advantages of participation are increased sales volume and elimination of some record-keeping costs.

Installment Accounts. The **installment account** is the vehicle of long-term consumer credit. A down payment is normally required, and it is typically 20 percent or more of the purchase price. Finance charges must be disclosed in accordance with the Truth-in-Lending Act. The most common payment periods are from 12 to 36 months, although in recent years automobile dealers have extended payment periods to 60 months. An installment account is useful for large purchases such as automobiles, washing machines, and television sets.

The seller must also determine, in view of the different state laws, whether the credit should be secured by a conditional sales contract or a chattel mortgage. Under a **conditional sales contract**, legal title to the product does not pass until the customer makes the last payment; immediate repossession is possible in case a payment is defaulted. When a **chattel mortgage** is used, legal title passes when the sale is made but is subject to the seller's lien. When a payment is defaulted, the seller can take court action to repossess and resell the goods.

Budget Accounts. The **budget account**, sometimes called a Major Purchase Account (MPA), might be defined as a short-term installment account. It results from charge purchases in amounts typically ranging from $200 to $400, and payment is ordinarily spread over a period of three months. A consumer may purchase a power lawn mower or a set of tires, for example, in this way. Budget accounts are readily extended by many small merchants, but a service charge normally is added to the price when payments are deferred over 90 days. Monthly statements are usually not sent; this eliminates billing cost and places the responsibility for adhering to payment schedules on the customers.

Revolving Credit Accounts. The **revolving credit account** is another variation of the installment account. The seller may grant a line of credit up to $400 or $500, for example, and the customer may then charge purchases at any time if purchases do not exceed this credit limit. A specified percentage of the outstanding balance must be paid monthly, which forces the customer to budget and limits the amount of debt that can be carried. Finance charges are computed on the unpaid balance at the end of the month.

Trade Credit. Business firms may sell goods subject to specified terms of sale, such as 2/10, n/30. This means that a 2 percent discount is given by the seller if the buyer pays within 10 days. Failure to take this discount makes the full amount of the invoice due in 30 days. Other discount arrangements in common use are shown in Table 10-2.

Sales terms in trade credit depend on the kind of product sold and the buyer's and seller's circumstances. The credit period often varies directly with the length of the buyer's turnover period, which obviously depends on the type of product sold. The larger the order and the higher the credit rating of the buyer, the better the sales terms that can be granted if individual sales terms are fixed for each customer. The greater the financial strength and the more adequate and liquid the working capital of the seller, the more generous

Table 10-2 Trade-Credit Terms

Sales Term	Explanation
3/10, 1/15, n/60	Three percent discount for first 10 days; one percent discount for 15 days; net on 60th day.
M. O. M.	Billing twice a month; for example, on the 10th and 25th.
E. O. M.	Billing at end of month, covering all credit purchases of that month.
C. O. D.	Amount of bill will be collected upon delivery of the goods
2/10, n/30, R.O. G.	Two percent discount for 10 days; net on 30th day—but both discount period and 30 days start from the date of delivery of the goods.
2/10, n/30, M. O. M.	Two percent discount for 10 days; net on the 30th day—but both periods start from the invoice date following the sales date.
2/10, n/30, E. O. M.	Two percent discount for 10 days; net on 30th day—but both periods start from the end of the month in which the sale was made.

the seller's sales terms can be. Of course, no business can afford to allow competitors to outdo it in reasonable generosity of sales terms. In many lines of business, credit terms are so firmly set by tradition that a unique policy is difficult, if not impossible.

The Decision to Sell on Credit

Nearly all small businesses can sell on credit if they wish, and so the entrepreneur must decide whether to sell for cash or on credit. In some cases this is reduced to the question, "Can the granting of credit to customers be avoided?" Credit selling is standard trade practice in many lines of business, and in other businesses credit-selling competitors will always outsell the cash-selling firm.

Factors That Affect the Credit Decision. Numerous factors bear on the decision concerning credit extension. The seller always hopes to increase profits by credit sales, but each firm must also consider its own particular circumstances and environment.

Type of Business. Retailers of durable goods, for example, typically grant credit more freely than small grocers who sell perishables. Indeed, most consumers find it necessary to buy big-ticket items on an installment basis, and the product's life makes installment selling possible.

Credit Policy of Competitors. Unless a firm offers some compensating advantage, it is expected to be as generous as its competitors in extending credit. Wholesale hardware companies and retail furniture stores are businesses that face stiff competition from credit sellers.

Income Level of Customers. The income level of customers is a significant factor in determining a retailer's credit policy. Consider, for example, a corner drugstore adjacent to a city high school. High school students are typically unsatisfactory credit customers because of their lack of maturity and income.

Availability of Adequate Working Capital. There is no denying the fact that credit sales increase the amount of working capital needed by the business. Money that the business has tied up in open-credit and installment accounts cannot be used to pay business expenses.

The Four C's of Credit. In evaluating the credit standing of applicants, the entrepreneur must answer the following questions:

1. Can the buyer pay as promised?
2. Will the buyer pay?
3. If so, when will the buyer pay?
4. If not, can the buyer be forced to pay?

Before credit is approved, the answers to questions 1, 2, and 4 must be "yes"; to question 3, "on schedule." The answers depend in part on the amount of credit requested and in part on the seller's estimate of the buyer's ability and willingness to pay. Such an estimate constitutes a judgment of the buyer's inherent credit worth.

Every credit applicant possesses credit worth in some degree so that extended credit is not necessarily a gift to the applicant. Instead, a decision to grant credit merely recognizes the buyer's earned credit standing. But the seller faces a possible inability or unwillingness to pay on the buyer's part. In making credit decisions, therefore, the seller decides the degree of risk of nonpayment that must be assumed.

Willingness to pay is evaluated in terms of the four C's of credit: character, capital, capacity, and conditions.[12] *Character* refers to the fundamental integrity and honesty which should underlie all human and business relationships. In the case of a business customer, it takes shape in the business policies and ethical practices of the firm. Individual customers who apply for credit must also be known to be morally responsible persons. *Capital* consists of the cash and other assets owned by the business or individual customer. In the case of a business customer, this means capital sufficient to underwrite planned operations, including adequate owner capital. *Capacity* refers to the business customer's ability to conserve assets and faithfully and efficiently follow financial plans. The business customer with capacity utilizes the invested capital of the business firm wisely and capitalizes to the fullest extent on business opportunities. *Conditions* refer to such factors as business cycles and changes in price levels which may be either favorable or unfavorable to the payment of debts. Other adverse factors which might limit a customer's ability to pay include fires and other natural disasters, new legislation, strong new competition, or labor problems.

Credit Investigation of Applicants. In most retail stores, the first step in credit investigation is the completion of an application form. The information obtained on this form is used as the basis for examining the applicant's financial responsibility.

---

12. Around the turn of the century, a noted financier and venture capitalist said that he would provide anyone having CHARACTER and CAPACITY with the necessary capital for launching a business, thus suggesting that only two factors are really needed. However, the borrower's capital position and the prevailing economic conditions would either facilitate payment or make it difficult.

Nonretailing firms should similarly investigate credit applicants. One small clothing manufacturer has every sales order reviewed by a Dun & Bradstreet-trained credit manager who maintains a complete file of D&B credit reports on thousands of customers. Recent financial statements of dealer-customers are filed also. These, together with the dealer's accounts-receivable card, are the basis for decisions on credit sales, with major emphasis on the D&B credit reports.

Credit Limits. Perhaps the most important factor in determining a customer's credit limits is the customer's ability to pay the obligation when it becomes due. This in turn requires an evaluation of the customer's financial resources, debt position, and income level.

The amount of credit required by the customer is the second factor that requires consideration. Customers of a drugstore need only small amounts of credit. On the other hand, business customers of wholesalers and manufacturers typically expect larger amounts of credit. In the special case of installment selling, the amount of credit should not exceed the repossession value of the goods sold. Automobile dealers follow this rule as a general practice.

Sources of Credit Information. One of the most important and frequently neglected sources of credit information is found in the accounts-receivable records of the seller. Properly analyzed, these records show whether the customer regularly takes cash discounts and, if not, whether the customer's account is typically slow.

Manufacturers and wholesalers frequently can use the financial statements submitted by firms applying for credit as an additional source of information. Obtaining maximum value from financial statements requires a careful ratio analysis which will reveal working-capital position, profit-making potential, and general financial health of the firm.

Pertinent data may also be obtained from outsiders. For example, arrangements may be made with other suppliers to exchange credit data. Such credit interchange reports are quite useful in learning about the sales and payment experiences of others with one's own credit customers or applicants.

Another source of credit data, on commercial accounts particularly, is the customer's banker. Some bankers are glad to supply credit information about their depositors, considering this a service in helping them to obtain credit in amounts they can successfully handle. Other bankers feel that credit information is confidential and should not be disclosed in this way.

Organizations that may be consulted with reference to credit standings are trade-credit agencies and local credit bureaus. **Trade-credit agencies** are privately owned and operated organizations which collect credit information on business firms. After they analyze and evaluate the data, they make credit ratings available to client companies for a fee. These agencies are concerned with trade-credit ratings only, having nothing to do with consumer credit. Dun & Bradstreet, Inc., is a general trade-credit agency serving the nation. Manufacturers and wholesalers are especially interested in its reference book and credit reports. The reference book covers all United States businesses and shows credit rating, financial strength, and other key credit information. It is available to subscribers only.

A **credit bureau** serves its members—retailers and other firms in a given community— by summarizing their credit experience with particular individuals. A local bureau can also broaden its service by affiliation with either the National Retail Credit Association or the Associated Credit Bureaus of America. This makes possible the exchange of credit information on persons who move from one city to another. A business firm need not be a member of some bureaus in order to get a credit report. The fee charged to nonmembers, however, is considerably higher than that charged to members.

Collection of Past-Due Accounts

Slow credit accounts are a problem because they tie up the seller's working capital, prevent further sales to the slow-paying customer, and lead to losses from bad debts. Even if the slow-paying customer is not lost, relations with this customer are strained for a time at least.

Inadequate records and collection procedures often fail to alert the small firm in time to permit prompt collections. Also, the personal acquaintance of seller and customer sometimes tempts the seller to be less than businesslike in extending further credit and collecting overdue accounts. Conceding the seriousness of the problem, the small firm must know what steps to take and how far to go in collecting past-due accounts. It must decide whether to undertake the job directly or to turn it over to an attorney or a collection agency.

Collection Procedure. Perhaps the most effective weapon in collecting past-due accounts is the debtors' knowledge of possible impairment of their credit standing. This impairment is certain if an account is turned over to a collection agency. Delinquent customers who foresee continued solvency will typically attempt to avoid damage to their credit standing, particularly when it would be known to the business community generally. It is this knowledge that lies behind and strengthens the various collection efforts of the business.

Most business firms have found that the most effective collection procedure consists of a series of steps, each of which is somewhat more forceful than the preceding one. Although these typically begin with a gentle written reminder, they may include additional letters, telephone calls, registered letters, personal contacts, and referrals to collection agencies or attorneys. The timing of these steps may be carefully standardized so that step two automatically follows step one in a specified number of days, with subsequent steps similarly spaced.[13]

The Bad-Debt Ratio. In controlling expenses associated with credit sales, it is possible to use various expense ratios. The best known and most widely used ratio is the **bad-debt ratio**, which is computed by dividing the amount of bad debts by the total credit sales.

The bad-debt ratio reflects the efficiency of credit policies and procedures. A small firm may thus compare the effectiveness of its credit management with that of other firms. There is a relationship between the bad-debt ratio on the one hand and the type of business, profitability, and size of firm on the other. Small profitable retailers have a much higher loss ratio than large profitable retailers. The bad-debt losses of all small-business firms, however, may range from a fraction of one percent of net sales to percentages large enough to put them out of business!

LOOKING BACK

1. The four main functions of channel intermediaries are breaking-bulk, assorting, providing information, and risk taking. A channel of distribution with no intermediaries is a direct channel. An indirect channel is one that uses intermediaries such as retailers, industrial distributors, agents, or merchant wholesalers.
2. Choosing a distribution system involves considerations of costs, coverage, and control. The main components of physical distribution are transportation, storage, materials handling, delivery terms, and inventory management.
3. Small business is becoming more and more involved in exporting. The small business can learn about foreign markets through available publications, personal visits to the country, and talks with people who have visited the market. Numerous channel options are available to exporters.
4. Cost considerations in pricing involve an understanding of the components of total variable costs and of total fixed costs. Demand considerations involve such factors as product appeal, marketing effort, and product price, all of which exert an influence on demand. An understanding of elastic demand and inelastic demand is also important.

   Break-even analysis in pricing entails a formal comparison of cost and demand for purposes of determining the acceptability of alternative prices.

13. An excellent article on managing accounts receivable is Steven D. Popell, "Effectively Manage Receivables to Cut Costs," *Harvard Business Review*, Vol. 59, No. 1 (January-February, 1981), pp. 58-64.

Fixed and variable costs are used to construct a cost break-even chart. Demand factors can be incorporated to construct a cost-adjusted break-even chart.

5. By extending credit, sellers can increase sales volume and expect the increased revenue to more than offset credit costs so that their profits will increase. Benefits from the use of credit by buyers consist of deferred-payment privileges, convenience, and a supply of working capital. The small business should consider several factors, such as the type of business, the credit policy of competitors, the income level of customers, and the availability of adequate working capital, before deciding to sell on credit. It should evaluate the credit standing of applicants in terms of the four C's of credit—character, capital, capacity, and conditions.

DISCUSSION QUESTIONS

1. How does physical distribution differ from a channel of distribution?
2. Discuss the major considerations in structuring a channel of distribution.
3. What are the major components of a physical distribution system?
4. If a small business has conducted its break-even analysis properly and finds break-even at a $10 price to be 10,000 units, should it price its product at $10? Discuss.
5. What is the psychology behind price lining?
6. What is the difference between consumer credit and trade credit?
7. What is meant by the terms 2/10, n/30? Does it pay to take discounts?
8. If the small-business owner has adequate investment to cover all working-capital needs, does it cost as much to sell on credit as it costs to borrow? Why?
9. Which of the "four C's" seems most important in considering extension of credit to an ultimate consumer? Is the same true in extending credit to a manufacturer or wholesaler?
10. Does the fact that a business is small make personal contact superior to letters in collecting past-due accounts?

REFERENCES TO SMALL BUSINESS IN ACTION

"Arrow Electronics: On Target." *Financial World*, Vol. 148, No. 19 (October 1, 1979), pp. 49-50.

This article explains how three Harvard Business School students, upon graduation, successfully entered the field of electronics distribution.

Buckley, Jerry. "Timesharing, 1980's Style." *Venture*, Vol. 2, No. 8 (August, 1980), pp. 32-36.

The time-sharing of resort condominiums is rooted in the price escalation of building. Several pricing plans are included in this report of a new venture.

Gupta, Udayan. "A New Breed of Sales Rep." *Venture*, Vol. 3, No. 3 (March, 1981), pp. 57-58.

The experiences of several women sales representatives are related in this report. Some advantages of starting a sales organization are included in the discussion.

Marion, Larry. "Exporting Without Tears." *Forbes*, Vol. 127, No. 8 (April 13, 1981), pp. 62-66.

Interesting accounts of the exporting experiences of four small businesses are provided in this article.

Rose, Carol. "Extending and Collecting—Exercises in Credit." *In Business*, Vol. 3, No. 2 (March-April, 1981), pp. 44-45.

The collection experiences of several small businesses are related in this article, which also describes the use of collection services.

Chapter 11

Personal Selling, Advertising, and Sales Promotion

LOOKING AHEAD

Watch for the following important topics:

1. Considerations in developing a promotional mix.
2. Methods of determining promotional expenditures.
3. Preparing and making a sales presentation.
4. Advertising options for the small business.
5. Uses and tools of sales promotion.

Despite the old adage, "Build a better mousetrap and the world will beat a path to your door," the entrepreneur must turn to promotion. Why? Because potential customers, at the very minimum, must be informed of the new, improved "mousetrap" and how to get to the door! They may even need to be persuaded that the mousetrap is better. This process of informing and persuading is one of communication. **Promotion** is communication between the small business and its target market.

Naturally, small businesses use promotion in varying degrees. Any given firm can use all or part of the many available promotional tools. The three groupings of promotional methods presented in this chapter are personal selling, advertising, and sales promotion.

PROMOTIONAL PLANNING

Small businesses sometimes stand in awe of promotional planning. They are confused by rate schedules, reach, and frequency terminology, as well as the numerous options which are available. Promotion is admittedly a complex area, and most entrepreneurs are not "turned" in that direction. But understanding promotion can begin by realizing the simple fact that promotion is largely communication. In fact, promotion is worthless unless it communicates. Let's briefly look at the communication process and see how promotion needs to be built on these ideas.

The Communication Process

All of us communicate each day. However, we may not have stopped to analyze our communications to realize that communication is a process with identifiable parts. Figure 11-1 depicts the various parts of communication. Part A in the figure represents a personal communication. Part B represents a small-business communication (promotion).

As you can see, the differences between Parts A and B in Figure 11-1 are in form, not in basic structure. Each communication involves a source, a channel, and a receiver. In Part B the receiver for the small-business communication from the XYZ Company is the customer. The receiver for Gwen Doe's personal communication is Charles Buck. She has used three different channels for her message: personal conversation, the telephone, and a special window message. The XYZ Company has used similar message channels: face-to-face communication (personal selling), the radio (advertising), and a hot air balloon circling the city (sales promotional tool).

At this point your understanding of promotion and its roots in personal communication should be clearer. We now will turn to the particulars of molding a strong promotional plan. A good promotional plan must consider three major topics: which promotional tools to mix together, how much to spend, and how to create the messages for the tools.

The Promotional Mix

The mixture of the various promotional methods—personal selling, advertising, and sales promotion—is influenced by two major factors. First—and always more important—is the nature of the market to be reached. A widely dispersed market tends to favor mass coverage by advertising, in contrast to the more costly individual contacts of personal selling. On the other hand, if the market is local with a relatively small number of customers, personal selling will be more feasible.

A small business must also understand (as discussed in Chapter 5) who its customers are. It is expensive to use shotgun promotion, which "hits"

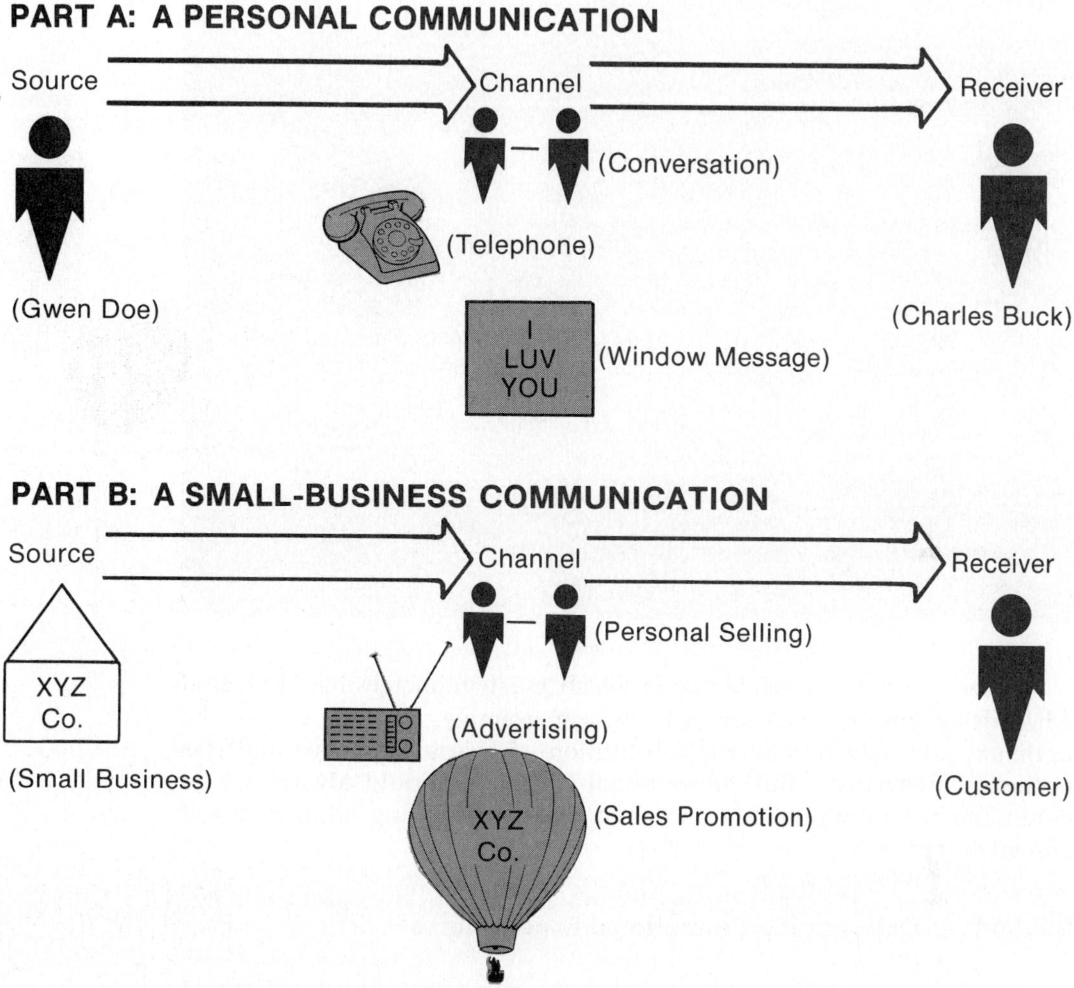

Figure 11-1 An Analogy of Personal and Small-Business Communication

potential customers and nonpotential customers alike. This error can be minimized by knowing media audiences. The media are extremely helpful in profiling their audiences. But a small business cannot obtain a media match until it has specified its target market carefully. Personal selling is more widely used for marketing to industrial markets than to consumer markets.

The second factor that influences the promotional mix is the product's own characteristics. If a product is of high unit value, personal selling will be a vital ingredient in the mix. Personal selling will also be prominent for promoting highly technical products. On the other hand, sales promotion will more likely be used on an impulse good than on a shopping good.

ACTION REPORT: Shotgun Approach Backfires

Too often, it seems, a small business will spend money to promote its products without understanding its market. A West Coast industrial design firm is an unfortunate example of this tendency.

The company spent $25,000 in a special campaign encompassing virtually every type of media to attract new clients to its design service. It "got a lot of exposure, but very few new clients." The problem was recognized as "going everywhere and anywhere with a 'blitzkrieg' approach."

The company's shotgun approach was dropped and replaced by one "directed only to companies that really needed their services." Direct mail, trade magazines, and special seminars were blended into the new promotional mix.

The market was reached successfully. An inquiry list of more than 50 potential customers was obtained, as well as 8 new clients. All of this occurred in three months.

Source: John E. Shea, "Target Your Market to Rake in Profits," *Industrial Marketing*, Vol. 64, No. 12 (December, 1979), pp. 66–68.

There are other considerations which must ultimately be considered when developing the promotional mix. For example, the high cost of the optimum mix may necessitate substitution of a less expensive and less optimum alternative. But promotional planning should always try to determine the optimum mix and then make cost-saving adjustments if absolutely necessary.

Methods of Determining Promotional Expenditures

There is no simple formula to answer the question, "How much should a small business spend on promotion?" There are, however, some helpful approaches to solving the problem. The most common methods of earmarking funds for promotion are:

1. A percentage of sales (APS).
2. What can be spared (WCS).
3. As much as competition spends (ACS).
4. What it takes to do the job (WTDJ).

A Percentage of Sales (APS). Earmarking a percentage of sales is a simple method for a small business to use. A company's own past experiences are evaluated to establish a promotional-sales ratio. If 2 percent of sales, for example, has historically been spent on promotion, the business would budget 2 percent of forecasted sales. Secondary data can be checked to locate industry ratio averages for comparison.

The major shortcoming of this method is its inherent tendency to spend more dollars when sales are increasing and less when they are declining.[1] If promotion stimulates sales, the reverse would seem desirable.

What Can Be Spared (WCS). The most widely used approach to promotional funding is to spend what is left over when other activities have been completed. Or a budget may be nonexistent and spending is determined only when a media representative sells the entrepreneur on a special deal. Such a piecemeal approach to promotional spending should be avoided.

As Much as Competition Spends (ACS). If the small business can duplicate the promotional mix of close competitors, it will be spending approximately as much as competition. This approach is generally unworkable for planning the entire promotional budget. However, it can be used to react to a special short-run effort by close competitors.

What It Takes to Do the Job (WTDJ). The preferred approach to estimating promotional expenditures is to decide what it takes to do the job. This method requires a complete analysis of the market and promotional alternatives. Assuming reasonably accurate estimates, this approach determines the amount that truly needs to be spent.

Our recommendation to a small business for estimating promotional expenditures involves all four approaches. Start with an estimate of what it takes to do the job (WTDJ). If this estimate is equal to or smaller than any of the other three estimates, proceed to invest that amount in promotion. If the WTDJ estimate is larger than any of the others, compute the average of the four estimates [(WTDJ + APS + WCS + ACS)/4]. Then compare the WCS estimate with this average. If WCS equals or exceeds the average estimate, proceed to develop the promotion at the average estimate. On the other hand, if the WCS is less than the average, additional funds for promotion should be sought. The logic of these steps is represented by the flowchart in Figure 11-2.

Sources of Promotional Expertise

Most small businesses must rely on others' expertise in creating promotional messages. There are two main sources for this specialized assistance: the advertising media and the advertising agency.

---

1. A strong case for maintaining or increasing advertising efforts in times of business downturns is made in J. Wesley Rosberg, "Is a Recession on the Way? It's No Time to Cut Ad Budgets," *Industrial Marketing*, Vol. 64, No. 4 (April, 1979), pp. 64-79.

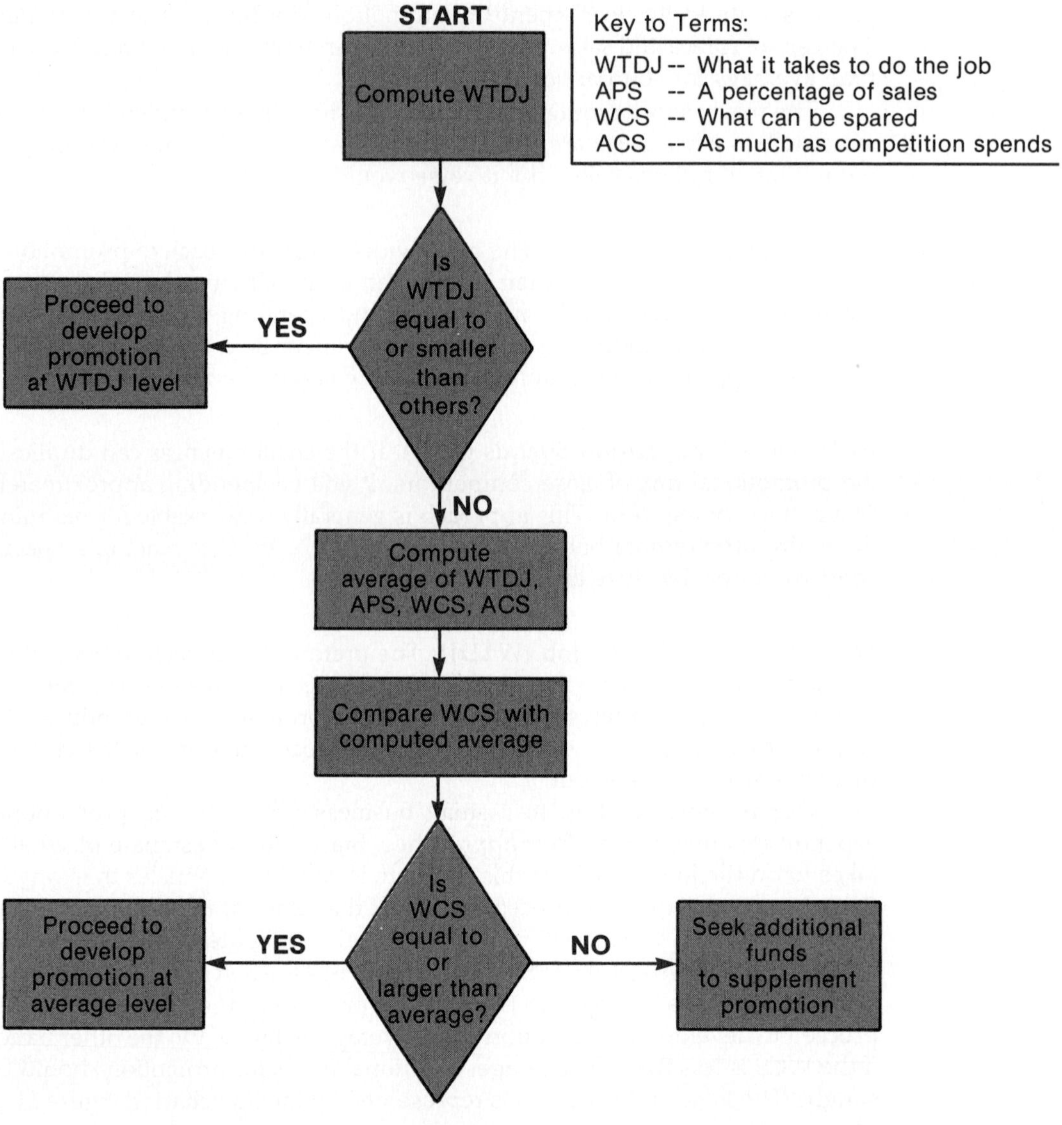

Figure 11-2 A Flowchart for Comparing Alternative Promotion Expense Estimates

Some of the services that advertising agencies provide are:

1. To furnish design, artwork, and copy for specific advertisements and/or commercials.
2. To evaluate and recommend the advertising media with the greatest "pulling power."

3. To evaluate the effectiveness of different advertising appeals.
4. To advise on sales promotions and merchandise displays.
5. To make market-sampling studies for evaluating product acceptance or area sales potentials and to furnish mailing lists.

Since an advertising agency may charge a fee for its services, the advertiser must make sure that the return from those services will be greater than the fees paid. Only a competent agency can be of real aid to the advertiser.[2]

Other outside sources may also provide assistance in formulating and carrying out promotional programs. Suppliers often furnish display aids and even complete advertising programs to their dealers. Trade associations also are active in this area. Finally, the advertising media can provide some of the same services offered by an ad agency.

PERSONAL SELLING

Many products require personal selling. Sales procured via catalogs, direct mail, and other impersonal techniques are merely exceptions to the general rule. **Personal selling** is promotion delivered in a one-on-one environment. It includes the activities of both the inside salespersons of retail, wholesale, and service establishments and the outside sales representatives who call on business establishments and ultimate consumers.

Importance of Product Knowledge

Effective selling must be built upon a foundation of product knowledge. If salespeople know the product's advantages, uses, and limitations, they can educate the customers and successfully meet objections. Most customers look to the salesperson for such information—whether the product is a camera, a suit of clothes, an automobile, paint, a machine tool, or an office machine. Customers seldom are specialists in the products they buy; however, they immediately sense the knowledge or the ignorance of the salesperson. The significance of product knowledge is revealed by the fact that personal selling degenerates into mere order-taking where such knowledge is not possessed by the salesperson.

The Sales Presentation

The heart of personal selling is the sales presentation to the prospective customer. At this crucial point the order is either secured or lost. The first

2. Some ideas on selecting an agency are found in Leland J. Katz, "Guide to Marketing Communications for New and Small Business Advertisers," *Industrial Marketing*, Vol. 62, No. 6 (June, 1977), p. 107.

step in preparing an effective sales presentation is **prospecting**, a systematic process of continually looking for new customers. The time to look is before you need them.[3]

Techniques of Prospecting. One of the most efficient techniques of prospecting is through *personal* referrals. Referrals come from personal friends, customers, and other businesses. The initial contact with a potential customer is greatly facilitated by the ability to mention that, "You were referred to me by . . ."

Another technique of prospecting is through *impersonal* referrals. Examples of impersonal referrals are media publications, public records, and directories. Newspapers and magazines, particularly trade magazines, also help identify prospects. These publications report on new companies entering the market, as well as on new products. Prospects can be derived from this information. For example, wedding announcements in the newspaper are impersonal referrals for a local bridal shop.

Public records of property transactions and building permits can also provide prospects. For example, a garbage pick-up service might find prospective customers from those who are planning to build houses or apartments.

Prospects can also be identified without referrals through marketer-initiated contacts. Telephone calls or mail surveys, for example, isolate prospects. One market survey conducted for a small business by an author of this text used a mail questionnaire to identify prospects. The questionnaire, which asked technical questions about a service, concluded with the following statement: "If you would be interested in a service of this nature, please check the appropriate space below and your name will be added to the mailing list."

Prospects can also be identified by recording customer-initiated contacts. Inquiries by a potential customer which do not conclude in a sale would classify that person as a "hot" prospect. Small furniture stores will often require their salespeople to create a card for each person visiting the retail store. These prospects are then systematically contacted over the telephone, and records of these contacts should be updated periodically.

Practicing. The old saying that "practice makes perfect" applies to the salesperson prior to making the sales presentation. If you are a salesperson, make the presentation to your spouse, a mirror, or a tape recorder. You may feel a little silly the first few times, but this method will improve your success rate. One sales textbook emphasizes the importance of practice with the following comments:

---

3. For an interesting analysis of the importance of "setting the stage" in a sales presentation, see "Why First Impressions Count," *Industrial Distribution*, Vol. 70, No. 1 (January, 1980), pp. 79-80.

Prepare . . . A Houston salesman accepted the challenge to spend as much as twice the time preparing for his sales presentation as he had been spending on making the presentation. He reported that he cut his selling time in front of the prospect from an hour and a half to eight minutes! Plus, he increased the size of the sale by over 50 percent.[4]

The salesperson should also be aware of possible objections and should prepare how to handle them. Experience is the best teacher here; however, there are ten frequently used techniques which have proven helpful.[5] These are listed and briefly discussed below.

1. *Product comparison*. When the prospect is mentally comparing a product being used now or a competing product with the salesperson's product, the salesperson may make a complete comparison of the two. The salesperson lists the advantages and disadvantages of each.
2. *Relating a case history*. Here the salesperson describes the experiences of another prospect similar to the prospect to whom he or she is talking.
3. *Demonstration*. A product demonstration gives a quite convincing answer to a product objection because the salesperson lets the product itself overcome the opposition.
4. *Giving guarantees*. Often a guarantee will remove resistance from the prospect's mind. Guarantees assure prospects that they cannot lose by purchasing. The caution, of course, is that guarantees must be meaningful and must provide for some recourse on the part of the prospect if the product does not live up to the guarantee.
5. *Asking questions*. The "why" question is of value in separating excuses from genuine objections and in probing for hidden resistance. The same question is useful in disposing of objections. Probing or exploratory questions are excellent in handling silent resistance. They can be worded and asked in a manner that appeals to the prospect's ego. In making the prospect do some thinking to convince the salesperson, questions of a probing nature get the prospect's full attention.
6. *Showing what delay costs*. A common experience of salespeople is to obtain seemingly sincere agreements to the buying decisions concerning need, product, source, and price, only to find that the prospect wants to wait some time before buying. In such cases, the salesperson can sometimes take pencil and paper to show conclusively that delay of the purchase is expensive.
7. *Admitting and counterbalancing*. Sometimes the prospect's objection is completely valid because of some limitation in the salesperson's product. The only course of action in this case is for the salesperson to agree that the product does have the disadvantage to which the prospect is obviously objecting. Immediately after the acknowledgement, however, the salesperson should direct the prospect's attention to the advantages which overshadow the limitation of the product.
8. *Hearing the prospect out*. Some prospects object mainly for the opportunity to describe how they were once victimized. The technique recommended for

---

4. James F. Robeson, H. Lee Mathews, and Carl G. Stevens, *Selling* (Homewood, IL: Richard D. Irwin, Inc., 1978), pp. 85-86.

5. Charles A. Kirkpatrick and Frederick A. Russ, *Effective Selling* (7th ed.; Cincinnati: South-Western Publishing Co., 1981), pp. 254-255. Reproduced with permission.

this type of resistance is that of sympathetic listening.

9. *Making the objection boomerang*. Once in a while the salesperson can take a prospect's reason for not buying and convert it into a reason for buying. This takes expert handling. Suppose the prospect says, "I'm too busy to see you." The salesperson might reply, "That's why you should see me—I can save you time."
10. *The "Yes, but" technique*. The best technique for handling most resistance is the indirect answer known as the "Yes, but" method. Here are two examples of what salespeople might say when using this technique: (1) "Yes, I can understand that attitude, but there is another angle for you to consider." (2) "Yes, you have a point there, but in your particular circumstances, other points are involved, too." The "Yes, but" method avoids argument and friction. It respects the prospect's opinions, attitudes, and thinking, and operates well where the prospect's point does not apply in a particular case.

Making the Sales Presentation. Salespersons must adapt their sales approach to the customer's needs. A "canned" sales talk will not succeed with most buyers. For example, the salesperson of bookkeeping machines must demonstrate the capacity of the equipment to solve a customer's particular bookkeeping problems. Similarly, a boat salesperson must understand the special interests of particular individuals in boating and talk the customer's language. Every sales objection must be answered explicitly and adequately.

There is considerable psychology in successful selling. The salesperson, as a psychologist, must know that some degree of personal enthusiasm, friendliness, and persistence is required. Perhaps 20 percent of all salespersons secure as much as 80 percent of all sales made. This is because they are the 20 percent who persist and who bring enthusiasm and friendliness to the task of selling.

Some salespersons have special sales "gimmicks" which they use with success. One automobile salesperson, for example, offered free driving lessons to people who had never taken a driver's training course or who needed a few more lessons before they felt confident enough to take the required driving tests. When such customers were ready to take the driving tests, this salesperson accompanied them to the driver examination grounds for moral support. Needless to say, these special efforts could hardly be turned down by new drivers who were in the market for cars.

Cost Control in Personal Selling

There are both economic and wasteful methods of achieving the same volume of sales. For example, the efficient routing of traveling salespersons and the making of appointments prior to arrival can conserve time and transportation expense. The cost of an outside sales call on a customer may be considerable—perhaps $80 or more. This emphasizes the need for efficient, intelligent scheduling. Moreover, the salesperson for a manufacturing firm can contribute to cost economy by stressing products which most need selling in order to give the factory a balanced run of production.

Profitability is increased to the extent that sales are made on the basis of quality and service rather than price-cutting. All products do not have the same margin of profit, however, and the salesperson can maximize profits by emphasizing high-margin lines.

Compensating the Salespeople

Salespeople are compensated in two ways for their efforts: financially and nonfinancially. The goals of salespeople may differ from those of the entrepreneur. For example, the entrepreneur may be seeking nonfinancial goals, but the salespeople may not. A good compensation program will allow its participants to work for both forms of rewards.

Nonfinancial Rewards. Personal recognition and the satisfaction of reaching a sales quota are examples of nonfinancial rewards. A person can be motivated by these goals. Many retail small businesses will post the photograph of the top salesperson of the week on the bulletin board for all to see. Plaques are also used for a more permanent record of sales achievements.

Financial Rewards. Nonfinancial compensation is important to salespeople, but it doesn't put bread on the table. Financial compensation is typically the more critical issue. There are two basic plans of financial compensation: commissions and straight salary. Each has specific advantages and limitations.

Most small businesses would prefer to use a commission plan of compensation, which is simple and directly related to productivity. A certain percentage of the sales generated is the salesperson's commission. A commission plan incorporates a strong incentive into the selling activities—no sale, no income! With this type of plan, there is no drain on cash flow until there is a sale.

With the straight salary form of compensation, salespeople have more security because their level of compensation is assured regardless of personal sales made. However, this method can tend to make a salesperson lazy.

A combination of the two forms of compensation can give the small business the "best of two worlds." It is a common practice to structure the combination plan so that salary represents the larger part for new salespeople. As the salesperson gains experience, the ratio is adjusted to provide a greater share from commissions and less from salary.

Building Customer Goodwill

The salesperson must look beyond the immediate sale to build customer goodwill and to create satisfied customers who will patronize the company in the future. One way to accomplish this is to preserve a good appearance, display a pleasant personality, and demonstrate good habits in all contacts with the customer. One can also help build goodwill by understanding the customer's point of view. Courtesy, attention to details, and genuine friendliness will help to gain acceptance with the customer.

Of course, high ethical standards are of primary importance in creating customer goodwill. This rules out misrepresentation and calls for confidential treatment of a customer's plans. Certainly the salesperson who receives secret information from a buying firm should preserve the confidence of that firm.

ADVERTISING

Advertising is the impersonal presentation of an idea which is identified with a business sponsor and is projected through mass media. The media used include television, radio, magazines, newspapers, and billboards. Advertising is a vital part of every small-business operation. As Steuart Henderson Britt has expressed it, "Doing business without advertising is like winking at a girl in the dark." You know what you are doing, but no one else does.

Objectives of Advertising

The primary goal of advertising is to draw attention to the existence or superiority of a firm's product or service. To be successful, it must rest upon a foundation of product quality and efficient service. Advertising can bring no more than temporary success to an inferior product. For example, through advertising a restaurant may entice customers to give it a trial; but only good food, fair prices, and prompt service can build repeat business. Advertising may also accentuate a trend in the sale of an item or product line, but it seldom has the power to reverse such a trend. It must, consequently, be closely related to changes in customer needs and preferences.

Used superficially, advertising may appear to be a waste of money. It seems expensive, while adding little utility to the product. Nevertheless, the major alternative is personal solicitation of potential customers, which is often more expensive and time-consuming.

Types of Advertising

There are two types of advertising—product advertising and institutional advertising. **Product advertising** is designed to make potential customers aware of a particular product or service and of their need for it. **Institutional advertising**, on the other hand, conveys an idea regarding the business establishment. It is intended to keep the public conscious of the company and of its good reputation.[6] Figures 11-3 and 11-4 illustrate the differences between product advertising and institutional advertising.

No doubt the majority of small-business advertising is of the product type. Retailers' advertisements, for example, stress products almost exclusively, whether those of a supermarket featuring weekend specials or a wom-

Source: Dillon Construction Company, 125 N. Lafayette Avenue, Ventnor, New Jersey. Reproduced with permission.

Figure 11-3 Example of Product Advertising

---

6. Some practical advice for creating newspaper advertising consistent with store image is found in L. Lee Manzer, R. Duane Ireland, and Philip M. Van Auken, "Image Creation in Small Business Retailing: Applications of Newspaper Advertising," *Journal of Small Business Management*, Vol. 18, No. 2 (April, 1980), pp. 18-23.

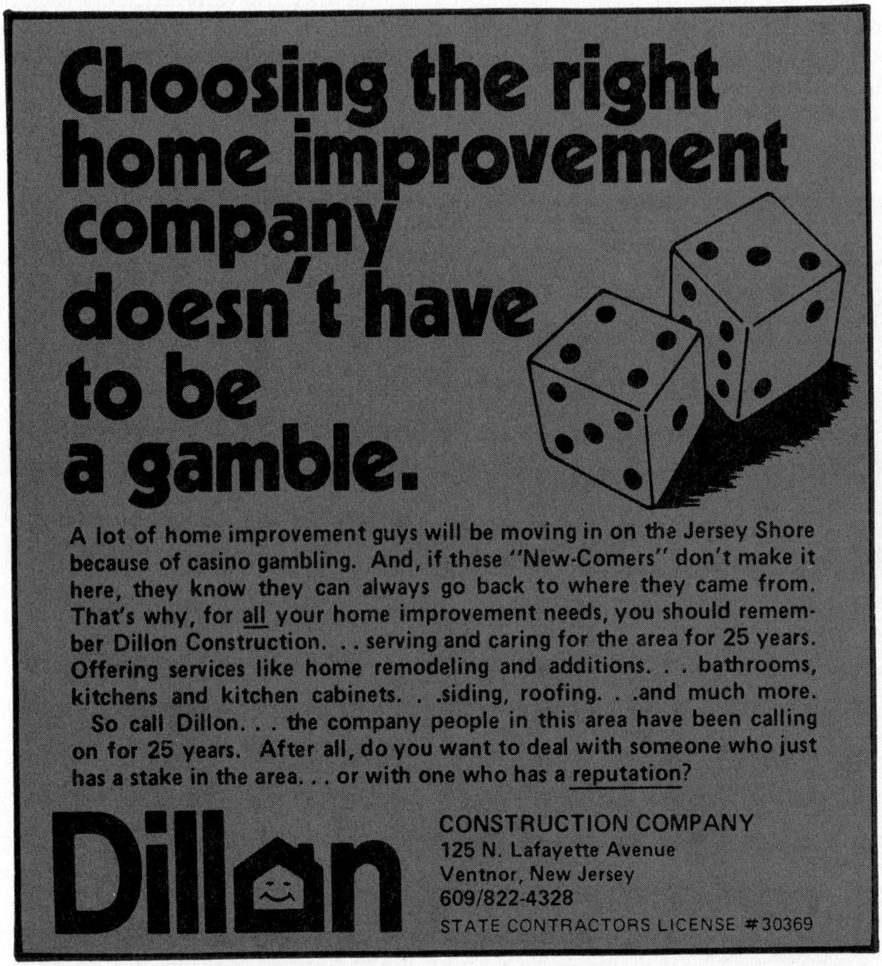

Source: Dillon Construction Company, 125 N. Lafayette Avenue, Ventnor, New Jersey. Reproduced with permission.

Figure 11-4 Example of Institutional Advertising

en's shop focusing upon sportswear. At times the same advertisement carries both product and institutional themes. Furthermore, the same firm may stress product advertising in newspapers and, at the same time, use institutional appeals in the Yellow Pages of the telephone book. Decisions regarding the type of advertising used should be based upon the nature of the business, industry practice, media used, and objectives of the firm.

When to Advertise

Frequency of advertising is an important question for the small business. Institutional advertising should be done regularly. Attempts to stimulate interest in a company's products or services should be part of a continuous advertising program. One-shot advertisements which are not part of a well-planned advertising effort lose much of their effectiveness in a short time.

Some noncontinuous advertising, of course, may be justified. This is true, for example, of advertising to prepare consumers for acceptance of a new product. Similarly, special advertising may be employed to suggest to customers new uses for established products. This is true also in advertising special sales.

Where to Advertise

Most small firms are restricted either geographically or by class of customer. Advertising media should reach—but not overreach—the present or desired market. From among the many media available, the small-business entrepreneur must choose those that will provide the greatest return for the advertising dollar.

The selection of the right combination of advertising media depends upon the type of business and its governing circumstances. A real estate sales firm, for example, may rely almost exclusively upon classified advertisements in a local newspaper, supplementing these with listings in the Yellow Pages of the telephone book. A transfer and storage firm may use a combination of radio, billboards, and telephone directory advertising to reach individuals planning to move household furniture. A small toy manufacturer may place greatest emphasis on television advertisements and participation in trade fairs. A local retail store may concentrate upon display advertisements in a local newspaper. The selection should be made not only on the basis of tradition but also upon an evaluation of the various ways to cover the particular market.

The best way to build a media mix is to talk with representatives from each medium. The small-business manager will usually find these representatives willing to recommend an assortment of media and not just the one they represent. Before you meet with these representatives, read as much as possible about advertising so you will know both the weaknesses and the strengths of each medium. The next two pages give a concise summary of several important facts about media.[7] Study these pages carefully. Note particularly the advantages and disadvantages of each medium. Recognize that space costs vary from place to place and will change over time.

---

7. Reprinted with permission from Bank of America, NT&SA, "Advertising Small Business," *Small Business Reporter*, Vol. 15, No. 2, Copyright 1976, 1978, 1981.

Medium	Market Coverage	Type of Audience	Sample Time/Space Costs
Daily Newspaper	Single community or entire metro area; zoned editions sometimes available.	General; tends more toward men, older age group, slightly higher income and education.	Per agate line, weekday; open rate: Circ: 8,700: $ .20 19,600: $ .35 46,200: $ .60 203,800: $ 1.60
Weekly Newspaper	Single community usually; sometimes a metro area.	General; usually residents of a smaller community.	Per agate line; open rate: Circ: 3,000: $ .35 8,900: $ .50 17,100: $ .75
Shopper	Most households in a single community; chain shoppers can cover a metro area.	Consumer households.	Per agate line; open rate: Circ: 10,000: $ .20 147,000: $ 2.00 300,000: $ 3.20
Telephone Directories	Geographic area or occupational field served by the directory.	Active shoppers for goods or services.	Yellow Pages, per half column; per month: Pop: 14-18,000: $ 15.00 110-135,000: $ 35.00 700-950,000: $ 100.00
Direct Mail	Controlled by the advertiser.	Controlled by the advertiser through use of demographic lists.	Production and mailing cost of an 8½″ × 11″ 2-color brochure; 4-page, 2-color letter; order card and reply envelope; label addressed; third class mail: $.33 each in quantities of 50,000.
Radio	Definable market area surrounding the station's location.	Selected audiences provided by stations with distinct programming formats.	Per 60-second morning drive-time spot; one time: Pop: 400,000: $ 35.00 1,100,000: $ 90.00 3,500,000: $ 150.00 13,000,000: $ 300.00
Television	Definable market area surrounding the station's location.	Varies with the time of day; tends toward younger age group, less print-oriented.	Per 30-second daytime spot; one time; nonpreemptible status: Pop: 400,000: $ 100.00 1,100,000: $ 300.00 3,500,000: $ 500.00 13,000,000: $ 600.00
Transit	Urban or metro community served by transit system; may be limited to a few transit routes.	Transit riders, especially wage earners and shoppers; pedestrians.	Inside 11″ × 28″ cards; per month: 50 buses: $ 125.00 400 buses: $1,000.00 Outside 21″ × 88″ posters; per month: 25 buses: $ 1,850.00 100 buses: $ 7,400.00
Outdoor	Entire metro area or single neighborhood.	General; especially auto drivers.	Per 12′ × 25′ poster; 100 GRP* per month: Pop: 21,800: $ 125.00 386,000: $ 135.00 628,900: $ 150.00
Local Magazine	Entire metro area or region; zoned editions sometimes available.	General; tends toward better educated, more affluent.	Per one-sixth page, black and white; open rate: Circ: 25,000: $ 310.00 80,000: $ 520.00

*Several boards must be purchased for these GRPs.

Particular Suitability	Major Advantage	Major Disadvantage
All general retailers.	Wide circulation.	Nonselective audience.
Retailers who service a strictly local market.	Local identification.	Limited readership.
Neighborhood retailers and service businesses.	Consumer orientation.	A giveaway and not always read.
Services, retailers of brand-name items, highly specialized retailers.	Users are in the market for goods or services.	Limited to active shoppers.
New and expanding businesses; those using coupon returns or catalogs.	Personalized approach to an audience of good prospects.	High CPM.
Businesses catering to identifiable groups; teens, commuters, housewives.	Market selectivity, wide market coverage.	Must be bought consistently to be of value.
Sellers of products or services with wide appeal.	Dramatic impact, wide market coverage.	High cost of time and production.
Businesses along transit routes, especially those appealing to wage earners.	Repetition and length of exposure.	Limited audience.
Amusements, tourist businesses, brand-name retailers.	Dominant size, frequency of exposure.	Clutter of many signs reduces effectiveness of each one.
Restaurants, entertainments, specialty shops, mail-order businesses.	Delivery of a loyal, special-interest audience.	Limited audience.

SALES PROMOTION

Sales promotion is promotion which serves as an inducement to perform a certain act while also offering value to recipients. The term *sales promotion* includes all promotional techniques which are neither personal selling nor advertising.

When to Use Sales Promotion

The small firm can use sales promotion to accomplish varied objectives. For example, small-business manufacturers can use sales promotion to stimulate commitments among channel intermediaries to market their product. Wholesalers can use sales promotion to induce retailers to buy inventories earlier than normally needed. Finally, with varied sales promotional tools, retailers can induce final consumers to make a purchase.

Sales Promotional Tools

Sales promotion should never represent the entire promotional effort of a small business. It should always be interlaced with advertising and personal selling. A partial list of sales promotional tools is given below:

1. Specialties.
2. Publicity.
3. Exhibits.
4. Sampling.
5. Coupons.
6. Premiums.
7. Contests.
8. Point-of-purchase displays.
9. Cooperative advertising.
10. Free merchandise.

The scope of this book does not allow us to comment on each of the sales promotional tools listed above. However, we will examine the first three on the list—specialties, publicity, and exhibits.

Specialties. The most distinguishing characteristic of specialties is the enduring nature and tangible value of the specialty items themselves. Specialties are referred to as the "lasting medium." They are also worth something to recipients as functional products.

The most widely used specialty item is the calendar. Other examples are pens, key chains, and shirts. Actually, almost anything can be used as a

ACTION REPORT: Specialties Give Company a Lift

Sales promotion specialties can be used individually or collectively as a campaign. In the latter case, a common theme will often be imprinted on every item.

A small materials-equipment distributor, Central Texas Clarklift Corporation in Waco, TX won an industry award for its specialty promotion designed to secure more business for its service department.

A new logo and a new service philosophy were established by a dealership that had been burdened with a poor customer relations reputation under previous ownership. A serial promotion was undertaken to establish that the new owner's service department would really hustle to satisfy customers. The first mailing to the target audience of 425 companies contained a card that introduced "Super Hustler," a cartoon character depicted in a forklift and described as being "faster than a speeding piston, more powerful than a C-500, and able to cut overhead in a single call." The second mailing guaranteed a repair man on the scene within three hours of a call; imprinted on the enclosed soft-shoulder phone rest was the phone "Super Number" to call for service. Two more "Super Grams" followed, the last promising a coffee mug for those who returned an enclosed reply card.

The advertiser's service business was said to have increased 27 percent; total business, including sales, rose 32.5 percent. Redemption rate for the reply cards was approximately 50 percent, and the coffee mugs were distributed in person by salespeople.

Source: *How to Play Championship Specialty Advertising* (Rolling Meadows, IL: Specialty Advertising Association International, 1977), p. 20.

specialty promotion. Every specialty item will be imprinted with the firm's name or other identifying slogan.

Specialties can be used to promote a product directly or to create company goodwill. Specialties also are excellent reminder promotions. For example, a small appliance repair shop can position its name and telephone number at the customer's phone with a specialty item related to dialing.

Finally, specialties are personal. They are distributed directly to the consumer in a personal way, they are items which can be used personally, and they have a personal message. Since the small business needs to retain its personal image, entrepreneurs can use specialties to achieve this objective.

Publicity. Of particular importance to retailers because of their high visibility is the type of promotion called publicity. Publicity can be used to promote both

ACTION REPORT: Public Opinion Tips Coffee Shop

Small business can benefit from public opinion. Publicity can be instrumental in building a favorable or unfavorable image.

Barry Warfel attributes the loss of his small business to bad publicity. Business at his Roseland, NJ coffee shop was "perking" until a competitor set up business. The competitor was aggressive and often insulted Warfel's food and prices. But Warfel fought back. He chased the competitor from his coffee shop entrance and even turned him in to the local health inspector.

The public reacted negatively to Warfel's tactics. "People shunned his coffee shop, sales plunged, the Warfel family got nasty phone calls. 'I knew I couldn't stay,' Mr. Warfel says. He sold his shop. Today he manages a fast-food outlet in another town."

The competitor became a hero and last year received an award at the White House Conference on Small Business. By the way, Warfel's competitor operated his business in a red wagon outside Warfel's coffee shop. The competitor's name was Billy. He was 11 years old.

Source: Reprinted by permission of *The Wall Street Journal* (June 15, 1981), © Dow Jones & Company, Inc. (1981). All rights reserved.

a product and a firm's image and is a vital part of good public relations for the small business. A good publicity program must maintain regular contacts with the news media.

Although publicity is considered to be "free" advertising, this is not always an accurate profile of this type of promotion. A cost is associated with this effort. Examples of publicity efforts which entail considerable expense are involvements with school yearbooks or summer baseball programs. While the benefits are difficult to measure, publicity is nevertheless important to a small business and should be exploited.

Exhibits. The use of exhibits permits product demonstrations, or "hands-on" experience with a product. The customer's place of business is not always the best environment for product demonstrations in normal personal selling efforts. And advertising cannot always substitute for try-out experiences with a product.

Exhibits are of particular value to manufacturers. The greatest benefit of exhibits is the potential costs savings over personal selling. Trade-show groups claim that the cost of exhibits is less than half the cost of a sales call.[8] Small manufacturers also view exhibits as offering a savings over advertising.

8. See Bob Donath, "Show and Sell by the Numbers," *Industrial Marketing*, Vol. 65, No. 3 (March, 1980), p. 70.

ACTION REPORT: Consumers "Dig" Contest

The most successful contests are those which generate excitement. An attractive prize is one way to stimulate enthusiasm and excitement.

The promotion manager of the *Ottawa Citizen* newspaper, Ben Babelowsky, knows how this can be done. He organized a "gold rush" contest in which the prize was gold wafers valued at over $4,000. The contest instructions were, "The gold is in a public place, and it isn't necessary to dig or damage anything to find it."

The contest inspired several escapades:

- A hunter who was convinced the gold was in a bird's nest checked every tree along the city's seven-mile canal.
- Jailkeepers had to call police to clear the district jail of treasure hunters after a newspaper drawing indicated the prison might be a hiding place.
- Police headquarters also was a target. Before searchers were cleared from there, they had pulled insulation from the crevices of the building's exterior walls.

Where were the golden wafers? They were found in a tree near a cross-country snow trail. But before the contest ended, the newspaper was selling 1,500 more copies a day!

Source: Reprinted by permission of *The Wall Street Journal* (March 3, 1981),

For example, Virginia V. Ness, owner of a small company in San Rafael, CA, says, "You might not write many orders, but this sure costs less than advertising as a way of making the product known in the industry."[9]

LOOKING BACK

1. The promotional mix includes personal selling, advertising, and sales promotion. The exact mixture is influenced by the nature of the market and the nature of the product. The optimum promotional mix may be modified because of cost limitations.
2. The four techniques used to estimate promotional funding needs are: a

9. Thomas J. Lueck, "Innovators Vie for Attention at Trade Shows," *The Wall Street Journal*, July 20, 1981, p. 19.

percentage of sales, what can be spared, as much as competition spends, and what it takes to do the job.

3. The two major steps in preparing a sales presentation are prospecting and practicing. In making the sales presentation, salespersons must adapt their sales approach to the customer's needs and must show some degree of enthusiasm, friendliness, and persistence.
4. The two general types of advertising are product advertising and institutional advertising. Each available form of advertising has certain advantages and disadvantages. The majority of small-business advertising is product advertising.
5. Sales promotion can be used by the manufacturer to stimulate commitments among channel intermediaries to market its product; by the wholesaler to induce retailers to buy inventories earlier than normally needed; and by the retailer to induce final consumers to make a purchase. Some sales promotional tools are specialties, publicity, and exhibits.

DISCUSSION QUESTIONS

1. Outline a promotional mix which you believe would be appropriate to help market this textbook to college bookstores. Which promotional element do you feel is the most essential to your mix?
2. What problems, if any, do you see in selecting television to promote dental laboratory services to dentists' clients? Be specific.
3. Discuss the advantages and the disadvantages of each of the methods of earmarking funds for promotion.
4. Outline a system of prospecting which could be used by a small camera store. Incorporate all the techniques presented in the chapter.
5. Why are the salesperson's techniques for handling objections so important to a successful sales presentation?
6. What are the advantages and disadvantages of compensating salespeople by salary? By commission? What is an acceptable compromise?
7. Refer to pages 278-279 and list five media that would give the small business the most precise selectivity. Be prepared to substantiate your list.
8. How does sales promotion differ from advertising and personal selling?
9. How do specialties differ from other sales promotional tools? Be specific.
10. Comment on the statement that "publicity is free advertising."

REFERENCES TO SMALL BUSINESS IN ACTION

Adler, Jack. "Staging an Exposition." *Venture*, Vol. 2, No. 4 (April, 1980), pp. 18-19.

This article tells how an entrepreneur organizes an exposition, and it describes his promotional budget and "prospecting" strategy.

Post, David. "How to Sell to Big Companies." *Inc.*, Vol. 3, No. 3 (March, 1981), pp. 66-70.

A young entrepreneur outlines what it takes to get started with a business. His personal sales presentation is described as a key ingredient.

Rose, Carol. "You Can't Turn Your Back on Selling." *Inc.*, Vol. 3, No. 6 (June, 1981), pp. 75-76.

The top salesman of this company is also its chairman and CEO. He makes sales calls in his $100,000 Silver Hawk limousine.

Shapiro, Irv. "Solving an Ad Riddle." *In Business*, Vol. 3, No. 2 (March-April, 1981), pp. 40-41.

In this article the simple and inexpensive direct mail campaign of a small delicatessen is described along with the promotional program of a furniture store.

Shea, John E. "Target Your Market to Rake in Profits." *Industrial Marketing*, Vol. 64, No. 12 (December, 1979), pp. 66-68.

Several case histories of communication failures in small businesses are examined in this article. The importance of evaluating a market prior to structuring a communications program is emphasized.

CASE C-1

The Expectant Parent Center*

Linking consumer behavior with a new service business

In February, 1980, Mrs. Ramona Caliban started the first profit-oriented childbirth education center in Scranton, PA. On the basis of eight years' hospital experience as a registered nurse in obstetrics, Ramona made the decision to establish herself as an entrepreneur in the fast-growing service area of childbirth education.

---

*This case was prepared by Steve R. Hardy and Philip M. Van Auken of the Center for Private Enterprise and Entrepreneurship at Baylor University.

Location and Facilities

Ramona conducted her first prenatal classes in the fellowship hall of her church, charging $20 per couple. She stated:

> At first my only clients were three ladies in the married's Sunday school class at church, so space and facilities were no problem. However, the popularity of my instruction and techniques soon grew to the point that I needed additional room and more professional facilities.

Ramona then rented a small office in a mini shopping center in May, 1980, and began operating as The Expectant Parent Center (EPC). She subsequently moved into a slightly larger facility in the same shopping center.

Nature and Growth of Services

The Expectant Parent Center provided childbirth preparation and instruction to expectant parents through four separate classes, as follows:

1. Childbirth preparation at $45 per couple (6 instructional sessions).
2. Prenatal hygienics and orientation at $20 per couple (2 sessions).
3. C-section at $50 per couple (5 sessions).
4. Prenatal and postpartum exercises at $25 per couple (5 sessions).

Ramona shared instructional duties with two other RNs, who were compensated on the basis of number of teaching contact hours and class size.

The Center had experienced steady growth in enrollments despite lack of advertising. Ramona commented, "We doubled enrollment from May, 1980, to January, 1981. Between January and August of 1981, we doubled once again, peaking at 35 couples per month. Enrollment figures for the last quarter of 1981 averaged 33 couples per month."

Potential Demand

Ramona felt that the Center had only scratched the surface of demand for childbirth education in the Scranton area. She said:

> For a city with more than 100,000 people, I know we could be doing a great deal more business than we are. I have been so busy over the last year with teaching and managerial duties that I really haven't had much time for growth planning. However, I feel that we offer a service very much in demand by enlightened couples. There's no reason why we can't continue to grow at a healthy pace. We'll need larger facilities and more teachers, but that will all come in time.

Marketing Issues

Ramona characterized her marketing strategy as a "bewildering bundle of unanswered questions and unstated assumptions." In particular, she was confused about pricing and advertising. She claimed:

> I just don't know what the market will bear in paying for prenatal education. I'm not even sure what the market is here in Scranton—to whom I should target my services.
>
> Only 2 hospitals in town offer any alternative childbirth education, and they do it for $25 for 2 sessions. However, their classes are typically overcrowded, poorly taught, and offered only sporadically. There is no doubt that most expectant couples are willing to pay for better instruction, but I just don't know how high they are willing to go. Right now I'm pricing pretty much at break-even, at least from the looks of my latest profit-and-loss statement. Now that the business has established itself locally, I want to start turning a decent profit. Prices will definitely have to go up, but I just don't know how far.
>
> Neither am I sure how to best market my services. Obviously our clients are fairly well-educated and somewhat affluent, or they wouldn't be interested in paying for first-class prenatal care. Beyond this reference point, however, my customer profile is fuzzy. If I had a better feel for which people are most interested in the Expectant Parent Center, I would know how to promote and diversify my services better.

Product Line

In addition to its four areas of childbirth instruction, the Center sold a limited line of child-care books, equipment, and educational toys. Included in the products inventory was a back massager invented by Ramona to aid mothers during labor. She explained:

> The massager helps the mother to relax during labor and minimizes muscle spasms in and around the back. The thing has a simple design consisting of a handle with two attached wooden doorknobs. When rolled up and down the back, the wooden wheels greatly counteract muscle tension.
>
> I subcontract out the manufacturing at a cost of $2.40 a unit. I sell them at the Center for $7.00, and they go like hotcakes. I'm currently in the process of getting a manufacturer's rep to circulate them at medical trade shows. He thinks they have a national potential if properly marketed.

Competitive Strength

Ramona summed up her perceived competitive edge as follows:

> The Expectant Parent Center offers the very finest in childbirth education, presented with tender loving care. We have good facilities, top-

notch instructors, auxiliary products, and an affordable price. Given the right marketing, the Center's growth should really explode. To use a bad pun, we're really in a growth business!

Questions

1. Evaluate Ramona Caliban's pricing concerns and her firm's name in the light of consumers' perceptions of marketing stimuli. Recommend an appropriate pricing strategy.
2. What social and cultural influences may impact on the demand for Ramona's services?
3. What types of social power can Ramona use if she begins to promote her services more actively? Be specific. Give an example.
4. How important do you think opinion leadership would be in "selling" Ramona's services? Why?
5. Would you recommend that Ramona continue to pursue the marketing of auxiliary products through the Center? Why or why not?

CASE C-2

Aureal Stereo and Electronics*

Pricing the speakers after a break-even analysis

Aureal Stereo and Electronics was a partnership owned by Dick K. Philips and Gary Cahners. Located in La Mirada, CA, the company manufactured three lines of custom-made, high-performance loudspeakers. Dick was the active partner who managed the company with the assistance of his wife, Megan. Gary, the silent partner, was an attorney in Los Angeles.

Dick had been described variously as an electronics whiz kid, stereo fanatic, and physics wonder child. Twenty-nine years old, he held a bachelor's degree in physics and was an experienced electronics repairman. He started his own company two years ago, with Gary's financial backing, in order to realize his dream of designing the "world's perfect stereo speaker." Dick said, "I'd like Aureal speakers to be recognized as the very best going—the connoisseur's speaker!" He commented further that, even though quality doesn't necessarily sell itself, the quality of Aureal speakers should be obvious to the sophisticated stereo consumer. He added, "Once the discriminating listener hears my product, he or she will never be satisfied with anything else."

Aureal speakers were distinguished technically by four features:

---

*This case was prepared by Steve R. Hardy and Philip M. Van Auken of the Center for Private Enterprise and Entrepreneurship at Baylor University.

1. Full-bodied sonics, especially in bass ranges.
2. High wattage capacity.
3. A patented automatic overload cut-off system which prevented the speaker from ever being "blown."
4. Handmade walnut cabinets.

To demonstrate the stability of his speakers, Dick loved to show visitors how a nickle propped on its side atop a speaker would not show a trace of vibration even when the speaker was played at ear-splitting volume!

The 3 lines of Aureal speakers were being sold by 14 distributors in 5 states and by 1 retailer in Johannesburg, South Africa. Although Aureal had not been in business long enough to establish national distribution, Dick was impatient to expand. He explained:

> Our volume is currently too small for us to break even financially. We haven't been able to afford more than one salesman, so expansion has naturally been limited. To a certain extent, I realize that Aureal speakers are so expensive that many customers don't consider them. However, I feel certain that, with more exposure, a strong national market for our speakers will shape up. It's a matter of distribution and pricing.

Dick admitted his particular concern about pricing his speakers as follows:

> Not being well-versed in accounting, I'm frankly confused about how to optimally price the three lines. I'm not really certain what our break-even point is or what would be a fair price for unique, high-performance speakers. Naturally I can't completely ignore what my competitors price their speakers for, but I do expect to receive a reasonable return on my own investment in quality. If I can somehow crystalize my pricing strategy, I really feel that this company can generate a decent profit.

Questions

1. Using Exhibits 1, 2, 3, 4, and 5 on the next pages, calculate the break-even point for Aureal's total operation and for each of the 3 lines on a per-unit basis.
2. Determine the company's profit or loss on each line of speakers.
3. Design a pricing strategy for Aureal speakers. What do you feel is a fair profit margin for each line of speakers?

Exhibit 1 Aureal Stereo and Electronics Statement of Income for the Eight-Month Period Ending August 31, 1981 (Unaudited)

	August	Year to Date Dollars	Year to Date Percent
Gross sales	$19,946.23	$170,370.65	100.00%
Cost of goods sold:			
Beginning inventory	48,886.11	65,206.53	38.27%
Materials	2,378.17	64,437.74	37.82
Labor	137.70	26,696.85	15.67
Total	$51,401.98	$156,341.12	91.76%
Ending inventory	37,487.49	37,487.49	22.00
Total cost of goods	$13,914.49	$118,853.63	69.76%
Gross profit	$ 6,031.74	$ 51,517.02	30.24%
Operating expenses:			
Partner's salary	1,263.05	18,950.95	11.12%
Telephone	436.16	2,538.86	1.49
Utilities	291.62	1,706.96	1.00
Rent	600.00	4,800.00	2.82
Travel	636.61	8,109.73	4.76
CES — Rentals	0.00	3,500.00	2.05
Insurance	0.00	444.79	0.26
Miscellaneous	0.00	405.58	0.24
Advertising	0.00	3,265.17	1.92
Interest	1,222.79	7,754.70	4.55
Sales expenses — Commission	0.00	8,144.97	4.78
Payroll taxes	9.16	3,650.75	2.14
Depreciation	302.30	1,832.90	1.08
Freight	(1.41)	58.59	0.03
Legal and accounting	275.00	915.00	0.54
Maintenance and repair	0.00	96.93	0.06
Total operating expenses	$ 5,035.28	$ 66,175.88	38.84%
Net operating income (loss)	$ 996.46	$(14,658.86)	(8.60%)
Other expense:			
Discounts allowed	296.00	6,654.91	3.91
Net income (loss)	$ 700.46	$(21,313.77)	(12.51%)

Exhibit 2 Aureal Stereo and Electronics Balance Sheet, August 31, 1981 (Unaudited)

ASSETS		
Current assets:		
Cash in bank	$ 8,092.78	
Accounts receivable	13,618.19	
Inventory	37,487.49	
Total current assets		$59,198.46
Property and equipment:		
Furniture and equipment	$18,138.08	
Less: Accumulated depreciation	(1,832.90)	16,305.18
TOTAL ASSETS		$75,503.64
LIABILITIES		
Current liabilities:		
Note payable — First National Bank	$70,000.00	
Payroll tax payable	1,590.09	
Sales tax payable	593.90	
Lay-away	400.00	
Accrued interest	2,407.58	
Total liabilities		$74,991.57
PARTNERS' EQUITY		
John M. Davis, capital	$21,171.48	
William L. Weber, capital	654.36	
Net income (loss)	(21,313.77)	
Total partners' equity		512.07
TOTAL LIABILITIES AND EQUITY		$75,503.64

Exhibit 3 Direct Material Costs and Labor

	Super 200	Super 300	Deluxe 400
Cabinet	$35.00	$ 52.50	$ 84.50
10″ Woofer	15.00	15.00	
2 12″ Woofers			33.84
4″ Tweeter	5.60	5.60	5.60
Port hole	.10	.10	
Midrange		5.30	
Purple midrange			8.40
Plate	.98		
Backplate		.98	
Switchplate			.98
Piezo			3.97
Glass			.90
Wire	.20	.50	.50
Capacitor	.16	.67	.46
Spool and wire	.07	.50	.50
Circuit breaker	.63	.63	.63
Screws	.15	.15	.16
Grille cover	2.00		
Grille cover fabric		.65	
Grille cover frame		2.25	
Fabric			.75
Grille frame			2.75
Logo	.36	.36	.36
Shipping box	3.45	5.03	6.50
Base	5.35		
Dial plate		2.42	2.42
Light bulb	.25		
Miscellaneous	2.00	2.00	4.00
Total	$71.30	$ 94.64	$157.22
Labor	11.02	11.68	17.64
TOTAL COST	$82.32	$106.32	$174.86

Exhibit 4 Total Speakers Sold per Month in the Year 1981

Month	Super 200	Super 300	Deluxe 400
January	10	22	14
February	6	13	34
March	44	61	46
April	14	9	8
May	34	12	44
June	12	34	18
July	14	8	12
August	21	16	20
September	26	4	32
TOTAL	181	179	228

Exhibit 5 Aureal Stereo and Electronics Price Schedule (Effective January 1, 1981)

Product	2-4		6-8		10-14		16-over		Shipping Weight
	Dealer Cost Per Each	Cost After Discount	Dealer Cost Per Each	Cost After Discount	Dealer Cost Per Each	Cost After Discount	Dealer Cost Per Each	Cost After Discount	
Model Super 200	$165.00	$148.50	$155.00	$139.50	$145.00	$130.50	$140.00	$126.00	45 lbs.
Model Super 300	255.00	299.50	230.00	207.50	220.00	198.00	210.00	189.00	55 lbs.
Model Deluxe 400	460.00	414.00	420.00	378.00	395.00	355.50	380.00	342.00	105 lbs.

Note: 10% discount if paid within 20 days, net 30. To collect discounts, the remittance envelope must be postmarked no later than 20 days after invoice date. Freight is prepaid on all single orders to one point over 1,000 lbs. This price sheet supersedes all previous price sheets, and prices are subject to change without notice.

CASE C-3

The Jordan Construction Account*

Extending credit and collecting receivables

Bob McFarland was the president and principal stockholder of Iowa Tractor Supply Company, a farm and construction equipment distributor located in Marshalltown, IA. The firm employed 27 persons, and in 1981 sales and net profit after taxes reached all-time highs of $3.4 million and $81,500, respectively. The ending net worth for 1981 was slightly in excess of $478,000.

Bob was highly gratified by these figures as 1981 was the first full year since he had appointed Barry Stockton as general manager. Although the company had been in operation since 1957, it had prospered only from the time Bob had purchased it in 1969. Having been a territorial sales manager for the John Deere Company, he was able to obtain that account for Iowa Tractor, and it typically contributed two thirds or more of the annual sales volume. After struggling successfully for 10 years to build Iowa Tractor into a profitable firm, he decided that it was time to take things a little easier. Accordingly, he promoted Barry and delegated many of his day-to-day duties to him. Fortunately Barry seemed to do an outstanding job, and during the summer of 1982, Bob felt secure enough to spend six weeks in Europe with his wife.

One day shortly after Bob returned to work, he looked up from his desk and saw his accountant, Marvin Richter, approaching with several ledger cards in his hand. Marvin entered the office, carefully closed the door, and began to speak earnestly. Marvin said:

> Mr. McFarland, I think you should look at these accounts receivable, particularly Jordan Construction. I've been telling Barry to watch out for Jordan for two months, but he just says they're good for it eventually. I got the latest Dun & Bradstreet monthly report today which didn't look very good, so I've called Standifer Equipment in Ames and the Caterpillar branch at Cedar Rapids. Jordan seems to have run up some pretty good bills with both of them, and Carter at Standifer said some of the contractors in Des Moines think that the two jobs Jordan got on Interstate 80 are just too big for them to handle. If Jordan can't finish those jobs, we are going to be in trouble! Carter says they're probably going to put them on C.O.D. and call in the rental equipment.

Bob examined the data for a few minutes, asked Marvin several questions before dismissing him, and then summoned Barry to his office. The following dialogue took place between Bob and Barry:

*This case was prepared by John E. Schoen, Richards Equipment Company, Waco, TX.

Bob: Barry, I've just been looking over the sheets on Jordan and the amount really scares me. Apparently they are over 90 days on nearly $21,000, between 30 and 90 days on another $17,000, and the total due is more than $45,000. Payments on their account have been dropping off since April, and last month they barely covered the interest on the amount outstanding.
Barry: I know, Bob. I've been over to talk to old man Jordan twice in the last three weeks. He admits they are having some trouble with those jobs on the Interstate, but he claims it is only temporary. I hate to push him too hard because he has bought a lot of equipment from us over the years.
Bob: That's right, Barry, but we're talking about $45,000! At this rate, we'll soon have more money in Jordan's business than he does! I'm not so sure we shouldn't put Jordan on C.O.D. until he makes some substantial payments on their account.
Barry: I don't think so, Bob! Old man Jordan has a real mean streak, and the first time I went over there he really cussed me out for even questioning his account. He reminded me that he had been a good customer for more than 10 years, and he threatened to cut us off if we put any pressure on him.
Bob: Yes, but you've heard that before, Barry. Here we are contributing capital to his business involuntarily; we never get a share of his profits if he succeeds, but we sure get a share of the losses if he goes "belly-up." Barry, I don't want any $45,000 losses!
Barry: Well, I won't say that Jordan doesn't have some problems, but Harry thinks they'll be all right. It's just that if we put them on C.O.D. or pick up the rental equipment and they make it, I'm sure they'll never spend another dollar in here.
Bob: Harry thinks they'll be O.K.?
Barry: Yes, sir.
Bob: Get Harry in here!

In a few minutes Barry returned with Harry Reiser, the sales manager for Iowa Tractor. The following dialogue took place between Bob and Harry:

Harry: Barry says you wanted to talk to me?
Bob: That's right, Harry. We've just been discussing Jordan Construction, and I'd like to get any information you have on them.
Harry: Well, they're pretty good customers, of course. I rented them two tractor-backhoes last month. There are some rumors about their Interstate jobs, but I don't think there is much to it because Jordan was talking about buying a couple of crawler tractors last Friday. I think we have a good chance to get those crawlers if that joker over at Ames doesn't sell his below cost.
Bob: Just a minute. You rented them some backhoes last month?
Harry: Yes, sir, two model 310-A's.
Bob: How much are we getting for those units?

Harry: $1,400 a month each, and I think we have a good chance to convert them to a sale if Jordan gets 6 months' rent into them.
Bob: Did you check with anybody before you put those units out with Jordan?
Harry: Well, I think I asked Barry. No, I think he was busy that day. I'm really not certain, but Jordan Construction is one of our best accounts. Isn't it?
Bob: That's what we are trying to determine, Harry. Did you know that their accounts receivable is over $45,000?
Harry: No! That's great! I knew we'd really been selling them. I'm sure those rumors . . .
Bob: And did you know that $38,000 of the $45,000 is past due and that $21,000 is over 90 days?
Harry: Oh!

Then Bob turned to Barry and said:

"Barry, I think we've established what Harry knows about Jordan. Why don't we get Marvin in here and see what information he has. Then I think the four of us need to decide the best approach to getting as much of our money back as soon as possible."

Questions

1. Evaluate the quality of the information provided Bob McFarland by each of his subordinates.
2. Evaluate the alternatives in solving the Jordan situation.
3. What action should Bob take regarding the Jordan account?
4. How could Bob improve the credit and collections procedure of Iowa Tractor to minimize problems of this nature?
5. Evaluate the performance of Marvin Richter, Barry Stockton, and Harry Reiser in handling the Jordan account. Do the circumstances warrant any type of disciplinary action?

CASE C-4

Mitchell Interiors

Developing a promotional strategy

Joyce Mitchell, age 38 and married for 20 years, was a native Texan with 2 children. Her husband Joe, age 40, had recently taken a 20-year retirement from his firefighter's job in Dallas, TX. Together, Joyce and Joe operated an interior decorating business located on North Main Street in Corsicana, TX, a town of approximately 25,000 people.

Joyce's Background

During her early years of marriage, Joyce tried several jobs but was mainly a housewife. She was not content at being a housewife because, as she said, "I have a tendency to get everything done. I'm usually a pretty good organizer, and I just didn't feel fulfilled." When her children were older, she went back to school to pursue a home economics degree. During this time, she accepted a kindergarten teacher job at a private school.

Joyce soon found out she was not cut out to be a teacher. In her words, "I cannot train people. You know how some people play piano by ear—well, I'm that way. I feel I know how to do something, so why shouldn't you? So, teaching was frustrating to me." About this time, Joe and Joyce decided to move south of Dallas into the country. Joyce happily gave up her teaching.

Joe and Joyce decided to personally build their house on the land they purchased in Navarro County about 12 miles west of Corsicana. Therefore, the first year after Joyce had left teaching, she was busy helping with the construction project. "If I wasn't busy with a hammer and nails, wallpaper, or helping the plumber, I was running back and forth to Corsicana picking out interior decorations."

Working for a Large Chain

Joyce began helping friends with their decorating. A large chain store in Corsicana was a place Joyce would go for her decorating purchases. The store manager was always impressed by the well-organized clippings and folders that she would bring into the store. One day the manager offered Joyce an opportunity to work with the store in a newly created interior decorating job. This chain was just getting into this type of business activity. Joyce was not interested at that time because she had enrolled for 18 credit hours at a local college. The manager persisted, "I've been watching you for four months, and I know you are what I need." Finally, Joyce consented to work on Saturdays beginning in December after the semester concluded. The manager agreed, and Joyce continued for two months under this arrangement. Then, in January, she began working full time and set up the interior design department. During the next 5 years, she was highly successful and reached the point where she was earning more than $1,500 a month from salary and commissions. For the Corsicana area, this was a high income and an excellent supplement to Joe's salary.

One day Joyce realized she was "working around the clock for another company." She would get up at 5 a.m. to figure bids, report to the store at 8 a.m., oversee installations, and then come home to figure more bids at night. "I really had too many clients," she recalled. She was overloaded and uncomfortable with carrying heavy carpet samples and wallpaper samples in and out of clients' houses. The weight of these samples was also wearing on her personal car. Finally, she requested a company van to carry these samples. The request was received favorably, but the company never did buy the van.

Joyce was also being asked to train interior decorators from other stores in the chain organization. "When I was training these girls, I was missing out on store sales," Joyce recalled. "I was also getting behind in my other work. It was a nice compliment from the store, but I got to looking at it and decided they would have to compensate me or get me some help. I decided to resign." Later, Joyce was told the company was about to promote her to regional supervisor. This would have meant she would be teaching even more, something she didn't enjoy. Joyce decided, "I like decorating because that's my talent. That's the talent God gave me, so I'm going to stay with it."

Beginning Her Own Business

Since the lack of a van to transport decorating samples to clients' homes was a key issue in Joyce's departure from the chain store, Joe and Joyce decided to begin their own business with a used Dodge Motor Home. Mitchell Interiors was thus born in 1978. The business began smoothly. All of Joyce's suppliers were eager to help because they had observed her success with the large chain store. She had no trouble opening accounts with them because they knew she could sell.

After nine months, the van became crowded. Joyce told Joe, "If we are going to do this, let's do it big." So they bought a 28-foot Winnebago and Joyce personally designed a plush interior. Joe built the interior, and they had a decorating studio on wheels. "The type of clients I want need to see what you can do the minute they step into your place," Joyce commented. "I want them to think, 'If she can do this to a van, she can do my home to please me.'"

Opening the Mitchell Interiors Store

The Mitchell Interiors store opened in November, 1980. It was located in Corsicana and occupied 2,000 square feet of store and warehouse space. The store allowed for increased display of many items which were also for sale to walk-in customers. The location was leased and had three neighbor tenants: Prestige Realty, Clint's Jewelers, and Pat Walkers (a reducing salon). All these four businesses catered to the same type of clientele.

Joyce still used the Winnebago for travel to clients' homes. Business had been good. In fact, Joyce said, "I am so busy, I cannot take everything which comes in off the street. The first question I ask is: Have you been recommended? I cannot physically get to all the potential business. Therefore, I consider only those jobs I know I can get. I am really wasting time going out to bid on a job if they don't know whether they want me to do it or not."

Joyce was a strong believer in bringing the personal touch to a business. She always tried to bring this to her clients. Even Joe, who installed all drapes and supervised carpet installation, believed in the personal touch. Joyce said, "I hope our business never gets so big that we cannot personally oversee all our jobs."

The Product/Service Mix

Contract sales provided about 75 percent of the total business volume of Mitchell Interiors. Contract sales were those sales made to interior decorating clients—individual homeowners or business owners. Joyce occasionally contracted with builders for the decorating of new houses. Recently, however, because of high interest rates, there was little speculative building in the area. The main products which sold in contract jobs were carpet, vinyl floor covering, draperies, and wallpaper. Drapery sales constituted 60 percent of the contract sales, and Joyce was happy with this situation because of the higher markup associated with draperies. Since competition was much greater in carpeting and vinyls, these products produced a much lower markup. The remaining 25 percent of business volume came from in-store sales of tables, lamps, ceiling fans, and other decorative accessories.

Joyce saw her customers as upper-middle class and upper class, 35 to 50 years old, both in Corsicana and in surrounding towns.

Promotional Practices

Most of Joyce's promotion had been accomplished through the recommendations of satisfied customers. Customers who had known Joyce when she worked for the chain store recommended her to their friends. When Mitchell Interiors was initially "garaged" at Joe and Joyce's home, few people who had a cursory interest would call because of the long-distance telephone charges. Joyce would advertise such things as a drapery sale in the newspaper or on some other special occasion such as Mother's Day. Joyce also used radio advertising on the local FM country-western radio station. Joyce had done all the design work for the firm's stationery and for print advertising.

Joyce also used direct mail advertising. She felt very strongly that this was an effective medium for her business. These mail-outs were primarily a reminder that her store was there and that she was available. The mailing lists came mainly from an internal file of satisfied customers. This file was updated to remove customers who had not visited the store after about three mail-outs. Additional names were solicited from employees, the Corsicana telephone directory, new residents in the more elite parts of town, and listings of doctors and lawyers.

Yearly promotional expenditures were planned by Joyce at the beginning of the year when the master budget was finalized. Joyce forecasted the expenses and the sales needed to meet these expenses. Break-even sales were around $20,000 per month. In the master budget Joyce included an advertising budget because she believed that advertising was important. In 1981, she allowed approximately $300 of the total budget per month for promotion on newspaper advertising, radio, direct mail, business gifts, and specialty advertising. Most of her promotion emphasized accessory items. Joyce reasoned, "I want people to come in and buy accessories. I want people to get used to having a store like this in Corsicana."

The Store Employees

The business had only one full-time employee and four part-time helpers. According to Joyce, "Joe is the only person besides me who gets outside the business and works with clients." Joyce wanted to remain as the designer-buyer for the store but was willing to take on another designer. She was also looking for someone to manage the accessories area at the store. She wanted the manager to pre-interview other employees, but she wished to make the final hiring decisions.

Questions

1. What other types of promotion would "fit" Joyce Mitchell's customers?
2. Evaluate the promotional practices of Mitchell Interiors.
3. Should Joyce continue to advertise when she already has more business than she can handle? Why or why not?
4. How can Mitchell Interiors grow and also retain the personal touch that is so important to Joyce?

CASE C-5

Wild Water Coaster*

Promoting and advertising a water slide

The Wild Water Coaster was a two-chute water slide located on an interstate highway six miles outside Las Cruces, NM. Operated by Art Clemenson and his right-hand man Mark Chen, the slide was nearing the end of its fourth season of operation. On September 29, 1981, Art and Mark were having a final meeting to decide whether Art should buy the slide from Carl Slade, builder and owner of the slide. Art had been leasing the slide from Carl since July, 1981, and had an option to buy the slide at the end of the lease

*This case was prepared by David R. Hill.

period, September 30, 1981. So, Art and Mark started reviewing some key aspects of the slide in order to make a quick but well-thought-out decision.

Water Slide Operations

When Carl Slade was operating the business, the slide had been open only during the summer months — from Memorial Day to Labor Day. Art and Mark felt that the season could be extended, possibly from May 1 through September 30, because of the warm New Mexico weather. This would give them a five-month rather than a three-month season.

Carl had also kept the slide open from noon until midnight seven days a week. Art and Mark thought that they could attract more business by opening earlier, so they changed the schedule and operated from 10 a.m. till midnight Monday through Saturday, and noon till midnight Sunday.

At any given time, one manager and three or four slide attendants were needed to operate the slide. One employee was needed to work the concession stand. There were three managers and twelve attendants on the payroll.

The business also included a nine-hole miniature golf course at the same location. Although the golf course and the concession stand produced very little profit, these were more than self-supporting and contributed to customer goodwill.

Location Problems

Art and Mark were especially concerned with the location of the slide and the problems it presented. Although the slide was positioned right at one of the Interstate's exits, it was about 6 miles outside the city limits and roughly 8 miles from a key source of potential customers — a university with an enrollment of 10,000 students. Two other suburban communities (of 15,000 population each) were located within 3 miles of the slide and also constituted part of its potential market. The slide's out-of-town location had limited its impact on the city market. Many people apparently felt that it was too far out of town; therefore, they patronized instead the Lion's Park, an amusement park located inside the city limits. Lion's Park had a smaller, less exciting one-chute water slide, but it also had a swimming pool and putt-putt golf course to go with it. Art and Mark discussed the strengths and weaknesses of the location as follows:

Mark: We definitely have a superior product, but we don't get the business Lion's Park does because of their superior location and added attractions. I wonder why Carl built so far out of town. Art, did you ever ask him why he picked that location?

Art: No, but I did find out that he passed up a spot a mile outside the city that offered better long-term prospects but had a steeper price tag. I wish he would have built there. I think it would have made this decision a little easier. Right now I'm still undecided about the long-term prospects of the slide at its present location. How do you view the long-term prospects?

Mark: I think the crucial issue is deciding if the water slide is a fad or a viable long-term investment. The trampoline centers of the 50s and the big metal slides of the 60s proved to be fads, and one can't help but wonder if the water slides of the 70s and 80s will follow the same course. On the surface, it appears that they are viable long-term investments because more and more are being built as either part of an amusement park or as the single main attraction. But I've also heard of slides failing in the past, so it appears that in certain locales they could indeed be fads. Let's see if the slide's history gives us any clues.

Sales History

Carl Slade built the slide in early 1978 with an initial investment of $150,000. With gross revenue of $125,000 in 1978 and $95,000 in 1979, Carl was able to recover his initial investment in only 2 years (see Exhibit 1). In 1980, sales fell to $60,000; so Carl began to look for a buyer. When he opened in 1981, he was still looking for a buyer and began to devote less time to the slide. As a result, advertising and group bookings (very important for a sales base) were virtually nonexistent during the summer of 1981. Bad weather and lack of advertising really caused sales to plummet in 1981. Although Carl was still turning a profit, he decided to get out if he could and arranged a lease-buy contract with Art for the rest of the 1981 season. The lease called for Art to pay

Exhibit 1 Approximate Income Statements (Three months' operation)

	1980	1979	1978
Sales	$60,000	$95,000	$125,000
Less: Labor	14,500	13,200	12,500
Electric utilities	2,400	2,325	2,250
Water	500	450	400
Insurance	2,000	2,000	2,000
Misc./Maintenance	900	850	800
Depreciation*	10,000	10,000	10,000
Operating profit	$29,700	$66,175	$ 97,050

*Straight line depreciation: $150,000/15 years = $10,000 per year.

Carl a total of $20,000 for July through September and gave Art an option to buy the slide at the end of the lease period for another $20,000, which was due by March 1, 1982.

Looking at the Slide's Prospects

Both Art and Mark had been disappointed with the performance of the slide business since they took over in July. They continued their discussion of business prospects as follows:

Art: July was a fairly good month, but sales really fell off in August and September. So far this has been a losing venture for me. I've been able to cover my operating expenses quite adequately but fell about $5,000 short of covering my initial investment of $20,000. I had hoped the slide would be self-supporting in this venture, but it has actually been a drain on my other businesses. I feel the potential is there because of Carl's past success with the slide, but so far I've been very disappointed.
Mark: I've been very disappointed, too. But we must take into consideration the facts that we took over in the middle of the season and that Carl had not done very much advertising to build up his customer base early in the season. He was directing much of his effort at trying to sell the slide. Did he ever tell you his principal reason for selling the slide? I keep on wondering why he wanted to sell such a profitable venture.
Art: First of all, Carl was seeking to consolidate his entrepreneurial activity around Phoenix, where he makes his home and owns several other small businesses. He told me that the water slide was getting tough to handle because the Phoenix businesses were taking up more and more of his time. More important, though, there is little doubt in my mind that Carl was in it for the short run—to get a good return on his investment and then to sell the slide at a profit. This is what concerns me the most.

Questions

1. What should Art Clemenson and Mark Chen decide to do? Analyze the fad threat and long-range strategies for the slide.
2. Assuming that Art buys the slide, what short-range and long-range strategies would you suggest to overcome the location problem?
3. What sales promotional techniques would you suggest Art and Mark consider for the business? Could publicity be used to "promote" their business? If so, suggest how they could generate some publicity.
4. What type of advertising mix would be appropriate for this business? How would you suggest they determine an amount to spend on advertising?

Part D

MANAGING SMALL-BUSINESS OPERATIONS

Chapter 12

The Process of Management

LOOKING AHEAD

Watch for the following important topics:

1. The nature of management functions in small firms.
2. The relation of the management process to the growth cycle of a small business.
3. Special management problems of small entrepreneurial and family firms.
4. Effective use of managerial time.
5. Sources of management assistance.

Management consists of all activities undertaken to secure the accomplishment of work through the efforts of other people. Both large and small firms require good management in order to achieve success. In the typical small business that entails group effort, the manager provides direction by activities that are described as **management functions**.

MANAGEMENT FUNCTIONS IN SMALL BUSINESS

The general functions of management are: planning, organizing, directing, and controlling. Effective performance of these functions calls for the ability to lead and inspire other people. It is the manager who must integrate departmental and personal goals with those of the enterprise as a whole.

Planning

Planning is decision making regarding a future course of action. It is primarily the responsibility of the manager. This does not mean that employees never make decisions relative to their own daily tasks, but rather that their need to make decisions is minimized by good managerial planning.

Planning in business is concerned with the following:

1. Determination of company objectives.
2. Formulation of policies, programs, and procedures designed for attainment of company objectives.
3. Designation of performance and cost standards and their incorporation in a budget. This serves as a short-range plan of operations and as the basis for operating control during the budgetary period.
4. Long-range development of the company's line of products, services, and processes.

Since planning is primarily a thinking process, action-oriented entrepreneurs sometimes postpone it in favor of activities more directly related to operations. Because of the great importance of planning in small business, Chapter 13 is devoted to a review of this function.

Organizing

Organizing involves the assignment of functions and tasks to departmental components and to individual employees. It includes the delegation of authority to subordinate managers and operating employees so that they can properly carry out their duties. Thus, organizing establishes the pattern of relationships observed by all members of the organization.

A formal statement of structure ordinarily takes the form of an organization chart that shows all the managerial levels and positions. An example of an organization chart is presented in Figure 12-1. Some companies also prepare a supporting organizational manual to show the detailed functions assigned to each member of the management team.

A study of the organization chart serves to clarify organizational arrangements that may otherwise be hazy in the minds of employees. Whether the organization structure is reduced to writing or not, it is desirable that relationships among members of the organization be logically conceived and thoroughly understood by all. In the very small business, of course, this may be satisfactorily accomplished without a written chart or manual.

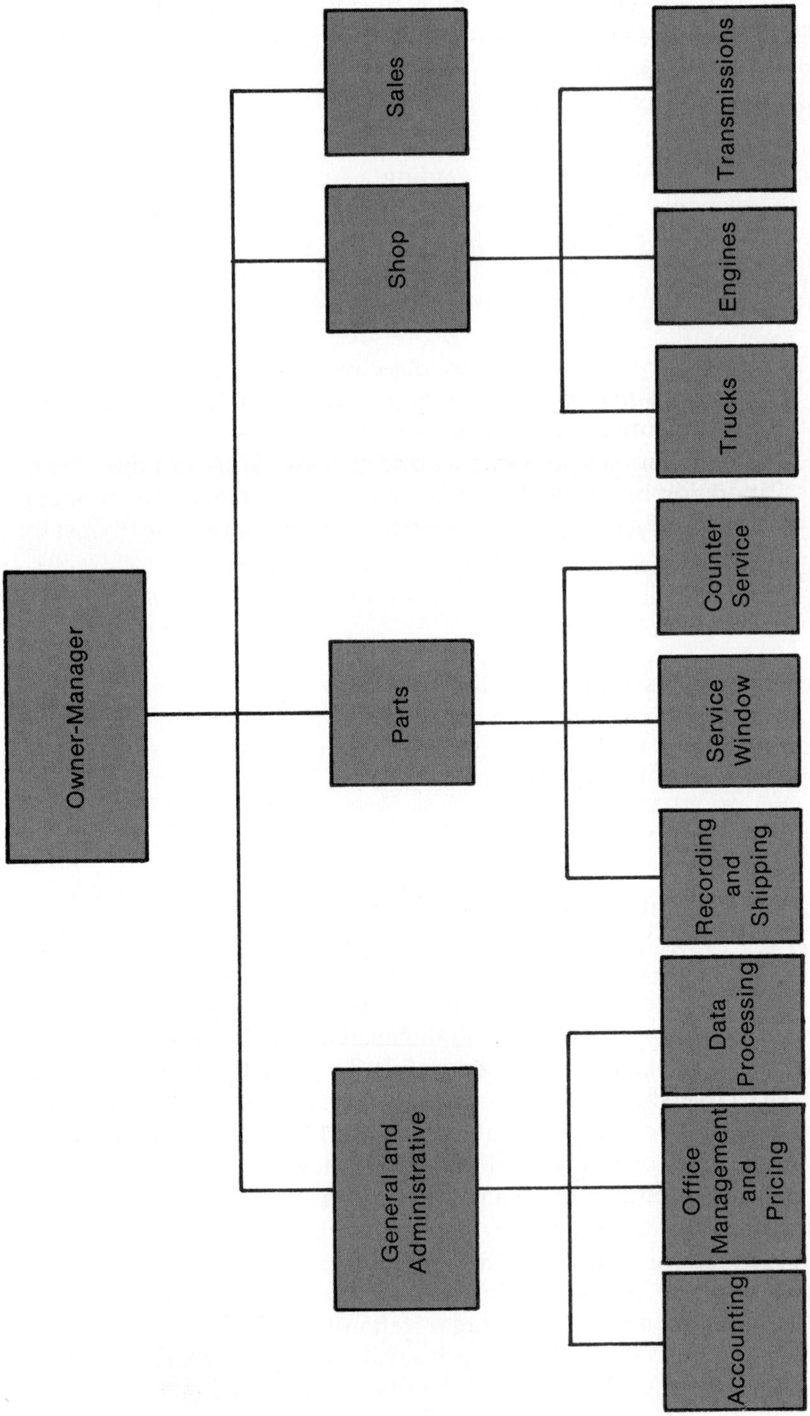

Figure 12-1 Organization of Diesel Engine Sales and Service Firm

For the typical small business, the management group may, and probably will, consist of very few persons. It will grow as the small business itself grows. Chapter 14 expands on the different forms of organization structure that the small firm may assume.

Directing

The **directing** function involves several activities whose purpose is to achieve the organization's objectives and at the same time build an organizational climate that is conducive to superior performance. The activities include order giving, supervising, leading, motivating, and communicating.

Order Giving. Orders may be given in person or in writing. Written orders may take the form of memos, notices on bulletin boards, or shop manuals. They may be addressed to a specific person or to groups of persons.

Supervising. Supervision is concerned with the training and discipline of the work force. It includes the checkups required to assure the prompt and proper execution of orders, and thus it is also a part of the controlling function. Supervising is performed by every member of a management team, from chief executive to first-line supervisors.

Leading. Leadership behavior serves to inspire and influence others to give maximum effort and cooperation, willingly and voluntarily, for the attainment of group objectives. The leader may find certain techniques helpful for getting people to do better work. Among these are:

1. Being a good listener and a ready, accurate communicator.
2. Being considerate of others.
3. Using suggestions or requests and explaining the reasons for the decisions reached.
4. Criticizing and reprimanding in private, but praising promptly and publicly.
5. Studying subordinates to find the most effective type of motivation for each.
6. Taking subordinates into plans and programs before decisions and commitments are made—and soliciting their suggestions and assistance, giving them credit for ideas used.
7. Developing the ability and judgment of subordinates for independent decision making.
8. Letting subordinates know where they stand.
9. Expecting and tolerating some "griping."
10. Admitting one's own mistakes promptly.
11. Delegating functions to subordinates.

Motivating. Creating a good work climate is a natural by-product of good leadership. But it also contributes materially to motivation of better work performance. Most people respond to a clear challenge and take pride in accomplishment. A number of motivating factors exist, including loyalty, challenging work, job and old-age security, fair pay, fair treatment, training and promotional opportunities, and only the necessary minimum of disciplinary action. Real loyalty depends upon pride in one's job, in the firm's product or service, and upon a personal sense of belonging—of "being on the team."

Communicating. Communicating with employees is a necessary part of the directing function. Communication occurs not only through established channels for communicating—up and down the chain of command—but also through the grapevine. Good communication depends upon prompt transmission of all pertinent facts and upon being a good listener to the subordinate with a gripe or a suggestion. Managers also communicate by well-timed silences and by either extending status symbols to subordinates or withholding them.

Controlling

Controlling involves the establishment of standards and the appraisal of operating results, followed by prompt remedial action when results deviate from the standard. Evaluation of operating results involves appraisal of managerial performance, audits of policy and employee relations, review of cost and performance control reports, and analysis of financial transactions.

Control is required in the areas of sales, costs, profits, output, quality, labor turnover, accidents, employee morale, and labor relations, among others. The cornerstone of financial control is the budget, in which accurately set cost and performance standards are incorporated. Cost and performance reports should go to all managerial personnel.

In the very small business, cost and performance standards may not be formally determined, and the budget may not always be reduced to writing. Nevertheless, the efficient manager will know what cost and performance should be, will keep track of actual results, and will investigate—looking toward prompt remedial action—whenever the actual results vary from what they should be.

Management Functions and Stages of Growth

The functions of a manager are performed differently in different situations. This is particularly true for very small firms. In considering management functions, therefore, we should think about their relationship to stages of business growth. Figure 12-2 identifies four stages of small-business growth.

ACTION REPORT: Controlling Performance of Sales Representatives

The managerial function of controlling can be applied to many types of business activity. One small firm, Dranetz Engineering Laboratories of Plainfield, NJ, has developed a system to track and control the performance of independent sales representatives (reps) who sell its electronic instruments and instrumentation systems. A writer notes:

> Graphs are also used to track reps' performances. After a quota is set for each rep, the projected sales levels are plotted on a graph to provide a base line for tracking sales in the next year. At the end of each month, a member of the sales staff plots the month's actual sales for each rep for each of the three product lines. As the year progresses, Orlacchio [sales vice-president] can tell at a glance how closely a rep is progressing towards his quota in each product line.
>
> The reps get photocopies of their charts each month, along with comments from Orlacchio about how he thinks each rep is doing. If one of them is significantly off his quota, Orlacchio or one of his regional managers contacts the rep to try to discover the reasons.

Source: David De Long, "Track Sales to Control Company Growth," *Inc.*, Vol. 2, No. 5 (May, 1980), p. 80.

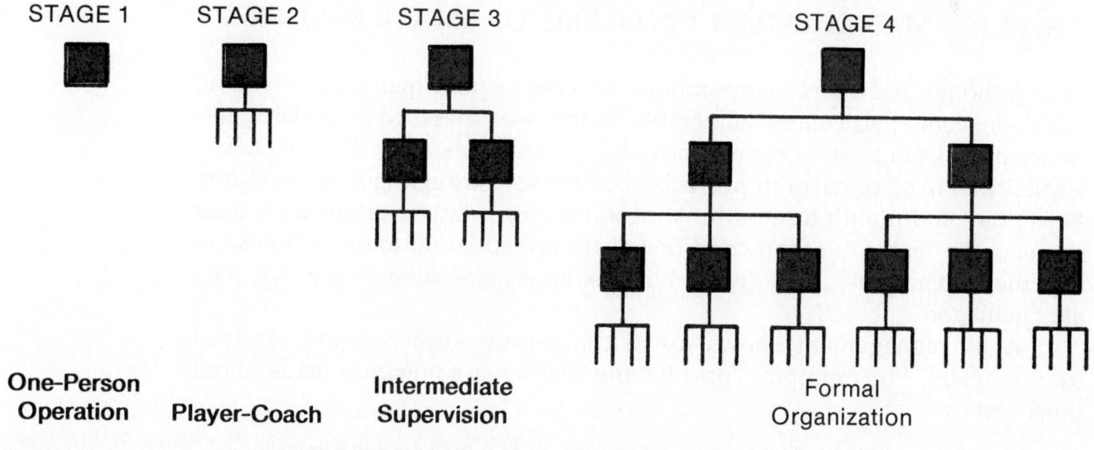

Figure 12-2 Stages of Small-Business Growth

In Stage 1 the firm is simply a one-person operation. Of course, not all firms begin at this level, but this situation is by no means rare. In Stage 2 the entrepreneur becomes a player-coach, which implies extensive participation in the operations of the business. In addition to performing the basic work—whether it be production, sales, writing checks, or record keeping—the entrepreneur must also coordinate the efforts of others.

In Stage 3 a major milestone is reached when an intermediate level of supervision is reached. In many ways this is a difficult, dangerous point for the small firm because the entrepreneur must rise above direct, hands-on management and work through an intermediate level of management.

Stage 4, the stage of formal organization, involves more than increased size and multi-layered organization. The formalization of management involves the adoption of written policies, preparation of plans and budgets, standardization of personnel practices, computerization of records, preparation of organization charts and job descriptions, scheduling of training conferences, institution of control procedures, and so on.

Some formal management practices may be adopted prior to Stage 4 of the firm's growth. Nevertheless, the stages of management growth describe a typical pattern of development for successful firms. The early flexibility and informality may be functional at the beginning, but growth necessitates greater formality in planning and control. A tension often develops as the traditional easy-going patterns of management become dysfunctional. Great managerial skill is required to preserve the "family" atmosphere while introducing professional management.

As shown in Figure 12-3, the entrepreneur's activities change drastically as the business grows from Stage 1 to Stage 4. In the very small firm, the entrepreneur is basically a "doer." As a firm grows, the entrepreneur must of necessity become less a doer and more a manager.

SPECIAL MANAGEMENT PROBLEMS OF SMALL BUSINESS

Although some large corporations experience poor management, small business seems particularly vulnerable to this weakness. Managerial inefficiency prevails in tens, or even hundreds, of thousands of small firms. Many small firms are marginal or unprofitable businesses, struggling to survive from day to day and month to month. At best, they earn only a pittance for their owners. The reason for their condition is at once apparent to one who examines their operations. They "run," but it is an exaggeration to say that they are "managed."

Weak management shows up in the service observed and received by customers. For example, consider the following comments made about hotel service:

> My guess, simply as one traveling man, is that the secret is primarily a secret of management. Capital may have something to do with it, of

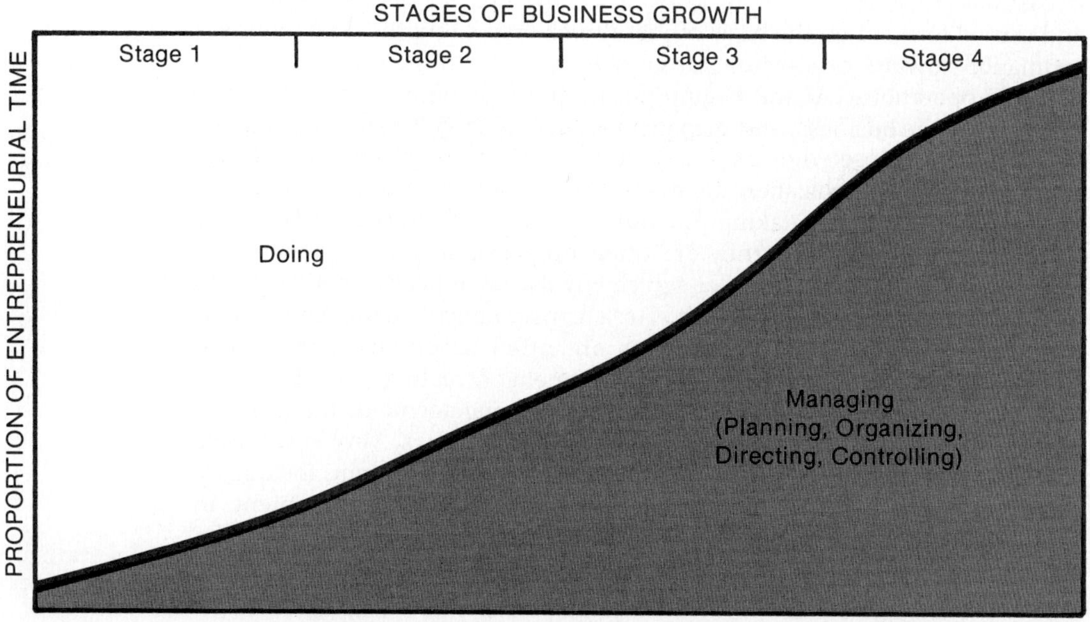

Figure 12-3 Management Functions and Stages of Growth

> course; architecture, interior decoration, location, the nature of the clientele—all these doubtless figure into the equation. At bottom, I suspect, the difference between a poor hotel/motel and a good one lies in the experience, the attitude, and the personal attention of the man or woman who runs the place. If a manager does a good job of training the maids, and pays them tolerable wages, and treats them with dignity, and praises them for doing well, that manager's rooms will be comfortable rooms—for the maids will have checked the light bulbs and tried the TV before they leave. If a manager insists upon friendly courtesy on the part of his desk clerks, he can get it—or he can get some new desk clerks.[1]

Even though management weakness is prevalent in small business, it is not universal. More important, poor management is by no means inevitable just because a firm is small.

Founders as Managers

The initial direction of a business by the founding entrepreneur is uniquely related to that entrepreneur and his or her interests. The entrepreneur's strengths may lie in production (in some cases the entrepreneur

1. James J. Kilpatrick, "Making Life More Bearable for the Traveler," *Nation's Business*, Vol. 65, No. 12 (December, 1977), p. 12.

is basically a tradesman) or in sales. The new business is often launched and carried forward on the basis of these functional strengths. The founder's inclination toward production or sales is typically influential in shaping business operations. At the beginning, the entrepreneur may be the only employee in the business, and management may be largely self-management.

Moreover, those who create new firms — the pure entrepreneurs — are not always good organization members. As we saw in Chapter 1, they are creative, innovative, risk-taking individuals who have the courage to strike out on their own. Indeed, they are often propelled into entrepreneurship by precipitating events, some of which involve a difficulty in fitting into conventional organizational roles. As a consequence, management and organizational precepts and practices are often secondary concerns of entrepreneurs who are caught up in the excitement of creating a new business.

Although business firms of all sizes require management, the need for effective management becomes more acute as a firm grows. Very small firms may survive in spite of weakness in management. To some extent, the quality of their products or services may offset deficiencies in their management. In the early days of business life, therefore, the firm may survive and grow even though its management is less than professional. Even in very small businesses, however, defects in management place strains on the business and retard its development.

Managers of Family Firms

Family relationships introduce special complications into the management process of the family firm. Some business decisions are also family decisions, and nonfamily managers may be surprised at the way in which family interests influence business operations. Rene Plessner, whose executive search firm specializes in finding executives for family-owned companies, explains how family decisions dominate the business:

> In a family company, you may have the title and the responsibility, and one day you walk into the office and you don't know that two cousins, a brother-in-law, sister, and the Papa had dinner over the weekend and made a decision upsetting what you expected to do .... Nobody was out to get you; it's simply, to be trite about it, blood is thicker than water. The family members talk among themselves. You have to be flexible enough to handle that.[2]

In some family businesses, key positions are reserved for family members. This, in turn, reduces the attractiveness of the firm for nonfamily members who have ambition for advancement. Family members may also be

2. Priscilla Anne Schwab, "Matchmaker Discourages Love at First Sight," *Nation's Business*, Vol. 69, No. 1 (January, 1981), p. 64.

retained in key positions because of their family relationship, even though they are professionally weak.

One family entrepreneur's attempt to correct a lack of management skills is described below:

> In one case the founder's son, who was in command, diagnosed the business' problem as a lack of specialized talent. His solution was to become the firm's all-purpose expert—lawyer, accountant, and personnel specialist all wrapped into one. And to implement his solution, he went to night school. Little did he know that hiring someone outside the family who already had the necessary knowledge would have been better. His choice had several negative consequences, including his own physical exhaustion. The lesson here is that when the money is available or the need is critical there is no substitute for genuine expertise.[3]

Thus, decisions which sacrifice efficiency in the interest of preserving family interests can easily destroy the vitality of the family firm's management.

Managers and Decision Making

A manager constantly faces the necessity of making decisions. Proper guidance of the enterprise requires decisions on business objectives, scale of operation, marketing policies, products and product cost, product quality, work assignments, pay rates, and employee grievances, among many others. Virtually every managerial activity involves a choice among alternatives, thereby requiring a decision by the manager.

In making decisions, the business manager is often tempted to rely upon intuition. Indeed, one may be forced to do so because of the intangibles involved or the absence of necessary information. The intuitive decision may be criticized, however, if it disregards factual information that is already available or that is easy to obtain. Another basis for decisions is past experience, which has both strength and weakness. There is an important element of practicality that comes from experience; but at the same time, past experience is no sure guide to the future. In making decisions, therefore, the manager should have a healthy respect for factual data and should utilize them as extensively as possible.

TIME MANAGEMENT

Much of the manager's time during the working day may be spent on the firing line—meeting customers, solving problems, listening to employee complaints, seeing outsiders interested in getting contributions for charity, and the like. The manager of the small firm faces the problems of

3. Elmer H. Burack and Thomas M. Calero, "Seven Perils of the Family Firm," *Nation's Business*, Vol. 69, No. 1 (January, 1981), p. 63.

management with the assistance of only a small staff. All of this means that the manager's energies and activities are diffused more than those of managers in large firms.

Problem of Time Pressure

Many managers work from 60 to 80 hours per week. One frequent and unfortunate result of overwork is the inefficient performance of those tasks for which the managers are responsible. They may be too busy to see traveling salespeople who can supply market information on new products and processes. They may be too busy to read the technical or trade literature in order to discover what others are doing and the improvements being created that might be adapted to their own use. Because managers are too busy, they fail to listen carefully to employee opinions and grievances or to reach an understanding with employees. Because managers are too busy to give instructions in a proper manner, employees may not know what to do or how to do it correctly.

Time-Savers for Busy Managers

One important answer to the problem of lack of time is a good organization of the work. This permits delegation of duties to subordinates, who are then permitted to discharge those duties without close supervision. Of course, this requires the selection and training of individuals to assume responsibility for the delegated functions.

Sometimes a manager must see visitors who may overstay the necessary time. Various devices have been tried by managers who have faced this problem, including the use of secretarial interruptions with reminders of other appointments. A more direct approach is simply to tell the visitor in advance that the manager is busy and can allot at most ten minutes, and then stick to this time limit. Another means of conserving time is to provide dictating equipment which permits dictation at convenient times and transcription by the secretary without frequent interruptions. In addition, the secretary can sort out unimportant mail, screen incoming phone calls, and keep a schedule of appointments.

Another major time consumer is the business conference with subordinates. Often these meetings just happen and drag on without any serious attempt to control them. The manager should prepare an agenda for such meetings, set starting and ending times, hold the conferences to the subjects to be discussed, and assign the necessary follow-through to specific subordinates. In this way the contribution of business conferences may be maximized and the manager's own time conserved, along with that of subordinates.

Perhaps the greatest time-saver of all is the effective use of time. If an individual flits from one task to another and back again, it is likely that little will be accomplished. Effective, sustained effort requires some planning to prevent the haphazard use of time that occurs if there is no planning. The first step in planning one's use of time should be a survey of time normally spent on various activities. Relying on general impressions is unscientific and is likely to involve considerable error. For a period of several days, or preferably several weeks, the manager should record the time spent on various types of activities during the day. Analysis of these figures will reveal the pattern of activities, those projects and tasks involving the greatest time expenditure, and factors responsible for waste of time.

OUTSIDE MANAGEMENT ASSISTANCE

In carrying out their managerial functions, managers of small firms often are less effective than they should be. Frequently they encounter problems that they themselves cannot solve. They should recognize that seeking outside counsel is not an admission of failure or incapacity, but rather a logical move to supplement and strengthen one's management abilities.

The value of management consultation does not vary directly with business size. The management problems of small firms may be fully as perplexing to their management staffs as are the problems of large corporations to their management teams. Many small firms clearly recognize this fact and regularly utilize outside management advisers. Even very small firms of the corner-grocery type consult with their bankers or public accountants.

By using consultants, entrepreneurs can overcome some of their own deficiencies in managerial capacity. Furthermore, an "insider" directly involved in a business problem often "cannot see the forest for the trees." To offset this limitation, the consultant brings an objective point of view and new ideas, supported by a broad knowledge of proved, successful, cost-saving methods. The consultant also can help the manager improve decision making through better organization of fact-gathering and the introduction of scientific techniques of analysis. Ideally the consultant should have an "on call" relationship with the small business, so that improved methods may be put into use as the need arises.

Sources of Management Assistance

The sources of management assistance given here are by no means exhaustive. No doubt there are numerous, less obvious sources of management knowledge and approaches to seeking needed help. For example, owner-managers may increase their own skills by consulting public and university libraries, attending evening colleges, or considering suggestions of friends and customers.

Small Business Institute (SBI) Programs. In 1972, the Small Business Administration implemented the Small Business Institute (SBI) program to make the consulting resources of universities available to small-business firms.[4] SBI teams of upper-division and graduate students, under the direction of a faculty member, work with owners of small firms in analyzing their business problems and devising solutions. The primary users of such SBI consulting assistance are applicants for SBA loans, although the services are not restricted to such firms.

The program has been one of mutual benefit in providing students with a practical view of business management and in finding answers for the problems of small firms. Students from a small-business, business-policy, or similar course are typically combined in teams that provide a diversity of academic backgrounds. Individual teams, for example, may have different members specializing in management, marketing, accounting, and finance. There has been an evident enthusiasm on the part of those participating in the program, and many feel it has been one of the most successful consulting programs for small business.

ACTION REPORT: SBI Students Salvage a Small Business

Although there is no way of evaluating the overall effectiveness of the SBI student consulting program, a few teams have produced sensational results. One team which received national attention consisted of students at the University of North Florida under the direction of their faculty project director, Dr. Lowell M. Salter.

The client firm, a building contractor, was in serious trouble. His bills were delinquent, his contractor's license was revoked, and the IRS was threatening to close his business.

Dr. Salter assigned two graduate business students as the SBI counseling team. Within four weeks, the business was turned around. Within ten weeks, payments were current, including obligations to the IRS. Within six months, the business had tripled.

How did the students do it? First, they generated $22,000 worth of business for their client. Then they managed to have his license restored, and they helped him recruit some qualified personnel. Dr. Salter appraised the team as follows: "We not only saved this man from going on welfare, we also helped him employ jobless people. He would not be in business today if it were not for the students."

Source: Small Business Administration, "SBI Story Brings Deluge of Calls, Letters to Director," *Insight*, Vol. 4, No. 1 (August, 1976), p. 6.

---

4. A series of articles on the Small Business Institute program appears in the *Journal of Small Business Management*, Vol. 15, No. 2 (April, 1977).

Service Corps of Retired Executives (SCORE). Small-business managers can obtain free management advice from a group called the Service Corps of Retired Executives (SCORE) by appealing to any Small Business Administration field office. SCORE is an organization of retired business executives who will consult on current problems with small-business managers. Functioning under the sponsorship of the Small Business Administration, this group provides an opportunity for retired executives to be useful again to society, and it helps the small-business managers solve their problems. Hence, the relationship is mutually beneficial. It may also encourage entrepreneurs to utilize paid consultants as their firms grow by demonstrating the worth of consulting service.

There are numerous stories of successful SCORE assistance to small firms. A race car driver, for example, went into the tire business but experienced problems with poor records and inadequate credit control. The SCORE counselor, a retired tire manufacturer and district sales manager, provided suggestions that led to an immediate increase in profits. Another firm, a small manufacturer, established a cost reduction/profit improvement program with the aid of a SCORE counselor. The enthusiastic owner reported increased sales volume, higher-than-industry profits, and improved financial standing.

Certified Public Accountant (CPA) Firms. CPA firms, both large and small, provide a range of financial and management services to small businesses. Deloitte Haskins and Sells, one of the major CPA firms, offers the services listed in Figure 12-4.

Management Consultants. General management consultants serve small-business firms as well as large corporations. The entrepreneur should regard the service of a competent management consultant as an investment in cost reduction. Many small firms could save as much as 10 to 20 percent of annual operating costs. The inherent advantage in the use of able consultants is suggested by the existence of thousands of consulting firms. They range from large, long-established firms to small one- or two-person operations. Two broad areas of service rendered by management consultants are:

1. To help a client get out of trouble.
2. To help prevent trouble by anticipating and eliminating its causes.

Business firms have traditionally used consultants to help solve problems they could not handle alone.[5] But an even greater service that manage-

5. Professor Herbert E. Kierulff of Seattle Pacific University has described a three-phase "turnaround" process successfully used by a consulting firm in helping more than 200 smaller companies. See Herbert E. Kierulff, "Turnaround vs. Bankruptcies," *In Business*, Vol. 3, No. 3 (May-June, 1981), pp. 37-38. This shows how consultants help small firms get out of trouble.

Accounting and Reporting Systems

1. Developing basic accounting systems and forms, and establishing related office procedures.
2. Designing and installing cost accounting systems.
3. Designing and installing systems for the control of production and inventories.
4. Designing financial reports.
5. Planning and coordinating the use of outside computer services.
6. Assisting in recruiting, training, and evaluating accounting and clerical personnel.

Audit Services

1. Conducting a general audit of the financial statements.
2. Evaluating systems and procedures for internal control.
3. Assisting in various filings with the Securities and Exchange Commission and other regulatory agencies.

Budgets and Forecasts

1. Preparing monthly and annual operating budgets.
2. Developing long-range operating plans.
3. Installing cash-flow and other specialized forecasting systems.
4. Computing material, labor, and overhead rates for use in bidding and pricing.

Consulting

Consulting with management on the various aspects of:

1. Capital needs and alternative methods of financing business growth.
2. Credit and collection policies, dividend policies, compensation plans, and insurance.
3. Changes in products, methods, facilities, markets, and product pricing.
4. Accounting for pension and profit-sharing plans, stock-option plans, and other contracts.
5. Applying for loans and credit.
6. Preparing government reports.
7. Preparing contract bids and proposals.

Financial Statements

1. Assisting in the preparation of unaudited interim and year-end financial statements.
2. Assisting management in the interpretation of interim and year-end financial statements.

Taxes

1. Preparing annual income tax returns.
2. Advising on tax planning for the organization, the individual, and the individual's estate.
3. Training personnel to prepare payroll, sales and use, and similar tax returns due throughout the year.

Source: *Services to Small and Growing Businesses* (Deloitte Haskins and Sells, 1978), pp. 7-9.

Figure 12-4 Financial and Management Services Offered to Small Businesses

ment consultants provide is their daily observation and analysis, which keep problems from becoming "big." This view of the role of consultants greatly enlarges their service potential. Figure 12-5 shows a diagnostic checklist to determine whether or not the small business has a need for consultants.

The questions below may be used by owners to determine the need for management assistance and by students and other consultants who wish to "size up" a particular firm as an initial step in providing management assistance.

Management

_____ 1. Does the firm have specific objectives?
_____ 2. Are its objectives written?
_____ 3. Does it have written long-range and short-range plans?
_____ 4. Are there clear position descriptions for all key jobs?
_____ 5. Are relationships among positions and departments well-defined?
_____ 6. Does it have an organization chart?
_____ 7. Are its controls adequate for decision making?

Marketing

_____ 1. What has been the sales trend for the past five years?
_____ 2. Does the firm have a seasonal sales pattern?
_____ 3. Has the potential market been analyzed?
_____ 4. Is the nature of the firm's customers changing?
_____ 5. What share of the market does it hold?
_____ 6. Is its market share growing or declining?
_____ 7. Have its product lines been defined?
_____ 8. Does it explore new lines and delete less effective ones?
_____ 9. Does it prepare sales forecasts?
_____ 10. Does it compare sales results to sales quotas or forecasts?
_____ 11. Has the firm analyzed the effectiveness of its advertising?
_____ 12. Are its personal selling practices satisfactory?
_____ 13. Does it use appropriate sales promotion methods?
_____ 14. Does it measure customer satisfaction?
_____ 15. Does it price its products competitively?
_____ 16. Are credit accounts offered to its customers in line with industry practices?

Production/Operations

_____ 1. Is the firm's product design suitable for efficient production?
_____ 2. Is its production equipment technologically adequate and in good condition?
_____ 3. Does its physical layout contribute to operating efficiency?
_____ 4. If it is a marketing firm, does its physical layout encourage sales?
_____ 5. Is there extensive idle time for either machines or personnel?
_____ 6. Can the handling and storage of raw materials, work in process, or finished goods be significantly improved?

Figure 12-5 Diagnostic Checklist to Determine Need for Consultants (Page 1)

_____ 7. Does it control quality adequately?
_____ 8. At what points does it check for quality?
_____ 9. Are its production operations scheduled carefully?
_____ 10. Is its plant housekeeping adequate?

Purchasing and Inventory Control

_____ 1. Does the firm buy the desired quality at the best price?
_____ 2. Does it use the best sources of supply?
_____ 3. Does it have a minimum of dead stock?
_____ 4. Is its inventory truly current and usable?
_____ 5. Does it use an effective inventory control system?
_____ 6. Does it experience frequent stock-outs?
_____ 7. Is its inventory turnover rate adequate?
_____ 8. How does it determine its reorder point?
_____ 9. How does it determine its minimum ordering quantities?

Personnel

_____ 1. What sources does the firm use for recruiting personnel?
_____ 2. Are its selection methods adequate to assure properly qualified personnel?
_____ 3. Does it provide sufficient training for its personnel?
_____ 4. What types of training does it use?
_____ 5. Are its compensation levels and fringe benefits competitive?
_____ 6. How does its personnel turnover rate compare with that of the industry?
_____ 7. Has it prepared written personnel policies?

Finance

_____ 1. What is the firm's rate of return on equity?
_____ 2. What is its debt-equity ratio?
_____ 3. What is its current ratio?
_____ 4. What is its acid-test ratio?
_____ 5. Are its cash balances and working capital adequate for its sales volume?
_____ 6. Are its financial statements prepared regularly? By whom?
_____ 7. Does its accounting system provide current information on accounts payable and accounts receivable?
_____ 8. Does it use an operating budget?
_____ 9. Are its operating results compared with budgeted amounts?
_____ 10. Does it use a cash budget?
_____ 11. Does it take all available cash discounts in purchasing?
_____ 12. Does it pay its current obligations promptly?

Figure 12-5 Diagnostic Checklist to Determine Need for Consultants (Page 2)

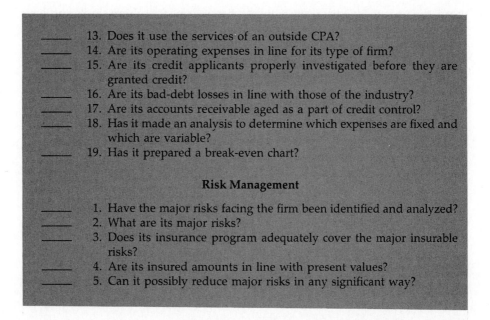

_____ 13. Does it use the services of an outside CPA?
_____ 14. Are its operating expenses in line for its type of firm?
_____ 15. Are its credit applicants properly investigated before they are granted credit?
_____ 16. Are its bad-debt losses in line with those of the industry?
_____ 17. Are its accounts receivable aged as a part of credit control?
_____ 18. Has it made an analysis to determine which expenses are fixed and which are variable?
_____ 19. Has it prepared a break-even chart?

Risk Management

_____ 1. Have the major risks facing the firm been identified and analyzed?
_____ 2. What are its major risks?
_____ 3. Does its insurance program adequately cover the major insurable risks?
_____ 4. Are its insured amounts in line with present values?
_____ 5. Can it possibly reduce major risks in any significant way?

Figure 12-5 Diagnostic Checklist to Determine Need for Consultants (Page 3)

Cost of Consulting Services

Management consultants may be hired on a fixed-fee basis (by the day or by the engagement) or on an annual retainer basis. Retained consultants are "on call" to the small firms that have contracted for their services, thus assuring their clients of regular assistance.

The direct cost of consulting service often appears high. While the cost savings may not be immediately measurable, they should be realized if competent counsel is obtained. Moreover, the small-business manager may propose a fee contingent upon demonstrable results (in the form of lower costs and higher profits). Small consulting firms can reasonably accept such an arrangement. Another possibility for the small firm is to let the consultant take a part of the fee in the form of company stock.

Selection of a Consultant

Management consultants may be located by talking with business friends, accountants, attorneys, bankers, and trade associations. Firms which have used a particular consultant may share their opinions and provide recommendations or warnings. By talking with these firms, it is possible to evaluate this consultant's work. To check a consultant's reputation, furthermore, the prospective user can request a list of firms for whom similar projects have been completed by this consultant.

The small business may well be wary of firms that use "high-pressure" approaches. An ethical consulting firm will not engage in offensive self-promotion any more than it will haggle over fees.

It is well also to learn some things about the consultant such as length of time engaged in business, training and experience, and financial status. Fees to be paid and time stipulated for the accomplishment of results should be contractually specified. And both consultant and client should require a clear definition of the consultant's task.

Cooperation between client and consultant is important. The small-business manager can contribute to the improvement of the consultant's service by throwing open the establishment and its business records to the consultant. Data requested should be promptly and accurately furnished—with no pertinent facts withheld. Problems noted by either client or consultant should be promptly called to the other's attention and full exploration made so that a solution may be found quickly. Promptness in taking remedial action reduces the scope and impact of many problems.

Common Criticisms of Consultants

One frequent criticism of management consultants is that even among the reputable ones there are charlatans who claim a background of skill and experience they do not possess. While this criticism may be valid occasionally, it does not warrant suspicion of able, ethical consulting firms. Instead, it calls for care in the selection of a consultant.

Another criticism is that management consultants, unlike doctors and public accountants, need not be licensed by the state to practice and are not subject to ejection from the profession in the event of unethical practice. There are, however, several associations whose members subscribe to a code of professional practice and ethics.

A third charge against management consultants is that they may insert themselves unduly into management and take over its responsibilities. Fulfillment of responsibilities is up to the managers themselves. They cannot be forced to turn responsibilities over to a consultant. Hence, if responsibilities shift from manager to consultant, it is the manager's own fault.

A fourth common criticism concerns lack of ability. Information on percentage of satisfied clients, like that on frequency of repeat engagements, is difficult to obtain. The growth of consulting services, however, makes it obvious that consultants have many satisfied customers.

LOOKING BACK

1. The management functions of planning, organizing, directing, and controlling are performed by all managers of both small and big businesses.
2. As small firms grow, they move from simple, informal management relationships to more complex, formalized management systems. This requires entrepreneurs to advance from "doers" to "player-coaches" to full-time managers.
3. A large proportion of small businesses is characterized by weak management. In part, this results from the lack of managerial expertise by entrepreneurs whose primary focus is creating a new business rather than managing. The managerial effectiveness of many family firms is also hampered by various family considerations which run counter to good management practice.
4. Small-business managers who are too busy to perform their managerial tasks efficiently should learn to delegate some duties to subordinates and to organize their work by careful planning.
5. Outside management assistance is provided by many types of consultants, including SBI student consultants, SCORE (retired executives), CPA firms, general management consultants, and various other organizations.

   The use of management consultants may be thought of as an investment in cost reduction. They may be employed for single projects, or they may be retained on a continuing basis for use as necessary. Owner-managers of small businesses can locate and screen consultants by talking with business friends, accountants, clients of particular consultants, and other business leaders.

DISCUSSION QUESTIONS

1. What are the general functions of management? Briefly describe the nature of each.
2. Is a budget more closely related to the function of planning or the function of controlling?
3. What are the activities involved in the function of directing?
4. What are the four stages of small-business growth outlined in this chapter? How do the managerial requirements change as the firm moves through these stages?
5. Is it likely that the quality of management is relatively uniform throughout the many types of small

businesses? What might account for any differences noted?

6. Evaluate founders as managers. Why is there a tendency toward managerial weakness in those who create new firms?

7. What special managerial problems exist in the family firm?

8. What practices can a small-business manager utilize to conserve time?

9. Is it reasonable to believe that an outsider coming into a business could propose procedures or policies superior to those of the manager who is intimately acquainted with operations? Why?

10. Explain the nature of the SBI student consulting program. Is this program of primary benefit to the client firm or to the students?

REFERENCES TO SMALL BUSINESS IN ACTION

"Entrepreneurial Trap." *Forbes*, Vol. 125, No. 7 (March 31, 1980), pp. 86-91.

The story of Lawter Chemicals, a growing business, explains the dilemma of an entrepreneur who tried to do too much of the work and who failed to practice delegation. Outside management consultants were employed to analyze the management problems of the firm.

Jakobson, Cathryn. "Putting Ideas to Work." *Inc.*, Vol. 3, No. 2 (February, 1981), pp. 90-96.

A new firm, National Singing Telegram Ltd., used the contributions of many creative persons but lacked proper management. This story tells how systematic management methods were applied to this small business.

"What Makes Tandem Run." *Business Week*, No. 2645 (July 14, 1980), pp. 73-74.

Tandem Computers, Inc., using a highly unorthodox management style, has grown rapidly and has prospered. Its people-oriented approach features Friday afternoon parties, flexible hours, a swimming pool open between 6 a.m. and 8 p.m., and a sabbatical for employees every four years.

"You've Got to Blow Your Horn." *Forbes*, Vol. 125, No. 3 (February 4, 1980), pp. 94-95.

Carl G. Sontheimer, inventor and marketer of the Cuisinart food-processing machine, has been highly successful. However, the firm has grown to the point that the entrepreneur's personal involvement in the details of the business is proving inadequate as a basis for effective management.

Chapter 13

Objectives, Strategy, and Operational Planning

LOOKING AHEAD

Watch for the following important topics:

1. Nature of profit, service, and growth objectives.
2. Social responsibilities and ethical standards of small firms.
3. Formulating strategy and finding the strategic niche.
4. The planning process in small business.
5. Quantitative tools to aid planning, and their limitations.

Someone has said, "If you don't know where you're going, any path will get you there." Unfortunately that statement describes many small firms—they don't know where they are going. This chapter directs attention to the planning process of deciding on objectives, formulating strategy, developing operating plans, and using quantitative tools to aid planning. The planning process enables the small firm to know *where* it is going and *how* it is going to get there.

SMALL-BUSINESS OBJECTIVES AND RESPONSIBILITIES

All privately owned businesses, large or small, are presumed to have at least three main objectives: to earn a profit, to perform economic service, and to achieve continued growth. In addition to these main objectives, small firms also have a more general objective involving social responsibilities to the community.

Profit Objective

A primary goal of every privately owned business is profit. Profits must be earned to reward the entrepreneur's acceptance of business risks and to assure business continuity. Without profit, a business firm can make no long-run contribution to employees, suppliers, customers, or the community.

Profit making is not a short-range concern but rather a matter of long-range significance. Hence, the owner cannot be unduly concerned with the net profit reported on the income statement each month, each quarter, or each year unless this is part of a long-run trend or condition. Undue concern with short-range profit making is somewhat like clock watching on the part of the employee. Profit maximization over the long run should be the major goal, with the periodic income statement regarded as a progress report.

Profit goals must be made specific if they are to be useful. These goals are part of the operational plans described on pages 339-344 of this chapter. In these plans the profit objective must be specified in terms of so many dollars of profit in a particular year, quarter, or month.

Service Objective

Rendering economic service to the community means providing a flow of goods and/or services to the public. Providing such service is necessary to earn the profits desired by the owner. In a broader sense, the service objective is also an obligation of the privately owned firm to the society which permits its existence.

The service goals of a business firm must be modified as consumer tastes change and as competitive products and services are developed. The most basic service objectives are part of a firm's strategy, which is discussed on pages 334-339. In the process of formulating strategy, the entrepreneur must contemplate the basic mission of the firm and the extent to which it will be similar to or different from competitors in serving customers.

Growth Objective

A business philosophy concerned with profit making and economic service must also be concerned with enterprise growth. Some persons have gone so far as to suggest that a business must either grow or die. In an expanding economy, growth is normal for a healthy, successful business. Growth envisions the need for additional operating facilities and calls for retained earnings or new investment by the owners. Growth demands an awareness of technological advances.

The importance attached to growth by different businesspersons varies. Some managers are inclined to accept the status quo and to feel little need for growth. The entrepreneur's age is an example of one variable that may affect the attitude toward growth. There are undoubtedly other factors, some of which are rooted in the personalities of the individuals. One research study of a small sample of business firms suggests the following three viewpoints concerning growth:

1. *The conservative operator's* major goal is survival. Growth in terms of production, revenue, or profit is not an objective. This person believes that the best way to remain relatively stable is to maintain the status quo.
2. *The industry stalwart's* goal is to seek an *acceptable* rather than an *optimum* rate of profit. This person merely strives to keep up with the industry.
3. *The aggressive, innovating operator's* goal is to maximize profit. This person views production and revenue growth as the means to this end.[1]

There is a danger in the assumption that all growth is good. Some owner-managers tend to prize growth for growth's sake without evaluating its impact on the profits of the business. One analyst has highlighted the problem in this way: "The most common cause of trouble is the widely held belief that the only road to success is through growth. Many businessmen see growth of sales as the solution to all problems. It seldom is."[2]

Growth objectives become specific as particular goals are built into the operating plans for the business. Plans may be developed, for example, to call for a doubling of sales volume over the next five years.

Social Responsibilities

In recent years public attention has been focused on the issue of social responsibilities of business organizations. Even business leaders have joined the chorus of those proclaiming the social obligations of the business community. These feelings of concern are seemingly rooted in a new awareness of the role of business in modern society. In a sense, managers now occupy a "trusteeship" position and must act accordingly to protect the new interests

---

1. Adapted from Chapter 5 of F. Parker Fowler, Jr., and E. W. Sandberg, *The Relationship of Management Decision-Making to Small Business Growth*, Small Business Management Research Report. Prepared by Colorado State University Research Foundation under a grant from the Small Business Administration, Washington, DC, 1964.

2. Herbert N. Woodward, "Management Strategies for Small Companies," *Harvard Business Review*, Vol. 54, No. 1 (January-February, 1976), p. 114.

of suppliers, employees, customers, and the general public, along with making a profit for the owners of the business.

Managers of small businesses have recognized the same responsibility as clearly, if not always as eloquently, as those who speak for big business.[3] In fact, many independent entrepreneurs speak of their satisfaction in serving the community as one of the major rewards from their businesses. Of course, this does not mean that all firms share this philosophy; some fail to sense or refuse to recognize any obligation beyond the minimum necessary to produce a profit.

A sense of social responsibility may be perfectly consistent with the firm's long-run profit objective. The firm which consistently fulfills certain obligations makes itself a desirable member of the community and may attract patronage. Conversely, the firm which scorns social responsibilities may find itself the object of restrictive legislation and may discover its employees to be lacking in loyalty. It seems likely, however, that the typical independent entrepreneur contributes to the community and other groups simply because it is a duty and a privilege to do so, and not because the profit potential in each such move has been cunningly calculated.

Recognition of a social responsibility does not change a profit-seeking business into a charitable organization. Earning a profit is absolutely essential. Without profits, the firm is in no position to recognize social responsibilities toward anyone. The point is that profits, although essential, are not necessarily the only factor of importance to the businessperson.

Environmentalism and Small Business. In recent decades the deterioration of the environment has become a matter of widespread concern.[4] One source of pollution has been business firms that discharge waste into streams, contaminants into the air, and noise into areas surrounding their operations. Efforts to preserve and redeem the environment thus directly affect business organizations, including small-business firms.

The interests of small-business owners and environmentalists are not necessarily or uniformly in conflict. Some business leaders, including those in small business, have worked and acted for the cause of conservation. For example, many small firms have taken steps to remove eyesores and to landscape and otherwise improve plant facilities. Others have modernized their equipment and changed their procedures to reduce air and water pollution. In a few cases, small business has been in a position to benefit from the emphasis

---

3. For another discussion of social responsibility in small businesses, see Fred L. Fry, "Social Responsibility in the Smaller Firm: A Model," *American Journal of Small Business*, Vol. 1 (January, 1977), pp. 25-32.

4. For further information, see Charles G. Leathers, "Environmentalism and Small Business," *Journal of Small Business Management*, Vol. 10, No. 4 (October, 1972), pp. 16-20; and James A. Commins and Alfred Stapler for the U. S. Small Business Administration, *Reducing Air Pollution in Industry*, Management Aid No. 217 (Washington: U. S. Government Printing Office, February, 1973).

on ecology. Those companies whose products are harmless to the environment gain an edge over competitive products that pollute. Also, small firms are involved in servicing pollution-control equipment. The auto repair shop, for example, services pollution-control devices on automobile engines.

Some small firms are adversely affected by efforts to protect the environment. Livestock feeding lots, cement plants, pet-food processors, and iron foundries are representative of industries that are especially vulnerable to extensive regulation. The cost impact in businesses of this type is often severe. Indeed, the required improvements can force the closure of some businesses.

The ability to pass higher costs on to customers is dependent upon the market situation and is ordinarily quite difficult for the small firm. Resulting economic hardships on small business must, therefore, be recognized as a cost of pollution control and evaluated accordingly. In some instances the controls are hardest on the small, marginal firm with obsolete equipment. Environmental regulation may merely hasten the inevitable demise of the firm.

The level of government regulation poses another potential problem for small business. Legislation, whether state or local, may prove discriminatory by forcing higher costs on a local firm than on competitive firms outside the regulated territory. The immediate self-interest of a small firm, therefore, is served by regulations that operate at the highest or most general level. A federal regulation, for example, applies to all United States firms and thereby precludes competitive advantages to low-cost polluters in other states.

Consumerism and Small Business. The concept of customer satisfaction has become increasingly critical in the last few years. At one time the accepted philosophy was expressed as "Let the buyer beware." In contrast, today's newer philosophy holds—"Let the seller beware." Today's sophisticated buyers feel that they should be able to purchase products that are safe, reliable, durable, and honestly advertised. This theme has influenced various types of consumer legislation. The Magnuson-Moss Warranty Act, for example, imposes special restrictions on sellers—such as requiring warranties to be available for inspection rather than be hidden inside a package.

Small firms are directly involved in the consumerism movement. To some extent they stand to gain from it. Attention to customer needs and flexibility in meeting these needs have traditionally been strong assets of small firms. Their managers have been close to customers and thus able to know and respond easily to their needs. To the extent that these potential features have been realized in practice, the position of small business has been strengthened. And to the extent that small firms can continue to capitalize upon customer desires for excellent service, they can reap rewards from the consumerism movement.

Consumerism also carries threats to small business. It is hard to build a completely safe product and to avoid all errors in service. Moreover, the growing complexity of products makes their servicing more difficult. The mechanic or repairer must know a great deal more to render satisfactory service today than was needed two or three decades earlier. Rising consumer expectations, therefore, provide a measure of danger as well as opportunity for small firms. The quality of management will determine the extent to which opportunities are realized and dangers avoided.

Ethical Practices and Small Business. The fact that an individual can enter business at will does not endow that person with the right to do anything and everything without restraints. Although our competitive system and governmental action are both policing forces that tend to regulate business conduct, they are not enough. Society needs entrepreneurs who voluntarily observe ethical standards which exceed the requirements of the law.

Development of Business Ethics. For years many business leaders failed to take seriously the matter of ethical business practice. Even now, some dismiss it as impractical for a firm seeking optimization of profits. Others consider ethical practices and governmental regulation to be virtually synonymous. Nevertheless, we have slowly attained a widespread acceptance of the view that business must act in the interest of its customers, employees, suppliers, and others affected by its operations, while also acting in its own interest.

In part, this moral progress has been fostered by competition. Ethical business practices, in other words, have been found to be good business. Enlightened self-interest has thus no doubt motivated much ethical behavior. It is true also that the government, through pure food and drug laws, Federal Trade Commission activities, and the like, has made a contribution to better business morals.

Nevertheless, much remains to be done. Our concern is not primarily with illegal practices. Legal conduct is assumed as the bare minimum for ethical behavior. In addition, management must be concerned with the borderline areas of ethical behavior. For example, the salesperson's expense account tends to become a "swindle sheet." Purchasing agents may accept expensive gifts from order-seeking firms. Unquestionably, this imposes some sense of obligation on their part and may create a conflict of loyalties.

Consistency in Business Ethics. A manager cannot be honest in big things and dishonest in little things. If one tries this, the cumulative effect of little dishonesties will pervert one's perspective of life and management. The manager is in a position of power; business success generates a sense of power and infallibility of action. The manager is often tempted to engage in small violations of ethical practice for immediate gain. But taking advantage of others in the small case leads eventually to total moral irresponsibility and improper use of administrative power.

It is indeed remarkable how those employed by a given firm can sense the manager's moral code. Insincerity and a lack of integrity on the manager's part cannot long be concealed from subordinates. The manager's moral code must have a sound basis so that fair play and honesty in all relationships with workers, customers, and others become instinctive acts. The crux of the matter is that restraint cannot come entirely from law but requires conscience in the management of business. When self-imposed restraints fail, people turn to the government for a restraint which the collective conscience failed to provide.

Formal Code of Ethics. In some industrial and professional fields, group action has been taken to adopt formal codes of ethics. Doctors, lawyers, and public accountants are typical examples of professional groups that are closely regulated by self-imposed ethical codes. A few years ago, owners of automobile repair shops in a small city met and formulated a code of ethics stressing the principle of fair play with employees and good service for customers. This is significant as an attempt to do something constructive about ethics in the business field and raise it to a professional level.

A special reference should be made to the work of trade associations and the Federal Trade Commission, often acting cooperatively, in formulating ethical codes for various industrial fields. The Federal Trade Commission sponsors trade-practice conferences in which representative business leaders attempt to develop codes to prevent unfair methods of competition. They are encouraged to discuss openly the practices and problems of their industries in arriving at codes of fair competition.

Ethical Advertising. Unethical business behavior has perhaps been more apparent in advertising than in any other area. The public has the right to expect ethical advertising, however, because of its importance to the individual and its great persuasive power in the economy. Advertising is a form of communication, and untruthfulness or other breaches of ethical behavior are as objectionable there as they are elsewhere.

Because of advertising's far-reaching influence, the advertiser must assume some social responsibility and must abide by ideals of honesty, reliability, and integrity. Advertising must be truthful without omitting material facts. For example, if only one or two items are being offered at a reduced price, this fact should be clearly stated. The claim that a soft drink is healthful would be unreliable advertising if there are *any* ill effects. Merchandise represented as "formerly $10.98" should have been sold by the advertiser at that price for a period of time if the advertiser has integrity.

There is also the question of good and bad taste in advertising. Advertisements bordering on the vulgar and immoral should certainly be avoided. Advertisements which reflect adversely on religious beliefs or minority groups should also be avoided because they tend to create resentment toward both the company and the product which it advertises.

Better Business Bureaus. Better Business Bureaus have been established by privately owned business firms in many cities to promote ethical conduct on the part of all business firms in the community. Specifically, a Better Business Bureau's function is two-fold: (1) it provides free buying guidelines and information about a company that the consumer should know *prior* to completing a business transaction, and (2) it attempts to solve questions or disputes concerning purchases. As a result, business swindles often decline in a community served by a Better Business Bureau. Figure 13-1 presents a small section from a code of advertising ethics developed by the Better Business Bureau.

SMALL-BUSINESS STRATEGY

Planning for the small firm's future should begin with a basic strategy—an overall plan that relates the firm's products and/or services to the needs of the marketplace and the offerings of competitors. Entrepreneurs formulate strategy by sizing up the general situation pertaining to the business as a whole and deciding upon necessary changes of a fundamental nature.

Formulating Strategy

Business strategy is concerned with decisions which shape the very nature of the firm. Decisions affecting such issues as breadth of product line, geographical expansion, quality level, and orientation toward growth are strategic decisions. A restaurant's strategy, for example, is determined by its decisions regarding menu (steaks versus hamburgers), motif (modern coffee shop versus old waterfront theme), location (shopping center versus resort area), and other choices of this type. Small-business strategy may just "happen," or it may result from careful thought about the mission of the firm. The latter is obviously preferable in building a profitable business.

The process of strategic decision making is depicted in Figure 13-2. The beginning step involves an identification of environmental opportunities and risks. The world constantly changes, and the changes provide challenges and opportunities. If the business location begins to deteriorate, for example, the entrepreneur must decide how to adapt to the changing situation. Environmental changes may be either positive or negative, and they may occur either slowly or quickly.

Bait Advertising and Selling

A "bait" offer is an alluring but insincere offer to sell a product or service which the advertiser does not intend to sell. Its purpose is to switch consumers from buying the advertised merchandise or service, in order to sell something else, usually at a higher price or on a basis more advantageous to the advertiser.

a. No advertisement should be published unless it is a bona fide offer to sell the advertised merchandise or service.

b. The advertising should not create a false impression about the product or service being offered in order to lay the foundation for a later "switch" to other, more expensive products or services, or products of a lesser quality at the same price.

c. Subsequent full disclosure by the advertiser of all other facts about the advertised article does not preclude the existence of a bait scheme.

d. An advertiser should not use nor permit the use of the following bait scheme practices:

—refusing to show or demonstrate the advertised merchandise or service;
—disparaging the advertised merchandise or service, its warranty, availability, services and parts, credit terms, etc.;
—selling the advertised merchandise or service and thereafter "unselling" the customer to make a switch to other merchandise or service;
—refusing to take orders for the advertised merchandise or service or to deliver it within a reasonable time;
—demonstrating or showing a defective sample of the advertised merchandise; or
—having a sales compensation plan designed to penalize salespersons who sell the advertised merchandise or service.

e. An advertiser should have on hand a sufficient quantity of advertised merchandise to meet reasonably anticipated demands, unless the advertisement discloses the number of items available. If items are available only at certain branches, their specific locations should be disclosed. The use of "rainchecks" is no justification for inadequate estimates of reasonably anticipated demand.

f. Actual sales of the advertised merchandise or service may not preclude the existence of a bait scheme since this may be merely an attempt to create an aura of legitimacy. A key factor in determining the existence of "bait" is the number of times the merchandise or service was advertised compared to the number of actual sales of the merchandise or service.

Source: Council of Better Business Bureaus, Inc., *Code of Advertising* (1981), pp. 6-7. Reproduced with permission.

Figure 13-1 Better Business Bureau Code of Advertising

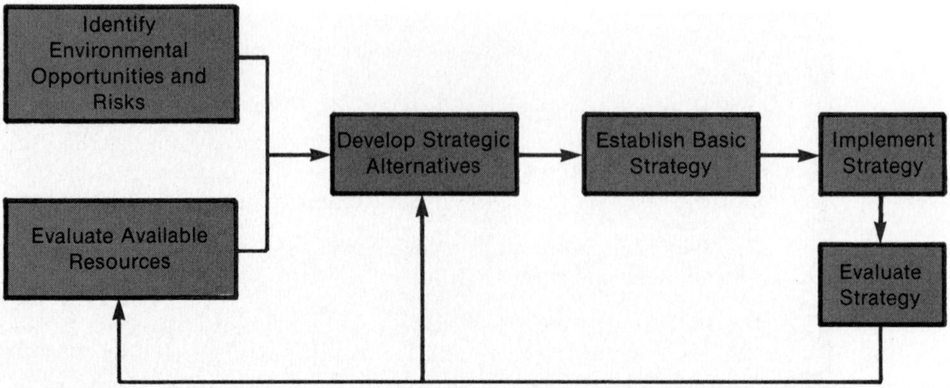

Source: Justin G. Longenecker and Charles D. Pringle, *Management* (5th ed.; Columbus: Charles E. Merrill Publishing Company, 1981), p. 72. Reproduced with permission.

Figure 13-2 Strategic Decision Making

The evaluation of resources, another important part of strategic decision making, is concerned with the firm's strengths and weaknesses and the extent to which its resources are committed to long-term projects. Firms with little debt and a strong line of credit, for example, have superior resources for expansion. The depth of managerial and professional talent is another significant variable which affects the resources of the business.

After examining opportunities, risks, and resources, the strategist must then develop alternatives and select a basic strategy. Following the adoption of the strategy, the entrepreneur must implement and then periodically evaluate the strategy in a new round of strategic decision making. In many small firms, strategy results from management by default. The entrepreneur can act professionally, however, by devoting specific attention to strategy rather than reacting haphazardly to environmental change.[5]

Finding the Strategic Niche

In a pluralistic economy there is a place for both large and small firms. Head-on competition with large competitors is difficult and may be fatal, however, unless the small firm has some natural advantages going for it. If possible, it is preferable for the small firm to capitalize on its potential strengths and to operate in the crack between larger firms.

5. See William L. Trombetta, "An Empirical Approach to Marketing Strategy for the Small Retailer," *Journal of Small Business Management*, Vol. 14, No. 4 (October, 1976), pp. 55-58, for a report on a "sick" retail business that had once been prosperous. The author of the article served as consultant to the firm and developed strategic recommendations based on his analysis of that firm's resources and opportunities.

ACTION REPORT: Environmental Opportunities for Jelly Beans

Environmental change is often subtle and gradual, but occasionally it is swift and dramatic. The election of President Ronald Reagan created a tremendous change in the market for one small firm. Herman Goelitz, Inc., a 59-year-old family-owned company in Oakland, CA, is the supplier of the President's favorite jelly beans.

According to Herman Rowland, 40, manager of the firm, the undelivered backlog skyrocketed in 1981 to 300,000 cases versus an average 15,000 cases before the inauguration. Sales were expected to double in 1981. To meet the need, Rowland installed $600,000 worth of new production equipment and hired 80 more employees. Although Rowland kept many customers on allocation, he continued to ship 60 cases per month to his steady client in the White House.

Source: "In the News (Jelly Boon)," *Fortune*, Vol. 103, No. 11 (June 1, 1981), p. 10.

The small firm should look for and emphasize the special niche it can best fill. If it can get a corner on the market for a particular specialized product, it will be in an unusually advantageous position. For example, some retailers specialize in children's clothing, fashions for tall people, formal wear, maternity clothes, blue jeans, or discount apparel. Some restaurants likewise specialize in baked potatoes, health foods, salads, spaghetti, Chinese food, Korean food, Greek food, and so on. By selecting the right specialty, a small firm can often compete effectively with large chain organizations.

Not all of the special niche cases are confined to the field of retailing. Small manufacturers can better their larger rivals by finding a new use for existing products or by altering production to meet peculiar requirements of an ethnic or minority group.

Finding the Appropriate Starting Point

Getting started with a study of strategy often seems difficult, and the owner-manager may find the experience frustrating! Being unaccustomed to systematic investigation of this type, the entrepreneur has difficulty finding an appropriate starting point. One approach is to begin by asking a number of fundamental questions about the firm and then to thoughtfully produce answers to these questions. The questions in Figure 13-3 have been proposed by Frank F. Gilmore as a framework for small-business strategic planning sessions.

1. *Record current strategy:*
   a. What is the current strategy?
   b. What kind of business does management want to operate (considering such management values as desired return on investment, growth rate, share of market, stability, flexibility, character of the business, and climate)?
   c. What kind of business does management feel it ought to operate (considering management's concepts of social responsibility and obligations to stockholders, employees, community, competitors, customers, suppliers, government, and the like)?
2. *Identify problems with the current strategy:*
   a. Are trends discernible in the environment that may become threats and/or missed opportunities if the current strategy is continued?
   b. Is the company having difficulty implementing the current strategy?
   c. Is the attempt to carry out the current strategy disclosing significant weaknesses and/or unutilized strengths in the company?
   d. Are there other concerns with respect to the validity of the current strategy?
   e. Is the current strategy no longer valid?
3. *Discover the core of the strategy problem:*
   a. Does the current strategy require greater competence and/or resources than the company possesses?
   b. Does it fail to exploit adequately the company's distinctive competence?
   c. Does it lack sufficient competitive advantage?
   d. Will it fail to exploit opportunities and/or meet threats in the environment, now or in the future?
   e. Are the various elements of the strategy internally inconsistent?
   f. Are there other considerations with respect to the core of the strategy problem?
   g. What, then, is the real core of the strategy problem?
4. *Formulate alternative new strategies:*
   a. What possible alternatives exist for solving the strategy problem?
   b. To what extent do the company's competence and resources limit the number of alternatives that should be considered?
   c. To what extent do management's preferences limit the alternatives?
   d. To what extent does management's sense of social responsibility limit the alternatives?
   e. What strategic alternatives are acceptable?
5. *Evaluate alternative new strategies:*
   a. Which alternative *best* solves the strategy problem?
   b. Which alternative offers the *best* match with the company's competence and resources?
   c. Which alternative offers the *greatest* competitive advantage?
   d. Which alternative *best* satisfies management's preferences?
   e. Which alternative *best* meets management's sense of social responsibility?
   f. Which alternative *minimizes* the creation of new problems?
6. *Choose a new strategy:*
   a. What is the *relative significance* of each of the preceding considerations?
   b. What should the new strategy be?

Source: Frank F. Gilmore, "Formulating Strategy in Smaller Companies," *Harvard Business Review,* Vol. 49, No. 3 (May-June, 1971), p. 80. Reproduced with permission.

Figure 13-3 Questions to Use in Formulating Strategy

Strategic decisions should be reduced to writing to insure completion of the strategy-determination process and to provide a basis for subsequent planning. The firm's strategy, moreover, should be incorporated into more specific plans of action. Periodic review and evaluation sessions could be devoted to measuring progress in following strategic guidelines and to dealing with problems that might emerge.

OPERATIONAL PLANNING IN SMALL FIRMS

Decisions about objectives and strategy, as explained earlier in this chapter, constitute the first stage of the planning process. Let us now turn to operational plans, policies, and procedures for the small business.

Sometimes the entrepreneur neglects the planning function as a result of severe business pressures. If he or she becomes too entangled in day-to-day operations, it becomes easy to put off the policy making and planning that is so essential to continuing success. For example, when a choice is to be made between getting out an order and planning operations for the next six months, the owner usually attends to the order. As a result, the time left for reflecting upon the future course of the business is reduced. In this case, a lack of appreciation of planning may be coupled with the limited time available. Planning becomes "postponable" and may not appear to be an absolute necessity. This situation is dangerous because failure to plan results in ineffective, undirected action.

Meaningful planning requires a commitment by the entrepreneur to devote time and energy to the planning process. According to Van Auken and Ireland:

> As a result of making the commitment to engage actively in planning, the small-business manager is ready to set aside and carefully preside over a specified time period for developing business plans. Nagging interruptions must be guarded against or "Gresham's law of planning" will inevitably prevail: daily brushfires push aside planning until it is forgotten altogether.[6]

Delegation of Some Planning Tasks

The small-business owner is directly and personally responsible for planning. Typically he or she does not have, and cannot have, a full-time planning staff, such as many large firms have. Neither the money nor the personnel are available for such a staff. Consequently, the owner must do the planning, and a great proportion of the owner's time will be spent in it. Nevertheless, this

6. Philip M. Van Auken and R. Duane Ireland, "An Input-Output Approach to Practical Small Business Planning," *Journal of Small Business Management*, Vol. 18, No. 1 (January, 1980), p. 45.

ACTION REPORT: Strategy and Planning by a Small Manufacturer

In 1973, Oliver O. Ward and three colleagues purchased the germanium division of an electronics manufacturer and began producing germanium-based semiconductors. The new company, Germanium Power Devices Corporation (GPD), succeeded and grew even though the big semiconductor manufacturers switched from using germanium to using silicon, a cheaper material. GPD's special success is apparently linked to its strategy and planning, described by a writer as follows:

GPD's Strategy

After he [Ward] and his co-founders had looked at the marketplace, they did some long-range planning. The strategy they proposed was to get an increasing share of the declining market by acquiring germanium divisions as the big companies got out of the business.

Ward and his colleagues also felt that new fields might open up for germanium.

GPD's Planning

To make that future as successful as possible, Ward and his three colleagues sit down once a week for an informal planning session. And they do a minimum of four days of long-range planning a year, which Ward considers invaluable. "When we sit down for two days each in the spring and the fall, we're trying to take a much broader view. In any area—whether it's a family or a business—it doesn't do any harm to sit back and take an objective look at where you are, where you're going, how you're going to get there, and what your needs and problems are."

Source: Susan E. Currier, "This Rare Bird Prospers in a Declining Market," *Inc.*, Vol. 2, No. 5 (May, 1980), pp. 93-98.

responsibility may be delegated to some extent because some planning is required of all the members of the enterprise. If the organization is of any size at all, the owner can hardly specify in detail the program for each department. Furthermore, there is a need for some factual information which can be supplied only by other members of the organization.

The concept that the boss does the thinking and the employee does the work is rather misleading. Progressive management has discovered that employees' ideas are often helpful in developing solutions to company problems. The salesperson, for example, is closer to the customer and usually best able to evaluate the customer's reactions. It is not enough for employees to call attention to problems—they must also turn up recommendations and solutions.

Kinds of Plans

Business plans may be classified in several ways. When classified according to the time period for which they are established, they are called *long-range* or *short-range* plans. When classified according to their frequency of use, they are known as *standing* plans (such as policies and procedures) or *single-use* plans (such as special projects and budgets). More detailed functional plans are also developed in production, marketing, finance, and other areas.

Long-Range and Short-Range Plans. To make current decisions intelligently, a manager must know what a firm will be doing several years in the future. Without some contemplation of the distant future, the business may find itself on a "dead-end street." The basic objectives and broad strategies discussed earlier in this chapter are examples of long-range plans.

One of the best-known and most used short-range, single-use plans is the budget. A **budget** is a device for expressing future plans, usually in monetary terms. It is also usually prepared for one year in advance, with a breakdown by quarters or months. As a plan of action, the budget provides a set of yardsticks by which operations can be controlled. To be effective, the budget must be based on a realistic estimate of sales volume, with appropriate expense levels determined accordingly. The budget is discussed in greater detail in Chapter 18.

Policies. Business policies are defined as fundamental statements which serve as guides to management practice. Some policies are general in that they affect the whole business, while other policies affect only particular departments or portions of the operation. In a small manufacturing firm there are product policies, sales policies, manufacturing policies, financial policies, expansion policies, personnel policies, and credit policies, among others. For example, any small firm establishes a personnel policy when it determines the amount of vacation to which its employees are entitled. Similarly, sales policy is established when a firm determines the geographical scope of its market and the type of customer it will seek.

An already-decided policy permits a prompt decision on a specific problem. This does not mean that the policy dictates the decision—a policy should allow a certain latitude for judgment in individual cases. Nevertheless, an established policy makes it unnecessary for the manager to analyze a specific problem each time it arises. For example, an employer need not decide each year the amount of vacation each employee should receive. The general statement of vacation policy is simply applied to individual cases.

Saving time is only one of the advantages in the use of definite policies in a small firm. Policies are established on the basis of a careful consideration of all pertinent factors and are thus arrived at logically. Without policy in particular areas, the manager is forced to make decisions under pressure and without the opportunity to think through the implications of those decisions. Finally, policies also provide consistency of action from one time to another. This is a matter of value to both customers and employees of the firm.

Procedures. A standard operating procedure is similar to a policy in that it is a standing or continuing plan. Once a method of work or a procedure is worked out, it may be standardized and referred to as a standard operating procedure. For example, the steps involved in taking a credit application, investigating the applicant, approving or disapproving the request, and subsequent authorizations of particular purchases by approved customers may be completely standardized.

Steps in Planning

The steps in planning may be thought of as steps in problem solving. This series of steps includes: recognizing the problem, collecting and analyzing the facts, making a tentative decision among the possible alternatives, testing the practicality of the tentative plan, and selecting and announcing the final plan.

Recognizing the Problem. Until the issue at hand is clear, it is impossible to develop a sound plan which will provide an adequate solution. Although this sounds easy, the true nature of a problem is not always evident on the surface. For example, a complaint about wages may be completely misleading and only a camouflage for another grievance. To assume that wages is the problem might lead to a plan that misses the mark completely.

Not all planning is problem-centered, however. For example, the mere act of carrying out organizational objectives requires planning. The first step in opening a restaurant, for example, would involve recognition of a need to plan the location, physical facilities, personnel requirements, financial structure, operating procedures, and so on. After the restaurant is under way, the manager would recognize a need to plan menus and purchasing even though these matters are not visualized as "problems."

Collecting and Analyzing the Facts. The second step in planning involves the collection and analysis of pertinent facts. Prior to opening the business, a prospective entrepreneur cannot obtain precise information on what conditions will be like after operations are under way. He or she must resort to trade publications, government and trade association data, and knowledge gleaned from personal experience and counseling with others.

Not all facts are significant to particular issues and, therefore, to particular planning activities. In this preliminary analysis, the entrepreneur must distinguish the significant facts, classify them, and note causal relationships. Moreover, gaps in the available data must be noted and arrangements made to secure the needed facts. However, time and cost pressures, among other factors, may make it difficult or impossible to obtain these additional pertinent facts.

In planning physical equipment of a restaurant, for example, the entrepreneur would investigate the types of equipment available and the various possibilities for its arrangement. Some of this information would no doubt be derived from past experience and supplemented by discussions with equipment suppliers, visits to other restaurants, contacts with a trade association, and the reading of trade publications. From these various sources, detailed information regarding the initial cost, durability, operating cost, efficiency, appearance, and size of the different types of equipment might be obtained. The effects of and demands for various types of equipment would be particularly noted, as would the types of financial arrangements available. For example, a particular unit might provide exceptional convenience of operation for personnel and require a down payment of one half its total cost.

Making a Tentative Decision Among Possible Alternatives. As factual information is collected and examined, various possible courses of action begin to suggest themselves. If planning is thorough, each of the major practical solutions or courses of action will be carefully identified. Here again, the process seems simple, but creative thinking is required to visualize possibilities that are not immediately apparent. Many times the obvious solution is not the best.

Returning to our example of the proposed restaurant, no doubt many alternatives exist with regard to the physical equipment that might be installed. Possible hypothetical alternatives might be:

1. Purchase of new Type A equipment from Supplier A at a cost of $1,500.
2. Purchase of new Type A equipment from Supplier B at a cost of $1,450 but with slower delivery.
3. Purchase of new Type B equipment from either supplier for $2,200.
4. Purchase of used Type A equipment from Supplier C for $950.

It should be clear that the possible alternative actions existing in other situations would be numerous. Only the most likely possibilities should be retained for further consideration.

Testing the Practicality of the Tentative Plan. Research and experimentation may sometimes be used to see what would happen under given circumstances. Insofar as experimentation can be utilized, it is well to do so because it will save hours of analysis and discussion, much of which might prove fruitless. For example, the prospective restaurant owner might be able to visit another restaurant, observe Type B equipment in operation, and talk with its operator. Of course, if research and experimentation are too costly or simply cannot be undertaken, one is thrown back upon the discussion of the pros and cons of the situation and upon analysis by mental trial and error.

Selecting and Announcing the Final Plan. The final step in planning is twofold: (1) selecting one of the alternatives after reflecting upon all the tangible and intangible factors in the case, and (2) announcing the final plan and its effective date to all concerned. The entrepreneur cannot postpone decisions merely because uncertainties and unknowns exist.

The final step in planning should flow naturally from the preceding steps. If alternatives have been clearly stated and carefully examined, the most desirable choice is usually apparent. Applying this step to our example of planning restaurant equipment, it is at this point that the prospective entrepreneur would decide, perhaps, to buy Type B equipment.

QUANTITATIVE TOOLS TO AID PLANNING

In both large and small businesses, certain quantitative tools may be utilized to improve decision making. Most owners of independent businesses associate these quantitative tools with big business, considering them quite inapplicable to small firms. However, the potential usefulness of quantitative tools to the small firm should not be overlooked.

Most of the quantitative tools discussed below depend, in part, on the **theory of probability**, which deals with the rational calculation of chances of specific outcomes from a contemplated course of action. Much has been said about the taking of calculated risks in business. Nevertheless, relatively few decision makers calculate the risks involved in a specific course of action. All of the quantitative tools available to planners, however, take account of determinable risks, thus leading to better decision making.

As a practical matter, few owners of small firms have sufficient knowledge of advanced mathematics and statistical theory to apply these tools personally. A consideration of these tools is pertinent, however, for at least two reasons. First, the small-business owner should know that such tools exist and that they can be applied to certain problems that are referred to management consultants. Second, the growing use of these techniques points up the need for increased training in quantitative methods on the part of small-business managers. Even though an individual lacks the necessary technical knowledge for using the tools, it is desirable that he or she appreciate their possibilities, advantages, and limitations.

Sampling Theory

Sampling theory is concerned with the selection of samples of adequate size which are truly representative of the underlying population. A sample is *random* if every item in the population (totality of data) has a known chance of being included in the sample. A sample is *representative* when it retains the population proportions for all significant variables such as occupation, income level, etc. An adequate sample is one large enough to yield a dependable answer.

Sampling is essential for the simple reason that the entire population of data can hardly ever be investigated. Cost and time pressure make this prohibitive. One useful application of random sampling in the small factory lies in quality control problems. The final acceptance of entire lots or batches of product may be based upon inspection of a properly selected sample.

Linear Programming

Linear programming involves the use of mathematical formulas for evaluating the results from several alternative courses of action, each of which contains a number of variables. This tool is used to discover the exact solution that will minimize costs or maximize gains. It is beyond the scope of this text to illustrate advanced statistical theories in solving problems by linear programming. Suffice it to say that this tool can be used to analyze manufacturing problems that involve the production of several products for which basic, but scarce, raw materials are used. Linear programming would determine the following for such a problem:

1. The amount of each raw material needed for each product.
2. The profit per unit for each product.
3. Which product or combination of products to produce in order to maximize profits.
4. How much of each product should be produced.
5. How much of a low-profit product to produce in order to "take care" of certain loyal customers.

Queuing Theory

Queuing theory is waiting-line theory. It consists of the use of calculated probabilities for determining the number of persons who will stand in a line. Examples of problems that may be solved by applying this theory might include the number of depositors who will stand in line for service at a bank teller's window, customers who will stand in line at checkout counters in a supermarket, or car owners who will wait in line at car wash establishments.

Take the case of a barber facing retirement at age 65 in order to draw a social security pension. The alternatives considered were: (1) to sell out, (2) to trade the two-chair shop for a one-chair shop to be operated on weekends only, and (3) to keep the two-chair shop open on Fridays and Saturdays only. Using the queuing theory for Alternative No. 2 showed that the barber would work continuously, without rest breaks or meals, from 8:00 a.m. to 10:00 p.m. if all arriving customers waited until served—even though the shop was locked for an hour at noon and after 5:00 p.m. Because this was untenable, the possibilities of Alternative No. 3 were simulated. This alternative proved to be workable, except that the barber would still make too much money to be legally entitled to the social security checks. Hence, the waiting-line simulations suggested a different solution: the barber sold out and contracted to work for another barber on Fridays and Saturdays only, taking full pay for services up to the limiting monthly amount and letting the shop owner take everything over that figure. This case exemplifies the application of waiting-line theory for the guidance of a small-business owner's decision to sell out.

Simulation Technique

Another tool for the improvement of decision making is **simulation**, which makes possible the inexpensive, rapid reproduction of large-scale events over a considerable period of time through the use of a "model." Ordinarily the use of the simulation technique also requires the availability and utilization of a digital computer. The small-business owner might get around this costly factor, however, through the use of a rented computer.

The simulation technique requires input to the computer of the actual business situation in terms of marketplace pricing, inventory data, production capacity, and all other pertinent factors which can be included in the business model. If all of the possible factors are included in the model, all alternative decisions can be outlined. Then a business game can be played. Each player would be faced with a limited range of possible decisions including:

1. Raising or lowering prices.
2. Buying or selling productive equipment to increase or decrease capacity.
3. Investing (or failing to invest) in research and development.
4. Obtaining information about competitors' actions.

When a particular decision is fed into the computer, the computer calculates its effects. Thus, all participants in the game see the consequences of their specific decisions. The computer forecasts actual results of given decisions and thereby guides the making of sound decisions. The simulation technique can broaden the entrepreneur's experience in days, or even hours, instead of years of hit-and-miss operations.

Game Theory

Game theory is concerned with the formulation of a strategy against the competition. This theory assumes that business situations have a strong resemblance to games, with both involving elements of competition, chance, and strategy.

The game may be played by two or more players. Each player is given a set of directions, or strategy, for playing the complete game—including instructions on what moves to make during the course of the game. Before the game is played, one must assume that a competitor either knows or does not know one's strategy. If a competitor is assumed to know one's strategy in advance, game theory may then be utilized to formulate a new strategy that will provide maximum countering action. On the other hand, one's moves are governed by the given strategy as long as one assumes that a competitor is unaware of it. The outcome of the game for each player is, of course, predictable even before the game is played when there is *perfect* information; that is, each player knows exactly what a competitor's strategy is, as well as the outcome of every possible move that a competitor can make.

Limitations of Quantitative Tools

Quantitative tools do not preclude the exercise of managerial judgment, which is definitely required because of the human factor in any problem situation. The tools are a means to an end, not the end itself. The manager's judgment remains the decisive factor in planning.

Neither does the use of quantitative tools preclude the requirement of feedback. Any information about operating results must be fed back to the planner so that plans, programs, and instructions may be modified when necessary. For example, when feedback reports describe deviations from an existing budget, the budget may have to be modified as a means of corrective action.

It must be emphasized that quantitative tools are just that—they are tools, and no more. When used properly, they tend to improve managerial decision making. These decision-making tools do not eliminate business risk totally. Risk is inherent in the use of present resources and production facilities for the creation of new goods. It is inherent also in the purchase of merchandise for resale. Decision-making tools are designed merely to minimize risk by providing a rational approach to business problems.

LOOKING BACK

1. The main objectives of a privately owned business are: profit, economic service, and growth. Profits must be earned to reward the entrepreneur's acceptance of business risks and to assure continuity of the business. The service objectives must be modified as consumer tastes change and as competitive products and services are developed. The growth objective envisions the need for additional operating facilities and calls for retained earnings or new investment by the owners.
2. A sense of social responsibility characterizes many modern business leaders. Entrepreneurs, in particular, often speak of their service to the community as one of the major rewards of their business activity. Consistency and sincerity in adherence to ethical codes are obligatory if ethical business practices are to remain effective. Ethical advertising is especially important, and local Better Business Bureaus have been established to advise consumers about unethical advertising and other objectionable business practices.
3. In strategic planning, entrepreneurs identify environmental opportunities and risks, evaluate the firm's resources, and make necessary changes in the basic nature of business operations. The small firm can maximize its competitive strength by avoiding head-on competition with big business, emphasizing its natural advantages, and finding a strategic niche.
4. The various kinds of plans include long-range and short-range plans, policies, and standard operating procedures. The steps in planning include: recognizing the problem, collecting and analyzing the facts, making a tentative decision among possible alternatives, testing the practicality of the tentative plan, and selecting and announcing the final plan.
5. Quantitative tools useful for the improvement of decision making include sampling theory, linear programming, queuing theory, simulation technique, and game theory. The limitations of quantitative tools should be known to the entrepreneur. As tools, they assist in reaching a decision but do not preclude the use of personal judgment.

DISCUSSION QUESTIONS

1. What stake do the employees of a small firm have in the attainment of its profit objective?
2. Why must a business firm recognize and fulfill its service objective? Is this equally true in all types of

businesses? Is the service objective equal to the firm's profit objective, or subordinate to it?

3. A men's clothing store has been opened by an extremely ambitious young person who is strongly growth-oriented. How might this affect the operating methods and policies of the business?

4. Is it necessary for the entrepreneur to be a philanthropist to some degree to adhere to the social objectives of the business? Why?

5. Suppose that a used car dealer has just made an oral commitment to sell a car at a particular price. Before the deal is completed, another customer indicates a willingness to pay a substantially higher price. What is the ethical thing to do? Is it also practical and good business?

6. Give some examples of strategic moves that might be made by an independently owned service station.

7. What is the concept of the "strategic niche," and what are its values for the small firm?

8. Do small firms too often neglect the managerial function of planning? If so, what accounts for its neglect?

9. What major blunders might result from a lack of long-range planning on the part of a small manufacturing firm?

10. To what extent are sophisticated, quantitative decision-making tools actually applicable to small-business management?

REFERENCES TO SMALL BUSINESS IN ACTION

"Feasting on Crumbs." *Forbes*, Vol. 124, No. 13 (December 24, 1979), pp. 61-63.

Apoges Enterprises, a small business, has succeeded and grown by producing a number of products which are in various market niches. This company has constantly sought for the little niches that others disdain.

"It Won't Be a Picnic Trying to Copy Us." *Forbes*, Vol. 124, No. 8 (October 15, 1979), pp. 113-115.

Small firms are strong in furniture manufacturing. In this article the special strategy of a highly successful firm, Henredon Furniture of Morgantown, NC, is described.

"A Short-Haul Trucker Drives Hard to Expand." *Business Week*, No. 2651 (August 25, 1980), pp. 33-34.

A family-owned, short-haul trucking firm discovered opportunities for expansion as the Interstate Commerce Commission eased trucking rules. Careful planning is being used to exploit those opportunities.

"Softsoaping P & G." *Forbes*, Vol. 125, No. 4 (February 18, 1980), pp. 97-99.

Minnetonka, Inc., was founded in 1964 to compete with major corporations in the production of soap. The launching of a liquid soap product called Softsoap, which is pumped from a dispenser, has given this small company a remarkable competitive advantage.

Chapter 14

Organizing the Small Firm

LOOKING AHEAD

Watch for the following important topics:

1. The unplanned organization structure.
2. Line-and-staff organization and the chain of command.
3. Informal organization.
4. Fundamentals of the organizing function.
5. Boards of directors in small corporations.

"Next week, we've got to get organized!"

This sign on a desk is intended to be facetious, but it expresses the real plight of many small firms. They are not well-organized, and they would like to do something about it. In this chapter we will look at organizational relationships, both formal and informal, and the way in which these can best be structured for effectiveness and growth of the small firm.

TYPES OF FORMAL ORGANIZATION STRUCTURE

More than one type of organization structure is available to the small firm. The structures range from one that is unplanned to a line organization and a line-and-staff organization.

The Unplanned Structure

In small companies the organization structure tends to evolve with little conscious planning. Certain employees begin performing particular functions when the firm is new and retain those functions as the company matures. Other functions remain diffused in a number of positions, even though they have gained importance as a result of company growth.

This natural evolution is not all bad. Generally a strong element of practicality exists in organizational arrangements which evolve in this way. The structure is forged in the process of working and growing, not derived from a textbook. Unplanned structures are seldom perfect, however, and growth typically creates a need for organizational change. Periodically, therefore, the entrepreneur should examine structural relationships and make adjustments as needed for effective teamwork.

Assuming that the business is more than a one-person operation, the entrepreneur must decide whether a line organization is appropriate or whether a more complex form of organization is desirable.

Line Organization

In a **line organization** each person has one supervisor to whom he or she reports and looks for instructions. Thus, a single, specific chain of command exists. All employees are engaged directly in getting out the work—producing, selling, or arranging financial resources. Most very small firms—for example, those with fewer than ten employees—use this form of organization. A line organization is illustrated in Figure 14-1.

The phrase *chain of command* implies a superior-subordinate relationship with a downward flow of orders, but it involves much more. The chain of command is also a channel for two-way communication, although this does not mean that communication among employees at the same level is forbidden. Informal discussion among employees is inevitable. However, the chain is the *official, vertical* channel of communication. Even so, not all of the communication between superior and subordinate is official, and not all of the superior's statements are orders. There is normal social interaction between superior and subordinate, as well as order giving. When orders are given, the subordinate's line of responsibility or obligation to the superior to carry out the orders becomes evident.

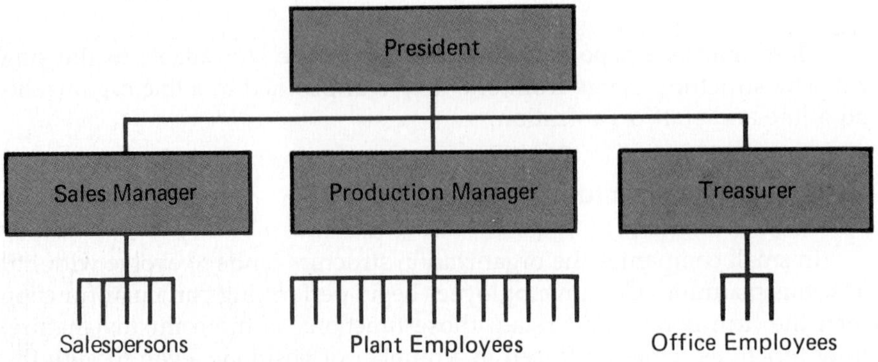

Figure 14-1 Line Organization

An organizational problem occurs when managers or employees ignore organization lines. In small firms the climate of informality and flexibility makes it easy to short-circuit the formal chain. A president and founder of the business, for example, may get in a hurry and give instructions to salespersons or plant employees instead of going through the sales manager or the production manager. Similarly, an employee who has been with the entrepreneur from the beginning tends to maintain that direct person-to-person relationship rather than observe newly instituted channels of communication.

As a practical matter, adherence to the chain of command can never be complete. An organization in which the chain of command is rigid would be bureaucratic and inefficient. Nevertheless, frequent and flagrant disregard of the chain of command quickly undermines the position of the bypassed manager. This is a particular danger for the small firm, and only the entrepreneur can make sure that the integrity of the structure is maintained. Occasionally, for example, the entrepreneur may need to say, "Why don't you talk with your supervisor about that first?"

Line-and-Staff Organization

The **line-and-staff organization** is similar to a line organization in that each person reports to a single supervisor. However, in a line-and-staff organization there are also staff specialists who perform specialized services or act as management advisers in special areas. Examples of staff specialists include a personnel manager, a production control technician, a quality control specialist, or an assistant to the president. Small firms ordinarily grow quickly to a size requiring some staff specialists. Consequently, this is a widely used type of organization in small business. Figure 14-2 shows a line-and-staff organization.

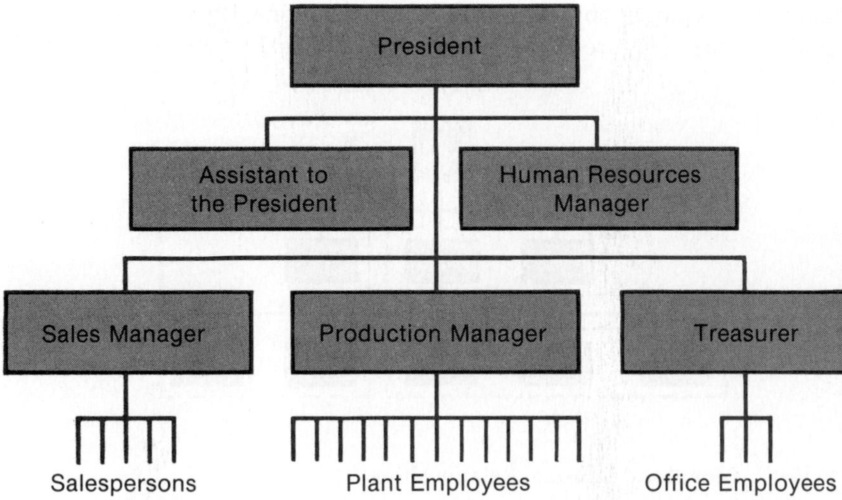

Figure 14-2 Line-and-Staff Organization

Line activities are those that contribute directly to the primary objectives of the small firm. Typically, these are production and sales activities. **Staff activities**, on the other hand, are the supporting or helping activities. Although both types of activities are important, the focus must be kept on line activities—those which earn the customer's dollar. The owner-manager must insist that staff specialists function primarily as helpers and facilitators. Otherwise the firm will experience confusion as employees receive directions from a variety of supervisors and staff specialists. Unity of command would be destroyed.

Committee Organization

The **committee organization** is a variation of the line-and-staff structure. Superimposed on the line-and-staff organization is a set of committees such as executive and finance committees. Committees are designed to help managers reach necessary decisions by exploring the pros and cons of a given situation. In a very small firm, only the entrepreneur and perhaps one or two assistants are empowered to make major decisions. As a result, the extensive use of committees in small business is unnecessary and often inefficient.

INFORMAL ORGANIZATION

The types of organization structure previously discussed are concerned with the formal relationships among members of an organization. In any organization, however, there are informal groups that have something in common such as job, hobby, carpool, age, or affiliation with a civic association. The dotted areas in Figure 14-3 represent informal groups in an organization.

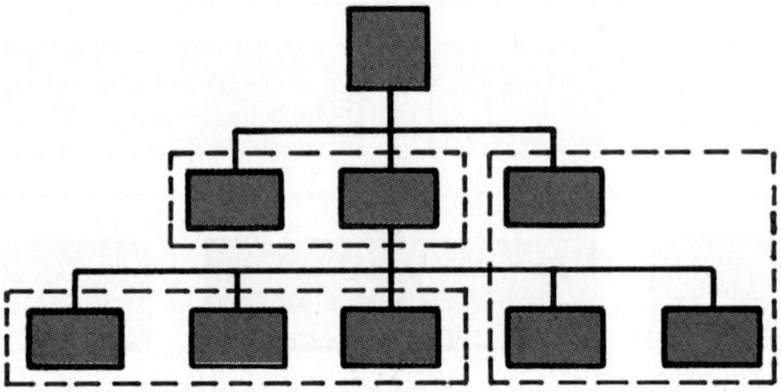

Figure 14-3 Formal and Informal Relationships

Although informal groups are not a part of the formal organization, the manager should observe them and evaluate their effect on the functioning of the total organization. Ordinarily no serious conflict arises between informal groups and the formal organization. It is probable, of course, that an informal leader or leaders will emerge who will influence employee behavior. The wise manager understands the potentially positive contribution of the informal organization and the inevitability of such informal leadership. Of course, if a leader were to persist in influencing other employees to behave contrary to the wishes of management, it might become necessary to discharge such an employee.

Informal interaction among employees and managers can facilitate work performance and also can make life in the workplace more enjoyable for everyone. The value of compatible work groups to the individual became painfully clear to one college student who worked on a summer job and said:

> I was employed as a forklift driver for one long, frustrating summer. Soon after being introduced to my work group, I knew I was in trouble. A clique had formed and, for some reason, resented college students. During lunch breaks and work breaks, I spent the whole time by myself. Each morning I dreaded going to work. The job paid well, but I was miserable.

FUNDAMENTALS OF THE ORGANIZING FUNCTION

Several time-tested guidelines to promote effective organization and management are particularly applicable to the small business. These concepts are relevant not only to initial organizational decisions, but also to subsequent organizational changes.[1]

Human Factors and Organization Design

At times, conflicts arise between organizational ideals and human considerations. Suppose some otherwise desirable employees have certain limitations which prevent the assignment of responsibility that they should theoretically bear. Must the manager dismiss such employees? There is, of course, no hard-and-fast answer. Although the manager cannot flagrantly disregard the important principles of organization, he or she will find it necessary to bend these principles at times in the interest of enabling the firm to operate effectively. The important thing is that departures from an ideal structure be supported by logical thinking and that they be recognized for what they are—temporary deviations from the theoretically desirable arrangement.

It is also well to recognize that some members of an organization have personal interests which can affect organizing decisions. Even in a small organization, managers may be guilty of "empire building" to enhance their own status. The entrepreneur needs to examine each organizational change to be sure it enhances the overall organizational effectiveness and not merely the welfare of one individual.

Departmentation

In grouping activities into positions and departments, similarity of work provides a practical guiding principle. Obviously production activities would be placed under a shop supervisor while sales activities would be directed by a sales manager. Such homogeneous assignments of work facilitate effective operation.

As a small firm grows, other patterns of departmentation become possible. If the business has more than one location, for example, a geographic pattern may be used, with employees in each area reporting to a branch supervisor. Or, if the sales force expands sufficiently, sales personnel may be grouped according to product categories or geographic areas.

Delegation of Authority

Given a proper concept of delegation of authority, a superior will grant to subordinates, on the basis of competence, the right to act or to decide. By

---

1. Unfortunately most organization theory has been developed in large organizations. See Thomas C. Dandridge, "Children Are Not 'Little Grown-Ups': Small Business Needs Its Own Organizational Theory," *Journal of Small Business Management*, Vol. 17, No. 2 (April, 1979), pp. 53-57.

delegating authority, the superior can perform more important tasks after turning over less important functions to subordinates.

Failure to delegate may well be the weakest point in small-business organizations generally. Although the problem is found in all organizations, it is a special problem for the independent entrepreneur, whose background usually contributes to this situation. Frequently the entrepreneur has

ACTION REPORT: Learning to Delegate at Flambeau Corporation

Founders of business firms find it difficult to delegate authority, and Bill Sauey, founder of Flambeau Corporation, was no exception. Eventually he learned, however. "My biggest regret," he says, "is that I didn't do it sooner." The company, which manufactures plastic products, was started by Sauey in 1947. His single-handed control of the firm is described as follows:

> Sauey signed all the checks, bought all the plant equipment, interviewed all potential employees, and played a role in developing and selling all of Flambeau's products. The company was a testament to his persistence and his conviction that he could solve any business problem. So he continued to manage the company in his own tightly controlled way even though there were signs that this style wasn't working so well anymore.
>
> "My biggest weakness was my inability to listen," he says. "When I felt strongly about something, like my business, I wasn't really hearing what others were saying."

Sauey discouraged decision making by others by flying into a rage when others acted independently, as evidenced by the following:

> One manager remembers a typical incident back in 1975. Sauey was out of town when his company received an unusually large parts order from Chrysler. In his absence, the managers at the Baraboo, Wis., plant reviewed their already tight production schedule and accepted only half the order. When Sauey returned and heard the news, he went wild. "No one turns down business around here except me," he shouted. "No matter what!"

When the work load became too heavy, Sauey simply made himself change and then found it worked better than expected. He said, "I feel more in control now than I ever did. The divisions are really separate companies now. I have very little direct control over them, and the surprise is, I like it!"

Source: David De Long, "They All Said Bill Sauey Couldn't Let Go," *Inc.*, Vol. 3, No. 5 (May, 1981), pp. 89-91.

organized the business and knows more about it than any other person in the firm. Thus, to protect the business, the owner is inclined to keep a firm hold on the reins of leadership.

Inability or unwillingness to delegate authority is manifested in numerous ways. Employees find it necessary to "clear it with the boss" before making even a minor decision. A line of subordinates is constantly trying to get the attention of the owner to resolve some issue which the subordinates lack authority to settle. This keeps the owner exceptionally busy, rushing from assisting a salesperson to helping iron out a production bottleneck to setting up a new filing system.

Delegation of authority is important for the satisfactory operation of a small firm and is an absolute prerequisite for growth. This factor alone is the reason why many firms can never grow beyond the small size that can be directly supervised in detail by the owner. One owner of a small restaurant operated it with excellent profits. As a result of this success, the owner acquired a lease on another restaurant in the same area and proceeded to operate it for one year. During this time, the owner experienced constant "headaches" with the second restaurant. Working long hours and trying to supervise both restaurants finally led the owner to give up the job. This person had never learned to delegate authority.

The independent entrepreneur may find delegation as painful as pulling teeth, but it is fully as necessary. Admittedly, if subordinates are incompetent or untrained, difficulties will be experienced. In such a situation, the manager should work to eliminate the basic weakness and proceed with the delegation of authority. If the manager succeeds in doing this, the morale and interest of most employees will improve. This will also provide a means for developing personnel.

Parity of Authority and Responsibility

A frequent criticism which relates to authority and responsibility is that the authority delegated is not equal to the responsibility assigned. A manager may expect the subordinate to produce or to achieve a given volume of sales but may limit the latter by unreasonable financial or personnel restrictions. Equity demands that the subordinate be held responsible only for that which is within the given range of authority.

Having acknowledged this ideal of equal responsibility and authority, we must realize that the ideal is seldom fully achieved. It is difficult to spell out authority in detail, and key employees are often expected to get a job completed without worrying about the precise degree of their authority. Moreover, a capable employee may gain cooperation from other employees by positive persuasion as well as by wielding a stick. Nevertheless, substantial differences in authority and responsibility would contribute to poor morale.

Span of Control

The optimum **span of control** is the number of subordinates who can be effectively supervised by a given manager. Although some authorities have stated that six to eight people are all that one individual can supervise effectively, the proper span of control actually is a variable depending upon a number of factors. Among these are the nature of the work and the superior's knowledge, energy, personality, and abilities. In addition, if the abilities of subordinates are greater than average, the span of control may be enlarged accordingly.

In a business organization there is a limit on the number of operative employees who can be effectively supervised. Of course, the span of control is greater in the case of personnel performing routine assignments than in the case of technical, professional, or administrative personnel.

As a very small firm grows and adds employees, the entrepreneur's span of control is extended. There is a tendency to stretch the span too far—to supervise not only the first 5 or 6 employees but later to supervise all 10 or 12 as they are added. Eventually a point is reached at which the attempted span exceeds the entrepreneur's reach—the time and ability he or she can devote to the business. It is at this point that the entrepreneur must establish intermediate levels of supervision, devoting more time to management and moving beyond the role of player-coach.

Organization Principles and Small-Business Success

A study of 20 Cuban-owned businesses in Miami, FL was made to determine whether organization principles were related to business success. The principles examined were the following:

1. Unity of objectives.
2. Organizational balance.
3. Responsibility.
4. Flexibility.
5. Parity of authority and responsibility.
6. Unity of command.
7. Span of management.
8. Delegation of authority.
9. Stability.[2]

Overall, the study concluded that as a group these principles of organization did relate to business success, although some of them were not significantly

2. Leonardo Rodriguez, "Organization Principles and Financial Measures of Success in Cuban-Owned Businesses in Miami, Florida," *American Journal of Small Business*, Vol. 1 (October, 1976), pp. 23-29.

related. This study lends support to our argument that the entrepreneur should devote careful attention to organizational relationships.

THE BOARD OF DIRECTORS IN SMALL CORPORATIONS

All too often, the majority stockholder (the entrepreneur) in a small corporation appoints a board of directors merely to fulfill a legal requirement. Such owners make little or no use of directors in managing their companies. In fact, an entrepreneur may actively resent efforts at managerial assistance from directors. When appointing directors, the entrepreneur tends to select personal friends, relatives, or other managers who are too busy to analyze situations and are not inclined to argue. In directors' meetings, the entrepreneur and other directors may simply engage in long-winded, innocuous discussions of broad general policies, leaving no time for serious, constructive questions.[3] Some entrepreneurs, however, have found an active board to be both practical and beneficial.

Contribution of Directors

A properly assembled board of directors can bring supplementary knowledge and broad experience to corporate management. The board should meet regularly to provide maximum assistance to the chief executive. Such board meetings should be conferences in which ideas are debated, strategies determined, and the pros and cons of policies explored. In this way, the chief executive is assisted by the combined experience of all the board members. Their combined knowledge makes possible more intelligent decisions on major issues.

Utilizing the combined experience of a board of directors does not mean that the chief executive of a small corporation is abdicating active control of its operations. Instead, it means merely that the chief executive is consulting with, and seeking the advice of, the board's members in order to draw upon a larger pool of business knowledge.

The active board of directors serves management in several important ways. The first of these, of course, is the board's review of major policy decisions. But there is also the matter of advice on external business conditions and on proper reaction to the business cycle. Moreover, some directors are willing to provide individual advice informally, from time to time, on specific problems that arise.

Outside directors may also serve the small firm by scrutinizing and questioning its ethical standards. S. Kumar Jain notes that "operating execu-

---

3. For a review of this topic as it applies to business organizations in general, see Milton C. Lauenstein, "Preserving the Impotence of the Board," *Harvard Business Review*, Vol. 55, No. 4 (July-August, 1977), pp. 36-38, 42, 46.

ACTION REPORT: A Director's Valuable Counsel

Directors of small firms are supposed to offer valuable counsel to management. Here is the story of one small company which received this type of assistance from a company director:

> In early 1978, Joseph D. Simons, chief executive officer of Badgerland Equipment Inc., of Waukesha, Wis., faced a dilemma. Salesmen were pressuring him to reduce prices of the company's aerial work platforms and other high-reach equipment, leased or purchased by contractors to lift workers and supplies at construction sites. But Simons's late brother Peter, who had founded the firm in 1969, had built Badgerland by providing prompt, excellent service, which allowed the firm to charge 10% to 15% more than competitors. Simons's instincts told him to continue that policy, but he had doubts. One salesman, for instance, complained that Badgerland had lost a $40,000 contract because its prices were too high. . . .
>
> When Simons faced his pricing strategy dilemma, he turned to John Komives, one of Badgerland's three outside advisers. If Badgerland cut prices, it would have to lower quality, Komives reasoned. And if it did that, the firm could destroy an image that had taken five years to establish. "Komives headed me off at the pass," says Simons. "I saw that it would be foolhardy not to keep our standards and our prices high."

Source: Bill Hendrickson, "Who Do You Turn to When You're the Boss?" *Inc.*, Vol. 3, No. 1 (January, 1981), pp. 69-74.

tives, without outside directors to question them, may rationalize unethical or illegal behavior as being in the best interest of the company."[4] With a strong board, the small firm gains greater credibility with the public as well as with the business and financial community.

Selection of Board Members

Many sources are available to the owner attempting to assemble a cooperative, experienced, able group of directors. The firm's attorney, banker, accountant, other business executives, and local management consultants might all be considered as potential directors. Peter Drucker has questioned the independence of auditors and attorneys, however, in view of the fact that they are retained by the firm.[5] Thus, they may not be free to be as critical of management's policies as they should be.

---

4. S. Kumar Jain, "Look to Outsiders to Strengthen Small Business Boards," *Harvard Business Review*, Vol. 58, No. 4 (July-August, 1980), p. 166.
5. "Conversation with Peter F. Drucker," *Organizational Dynamics* (New York: AMACOM, a division of American Management Associations, Spring, 1974), p. 49.

The importance of selecting an independent board of directors is expressed in these comments by Drucker:

> Therefore, the small and medium-size company needs an effective board of directors even more than the big one and usually has one that is even less effective. If I were chief executive officer of a medium-size company, I would spend a fair amount of time thinking through what I want my board to do, what I need from a board—including, let me say, somebody who will look at my proposal and say flatly, "This is not good enough." One doesn't need a rubber stamp; one needs people on a board who can ask the right questions. You need people who can say, "Jim, you are moving into the toy business and you don't know a thing about it. Have you really thought it through? Or do you want to make this acquisition just because it's available at a good P-E ratio?"[6]

Business prominence in the community is not essential for the small-corporation director. Rather, it is desirable that this individual be one who really understands small business and sympathizes with its problems. Moreover, he or she should be interested in sharing knowledge and have the personality and ability to transmit knowledge to the chief executive.

Compensation of Directors

The amount of compensation paid to board members varies greatly, and some small firms pay no fees whatever. One survey of small-company director compensation reported the following compensation levels in 1980:

1. 45 percent of the responding companies offered no compensation to board members.
2. 15 percent paid annual retainers ranging from $600 to $5,000 and averaging $2,000.
3. 15 percent paid annual retainers ranging from $600 to $5,000 and averaging $1,900; in addition, they paid meeting fees ranging from $35 to $500 and averaging $275 per meeting.
4. 25 percent paid only meeting fees, which ranged from $25 to $500 and averaged $210 per meeting.[7]

The fact that many companies can attract directors without paying directors' fees indicates that money is not the only factor involved. This may be somewhat misleading, however, because compensation rates for outsiders and nonfamily members in the study exceeded the rates for insiders and family members. This tended to bring down the average compensation level that was reported. Nevertheless, the compensation levels appear modest,

---

6. *Ibid.*
7. Jain, *op. cit.*, p. 169.

assuming the directors provide a meaningful contribution to the management of the firm.

An Alternative: A Board of Advisors

In recent years, increased attention has been directed to the legal responsibilities of directors. Under the law, outside directors may be held responsible for illegal company action even though they are not directly involved in wrongdoing. As a result of such legal pressures, some individuals are now reluctant to accept directorships.

One alternative that is used by some small companies is a board of advisors.[8] Rather than being elected as directors, qualified outsiders are asked to serve as advisors to the company. The group of outsiders then functions in much the same way as a board of directors does.

LOOKING BACK

1. The unplanned structure refers to the organization structure of small firms which often evolves with little conscious planning.
2. Line organization involves a single chain of command, and all employees and managers are expected to go through channels as much as possible. In a line-and-staff organization, specialists are added to help or advise line personnel.
3. Informal relationships in an organization arise spontaneously and supplement formally prescribed relationships. The wise manager understands the potentially positive contribution of the informal organization and informal leaders.
4. Among the basic organizational concepts that are relevant to the organizing function are: human factors and organization design, departmentation, delegation of authority, equality of authority and responsibility, and span of control.
5. Boards of directors can contribute to small corporations by offering counsel and assistance to their chief executives. To be most effective, selected members of the board must be properly qualified and be independent outsiders.

---

8. See Harold W. Fox, "Advisory Board: Resource for Closely Held Companies," *MSU Business Topics*, Vol. 27, No. 3 (Summer, 1979), pp. 25-30; and Eugene M. Zuckert and John H. Quinn, Jr., "Small Company Advisors: Substitute for Outside Directors," *Michigan Business Review*, Vol. 26, No. 3 (May, 1974), pp. 18-23.

DISCUSSION QUESTIONS

1. How large must a small firm be before it encounters problems of organization? As it grows, do its problems become more difficult to solve? Explain.

2. What type of small firm might properly use the line type of organization? When should its type of structure require change? To what type? Why?

3. Is the chain of command more than a conduit for orders? Explain.

4. What are the reasons for—and the dangers in—going outside of formal channels in small firms?

5. In a line-and-staff organization, which positions are line positions? What is the proper relationship between line departments and staff departments?

6. When one employee becomes the recognized leader of an informal organization and has goals at variance with those of management, what should the manager do to correct the situation?

7. Should a manager disregard human considerations when an ideal organization structure is threatened? Explain.

8. What are the two most likely causes of failure to delegate authority properly? Is delegation important? Why?

9. Explain the relationships, if any, between span of control and proper delegation.

10. How might a board of directors be of real value to management in a small corporation? What are the qualifications essential to a person chosen as a director in a small corporation? Is stock ownership in the firm a prerequisite?

REFERENCES TO SMALL BUSINESS IN ACTION

Churchill, Neil. "I Was an Expert on Small Companies (Until I Tried to Run One)." *Inc.*, Vol. 3, No. 2 (February, 1981), pp. 84-88.

This article presents the experiences of a business professor who became the chief operating officer of a small business. He describes some of the organizational and managerial problems he encountered.

"Phoenix." *Forbes*, Vol. 125, No. 8 (April 14, 1980), pp. 122-125.

This report explains how the founder of a young and growing firm experienced and solved, among other difficulties, the organizational problems of the business.

Rose, Carol. "Strong Managers Made His Business Bloom." *Inc.*, Vol. 3, No. 2 (February, 1981), pp. 79-82.

Dick Hutton, manager of a family-owned nursery business, concluded that he was the company's biggest impediment because he was spending too much time solving his subordinates' problems. Hutton's solution to this situation is described.

Chapter 15

Managing Human Resources in Small Firms

LOOKING AHEAD

Watch for the following important topics:

1. Recruiting and selecting applicants.
2. Steps in evaluating applicants.
3. Training, development, and management succession.
4. Compensation, including financial and nonfinancial incentives, in small firms.
5. Effective human relationships in small firms.

Smallness creates a unique situation in the management of human resources. For example, the owner of a small retail store cannot adopt the personnel program of Sears, Roebuck and Company, which has 400,000 employees, by merely scaling it down. The atmosphere of a small firm also creates distinctive opportunities to develop strong relationships among its members. In view of the special employment characteristics associated with smallness, the entrepreneur needs to develop a personnel program which is directly applicable to a small firm.

RECRUITING AND SELECTING

The initial step in a sound personnel program is the recruitment of capable employees. In recruitment the small firm competes with both large and small businesses. It cannot afford to let competitors take the cream of the crop. Aggressive recruitment requires the employer to take the initiative in locating applicants and to search until enough applicants are available to permit a good choice.

Sources of Employees

To recruit effectively, the small firm must know where and how to secure qualified applicants. The sources are numerous, and one cannot generalize about the best source in view of the variations in personnel requirements and quality of sources from one locality to another. Some major sources of employees are discussed below.

Unsolicited Applicants. A firm may receive any number of unsolicited applications from acceptable or unacceptable individuals of various backgrounds. If qualified applicants cannot be hired immediately, their applications should be kept on file for future reference. In the interest of good public relations, all applicants should be treated courteously.

Schools. Secondary schools, trade schools, colleges, and universities are desirable sources for certain classes of employees, particularly those who need no specific work experience. Secondary and trade schools provide applicants with a limited but useful educational background. Colleges and universities can supply candidates for positions in management and in various technical and scientific fields. In addition, many colleges are excellent sources of part-time employees.

Public Employment Offices. State employment offices, which are affiliated with the United States Employment Service, offer, without cost, a supply of applicants who are actively seeking employment. These offices attempt to place applicants on the basis of work experience, education, and extensive psychological testing. There are over 2,400 public employment offices throughout the United States and its territories.

Private Employment Agencies. Numerous private agencies offer their services as employment offices. In most cases an employer receives their services without cost because the applicant pays a fee to the agency. However, some firms pay the fee if the applicant is highly qualified. Whether private employ-

ACTION REPORT: Hiring Interns from a State University

Cleveland State University sponsors a cooperative education program which allows business firms to employ interns for three months of the year. Kalcor Coatings Company, a small manufacturer in Willoughby, OH, has found the program useful in obtaining short-term employees with technical training and also in sizing up students as prospects for subsequent full-time employment. A representative of Kalcor states:

> Since joining the program, we've employed five interns, with mixed results. Two students were downright lazy, one was mediocre, and two were excellent.
>
> Jack and Steve (the names are fictitious) both had a bad habit of sleeping on the job. Jack, however, was industrious—at avoiding work. He decided to test random samples at the quality control station and, at times, fudge the results on the rest. In his spare hours, he dozed, neglecting the R&D labs. Jack and Steve received poor evaluations for their efforts.
>
> Bill and Ellen, on the other hand, showed enough initiative to finish their scheduled work early and seek out work in other departments. Bill became a company "utility" person, helping out wherever he was needed. Ellen was so helpful in the lab that we hired her again for another term just to do lab work. We hope to hire her when she reaches the job market—we know what kind of worker we'd be getting.
>
> Overall, we're pleased with the results. The way we look at it, we got to look over five prospective employees without making any commitment. We were able to benefit from some fresh ideas and genuine enthusiasm. And we were able to see what kind of people are available while getting a glimpse of the training they are likely to receive.

Source: M. Cory Zucker, "School Interns Get High Marks from Us," *Inc.*, Vol. 2, No. 9 (September, 1980), p. 38.

ment agencies can be used profitably depends upon their services and the quality of the applicants listed with them.

Some private agencies, such as Kelly Services ("Kelly Girls") and Manpower, specialize in recruitment of temporary personnel. By paying a fee based upon the number of hours worked, a small firm can obtain qualified people on short notice to help with emergency projects or to fill in for vacationing employees.

Employee Referrals. If current employees are good employees, their recommendations may provide excellent prospects. Ordinarily, current employees will hesitate to recommend applicants thought to be inferior in ability. Many small-business owners say that this source provides more of their employees than any other source.

Help-Wanted Advertising. The "Help Wanted" sign in the window of a business establishment is one form of recruitment used by small firms. More aggressive recruitment takes the form of advertisements in the classified pages of local newspapers. Although the effectiveness of this source has been questioned by some, the fact remains that many well-managed organizations recruit in this way. Advertising in newspapers is particularly useful when there is a shortage of highly skilled personnel, scientists, or professional employees.

Selection Guidelines

The small-business manager should analyze the functions required and determine the number and kinds of jobs to be filled. Knowing the job requirements and the capacities and characteristics of the individual applicants permits a more intelligent selection of persons for specific jobs. In particular, the small business should attempt to obtain individuals whose capacities and skills complement those of the owner-manager.

Certainly the owner-manager should not select personnel simply to fit a rigid specification of education, experience, or personal background. Rather, the employer must concentrate upon the ability of an individual to fill a particular position in the business.

ACTION REPORT: Equal Employment Opportunity Regulation

Small business faces many of the same employment regulations that apply to big business. According to one source:

> One Philadelphia area contractor, Dane DiGaetano, became a classic example when, with only three employees (one black), and a modest federal contract for $112,000, he was hounded by contract compliance officers for failure to fill in reports correctly, for not having separate toilets for women, and for failure to set a hiring goal for women. He finally had a "conciliation agreement" forced on him that puts the burden of proof on him, not the government, that he is obeying the law.

Source: Reprinted from the May 25, 1981 issue of *Business Week* by special permission, ©1981 by McGraw-Hill, Inc., New York, NY 10020. All rights reserved.

Finally, some legal requirements must be met when selecting applicants for employment. Age, sex, minority status, and physical handicaps are employment factors that are covered by federal laws and, in many cases, state laws as well. An excellent outline of the basic requirements of the major federal employment rules and regulations appears in a publication of the Bank of America.[1]

Evaluation of Applicants

Many techniques for evaluating applicants are available to the small business. An uninformed, blind gamble on new employees may be avoided by following the series of steps described below.

Step 1—Use of Application Forms. The value of having an applicant complete an application form lies in its systematic collection of background data that might otherwise be overlooked. The information recorded on application forms is useful in sizing up an applicant and serves as a guide in making a more detailed investigation of the applicant's experience and character.

An application form need not be elaborate or lengthy. In fact, it need not even be a printed sheet. A simple application form is illustrated in Figure 15-1. In drawing up such a form, the employer should remember that questions concerning race or religion are prohibited by the Civil Rights Act of 1964. Even questions about education must be demonstrably job-related.

Step 2—Interviewing the Applicant. An employment interview permits the employer to get some idea of the applicant's appearance, job knowledge, intelligence, and personality. Any of these factors may be significant in the job to be filled. Although the interview is an important step in the process of selection, it should not be the only step. Some individuals have the mistaken idea that they are infallible judges of human nature on the basis of interviews alone.

The profitability of the interview depends upon the interviewer's skill and methods. Any interviewer can improve the quality of interviewing by following these generally accepted principles:

1. Determine the questions you want to ask before beginning the interview.
2. Conduct the interview in a quiet atmosphere.
3. Give your entire attention to the applicant.
4. Put the applicant at ease.
5. Never argue.

---

1. See "Personnel Guidelines," *Small Business Reporter*, 1981, published by the Bank of America, San Francisco, CA.

APPLICATION FORM

1. **PERSONAL DATA**

    Name ______________________ Social Security No. __________

    Address ______________________________ Tel. No. __________

2. **WORK EXPERIENCE**

    Present or last job:

    Name and address of employer ______________________
    Dates of employment ______________________
    Title of your job ______________________
    What kind of work did you perform? ______________________
    ____
    Why did you leave? ______________________

    Next-to-last job:

    Name and address of employer ______________________
    Dates of employment ______________________
    Title of your job ______________________
    What kind of work did you perform? ______________________
    ____
    Why did you leave? ______________________

3. **EDUCATION**

    High School:

    Name and address of school ______________________
    Did you graduate? __________ When? __________

    College or Specialized School:

    Name and address of school ______________________
    Did you graduate? __________ When? __________
    Nature of course ______________________

4. **REFERENCES (List three references not mentioned above)**

NAME	*ADDRESS*	*OCCUPATION*

Figure 15-1 Simplified Application Form

6. Keep the conversation at a level suited to the applicant.
7. Listen attentively.
8. Observe closely the applicant's speech, mannerisms, and attire if these characteristics are important to the job.
9. Try to avoid being unduly influenced by the applicant's trivial mannerisms or superficial resemblances to other people you know.

To avoid the possibility of running into legal problems with the Equal Employment Opportunity Commission (EEOC), the interviewer should refrain from:

1. Direct or indirect inquiries that will reveal the applicant's national, ethnic, or racial origin.
2. Questions to female applicants on marital status, number and age of children, pregnancy, or future child-bearing plans.
3. Inquiries about arrest or conviction records, unless such information is demonstrably job-related.

Step 3—Checking References and Further Investigation. When contacted, most references listed on application forms give a rose-colored picture of the applicant's character and ability. Nevertheless, careful checking with former employers, school authorities, and other references can be most constructive. A written letter of inquiry to these references is probably the weakest form of checking because people hesitate to put damaging statements in writing. However, individuals who provide little useful information in response to a written request often speak more frankly when approached by telephone or in person.

For a fee, an applicant's history (financial, criminal, employment, and so on) may be supplied by personal investigation agencies or local credit bureaus. The address of the nearest local bureau may be obtained from the Associated Credit Bureaus of America, Inc., Publications Department, 7000 Chippewa St., St. Louis, MO. If an employer needs this investigative consumer report to establish the applicant's eligibility for employment, the Fair Credit Reporting Act requires that the applicant be notified in writing prior to the request for such a report.

Step 4—Testing the Applicant. Many kinds of jobs lend themselves to performance testing. For example, a typist may be given some material to type to verify the typing speed and accuracy previously reported. With a little ingenuity, employers may improvise practical tests pertinent to most of the positions in their businesses.

Psychological examinations may also be used by small-business firms, but the results can easily be misleading because of difficulty in interpretation or in adapting the tests to a particular business. In addition, the United States Supreme Court has approved the EEOC's requirement that *any* test used in making employment decisions must be job-related.

Step 5—Physical Examinations. Though frequently neglected, physical examinations of applicants are of practical value to the small business. Few small firms have staff physicians, but arrangements can be made with a local doctor to administer the examinations. The employer, of course, should pay for the cost of the physical examination. In a few occupations physical examinations are required by law, but it is wise to discover physical limitations and possible contagious diseases of all new employees.

TRAINING AND DEVELOPMENT

There are very few positions in industry for which no training is required. It would be a rare individual who had an adequate background when applying for employment. To develop skill and knowledge, the employee is usually trained by the manager or a senior employee. If the employer fails to provide training, the new employee must proceed by trial and error, frequently with a waste of time, materials, and money.

Training to improve skills and knowledge is not limited to newcomers. The performance of current employees may often be improved through additional training. Furthermore, a different type of training designed to prepare a current employee for promotion is advisable.

In view of the fact that personal development and advancement are prime concerns of able employees, the small business can profit from careful attention to this phase of the personnel program. If the opportunity to grow and move up in an organization exists, it not only improves the morale of current employees but also offers an inducement for outsiders to accept employment. For all classes of employees in a small business, more training is accomplished on the job than through any other method.

Training Nonmanagerial Employees

The weakness of on-the-job training in small firms results from the use of haphazard learning in contrast to planned, controlled training programs. A system designed to make on-the-job training more effective is known as Job Instruction Training (JIT). The steps of this program, listed below, are intended to help the manager who is not a professional educator in "getting through" to the nonmanagerial employee.

1. *Prepare the employee*. Put the employee at ease. Find out what he or she already knows about the job. Get the employee interested in learning the job. Place the employee in an appropriate job.
2. *Present the operations*. Tell, show, illustrate, and question carefully and patiently. Stress key points. Instruct clearly and completely, taking up one point at a time—but no more than the employee can master.
3. *Try out performance*. Test the employee by having him or her perform the job. Have the employee tell, show, and explain key points. Ask questions and correct errors. Continue until the employee knows that he or she knows how to do the job.

4. *Follow up*. Check frequently. Designate to whom the employee should go for help. Encourage questions. Get the employee to look for the key points as he or she progresses. Taper off extra coaching and close follow-up.

Developing Managerial and Professional Employees

The small business faces a particularly serious need for developing managerial and professional employees. Depending on the size of the firm, there may be few or many key positions. Regardless of the number, individuals must be developed in or for these key positions if the business is to function most effectively. Incumbents should be developed to the point that they can adequately carry out the responsibilities assigned to them. Ideally, potential replacements should also be available for key individuals who retire or leave for other reasons. The entrepreneur often postpones grooming a personal replacement, but this step is likewise important in assuring a smooth transition in the management of a small firm.

In accomplishing management training, the manager should give serious consideration to the following factors:

1. *Determine the need for training*. What vacancies are expected? Who needs to be trained? What type of training and how much training does each of them need?
2. *Develop the plan for training*. How can the individuals be trained? Do they currently have enough responsibility to permit them to learn? Can they be assigned additional duties? Should they be given temporary assignments in other areas—for example, should they be shifted from production to sales? Would additional schooling be of benefit?
3. *Establish a timetable*. When should training be started? How much can be accomplished in the next six months or one year?
4. *Counsel with employees*. Do the individuals understand their need for training? Are they aware of the prospects for them in the firm? Has an understanding been reached as to the nature of training? Have the employees been consulted regularly about progress in their work and problems confronting them? Have they been given the benefit of the owner's experience and insights without having decisions made for them?

Management Succession in the Family Firm

Family relationships tend to complicate the process of management development and succession. For example, one or more employees or managers may be related to the entrepreneur. Such a situation can discourage other

ACTION REPORT: Son-in-Law Marvin

Promoting family members of a business, according to the following report, should be handled in a manner that will minimize anxiety among nonfamily members:

> Marvin was sharp, ambitious, and a graduate of a good business school. When Ruthie married Marvin, the family beamed with delight. And when his father-in-law, the president, offered Marvin the vice-presidency after a one-year apprenticeship, it was not true that he had gotten a job he didn't deserve.
>
> Of course, he got it sooner than he might have otherwise. But he worked hard, and he was competent.
>
> What, then, was the problem? As I found when I ran across this situation in a company we once considered for acquisition, the problem was disgruntlement in the ranks.
>
> Marvin's job, with its prestige and fat salary, was a plum sought after by a whole field of contenders. When Marvin won out, the inevitable conclusion was that he had been smiled upon not because of his ability, but because he had married the boss's daughter. What followed was an exodus of talented managers and seething bitterness among many who remained. One of them summed up the feelings of all: "The only way to get ahead in this outfit is to marry into the family."
>
> Care must always be taken in promoting family members. In this case, management should have tried for two objectives. One was to get the message across that, son-in-law or not, Marvin was good for the firm.
>
> At the same time, management should have made it clear that you did not have to be a relative to get ahead in the company. It is important to design an attractive management development and advancement program that includes nonfamily members as well as those in the family.

Source: Robert E. Levinson, "What to Do About Relatives on the Payroll," *Nation's Business,* Vol. 64, No. 10 (October, 1976), p. 56.

capable individuals who aspire to positions of greater responsibility but who believe relatives have the "inside track" for promotion. To avoid a stifling atmosphere, the entrepreneur should make clear the extent of opportunity that does exist and identify the positions, if any, that are reserved for members of the family.

The task of preparing family members for careers in the business is difficult and sometimes frustrating. The professional and managerial requirements tend to become intertwined with family feelings and interests. Indeed,

Table 15-1 Stages of Father-Son Succession

Pre-business	Introductory	Introductory-Functional	Functional	Advanced Functional	Early Succession	Mature Succession
		Entry of Successor		Transfer of Presidency		
Successor may be aware of some facets of the organization or industry. Orientation of successor by family members, however, is unplanned or passive.	Successor may be exposed by family members to jargon, organizational members, and environmental parties prior to part-time employment in firm.	Successor works as part-time employee in organization. Gradually, the work becomes more difficult and complex. Includes education and work as full-time employee in other organizations.	Successor enters organization as full-time employee. Includes first and all subsequent nonmanagerial jobs.	Successor assumes managerial position. Includes all supervisory positions prior to becoming the president.	Successor assumes presidency. Includes time successor needs to become leader of organization or more than *de jure* head of organization.	Successor becomes *de facto* leader of organization.

Source: Justin G. Longenecker and John E. Schoen, "Management Succession in the Family Firm," *Journal of Small Business Management*, Vol. 16, No. 3 (July, 1978), p. 4. Reproduced with permission.

the preparation of a son to take over a family firm has been described as a long-term process of socialization by which family successors are gradually prepared for leadership.[2] The stages in this process are outlined in Table 15-1.

Preparation for management succession is not necessarily smooth in any organization. In the family firm, however, the emotions of the various parties are involved to an unusual degree, as shown in the following:

> In one firm, for instance, family feuds had reached the battle pitch; various family representatives were no longer speaking to one another. As a result, each group brought its own lawyer to the company board meetings. Simulating deaf mutes, family members passed hastily written questions to their attorney who, in turn, would ask an opposing attorney for the desired information.[3]

The error of appointing incompetent managers on the basis of family relationship is obvious, although avoiding this error may be difficult. Family

2. Justin G. Longenecker and John E. Schoen, "Management Succession in the Family Firm," *Journal of Small Business Management*, Vol. 16, No. 3 (July, 1978), pp. 1-6.

3. Bank of America, "Management Succession," *Small Business Reporter*, Vol. 10, No. 12 (1972), p. 13.

members should never be designated as chief executives or even appointed to other critical management positions if they lack the necessary ability. The appointment of competent outsiders to these jobs, if necessary, increases the value of the firm to all members of the family who have an ownership interest in it.

COMPENSATION AND INCENTIVES FOR SMALL-BUSINESS EMPLOYEES

Financial incentives are important to all employees, and the small firm must acknowledge the central role of the paycheck in attracting and motivating personnel. In addition, small firms can also offer several nonfinancial incentives which appeal to both managerial and nonmanagerial employees.

Legislation Affecting Wages

Various external influences affect the setting of compensation levels for employees. For example, wages cannot be established on an individual basis when employees are represented by a union. Furthermore, the small firm cannot afford to pay more than its competitors unless the higher wage stimulates greater productivity. Perhaps the most important external influence on wage-setting is the applicable federal and state legislation.

Compensation levels are subject to various federal statutes. The most comprehensive law is the Fair Labor Standards Act, which establishes minimum wage rates and requires the payment of overtime rates for hours over 40 per week. The Equal Pay Act of 1963 specifies that women and men shall be paid at the same rate "for equal work on jobs requiring equal skill, effort, and responsibility which are performed under similar working conditions within the same establishment."

Many states have also legislated in the field of wages and hours, and those with comprehensive fair employment practice laws now include sex discrimination among the prohibitions. The minimum wage provisions of state laws, however, are generally lower than those of the Fair Labor Standards Act. In cases where state fair employment practice laws have been found to conflict with state "protective" laws prohibiting the employment of women in certain types of work and/or regulating the hours they work, the fair employment laws have been consistently upheld in both state and federal courts.

Financial Incentives

Wages or salaries paid to employees either are based on increments of time—such as an hour, a day, a month—or vary directly with their output. Compensation based on increments of time is commonly referred to as

daywork. The daywork system is most appropriate for types of work where performance is not easily measurable. It is the most common compensation system in American industry and is easy to understand and administer.

In order to motivate employees to increase their productivity, incentive systems have been devised. Incentive wages may constitute an employee's entire earnings or may supplement regular daywork wages. Some financial incentive plans are the piecework system, the production bonus system, and the commission system, which is widely used to compensate salespersons.

Other types of compensation which are less directly related to employee output consist of profit-sharing plans and fringe benefits. Profit sharing provides more direct work incentive in small companies than in large ones because the connection between individual performance and company success can be more easily understood and appreciated by employees in small firms. On the other hand, fringe benefits (which usually include vacations, holidays, group insurance, pensions, and severance pay) are expensive for the small firm. Obviously the costs of these benefits add substantially to the direct wage costs, which may account for more than 50 percent of the small firm's operating expense. Nevertheless, the small firm cannot ignore fringe benefits if it is to compete effectively for good employees.

Nonfinancial Incentives

Although small firms must be competitive in levels of compensation, they can also emphasize their unique features as they attempt to attract well-qualified personnel. Not all of the recruiting advantages lie with large corporations.

Some small firms, for example, can offer their professional and managerial personnel greater freedom than they would have in big business. According to one writer, the president of a small electronics company in California, Marshall Fitzgerald, has emphasized this advantage of the small firm:

> Fitzgerald says he has managed to win in the Silicon Valley bidding wars not by offering more money than his better-financed rivals, but by better understanding what motivates and attracts the different kinds of employees his company needs.
>
> "We start by identifying an expert in a key area where we need superior talent," explains Fitzgerald. "We lure him into the company by offering him more freedom than he'll probably ever get in a large bureaucracy. And then we use him as a magnet to attract a supporting staff of people who want an opportunity to work with a superstar.
>
> "Good people are motivated as much by creative challenges, by a chance to learn and grow, as they are by paychecks," Fitzgerald adds. "Here's where a small company actually has an advantage over a large organization. We can give a person a job and let him run with it."[4]

---

4. James Fawcette, "Money Alone Can't Buy Top Talent," *Inc.*, Vol. 3, No. 3 (March, 1981), p. 92.

In the small firm, key personnel may also have the opportunity for a more diversified type of experience. Their positions or assignments are often broader in scope, and their impact on the business is more evident.

A vice-president of an international executive search firm, Kieran J. Hackett, has described the type of person who may be attracted to the smaller company as follows:

> The best small-company managers are entrepreneurial personalities—people who are willing to bank on themselves and their efforts. They don't want to turn around and blame somebody else if something goes wrong. The right kind of person likes doing things himself. He hates watching his plans filter through layers of management, and he hates carrying out other people's plans even more.[5]

In lower-level positions, the advantages cited above are less persuasive, and wage rates are relatively more important. Even here, however, small-firm flexibility may be attractive.

EFFECTIVE HUMAN RELATIONSHIPS IN THE SMALL FIRM

Satisfactory compensation, company picnics, and fringe benefits do not guarantee harmony in employer-employee relationships. These elements of a personnel program are only part of the total fabric of interpersonal relationships. Some of the more general concerns which are significant in building effective teamwork are noted below.

Effective Communication

The key to healthy interpersonal relationships lies in effective communication. To be sure, much communication flows in the form of orders and instructions to employees. But communication is a two-way process, and it is difficult for employees to be either intelligent or enthusiastic teamworkers if they do not know the reasons for such orders and instructions. Furthermore, the opportunity to contribute ideas and opinions *before* the manager decides an issue adds dignity to the job in the eyes of most employees.

Other aspects leading to effective communication include telling employees where they stand, how the business is doing, and what plans are for the future. Negative feedback to employees may be necessary at times, but positive feedback is the primary tool for establishing good human relations. Perhaps the most fundamental concept to keep in mind is that employees are

---

5. "Can a Small Company Attract Top Managers?" *Inc.*, Vol. 3, No. 5 (May, 1981), p. 138.

ACTION REPORT: Effective Two-Way Communication

Hope's Windows, Inc., is a custom manufacturer of steel and aluminum windows located in Jamestown, NY. In 1977, the company experienced a drop in orders in one of its key markets, forcing the layoff of 23 of 35 employees. The problem was caused by the bidding process, which produced bids that were consistently too high.

To solve the problem, Hope's management appealed to employees who made the windows. The company created a bidding committee made up of managers and production workers which proved successful in winning most of their subsequent bids. Dale Mansfield, a ten-year veteran at Hope, commented as follows:

> In a lot of companies the managers act like they're too good to be speaking to a "nobody." Here they listen to people like me. No manager can do every job or understand every job. So how can he always know what needs to be done? I don't think managers are relinquishing anything by asking us what we think. We're just providing the information; management still has to make the decisions. But, with their ideas and our ideas, maybe we can come up with something that will really help the company.

Source: "Hope's Windows, Inc.: Surviving with the Workers' Help," *Inc.*, Vol. 3, No. 4 (April, 1981), pp. 82-84.

people. They quickly detect insincerity, but they respond to honest efforts to treat them as mature, responsible individuals.[6]

Personal Contact Between Employees and Entrepreneur

Employees of a small firm get to know the owner-manager personally within a relatively short period of time. As the result of day-to-day contact, the owner-manager can be understanding when employees have personal problems. If the employer-employee relationship is good, the employee develops a strong feeling of personal loyalty to the employer, coupled with a stronger sense of responsibility than is likely in a large business. How could one feel deeply about the president of a large corporation whom one has never seen?

On the other hand, there is a danger in the reluctance of an employer to discipline those employees who are also friends. For example, Miss Ash, the owner of a small supermarket, employs an old acquaintance, Mrs. Gray. Miss

6. For an excellent discussion of motivating people in organizations, see J. Clifton Williams, *Human Behavior in Organizations* (2d ed.; Cincinnati: South-Western Publishing Co., 1982), Chapters 3-5.

Ash is aware of Mrs. Gray's acute need of a job. Mrs. Gray's main duty is to be the cashier. In performing her work, however, she is extremely choosy about what she will do. When there are no customers to be checked out, for instance, Mrs. Gray refuses to arrange stock on the shelves or perform other work. The long-suffering Miss Ash permits this situation to exist because of her sympathy for Mrs. Gray as a friend.

Informal Personnel Relationships

Most small firms do not have the written personnel policies and formalized procedures that are found in large companies. The advantage of the small firm's informality lies in the manager's ability to devise solutions to fit particular personnel problems. Individual considerations may be taken into account, and problems that do not fit a rule book may be solved in the most appropriate manner.

The danger inherent in the informal solution of personnel problems on a case-to-case basis is that solutions may be improvised without proper thought. The quick answer may not be the right answer, and precedents established might prove to be embarrassing later. Placing some minimal set of policies in writing is usually desirable as a safeguard against the dangers of excessive informality.

Pervading Influence of the Entrepreneur

A large firm may need years to educate lower-level supervisors who may misunderstand or even sabotage any new personnel philosophy that needs to be introduced into the business. In contrast, a weakness in personnel philosophy may be seen and corrected immediately by the owner-manager of a small firm. Suppose, for example, that the decision has been made to change from fighting a union to cooperating with it. If the owner-manager is the only manager in the business, the new philosophy can be adopted completely without delay. Even if there are additional managers, the new philosophy can be quickly explained to them and relayed in turn to all other employees.

This pervading influence of the owner-manager can be a disadvantage, however, when the entrepreneur has a specialized background in one functional area of business, say, production management. In the day-to-day operations there looms a diversity of pressing production problems, sales problems, and financial problems. Personnel problems, in contrast, appear less critical—at least in their early stages. As a result, the entrepreneur may become so enmeshed in production, sales, or financial problems that human relations factors are inadvertently ignored.

Use of a Personnel Manager

A firm with only a few employees cannot afford a full-time specialist to deal with personnel problems. Some of the more involved personnel tools and techniques which are required in larger businesses may be unnecessarily complicated for this small business. As it grows in size, however, its personnel problems will increase in both number and complexity.

The point at which it becomes logical to hire a personnel manager cannot be specified precisely. Each entrepreneur must decide whether the type and size of the business could profitably pay for a personnel specialist. Hiring a part-time personnel manager might be a logical first step in some instances.

Some conditions that encourage the appointment of a personnel manager in a small business are:

1. When there is a substantial number of employees. (What is "substantial" varies with the business, but 100 employees is suggested as a guide.)
2. When employees are represented by a union.
3. When the labor turnover rate is high.
4. When the need for skilled or professional personnel creates problems in recruiting or selection.
5. When supervisors or operative employees require considerable training.
6. When employee morale is unsatisfactory.
7. When competition for operative personnel is keen.

Labor Unions and Small Business

Most entrepreneurs prefer to operate independently and to avoid unionization. Indeed, most small businesses are not unionized. To some extent, this results from the predominance of small business in such areas as services, where unionization is less common than in manufacturing. Also, unions typically concentrate their primary attention on large companies.

This does not mean, of course, that labor unions are unknown in small firms. Many types of firms—building and electrical contractors, for example—negotiate labor contracts and employ unionized personnel. The need to work with a union formalizes and, to some extent, complicates the relationship between the small firm and its employees.

If employees wish to bargain collectively, the law requires the employer to participate in such bargaining. The demand for labor union representation may arise from labor dissatisfaction with the work environment and employment relationships. By following enlightened personnel policies, the small firm can minimize the likelihood of labor organization and/or contribute to healthy management-union relationships.[7]

---

7. For a further discussion of this topic, see Linda A. Roxe, *Personnel Management for the Smaller Company* (New York: AMACOM, 1979), Chapter 10.

LOOKING BACK

1. To secure capable employees, the small firm must take the initiative in seeking applicants. Sources include unsolicited applicants, schools, public and private employment agencies, friends and acquaintances of current employees, and advertising. The selection process must conform to legislation applying to the hiring of minorities and other special employment groups.
2. Steps in the evaluation of applicants include the use of an application form, applicant interviewing, checking references and background investigation, testing, and physical examinations.
3. Nonmanagerial employees of small firms require training to develop skill and knowledge in their jobs and to prepare them for promotion. The need for developing personnel at the managerial and professional levels is particularly acute.

   Family relationships tend to complicate planning for management succession in the family firm. Family members should never be designated as chief executives or even appointed to other critical management positions if they lack the necessary ability.
4. Small firms must be competitive in wage and salary levels. They can also use both financial and nonfinancial incentives. As an example of the latter, freedom to operate with a minimum of bureaucratic control is appealing to many managerial and professional employees.
5. Effective teamwork in small firms can be developed by effective communication, close personal contact between the owner-manager and the employees, appropriate discipline, and informality in relationships. In some cases, the development of a personnel program also involves the use of a personnel manager and bargaining with a labor union.

DISCUSSION QUESTIONS

1. Discuss with the owner or manager of a small firm the sources that the firm uses for obtaining new employees. In particular, ask for the owner's opinion of the relative value of the available sources.
2. How might the manager of a small business be aggressive in recruiting new employees? Explain.
3. Do small firms that cannot afford elaborate employment procedures suffer a competitive disadvantage in comparison to larger companies? Why?
4. For what types of jobs would it be practical to inquire closely into the applicant's arrest and conviction record? Explain.

5. Consider the small business with which you are best acquainted. Has adequate provision been made to replace key management personnel? Is the firm using any form of executive development?

6. What problems are involved in using incentive wage systems in a small firm? Would the nature of the work affect management's decision concerning use or nonuse of wage incentives? Why?

7. Is the use of a profit-sharing system desirable in a small business? What major difficulties might be associated with its use when intended to provide greater employee motivation?

8. What types of nonfinancial incentives can be used by a small firm to attract highly qualified managers?

9. List the factors in small-business operation that encourage the appointment of a personnel manager. Should a personnel manager always be hired on a full-time basis? Why or why not?

10. It has been said that labor unions have been more successful in their organizing efforts in small manufacturing firms than in small merchandising firms. Why is this true?

REFERENCES TO SMALL BUSINESS IN ACTION

"Entrepreneurial Trap." *Forbes*, Vol. 125, No. 7 (March 31, 1980), pp. 86-91.

The founder of Lawter Chemicals experienced difficulty—but eventually succeeded—in hiring and delegating decision making to qualified professional assistants. However, he has still failed to designate a successor for his own position.

"How to Keep That Old Company Spirit Alive." *Inc.*, Vol. 2, No. 9 (September, 1980), pp. 40-54.

In this special section, *Inc.* presents the stories of three rapidly growing companies. Each of the firms followed a different route in trying to preserve the excitement and spirit that are found in new small firms.

Kinkead, Gwen. "Family Business Is a Passion Play." *Fortune*, Vol. 102, No. 1 (June 30, 1980), pp. 70-75.

Family relationships and conflicts in a Los Angeles life insurance agency are described.

Sambul, Nathan J. "Fine Tune Your Training Program." *Inc.*, Vol. 2, No. 8 (August, 1980), pp. 74-76.

The author describes the use of videotape equipment in the training programs of various small businesses.

Chapter 16

Managing Production Operations

LOOKING AHEAD

Watch for the following important topics:

1. Types of production processes and steps in production control.
2. Role of and types of maintenance.
3. Building and controlling product quality.
4. Methods of work improvement and measurement.
5. Industrial research for small plants.

In this chapter we will go to the very core of the business enterprise – the management of its production/operations process. If a firm is to be profitable, it must carefully control the various elements of this process which include: production/operations control, plant maintenance, quality control, work improvement and measurement, and industrial research.

PRODUCTION/OPERATIONS CONTROL

Every business firm has some production or operations process. This is true whether the business produces a physical product or an intangible ser-

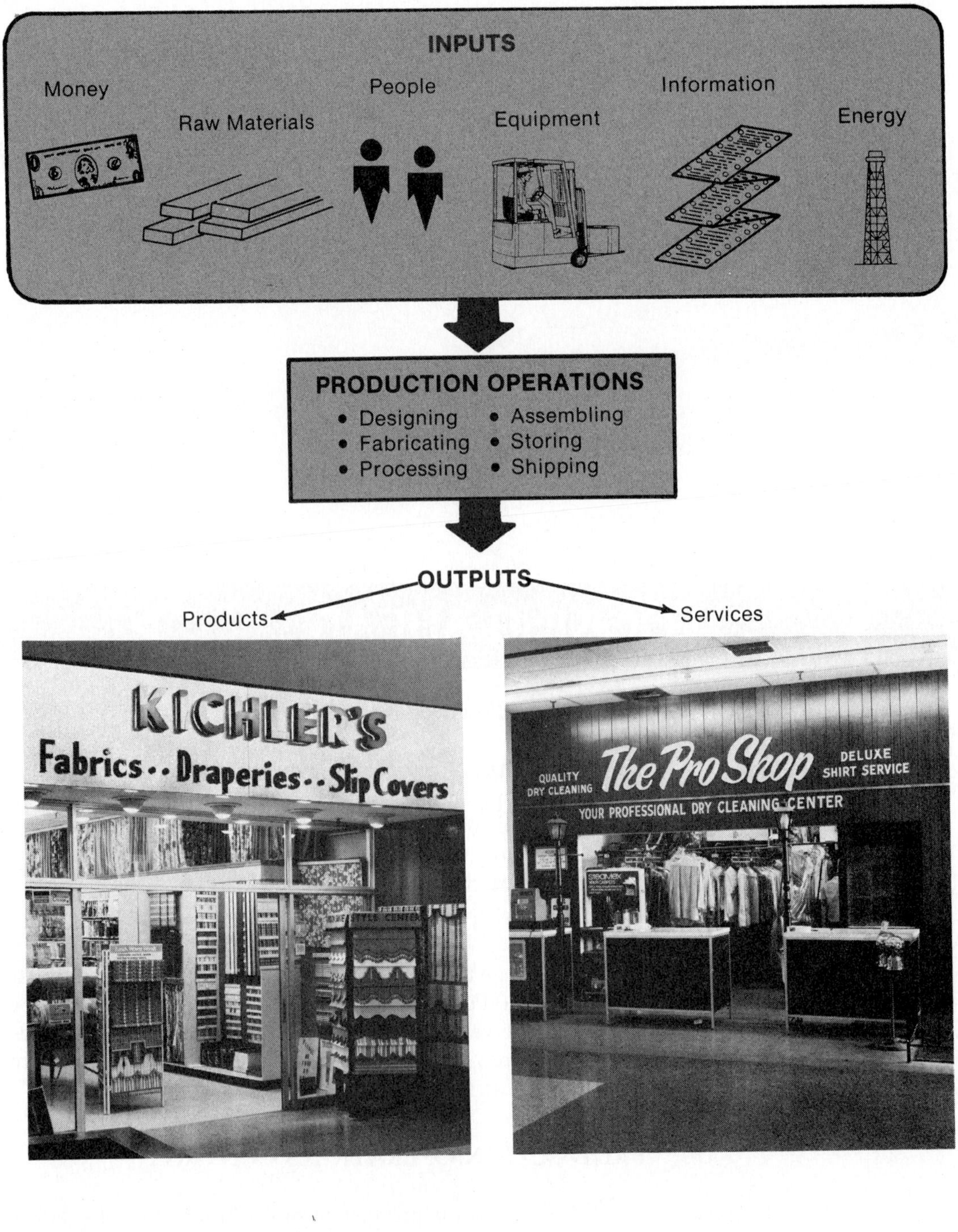

Figure 16-1 The Production/Operations Process

vice. The production/operations process, as pictured in Figure 16-1, is concerned with the conversion of inputs into outputs.

Inputs include raw materials, labor, and energy, which are combined to form the finished product or output. In Figure 16-1 it is the conversion activities that constitute the production process. In this chapter we will concentrate our attention upon control of production in a manufacturing plant, but the same underlying concepts are applicable to all types of businesses. If a business firm prepares tax returns for clients, for example, the inputs include financial data from the client, the analyst's knowledge, the applicable regulations, the tax forms, the typewriter, and so on. The completed tax return is the output.

Kinds of Manufacturing Processes

There are many variations in manufacturing processes. In considering the nature of production control, it may be helpful to identify two basic types of manufacturing processes. As a matter of fact, most production processes are a combination of these types.

Intermittent Manufacturing. Often described as job-order production, **intermittent manufacturing** involves short production runs with only one or a few products being produced before shifting to a different production setup. General-purpose machines are used for this type of production. Examples of businesses that use this type of process include print shops, machine shops, and automobile repair shops.

Continuous Manufacturing. Firms that produce a standardized product or a relatively few standardized products use the **continuous manufacturing** process, which involves long production runs. Highly specialized equipment can be used. A soft-drink bottling plant is an example of a continuous manufacturing process.

Figure 16-2 shows the layout of a small factory that produces a single, final product called ABC. This product is made from three machine parts: Part A, which is fabricated by the factory in three shop operations, and Parts B and C, which are purchased. The raw materials for Part A, as well as the purchased parts, flow to the plant from suppliers by rail and by truck. They are received, inspected, and then sent to the storeroom for subsequent issue.

To start a production run, the raw materials for Part A move lot by lot to the storage table and then to the machines for Shop Operation #1 through Shop Operation #3. Meanwhile, Parts B and C move by conveyor to the two assemblers near the end of the process. When each lot of Part A has passed inspection, it goes to the line loader, who places one part at a time on the

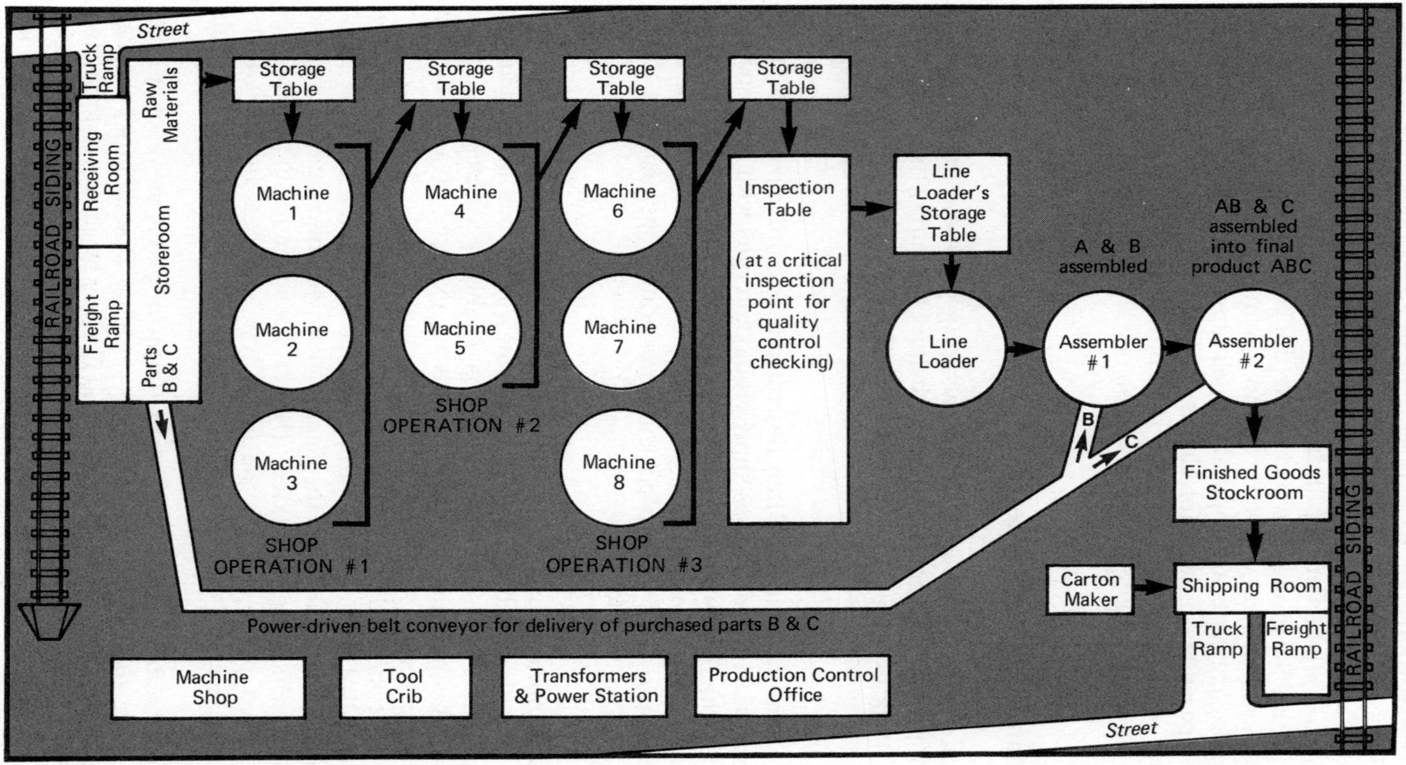

Figure 16-2 A Manufacturing Layout and Process

conveyor going to Assembler #1. Parts A and B are joined by Assembler #1 to form subassembly AB. Then subassembly AB goes to Assembler #2, who joins Part C to subassembly AB to produce the finished product ABC. Final inspection, storage, and shipping operations follow.

Steps in Production Control

Production control consists of securing the orderly sequential flow of products through the plant at a rate commensurate with scheduled deliveries to customers. To attain this objective, it is essential to avoid work stoppages, to eliminate production bottlenecks when they occur, and to utilize machines and personnel efficiently.

Simple, informal control procedures are frequently used in small plants. If a procedure is simple and the output small, the manager can keep things moving smoothly with a minimum of paperwork. Personal observation might even suffice. However, there comes a time in the growth of any manufacturing organization when formal procedures must be established to attain production efficiency. Each of the steps in formal production control is explained below.

Planning and Routing. Planning involves the determination of the basic manufacturing data needed. Among the most important data needed are:

1. Kinds of raw materials and fabricated parts required.
2. Number of fabricated parts and amounts of material of each kind required per unit of finished product.
3. Best sequence of processing operations for making each product.
4. Number of machines and operators needed on each processing operation.
5. Number and kinds of tooling items required to set up each machine.
6. Standard output rate of each machine.
7. Number of units of finished product that the plant can produce daily or yearly.

Once the manufacturing data are determined, two things can be prepared: (1) a bill of materials listing the raw materials, consumption standards, and other related information, and (2) a route list showing the sequence of processing operations and who will perform them.

In intermittent processing, machines are shut down rather frequently and retooled to produce a different product. Therefore, the basic manufacturing data are needed well in advance of the start of production. This allows management sufficient time to make any necessary changes in plant layout, to buy any new tooling items required, and to train workers.

In continuous processing, most or all of the machines run without stopping for long periods of time. Advance planning is even more essential; for once the machinery is set up and operations have begun, changes are both difficult and costly.

Scheduling and Dispatching. After a given process is planned and set up, timetables for each department and work center are established to control the flow of work. In continuous processing, which involves large-scale production and is done in very few small factories, flow control is fairly simple and involves little paperwork. This is because continuous processing assures a steady flow of finished products off the final assembly line. The dispatcher must keep all lines (subassembly and final assembly) operating all the time. If delays occur, rescheduling or other adjustment is required.

In intermittent processing, which involves small- to medium-volume production where lots are produced one at a time, there are different flow-control techniques. Where a lot is in process for several days, or is slow-moving, it is possible to use *visual control boards* to reflect both work assignments and the progress of work toward completion. For fast-moving processes where a lot clears each machine quickly, the *block control* technique clears the oldest blocks first on each processing operation.

Supervising and Performance Follow-Up. Keeping the work moving on schedule is the major responsibility of the shop supervisor. Schedule performance reports and necessary follow-up routines are established. After an order is completed, the schedules are terminated and the work records are filed for future use.

Balancing Sales Volume and Production Control

Planning, timing, and volume of output are all limited by the plant's capacity to produce. Typically the sales demand can be satisfied with production at less than capacity. However, an unexpected high sales volume may force a plant to produce at capacity. The plant then makes what it can when it can. Of course, if long-term increased sales are expected, the plant's capacity may be enlarged when it is financially feasible to do so.

PLANT MAINTENANCE

According to Murphy's Law, if anything can go wrong, it will! In operating systems which make extensive use of tools and equipment, there is indeed much which can go wrong. The maintenance function is intended to correct malfunctions of equipment and, as far as possible, to prevent such breakdowns from occurring.

Role of Maintenance in Small Firms

The nature of maintenance work obviously depends upon the type of operation and the nature of the equipment being used. In an office, for example, the machines that require maintenance may simply include typewriters, office copiers, and related office machines. Maintenance services are usually secured on a contract basis—either by calling for repair personnel when a breakdown occurs or by contracting for periodic servicing and other maintenance when needed.

In manufacturing firms that use more complex and specialized equipment, the maintenance function is much more important. For all types of firms, maintenance includes plant housekeeping as well as equipment repair. Plant housekeeping contributes to effective performance, moreover, even in those operations that use simple facilities.

It is easy to underestimate the importance of maintenance. Managers often think of it as janitorial-type work and postpone it as much as possible in order to concentrate upon the production process. The increased use of expensive, complex equipment, however, has made the maintenance role a much greater factor in the firm's overall effectiveness. A major breakdown in production equipment, for example, can interfere with scheduled deliveries and cause labor costs to skyrocket as personnel are idled.

In small plants, maintenance work often is performed by regular production employees. As the firm expands its facilities, it may add specialized maintenance personnel and eventually create a maintenance department.

Types of Maintenance

Plant maintenance activities fall into two categories. One is **corrective maintenance**, which includes both the major and minor repairs necessary to restore a facility to good condition. The other is **preventive maintenance**, which includes inspections and other activities intended to prevent machine breakdowns and damage to people and buildings.

Corrective Maintenance. Major repairs are unpredictable as to time of occurrence, repair time required, loss of output, and cost of downtime. Because of these characteristics, some small manufacturers find it desirable to contract with other service firms for major repair work.

In contrast, the regular occurrence of minor breakdowns makes the volume of minor repair work reasonably predictable. Minor repairs are completed easily, quickly, and economically. Therefore, many small plants use one or two of their own employees to perform such work.

Preventive Maintenance. A small plant can ill afford to neglect preventive maintenance. If a machine is highly critical to the overall operation, it should be inspected and serviced regularly to preclude costly breakdowns. Also, the frequent checking of equipment reduces industrial accidents, and the installation of smoke alarms and/or automatic sprinkler systems minimizes the danger of fire damage.

Preventive maintenance of equipment need not involve elaborate controls. Some cleaning and lubricating is usually done as a matter of routine. But for preventive maintenance to work well, more systematic procedures are needed. A record card showing cost, acquisition date, periods of use and storage, and frequency of preventive maintenance inspections should be kept on each major piece of equipment. On any given day, the machinist is handed the set of cards covering that day's required inspections. The machinist inspects each piece of equipment, makes necessary notations on the cards, and replaces worn parts.

Good Housekeeping and Plant Safety

Good housekeeping facilitates production control, saves time in looking for tools, and keeps floor areas safe and free for production work. Disregard for good housekeeping practices is reflected in a plant's production record, for good workmanship and high output are hard to achieve in an ill-kept plant.

According to the Occupational Safety and Health Act of 1970 (OSHA), employers are required to provide a place of employment free from hazards which are likely to cause death or serious physical harm. This means that the building and equipment must be maintained in a way that minimizes safety and health hazards. Although very small firms have been relieved from some of OSHA's record-keeping requirements, they are still subject to the requirements of the law.[1]

As far as safety of the premises is concerned, not all small manufacturers require a sophisticated security system. However, all should be aware of the security problem and of available security devices. Such devices include the use of fences to help deter intruders, security guards, burglar-alarm systems, and gates or doors equipped with access controls which are activated only by identification cards or keys given to authorized personnel.

QUALITY CONTROL

Most consumers view quality subjectively as a single variable ranging from very bad to very good. The manufacturer knows, however, that there is a set of objectively measurable physical variables—such as length or diameter—which *together* determine how good or bad a product is. To approach perfection on even one variable is very costly. To make a product

1. "Easing Regulatory Burdens on Small Business," *Business Week*, No. 2641 (June 16, 1980), pp. 156-159.

inferior to that of competitors, however, means that they will get the business. Thus, a product must be good enough so that it will be competitive, yet it must not be prohibitively expensive.

Building Quality into the Product

One company advertises, "The quality goes in before the label goes on." This slogan implies that quality does not originate with the inspection process that checks the finished product but with the earlier production process. Quality of a product begins, in fact, with its design and the design of the manufacturing process.

Other factors that contribute to product quality include the quality of the raw materials used. Generally the finished product is better if a superior grade of raw material is used. A contractor who uses lumber of inferior grade in building a house produces a low-quality house.

In many types of businesses, an even more critical variable is found in the performance of employees. Employees who are careful in their work produce products of a better quality than those produced by careless employees. You have probably heard the admonition, "Never buy a car which was produced on Friday or Monday!" The central role of personnel in producing a quality product suggests the importance of human resources management—properly selecting, training, and motivating production personnel.

Inspection: The Traditional Technique

Inspection consists of scrutinizing a part or a product to determine whether it is good or bad. An inspector typically uses gauges to evaluate the important quality variables. For effective quality control, the inspector must be honest, objective, and capable of resisting pressure from shop personnel to pass borderline cases.

Inspection Standards. In manufacturing, inspection standards consist of design tolerances that are set for every important quality variable. These tolerances show the limits of variation allowable above and below the desired dimension of the given quality variable. Tolerances must satisfy the requirements which customers will impose on finished products.

Points of Inspection. Traditionally, inspection occurs in the receiving room to check the condition and quantity of materials received from suppliers. Inspection is also customary at critical processing points—for example, *before* any operation that would conceal existing defects, or *after* any operation that produces an excessive amount of defectives. Of course, the final inspection of finished products is of utmost importance.

ACTION REPORT: Employee Performance and Product Quality

The work of production employees is often crucial in determining the quality of a company's products. This was the case with Chester Cable Corporation, a small wire manufacturer in Chester, NY. Unfortunately much of its wire came back as fast as it went out. An average of $70,000 worth of wire was returned monthly because of poor workmanship.

Quality control supervisor Steve Rodvansky tried, with little success, to get production workers to take quality seriously. Ms. Carol Rose writes:

> Rodvansky knew his problem had to be solved by the workers who actually produced the wire at the company's Chester, NY, plant. "You can't inspect quality into a product," Rodvansky says. "You've got to build it into the product in the first place."

Rodvansky finally got his point across when he brought into the plant a TV game manufactured by one of Chester Cable's customers and recalled as follows:

> Suddenly everyone got very excited. I was demonstrating the game plan to Pam Van Dunk, an extrusion operator who made the hair-thin wires that went into the game's connector cable. She showed it around the plant and insisted I get samples of other products that used our wire.
>
> I know it sounds too simple to be true, but that demonstration turned out to be the beginning of an answer to our quality control problems.

Source: Carol Rose, "You Can't Inspect Quality into Your Products," *Inc.*, Vol. 2, No. 10 (October, 1980), pp. 123-125.

Reduction of Inspection Costs. To reduce costs, the manufacturer must be alert to possibilities for mechanization or automation of inspection. Automated inspection requires only first-piece inspection and periodic rechecks. So long as the setups remain satisfactory, the production run continues without other inspection.

100 Percent Inspection. When each item in every lot processed is inspected, this is called **100 percent inspection**. Supposedly it assures the elimination of all bad materials in process and all defective products prior to shipment to customers. Such goals are seldom reached, however. In addition, this method of inspection is not only time-consuming but also costly. Furthermore, inspectors often make honest errors in judgment. A reinspection of lots that have been 100 percent inspected, for example, will show that inspectors err by placing good items in the scrap barrel, and bad items or rework items in the good-item barrel. Also, some types of inspection—for example, opening a can of vegetables—destroy the product, making 100 percent inspection impractical.

Statistical Quality Control

To avoid the cost and time of 100 percent inspection, small firms can use statistical methods to devise sampling procedures for quality control. In this way, the small firm can inspect a small number of items in a group and make an inductive decision about the quality level of the entire group.

Attributes Sampling Plans. Some products are judged to be either acceptable or unacceptable, good or bad. For example, a light bulb either lights up or it doesn't. Likewise, a manufactured part either falls within the tolerance size limits or it doesn't. In these cases, control of quality involves a measurement of *attributes*.

Suppose a small firm receives a shipment of 1,000 parts from a supplier. Rather than evaluating all 1,000 parts, the purchaser can check the acceptability of a small sample of parts and decide about the acceptability of the entire order. The size of the sample—for instance, a sample of 25 of the 1,000 parts—affects the discriminating power of an attributes sampling plan. The smaller the sample, the greater the danger of either accepting a defective lot or rejecting a good lot due to sampling error. A larger sample, on the other hand, reduces this danger but increases the inspection cost. An attributes sampling plan must strike a balance between these two forces, avoiding excessive inspection costs and simultaneously avoiding an unreasonable risk of accepting a bad lot or rejecting a good lot.

Variables Sampling Plans. A variables sampling plan measures many degrees of an item, rather than simply judging the item as acceptable or unacceptable. If the characteristic being inspected is measured on a continuous basis, a variables sampling plan may be used. For example, the weight of a box of candy—which is being manufactured continuously throughout the day and week—may be measured in pounds and ounces. The process can be monitored to be sure it stays "in control." Periodic random samples are taken and plotted on a chart to discover if the process is out of control, thus requiring corrective action.

The variables control chart used for this purpose has lines denoting the upper and lower control limits. For example, a shop might produce wooden pieces averaging 42 inches in length. The upper control limit might be 43 inches and the lower control limit 41 inches. A signal of a lack of control would be given by a measurement falling outside either control limit, by a trend run of points upward or downward, and by various other indicators.

To establish a specific variables or attributes sampling plan, the small-business manager may consult more specialized publications in production/operations management or statistical quality control. Or, more likely, the manager may consult a specialist in quantitative methods for assistance in devising a sound sampling plan. The savings possible by using an efficient quality control method can easily justify the consulting fees required in devising a sound quality control plan.

Quality Control in Service Businesses

The discussion of quality control typically centers on a manufacturing process involving a tangible product which can be inspected or measured in some way. The need for quality control, however, is not limited to producers of physical products. Service businesses, such as motels, dry cleaners, accounting service firms, and automobile repair shops, also need to maintain an adequate control of quality. In fact, many firms offer a combination of a tangible product and intangible services and, ideally, wish to control quality in both areas.

Measurement problems are greater in assessing the quality of a service, however. One can measure the length of a piece of wood more easily than the quality level of motel accommodations. Nevertheless, methods can be devised for measuring the quality of services. Customers of an automobile repair shop, for example, may be sampled to determine their view of the service they received. And a motel can maintain a record of the number of "foul-ups" in travelers' reservations, complaints about cleanliness of rooms, and so on.

For some types of service firms, control of quality constitutes the single most important managerial responsibility. All that such firms sell is service, and the future of the business rests upon the quality of its service as perceived by customers.

WORK IMPROVEMENT AND MEASUREMENT

Work improvement means finding work methods that demand the least physical effort and the shortest execution time at the lowest possible cost. Most large manufacturing plants employ industrial engineers who specialize in work improvement methods. In the small plant, however, the manager may have to initiate and carry out a work improvement program with the help of shop supervisors.

Nature of Work Study

When conducted for the entire operation of a plant, work study and improvement involves an analysis of equipment and tooling, plant layout, working conditions, and individual jobs. It means finding the answers to such questions as:

1. Is the right machine being used?
2. Can one employee operate two or more machines?
3. Can automatic feeders or ejectors be utilized?
4. Can power tools replace hand tools?
5. Can the jigs and fixtures be improved?
6. Is the workplace properly arranged?
7. Is the operator's motion sequence effective?

To be successful, work improvement and measurement require the collaboration of employees and management. Figure 16-3 outlines the procedures to be followed in devising and installing new work methods. Note that two steps toward the end of the procedure — "sell" and "install" — call for convincing and training employees who must use the new methods.

The competitive pressures on today's small-business firms provide the incentive for work improvement. Small firms can improve their productivity and stay competitive. To the extent that methods can actually be improved, there will be increased output from the same effort (or even reduced effort) on the part of production employees.

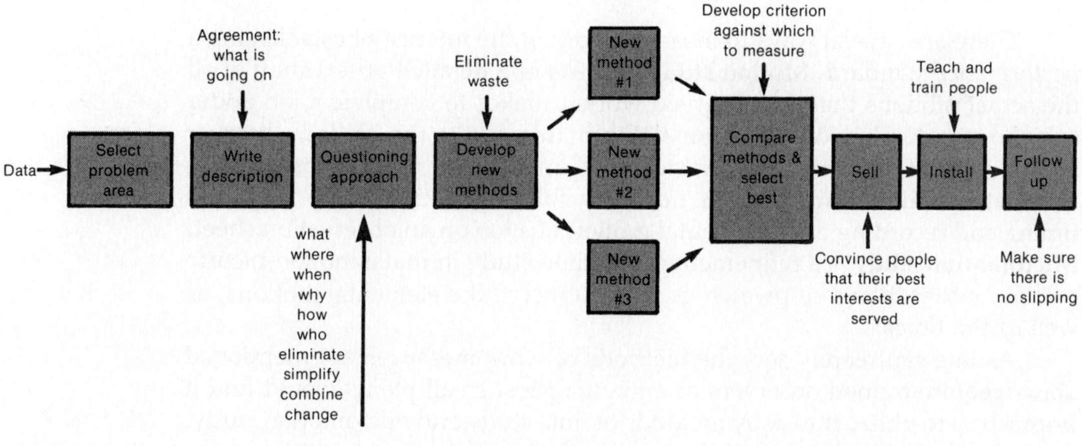

Source: Figure from MANAGING THE PRODUCTIVE PROCESS, by Joel Corman © 1974 General Learning Corporation. Reprinted by permission of Silver Burdett Company.

Figure 16-3 Procedure for Developing and Installing New Work Methods

Laws of Motion Economy

Underlying any work improvement program—whether it be for the overall operations of a plant or for a single task—are the laws of motion economy. These laws concern work arrangement, the use of the human hands and body, and the design and use of tools. Some of these laws are:

1. If both hands start and stop their motion at the same time and are never idle during a work cycle, maximum performance is approached.
2. If motions are made simultaneously in opposite directions over similar paths, automaticity and rhythm develop naturally, and less fatigue is experienced.
3. The method requiring the fewest motions generally is the best for performance of a given task.
4. When motions are confined to the lowest practical classification, maximum performance and minimum fatigue are approached. Lowest classification means motions involving the fingers, hands, forearms, and trunk.

A knowledge of the laws of motion economy will suggest various ways to improve work. For example, materials and tools should be so placed as to minimize movement of the trunk and the extended arms.

Methods of Work Measurement

There are several ways to measure work in the interest of establishing a performance standard. **Motion study** consists of a detailed observation of all the actual motions that the observed worker makes to complete a job under a given set of physical conditions. From this study the skilled observer should be able to detect any wasted movements that can be corrected or eliminated. **Time study**, which normally follows motion study, involves timing and recording each elemental motion of a job on an observation sheet. **Micromotion study** is a refinement of the time study in that a motion-picture camera, rather than a stopwatch, is used to record the elemental motions, as well as the times.

As one can readily see, the methods of work measurement mentioned above require trained observers or analysts. Most small plants would find it impractical to utilize the costly methods of time study and micromotion study. A more practical method of work measurement, which provides little operating detail but estimates the ratio of actual working time and downtime, is **work sampling.** This method was orginated in England by L. H. C. Tippett in 1934. Work sampling involves random observations in which the observer simply determines whether the observed worker is working or idle. The numbers of observations are tallied in "working" and "idle" classifications; the percentages of the tallies are estimates of the actual percent of time that the worker was working and idle.

INDUSTRIAL RESEARCH FOR SMALL PLANTS

In small companies, industrial research is aimed at improving manufacturing processes or products. Some small manufacturers, however, believe that research of this type is too expensive to undertake. And still others equate research with experimentation conducted in an expensively equipped laboratory, when sometimes all it requires is a questioning attitude which seeks to improve existing methods and products.

Problems of the Small Manufacturer

There is no question that industrial research requires the expenditure of both money and management time. Yet the small manufacturer cannot ignore it because competitive firms are continually introducing new products and processes which pose a challenge to existing ones. The money spent for productive research can easily be outweighed by the profits from successful new products or the cost savings from improvements achieved. And if a lack of management time is the problem, the manager can assign special responsibility for keeping abreast of research in the firm's area of interest to its most technically proficient employees. Such employees should review the current trade literature, attend professional and technical conferences, and contact suppliers who engage in research and development. Furthermore, the manager can utilize the following external resources:

1. Individual members of university faculties—as research consultants.
2. University research bureaus—for the completion of research projects.
3. Private research agencies—to which research problems can be referred.
4. Trade associations serving the given industry with a research program—in which participation through membership is open.

Possibilities for Research

The possibilities for industrial research and development are almost endless. Here are just a few of them:

1. Checking on old, but still useful, inventions which have been thrown open for use by the general public.

ACTION REPORT: Docutel's R and D Problems and Progress

To stay competitive, producers of high-technology products must maintain an active research and development program. Docutel Corporation, which introduced the first automatic bank teller machine in 1971, came close to losing out to its larger corporate competitors — Diebold, IBM, and NCR. Its weakness was technological sluggishness. As a result, "the tiny Dallas company was slow to incorporate technological advances into its machines and quickly lost its market dominance to powerful new entrants."

After losing ground to competitors, Docutel sought to correct its problems. It survived, in fact, by bringing out a low-cost retrofit unit for its aging machines. As of 1981, many bankers ranked Docutel's unit as the best on the market — a tribute to its revitalized research and development effort.

Source: Reprinted from the July 27, 1981 issue of *Business Week* by special permission, © 1981 by McGraw-Hill, Inc., New York, NY 10020. All rights reserved.

2. Reclamation of waste materials.
3. Recycling of already used materials.
4. Finding substitute raw materials for those that are scarce and in current use.
5. Devising equipment to control air and water pollution.

We might emphasize that public awareness of air and water pollution is forcing today's small manufacturer to conduct research in this area.

LOOKING BACK

1. Two basic types of manufacturing processes are intermittent manufacturing and continuous manufacturing. Intermittent manufacturing involves short production runs, with only one or a few products being produced before shifting to a different production setup. Continuous manufacturing involves long production runs and is used by firms that produce one or a few standardized products.

Production control provides for the orderly, efficient flow of production operations. It includes the steps of planning and routing, scheduling and dispatching, and supervising and follow-up.

2. The maintenance function is critical for firms that use complex and highly specialized equipment. Plant maintenance includes corrective maintenance to restore a facility to good condition and preventive maintenance to minimize breakdowns. Plant housekeeping and safety engineering are also part of the maintenance function.
3. Quality is built into a product during the production process, not at the inspection stage. The quality of a product is influenced by its design, the quality of raw materials used, and the performance of employees.

   Inspection is the method traditionally used to maintain control of quality. Modern quality control involves the use of two statistical techniques: attributes sampling plans and variables sampling plans. Quality control is important in service businesses as well as in manufacturing.
4. Work improvement and measurement are accomplished by the use of motion study, time study, work sampling, and other tools of industrial engineering.
5. Industrial research to improve products and processes is important for most small manufacturers in order to maintain a competitive position. Although such research is difficult for a small business, the methods may be adapted to fit the resources of the small firm.

DISCUSSION QUESTIONS

1. What is the difference between intermittent manufacturing and continuous manufacturing?
2. What are the proper objectives of production planning and control in a small manufacturing establishment?
3. Explain the difference between preventive and corrective maintenance. Stipulate also the relative importance of each of the above when (a) one or more major breakdowns have occurred in a small plant, and (b) shop operations are running smoothly and maintenance does not face any major repair jobs.
4. The breakdown of machines during their use is a result of failure to exercise preventive maintenance. Why should these breakdowns always be investigated promptly? What should be the outcome of such investigations? Are cost considerations or lost production of paramount importance in such situations? Why?
5. What is meant by the saying, "You can't inspect quality into a product"?
6. It is said that the major problems of manufacturing inspection are where to inspect, how much to in-

spect, and the cost of inspection. Explain each of these inspection problems concisely.

7. A small manufacturer does not believe that using statistical quality control charts and sampling plans would be useful in his plant. Can traditional methods suffice? Can 100 percent inspection by final inspectors eliminate all defectives? Why?

8. How can a service business, such as a dry cleaner, use the concept of quality control?

9. What is meant by the "laws of motion economy"?

10. Discuss the following concisely: (a) goals of industrial research in small industrial firms, (b) techniques available, and (c) types of research that can be done.

REFERENCES TO SMALL BUSINESS IN ACTION

Burck, Charles G. "The Micro-I. T. T. in Sam Stone's Basement." *Fortune,* Vol. 98, No. 2 (July 31, 1978), pp. 124-125.

In a tiny family manufacturing business, the entrepreneur struggles with problems of quality control, cost control, and production control.

"Miss Enid Stays Put." *Forbes,* Vol. 126, No. 6 (September 15, 1980), p. 194.

The Nacona Boot Company produces custom-made boots that can cost as much as $2,500. Some of its production process is standardized, but it also has expert craftsmen who will make specialty products for those willing to pay the price.

Moore, Harrison L. "From Made-to-Order Failure to Off-the-Shelf Success." *Inc.,* Vol. 2, No. 9 (September, 1980), pp. 82-85.

A small computer company achieved success by standardizing its product line and avoiding products designed for the unique needs of particular customers.

Chapter 17

Purchasing and Managing Inventory

LOOKING AHEAD

Watch for the following important topics:

1. The purchasing cycle.
2. Purchasing policies.
3. Factors to consider in selecting suppliers.
4. Objectives and control of inventory.
5. Quantification in inventory control.

A saying goes, "nothing ventured, nothing gained." The justification for this chapter is described by a slight modification of this phrase to "nothing bought, nothing sold." Raw materials and merchandise do not automatically appear in warehouses and stores. They must be purchased and managed. In this chapter we will examine how small firms should purchase and manage their inventories of raw materials and merchandise.

PURCHASING

Purchasing includes the procurement of both materials and merchandise. The manufacturer buys raw materials, parts and subassemblies, and factory and office supplies. The wholesaler or retailer purchases merchandise for resale to customers.

Importance of Effective Purchasing

There is a direct correlation between the quality of finished products and the quality of the raw materials placed in process. For example, if tight tolerances are imposed on a manufacturer's product by design requirements, this in turn requires the acquisition of high-quality materials and component parts. Then, given an excellent process, excellent products will be produced. But even a superior process will not compensate for inferior materials or components. Therefore, purchasing is crucial in the manufacturing process. Similarly, in merchandising the acquisition of quality merchandise makes sales to customers easier and reduces the number of markdowns required.

It is also desirable that the delivery of goods be timed to meet the exact needs of the customer. In a small factory, failure to receive materials, parts, or equipment on schedule is likely to cause costly interruptions in production operations. Machines and personnel are idled until the items on order are finally received. And in the retail business, failure to receive merchandise on schedule may mean the loss of one or more sales and, possibly, the permanent loss of disappointed customers.

Recent developments in our economy have placed even greater importance on purchasing and managing inventory. Shortages of materials, inflation, and high interest rates have forced the small business to emphasize purchasing and inventory activities.

The Purchasing Cycle

Purchasing is a process, and therefore it involves steps. It is essential that all steps be followed and in the sequence required. In general terms the purchasing cycle consists of the following steps:

1. Receipt of a purchase request.
2. Evaluation of the purchase request.
3. Issuance of the purchase order.
4. Maintenance of buying and warehousing records.
5. Follow-up of purchase order.
6. Receipt of goods.

Receipt of a Purchase Request. A **purchase requisition** is a formal, documented request from an employee or a manager of the firm for something to be bought for the business. In a small business, a purchase request is not always documented. But financial control is improved by requiring the purchasing agent to buy only on the basis of purchase requests.

ACTION REPORT: A Purchasing Yarn

Profitable selling for some firms requires purchasing raw materials at low prices. This is one key to success for Oneita Knitting, a family business which earns a return on investment comparable to or greater than that of larger competitors such as Levi Strauss and Spring Mills. Oneita's president, a third-generation family member, explains how Oneita keeps its sales prices low:

> The trick is know when to buy yarn—that's our commodity.... In 1971...I heard that there was a good, inexpensive yarn to be had in Portugal—the government there wanted to export it. So, I spent a month going through every yarn mill in Portugal and had the stuff shipped over here at a savings to us of about 20 percent over U.S. prices. I think we were the first U.S. firm to buy yarn in Portugal.

Efficient purchasing, along with other modern management practices, permits Oneita Knitting to price its products competitively and to retain four major firms as customers—Sears, K mart, J. C. Penney, and Montgomery Ward.

Source: "The Generation Syndrome," *Forbes,* Vol. 126, No. 3 (August 4, 1980), pp. 48-50.

Evaluation of the Purchase Request. The purchasing agent needs to scrutinize each purchase request carefully. On some occasions it may be necessary to contact the individual requesting supplies for additional information. Other experts might also be consulted. In a manufacturing concern, for example, the purchasing agent might collaborate with engineering and production managers for an accurate determination of consumption standards applicable to the raw materials. Joint setting of the standard amount of raw materials required per unit of finished product will produce a better standard than individual standard setting by the product designer. The purchasing agent is also in a position to discover new materials on the market and bring them to the attention of the engineering department.

Issuance of the Purchase Order. The next step in purchasing is the issuance of a purchase order. A standard form, such as that shown in Figure 17-1, should be used in all buying operations. When the signed order is accepted by a vendor (supplier), it becomes a binding contract. In the event of a serious violation, the written purchase order serves as the basis for adjustment.

PURCHASE ORDER
THE RED WING COMPANY, INC.
Fredonia, NY 14063-4925

June 27, 19--
DATE OF ORDER

No. 05202
SHOW THIS NUMBER ON INVOICE

BYRON JACKSON & COMPANY
4998 Michigan Avenue
Chicago, IL 60615-2218

SHIPPING INSTRUCTIONS:
Mark purchase order number on each piece in shipment

DELIVERY REQUIRED	F.O.B.	ROUTING	TERMS
July 24	Chicago	via NYC-Buffalo	2/10 net 30

ITEM	QUANTITY & UNIT	DESCRIPTION	PRICE & UNIT
622	35 each	Spring assembly	14.35 ea
230	200 each	Bearings	3.35 ea
272	70 each	Heavy duty relay 50V	7.50 ea
478	490 each	Screw set	.03 ea

ORIGINAL BILL OF LADING MUST ACCOMPANY ALL INVOICES FOR GOODS SHIPPED BY FREIGHT.
2% DISCOUNT FOR PAYMENT IN 10 DAYS WILL BE DEDUCTED FROM FACE OF INVOICE UNLESS OTHERWISE SPECIFIED.

INVOICE IN DUPLICATE BY J. Gromboski
Purchasing Agent

Figure 17-1 A Purchase Order

Buying Stock Items. In small manufacturing firms each regularly stocked kind of material or part normally has a **stores card** showing the reorder point. In small wholesale and retail firms, basic stock lists and model stock lists are used. When the inventory balance is brought down to the reorder point, the stores clerk or the shop supervisor notifies the purchasing agent of the need to reorder. The purchasing agent then prepares and mails the purchase order.

Buying Nonstock Items. If special orders which require materials not normally carried in stock are accepted, the manufacturer must prepare a bill of materials which shows the kinds and amounts of special materials required for the particular order. The purchase orders are then prepared and mailed.

Maintenance of Buying and Warehousing Records. Small firms should keep buying and warehousing records for all purchased items. As mentioned above, stores cards show the supply of each kind of raw material, purchased part, and supply item carried in the storeroom. Other records include the following:

1. Price quotations and credit terms—by suppliers and by kinds of materials or parts.

2. Purchase records showing outstanding orders and receipts from suppliers for each commodity.
3. Record of contract commitments.
4. Vendor quality and yield ratings.
5. Miscellaneous supplier data records, showing such things as willingness to inform the buying firm of new materials developed, cooperativeness in meeting delivery schedules and in improvement of quality control over purchased materials and parts, and attempts at bribery to procure orders.

Purchase records should be so filed as to facilitate traffic expediting of inbound shipments and to assure the prompt arrival of the goods or equipment orders. While price quotations received should be retained in a "price quote" file, the purchasing agent should obtain price confirmations before mailing any major purchase order. Some suppliers' prices are "subject to change without notice." Price confirmation avoids the receipt of a shipment and invoice at a higher unit price than expected.

Follow-Up of Purchase Order. The follow-up of purchase orders is necessary to assure delivery on schedule. It is also important that merchants follow up merchandise purchases to see how they are selling. This improves subsequent purchasing by eliminating slow-selling items.

Among the sources of follow-up data will be rates of turnover, customer complaints, markdowns, and customer returns. Annually, perhaps, small retailers should "age" their inventories so that nonselling items can be removed from stock.

Receipt of Goods. The receipt and inspection functions are usually assigned to the purchasing agent as administrative responsibilites. Such assignments should not be made blindly, however, because the separation of some functions permits cross-checking to eliminate errors and fraud.

The receiving clerks take physical custody of incoming materials and merchandise, check their general condition, and sign the carrier's release. Inspection follows to assure an accurate count and the proper quality and kind of items. The quality check may be performed on a sampling inspection basis by a representative of the firm's quality control department. Figure 17-2 shows a weekly or quarterly summary analysis of the quality of a given material.

Purchasing Policies

Purchasing policies can significantly affect the cost of purchasing, but they may be even more important for the preservation of good relationships with suppliers. Whenever possible, purchasing policies should be written.

Materials Yield Summary
The Iowa Manufacturing Company

Stores Item ______________________ Week Ending ______________________

Stores Item Number ______________________ Quarter Ending ______________________

Supplier	Units of Product Put in Process	Allowance per Unit of Finished Product	Total Units Allowed	Actual Units Used	Usage as % of Units Allowed
1	2	3	4 = 3•2	5	6 = 5/4 (100) (Quotient) = %

The materials yield summary provides an analysis of the quality of the given material (or part), as supplied by each vendor, for the given week (or quarter). Both weekly and quarterly summaries are made for each major stores item, using this same form. Since the standard usage percent of units allowed = 100, actual percentages for each supplier afford the purchasing agent concrete evidence of which suppliers are good and which are bad.

Percentages under 100 (given high-quality output) are favorable yield ratings; percentages over 100 are unfavorable.

Figure 17-2 Materials Yield Summary

This will assure that the policies are understood and will eliminate the need for repetitive decisions.

Reciprocal Buying. Some firms try to sell to others from whom they also purchase. This policy of **reciprocal buying** is based on the premise that one company can secure additonal orders by using its own purchasing requests as a bargaining weapon. Although the typical order of most small companies is not large enough to make this a potent weapon, there is a tendency for purchasers to grant some recognition to this factor. Of course, this policy would be damaging if it were allowed to obscure quality and price variations. Otherwise, there is probably little to be lost or gained from this policy.

Making or Buying. Whether to make or to buy component parts is a manufacturer's problem. The arguments in favor of *making* the component parts are:

1. Uses otherwise idle capacity, thus permitting more economical production.
2. Makes the buyer more independent of suppliers so that there are fewer delays and interruptions resulting from difficulties with suppliers.
3. Protects a secret design.
4. May be cheaper by avoiding payment of the supplier's selling expense and profit factors.
5. Permits closer coordination and control of total production operations, facilitating scheduling and quality control.
6. Permits better control over timing of design changes.

Some of the arguments for *buying* the component parts are:

1. May be cheaper, as shown by cost studies, due to the supplier's concentration on production of the given part, which makes possible specialized facilities, added know-how, and greater efficiency.
2. A shortage of space, equipment, personnel skills, and working capital may exist, thus precluding "in-plant" manufacture of the part.
3. Requirement of less diversified managerial experience and skills.
4. Greater flexibility; for example, seasonal production of a given item makes its manufacture risky.
5. Frees "in-plant" operations for concentration on firm's specialty (finished products).
6. Partial purchase of components serves to check the efficiency of one's own parts-fabricating operations.
7. The increasing impact of technological change enhances the risk of equipment obsolescence, making diversion of this risk to outsiders a sound procedure.

The decision to make or to buy may be expensive to reverse. It should certainly be based on long-run cost and profit optimization. The underlying cost differences need to be analyzed very carefully since small savings in buying or making may greatly affect profit margins.

The entrepreneur in a small firm should approach this policy decision with an open mind and should be receptive to the arguments on both sides of the question. In particular, the entrepreneur should be perceptive of the supplier's added costs (and profit factor) as compared with the buying firm's ability, capacity, and costs (overhead, administration, records and payroll, materials, design, tooling, equipment, and supervision). There is no definitive formula to guide one's decision.

Substituting Materials or Merchandise. New types of materials and merchandise are constantly being developed. Some of them may be both cheaper and better than older products. For example, certain upper leathers stretch just right to make shoes feel comfortable and last effectively, while others cannot possibly "last" without wrinkling the vamps. Nevertheless, the purchaser must consider not only the impact on the product and its cost but also the effect upon the process. A change in materials may alter the sequence of operations or may even cause the deletion or addition of one or more operations.

The small merchandising firm may be forced to drop a given product in its line. Consider the case of a small wholesaler of appliances, who also provided a repair service for the units sold by retail outlets. One day the wholesaler was notified by the foreign manufacturer of a certain type of tape recorder that it would henceforth accept and ship only a minimum order of 20 units. Such an order involved an investment of about $2,500, and the whole-

ACTION REPORT: Buy with Savvy

A good retail purchasing agent must first know what will sell and then must make a good buy. Leon Levine can do both. He is the founder and chief officer of Family Dollar Stores in North Carolina, which operates small self-service outlets selling "everything from soap to blue jeans to toys."

One of Levine's golden rules for good buying is expressed as follows:

> In order to buy well yourself, you must keep shopping the competition to see what they're carrying and for how much. One company manager put my pictures up in his stores.... And I've been asked to leave some stores.

Levine is always alert to a good buy. One of his deals was:

> ...with this gentleman in Chicago, who had a plant in Mississippi.... He would go to General Motors and Ford plants and buy their carpet remnants for next to nothing to use for coat linings. And they were *warm*. We'd get them for $2 apiece and sell them for $2.99. Other stores would come in and buy them from us—48 and 60 at a time—to sell at $5 or $6. Finally, we had to limit the sales to two per customer to keep enough in stock for our regular customers.

Source: "The Leon and Al Show," *Forbes*, Vol. 126, No. 7 (September 29, 1980), pp. 52-56.

saler had to discontinue selling that kind of tape recorder. Turnover of the recorder was too low to justify a substantial investment.

Purchasing policy should be sufficiently flexible to permit ready consideration of new or different materials or merchandise. Of course, a change must be based upon the possibility of producing or selling a better, cheaper product. However, as noted in the tape recorder case, circumstances may sometimes force a decision for a given change.

Taking All Purchase Discounts. One argument in favor of taking all purchase discounts available is that this evidences financial strength to suppliers and tends to promote good relationships with them. Even more important is the fact that discounts provide a source of savings. If the discount is taken on terms of 2/10, n/30, the savings are equivalent to interest at the rate of 36 percent per year (under the banker's rule for interest calculation). This is such a good rate that it pays to borrow if necessary in order to take the discount.

Diversifying Sources of Supply. In the purchase of a particular item, there is a question of whether it is desirable to use more than one supplier. Division of orders among several suppliers can be a form of insurance against difficulties with a sole supplier. For example, a strike or a fire might eliminate the supply for a time. The purchaser would then experience the delays involved in placing initial orders with a new source of supply. Moreover, if there is only one source, the purchaser is limited to just one quality of goods. This might eliminate the use of the best available raw material by a small manufacturer or prevent a small retailer from meeting competition effectively. An even greater danger is the fact that failure to "shop" may result in a loss of the lower prices and superior service offered by other suppliers.

Nevertheless, the arguments on this problem do not all favor diversification of sources of supply. With centralized buying from one firm, the purchaser may acquire the right to special quantity discounts and other favorable terms of purchase. Special service, such as prompt treatment of rush orders, is readily granted to established customers. Moreover, the single source of supply may provide financial aid to the regular customer who encounters financial stress. It will also provide management advice and market information. It may even grant an exclusive franchise or dealership for the merchandising of certain branded goods.

Some firms follow a compromise policy by which they concentrate enough purchases to justify special treatment. At the same time they diversify purchases sufficiently to provide alternative sources of supply.

Hand-to-Mouth Buying. The policy of **hand-to-mouth buying** involves buying small amounts as needed. For example, a firm might buy just what it requires for one week's operations. Hand-to-mouth buying presumes that the goods will be readily available and that transit time for inbound shipments will be at a minimum. Among the advantages of this purchasing policy are:

1. Simple determination of purchase requirements.
2. Avoidance of loss from price decline on inventory.
3. Reduction of dollar investment in inventory.
4. Shorter time cycle from purchase to use or sale, providing increased inventory turnover and reduced deterioration or obsolescence.

Correspondingly, hand-to-mouth buying presents certain disadvantages. They include:

1. Higher cost of procurement due to loss of quantity discounts, higher freight cost of LCL (less than carload) shipments, and repeated order costs.
2. Higher receiving and stores warehousing costs of handling small quantities per order.
3. Lower reserve stock with possible tie-up of production operations if deliveries are not made on schedule.

Speculative Buying. Buying substantially in excess of quantities needed to meet actual use requirements is called **speculative buying.** This is done in the expectation that prices are going up. Price appreciation produces inventory profits. The great danger is that speculative buying entails gambling on the continued rise of prices. Broad price declines subsequent to heavy speculative buying could bankrupt the speculator. Unless one is very stable financially and very wise, speculative buying should be avoided. It is typically used when the business cycle is on the way up; its use during a depression would be suicidal.

Scheduled Budget Buying. Buying to meet anticipated requirements is planned buying, or **scheduled budget buying**. This policy involves the adjustment of purchase quantities to estimated production or sales needs. Budget buying in suitable quantities will assure the maintenance of planned inventories and the meeting of product schedule requirements without delays in production due to delayed deliveries. It strikes the middle ground between hand-to-mouth buying, with its planned understocking of materials and its occasional delays due to late deliveries, and speculative buying, with its careful overstocking which entails risks as it seeks speculative profits. It represents the best type of buying for the conservative small firm.

Selection of and Relations with Suppliers

Before making a choice of suppliers, the purchaser must know the materials or merchandise to be purchased, including details of construction, quality and grade, intended use, maintenance or care required, and the importance of style features. The purchaser must also know how different grades and qualities of raw materials affect various manufacturing processes.

Factors to Consider in Selecting Suppliers. The small firm can locate suppliers in a number of ways. On important purchases the purchaser should actively search for new sources of supply. For many firms the best lead to new suppliers is the supplier's traveling representative. Other leads include trade association listings, the purchaser's advertising for bids, advertisements in trade literature, and directories of manufacturers.

Price Quotations. Quantity price discounts and shipping charges require attention in the comparison of price quotations. Price differences are significant if other factors are equal or do not offset price advantages.

Quality Ratings. Some quality differences are difficult to detect, and a number of items varying in quality may all be satisfactory. On some types of materials, statistical controls may be utilized by computing and recording the ratio defective of all inbound shipments from a specific vendor. In this way, the purchaser obtains an overall or average quality rating for each supplier. It also enables the purchaser to work with the supplier to upgrade quality or to cease buying from that supplier if quality improvement is not achieved.

General Reputation. The supplier's general reputation is gauged by certain abilities and services. For example, can the purchaser depend upon the supplier's ability to meet delivery schedules promptly?

Services provided by the supplier must also be considered. The extension of credit by suppliers provides a major portion of the working-capital requirements of many small firms. Some suppliers provide merchandising aids, plan sales promotions, and furnish management advice. In times of depression, some small retailers have even received direct financial assistance from major suppliers of long standing. Another important service is the provision of repair work by the supplier.

Importance of Good Relations with Suppliers. Good relations with suppliers are essential for firms of any size, but they are particularly important to small businesses. Perhaps the cornerstone of good supplier relationships is the buyer's realization that the supplier is more important to the buyer than the buyer (as a customer) is to the supplier. The buyer is only one among dozens, hundreds, or perhaps thousands buying from that supplier. Moreover, the buyer's volume of purchases over a year and the size of the individual orders are often so small that the business could be eliminated without great loss to the supplier. Hence, in the interest of improving supplier relationships, the small firm should buy in as large a quantity as is consistent with its own sales volume and inventory turnover rate.

To implement the policy of fair play and to cultivate good relations, the small buying firm should try to observe the following practices:

1. Pay all bills promptly.
2. See all traveling sales representatives promptly, according them a full, courteous hearing.
3. Do not summarily cancel orders merely to gain a temporary advantage.
4. Do not argue over prices, attempting to browbeat the supplier into special concessions and unusual discounts.
5. Cooperate with the supplier by making suggestions for product improvement and/or cost reduction whenever possible.
6. If gifts are returned or reciprocal purchase contracts refused, give a courteous explanation of the reasons underlying the decision.

Small buyers must remember that it takes a long time to build good relationships with a supplier but that good relations can be destroyed by one ill-timed, tactless act.

INVENTORY CONTROL

For many firms, inventory control can make the difference between success and failure. The larger the inventory investment, the more vital is its proper use and control. The importance of inventory control, particularly in small retail or wholesale firms, is attested by the fact that inventory typically represents these firms' major dollar investments.

Objectives of Inventory Control

Both purchasing and inventory control have the same general objective: *to have the right goods in the right quantities at the right time and place.* This general objective requires other, more specific subgoals of inventory control.

Assured Continuous Operations. Efficient manufacturing requires work in process to be moved on schedule. A delay caused by lack of materials or parts can cause the shutdown of a production line, a department, or even the whole plant. Such interruption of scheduled operations is both serious and costly. Costs jump when skilled workers and machines stand idle. Given a long delay, the fulfillment of delivery promises to customers may become impossible.

Maximum Sales. Assuming adequate demand, sales are greater if goods are always available for display and/or delivery to the customer. Most customers desire to choose from an assortment of merchandise. Customers who are forced by a narrow range of choice and/or stockouts to look elsewhere may be lost permanently. On the other hand, the small store might unwisely go to the other extreme and carry too large an inventory. Management must walk the chalk line, so to speak, between overstocking and understocking in order to retain customers and maximize sales.

Protection of Assets. One of the essential functions of inventory control is to protect inventories against theft, shrinkage, or deterioration. The efficiency or wastefulness of storeskeeping, manufacturing, and handling processes affect the quantity and quality of usable inventory. For example, the more often an article is picked up and physically handled, the more chance there is for

ACTION REPORT: Inventory — A Hot Potato

To a business, inventory is like a hot potato — no one wants to hold it. In the furniture industry, long setup and production times fuel the problem. Bill Smith, president of Henredon Furniture, has felt the heat at the company's plant in Morgantown, NC. Smith explains:

> The big department stores and the chains don't give you an order at the trade fair. They have to go back home and check inventory first. . . . Only trial and error will tell you whether to multiply the orders you write at the market by three and one-half or four or five to arrive at the proper cutting.
>
> . . . For a store, the ideal is to sell against stock coming. . . . They'd like not to carry inventory. But we have almost compelled them to buy inventory now.

Henredon has one new design which takes from nine to ten months to deliver. Smith concedes, "We haven't shown it because we couldn't make it in time to have the same buyer alive when he received it."

Source: "It Won't Be a Picnic Trying to Copy Us," *Forbes,* Vol. 124, No. 8 (October 15, 1979), pp. 113-115.

physical damage. Inventory items that need special treatment can also spoil or deteriorate if improperly stored.

Minimum Inventory Investment. Effective inventory control permits inventories to be smaller without causing disservice to customers or to processing. This means that the inventory investment is less. It also means lower costs for storage space, taxes, and insurance. And inventory deterioration or obsolescence is less extensive as well.

Administrative Uses of Inventory Records. The inventory records provide data useful for various administrative uses. For example, the records provide information for determining proper purchase quantities and ordering dates. They also provide information useful for evaluating managerial performance. For example, a business with an inventory turnover ratio that is lower than normal may be considered less efficient than the competition. Finally, the inventory records may be used to audit clerical work. If the audits reveal too many clerical errors, remedial action or mechanization of inventory record keeping should be implemented.

Inventory Accounting Systems

A small business needs a system for keeping tabs on its inventory. The bigger the small business, the greater is the need. Also, since manufacturers are concerned with three broad categories of inventory (raw materials and supplies, work in process, and finished goods), their accounting for inventory is more complex than that for wholesalers and retailers.

Although some record keeping is unavoidable, small firms should emphasize simplicity of control methods. Too much control is as wasteful as it is unnecessary.

Physical Inventory Method. The traditional method of taking physical inventory is for two people to go from item to item, with one calling off the kind of item and the number of units on hand while the other records this information.[1] Others have improved on this system by using only one clerk, who counts off the items into a dictating machine or a tape recorder. The inventory data sheets can then be typed directly from this recording. Making a single employee responsible for inventory may enhance the efficiency of inventory control. Although manual control systems are customarily adequate, the use of computer-aided systems should be adopted by small firms if at all possible.

---

1. The use of two persons supposedly guarantees the honesty, accuracy, and completeness of the physical inventory, *as recorded*.

STORES CARD

SHAFER SHOE COMPANY

Item: Metal Eyelets

Maximum No. of Pairs 60,000
Reorder Point No. of Pairs 24,000
Minimum No. of Pairs 12,000

	Receipts			Issues			Balance on Hand		
Date	Pairs	Price per Pair	Cost	Pairs	Price per Pair	Cost	Pairs	Price per Pair	Cost*
Jan. 1							14,000	$.00400	$ 56.00
2				2,500	$.00400	$10.00	11,500	.00400	46.00
3	48,000	$.00420	$201.60				59,500	.00416	247.60
3				2,000	.00416	8.32	57,500	.00416	239.28
4				2,100	.00416	8.74	55,400	.00416	230.54
7				2,000	.00416	8.32	53,400	.00416	222.22

*Minor discrepancies in this column are due to 5-place rounding in the preceding column.

The stores card is used by routing and planning clerks to assure an adequate supply of materials and parts to complete any given factory order.

Figure 17-3 A Stores Card

Perpetual Inventory Method. A perpetual inventory system provides a current record of inventory items. It does not require a physical count of inventory. Periodically, a physical count can be made to assure the accuracy of the perpetual system and to make adjustments for such factors as theft. The stores card illustrated in Figure 17-3 is the basic control tool in a perpetual inventory system covering raw materials and supplies.

With a separate perpetual inventory card for each raw material or supply item, the firm will always know the number of units on hand. If each receipt and issue is costed, the dollar value of these units is also known.

Use of a perpetual inventory system may be justified in the small factory or the wholesale warehouse. In particular, this is desirable for expensive and critical items – for example, those which could cause significant losses through theft or serious production delays.

Perpetual inventory control for finished goods is similarly available, but the cards used in this case are known as **stock cards** rather than stores cards. Techniques for the use of stock cards are the same as for stores cards.

Quantification in Inventory Control

Mathematical computations are an aid to effective inventory management. They help provide the answers to such questions as how much to purchase, how much should be stocked, how long did merchandise stay on the shelves, and what is the value of the merchandise at the selling price. We will examine some simple methods of answering these questions.

Economic Order Quantity. If a firm could place a merchandise order without expense (other than the cost of the merchandise) and incur no expenses while maintaining items in the firm's inventory, it would be less concerned about ordering the proper inventory size. However, every firm incurs order costs and inventory-carrying costs. **Order costs** include the preparation of a purchase order, follow-up, and all related bookkeeping expenses. If 1,000 units are ordered at one time, the order costs will be less than if 10 orders are placed to accumulate 1,000 units. Thus, the order-costs curve shown in Figure 17-4 decreases as the order quantity increases.

Inventory-carrying costs include interest, insurance, storage, obsolescence, and pilferage. Figure 17-4 portrays the behavior of these costs, which increase with the amount stocked. The total-costs curve is simply the sum of the carrying and order costs at any given quantity.

The **economic order quantity** is the quantity to be purchased which minimizes the total costs of ordering and carrying the inventory.[2] It is the point labeled "EOQ" in Figure 17-4. Notice that it is the lowest point on the total-cost curve. It also coincides with the intersection of the carrying-costs and order-costs curves.

Retail Inventory Valuation. Retailers can value their inventories at cost or at retail. The retail inventory method requires that starting inventory and purchases be recorded at both cost and retail; sales, net markdowns, and net added markups are to be entered at retail only.[3] For example, here are some data from a small department store recorded for the month of April:

Sales	$75,000	
Added markups	6,000	
Markdowns	2,500	
Markdown cancellations	1,800	
Purchases	45,000 at cost	$81,000 at retail
Freight in	500	
Starting inventory	1,000 at cost	$1,800 at retail

To find the *retail value* of ending inventory for this department store, first tabulate the data so that starting inventory, purchases, and net added mark-

2. The EOQ formula is derived from Norman Gaither, *Productions and Operations Management* (Hinsdale, IL: The Dryden Press, 1980), Chapter 12.

3. Initial markup is the excess of initial sales price over the purchase cost of the goods and the pertinent transportation cost. Added markups are increases in selling price above initially marked prices. These may later be cancelled, in part, in which case the difference is the net added markup. Markdowns are reductions below original sales prices. These may be subsequently cancelled, in part, in which case the difference is the net markdown.

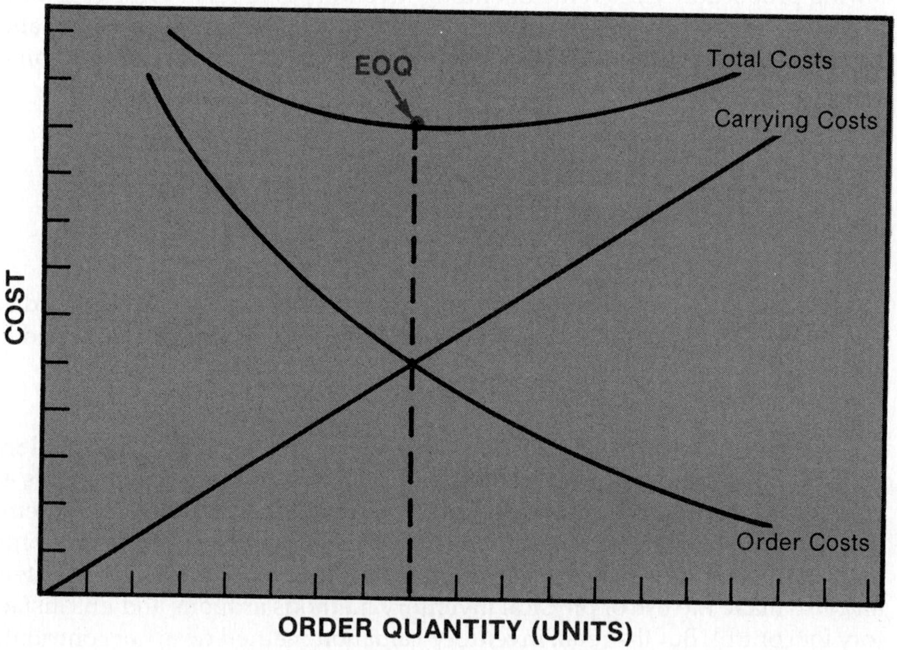

Figure 17-4 Carrying Costs, Order Costs, and EOQ

ups can be totaled to provide cost and retail values of goods available for sale during April. Then deduct the total of sales and net markdowns, which are separately recorded at retail, from the total retail value of starting inventory, purchases, and net added markups. The resulting tabulation is shown below, with $13,100 as the retail value of ending inventory.

	Cost		Retail
Starting inventory	$ 1,000		$ 1,800
Purchases	45,000		81,000
Freight in	500		
Net added markups			6,000
Goods available for sale	$46,500		88,800
Sales		$75,000	
Net markdowns		700	75,700
Ending inventory (retail value)			$13,100

For balance-sheet purposes, the *cost value* of ending inventory is needed. This unknown amount in dollars can be calculated algebraically by using the following proportion: Cost value of ending inventory is to retail value of ending inventory as cost of goods available for sale is to retail value of goods available for sale. Using X to represent the cost of ending inventory, this proportion is figured out as follows:

$$X : 13{,}100 :: 46{,}500 : 88{,}800$$
$$88{,}800X = 13{,}100 \times 46{,}500$$
$$88{,}800X = 609{,}150{,}000$$
$$X = 609{,}150{,}000 \div 88{,}800 = 6{,}859.80$$

The balance sheet of this department store would show the merchandise inventory at $6,860 (rounded to the closest dollar), which is its value stated in cost dollars.

Primary Use of the Retail Inventory Valuation Method. The retail inventory valuation method was developed primarily for department stores as a basis for *dollar control* of merchandise stocks involving a multiplicity of items in a number of departments. Such inventory conditions, together with a high volume of sales, preclude the use of perpetual inventory cards for each item and also make the use of physical inventory methods arduous and unsatisfactory for control. But the retail inventory valuation method does not contribute to *unit control*.

Advantages of the Retail Inventory Valuation Method. The retail inventory valuation method is approved for income tax reporting. It facilitates the preparation of monthly financial statements, which would be prohibitively expensive if physical inventories were required as their basis. Moreover, this method gives a more conservative balance-sheet evaluation than historical cost data would provide because it relates the inventory values to current sales prices. Hence, the retail inventory valuation method gives valuations equivalent to the lower of cost or market value.

Weaknesses of the Retail Inventory Valuation Method. The retail inventory valuation method has the following weaknesses:

1. Being based on averages and applied on a department-wide or class-of-merchandise basis, this method tends to overvalue certain merchandise items and undervalue others. That is, the inventory value on the balance sheet shows a cost value for total inventory which assumes that all inventory items have the same relation between cost and sales price; this is frequently untrue.

   The retailer ordinarily finds it desirable or necessary to sell merchandise with different gross margins. To the extent that sales are not proportional among the merchandise groups carrying different gross margins, the inventory value computed by the retail inventory valuation method may be distorted. That is, separate inventories, using this method, are required for each "gross margin" class for complete accuracy.

2. Given very frequent markups and markdowns, the record keeping for the retail inventory valuation method becomes arduous and costly. This is particularly true if separate "gross margin class" inventories are maintained individually under this method.
3. The system also ignores stock shortages and employee discounts, and suffers disadvantages in the proper handling of trade-ins and customer discounts. Of course, physical inventory, used along with this method, helps reveal the "ignored" stock shortages.

The retail inventory valuation method may be an effective system, and it is certainly a unified, integrated system of inventory control in a retail store. Nevertheless, its disadvantages may sometimes outweigh its advantages. Hence, the small retailer should consider carefully both its strengths and its limitations before reaching a decision on its use.

Inventory Ratios. A number of inventory ratios help in the management of inventory by a business. Among these is the inventory turnover ratio. The calculation of this ratio is discussed in Chapter 18.

The **inventory turnover ratio** is a measure of how quickly merchandise was brought into inventory and then sold. A low rate of turnover means that the merchandise was in inventory for a long period. It is important to know the normal inventory turnover ratio for a particular line of business in order to have a standard for measurement. Too high a turnover, as well as too low a turnover, can be bad. The best turnover ratio is above, but not too far above, the industry standard.

LOOKING BACK

1. The purchasing cycle includes the receipt and evaluation of a purchase request, issuance of the purchase order, maintenance of buying and warehousing records, follow-up of purchases, and receipt and inspection of purchased items.

2. Policies related to purchasing include reciprocal buying, making or buying parts, substituting materials or merchandise, taking all purchase discounts, diversifying sources of supply, hand-to-mouth buying, speculative buying, and scheduled budget buying.
3. Choice of a supplier entails consideration of the supplier's price, quality rating, ability to meet delivery schedules, quality of service, and general reputation. Good relations with suppliers are particularly valuable to small firms.
4. The objectives of inventory control include: assured continuous operations, maximum sales, protection of assets, minimum inventory investment, and administrative uses of inventory records.

   The physical inventory system consists of taking actual count of items on hand and recording the information. The perpetual inventory system does not require a physical count but provides a current record of inventory items through the use of stores cards or stock cards.
5. Examples of quantification in inventory control are economic order quantity, retail inventory valuation, and inventory ratios.

DISCUSSION QUESTIONS

1. What conditions make purchasing a particularly vital function in any given business? If it is important, can the owner-manager of a small firm safely delegate the authority to buy to a subordinate? Explain.
2. Of what value are purchasing records to a small firm?
3. Is reciprocal buying ethical? Wise? Necessary? Explain, with special reference in your answer to a (a) jewelry store, (b) plumbing contractor, and (c) small manufacturer who produces plywood pallets.
4. Under what conditions should the small manufacturer make component parts or buy them from others?
5. Compare the arguments for and against the concentration of purchases with only one or two suppliers.
6. State the factors governing a small manufacturer's selection of a supplier of a vitally important raw material.
7. Does the maximization of inventory turnover also result in the maximization of sales? Explain.
8. Explain the nature of the following types of factory inventories: (a) raw materials and supplies, (b) work in process, and (c) finished goods.
9. What are the advantages and disadvantages of a perpetual inventory system in contrast to a physical inventory system?
10. Explain the retail inventory valuation method as it would be applied in a small department store.

REFERENCES TO SMALL BUSINESS IN ACTION

Ford, Joan G. "How to End the Inventory Poker Game." *Inc.*, Vol. 3, No. 5 (May, 1981), pp. 76-79.

A company president realized that customers were maintaining inventories beyond their needs. This article tells how he developed a computer program to reduce these inventories.

"Phoenix." *Forbes*, Vol. 125, No. 8 (April 14, 1980), pp. 122-124.

The inventory experiences of the new Shopsmith Company demonstrate the need for tight inventory control.

Slutsker, Gary. "When Quick Success Is a Mixed Blessing." *Venture*, Vol. 2, No. 10 (October, 1980), pp. 67-69.

The importance of an inventory control system is demonstrated by the experiences of a small photographic service. The system keeps track of rolls of film while they are being processed by different labs.

CASE D-1

Central Engineering

How the entrepreneur's managerial practices hampered decision making

Henry and Jami Wolfram, a husband-and-wife team, owned and operated Central Engineering, a heating and air-conditioning firm located in Huntsville, AL. The business had prospered during the six years they had owned it, and it served both residential and commercial accounts.

Organizational Structure

Henry served as general operations manager. (Figure D-1 shows the simple organization structure of the firm.) As the business grew, more and more responsibility fell on Henry's shoulders. Although Jami assumed some of the burden by acting as treasurer and supervising the office work, Henry was personally involved in most of the key decisions. Henry's son, Jeff Wolfram, had started work on an installation crew. Later he moved into the position of estimator-salesman and acted as manager on those occasions when his father was away.

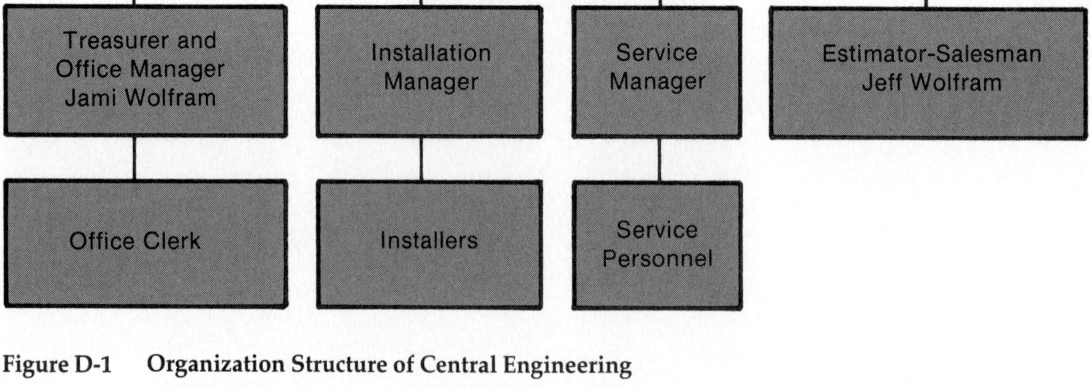

Figure D-1 Organization Structure of Central Engineering

The Bottleneck

An unfortunate consequence of Henry's growing work load was the creation of a bottleneck at the very top of the business. Since he was a key person, his judgment seemed indispensable in many actions. As a result, decisions were sometimes delayed while waiting for his attention. Others in the organization sometimes found themselves waiting in line to get a chance to talk with him. And Henry found himself rushed, with insufficient time to think carefully about some aspects of the business. In addition, he would have liked to devote a little more time to family, church, and personal interests.

Review of Customer Billing

One task that required Henry's attention was his personal review of bills before they were sent to customers. When a management consultant asked why this was necessary, the following dialogue took place:

Henry: I really need to take a last look before bills are sent out. For example, on construction jobs there may be additions or extras that were included after we had made the original bid.
Consultant: On regular service calls, is there a similar chance of an error?
Henry: That's right. For instance, maybe the worker has left something off the work order. The worker may say he has done this and this and this, but over here on the material list he has some items that don't match up or that are missing from what he said he's done.
Consultant: Can you tell me how many hours in a day or week are required for this?
Henry: Well, it cuts into a lot of time. This is part of another problem. The office is too open, with Jeff and his customers in the same office with me. I just don't have any place where I can concentrate on this type of work. I think that, when we get that physical arrangement changed, it will help some.
Consultant: So, how many hours a week does this take?
Henry: Sometimes we stay here at night or come in Saturday to do this. But I suppose it might run 8 or 10 hours a week.
Consultant: Is there anybody else who could do this?
Henry: Well, on service calls Jami can usually spot such discrepancies. She is getting enough experience that she can recognize them.
Consultant: What is Jeff's role? Could he do this?
Henry: He's an estimator and does sales work. He doesn't quite have the experience yet. Well, he might be close to being capable. But he's pretty busy. Also, I have a service manager who could catch a lot of this when the orders are turned in. But he does not manage that carefully. I have a more aggressive manager in installation who is better at catching things like this.

The general theme in Henry's discussion with the management consultant was the difficulty of resolving the time-management problem. Henry recognized the burden this placed on him personally and on the business, but there seemed to be no obvious answer at this stage in the life of the firm.

Review of Accounts Payable

Henry also tried to look over all payments being made on trade accounts payable. His discussion with the management consultant regarding this function ran as follows:

Henry: These payments need to be checked over because we may be charged too much on some bills.
Consultant: How does this happen?
Henry: On particular jobs we may get special pricing. Say I'm working on a bid. I may pick up a phone and say to the supplier, "We need some special pricing. Here's what we're up against, and we need the special pricing to get this job." And if they give us the special pricing, we should pay accordingly.
Consultant: And you can't depend on them to bill you at that special price?
Henry: I don't think it is anything intentional. But they give it to their clerks to bill, and they may overlook the special pricing that was promised. So, if we don't catch it, we would lose it.

Henry's Dilemma

The responsibilities relative to accounts receivable and accounts payable were typical of the overall situation. In many aspects of the business, Henry felt compelled to give his personal attention to the issues and the decisions which needed to be made. In a sense he felt trapped by the very success and work that accompanied the operation of the business. He enjoyed the work, every minute of it, but occasionally he wondered why there was no obvious solution to his dilemma.

Questions

1. Is Henry Wolfram's personal involvement in the various specific aspects of the business necessary, or is it a matter of habit or of simply enjoying doing business that way?
2. What changes would be necessary to extricate Henry from the checking of customer bills before they are mailed?
3. If you were the consultant, what changes would you recommend?

CASE D-2

Sun-Brite Painting

Are the owner's objectives, ethics, and strategy geared to expansion?

Jim Colwell had reached the point of stability and profitability after two years in the painting-contracting business. The business was going smoothly and providing a reasonably good income for the family. The big question facing Jim was the possibility of expansion. Should he continue with a moderately successful business, or should he double, triple, or otherwise expand the business?

The Owner's Background

Jim's formal education included a bachelor's degree in business administration (marketing major) from a major state university. After graduation, he had worked for three different companies, primarily in sales work. Six years before starting the painting-contracting business, Jim and his wife had acquired a small resort hotel and operated it for several years as a "retreat" center, mostly for religious groups. In the process of maintaining the property, he acquired skills and equipment related to painting. Eventually he did a little independent painting-contracting as a sideline to the operation of the retreat center. When he sold the resort hotel and entered a seminary, he took his painting equipment with him. After attending the seminary for a year, Jim, age 35, launched the Sun-Brite business in Whittier, CA. Family finances seemed to preclude further seminary training at the time, and painting offered a way to get started again.

The business prospered, and Jim felt no particular pressure to return to the seminary. He realized that he could make a valuable contribution in business, as well as in some type of church ministry. However, he wondered whether he should limit himself to his present one-crew operation.

Personal and Company Objectives

As an entrepreneur, Jim placed great emphasis on service and always mentioned this ahead of profits. In fact, he frequently described his obligations both to customers and to employees in the context of his own religious faith. He once expressed his viewpoint in these words: "My philosophy of business is that we are in business to provide a service. In the process of doing that, we are to grow as individuals. I try to help people grow, and the Lord seems to take care of the business."

As a part of "helping people to grow," Jim employed a number of college students, both male and female, on a part-time basis. This enabled him to meet his fluctuating work load and permitted the students to learn a trade while meeting their college expenses.

Underlying Sun-Brite's philosophy was Jim's personal philosophy of life. He stated it as follows:

> My whole life is based on Jesus Christ being the Lord of it. He provides the work, the customers, and people, and I work with what he provides. We can try to own property and try to own our business and own all these good things, but they are things he gives us. With any business and with any kind of activity as human beings, we are stewards.

Jim recognized the implications of his philosophy with respect to the ethical standards in painting-contracting. He spoke thus of the practice of cash payments made by some types of small business to avoid payment of taxes:

> In construction, a tremendous amount of labor is paid "under the table." Union laborers, for instance, work five days a week and get a paycheck. They work overtime or on Saturdays and get cash. That way, they avoid taxes on overtime income.

When asked about competing for labor, Jim admitted he was limited to hiring employees who were willing to have all of their income recorded. He said, "I've had employees go to work for other people and make the same amount of money they would make with me but not have to pay taxes." Jim regarded off-the-books payments as totally wrong and showed no inclination to engage in such practices regardless of the consequences.

Sun-Brite's Strategy

In formulating a business strategy, Jim had avoided painting related to new construction. He concentrated primarily on repainting old buildings and served as prime contractor on the jobs accepted.

The painting business was divided almost equally between commercial and residential buildings. Initially it was mostly residential. However, the profit margin was better on commercial projects, and Jim had been gradually shifting to a higher proportion of commercial business.

Jim had confined the business to a restricted geographical area—approximately a five-mile radius. This was done for two reasons. First, it permitted greater efficiency of work and better coordination of projects by reducing travel time. Second, this practice reduced transportation expenses, which were becoming heavy with increasing energy costs.

Possibilities for Expansion

Although the business had grown, the company still used only one painting crew. This permitted Jim to do some of the painting personally, as well as to supervise operations. He also used one or two full-time painters in addition to the part-time college students. By careful scheduling, he was able to assign the students to less skilled work and thereby raise the productivity of the other painters.

Expansion of the business would involve the use of one or more additional crews. This would necessitate the use of one experienced, dependable individual to serve as lead painter and supervisor for each crew. Unfortunately the number of individuals capable of assuming such responsibility was quite limited.

One of the full-time painters on Jim's present crew might serve as a crew supervisor. This person's qualifications, however, were less than ideal for such a position. Jim would need to serve as a full-time manager if he created as many as three crews. To provide coordination, he would not be able to do the work of a painter, and he would need to remove himself from the direct supervision of any one crew. The scarcity of good supervising talent created a real dilemma. Where could he find competent personnel for this purpose?

One area of possible expansion involved the city of Arcadia. This would involve an additional driving time of 25 or 30 minutes plus the additional expense.

Sales Promotion for Expansion

Another question related to the marketing of painting-contracting services. Expansion would require additional customers, and this would necessitate some type of sales promotion.

Most of Sun-Brite's work came originally from referrals by paint stores. In addition, the firm advertised in the Yellow Pages of the telephone book—a space of approximately one column inch. Although some inquiries originated as a result of these ads, the number was insufficient for expansion of the business.

Jim had also experimented very tentatively with newspaper advertising. Several ads in a free "shopper" paper had produced no inquiries. However, several ads in the local Whittier newspaper stimulated a number of inquiries.

The *Los Angeles Times* provided another possibility for advertising. This paper would accept advertising directed to one specific part of the metropolitan area. Jim did not know the cost of such advertising. He assumed that the *Times* might appeal to a higher-income class of reader and might, therefore, get his message to an ideal type of potential customer.

Jim also considered the possibility of soliciting business by making personal sales calls. He might call on prospective commercial customers. One paint manufacturer provided an attractive color deck costing $6 that might be used as a gift in connection with such sales calls. The deck could be used to identify various interior colors and could be folded to fit into a pocket or a woman's purse.

Financial Considerations for Expansion

Sun-Brite had always been subjected to conservative financial management. Jim had avoided premature expansion, had purchased used equipment whenever possible, and had carefully watched the cash flow of the business. As a result, the business was in sound financial condition, having no significant debt.

To expand the business, Sun-Brite would need to purchase an additional panel truck (which would require a cash down payment) for each new crew plus additional ladders and related equipment. Assuming that some used equipment could be obtained, the immediate cash outlay for each additional crew might amount to $3,500.

Need for Decision

Jim knew that the business was providing a good income for the family. However, the prospect of expansion was exciting because a growing business would provide not only more profits, but also more employment opportunities for students, painters, and painting supervisors. Expansion also involved many uncertainties and would certainly take the business beyond the scope of Jim's previously demonstrated managerial capacity.

Questions

1. Identify the objectives of Sun-Brite, using the framework provided in Chapter 13. Is there conflict or potential conflict in these objectives?
2. How ethical does Jim Colwell seem to be? Do you feel his standards may be inflexible? Do you think he can hold to his standards when business is most difficult?
3. Outline and evaluate Jim's business strategy.
4. What is the major deterrent to growth in this business?
5. Discuss the marketing programs or policies you would recommend as part of any expansion plan.

CASE D-3

Fourt Furniture Incorporated*

Uncharted organizational relationships

Fourt Furniture Store was founded in 1965 by Mr. and Mrs. Millard Fourt. The original store occupied a space of 5,000 square feet and was operated by the Fourts and 2 employees. Ben Lonsberry joined the business in 1974 as the general manager and then was elected president in 1978.

Corporate Growth

In 1974, Fourt Furniture had a sales volume of $400,000 and operated with 5 employees, including the Fourts and Lonsberry. Merchandise was warehoused in a separate location where the firm leased 8,000 square feet of space. The business was incorporated in May, 1975, as a Subchapter S corporation. In June of 1979, it elected to become a regular corporation.

Construction began on a second store location to be named Lonsberry's Home Furnishings in August, 1978. This location opened for business on December 20, 1978. By November, 1979, all administrative and accounting offices had been moved to the new location and all paperwork was being processed at Lonsberry's. Together, the 2 store locations had a total of 60,000 square feet of sales space and 52,000 square feet of warehousing space. In addition to retail furniture and accessory sales, the business included an interior design sales division and a contract furniture sales division.

The total annual sales volume of Fourt Furniture Incorporated had grown from $400,000 in 1974 to $3,250,000 in 1980; and the number of employees had grown from 5 to 46 (including 8 part-time employees) in the same time period. The firm's departments and number of employees were as follows:

Department	Number of Employees
Sales	15
Design	7
Accounting	5
Warehousing	11
Administrative and Support	8

*This case was prepared by Professor Kenneth A. Middleton of Baylor University.

Organizational Structure

No formal organizational chart had been formulated for the firm. The lines of power, authority, and delegation were defined only in the minds of each employee. However, each employee realized that Ben Lonsberry was the president and chief executive officer and that all decision-making power came from him.

Ben hired Don Baker in September of 1978 as company manager and general merchandise manager. Prior to 1978, Don had been employed as an engineer in a high-technology electronics firm. Don's responsibility as company manager and general merchandise manager was to oversee daily operations and coordinate the purchase of inventory. A very good working relationship had existed between Ben and Don from the very beginning.

In 1978, when Ben was elected president and chief executive officer, Millard Fourt had retired from active management of the corporation due to ill health. Mrs. Fourt, however, retained her position as corporate secretary-treasurer. The principal stockholders of Fourt Furniture Incorporated were:

Stockholder	Position
Ben Lonsberry	President & Chief Executive Officer
Jane Fourt	Secretary-Treasurer
Ray Sands	Vice-President

Ray Sands, who held the position of corporate vice-president, had no active role in the daily operations of the company. He acted as a voting member of management only and was active in the operation of his own other businesses.

If a chart of the firm's organizational structure were drawn, it would resemble a hub-and-wheel configuration as illustrated in Figure D-2.

Management Style

Ben Lonsberry retained total control of daily operations in all phases of the corporation. It was not uncommon to see him building merchandise displays, moving inventory on the sales floor, and loading delivery trucks on any given day. He actively participated in the sale of merchandise and in routine housekeeping duties. He also instructed new sales personnel in sales techniques and helped store designers in color and fabric coordination and display.

Don Baker participated in the selection of merchandise and coordinated its delivery to the display floors and warehouse. Don was also involved in the training of new sales personnel and all general corporate personnel. He would

Figure D-2 Organizational Relationships at Fourt Furniture Incorporated

also be observed loading and unloading delivery trucks, moving displays, selling merchandise, and answering the phone.

It can be said that each of these managers became totally involved in each facet of daily operations and that each gave daily directions to the other employees. Ben and Don were the type of individuals who are motivated by self-competition and do not need outside feedback or reinforcement concerning their job performance.

Organizational Problems

The lack of a formal organizational chart created an overlap of power and authority centers within the firm. Employees were unable to identify who their immediate supervisors were and whose directions and instructions should be followed. One person employed as a merchandise stocker identified nine individuals who gave him job instructions. This situation was shown to exist at all levels within the organization. The impression of the majority of employees was that no one really knew to whom he or she was accountable.

Mrs. Lonsberry and Mrs. Baker, the wives of the managers, frequently visited the two store locations. When they visited, they would suggest methods of merchandise display and fabric coordination to the design administrator. They would tell the merchandise stockers what needed to be done and what displays were to be rearranged. They would also assist the sales personnel in the selling of merchandise and indicate which product lines should be promoted.

The employees within this organization did not know how their job performance was viewed by top management (Ben and Don). No formal evaluation or job reviews were utilized, and little verbal feedback was given. This frustration was evident when Ben was asked how he viewed Leo (a top salesperson) and when Leo was asked about his perceived status within the organization. Their respective comments illustrated the situation when Ben said, "Leo is one of our best. I couldn't be more pleased. I hope that he'll be with us for a long time because we sure need him." And Leo's reply was: "I feel that if I make a mistake today—I'm gone. I try to do my job, and the money isn't bad. But I'm not too sure if they like me. I'd like to know if I'm doing a good job or not. I may leave at the end of the month." It must be noted that this was not an isolated case because this situation existed at all levels within the organization.

Questions

1. Evaluate the overall performance of Fourt Furniture Incorporated. What does this show about the effectiveness of its management?
2. Identify the various organizational problems in this business. Which appears most serious? Why?
3. What are the probable causes of Ben Lonsberry's practices regarding delegation of authority? As a consultant, what changes, if any, would you recommend? How would you suggest that these changes be effected?
4. Outline an organizational plan for the firm, and defend any changes you propose.

CASE D-4

Gibson Mortuary

Personnel problems in a small family business

Gibson Mortuary was founded in 1929 and grew to become one of the best-known funeral homes in Tacoma, WA. One of its most persistent problems over the years had been the recruitment and retention of qualified personnel.

Background of the Business

Gibson Mortuary was a family business headed by Ethel Gibson, who owned 51 percent of the stock. As an active executive in the business, Ethel had become recognized as one of the community leaders. She had served in various civic endeavors, had been elected to the city council, and had served one term as mayor.

The mortuary had built a reputation as one of the finest funeral homes in the state. The quality of its service over the years had been such that it continued to serve families over several generations. While large corporations had bought up many mortuaries in recent years, Gibson Mortuary continued to remain competitive as an independent family firm—a "family serving families." Funeral homes in general had become the target of public criticism, and books such as *The American Way of Death* had reflected adversely on this type of business. Nevertheless, Gibson Mortuary had withstood this threat by its determined, consistent effort to provide the best possible customer service. In its most recent year it had conducted 375 funerals, which placed it in the top 9 percent of all funeral homes in the nation when measured in terms of volume of business.

Ethel's son, Max Gibson, had entered the business after completing military service and had become general manager of the firm. He was a licensed funeral director and embalmer. Both mother and son were active in the day-to-day management of the firm.

Recruitment and Retention Problem

Perhaps the most difficult problem facing Gibson Mortuary was the recruitment and retention of qualified personnel. The image of the industry made it difficult to attract the right caliber of young people as employees. Many individuals were repelled by the idea of working for an organization in which they daily and personally faced the fact of death. In addition, the challenges raised by social critics reflected poorly on the industry and conveyed to many youth the impression that funeral homes were profiteering on the misery of those who suffered bereavement.

One source of employees was walk-in applicants. Also, Gibson Mortuary worked through sales representatives who sold throughout that geographical area. They often knew of people who might be considering a change in their career.

As a small business, Gibson Mortuary also presented fewer total opportunities than a larger company or even a funeral home chain. The fact that it was a family business also suggested to prospective employees that top management would remain in the family. It was apparent to all that the two top management spots were family positions. However, Ethel and Max were the only family members employed, so there was some hope for the future for nonfamily employees. Max was 49 years old.

Training Problem

Gibson Mortuary used two licensed embalmers — Max and another individual. The pressure of other managerial work made it difficult for Max to devote sufficient time to this type of work. To become a licensed embalmer, one had to attend mortuary college and serve a two-year apprenticeship. (Mortuary science programs were part of some community-college programs.) The apprenticeship could be served either prior to or after the college training. Gibson Mortuary advised most individuals to take the apprenticeship prior to the college training so that they could evaluate their own aptitude for this type of career.

Gibson Mortuary preferred its personnel to be competent in all phases of the business. The work involved not only embalming, but also the making of funeral arrangements with families and conducting funerals and burials. However, some part-time employees assisted only in conducting funerals and did not perform preparatory work.

Personal Qualifications for Employment

All employees who met the public and had any part in the funeral service needed the ability to interact with others in a friendly and relaxed but dignified manner. The personalities of some individuals were much better suited to this than those of others. Ethel described one of the problem personalities she had encountered at Gibson Mortuary as follows:

> In the first place, he didn't really look the part for our community here. He was short and stocky, too heavy for his height. His vest was too short, and he wore a big cowboy buckle! Can't you see that going over big in a mortuary! He wanted to stand at the door and greet people as they came. We do furnish suits, so we tried to polish off some of the rough edges.
>
> But he was still too aggressive. He became upset with me because I wouldn't get him any business cards immediately. One day I had to send him to the printers, and he came back and said, "While I was there, I just told them to make some cards for me. I'll pay for them myself." I said to him, "Willis, you go right back there and cancel that order! When you are eligible for cards, I'll have them printed for you." We couldn't have him at that point scattering his cards with our name all over town.

Ethel also discussed a young applicant who made an impressive appearance but who lacked polish. His grammar was so poor that he lacked the minimal skills necessary for any significant contact with the public.

A characteristic of employment that discouraged some applicants was the irregular hours and the constant interruptions that were part of the life of a funeral director. A funeral director might start to do one thing and then find it necessary to switch over to another, more urgent matter. Then there was the requirement for including some night and weekend duty in the work schedule.

Solving the Personnel Problems

Although Gibson Mortuary had not completely solved its need for qualified personnel, the business was working at it. While waiting for the right person to come along, Gibson Mortuary had started another apprentice prior to any college training. In addition, it was following up on a former apprentice who was attending mortuary college and working during summer vacations. The business also employed a part-time minister as an extra driver. In these ways Gibson Mortuary was getting along but was still seeking to do a better job in personnel staffing.

Questions

1. Evaluate the personnel problems facing this firm. Which of these appears most serious?
2. How can Gibson Mortuary be more aggressive in recruitment? How can it make such a career attractive to applicants?
3. Does the fact that Gibson Mortuary is a family firm create a significant problem in recruitment? How can the firm overcome any problems that may exist in this area?
4. Assuming you are the proper age to consider such employment, what is the biggest question or problem you would have in considering employment with Gibson Mortuary? What might the Gibsons do, if anything, to deal with that type of question or problem?

CASE D-5

Concessionaire Trailers*

Production planning in trailer manufacturing

Concessionaire Trailers, a sole proprietorship, was owned and operated by Ty Bedmore since February, 1981. Located in Rock Island, IL (population

*This case was prepared by Steve R. Hardy and Philip M. Van Auken of the Center for Private Enterprise and Entrepreneurship at Baylor University.

48,000), the firm custom-manufactured concession trailers for mobile refreshment stands used at carnivals, fairs, amusement parks, and sporting events. Its manufacturing facilities consisted of 2 buildings (1100 square feet and 650 square feet) which had a combined monthly rental cost of $475.

Production Operations in 1981

According to Ty, his first year in business seemed to be an unending succession of 12 to 16-hour days and 7-day weeks, shared with 2 other employees. Notable production achievements during the first year included narrowing down the product line to three basic trailer prototypes (with a variety of customized options), engineering standardized and interchangeable parts, and finalizing pricing parameters. Unfortunately Ty was unable to establish an efficient production layout system during the first year, even though 30 trailers were produced.

Production Operations in 1982

Business picked up considerably for Concessionaire during 1982, with 66 trailers sold during the first 9 months alone. Sales orders for the fourth quarter of 1982 called for the production of an additional 32 trailers. Ty was also studying a contract offer from a major customer to produce 80 Concessionaires during the first quarter of 1983.

Some progress was made during the first three quarters of 1982 toward more efficiently systematizing the trailer manufacturing process. However, Ty recognized the need for further work-flow improvements before large customer contracts could be accommodated. Under the production set-up shown in Figure D-3, trailers were built from the ground up on each of the three production stations. Assembly was done in the larger building (Building 1); and painting and finishing, in the smaller facility.

Production Specifications

All three Concessionaire trailer models were constructed from the same materials: sheet metal, paint, wheels, tires, axles, and braces (see Exhibit 1). On the average, each trailer required a total production time of 48 labor hours. On extremely humid days (70 percent humidity or greater), paint-drying considerations necessitated operating at 75 percent capacity. Based on past experience, Ty estimated that humidity was a factor during 30 to 40 days annually, mainly during the spring and summer quarters.

Concessionaire's plant had raw-material storage facilities for 22 trailers. Six in-process or finished trailers could be inventoried. Ty felt that labor could

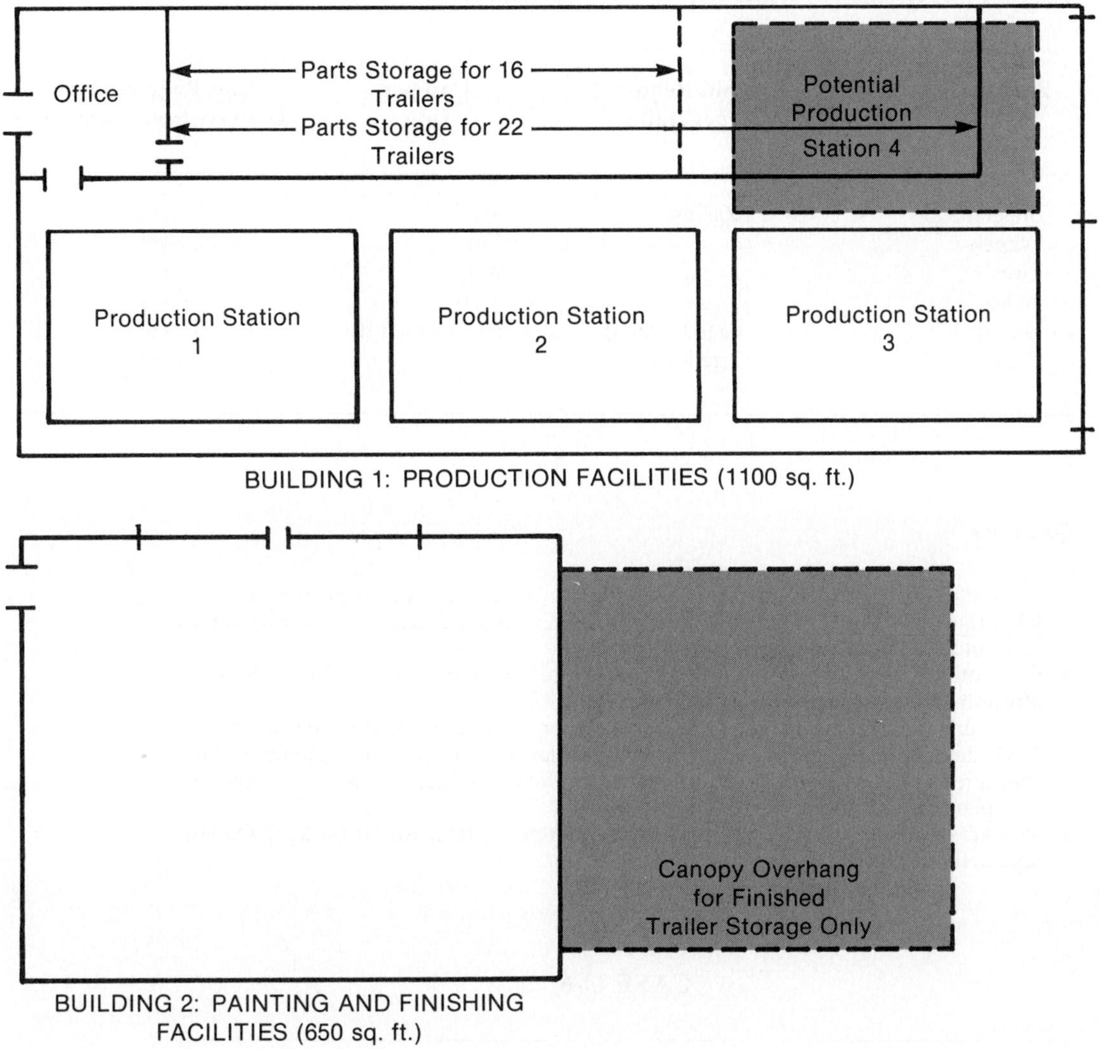

Figure D-3 Plant Layout of Concessionaire Trailers

be reduced from 48 hours per trailer to 36 if raw-material storage space were reduced to accommodate only 16 trailers. The freed-up floor space would be used to effect production-flow efficiencies, culminating in reduced labor hours per trailer.

Exhibit 1 Production Specifications for Concessionaire Trailers

Production Part or Material	Units Required per Trailer	Cost per Unit	Time Required for Delivery from Supplier
Sheet metal	600 lbs.	$1.45/lb.	5 weeks
Wheels	2	$10	6 weeks
Tires	2	$45	1 day
Axles	1	$200	2 days
Braces	16 (6 ft. each)	$0.15/linear ft.	5 weeks
Paint	2 gallons	$12	1 week

Questions

1. Compute the direct manufacturing cost of a Concessionaire trailer given an average labor rate of $6.15 per hour. How much would this cost be reduced if average hours of production were reduced from 48 to 36?
2. Can you see ways in which Concessionaire's production setup can be made more efficient? Make appropriate recommendations.
3. Assuming Ty Bedmore signed the contract for 80 trailers for the first quarter of 1983, develop a comprehensive production plan for the period September, 1982 through April, 1983. Include requirements for the following: raw materials, personnel, plant capacity, and inventory planning.
4. In your opinion, should Ty sign the first-quarter contract for 80 trailers? Explain and defend your reasoning.

CASE D-6

Mather's Heating and Air Conditioning

Selecting and dealing with suppliers

Fred Mather operated a small heating and air-conditioning firm which sold and serviced heating and air-conditioning systems. Over the years the firm had changed from primary reliance on one manufacturer—Western Engineering—as the major supplier to a more balanced arrangement involving three suppliers. In the following discussion with a consultant, Fred described some points of friction in dealing with Western Engineering:

Fred: Western Engineering is so big that it can't be customer-oriented. Why, with my firm they've probably lost $600,000 or $700,000 worth of business just because of their inflexibility!

Consultant: They can't bend to take care of your needs?

Fred: Right. They're not flexible. And part of it, of course, is due to the sales reps they have. They just blew the Mather account. We sold Western equipment mostly until we just got disgusted with them.

Consultant: Did the situation just deteriorate over time?

Fred: True. Finally, after a good period of time, I started getting on them. I'm kind of temperamental. I finally just made up my mind—although I didn't tell them—that in the future our policy will be to sell other equipment also. In essence, what we've done since then is sell more Marshall Corporation and Solex equipment than we have Western.

Consultant: What bothered you about Western Engineering?

Fred: It is really a combination of things. The sales rep, for example. Instead of creating a feeling that he was going to try to take care of you and work with you and be for you, he was always on the opposite side of the fence. It was really strange. Western had certain items that were special quotes to help us be competitive. Well, he was always wanting to take different items off the special quote list every time there was a price change. But we needed every item we could get. This is a very competitive area.

Consultant: What other kinds of problems did he create?

Fred: On paperwork, he would not get it done. Let me give you an example about this sign in front of the business. We bought that sign when we bought the business, and we paid Western for it. About a year later, he came back and said, "Western has a new policy. The sign can no longer belong to the owner, so we will return the money you paid for the sign." I said, "Now that you have operated on my money for a year, the sign doesn't belong to me?" I went along with it, but it was the idea of the thing. They tell you one thing and then do something else.

Consultant: Were there other special incidents that occurred?

Fred: One time we got a job involving $30,000 or $40,000 worth of equipment. I told the rep it *appeared* that we had the job. We had a verbal contract, but that wasn't final. The next thing I knew, the equipment was sitting in Central Truck Lines out here. I hadn't ordered the equipment or anything. Fortunately we did get the contract. But we weren't ready for the equipment for two more months and had no place to put it. And I ended up paying interest. It irritated me to no end.

Consultant: Was that what made you lean toward the other suppliers?

Fred: The final straw was the Park Lake project—a four-story renovation. I had designed the heating and air-conditioning system myself. I called the rep, intending to use Western equipment, and requested a price. So he called back and gave me a lump sum. There were lots of different items, and they were broken down into groups. I asked him to price the items by groups to provide various options to the purchaser. He replied, "We can't break it out." I said, "What do you mean, you can't break it out?" He said something about company policy. I really came unglued, but he never knew.

Consultant: What did you do about it?

Fred: As soon as I quit talking with him, I picked up the phone and called the Marshall Corporation rep. In just a few hours, we had prices that were broken down as I wanted them. The total price turned out to be about $2,500 more, but I bought it! That was the end of Western Engineering as sole supplier.

Questions

1. What services did Fred Mather expect from the supplier? Were these unreasonable expectations?
2. Evaluate Fred's reaction when the Western Engineering rep declined to give him a breakdown on the price. Was Fred's decision to pay $2,500 more for the other equipment a rational decision?
3. Was Western Engineering at fault in shipping the large $30,000 or $40,000 order on the basis of an oral commitment and in the absence of an order? What should Fred have done about it?
4. Are the deficiencies that bother Fred caused by weaknesses of Western Engineering or merely the sales rep who sells for them?
5. Should Fred continue to use three separate suppliers or concentrate more purchases with one of them?

Part E

FINANCIAL AND ADMINISTRATIVE CONTROLS

Chapter 18

Accounting Statements, Ratio Analysis, and Budgeting

LOOKING AHEAD

Watch for the following important topics:

1. Basic considerations in establishing an accounting system.
2. Typical accounting statements prepared by a small business.
3. Classification of financial ratios.
4. Components of the master budget.
5. Using the budget to control expenses.

A strong accounting system provides valuable information for planning, controlling, and evaluating the performance of a small business. Outwardly a business may appear sound, but actually it may be in poor health. Accounting information is the firm's X ray which allows the entrepreneur to monitor the "medical condition" of the business. Accounting statements, financial ratios, and budgets are important aspects of a complete accounting system. We will examine each of these in this chapter.

MAJOR CONSIDERATIONS IN ESTABLISHING AN ACCOUNTING SYSTEM

Most modern accounting systems are based on an accrual, rather than a cash, system. In a *cash system* the accounts are debited and credited as cash is received and paid out. In the *accrual system* the income earned and the expenses incurred are recorded at the time the sale is made or the expense is incurred. The use of the accrual method is preferable because it provides a more nearly accurate and up-to-date statement of profits.

Any accounting system should accomplish the following objectives for a small business:

1. The system should yield an accurate, thorough picture of operating results.
2. The records should permit a quick comparison of current data with prior years' operating results and with budgetary goals.
3. The records should provide financial statements for use by management, bankers, and prospective creditors.
4. The system should facilitate prompt filing of reports and tax returns to regulatory and tax collecting agencies of the government.
5. The system should reveal employee frauds, thefts, waste, and record-keeping errors.

Consistency with Accepted Principles of Accounting

An accounting system must be consistent with accepted principles of accounting theory and practice. This means that a business must be consistent in its treatment of given data and given transactions. Since designing an accounting system is seldom done well by the amateur, the services of a certified public accountant ordinarily are required for this purpose.[1]

Availability and Quality of Accounting Records

An accounting system provides the framework for managerial control of the firm. The effectiveness of the system rests basically on a well-designed and managed record-keeping system. The major types of accounting records and the financial decisions to which they are related are briefly described on pages 444-445.

---

1. The entrepreneur who wishes to develop an accounting system should see Bob L. Meisel, *Record Keeping for Small Business* (Houston: Small Business Publications, 1980); and Rick Stephen Hayes and C. Richard Baker, *Simplified Accounting for Non-Accountants* (New York: John Wiley & Sons, 1980). However, a professional review of self-developed systems is recommended.

ACTION REPORT: GAAP and Small Business

Generally Accepted Accounting Principles (GAAP) must be observed by large and small businesses. However, many people believe it is harder for a small business to develop accounting procedures within GAAP standards. For example:

> Privately held Dierckx Equipment Corp . . . does a lot of leasing as part of its equipment business. GAAP requires that these leases be capitalized, and that has placed Dierckx in the middle of a catch-22 with the banks. If it doesn't capitalize its leases, it's not in compliance with GAAP, and the bank may not like that. If it does capitalize leases, its leverage ratio looks a lot worse, and the banks may not like that. Not only does this GAAP requirement endanger Dierckx' credit rating, but the cost of complying with that *one* requirement is $7,500 annually. Says Financial Vice-President Ray Romano: "It's just a paper entry. It's immaterial. But it adds a lot of bookkeeping time. Our auditors must spend at least three days just going through the lease transactions, and without that requirement that wouldn't be necessary."

There are many proponents for a separate set of standards for small companies. The American Institute of Certified Public Accountants is aware of the problem. Dan Guy, director of auditing research, says, "You can't apply a large-client audit approach in a small-business setting. It doesn't work."

Source: "The World According to GAAP," by Jay Gissen, *Forbes*, Vol. 127, No. 12 (June 8, 1981), pp. 148-149.

1. *Accounts-receivable records.* Records of receivables are vital not only to decisions on credit extension but also to accurate billing and to maintenance of good customer relations. An analysis of these records reveals the degree of effectiveness of the firm's credit and collection policies.
2. *Accounts-payable records.* Records of liabilities show what the firm owes, facilitate the taking of cash discounts, and allow payments to be made when due.
3. *Inventory records.* Adequate records are essential to the control and security of inventory items. In addition, they supply information for use in purchasing, maintenance of adequate stock levels, and computation of turnover ratios.
4. *Payroll records.* The payroll records show the total payments to employees and provide the base for computing and paying the various payroll taxes.

5. *Cash records.* Carefully maintained records showing all receipts and disbursements are necessary to safeguard cash. They yield a knowledge of cash flow and balances on hand. Such information is essential for the proper timing of loans and for the assurance of cash available to pay maturing obligations.
6. *Other records.* Among other accounting records which are vital to the efficient operation of the small business are the insurance register, which shows all policies in force; records of leaseholds; and records covering the firm's investments outside of its business.

To safeguard business assets and prevent errors, the accounting records should be accurately maintained, transaction by transaction. No one employee should completely control any given business transaction. For example, cashiering and account collections should be divorced from bookkeeping, and the bookkeeper should never be allowed to authorize purchases.

In addition, data analyses and reports should ordinarily depend upon the efforts of at least two persons. Of course, in a small business using cash registers, the cash register tape provides a double check on cash received by the cashier. Such procedures tend to prevent fraud and errors.

As an alternative to account keeping by an employee or a member of the owner's family, a firm may have its financial records kept by a certified public accountant or by a bookkeeping or computer service agency that caters to small businesses. Very small businesses often find it convenient to have one and the same firm keep the books, prepare the statements and tax returns, and make the periodic audits. Numerous small accounting firms offer a complete accounting service to small businesses. Their services have been supplemented in recent years by the development of national firms which provide bookkeeping service on a mass-production basis to thousands of small businesses. Data are submitted by mail, and reports prepared by the agency are mailed back to the client firm.

Retention of Accounting Records

The life of an accounting record is not necessarily long. Nevertheless, some firms habitually keep all records without considering the future need for them. If a business is quite small and the records can be housed in just a few filing cabinets, the problem is not serious. For most firms, however, there are two weaknesses in such a policy. First, the excess storage equipment and the unnecessary handling of records are wasteful. Second, loading the files with unnecessary material makes it difficult and time-consuming to locate important information when it is needed.

Essential records, including those legally required for possible government audit, must be maintained as long as the actual need exists. The records may have to be kept for three, five, or ten years—or even longer. Nevertheless, every firm should study its needs and retain essential records only for the requisite time periods.

Once retention needs have been determined, the additional problem of reducing the cost of maintaining records should be resolved. For example, microfilming is widely used by firms that have a large volume of records, and it greatly reduces the space required for records retention. A manufacturer with 100 employees, for example, might record a complete weekly payroll, including all supporting documents, on less than one spool of film. Magnetic disks, which are used as part of computer systems, also conserve storage space.

Physical Protection of Accounting Records

Fires, floods, tornadoes, and other disasters can occur at any time. The loss of all business records in one such disaster could bankrupt a firm. Some precautions are clearly desirable to minimize such dangers. How extensive these should be necessarily depends upon the importance of the records. Financial records may be stored in fireproof safes or cabinets on the premises. Microfilmed copies of the originals, along with other important business documents, might be stored in the firm's safety-deposit box. The firm could also build a subsurface storeroom on company premises, separated from the main office and plant, for storing basic or duplicate records. This will involve some expense, but the precautionary measures afford a protection that may be viewed as a type of business insurance.

TYPICAL FINANCIAL STATEMENTS

The preparation of financial statements is made possible by the existence of accurate and thorough accounting records. Four major financial statements of the BLM Manufacturing Company, a hypothetical small corporation, are illustrated in this section. Two of these statements—the income statement and the balance sheet—will be referred to in the discussion of financial ratios later in the chapter.

Income Statement

The **income statement** shows the results of a firm's operations over a period of time, usually one year. Figure 18-1 shows the income statement of the BLM Manufacturing Company. A minor variation would be involved in preparing an income statement for a retailing or wholesaling, rather than a manufacturing, firm. Specifically, the "Cost of goods sold" section in Figure 18-1 would make reference to purchases rather than to manufacturing costs.

The BLM Manufacturing Company
Income Statement
For Year Ended Dec. 31, 1982

Sales			$830,200
Cost of goods sold:			
Finished goods inventory, Jan. 1, 1982		$ 77,000	
Cost of goods manufactured		589,350	
Total cost of finished goods available for sale		$666,350	
Less finished goods inventory, Dec. 31, 1982		102,000	
Cost of goods sold			564,350
Gross profit on sales			$265,850
Operating expenses:			
Selling expenses:			
Sales salaries and commissions	$57,150		
Advertising expense	38,600		
Miscellaneous selling expense	5,000		
Total selling expenses		$100,750	
General expenses:			
Officers' salaries	$46,120		
Office salaries	16,600		
Depreciation—office equipment	3,600		
Bad-debts expense	4,100		
Miscellaneous office expense	5,580		
Total general expenses		76,000	
Total operating expenses			176,750
Operating income			$ 89,100
Other expense:			
Interest expense			10,000
Net profit before income tax			$ 79,100
Income tax			17,390
Net profit			$ 61,710

Figure 18-1 Income Statement

The BLM Manufacturing Company
Balance Sheet
Dec. 31, 1982

ASSETS

Current assets:				
Cash			$ 44,480	
Accounts receivable		$ 83,000		
Less allowance for uncollectible accounts		5,000	78,000	
Inventories (at lower of cost or market):				
Finished goods		$102,000		
Work in process		52,000		
Raw materials		57,450	211,450	
Factory supplies			8,000	
Prepaid insurance			5,800	
Total current assets				$347,730
	Cost	Accumulated Depreciation	Book Value	
Plant assets:				
Office equipment	$ 36,000	$ 16,200	$ 19,800	
Factory equipment	552,000	327,000	225,000	
Buildings	250,000	40,000	210,000	
Land	70,000	—	70,000	
Total plant assets	$908,000	$383,200		524,800
Intangible assets:				
Patents				55,000
TOTAL ASSETS				$927,530

LIABILITIES AND STOCKHOLDERS' EQUITY

Current liabilities:			
Accounts payable	$ 77,200		
Estimated income tax payable	17,390		
Salaries and wages payable	3,930		
Interest payable	2,500		
Total current liabilities		$101,020	
Long-term liabilities:			
First mortgage 10% notes payable (due 1987)		200,000	
Total liabilities			$301,020
Common stock, no-par (30,000 shares authorized and issued)		$300,000	
Retained earnings		326,510	
Total stockholders' equity			626,510
TOTAL LIABILITIES AND STOCKHOLDERS' EQUITY			$927,530

Figure 18-2 Balance Sheet

Balance Sheet

The **balance sheet** is a statement that shows a firm's financial position at a specific date. Figure 18-2 shows the balance sheet of the BLM Manufacturing Company as of December 31, 1982. If this firm were a proprietorship or a partnership, the term "Stockholders' Equity" would read "Capital." And the items listed in this section would show individual ownership investments.

Statement of Cost of Goods Manufactured

The **statement of cost of goods manufactured** is a supporting, detailed schedule of the "cost of goods manufactured" entry in the income statement. Figure 18-3 shows the BLM Manufacturing Company's statement of cost of goods manufactured. If this company were a retailing or wholesaling firm, no supporting schedule comparable to Figure 18-3 would be required.

The BLM Manufacturing Company
Statement of Cost of Goods Manufactured
For Year Ended Dec. 31, 1982

Work-in-process inventory, Jan. 1, 1982			$ 40,000
Raw materials:			
Inventory, Jan. 1, 1982		$ 64,000	
Purchases		241,600	
Cost of materials available for use		$305,600	
Less inventory, Dec. 31, 1982		57,450	
Cost of materials placed in production		$248,150	
Direct labor		197,500	
Factory overhead:			
Indirect labor	$38,600		
Factory maintenance	16,000		
Heat, light, and power	23,600		
Property taxes	10,000		
Depreciation of factory equipment	35,200		
Depreciation of buildings	6,000		
Amortization of patents	5,000		
Factory supplies expense	12,000		
Insurance expense	5,200		
Miscellaneous factory expense	4,100		
Total factory overhead		155,700	
Total manufacturing costs			601,350
Total work in process during period			$641,350
Less work-in-process inventory, Dec. 31, 1982			52,000
Cost of goods manufactured			$589,350

Figure 18-3 Statement of Cost of Goods Manufactured

Statement of Changes in Financial Position

Formerly known as the "statement of sources and uses of funds," the **statement of changes in financial position** shows how a firm acquired working capital and employed it over the same period covered by the income statement. Figure 18-4 shows the BLM Manufacturing Company's statement of changes in financial position for the year ended December 31, 1982.

The BLM Manufacturing Company
Statement of Changes in Financial Position
For Year Ended Dec. 31, 1982

Increases in working capital were provided by:		
Operations:		
Net profit (per income statement)	$61,710	
Add: Depreciation expense charged to operations	44,800	
Amortization of patents	5,000	$111,510
Working capital was applied to:		
Dividends	$18,000	
Purchase of equipment	46,200	
Retirement of long-term notes payable	40,000	104,200
Increase in working capital		$ 7,310

The net increase in working capital is accounted for as follows:

	Jan. 1, 1982	Dec. 31, 1982	Working Capital Increase	Working Capital Decrease
Cash	$ 38,000	$ 44,480	$ 6,480	
Accounts receivable (net)	92,000	78,000		$14,000
Inventories	181,000	211,450	30,450	
Prepaid expenses and supplies	17,800	13,800		4,000
Accounts payable	56,400	77,200		20,800
Income taxes payable	29,000	17,390	11,610	
Other payables	4,000	6,430		2,430
			$48,540	$41,230
Net increase in working capital			—	7,310
			$48,540	$48,540

Figure 18-4 Statement of Changes in Financial Position

ANALYSIS OF FINANCIAL STATEMENTS

A single item from a financial statement has only limited meaning until it is related to some other item. For example, current assets of $10,000 mean one thing when current liabilities are $5,000 and another when they are $50,000. For this reason ratios have been developed to relate different income-statement items to each other, different balance-sheet items to each other, and income-statement items to balance-sheet items.

Although numerous financial statement ratios can be computed, only those that are the most practical and widely used for small businesses will be explained here. These ratios will be grouped into four classifications, using the financial statements of the BLM Manufacturing Company for illustrative purposes. It must be emphasized that a careful interpretation of ratios is required to make them useful to a particular firm. A ratio may indicate potential trouble, but it cannot explain either the causes or the seriousness of the situation. Most small firms find it profitable to compare their ratios with their own past experience and with industry standard ratios.

Ratios Related to Working-Capital Position

Adequacy and liquidity of working capital are measured by two ratios: the current ratio and the acid-test (or quick) ratio.

Current Ratio. To compute the current ratio, divide current assets by current liabilities. The "banker's rule" for this ratio is "at least two to one" for working capital to be judged adequate. Actually the proper size of this ratio depends upon the type of industry, the season of the year, and other factors. The current ratio of the BLM Manufacturing Company is:

$$\frac{\text{Current assets}}{\text{Current liabilities}} = \frac{\$347{,}730}{\$101{,}020} = 3.44 \text{ times}$$

From this it appears that the BLM Manufacturing Company has sufficient cash and other assets which will be quickly converted into cash to pay all maturing obligations.

Acid-Test (or Quick) Ratio. A more severe test of adequacy of working capital is provided by the acid-test, or quick, ratio. To compute this ratio, divide current assets less inventories by current liabilities. The exclusion of inventories from current assets is necessary because inventories are in part a fixed capital investment and are less liquid than other current assets. The BLM Manufacturing Company's acid-test ratio is:

$$\frac{\text{Current assets less inventories}}{\text{Current liabilities}} = \frac{\$347{,}730 - \$211{,}450}{\$101{,}020} = 1.35 \text{ times}$$

The traditional rule of thumb is a minimum of 1 to 1 acid-test ratio. Again it appears that the BLM Manufacturing Company's working-capital position is sound.

Ratios Related to the Sales Position

Comparisons between the level of sales and the investment in various asset accounts involve the use of three ratios: inventory turnover, average collection period, and fixed-asset turnover. These ratios indicate the need for a proper balance between sales and various asset accounts.

Inventory Turnover. The inventory turnover rate shows whether or not a company is holding excessive stocks of inventory. When this ratio is computed for a going concern, two questions arise: (1) Since sales are at market prices and inventories are usually carried at cost, which is more appropriate to use as the numerator in the ratio: sales or cost of goods sold? and (2) Which inventory figure should be used: an average inventory or an inventory at one point in time?

Logic dictates that the inventory turnover should be computed by comparing cost of goods sold to inventory. As a rule, however, it is better to use the ratio of sales to inventories carried at cost because established compilers of financial ratios, such as Dun & Bradstreet, do this. Thus, the firm can compute a ratio that can be compared to the standard ratio developed by Dun & Bradstreet. It is also better to use an average inventory figure (computed by adding the year's beginning and ending inventories and dividing by 2) if there has been a marked upward or downward trend of sales during the year. The BLM Manufacturing Company's inventory turnover rate is:

$$\frac{\text{Sales}}{\text{Average inventory}} = \frac{\$830{,}200}{\$89{,}500} = 9.28 \text{ or } 9.3 \text{ times}$$

If the industry average is 9, for example, it is obvious that the BLM Manufacturing Company is not carrying excessive stocks of inventory. Excessive inventories are unnecessary and would reduce business profits.

Average Collection Period. The average collection period is a measure of accounts-receivable turnover. A two-step procedure for finding the average collection period for the BLM Manufacturing Company, using 360 as the number of days in a year, is:

$$\text{Step 1: } \frac{\text{Sales}}{360} = \frac{\$830{,}200}{360} = \$2{,}306 \text{ average daily sales}$$

$$\text{Step 2: } \frac{\text{Receivables}}{\text{Average daily sales}} = \frac{\$78{,}000}{\$2{,}306} = 33.8 \text{ or } 34 \text{ days}$$

If the industry average collection period is 20 days, then it would appear that the BLM Manufacturing Company is experiencing serious collection problems.

Fixed-Asset Turnover. The fixed-asset turnover measures the extent to which plant and equipment are being utilized. For the BLM Manufacturing Company, the fixed-asset turnover is:

$$\frac{\text{Sales}}{\text{Fixed assets}} = \frac{\$830{,}200}{\$524{,}800} = 1.58 \text{ times}$$

If the industry average is 4 times, this means that BLM's plant and equipment are not being used effectively. This should be borne in mind when considering requests for additional production equipment.

Ratios Related to Profitability

Profitability is the net result of a firm's management policies and decisions. The ratios that may be used to measure how effectively the firm is being managed are: profit margin on sales, return on total assets, and return on net worth (or equity).

Profit Margin on Sales. The profit margin on sales gives the profit per dollar of sales. To compute this ratio, divide net profit by sales. For the BLM Manufacturing Company, the profit margin on sales is:

$$\frac{\text{Net profit}}{\text{Sales}} = \frac{\$61{,}710}{\$830{,}200} = .0743 \text{ or } 7.43 \text{ percent}$$

If the industry average is 7 percent, BLM's slightly higher profit margin indicates effective management of sales and operations.

Return on Total Assets. The return on total assets, or asset earning power, measures the return on total investment in the business. To compute this ratio, divide net profit by total assets. The BLM Manufacturing Company's return on total assets is:

$$\frac{\text{Net profit}}{\text{Total assets}} = \frac{\$61,710}{\$927,530} = .0665 \text{ or } 6.65 \text{ percent}$$

If the industry average is 8 percent, BLM's low rate may indicate an excessive investment in fixed assets even though its profit margin on sales is slightly better than the industry's average.

Return on Net Worth. The return on net worth, or return on equity, measures the rate of return on stockholders' investments in the business. To compute this ratio, divide net profit by net worth. For BLM's stockholders the return on net worth is:

$$\frac{\text{Net profit}}{\text{Net worth}} = \frac{\$61,710}{\$626,510} = .0985 \text{ or } 9.85 \text{ percent}$$

If the industry average is 12 percent, it would appear that BLM's return is unsatisfactorily low. It is possible that BLM's return on net worth may be improved by using more leverage, or debt.[2]

Ratios Related to Debt Position

One of the most critical aspects of the financial structure of a firm is the relationship between borrowed funds and invested capital. If debt is unreasonably large when compared with equity funds, the firm may be skating on thin ice. According to the conservative rule of thumb, two thirds of the total capital in a business should be owner-supplied. In most lines of business, however, the industry standard is somewhat lower.

The ratios that may be used to measure the debt position of a firm are debt to total assets and times interest earned.

Debt to Total Assets. The debt to total assets is a ratio that measures the percentage of total funds that have been provided by a firm's creditors. To compute this ratio, divide the total debts (current liabilities and long-term liabilities) by total assets. The BLM Manufacturing Company's debt ratio is:

$$\frac{\text{Total debts}}{\text{Total assets}} = \frac{\$301,020}{\$927,530} = .3245 \text{ or } 32.45 \text{ percent}$$

---

2. For a discussion of how this rate can be broken down into its underlying components, see Kenneth R. Van Voorhis, "The Dupont Model Revisited: A Simplified Application to Small Business," *Journal of Small Business Management,* Vol. 19, No. 2 (April, 1981), p. 45.

It is evident that BLM's debt ratio conforms to the conservative rule of thumb. This means that BLM should be able, if desired, to borrow additional funds without first raising more equity funds.

Times Interest Earned. The times-interest-earned ratio measures the extent to which a firm's earnings can decline without impairing its ability to meet annual interest costs. To compute this ratio, divide operating income by interest charges. The BLM's times-interest-earned ratio is:

$$\frac{\text{Operating income}}{\text{Interest charges}} = \frac{\$89,100}{\$10,000} = 8.9 \text{ times}$$

If the industry average is 8 times, it is obvious that BLM's position is strong and that it can cover its interest charges even with a substantial decline in its earnings. This reinforces the previous conclusion that BLM should have little difficulty if it tries to borrow additional funds.

Observance of Accounting Principles and Conventions

In seeking to analyze and interpret statements, a manager must realize that certain principles and accounting conventions govern the preparation of financial statements. For example, conservatism is a principle that guides accountants, and the most conservative method available is the one an accountant will typically choose. Another principle governing the preparation of statements is consistency. This means that a given item on a statement will be handled in the same way every month and every year so that comparability of the data will be assured. Also, the principle of full disclosure compels the accountant to insist that all liabilities be shown and all material facts be presented. This is intended to prevent misleading any investor who might read the firm's statements.

Certain accounting conventions also regulate, in part, the preparation of financial statements. One of these concerns the accrual accounting system mentioned earlier in this chapter. Again, there is a convention governing the balance-sheet valuation of inventory, which may be based on the last-in, first-out (LIFO) method or the first-in, first-out (FIFO) method. Similarly, receivables are valued at their cash value less an allowance for possible bad debts, while fixed assets other than land are valued at their depreciated value based on original cost.

BUDGETING

The budget is the principal short-range plan for any business. When a business is departmentalized, it usually has a master budget which covers the departmental budgets that constitute the component parts of the master budget. The departmental budgets include those for sales, production, purchases, and so on. The master budget yields budgeted financial statements covering the expected operating results and shows the impact of operations upon the firm's asset values and equity interests.

The Master Budget

An entrepreneur must predetermine expected normal performance in order to establish performance standards for the firm's various divisions and departments. Performance standards make possible the evaluation of operating results. To be functional for such evaluations, the standards must be reasonable and attainable in the light of expected business conditions. The only alternative is the creation of ideal standards, envisioning optimum operating conditions. But ideal standards would be difficult to attain because actual business conditions are seldom ideal. Hence, ideal standards must be rejected in favor of expected attainable performance.

Cost and Performance Standards. In view of the central role of standards in budgeting, attention is directed at this point to the process of constructing cost and performance standards. These standards should be developed for the areas of production, sales, and administrative management.

Manufacturing Standards. In manufacturing, certain items can be subjected to objective cost and performance standards. Some of these are:

1. Raw materials.
2. Finished products.
3. Manufacturing methods or processes.
4. Plant equipment.
5. Product designs.
6. Labor.

The dollar cost budgeted for materials depends upon the quality and quantity required for the entire production, as well as the cost of each type of material. The dollar cost budgeted for labor depends upon the standard hourly rates that are paid to machine operators on the various processing operations.

Some manufacturing overhead expenses, such as depreciation and utility costs, are less susceptible to objective standards. But the proper dollar amounts for these items can be determined in the light of past experience and of the percentage of capacity operation expected.

Selling and Administrative Standards. In the area of selling and administration, various expense items can be predetermined according to standards which are reasonably accurate and capable of attainment. Such expense standards might be based on the firm's past experience or on industry standards compiled by several agencies, notably Dun & Bradstreet.

The traditional accounting breakdown of selling and administrative expenses has been by *kind*, such as taxes, interest, office supplies, rent, and so on. Such a breakdown of expenses is imperfect because it does not provide a basis for functional expense control. Logically, a retailer requires the following functional-expense breakdown:

1. Merchandising
   a. Buying
   b. Selling
2. Sales promotion
   a. Advertising
   b. Window display
   c. Point-of-purchase display
   d. Premiums and trading stamps
3. Store operation
   a. Store protection
   b. Employee training
   c. Switchboard operation
   d. Cashiering
   e. Delivery
   f. Receiving, checking, and marking
   g. Warehousing
   h. Elevator operation
   i. Utilities
4. Control
   a. Accounting
   b. Statistical tabulations
   c. Payroll preparation and distribution
   d. Auditing
   e. Credit investigation
   f. Collections
5. Management (only those portions of the expenses which cannot be allocated to other categories)
   a. Executive salaries
   b. Rent
   c. Taxes
   d. Insurance
   e. Depreciation

In setting standards for selling and administrative expenses, several rules must be observed. First, the units of measurement used must be objective and clear-cut. For example, the expense standard for procuring orders by a salesperson might be expressed in terms of the dollars spent per sales call. Second, a separate classification should be made for each expense item, accumulating these items in terms of functional categories. Finally, expense classification should not be carried too far – that is, to the point where each minute kind of expense is identified and the amount separately accumulated regardless of its importance. A miscellaneous classification should be established for minor expenses.

Variables in Setting Standards. In manufacturing, the volume of production is obviously a major factor affecting cost. Frequently, however, the budget is constructed as though volume were the sole determinant of cost variation. It is not. For example, the following are sources of cost variation for a given accounting period:

1. Introduction of new products.
2. Variation in the size of production runs.
3. Variation in quality of raw materials available.
4. Rate of labor turnover.
5. Changes in labor efficiency.
6. Changes in handling or processing equipment.

Similarly, in setting standards for selling and administrative expenses, the following are sources of cost variation:

1. Changes in the product mixture of sales.
2. Changes in intensity of competition.
3. Entry into new territories and deletion of old ones.

Moreover, in establishing standards for administrative expenses, many so-called fixed expenses, such as rent, are fixed only for a given period of time. With a sufficient change in sales and production volume and/or mixture, these expenses must be varied upward or downward to a new fixed level.

Reports on Actual Results. Cost and performance standards are useless in themselves. Their effective use requires the prompt reporting of actual results, showing variations between these results and those anticipated. Concentrating upon insignificant or uncontrollable cost variations is a waste of time, however. In fact, minor discrepancies may reflect the inaccuracy of the standard itself rather than management inefficiency.

All significant cost and performance variances must be investigated immediately to locate and eliminate the unfavorable ones, if possible. Such analyses may reveal loose standards, changed external conditions, or superior performance. If unusually good performance is noted, it may be possible to apply the better methods in other sectors of the organization. Obviously immediate action to correct significant adverse variations is desirable.

Budget Revision During the Budget Year. Business operation is always full of uncertainties. Thus, actual operations seldom correspond exactly, and sometimes not even closely, to the budgeted operating level. A need for budget revision during the budget year consequently arises. For example, a manufacturer budgets a given product mixture and volume for sales. If actual sales do not conform in total amount and in product mixture, the budgeted sales and the corresponding expense budgets must be revised. Even if actual sales volume is achieved, a different mixture may require budget revision. Moreover, to obtain sales in a competitive market, anticipated prices may have to be changed. This, too, may occasion a need for budget revision.

In the retail or wholesale establishment, changes in advertising and sales promotion emphasis, changes in style trends, changes in customer clientele, and other changes lead to a similar need for budget revision.

Components of the Master Budget

Even in a small firm, the master budget is not prepared by one person alone, nor is it a task which is accomplished quickly. Weeks or months of effort are required. The small manufacturer should meet with heads of departments frequently before the amounts and standards to be incorporated in the budget are determined. Then the budget must be broken down by months. Finally, it must be typed, with copies for distribution to the department heads, each of whom will also have reviewed and agreed in advance to the annual and monthly figures.

Sales Budget. Since most business activities must be geared to the level of expected sales, it is customary to begin with the sales budget, which serves as the cornerstone of the master budget. The sales budget must be as nearly accurate as care and good judgment can make it because all of the other departmental budgets depend on the sales budget.

Suppose a small firm manufacturing a single product is preparing a sales budget for its eighth year of operations.[3] By years, the firm's market share has been .05, .055, .06, .065, .07, .075, and .08. Accordingly, the firm estimates a market share for Year 8 of .085 since its market share has been growing by .005, or .5 percent every year. Industry sales in the latest year were 4,159,934 units, and the industry has also reflected a .5 percent annual growth for the

3. If the firm makes two or more products, it would carry out the described procedure separately for each product.

last decade. Since the industry sales anticipated for the next year are expected to coincide with the past sales trend, the business cycle index (or ratio) is expected to be 100 percent, or 1. To budget the firm's sales (in units) for Year 8, the following formula is applied:

Year 8 sales in units = Estimated market share × (1 + Annual trend increase) × Latest industry sales × Estimated business cycle ratio

= .085 × 1.005 × 4,159,934 × 1.0

= 355,362

Now, with increasing costs of labor and raw materials, the firm decides to increase the selling price of its product from the current $30 to $33. Hence, the firm's budgeted sales revenue for Year 8 will be $33 × 355,362 = $11,726,946.

If the sale of the firm's product is nonseasonal, the monthly sales budgets—both in units and in dollars—will be 1/12 of the annual amounts budgeted. Given seasonal sales, each month's budgeted amounts are determined by the following formula (with seasonal indexes established by month):

$\frac{1}{12}$ × Annual total × Monthly sales seasonal index ratio

The sales budget will be complete when monthly budget amounts are distributed for each month by sales territories.

Production Budget. The production budget is tied closely to the sales budget and to the finished-goods inventory level planned. The formula for budgeting units to be produced during the year is:

Budgeted production = Budgeted sales less Expected starting inventory of finished goods plus Planned ending inventory of finished goods

Given nonseasonal production, the monthly production will be exactly one twelfth of the annual budgeted production. If the sales pattern has seasonal fluctuations, adjustments must be made.

Production must be budgeted separately for each product in the line. When the total monthly production in units has been determined for all products, the production budget is complete.

Purchases Budget. Differences between monthly materials requirements and materials available in the storeroom will necessitate a purchases budget.

The formula for determining the units of each kind of raw material to be purchased is:

Units of each raw material to be purchased = Units of material required for production plus Planned ending inventory of raw materials less Expected starting inventory of raw materials

Obviously this computation must be made separately for each kind of raw material for each month. Annual purchases in units for each kind of raw material are then obtained by adding the monthly figures. Budgeted purchases, in units, for each kind of material may be multiplied by the price per unit to arrive at the dollar figure.

Supporting Budget Schedules

Certain budget schedules are prepared to support the total budgeted amounts of specific items in the master budget. These budget schedules are explained below.

Materials Budget Schedule. The materials budget schedule specifies by months the amounts of each kind of material required to meet production schedules. It must be noted, however, that the budgeted monthly production for each kind of product is not equal to the units to be placed in process for those months because of the planned work-in-process inventory variation. Hence, units to be produced must first be translated into units to be placed in process, using the following formula:

Units to be placed in process = Units to be produced as budgeted less Units in expected starting inventory in process plus Units in planned ending inventory in process.

Once the units of each product to be placed in process monthly have been determined, it is possible to estimate the number of units of each kind of raw material required.

Direct-Labor Budget Schedule. In the direct-labor budget, estimates of *direct* labor to be used in production during the coming 12 months are made. Time and motion studies provide a standard rate of output per hour. To find the standard hours of direct labor, divide the number of budgeted production units by the standard hourly output rate. If time and motion studies have not been used, the total labor hours required must be estimated on the basis of past experience.

A separate computation of direct-labor hours is required for each product in the line and for each labor operation. When all the computations are completed, the results are totaled to give the total budgeted direct-labor hours (by departments, by months, and for the year). To find the standard labor cost, multiply the total number of direct-labor hours for each operation by the standard hourly wage rate. The sum of the direct-labor costs for all operations is the firm's total direct-labor cost in dollars.

Manufacturing-Expense Budget Schedule. Manufacturing expense is also known as "burden" or "factory overhead." One of the most important items in this schedule is *indirect* labor. To compute the indirect-labor expense, one must determine the desired number of such personnel as stores clerks, stock and shipping clerks, model makers, shop supervisors, timekeepers, inspectors, mechanics, boiler-room operators, and office clerks — most of whom typically are on straight salary. If so, their monthly salaries can be entered at once on this schedule.

Other items in the manufacturing-expense budget schedule include the following: property taxes, which are budgeted at the latest year's actual taxes and modified by any expected changes in property valuations or tax rates; fire and insurance premiums; depreciation of buildings and machines; repairs; tools and fixtures; factory supplies; utilities; freight and express; models and patterns; blueprints; and many others. Each factory-overhead expense must be separately budgeted by months and for the year.

Cost-of-Goods-Manufactured-and-Sold Budget Schedule. The materials budget schedule specifies the quantity of material required for monthly production schedules, but it does not specify the dollar value of the materials. Hence, the number of required units of each type of material must be multiplied by the standard cost price per unit. The total cost of materials, plus the dollar value of direct-labor hours and of factory-overhead expenses, gives the *cost of goods manufactured* — again by month and by year. Appropriate adjustments for expected variation in both starting and ending inventories of finished goods will give the *cost of goods sold* by month and by year. The figures calculated for the cost-of-goods-manufactured-and-sold budget schedule are used in preparing the budgeted income statement.

Selling- and Administrative-Expense Budget Schedules. The selling- and administrative-expense budget schedules should be separately prepared by month and by year. The selling-expense budget schedule covers salespersons' salaries and commissions, travel expenses, sales promotion and advertising, and the like. The amounts budgeted for each item tend to vary with business volume to a greater extent than those for administrative expenses. For example, assuming that prices are constant, greater expenditures for both advertising and personal selling are normally required to achieve a higher level of sales.

The administrative-expense budget schedule covers such items as salaries of administrative and clerical personnel, payroll taxes, office supplies, contributions, telephone and telegraph, depreciation of office equipment, and other office administrative expenses.

Accounts-Receivable and Cash Budget Schedules. Assuming that the firm's fiscal year coincides with the calendar year, the expected starting balance of accounts receivable is entered as the first item on the January accounts-receivable budget schedule. Credit sales for the month (the normal fraction of total budgeted sales) are then recorded. Collections from receivables, as well as losses on bad debts, must be estimated and entered before the ending balance can be determined. (Losses on bad debts are calculated from past experience and from an accounting method called "aging of accounts receivable.") This entire process is repeated to get each of the other eleven monthly accounts-receivable budget schedules.

Collections from accounts receivable are also entered on the cash budget schedule. The starting point of the cash budget schedule is the expected January 1 cash balance, to which collections from accounts receivable and other budgeted cash receipts are added. All budgeted cash receipts must be itemized separately. Then disbursements are budgeted and listed by kinds, such as accounts payable, payrolls, taxes, dividends, machines, tools and fixtures, supplies, insurance, utilities, and the like.[4] With the total disbursement figure, the ending cash balance can then be budgeted.[5] This process is repeated for each month of the year.

Budgeted Financial Statements

The budgeted income statement is constructed like an actual income statement except that both income items and expense items are estimates derived from the budget schedules discussed above. An estimated balance sheet is also prepared to reflect the expected net results of operations. Finally, the budgeted statement of changes in financial position is prepared to show the expected sources and applications of working capital during the budget year. Each of these budgeted financial statements is prepared by the month and year.

After the budgeted financial statements are prepared, they should be evaluated by the use of key financial ratios such as those that were discussed

4. Some of these items will have appeared on other budget schedules.

5. Working-capital bank loans will be required during the month if there is a negative ending cash balance. The loans and scheduled repayments (as disbursements) must then be incorporated in a revised cash budget for this month and in the months when repayments are scheduled.

ACTION REPORT: Knowing Your Accounting Options

Not every small-business manager can expect to be an expert accountant. But every entrepreneur should know enough about the income statement and the balance sheet to recognize optional accounting methods which will work to the advantage of the business's goals. For example, consider the president of a helicopter transportation company who was getting loan rejections due to his negative net worth shown on the balance sheet. The president had left all accounting matters to "a really good tax accountant . . . It turned out that the company's accountant was 'expensing'—that is, writing off in one year—the entire cost of the major overhauls the company did on its helicopters."

Although the write-off by the accountant was legitimate and helped reduce current taxable income, it was negatively affecting the balance sheet. The company went to another CPA for advice. "The new CPA redid the financial statement for the previous three years, and almost magically the retained earnings account turned positive."

This entrepreneur learned that it is good business to prepare financial statements tailored to the user's needs.

Source: Reprinted by permission of the *Harvard Business Review.* Excerpt from "Managing Financial Statements—Image and Effect" by James McNeill Stancill (March/April 1981). Copyright © 1981 by the President and Fellows of Harvard College; all rights reserved.

in the early part of this chapter and others found in financial management textbooks. If the ratio analysis indicates that the budgeted operations will produce unsatisfactory results, the master budget and all supporting schedules must be revised at once. But this revision must still be predicated upon reasonable expectations for next year's operations. On the other hand, if the ratio analysis indicates that the budgeted operations will produce satisfactory results, the master budget may be considered completed. Copies can then be prepared and issued to all persons concerned.

Flexible Budgets

As an alternative to the "static" budget procedures described above, it is possible to utilize a "flexible" budget plan. This entails a series of monthly budgets for each of several volume levels—for example, 50 percent, 60 percent, 70 percent, 80 percent, 90 percent, 100 percent, 110 percent, and 120 percent of normal capacity. Monthly normal capacity equals one twelfth of the average annual sales in units, attained over a complete business cycle. Typically the physical capacity of a plant is about 120 percent of normal capacity, which is why we stop at 120 percent. For each such level, a master budget and supporting budget schedules are prepared as in the case of the static budget. Data in units must be translated into dollar data. The annual budget is 12 times the monthly budget for any volume level. Seasonality of sales and production is ignored, except in selecting the appropriate budget level for each month.

One weakness in flexible budgeting lies in the fact that it presumes that volume change is the only cost-differentiating factor acting on a budget. This is untrue, as has already been noted.

Using the Budget to Control and Reduce Expenses

The budget, when properly used, is perhaps the most effective tool in controlling expense. By providing a set of standards for expenses of each kind, the budget points up overspending or underspending. To examine the possibilities for controlling expenses, we must first understand the different classifications of expenses discussed below.

Actual *vs.* Imputed Expenses. Those expenses that in fact accrue and require cash outlays are called **actual expenses. Imputed expenses** do not exist in the sense that they can be entered on the books of account and appear on the income statement. Consider, as an example, the interest on the owner's investment in a business. If the owner had invested the money in the stocks or bonds of other corporations or in government bonds, he or she would have received an income in the form of dividends or interest. The theory of imputing the interest expense on the owner's investment lies in the fact that an income which could have been received from another source is lost if the money is tied up in one's own assets. This lost income is the imputed interest expense. The economist refers to imputed expenses as *opportunity costs.* Certainly such imputed expenses cannot properly be included in the income statement. Consideration must be given to them, however, in many business decisions.

Fixed *vs.* Variable Expenses. Those expenses that do not vary in total amount for the accounting period are called *fixed expenses.* For example, a rental charge of $500 per month or a property tax of $1,000 per year are fixed expenses. **Variable expenses** are fixed on a per-unit basis but vary in total amount for month and year with the volume of goods manufactured or sold. As an example of a variable expense, consider machine operators in a factory who work on piece rates and receive a specified amount in dollars and cents per unit of product processed by them. If they process 100,000 units at 5 cents per unit, they receive $5,000. If they process 10,000 units at 5 cents per unit, they receive $500. Thus, the amount of the variable expense—in this case, direct labor—depends upon the number of units made. This distinction is also important in business decisions. For example, an order might be accepted under some circumstances at a price which would cover variable costs but fail to cover all fixed costs. As a practical matter, many expenses are neither completely fixed nor completely variable in nature.

Functional Expenses. On page 457 a functional-expense breakdown for a retailer was suggested. **Functional expenses** are those that relate to specific selling and administrative activities of a business. If the amounts recorded by *kinds* of expense in the books of account can be equitably distributed to the functional-expense categories, then expense control can be achieved. Consider, for example, the expense of "payroll preparation," which is charged to the functional category of "control." This expense does not include the production payroll itself; rather, it involves costs of payroll preparation, distribution of paychecks, and audit. (The payroll cost itself would be distributed to the various pertinent categories.)

A unit of measurement is required for control; this is afforded best, perhaps, by the number of payroll checks written. If the average payroll preparation expense over the past year is taken as standard for budgeting purposes, the actual expense for a given pay period can be compared and discrepancies evaluated. Certainly total payroll expense is not controllable as such, but it can be controlled if allocated equitably to various functional-expense categories.

Controllable vs. Noncontrollable Expenses. It is important that managers of small firms stress controllable expenses almost to the exclusion of noncontrollable expenses. Consider a lease with a flat rental. Once a lease has been signed, rental expense is not controllable during the life of the lease. Hence, attention should then be directed to other items of expense which are controllable.

In the small factory, for example, if a further mechanization of materials handling is possible and the capital expenditure is not prohibitive, the necessary equipment can be installed to reduce expenses. For a given system, however, expense control means that the system must be used more efficiently. For example, employees on hourly rates may be sent home when work is light.

Similarly, delivery expense is controllable to some extent. The truck driver's salary, truck depreciation, and operating cost can be more effectively used and better controlled if the truck is provided with a two-way radio. In contrast, a retailer subscribing to a delivery service at a fixed amount per month is committed to a noncontrollable expense. Accordingly, there is little need for attention to it until time to renegotiate the delivery service contract.

Areas for Expense Control. Greater attention should be given to major rather than to minor items of expense. Perhaps the most important expenses to the retailer are those of advertising and sales promotion, rent, buying and receiving merchandise, and inventory-carrying charges. The store's biggest investment is typically in merchandise inventory. The productivity of labor can also be so variable as to make labor the most important expense category.

The small manufacturer does not face the same important areas for expense control as does the retailer. For the manufacturer, the typically important areas for expense control are materials and supplies, direct-labor cost, and the cost of equipment and its operation, together with the costs of financing receivables and of freight. If the manufacturer uses traveling salespersons, their salaries and travel expense allowances may also be important categories of expense control.

Consider the small factory which employs traveling salespersons who carry models and samples of the product to dealer customers. For car transportation expense, expense standards may be developed in terms of mileage allowances. Actual expenses then can be compared with, and controlled in terms of, these standards. The so-called traveling expenses other than the cost of car operations are not so easily determinable and controllable, however. For example, a salesperson may report hotel costs, meal costs, tips, entertainment of customers, and other expenses on a weekly sheet. This individual could pad the expense account. To combat this danger, it is possible to supply all the firm's salespersons with credit cards for expenses incidental to travel. Thus, for a small amount per year, the firm gets a part-time bookkeeper and prevents the juggling of expense accounts in such a way as to give the salespersons additional income.

Expense Reduction. Expense control is frequently more important than expense reduction. Expense control may include expense reduction, but it may also involve the increase of expenditures for a given type of expense rather than either constant outlay or reduced outlay. However, a program of expense reduction, *superimposed upon one of expense control*, is invaluable if it can be achieved without reducing sales volume, eliminating customer services, or losing operating efficiency. Expense reduction can make possible price reductions or profit expansion, or both. Most business executives and management consultants will admit that a 5 percent or greater reduction in expenses could be achieved by almost any business, large or small.

Expense reduction may be achieved by recruitment and retention of superior personnel perhaps more effectively than by any other means. Even at a higher salary cost, superior employees more than make up the difference by their greater contribution to the firm's production and distribution effort. Because of their greater efficiency, expense per unit of product or service or per item sold is reduced.

Common Budgetary Control Deficiencies in Small Businesses

Even though budgets are designed to facilitate effective management, they sometimes fail to do so, particularly in the small business. Here are several reasons why small businesses suffer from unsatisfactory budgetary control.

1. *Inaccurate determination of budget standards.* When inaccurate budget standards are set, comparisons of actual results with budgeted amounts are misleading. Management may be lulled into the belief that all is well when, as a matter of fact, costs are uncontrolled and performance is inefficient.
2. *Failure to include all key business activities in the budget.* If desired overall results are to be attained, all business activities of the firm must be incorporated in the budget.
3. *Lack of full support for the budget.* When preparing the budget, managers should consult their subordinates so that the latter will feel that the budget is theirs, too. And when the budget is completed, top management must back it up and convince all employees of the value of the budget as a control system. Subordinates can show their full support by promptly submitting control reports, especially when the budget needs to be revised. Of course, any budget revisions should also be communicated promptly to the subordinates.
4. *Inability to interpret control reports.* Sometimes the manager and the employees find control reports difficult to interpret. Thus, they may fail to detect and to act on controllable expenses that have significant variations between actual and budgeted amounts.

LOOKING BACK

1. A well-conceived accounting system may require the expertise of an accountant. It should be consistent with generally accepted accounting principles and include as a minimum certain accounting records. The retention and physical protection of accounting records are necessary for the proper functioning of the accounting system.
2. The four accounting statements most typically prepared by a small business are the income statement, the balance sheet, the statement of cost of goods manufactured, and the statement of changes in financial position. The income statement shows the results of a firm's operations over a period

of time, usually one year. The balance sheet is a statement that shows a firm's financial position at a specific date. The statement of cost of goods manufactured is a supporting, detailed schedule of the cost of goods produced. The statement of changes in financial position accounts for changes in working capital.

3. Financial statements serve as the basis for computing financial ratios. These ratios can be grouped into those relating to working-capital position, sales position, profitability, and debt position.
4. The major components of a master budget are a sales budget (the customary starting point in preparing the master budget), a production budget, and a purchases budget. Certain supporting budget schedules which are used to develop the master budget cover estimates for materials, direct labor, manufacturing expense, cost of goods manufactured and sold, selling and administrative expense, accounts receivable, and cash.
5. The budget, when properly used, is an effective tool in controlling expenses. In this regard, first it is important to know which expenses can be controlled and/or reduced. Second, the standards for expenses of each kind must be set so that the manager will know whether overspending or underspending is occurring. Greater attention should be given to major items of expense rather than to minor items.

DISCUSSION QUESTIONS

1. Explain the accounting convention that income is realized when earned whether or not it has been received in cash.
2. Should entrepreneurs have an accounting system set up for their proposed small firm—or do it themselves? Why?
3. What is the relationship between the income statement and the balance sheet?
4. What is the disadvantage of having too low an inventory turnover?
5. Explain the danger in having too high a debt-to-total-assets ratio in a small firm.
6. What factors might lead to a requirement for budget changes during the budget period? Explain.
7. If a business firm could predict its sales volume quite accurately, would there be any point in budgeting? Explain.
8. What are the relationships between a firm's production budget and its sales and purchases budgets?
9. Can "fixed" expenses be controlled? Are they really always "fixed"? Cite some examples for answers to both questions.
10. What is the nature of an expense classification by function? Of what value is it to the manager?

REFERENCES TO SMALL BUSINESS IN ACTION

Blotnick, Srully. "Ask the Man Who Hates One." *Forbes,* Vol. 125, No. 2 (January 21, 1980), pp. 94-95.

The author reports how the financial statements of a small business may distort profitability due to poor record-keeping practices.

Grabowsky, Alex L. "What to Monitor to Stay in Control." *Inc.,* Vol. 3, No. 3 (March, 1981), pp. 74-76.

A chief executive officer explains a practical internal monitoring system which has helped him keep track of business operations.

Rashkow, Bertram R. "How to Set the Right Price." *Inc.,* Vol. 3, No. 2 (February, 1981), pp. 54-58.

This article demonstrates how to re-format the traditional income statement for purposes of comparing alternative price changes.

Chapter 19

Working-Capital Management and Capital Budgeting

LOOKING AHEAD

Watch for the following important topics:

1. Definitions of key financial terms.
2. The cash-flow system in a small business.
3. Managing accounts receivable, inventory, and accounts payable.
4. Capital-budgeting methods in the small business.
5. Considerations in evaluating expansion opportunities.

Sound working-capital management must be practiced by a small business so that its working capital will be available to meet all obligations in a timely fashion. In addition, the small business will lose profitable expansion opportunities if it does not engage in capital budgeting. Too often the financial planning of a small business is neglected, compounding the problems of an already weak capital structure. Unfortunately much of the financial theory subscribed to by big business is too complex and overwhelming for a small-business manager and is therefore inappropriate. In this chapter we will present a more practical orientation to working-capital management and capital budgeting for the small firm.

DEFINITIONS OF KEY FINANCIAL TERMS

The student of financial management is quickly confused in a sea of inconsistently applied financial terms. This problem is noted in a leading financial management textbook with the following comment on the definition of "funds":

> Funds may be defined in several different ways, depending upon the purpose of the analysis. Although they are often defined as cash, many analysts treat funds as working capital–a somewhat broader definition. Other definitions are possible, although the two described are the most common by far. Depending upon the analyst's objective, the definition can be broadened or narrowed.[1]

Another important financial term, "capital," is also used to mean different things. A quick glance at a dictionary will reveal several definitions for this term.

Why so much confusion? The answer probably lies in the differing perspectives of accountants and financial managers. For our purposes in this chapter, the following financial terms will be used as defined below.

1. **Capital** denotes all the possessions of a small business which are devoted to the earning of income. It consists of two types: current-asset capital and fixed-asset capital.
2. **Current-asset capital** includes cash and those assets that will be converted to cash within the near future. Accountants generally consider the "near future" to be one year, and we accept this meaning.
3. **Fixed-asset capital** consists of assets intended for long, continued use such as buildings and equipment.
4. **Working capital** is the difference between current assets and current liabilities.
5. **Funds** include money, checks received but not yet deposited, and balances on deposit with financial institutions. A firm's funds do not include such noncash current assets as accounts receivable and inventory.
6. **Working-capital management** concentrates on the management of current-asset capital and current liabilities.
7. **Capital budgeting** is the process of planning expenditures whose returns are expected to extend well into the future.

---

1. James C. Van Horne, *Financial Management and Policy* (5th ed.; Englewood Cliffs, NJ: Prentice-Hall, Inc., 1980), pp. 743-744.

WORKING-CAPITAL MANAGEMENT

The excitement of day-to-day business operations can isolate a small-business manager from potential working-capital problems. Failure to manage working capital usually has devastating consequences. For example, Dun & Bradstreet's 1975 study of business failures found that more than one in three had mismanaged operating expenses, receivables, and inventory accounts.[2]

Working capital is a concept representing the *net value* of tangible current assets since, by definition, working capital is current assets minus current liabilities. Therefore, the most logical approach to understanding working-capital management is one which analyzes the individual components of working capital: cash, accounts receivable, inventory, and accounts payable.[3]

ACTION REPORT: Profit You Can Spend

Cash problems often seem more troublesome to small firms than to large ones. Two businessmen with big-business backgrounds learned this lesson as they teamed up to run Omega Sports in St. Louis, MO.

Stanley Anonsen, chief executive officer of Omega, previously had 23 years of experience in a $400 million company. Anonsen's partner, John Prentis, had left the presidency of United Missouri Bank to manage Omega.

By 1977, Omega racquetball racquets had sold so well that the company had a cash crisis. Prentis says:

> As the presidents of large corporations, we had become used to looking at profit-and-loss statements. Unless there was a problem, we never bothered about cash flow. There was a whole financial staff to monitor specifics. When we tried to run our own business, we had to learn the difference between profit and profit-you-can-spend. We had a terrific P&L, but we had to borrow money to pay our bills.

Omega's major cash-flow problem centered around accounts receivable. Their customers were big enough to demand more time for payment. Omega's short-term solution included additional capital contributions by the partners and an additonal bank loan.

Source: Louise Melton, "He Tried to Play the New Game by the Old Rules," *Inc.*, Vol. 2, No. 10 (October, 1980), pp. 68-72.

---

2. "Survival Tips for Rough Times," *Nation's Business*, Vol. 68, No. 10 (October, 1980), p. 21.

3. Short-term investments (such as securities) and short-term liabilities (such as notes payable) are additional components of the working-capital equation but are ignored here as they are not a part of the capital requirements for the normal operating cycle.

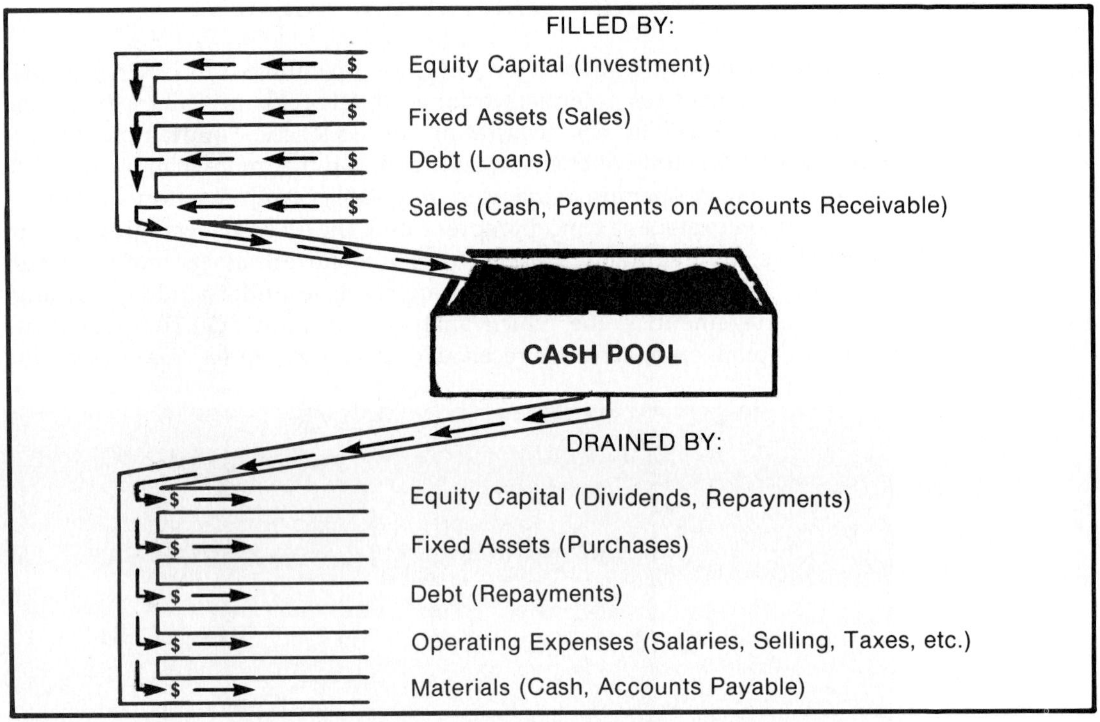

Figure 19-1 Major Determinants of the "Cash Pool" Level in Small Business

Managing the Cash Pool

Small-business managers can place undue emphasis on the income statement.[4] They must realize that a firm can "go under" with an income statement that shows a profit! Consider this situation: A firm has sales of $100,000 and expenses of $70,000. All sales and expenses are on credit. A simple income statement would show an exciting $30,000 profit. Nevertheless, the firm may be in trouble. If it cannot convert the $100,000 of accounts receivable into funds at the right time, it will be unable to pay the $70,000 accounts payable when due.

This simple scenario emphasizes the importance of understanding cash flow in a small business and the problems which occur when the flow is not managed properly. Cash must be cycled according to plans in order to make funds available when needed.

4. Stahrl W. Edmunds, "Performance Measures for Small Businesses," *Harvard Business Review,* Vol. 57, No. 1 (January-February, 1979), p. 174.

ACTION REPORT: Managing Cash with Common Sense

George Mason is president of Crossroads Press, Inc., a Hawaii publishing company, which was incorporated in 1963 with 3 employees. In 8 years, the company grew to employ 33 full-time people.

During these years, Mason encountered numerous money-management problems. He views money management with a common-sense perspective. Concerning his own money management, Mason says, "Last year more than 18% of our pretax profits were from earnings on company cash. Our daily average checking balance so far this year has been $4,300."

Regarding money management by others, he says:

> Strangely, many small- and medium-size businesses live with a lot of false impressions about money and banking. I have known some who keep $60,000 to $300,000 in checking accounts; others still haven't heard that a business can put idle money in money-market funds.

Mason was recently honored as Hawaii's Small-Business Person of the Year.

Source: Personal correspondence with George Mason, August 19, 1981.

In a cash-flow system, funds move constantly from one form of capital into another. The challenge for the small-business manager is to have this capital in the optimum form at the appropriate time. The "cash pool" is a vital component of the system. It can be equated to a swimming pool with the entrepreneur as the owner-swimmer. He cannot enjoy a cash pool which is empty or which is overflowing and wasting potential earning power.

The scope of cash management in small business can be visualized with the aid of Figure 19-1, which depicts the numerous demands on a cash pool and the sources which replenish its level. Notice that some sources of incoming funds seem similar to sources of cash depletion. For example, when a building is purchased, it requires cash; but when it is sold, it provides cash.

With proper financial monitoring, the "pipes" which fill and drain the cash pool can be kept unclogged and moving according to plans. For example, when inventories are lower than desired, they can be replenished with funds from the cash pool. If the pool is low, however, it may first need filling with a short-term loan. These tactics are possible when proper cash forecasting has been initiated. Figure 19-2 shows a simple cash forecast form which can aid in funds planning. The forecast form also allows space for recording actual cash receipts and disbursements, which may differ from the forecasted amounts.

	January		February		March		April	
	Est.	Act.	Est.	Act.	Est.	Act.	Est.	Act.
Cash balance beginning of month	____	____	____	____	____	____	____	____
RECEIPTS:								
Accounts-receivable collections	____	____	____	____	____	____	____	____
Bank loan proceeds	____	____	____	____	____	____	____	____
TOTAL CASH AVAILABLE	____	____	____	____	____	____	____	____
DISBURSEMENTS:								
Trade payables	____	____	____	____	____	____	____	____
Payroll—hourly	____	____	____	____	____	____	____	____
Payroll—salary	____	____	____	____	____	____	____	____
General expenses	____	____	____	____	____	____	____	____
Selling expenses	____	____	____	____	____	____	____	____
Capital additions	____	____	____	____	____	____	____	____
Income taxes, local, state, federal	____	____	____	____	____	____	____	____
Bank loan repayment	____	____	____	____	____	____	____	____
Total disbursements	____	____	____	____	____	____	____	____
CASH BALANCE END OF MONTH	____	____	____	____	____	____	____	____
Less minimum balances	____	____	____	____	____	____	____	____
ESTIMATED AMOUNT OF CASH AVAILABLE	____	____	____	____	____	____	____	____

Source: U. S. Small Business Administration, *Managing for Profits* (Washington: U. S. Government Printing Office, 1981), p. 81.

Figure 19-2 Cash Forecast Form

On those occasions when a small business has idle funds, the cash should be invested. The cash forecast is a basis of anticipating these occasions. If unexpected excess funds are generated, they can be invested also. Many short-term investment opportunities are available. Certificates of deposit and money market certificates are just two of the many vehicles for putting excess cash to work for the firm.

Managing Accounts Receivable

In Chapter 10 some credit activities of small businesses were discussed. At that point, we emphasized the types of credit and the granting of credit with a brief mention of credit-collection techniques. An effective collection system converts accounts receivable to cash at the earliest agreed-upon time. In this chapter we will treat two other aspects of accounts-receivable management–the aging of accounts receivable and the life cycle of accounts receivable.

Aging Accounts Receivable. Many small businesses can benefit from an aging schedule which divides accounts receivable into age categories based on the length of time they have been outstanding. Usually some accounts are current and others are past due. Various collection actions can be used for different-aged accounts. With successive scheduling, troublesome trends can be spotted and appropriate action taken. With experience, the probabilities of collecting accounts of various ages can be estimated and used to forecast cash conversion rates.

Table 19-1 Hypothetical Aging of Accounts Receivable

Account Status	Customer Account Number					Total
	001	002	003	004	005	
120 days	–	–	$50,000	–	–	$ 50,000
90 days	–	$ 10,000	–	–	–	10,000
60 days	–	–	–	$40,000	–	40,000
30 days	–	20,000	20,000	–	–	40,000
15 days	$50,000	–	10,000	–	–	60,000
Total Overdue	$50,000	$ 30,000	$80,000	$40,000	0	$200,000
Not Due (beyond-discount period)	$30,000	$ 10,000	0	$10,000	$130,000	$180,000
Not Due (still in discount period)	$20,000	$100,000	0	$90,000	$220,000	$430,000
Credit Rating	A	B	C	A	A	

Table 19-1 shows a hypothetical aging of accounts receivable. It shows that four customers have overdue payments totaling $200,000. Only Customer 005 is current. Customer 003 has the largest amount ($80,000) of overdue credit. In fact, the schedule shows that Customer 003 is overdue on all charges and has a past record of slow payment (a credit rating of "C"). Immediate attention to collecting from this customer is necessary. Customer 002 should be contacted also. The status of this customer is critical because, among overdue accounts, Customer 002 has the largest amount ($110,000) in the "Not Due" classifications. This customer could quickly have the largest amount overdue.

Customers 004 and 001 need a special kind of analysis. Customer 004 has $10,000 less overdue than Customer 001. However, Customer 004's overdue credit of $40,000, which is 60 days past due, may well have a serious impact on the $100,000 not yet due ($10,000 in the beyond-discount period plus $90,000 still in the discount period). On the other hand, even though Customer 001 has $50,000 of overdue credit, he or she is overdue only 15 days. Also, Customer 001 has only $50,000 not yet due ($30,000 in the beyond-discount period plus $20,000 still in the discount period) as compared to $100,000 not yet due from Customer 004. Both customers have a credit rating of "A". In conclusion, Customer 001 is a better potential source of cash; so, collection efforts need to begin with Customer 004 rather than with Customer 001. Customer 001 may simply need a reminder that he or she has an overdue account of $50,000.

The Life Cycle of Receivables. Even with timely payment by creditors, the conversion of accounts receivable into cash does not occur instantaneously. The stages in the billing and collection cycle consume a large amount of time. The small-business manager should understand these stages so that tactics can be planned and implemented to minimize the overall cycle time. One clear conceptualization of this life cycle identifies the following five stages.

1. Invoice preparation.
2. Mail transit.
3. Customer processing.
4. Funds remittance.
5. Collection.[5]

Problems may occur in each stage. As an example of stage 1 – invoice preparation – the president of a manufacturing company learned of a five-day lag in invoice mailing. The president found that "the shipping office at his plant was batching invoices before forwarding them to the administrative staff

5. William Barent Wemple, "Where Are Your Receivables Right Now?" *Inc.*, Vol. 3, No. 4 (April, 1981), pp. 86-88.

for processing and mailing."[6] By processing invoices immediately after they were written, time was reduced and the cash cycle expedited.

Each stage of the life cycle of receivables should be similarly scrutinized. One day saved at each stage means funds will be available five days sooner.[7]

Managing Inventory

Inventory is a "necessary evil" to the financial-management system. It is necessary because supply and demand cannot be manipulated to coincide precisely in day-to-day operations. It is an evil because inventory ties up funds which are not actively productive.

Inventory is a bigger problem to some small businesses than to others. For example, by and large, service firms create their "product" as it is sold. Inventories of supplies are, therefore, the only tangible inventory which they have. A manufacturer, on the other hand, has several inventories—raw materials, finished goods, and supplies. Also, retailers and wholesalers, especially those with high inventory turnover rates (such as those in grocery distribution), are continually involved in inventory-management problems.

In Chapter 17 we discussed several ideas related to purchasing and inventory management which were designed to minimize inventory-carrying costs and processing costs. At this point, we wish to emphasize practices which will minimize average inventory levels, thereby releasing funds for other applications. A correct minimum of inventory is the level needed to maintain desired production schedules or a required level of customer service. A concerted effort to manage inventory can trim inventory fat and pay handsome dividends. For example, the Boston-based Superior Pet Products Company tightened its inventory policies and freed up about $400,000 in capital. This released capital also meant a savings of $80,000 in interest expense, which was being paid to finance the inventory.[8]

Staying on Top of Inventory. One of the first tactics of managing inventory to reduce capital investment is to discover what is in inventory and how long it has been there. Too often, items are purchased, warehoused, and essentially lost! A yearly inventory for accounting purposes is inadequate for good inventory control. Items that are slow-movers may sit in a retailer's inventory beyond the time when markdowns should have been applied.

Computers can provide assistance in inventory identification and control. The use of physical inventories may still be required but only as a supplement to the computer system.

---

6. *Ibid.*

7. The advantages and disadvantages of several collection techniques are set out in John A. Welsh and Jerry F. White, *Administering the Closely Held Company* (Englewood Cliffs, NJ: Prentice-Hall, Inc., 1980), Chapter 2.

8. "How to Unlock Your Company's Hidden Cash," *Inc.*, Vol. 2, No. 7 (July, 1980), p. 64.

Holding the Reins on Stockpiling. Some small-business managers tend to overbuy inventory. There are several possible reasons for this behavior. First, the entrepreneur's enthusiasm may forecast greater demand than is realistic. Second, the personalization of the business-customer relationship may motivate the manager to stock everything customers want. Third, the price-conscious entrepreneur may overly subscribe to vendor appeal—"buy now, prices are going up."

Stockpiling is not bad per se. Improperly managed and uncontrolled stockpiling may, however, greatly increase carrying costs and place a heavy drain on the funds of a small business. Restraint must be exercised with stockpiling efforts.

Managing Accounts Payable

Small businesses are legally and ethically bound to pay their debts. This is not debatable. They are also expected to pay their bills when due. However, there may be some flexibility as to the timing of payments. Also, debt obligations can be renegotiated and payment rescheduled. Therefore, financial management of accounts payable hinges on negotiation and timing.

Negotiation. Any business is subject to emergencies, which may lead to a request for the postponement of its payable obligations. If a firm finds itself in this situation, it should so inform its creditors. Usually creditors will cooperate in working out a solution because they are interested in the firm and want it to succeed.

Table 19-2 An Accounts-Payable Timetable

Timetable (Days after invoice date)	Account Settlement Costs for a $100,000 Purchase (Terms: 3/10, net 30)
Day 1 through Day 10	$97,000
Day 11 through Day 30	$100,000
Day 31 and thereafter	$100,000 + possible late penalty + deterioration in credit standing

Timing. It would not be surprising to find the motto "Buy Now, Pay Later, Later, Later..." over all entrepreneurs' desks. By buying on credit, a small

ACTION REPORT: Stretching Payables for Cash

Small businesses can experience financial difficulties from rapid growth even with strong profit-and-loss statements. One of these financial difficulties centers on cash flow.

Derma Science Laboratory, Inc., is a manufacturer and retailer of organic cosmetics located near Dallas, TX. Luci Flint and her husband founded the company and "operated on the premise that paying her bills promptly was good business." As the company grew, Mrs. Flint "began to find she was increasingly strapped for cash." Her company was experiencing a classic cash-flow problem.

Her banker advised against a bank loan because it would provide only a temporary solution. Rather, the banker suggested that the Flints control accounts payable to loosen working capital. Mrs. Flint began to calculate how much delay she could build into accounts payable and still retain a good credit rating. A writer states:

> Flint's evaluation of her suppliers and the additional time she devoted to monitoring her payables carefully had impressive results. As the company has grown, accounts payable now average $130,000 and stretch for 45 days. By stretching payables from 22 to 45 days, Flint points out, she has in effect generated $65,000 in interest-free cash from her suppliers, an amount that will grow almost automatically as her purchases increase.

In stretching payments to improve cash flow, a debtor firm must be careful not to delay them beyond the specified due dates. This would violate the contracted agreement and damage the firm's credit standing.

Source: Harrison L. Moore, "Borrow from Stretched Payables," *Inc.*, Vol. 2, No. 7 (July, 1980), pp. 62, 64, 67.

business is using creditors' funds to supply short-term cash needs. The longer the creditors' funds can be "borrowed," the better. Payment, therefore, should seemingly be made as late as the agreement specifies.

Typically trade credit will include payment terms which contain a cash discount. For example, terms of 3/10, net 30 would offer a 3 percent potential discount. With trade discount terms, the entrepreneur's motto mentioned above may be inappropriate. As an explanation, begin by looking at Table 19-2, which shows the possible settlement cost over the credit period of 30 days. For a $100,000 purchase, a settlement of only $97,000 is required if payment is made within the first 10 days ($100,000 minus the 3 percent discount of $3,000). During the interim between day 11 and day 31, a settlement of $100,000 is required. After 30 days, the settlement cost may even exceed the original amount, as the table indicates.

The timing question is: Should the account be paid on day 10 or day 30? There is little support for paying $97,000 on day 1 through day 9 when the same amount will settle the account on day 10. Likewise, if payment is to be made after day 10, why not wait until day 30 to pay $100,000?

It is clear that payment should be made on day 30 if not on day 10. But why would payment be made on day 10 (taking the discount) rather than on day 30 (with no discount)? The answer lies in the concept of opportunity costs.[9] Consider carefully the following logic. If the business takes the discount, there is no opportunity cost for the use of the trade credit during the discount period. Likewise, there is no opportunity cost if the credit terms offer no cash discount. Therefore, the justification for taking the discount is in the "opportunity" to earn $3,000 for the 20-day period from day 10 to day 30.

Figures which develop the opportunity costs of a cash discount customarily compute an annualized interest rate which transforms the discount rate into a more meaningful percentage. This computation for the example in Table 19-2 is:

$$\text{Annualized rate} = \frac{\text{Days in year}}{\text{Net period} - \text{Cash discount period}} \times \frac{\text{Cash discount \%}}{100\% - \text{Cash discount \%}}$$

$$= \frac{365}{30 - 10} \times \frac{.03}{1.00 - .03}$$

$$= 18.25 \times .030928$$

$$= 56.4\%$$

By failing to take the discount, the business is losing the "opportunity" to earn the equivalent of 56.4 percent on its money. If funds are short and cannot be obtained easily, however, the small business may find itself paying on the last possible date and incurring the opportunity cost.

CAPITAL BUDGETING IN SMALL BUSINESS

The manager of a going concern must find time to search for alternative prospective investments if the business is to grow. After assessing the availability of expansion capital, the manager must determine the most profitable use of such funds by appraising the alternative investment opportunities open to the small firm.

Capital budgeting assumes that the firm's supply of capital is limited and that it should be rationed in such a way as to provide funds for the best

9. An opportunity cost is the value of a lost opportunity. If you see a dollar on the floor and pass it by, your "opportunity," which went unexercised, cost you one dollar!

investment proposals. In its broadest sense, capital budgeting includes investments of both a long-range and a short-range nature. In this chapter, however, our concern is with long-range financial commitments; and the discussion that follows deals exclusively with long-range movements of funds.

What are some typical investment proposals entailing an outlay of funds that a small manufacturer might be contemplating at one time? Below are some examples.

1. Development and introduction of a new product that shows promise but requires additional study and improvement.
2. Replacement of the company's delivery trucks with newer models.
3. Expansion of sales activity into a new territory.
4. Construction of a new building.
5. Employment of several additional salespersons for more intensive selling in the existing market.

Because capital is insufficient to finance all five investment proposals, the owner-manager must decide which of them must be postponed or rejected and which must be accepted. Both the cost of capital and the absolute limit on the volume of available funds require the rejection not only of proposals that would be unprofitable, but also of those that would be *least* profitable. A ranking of the alternative investment proposals according to their profitability can be made after each proposal has been evaluated.

Traditional Methods of Investment Valuation

Two rule-of-thumb methods of evaluating investment proposals are the payback-period method and the return-on-investment method. In using either of these methods, only net additions to costs or profits are considered. For example, if a partially depreciated machine is to be replaced, the book value of the old machine is ignored except for the purpose of calculating the tax impact of resale at a price differing from book value. Of course, any salvage or trade-in value of the old machine would be considered in computing the investment cost.

The greatest value of these traditional methods lies in their simplicity. They provide a rough check for evaluating an investment. Although they have definite limitations when compared with the more sophisticated valuation tools described later in this chapter, they are widely used and often provide satisfactory answers.[10]

10. Recent studies which show the widespread preference for these methods are: Rolf O. Christiansen and Crumpton Ferrell, "Survey of Capital Budgeting Methods Used by Medium-Size Manufacturing Firms," *Baylor Business Studies,* Vol. 11, No. 4 (January, 1981), pp. 35-43; and Donald M. Pattillo, "Capital Investment Practices of Small Manufacturers: America Versus Multinational," *Journal of Small Business Management,* Vol. 19, No. 2 (April, 1981), pp. 29-36.

Payback-Period Method. The **payback-period method** shows the number of years it takes to recover the original cost of an investment from annual net cash flows. Suppose that a firm is considering Project A and Project B, each of which requires an investment of $100,000. The estimated annual cash flows (profit plus depreciation) from the two projects are as follows:

Economic Life (Year)	Cash Flow Project A	Cash Flow Project B
1	$50,000	$10,000
2	40,000	20,000
3	10,000	30,000
4	10,000	40,000
5		50,000
6		60,000
	$110,000	$210,000

The payback period for Project A is three years; for Project B, four years. If the firm ordinarily sets three years as its standard payback period, then Project A will be accepted and Project B rejected.

Return-on-Investment Method. The simple **return-on-investment method** evaluates proposals by relating the expected annual profit from an investment to the amount invested. This method is expressed in the following equation:

$$\text{Rate of return} = \frac{\text{Annual profit}}{\text{Investment}}$$

If the expected return on an investment of $100,000 is $20,000, the rate of return will be 20 percent. Such an investment is justified if more lucrative investments are not available and if a return of 20 percent is reasonable in view of the risk involved.

Weaknesses of Traditional Methods. The payback-period method and the return-on-investment method are subject to two major weaknesses. First, they fail to recognize the time value of money.[11] For example, suppose Projects C and D, each of which costs $10,000, had net cash flows listed on page 485. Both projects have a three-year payback, which makes them equally attractive when judged by this criterion. But we know that a dollar today is worth more than a dollar a year from today because the dollar can earn interest during the year. Therefore, Project C with its faster cash flow is more desirable.

11. For an unusually clear explanation of the time value of money, see Bertram R. Raskon, "The Longer You Wait for Cash, the Less It's Worth," *Inc.*, Vol. 2, No. 5 (May, 1980), pp. 65-68.

Year	Cash Flow Project C	Cash Flow Project D
1	$ 5,000	$ 1,000
2	4,000	4,000
3	1,000	5,000
	$10,000	$10,000

The second weakness of the traditional methods is their neglect of the economic life of a project. Going back to the annual cash flows from Projects A and B listed on page 484, we note that the payback period of Project B is a year longer than that of Project A. But Project B's longer economic life of 6 years provides $100,000 more in total cash flow than Project A. In a similar manner, a simple rate-of-return method gives no indication of the length of time during which that rate of return may be expected to continue.

Theoretically Correct Methods of Investment Valuation

Two valuation methods designed to eliminate the defects of traditional methods are the net-present-value method and the internal-rate-of-return method.[12]

Net-Present-Value Method. **Present value** means the value today of a stream of expected net cash flows, discounted at an appropriate rate of interest. The **net-present-value method** is calculated by means of the following formula:

$$V = \left[\frac{Q_1}{(1+r)} + \frac{Q_2}{(1+r)^2} + \ldots + \frac{Q_n}{(1+r)^n} + \frac{S}{(1+r)^n}\right] - C$$

where V = excess present value over cost

Q_t = post-tax cash flow in year t (where t is 1, 2, 3, . . . n)

S = terminal salvage value

r = selected rate of interest

C = cost of asset/project

n = useful life of asset/project

12. The formulas presented in this text, used with permission of the publisher, are from Martin B. Solomon, Jr., *Investment Decisions in Small Business,* Small Business Management Research Report. Prepared by the University of Kentucky under a grant by the Small Business Administration, Washington, DC (Lexington: University of Kentucky Press, 1963), pp. 13-17.

Note that the present-value symbol, V, represents the net value of the investment over and above the cost of the project and the firm's cost of capital. The selected rate of interest, r, is usually a firm's cost of capital. When the net present value is negative, the project should be rejected. When it is positive, the project should be accepted because the value of the firm increases by the amount of the net present value of the project.

To illustrate, let us calculate the net present value of Projects A and B, previously cited, assuming a 10 percent cost of capital. Also assume that neither project has any salvage value. By using the above formula, the net present value of Project A is calculated as follows:

$$V = \left[\frac{Q_1}{(1 + r)} + \frac{Q_2}{(1 + r)^2} + \frac{Q_3}{(1 + r)^3} + \frac{Q_4}{(1 + r)^4}\right] - C$$

where Q_1 = cash flow in year 1 = \$50,000
Q_2 = cash flow in year 2 = \$40,000
Q_3 = cash flow in year 3 = \$10,000
Q_4 = cash flow in year 4 = \$10,000
r = 10%
C = \$100,000
n = 4 years

$$V = \left[\frac{50{,}000}{1.1} + \frac{40{,}000}{1.21} + \frac{10{,}000}{1.33} + \frac{10{,}000}{1.46}\right] - 100{,}000$$

$$V = [45{,}455 + 33{,}058 + 7{,}519 + 6{,}849] - 100{,}000$$

$$V = -\ 7{,}119$$

With a *negative* present value of \$7,119, Project A should be rejected.[13]

Calculating the net present value of Project B, the formula would be applied as follows:

$$V = \left[\frac{10{,}000}{1.1} + \frac{20{,}000}{1.21} + \frac{30{,}000}{1.33} + \frac{40{,}000}{1.46} + \frac{50{,}000}{1.61} + \frac{60{,}000}{1.77}\right] - 100{,}000$$

$$V = [9{,}091 + 16{,}529 + 22{,}556 + 27{,}397 + 31{,}056 + 33{,}898] - 100{,}000$$

$$V = 40{,}527$$

---

13. The use of interest factors found in present-value tables would facilitate the solution of these problems.

Since Project B yields a *positive* net present value of $40,527, this project should be accepted.[14]

Internal-Rate-of-Return Method. In using the **internal-rate-of-return method,** one first finds that rate of return which equates the cost of the investment project with the present value of its net cash flows. The formula to be applied is the following, which is basically the same as that of the net-present-value method:

$$C = \frac{Q_1}{(1 + r)} + \frac{Q_2}{(1 + r)^2} + \cdots + \frac{Q_n + S}{(1 + r)^n}$$

where Q_t = post-tax cash flow in year t (where t is 1, 2, 3, . . . n)
C = cost of asset/project
n = useful life of asset/project
r = unknown rate of return
S = terminal salvage value

The internal rate of return on the project may be found by trial and error, starting with any arbitrarily selected rate of interest. Then compute the present value of the cash flows and compare it with the cost of the project. If the present value is higher than the project's cost, try a higher interest rate and go through the procedure again. Conversely, if the present value obtained is lower than the project's cost, try a lower rate of interest and repeat the process. Continue this procedure until the present value obtained is approximately equal to the project's cost. The interest rate that brings about this equality is the internal rate of return of that particular project.

To calculate the internal rate of return for Project A, again assuming that there is no salvage value, we can start with the firm's cost of capital, which has already been given as 10 percent. By substituting 10 percent for r, we find that the present value of the net cash flows of Project A is less than its initial cost of $100,000.

$$V = \frac{50{,}000}{1.1} + \frac{40{,}000}{1.21} + \frac{10{,}000}{1.33} + \frac{10{,}000}{1.46}$$

$$V = 45{,}455 + 33{,}058 + 7{,}519 + 6{,}849$$

$$V = 92{,}881$$

14. Rounding off the denominators in the equation or rounding off interest factors in present-value tables would give slightly different answers.

By repeating the procedure with lower interest rates, we find that the interest rate which will equate the present value of the net cash flows with the project's initial cost is somewhere between 5 percent and 6 percent.

Once the internal rate of return of a particular project is calculated, it can be compared with the firm's current cost of capital (or cost of debt). If the particular project's internal rate of return is calculated to be the same as the firm's cost of capital, the firm would simply be breaking even if it went ahead with the project. If the calculated internal rate of return exceeds the firm's cost of capital, the project would be profitable. But if the calculated internal rate of return is less than the firm's cost of capital, as is the case for Project A, the result would be a loss.

Criticisms of Theoretically Correct Methods. Even though these methods are theoretically superior to the traditional ones, they are not widely used in small businesses. The typical small-business manager is unaware of the existence of these methods and would not readily understand the underlying reasoning and analysis involved. In addition, the solution of problems through these methods is often time-consuming and may require the use of an electronic computer.

Perhaps the greatest deterrent to the use of theoretically correct valuation methods is the extreme uncertainty that surrounds many investment decisions. If great uncertainty about future demands or costs exists, the use of sophisticated methods may provide little practical guidance. Instead, the small-business entrepreneur may prefer to base decisions on short-run prospects—for example, approving an investment that seems likely to return the invested capital in one or two years.

OTHER CONSIDERATIONS IN EVALUATING EXPANSION OPPORTUNITIES

Having focused on capital-budgeting methods for evaluating investments in expansion opportunities, let us now turn to other considerations that enter into expansion decisions. These considerations involve a firm's growth philosophy, search activity, and approach to financing the expansion.

Growth Philosophy

There are many entrepreneurs who prefer smallness. They are content with their past growth and intentionally ignore further expansion. For example, L. C. Martin, president and chief operating officer of "tiny" Aztec Manufacturing in Crowley, TX, says, "I never really wanted to be rich. What I

ACTION REPORT: Growth Pains

Successful growth provides its own unique problems for the small business. Growth strategy must be laid carefully to prevent undue stress on existing operations.

Sandy Ruby's Tech HiFi chain started in 1967 with a few stereo component sales to fellow MIT students. His first stores were all located next to the campuses where his young college customers lived and worked. One writer notes:

> To Ruby's delight, eager young customers snatched components off his store shelves almost faster than Tech HiFi's salespeople could replace them. "We began to think everything we tried would be a winner," he recalls. It was a reasonable assumption: By 1973, six-year-old Tech HiFi had mushroomed into a chain of 16 stores, with sales that topped $12 million.

Ruby's ambition was to grow and the time seemed right. Within a year, 15 new stores were opened near college campuses. However, sales faltered and profits dropped. "Ruby's new stores were scattered all over the map, some in markets too isolated to manage effectively, others in suburbs where Ruby belatedly discovered there was far less enthusiasm for stereo components than in Tech HiFi's usual college locations."

Ruby put a hold on expansion and began to bring overhead under control. The company recovered but not until, according to Ruby, he had lost his own net worth in the business.

Source: Jeffrey Tarter, "Can He Keep His Customers Tuned In?" *Inc.*, Vol. 2, No. 11 (November, 1980), pp. 73-78.

wanted was to work in a small-company environment, and that's what I've got."[15]

Many other small-business owners, however, carry growth ambitions from the very early days of starting their businesses. Growth is a continuing goal for these entrepreneurs. For example, Carl Karcher, who founded Carl's Jr. Hamburgers in California in 1941, expresses his personal growth philosophy by saying, "If your company decides not to grow, that's the beginning of the end."[16]

But growth is not without its potential problems. Expansion can strain a firm's capital position and damage current operations. It can also spread managerial skills too thinly.

---

15. Phyllis Berman, "Close to the Vest," *Forbes*, Vol. 127, No. 9 (April 27, 1981), p. 104.

16. Doris A. Byron, "Carl's Jr.: 306-Unit Restaurant Chain Began as a Hot Dog Cart," *Los Angeles Times*, May 26, 1981, p. 1.

Search Activity

All growth opportunities must be scrutinized carefully. For too long, small business has been saddled with the reputation of making growth decisions without extensive search. Small-business managers have often considered growth opportunities on a one-at-a-time basis. They have been less concerned with ranking a number of growth possibilities than with trying to determine the merit of one particular proposal. Moreover, in the analysis of a single proposal, they have often jumped to a conclusion on the basis of sketchy information. The following case illustrates a behavior pattern of this type:

> Mr. E, a dry cleaner, had an opportunity to open a branch dry cleaning store in a new shopping center. After looking at the center, talking to associates, and computing a break-even point, he decided to invest. His demand estimate was based on information given to him by the promoter of the shopping center.
>
> The search for information was both spontaneous and non-programmed. Mr. E had no predetermined approach to the collection of data. He devoted little time to finding sources of information for demand estimates, such as city planning and zoning maps of population. He had no time for such things because of involvement in the day-to-day details of his business. He did not delegate many routine tasks in maintenance, collections, and deliveries.
>
> Similarly, the search for alternatives was neither planned nor programmed. Mr. E did consider the possible purchase of common stock as an alternative to opening the branch store, but the search went no further. Instead of seeking out still other alternatives, he considered only proposals brought to his attention; this was true of the branch-store proposal itself. The issue in this case is whether the delegation of routine tasks would have profited Mr. E by providing him with time for more concentrated attention to investment alternatives.[17]

The apparent deficiencies in small-business search activity provide an opportunity for improvement in the quality of small-business investment decisions. By breaking out of the pattern of routine activity or by delegating such work to others, the small-business entrepreneur can make more time for the search activity that leads to more profitable expansion.

Friends and acquaintances who are in management positions with other firms are valuable sources of information about expansion opportunities. Many other professionals, such as lawyers and bankers, are also reliable sources of this type of information. Trade journals and publications, such as *The Wall Street Journal,* can also contain notifications of purchase opportunities which represent potential growth developments.

---

17. Solomon, *op. cit.*, p. 96.

Approach to Financing the Expansion

The financing of expansion is usually a major consideration in growth plans. Financing can be internal or external. Many of the sources of initial financing discussed in Chapter 7 also provide expansion funds. An entrepreneur's past success with a new venture will usually make the financing of expansion easier than start-up financing. However, there can be constraining factors which limit full funding of expansion opportunities. Harold Heinold, now a major marketer of hogs, grew from a small buyer by rapid and aggressive expansion. But still he says, "I never could raise enough money to do the things I wanted to do, never enough to take advantage of all the opportunities that came along."[18]

Realized profits that are plowed back into the business, or **retained earnings,** constitute a major source of funds for financing small-business expansion. Such internally generated funds may be invested in physical facilities or used to expand the firm's working capital. It is likely that the majority of small firms experience an annual growth in net worth as a result of retained earnings.

In using retained earnings, the rate of expansion is limited by the amount of profits generated by the business. In the case of a rapidly expanding small firm, these funds are often insufficient to meet the heavy capital needs.

Financing through retained earnings provides a conservative approach to expansion. The dangers of overexpansion or expansion that is too rapid are largely avoided. Because the additional funds are equity, the firm has no creditors threatening foreclosure and no due dates by which repayment must be made.

The lack of an interest charge on funds secured in this way may create the impression that there is no cost involved in their use. Even though there is no out-of-pocket cost, there is a definite opportunity cost involved. This opportunity cost is the dividend foregone by stockholders. Presumably the stockholders could have reinvested their dividends in other income-generating opportunities.

LOOKING BACK

1. *Capital* refers to the possessions of a business which are devoted to the earning of income. *Current-asset capital* consists of cash and assets that are normally converted to cash within a year's time. *Fixed-asset capital* consists

18. Dick Braun, "One in 17 Grunts Comes from a Heinold Pig," *Farm Journal*, Vol. 105, No. 11 (September, 1981), p. 43.

of assets intended for long, continued use such as buildings and equipment. *Working capital* is current-assets minus current liabilities. *Funds* refers to cash and includes checks received but not yet deposited and balances on deposit with financial institutions. *Working-capital management* concentrates on the management of current-asset capital and current liabilities. *Capital budgeting* is the process of planning expenditures whose returns are expected to extend well into the future.

2. The sources of funds which fill the cash pool are cash sales, payments on accounts receivable, loans, sales of fixed assets, and equity investments. The cash pool is drained by cash payment of material purchases, accounts payable, operating expenses, debt repayment, equity payment, and fixed-asset purchases.
3. An aging schedule provides a breakdown of receivables by age of the individual accounts. The five stages of the life cycle of receivables are: invoice preparation, mail transit, customer processing, funds remittance, and collection.

   Periodic inventorying is essential to good inventory control. Stockpiling should be monitored to avoid undue drains on funds.

   Accounts payable should be paid in accordance with prior agreements but can be negotiated to fit financial situations. Trade discounts can provide a profitable reward for paying accounts earlier than required.
4. The most popular capital-budgeting techniques among small businesses are the payback-period and the return-on-investment methods. The net-present-value method and the internal-rate-of-return method are additional techniques which are considered to be theoretically correct.
5. Small business has various expansion philosophies. Expansion success is facilitated by proper search activity and available financing. Most sources of initial financing can also be approached for expansion support. Retained earnings can be used to finance expansion.

DISCUSSION QUESTIONS

1. Explain the difference between fixed-asset capital and working capital. What is meant by the statement that "working capital is a concept representing the net value of tangible current items"?
2. Explain how a firm may be unable to pay its bills when its income statement shows a profit.
3. What is the principal purpose of aging accounts receivable? Why would an aging schedule show "net-due" credits as well as those which are past due?
4. Can you think of ways to expedite the life cycle of receivables? Give an example for each stage of this cycle.

5. Do you think a business has an obligation to pay its accounts payable before the net-due date if it has the funds? Why or why not?

6. Compute the annualized interest rate which represents the opportunity cost on credit terms of "3/10, net 50." Compare this rate with the one in the text on page 482. Explain the difference.

7. What appear to be the principal weaknesses of traditional capital-budgeting methods used by small-business firms?

8. What are the principal advantages of the internal-rate-of-return method and the net-present-value method as compared with the traditional methods of capital budgeting?

9. What is meant by "search activity," and how is it related to investment by small-business firms?

10. Explain the danger in considering investment expansion proposals one at a time (as is done by so many small-business owner/managers) instead of ranking a number of them.

REFERENCES TO SMALL BUSINESS IN ACTION

Bellegoni, Elvira, and Miriam Weisberg. "Forecast Your Cash Needs." *Inc.*, Vol. 2, No. 9 (September, 1980), pp. 64-67.

The process and benefits of making cash projection forecasts are demonstrated with data from a small company. The numbers representing cash-flow components are used to develop a 12-month forecast.

Kierulff, Herbert E. "Finding the Best Acquisition Candidates." *Harvard Business Review*, Vol. 59, No. 1 (January-February, 1981), pp. 66-68.

Ten criteria to help a small business evaluate an acquisition candidate are discussed. Additional information on search activities is also presented.

Paris, Ellen. "As the Twig Is Bent." *Forbes*, Vol. 127, No. 9 (April 27, 1981), pp. 131, 135.

This article explains how a conservative expansion philosophy enabled a family business, started in 1906, to become a leading manufacturer of clothing.

Rhodes, Lucien. "Confessions of a Risk-Taker." *Inc.*, Vol. 2, No. 12 (December, 1980), pp. 34-42.

This article provides an in-depth "diary" of the cash-flow problems that plagued an entrepreneur until he became a "businessman."

Wemple, William Barent. "Where Are Your Receivables Right Now?" *Inc.*, Vol. 3, No. 4 (April, 1981), pp. 86-88.

The author examines the life-cycle of receivables using the real-life experiences of several small businesses. Some suggestions for improving cash flow are provided.

Chapter 20

Computerizing the Small Business

LOOKING AHEAD

Watch for the following important topics:

1. Components of a business computer system.
2. Types of computers based on sophistication and size, and types of computer systems.
3. First-stage and second-stage applications of the computer.
4. Options for the small business that decides to computerize its operations.
5. Ten steps to take when obtaining a computer for the first time.

Computers have traditionally been affordable only by large governmental bodies and large businesses. This is changing rapidly. Now small firms can also reap the benefits of a computer. In this chapter we will give a brief background on the growth in use of the transistorized computer, explain some computer basics, and examine the different computer applications for small businesses.

THE COMPUTER REVOLUTION

The first transistorized computer was built in 1954 by Bell Laboratories. This invention has led to significant changes and advances in computer systems because the transistorized computer is not only faster than earlier-generation computers, but also smaller and less costly. Among the first computer manufacturers was IBM, the early leader in producing and installing computer systems. By 1964, IBM had a market share of 70 percent.

During the late 1960s, a major weakness in the computer industry was the incompatibility of computers produced by one manufacturer with those produced by another manufacturer. That is, computer programs (often called software) written for one computer would not run on a computer made by a different manufacturer. Errors made by inexperienced personnel were highly publicized by the news media. An example of the bad press that computers received is presented below.

The problem of computer incompatibility gave birth to a new industry—the software industry. Trained personnel who could write programs of instructions for computers were in great demand. However, the development

ACTION REPORT: Welfare Recipients Receive $80,000 in Duplicate Checks

The following report of a computer error illustrates the unfavorable publicity received by computers during the late 1960s and early 1970s. Even though the majority of problems were caused by inexperienced computer personnel, the computer gained a reputation for mistakes and unreliability.

> DETROIT—A computer in the state's Department of Social Services recently sent out $80,000 in duplicate checks to welfare clients throughout the state.
>
> According to Gerrold Brockmyre, assistant deputy director of the state agency, the duplicate checks resulted when the same batch of supplemental emergency payments was fed into the computer on two separate days. The error was discovered when merchants who were asked to cash two checks grew suspicious.
>
> Many of the 887 twice-paid recipients are cashing the second check under the mistaken impression that they are entitled to the money, but some clients "are sending the extra checks back," said Brockmyre.
>
> "Those who have spent the money have received a rather strong letter suggesting they make an arrangement to repay the money," he added.

Source: Copyright 1979 by CW Communications, Inc., Framingham, MA 01701–Reprinted from COMPUTERWORLD.

of software did not keep up with the development of hardware (computer machines) during the 1970s. Furthermore, some companies found that their computer systems were not economically feasible because computer specialists did not coordinate the development of computers and computer programs with business management.

With the development of smaller computer systems in the 1970s, applications of computers became more sophisticated. Since these smaller systems were also more affordable than the larger ones, many small businesses began to use them to maintain pace with competitors. However, the widespread use of computers has also spawned some social concerns. For example, the expansion of storage capacity enabled computers to store vast amounts of information about large numbers of individuals. Individual credit information and other personal data were kept by credit agencies, private organizations, and government bodies. Questions arose about the invasion of privacy by computer users and the way in which citizens could be assured that data about them were correct. Thus, the Privacy Act of 1974 was passed by the Congress of the United States. This act states that justification must be shown before federal agencies can view private information about citizens. The act also gives a citizen the right to review and correct personal information stored on computers.

One of the more controversial uses of computers in the banking industry is the procedure called **electronic funds transfer (EFT).** Through EFT, money is transferred from one account to another without the money ever being seen by the bank's customer. Stores can instantly connect to the customer's bank and adjust that customer's account by the amount of a purchase made. Again, the privacy issue lies at the root of the controversy about electronic funds transfer. So far, companies that have experimented with EFT have used it for direct deposit of payroll and preauthorized payments of insurance premiums.

Another social problem that emerged was that of computer crime. A few dishonest programmers used the computer to transfer company funds into their own private accounts at banks. Some were able to bill companies for merchandise that did not even exist! When discovered, this problem also received wide publicity in the news media. To minimize this problem, computer programs are now being written more carefully to insure that only appropriate users are given access to confidential information.

COMPUTER BASICS

A **computer** is a high-speed electronic machine that manipulates data by following sequential programmed instructions. A **computer system** consists of a computer and its related interactive components. Figure 20-1 shows a typical computer installation for a small business. The computer operator is working with the data and following the procedures she has learned through training. The unit on the right is a keyboard terminal with a screen for viewing input

Figure 20-1 A Computer Installation for a Small Business

and output. The unit on the extreme left is a printer which gives "hard copy" for permanent record keeping. The middle unit is a floppy disk drive used for input and external storage of data and programs.

Components of a Computer System

The five main components of a computer system are: hardware, software (programs), data, personnel, and procedures.[1] Figure 20-2 depicts these five components, each of which is essential to the total system.

Hardware. The hardware consists of the computer itself and items of peripheral equipment used for data input, data output, and data storage. Input units supply data to the central processing unit, and the processed information is channeled to output units. Some typical input and output units are card readers, floppy disk readers, magnetic tape readers, printers, and keyboard terminals.

---

1. These five components are identified in David M. Kroenke, *Business Computer Systems* (Santa Cruz, CA: Mitchell Publishing, Inc., 1980). This reference has an excellent discussion of the technical aspects of computers.

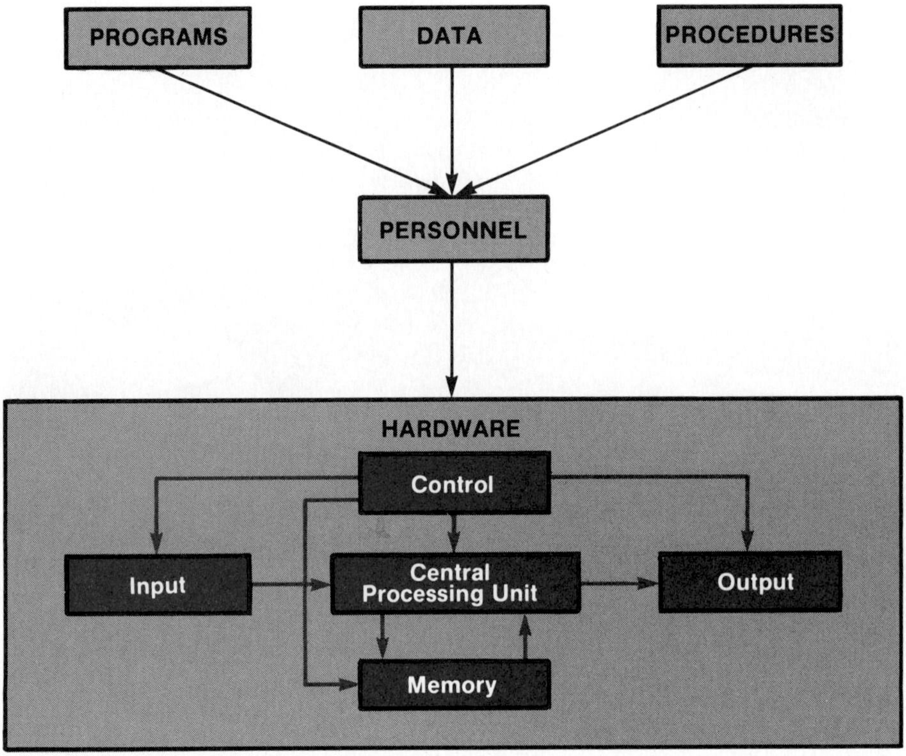

Figure 20-2 **Components of a Computer System**

Software. The programs (software) for a computer system are usually divided into two types: system programs and application programs. **System programs** control the internal operation of the computer system such as starting and stopping jobs, reading input data, and printing output data. **Application programs** are written for particular business needs. For example, an application program may instruct the computer to print payroll checks, to check the day's ending inventory, to perform certain accounting functions, and so on.

Several programming languages are used for application programs. Some of the more common languages are COBOL (COmmon Business Oriented Language), FORTRAN (FORmula TRANslator), BASIC (Beginner's All-purpose Symbolic Instruction Code), RPG (Report Program Generator), and PL1 (Programming Language 1).

Data. Before a computer can perform an operation, all relevant data must be collected and put in a form that the computer can interpret. The data may be punched onto cards, typed directly into the computer by the use of a keyboard, transmitted by a scanning light, or entered from magnetic tapes or disks.

Although computers operate at extremely high speed, they are unable to make judgmental decisions. Therefore, the data a computer uses must be as nearly accurate as possible. The computer information system is only as strong as its weakest data source. As a well-known saying in the computer industry goes, "Garbage in, garbage out."

Personnel and Procedures. Procedures and the personnel who follow these procedures are interrelated components of the computer system. Procedures are instructions on the use and operation of a computer system. The personnel are the people who bring the other four components together, and qualified personnel are the key to a smoothly operating business computer system.

Types of Computers and Computer Systems

Different types of nomenclature are given to computers, depending on their degree of sophistication and size. A **maxicomputer or mainframe** refers to a very large, expensive computer which costs more than $150,000. The next smaller computer is the **minicomputer**, whose cost ranges from $10,000 to $150,000. The development of the **microcomputer (or personal computer)**, which costs well under $10,000, has made computers economically feasible for the small business.

The so-called **turnkey system** in the computer industry refers to a package consisting of hardware, programs, and procedures that are produced by the vendor and sold as a unit. A **time-sharing system** refers to the sharing of one computer by several users. Terminals to collect data are located at the business place of each user, and the computer runs the programs for all users in sequence, switching rapidly from one program to the other and minimizing the waiting time for each user. The fee for each user is much lower than the cost of owning a computer system. Time-sharing is usually the logical first step for a small business moving from manual business operations to an automated computer system.

COMPUTER APPLICATIONS FOR SMALL BUSINESS

There are three basic reasons for the increasing use of computer systems in small businesses. First, a properly designed computer system can reduce the costs of operating a business. Second, the computer can assist in providing more timely, accurate information for managerial decisions. Third, the computer can improve customer service and thus pave the way for increased revenues.

The benefits of a computer system can be temporarily shrouded by problems which occur when small businesses first change to computer systems. For example, the use of a computer system requires discipline in following procedures, and some employees resist the change from traditional or their own ad hoc practices. Also, computer inventory coding often requires lengthy part numbers which may be confusing or time-consuming for salespersons when they record sales. However, the speed and efficiency of computers more than offset these temporary inconveniences. For the first-time users of a business computer system, therefore, it may be wise to acquire some years of experience in first-stage applications only.

First-Stage Applications

In the first stage, computers are used for highly repetitive procedures such as those used for payrolls, billing, accounts receivable, accounts payable, general-ledger systems, word processing, and inventory control. Usually payroll is the first operation to be computerized.

Payroll Application. The payroll application leads to the preparation of paychecks. The input documents to the computer are attendance and time records. The output documents from the computer, in addition to the paychecks, are statements showing earnings, amount of income taxes withheld, social security taxes, and other payroll deductions. Since computations required for payroll are repetitive, computers have been very satisfactory in performing this function.

Ordering and Billing Applications. Ordering and billing are other business functions that are quickly converted to computerized systems. A vendor may receive orders through a salesperson, by mail, by telephone, or by telegram. The computer can prepare the shipping order with customer codes, names, descriptions of items ordered, and prices in an accurate and very rapid manner. When the billing operation is due, the input document to the computer is a copy of the shipping order. The output document is the invoice prepared for mailing.

Accounts-Receivable Application. To control accounts receivable, management needs information on amounts owed by each customer and the length of time the accounts have been outstanding. The importance of accuracy is obvious. Errors cause loss of revenues and annoyance to customers. The accuracy and speed of computers reduce errors in this function and present a more professional appearance to customers.

Accounts-Payable and General-Ledger Applications. Computerized accounts-payable systems produce checks to pay company bills. Both payroll and accounts payable should have controls that allow only authorized personnel to operate these systems. Computerized general-ledger systems perform the company's bookkeeping function. The format of financial reports, balance sheets, and income statements—which varies widely from one small business to another—can be programmed easily.

Word-Processing Application. The term **word processing** refers to any process that involves textual information and uses such equipment as typesetters, copiers, and automatic typewriters. Once a document has been prepared, the text can be stored on magnetic disks. It can then be retrieved, edited, and printed. Word processing is particularly useful where documents go through several drafts before they are finished.

Inventory-Control Application. A computer system can compare stock levels with expected sales for a given period and automatically generate purchase or production orders for needed additional stock. It can keep accurate records of items that are selling rapidly and those that are selling slowly. Thus, it enables the manager to keep a current, accurate watch on inventory levels and avoid stockouts.

The goals of inventory control are a reduction of inventory investment and an elimination of stockouts. Somehow these goals seem contradictory since a reduction of inventory investment increases the probability of stockouts. With modern inventory-management techniques, the small firm may be able to overcome the contradictory aspects of these goals. Unfortunately many small businesses do not use modern inventory-management techniques. However, small businesses can achieve effective inventory control by having a computerized inventory system which uses the modern inventory-management techniques. Without increasing the probability of stockouts, the small firm can reduce inventory by 20 percent with computerized inventory controls. In addition, a computerized inventory system allows a significant savings in time required by personnel to perform the inventory-control function. Unquestionably, an inventory-control system is one of the most cost-effective systems placed on computers.

Examples of First-Stage Application Users. Small businesses that have successfully experienced first-stage applications of computers are found in various fields. Marcel Bernier, who owns six gas stations in California, has computerized the accounting functions in his business. He previously paid a CPA $600 each month to prepare profit-and-loss statements, and many days would elapse before he could see these statements. A new $20,000 microcomputer system now generates 7 income statements—one for each gas station plus one for the home office—as soon as the last day's figures are entered. The computer also maintains records on his bank balances, accounts payable, and accounts receivable.[2]

Bobby Hall, a dairy and row-crop farmer near McComb, MS, has found a computer to yield a higher profit than most farm-machinery investments. He uses the computer to maintain payroll records, to write paychecks for nine employees, to keep records for accounts receivable and accounts payable for the dairy, to record cash transactions, to prepare monthly reports on feed management, to keep track of depreciation schedules and investment credit details on each capital asset, and to complete herd records. Hall concludes that a dairy farmer who owns 125 milking cows and a feed mill could justify the purchase of a computer.[3]

Computerized billing is also found in the law profession. It is estimated that half of the law firms in the United States use computers for billing and other office functions.[4] Lawyers who use computers for billing are able to give more detailed statements on the bills. Some law firms use word-processing computers to search for past legal cases that are stored on computer information files. The word-processing computer searches are fast, and they improve the reliability and safety of legal research. The word-processing computers are also used to print lengthy case briefs.

Al's Auto Supply in Oklahoma City computerized approximately 30 percent of its 15,000 items in inventory. This store was able to reduce its average inventory investment by 25 percent and to reduce its stockout percentage from 6 percent to 3 percent. The savings quickly paid for the cost of the computer system.[5]

Another example of a business that computerized its inventory-control system is Southwest Tablets Manufacturing Company in Dallas. This business produces writing tablets and notebooks. For this low-profit-margin business, the computer has been helpful in the making of purchasing decisions, in the effective use of production facilities, and in the tabulation of available inventory.[6]

Grocery stores are also using computers to improve the efficiency of their checkout counters, to determine buying patterns, and to monitor inventory levels. The key to their operation is the Universal Product Code, which now appears on most grocery items. A scanner held by the checkout person inter-

---

2. Edward Goldfinger, "A Manager's Guide to Computer Systems," *Inc.*, Vol. 2, No. 5 (May, 1980), p. 103.

3. "Computer Is as Important as Milk Cows," *Progressive Farmer* (December, 1980), pp. 22-23.

4. "More Law Firms Put Computers to Work to Find Cases, Print Filings, Bill Clients," *The Wall Street Journal*, December 23, 1980, p. 32.

5. K. K. Moore's personal consulting experience. Name and location are fictitious, but the other facts are correct.

6. Goldfinger, *op. cit.*, pp. 105-106.

prets the code on the item and supplies the computer with the item's cost, department, and tax information. Not only is this method faster, but fewer mistakes are made. At the end of each day, the store managers can look at a computer read-out to determine inventory levels and total sales of each item in the store. This current information is also important in evaluating the effect of advertisements and specials.[7]

Second-Stage Applications

Second-stage applications involve more advanced uses of computers and usually follow several years of successful first-stage applications. Some second-stage applications involve financial planning, management of information, and market research. These applications would not be recommended for the first-time computer user.

Financial-Planning Application. Financial management involves the management of money. While accounting functions also involve the control of money, a major difference exists between computerized financial-planning systems and computerized accounting systems. The accounting system has many users; therefore, procedures for this system must be clearly defined in order to maintain proper control. On the other hand, financial operations are managed by fewer people—usually high-level personnel. Consequently, the computerized financial-planning system can be flexible and quite varied from one small business to another. Computerized financial-planning systems, though not widely developed, are being used by small businesses.

Like the sophisticated calculator, a computer can be used to calculate cash flow, interest rates, present values, and rates of return for capital budgeting. More important, through financial-planning computer software, the computer can aid in the following financial functions:

1. Forecasting revenues and expenses of the business operation over future years.
2. Analyzing capital expenditures by computing the costs and benefits for different plans of action.
3. Cash planning by keeping current records of cash flows, helping to avoid cash shortages, and properly investing any surplus cash.
4. Credit analysis, which is used primarily by banks and loan agencies to determine the creditworthiness of potential borrowers.

---

7. Joseph S. Coyle, "Scanning Lights up a Dark World for Grocers," *Fortune* (March 27, 1978), pp. 76-80.

Management-of-Information Application. Managers need to make decisions based on current, accurate information. They also want information quickly and in a summarized form. Computers can supply information quickly and in any form the managers desire. Computers can ease the burden of increased paperwork required by government legislation over recent years.

The management of information can be used for both long-range planning and operational planning. Long-range planning involves the future financial status of the business. Operational planning usually involves optimization and data analysis to organize daily activities such as the preparation of delivery schedules, truck routes, and purchase orders.

Market-Research Application. Through advanced methods, the computer can evaluate historical data and interpret results of statistical market surveys. These sophisticated procedures are likely to become invaluable to the progressive small-business manager of the future.

DECIDING TO COMPUTERIZE THE SMALL BUSINESS

If a small business is considering the use of a computer, it should analyze the potential benefits, estimate the costs, and work out an appropriate plan. There are no quick and easy procedures to follow in this decision process. Each business will have a unique set of problems.

The Feasibility Study

As a first step, the small business should make a feasibility study. This study should determine whether the firm has a sufficient work load or need for efficiency to justify the expense of a computer. The cost/benefit analysis is difficult to make, but it is the most important step in the decision-making process. This analysis can be performed by the business owner/manager or by an outside computer consultant.

The feasibility study may indicate that the business should not computerize. If the study shows that the business should computerize, the second step is to decide whether to use a service bureau, to opt for time-sharing, to lease a computer, or to buy a computer. If the firm decides to buy a computer, then it should select the best system for the business.

Service Bureaus

Service bureaus are computer firms which receive data from business customers, perform the data processing, then return the processed information to the customers. The service bureaus charge a fixed fee for the use of their computer. For a small firm desiring a single application and lacking computer experience, the service bureau represents a logical first choice.

Using a service bureau has several advantages. The user avoids an investment in equipment, which will soon become obsolete. The user also avoids the need for specialized computer personnel. Some service bureaus even provide guidance to make it easy for the user to start and expand computer usage. The disadvantages of a service bureau are: slow "turnaround" time in receiving processed information from the service bureau, divulgence of confidential information to outside parties, and difficulty in working with a group unfamiliar with the client company's procedures.

In the past there have been numerous small service bureaus. However, today the small service bureaus are having difficulty competing with bigger bureaus that have larger minicomputer systems. The competition between service bureaus will no doubt become even greater in the future.

Time-Sharing

Time-sharing allows a business to have the capabilities of a computer without buying or leasing it. The business pays a variable fee for the privilege of using a computer system. As indicated earlier in this chapter, the user of time-sharing must have at least one terminal in order to input data. The terminal is connected to the time-sharing computer via a telephone line with a device known as a **modem.**

Early time-sharing systems provided computer time for professionals who knew how to operate and to program a computer. With the advancement of software, time-sharing is used more to process data and information for a company by using existing programs. The time-sharing approach is often a good first or second step for small firms that decide to computerize.

The advantages of time-sharing include control of company records, more sophisticated applications of programs, and lower cost of installing a working system. The disadvantages include variable costs, waiting time when other customers are using the system, and the need for the user to have some computer ability.

Leasing a Computer

For most businesses, leasing a computer means acquiring possession and use of a computer without buying it. The most common leasing arrangement is the full payback lease. Usually the lease periods are fairly long-term (i.e., for around eight years). A shorter lease period may be more expensive, but it reduces the possibility of having to use outdated equipment. With the current rapid advances in computer technology, some computer users claim that computer equipment becomes outdated every two years!

ACTION REPORT: Mathis Equipment Converts to a Time-Sharing System

Mathis Equipment Company is an industrial supply business located in a city with a population of 100,000. The company has approximately 25,000 inventory items and over 1,200 accounts. Before the business converted to time-sharing, sales had increased at an average annual rate of 20 percent over the last 5 years. The office staff which handles invoicing, accounts receivable, accounts payable, and monthly billing had neither changed its procedures nor increased its size over this growth period. Output was slow (averaging five days to process a customer's monthly statement), and inventory was ordered when stockouts occurred.

A business computer system seemed to be the solution. The initial cost of a computer system and personnel was deemed too costly by management without proof that it would solve the company's problems. Moreover, the employees were reluctant to switch to a computer system. A solution was reached by entering a time-sharing agreement with a local computer firm.

A small monthly fee was paid for computer time via a time-sharing system, and Mathis purchased two terminals for data input and a printer for data output. The terminals and the printer were connected to the time-sharing computer, which was five miles away, via a leased telephone line. A program was used to process the accounts receivable.

The Mathis employees have access to the receivables information through the terminals on a real-time basis throughout the working day. All charges and payments are now posted directly to the proper account, using efficient, transaction-based procedures. Mathis can now process its monthly statements in one day, thus reducing the length of its cash cycle significantly. The employees also have become comfortable with computer technology, and management considers the transition a success. Joe Stone, manager-owner, sums up the conversion process by stating, "The time-sharing system was not without problems but was a good learning experience. Our next step to a larger computer will be much smoother as a result of this experience."

Source: Fred Hulme's personal consulting experience.

Two advantages of leasing are the use of a complete computer system without a large initial investment and the availability of consulting help through the leasing company's computer specialists. The disadvantages relate to the length of the lease period and the possibility of having to use outdated equipment. In addition, leasing a computer requires the lessee to have skilled computer personnel.

Buying a Computer

The advantages of buying a computer are obvious. The owner has total control and ownership of the computer. Also, the accompanying investment tax credits and depreciation expense reduce the business owner's taxable income. The disadvantages are the large expense of the computer system, the need for trained computer personnel to operate the programs and maintain the hardware, and the possible obsolescence of the equipment.

For small firms choosing to purchase a computer, the key to creating a successful computer system is a carefully planned approach. It is important for the first-time computer user to look first at the programs, not at the hardware. "The difference between the best and worst hardware is a lot less than it is between the best and worst programs."[8]

Edward Goldfinger lists ten steps for a company to take when considering the purchase of a computer.[9] Frank Greenwood also identifies ten rules of small-business computerization.[10] The ten steps described below involve a blending of these two persons' ideas.

Step 1. Learn About Computers. Visit other firms that are already using computers for similar applications. Ask for a vendor demonstration. Be aware that the changeover will require much time and thought. If possible, hire a "data-processing manager" with experience, or at least place someone in charge of the changeover. In summary, the computer is not an easy way out. If the business is in basic trouble, the computer system will not save it. The computer can help a successful business become more successful.

Step 2. Analyze the Present Manual System. Examine the transactions which involve routine actions. Restudy the routine manual actions to find a more efficient procedure if possible. Having established an efficient procedure, you are then ready to think about introducing a computer.

The detailed study of the business and the areas that might be computerized help to clarify computer needs. This is information that computer vendors need in order to propose ways to computerize a company efficiently.

Step 3. Clearly Define Your Expectations from the Computer System. Having reviewed your manual system, decide what you need in a computer system. Be specific in the functions you want the computer to perform. For example, you may decide to computerize mailing lists, accounting payroll,

---

8. "Picking a Small Computer," *Dun's Review,* Vol. 118, No. 2 (August, 1981), p. 72.

9. *Ibid.*

10. Frank Greenwood, "The Ten Commandments of Small Business Computerization," *Journal of Small Business Management,* Vol. 19, No. 2 (April, 1981), pp. 61-67.

inventory control, or sales analysis. These needs should be outlined for five years in the future. If you are unable to determine your exact needs, you may want to seek help. Possible sources are other small businesses, computer consultants, or an employee with computer experience.

Step 4. Compare Costs and Benefits. It is easy to estimate the costs of current manual systems, but it is difficult to estimate the cost of computerization. Estimates should be obtained from several vendors to help determine the cost of changeover. Also, there are hidden costs incurred. For example, the patience and endurance of employees are tested during the conversion.

Step 5. Establish a Timetable for Installing the System. A five-year schedule should be made to install the computer system. It is best to automate the simplest manual operations first. Each computerized operation should be working before going to the next. Be aware that transitions are slow. If possible, run the manual system in parallel with the automated system until the rough spots are smoothed out. Be willing to adjust the timetable from time to time as unexpected problems occur.

Step 6. Write a Tight Contract. Both the purchaser and the vendor should be willing to sign a formal agreement on the function the computer is expected to perform. The specifications should contain details rather than general summaries of expected performance. Service contracts should also be clearly specified. The contract should specify what the vendor must do before each step in the payment schedule.

Also, it is usually unwise to agree to field-test *new* equipment. It is best to obtain established equipment and programs that have been working in other small businesses.

Step 7. Obtain Programs First, Then Obtain the Computer. There are several options for obtaining computer programs.

1. Obtain programs that are already working at other similar small businesses.
2. Hire a programmer to write programs.
3. Hire a consultant who has programs which can serve most business functions.

The manager must make the decision about which alternative is best for the particular business. Once the needed programs are identified, the most economical hardware to run the programs can be obtained.

"I don't want to talk to a middleman . . . put me straight through to the computer!"

Source: From *The Wall Street Journal*, September 9, 1981, p. 25. Permission—Cartoon Features Syndicate.

Figure 20-3 The Importance of Computers in the Future

Step 8. Prepare Your Employees for Conversion. It is commonplace for employees to resist the move to computers. They may feel the computer is a threat to their jobs. Assure employees that the change will be beneficial to the business and consequently beneficial to them. People who are unwilling to become involved should be moved to other departments. A good attitude with interest in the computerization must prevail for a successful transition from manual power to computer power.

Step 9. Make the Conversion. First, assign the responsibilities carefully for the conversion process. The conversion period will require extra work because daily work must continue. Second, remember to convert operations one at a time. Again, if possible, keep the parallel manual system functioning as long as possible. Third, be patient, remembering that pitfalls will occur. Do not plan on using the system until it begins functioning.

Step 10. Reap the Benefits. The goal of the transition is to obtain the following benefits:

1. Earlier, more nearly accurate, and more extensive information.
2. Better organization of information because of the discipline the computer requires.
3. Current information on costs and sales.
4. Current information on inventory levels.
5. Better cash control.

THE FUTURE OF COMPUTERS

The use of computers is already evident in stores, airports, banks, libraries, newspaper plants, law enforcement agencies, hospitals, educational institutions, business offices, and recreation facilities. Computerized grocery checkout stands will increase. The stand-alone cash register will continue to be replaced by computer terminals in retail stores. And there is no reason to believe that improvements in computer technology will slow in the near future. Already computer robots are replacing workers in performing repetitive tasks in manufacturing assembly lines.

The future development of the computer will continue to reduce the time spent in performing manual tasks and to aid in the decision-making process. Computers may become as common as the television sets in our homes so that it will be possible to shop at home via a computer terminal. As transportation costs continue to rise, computers and video displays will be used for long-distance sales to customers. It is entirely possible that in the near future every desk, even in a small business, will have a computer terminal.

LOOKING BACK

1. The five components of a business computer system are: hardware, programs (or software), data, procedures, and personnel. The personnel bring the other four components together and are the key to a smoothly operating system.
2. The three basic types of computers based on sophistication and size are: mainframes (or maxicomputers), minicomputers, and microcomputers (or personal computers). The turnkey computer system consists of hardware, software, and procedures that are produced and sold as a package by the vendor. In the time-sharing computer system, terminals to collect data are located at the business place of each user of the system, and the computer runs the programs for all users in very rapid sequence.
3. First-time users of a business computer system should acquire some years of experience in first-stage applications before proceeding with second-stage applications. The first-stage applications involve highly

repetitive procedures such as those used for payrolls, billing, accounts receivable, accounts payable, general-ledger systems, word processing, and inventory control. More advanced uses of the computer (or second-stage applications) involve financial planning, management of information, and market research.

4. The small-business manager who decides that a computer is feasible for business operations has several options: using a service bureau, time-sharing, leasing a computer, or buying a computer.
5. The ten steps to take when obtaining a computer system for the first time are: learn about computers, analyze the present manual system, clearly define expectations from the computer system, compare costs and benefits, establish a timetable for installing the system, write a tight contract with the computer vendor, obtain programs first before obtaining the hardware, prepare employees for conversion, make the conversion, and reap the benefits.

DISCUSSION QUESTIONS

1. Discuss the social problems that arose with the advancement of computer technology.
2. List and define the five components of a business computer system.
3. What types of input units and output units are available in computer systems?
4. What are three types of computers?
5. What is a turnkey computer system?
6. Why have computers become more commonly used in small businesses?
7. Discuss the applications of computers in small businesses.
8. Discuss the advantages and disadvantages of (a) service bureaus, (b) time-sharing systems, (c) leasing computers, and (d) buying computers.
9. List and discuss the ten steps a business should take when obtaining a computer system for the first time.
10. Discuss the future of computers.

REFERENCES TO SMALL BUSINESS IN ACTION

"America's Newest Cottage Industry." *Output* (June, 1981), pp. 19-20.

The growth of computers has seen the flowering of a new breed of entrepreneur—the home-computer owner who turns a hobby to profit by writing software that businesses will buy.

"America's Offices Enter a New Age." *Nation's Business*, Vol. 69, No. 7 (July, 1981), pp. 49-54.

The role of electronic office equipment in increasing the productivity of office functions in small business is discussed in this article.

"A Manager's Guide to Computer Systems." *Inc.*, Vol. 2, No. 5 (May, 1980), pp. 101-106.

This article reports on small businesses that have computerized their business functions.

"Tapping the Mom and Pop Market." *Information Processing* (October 27, 1980), pp. 165-172.

This article describes the way in which computer makers seek to reach small-business buyers.

Chapter 21

Business Risks and Insurance

LOOKING AHEAD

Watch for the following important topics:

1. The concept of risk management.
2. Classifications of business risks.
3. Importance of adequate insurance coverage.
4. Requirements for obtaining insurance.
5. Types of insurance.

It is said that "nothing is certain except death and taxes." Entrepreneurs live with still another certainty—that of taking a risk when operating a small business. Even though most entrepreneurs are especially suited to cope with business risk, they nevertheless seek to minimize the tension that arises from it. The best way to reduce business-risk tension is by understanding the different types of business risks and alternatives for managing them.

Most types of business risk can be dealt with through the practice of risk management. **Risk management** is "an approach to management concerned with the preservation of the assets and earning power of a business against risks of accidental loss,"[1] The term "assets" in this definition includes not

---

1. Albert G. Giordano, *Concise Dictionary of Business Terminology* (Englewood Cliffs, NJ: Prentice-Hall, Inc., 1981), p. 157.

only accounting assets, such as inventory and plant, but also such assets as employees.

Risk management in the small firm differs from risk management in the large firm. The manager of a small business is also the risk manager. In contrast, a large firm may assign the responsibilities of risk management to a specialized staff manager. In practicing risk management, the small-business manager should be able to identify the different types of business risks and be able to cope with them. The three basic ways to cope with business risks are: (1) reduce the risk, (2) save to cover possible future losses, and (3) transfer the risk to someone else, whenever possible, by carrying insurance. The best solution often involves a combination of these three approaches.

COMMON BUSINESS RISKS

Business risks can be classified in several ways. One simple approach is to list the causes of accidental losses. Fire, personal injury, theft, and fraud would be items on such a list. Another system portrays business risks by grouping accidental losses into those which are generally insurable and those which are largely uninsurable. A fire loss would typify the first category; product obsolescence, the second category.

A third system, one which we will use in this text, emphasizes the asset-centered focus of the definition of risk management by grouping business risks into four categories: marketing-centered risks, property-centered risks, employee-centered risks, and customer-centered risks. This classification system encompasses four key "asset" groups for the small business. A substantial loss in any one category could mean devastation for the small business. We will examine the forms of risk associated with each category and identify the possible alternatives for coping with them.

Marketing-Centered Risks

Some of the most crippling forms of business risks are centered around the firm's marketing effort. Many marketing-centered risks involve opportunity losses which are intangible and, therefore, not very noticeable. Generally marketing-centered risks are uninsurable.

Business Recessions. During recessions, small businesses are particularly vulnerable to loss. Perhaps their major weakness lies in their failure to build reserves and increase ownership equity during a preceding period of business prosperity. As a practical alternative, the small firm should utilize profits in times of prosperity to increase its ownership equity and to build a strong working-capital position.

Price Fluctuations. Fluctuations in price levels may or may not contribute to losses. If the business carries a substantial inventory, however, price declines almost automatically result in inventory losses. The risk of price fluctuations can be minimized by a policy of hand-to-mouth buying, which was discussed in Chapter 17. However, to do this the manager must resist the lure of speculative profits from possible price increases.

Product and Process Obsolescence. Small manufacturers who cannot undertake extensive research often find their processes and products becoming obsolete. Product innovation is a key factor for the small business that stays competitive. The marketing risk of having to sell an obsolete product is increased when product innovation is lacking. About the only way to avoid this form of risk is for the small firm to have a progressive management which keeps up with industrial progress.

Property-Centered Risks

In contrast to marketing-centered risks, property-centered risks involve tangible and highly visible assets. When these physical assets are lost, they are quickly missed. Most property-centered risks, however, are insurable.

Fire Hazards. The possibility of fire is always present. Buildings, equipment, and inventory items can be totally or partially destroyed by fire. Of course, the degree of risk and the loss potential differ with the type of business. For example, industrial processes that are complex and hazardous or that involve explosives, combustibles, or other flammable materials enlarge this risk.

Fire not only causes a direct property loss, but also may interrupt business operations, resulting in a loss of profit to the firm. During the period when business operations are interrupted, such fixed expenses as rent, supervisory salaries, and insurance charges continue. To avoid losses arising from business interruptions, a business might, for example, have alternative sources of electric power, such as its own generators, for use in times of emergency.

Obviously the small firm needs to take every possible precaution to prevent fires. Among the possible precautions are the following:

1. *Use of safe construction.* The building should be made of fire-resistant materials, and electrical wiring should be adequate to carry the maximum load of electrical energy which will be imposed. Fire doors and insulation should be used where necessary.

2. *Provision of a completely automatic sprinkler system.* With an automatic sprinkler system available, fire insurance rates will be lower—and the fire hazard itself is definitely reduced.
3. *Provision of an adequate water supply.* Ordinarily this involves location in a city with water sources and water mains, together with a pumping system that will assure the delivery of any amount of water needed to fight fires. Of course, a company may hedge a bit by providing company-owned water storage tanks or private wells.
4. *Institution and operation of a fire-prevention program involving all employees.* Such a program must have top management support, and the emphasis must always be to keep employees fire-safety conscious. Regular fire drills for all employees, including both building-evacuation and actual fire-fighting efforts, may be undertaken.

Under some conditions, a large company can safely self-insure against major risks. A retail chain store with outlets in many different cities and states, for example, might act as its own fire insurance company. This would require the store management to determine the probability of loss through fire and then set aside a sum determined by the use of an actuarial method to meet those losses which are realized. It is clear that the risk would need to be spread so that any one fire would not destroy a substantial portion of the company's property. Self-insurance is seldom applicable to a small business.

Natural Disasters. Floods, hurricanes, tornadoes, and hail are often described as "acts of God" because of human limitations in foreseeing and controlling them. As in the case of fire, natural disasters may also interrupt business operations. Although a business may take certain preventive measures—for example, locating in areas not subject to flood damage—there is not much one can do to avoid natural disasters. Major reliance is placed upon insurance in coping with natural-disaster losses.

Burglary. The forcible breaking and entering of premises closed for business with the subsequent removal of cash or merchandise is called burglary. Although insurance should be carried against losses from burglary, it may prove helpful for a business to install burglar alarm systems and arrange for private security services.

Shoplifting. The theft of merchandise during store hours costs retail merchants alone upwards of $8 billion a year, and small business is not immune to this danger.[2] It is estimated that one out of three small-business

2. "How Shoplifting Is Draining the Economy," *Business Week,* No. 2607 (October 15, 1979), p. 119.

bankruptcies is a direct result of shoplifting by customers or employees.[3] Various precautionary measures may be taken by the small business to minimize shoplifting. These include:

1. Limiting access to certain areas of the business premises.
2. Screening employees carefully.
3. Laying out the facilities to provide good visual coverage.
4. Keeping high-unit-value items in special-security locations.
5. Monitoring shoplifting with special equipment such as closed-circuit television.
6. Educating potential offenders to understand that they will be prosecuted.

Employee-Centered Risks

Employee-centered losses occur indirectly due to employees' personal circumstances or directly through employee actions against the business. A physically sick or injured employee is an example of an indirect loss. Employee spying, on the other hand, is a direct action against the business and constitutes a major concern for many small businesses. Most employee-centered risks are insurable.

Employee Strikes. An employee strike can cause a business considerable trouble. For example, the United Mine Workers' coal strike which started on December 5, 1977 and ended on March 25, 1978 seriously affected the coal-rich states that depend on coal for 40 to 70 percent of their electrical energy requirements. Numerous businesses were required by the utility companies to curtail drastically their usage of electricity. To many small firms, this meant shortening office or store hours; to others, it was a matter of closing down and laying off employees. In the case of a strike threat among suppliers of goods, stockpiling is a widely used precautionary measure.

Business Frauds and Theft. Business swindles can amount to hundreds of millions of dollars a year. Small firms in particular are susceptible to swindles. Examples of these are bogus office-machine repairers, phony charity appeals, billing for listing in nonexistent directories, sale of advertising space in publications whose nature is misrepresented, and advance fee deals. Risks of this kind are avoidable only through the alertness of the business manager.

Thefts by employees may include not only cash but also inventory items, tools, metal scrap, stamps, and the like. Then there is always the possibility

3. *Ibid*.

ACTION REPORT: Making Employee Safety Pay

Employee-centered risks can be minimized with a formal program to reward safety. Parsons Pine Products, Inc., in Ashland, OR instituted two safety programs, and employees reaped the benefits.

Before these programs, the company was paying $.21 in Oregon's State Accident Insurance Fund (SAIF) for every dollar of wages. The company, which produces mouse and rat trap blanks, louver and venetian slats, and some furniture parts, employs about 75 people. The company had a cost of over $100,000 yearly for premiums and lost production time due to its extremely high accident rate.

The company's "Safety Pay" plan rewards each employee who works safely for one month with four hours of extra pay. This can amount to about $240 a year for the average employee.

Another plan, called "Safety Retro Plan," allows the company to get back a maximum of 90 percent of premiums paid to SAIF if there are no accidents during the year. In turn, Parsons Pine "guarantees that at least 50 percent of any returned premium would go to the Bonus Plan as cash dispersal." During the first year, this plan returned $89,000 in premiums. "Each employee that had worked safely for that year received about $1,000 and had a justified pride in being part of a team that had met the challenge and won."

Source: Terrence O. Brimhall originated these safety ideas. "Safety Through Positive Reinforcement," *National Safety News*, Vol. 123, No. 6 (June, 1981), pp. 29-30.

of forgery, raising of checks, or other fraudulent practices. The trusted bookkeeper may enter into collusion with an outsider to have bogus invoices or invoices double or triple the correct amount presented for payment. The bookkeeper may approve such invoices for payment, write the check, and secure the manager's signature. In addition to bonding employees, the firm's major protection against employee frauds is a system of internal checks or control.

Loss of Key Executives. Every successful small business has one or more key executives. These employees could be lost to the firm by death or through attraction to other employment. If key personnel cannot be successfully replaced, the small firm suffers appreciably and loses profits as the result of the loss of their services.

In addition to valuable experience and skill, there is also the possibility that the executive may have certain specialized knowledge which is vital to the successful operation of the firm. For example, a certain manufacturer was

ACTION REPORT: Computer Crime

Computer crime is not restricted to big business. One expert estimates small-business losses through computers to be around $15 billion a year.

Stephen Kennedy, a financial crimes expert with the FBI, sees the primary cause to be carelessness. He gives the following example:

> The company's financial records were stored in a minicomputer. None of the company's top executives, not even the controller, had access to the computer. Three relatively low-level employees enjoyed total control over the minicomputer and all its contents—including inventory control, payroll records, and financial accounts.

Kennedy has found small-business computer owners to be reluctant to report computer theft. They are "embarrassed that their systems have been penetrated," he says. Kennedy recalls one case where:

> ...a computer criminal "broke into" a firm's data bank, got information from customer files, then tried to extort money from the company by threatening to expose to customers the weakness of the firm's computer security.

There is good reason to believe that the more complex and possibly larger computer crimes have not yet been discovered.

Source: "Smaller Firms Can Feel Computer Crime's Sting," *Inc.*, Vol. 2, No. 10 (October, 1980), p. 42.

killed in an auto accident at the age of 53. His processing operations involved the use of a secret chemical formula which he had devised originally and divulged to no one because of the fear of loss of the formula to competitors. He did not reduce it to writing and place it in a safety-deposit box. Not even his family knew the formula. As a result of his sudden death, the firm went out of business within six months. The expensive special-purpose equipment had to be sold as junk. All that his widow salvaged was about $60,000 worth of bonds and the Florida residence which had been the winter home of the couple.

Two answers, at least, are possible to the small firm faced with this contingency. The first of these is life insurance, which is discussed later in this chapter. The second solution involves the development of replacement personnel. A potential replacement may be groomed for every key position, including the position of the owner-manager.

Customer-Centered Risks

Customers are the source of profit for small business, but they are also the center of an ever-increasing amount of business risk. Much of this risk is attributable to personal injury, product liability, and bad debts. Most customer-centered risks are insurable.

Personal Injury and Product Liability. Liability risks involve losses to third parties who make claims against a business. Personal injury liability, for example, is incurred when a customer breaks an arm by slipping on icy steps while entering a place of business. Personal injury suits can be reduced by practicing good business housekeeping.

A product liability suit may be filed when a customer becomes ill or sustains property damage in using a product made or sold by a company. Class-action suits, together with individual suits, are now widely used by consumers in product liability cases. And juries have been awarding increasingly larger amounts to plaintiffs in liability suits, particularly those that involve product liability.[4] To prevent the marketing of products that could be harmful to health or property, quality production standards and product safety design should be emphasized.

Richard S. Betterley, a consultant, suggests the following steps to help a small company reduce product liability losses:

1. Include thorough and explicit directions for the product's use with each product. Warn customers of potential hazards and keep an eye on promotional material to make sure advertising doesn't undo the company's precautions.
2. Develop procedures for handling consumers' complaints through distributors and at the home office. Prepare a plan to handle the worst possible kind of disaster.
3. Determine whether any of the company's products are too risky to sell, given the consequences of a suit.
4. Test products internally for possible safety problems. Then obtain a "second opinion" from others in the field and consult the company's insurer.
5. Acquaint all employees with the company's concern with product safety.
6. Stay current with legislation and litigation within the appropriate industries.[5]

---

4. For references dealing specifically with product liability, see "The Devils in the Product Liability Laws," *Business Week*, No. 2572 (February 12, 1979), pp. 72-78. See also Richard S. Betterley, "Liability Headaches: 12 Ways to Cope," *Journal of Applied Management*, Vol. 5, No. 1 (January-February, 1980), pp. 30-32.

5. "Proper Precautions Trim Product Liability Risks," *Inc.*, Vol. 2, No. 5 (May, 1980), p. 131.

Bad Debts. Bad debts are an unavoidable risk associated with credit selling. Most customers will pay their obligations with no more than a friendly reminder. A few customers will intentionally try to avoid payment. These accounts should be quickly turned over to a lawyer for litigation or be written off.

Customers who fall in between the two groups of "quick pay" and "no pay" are the ones who cause the most trouble. These customers may be good customers but, for various reasons, may temporarily experience difficulty and become slow payers. Every effort should be made in a firm but courteous manner to offer these customers options which will encourage payment.

RISK INSURANCE FOR THE SMALL BUSINESS

Insurance provides one of the most important means of transferring business risks. Too often in the past, the small firm has paid insufficient attention to insurance matters and has failed to acquire skill in analyzing risk problems. Today such a situation is untenable. A sound insurance program is imperative for the proper protection of a business.

ACTION REPORT: Tightening a Credit Policy

Credit is a valuable marketing tool for making a sale but can be counterproductive when an account is uncollectible. A small business must monitor its accounts receivable and get tough when necessary. Two Chicago small-business manufacturers have learned to manage their accounts with "tough" language.

Payson Coasters in Chicago sets 60 days as the signal to act aggressively to collect customers' accounts. If an account goes beyond 90 days, the firm will use COD or CBS (Cash Before Shipping). President Harry Sullivan says, "We've been burned on COD . . . so we prefer CBS." The result of this policy is that "receivables are in fairly good shape" because Sullivan has found that "it's too expensive to carry nonpaying accounts these days."

The 90-day limit is imposed by Better Containers, another Chicago firm. Bill Wilson, vice-president and sales manager, takes an even stronger position. They do not use COD or CBS. "We tell them to pay for what they've got on the books, and then we'll take another order—with a promise they'll be a little more diligent about paying their bills."

Wilson does make it clear that they "work with customers who have been good in the past."

Source: "Slow Payments: The Small Business Counterattack," *Managing*, Vol. 8, No. 8 (June 8, 1981), p. 2. ©1981 by HBJ Newsletters, Inc., 757 Third Avenue, New York, NY 10017.

Insurance coverage is available for almost anything. Consider these unusual coverages:

1. A graveyard in Pennsylvania insures its tombstones against vandalism.
2. Clergymen carry insurance against suits for giving advice.
3. A nine-foot-long alligator (stuffed) in front of a general store in Ponchatoula, LA is insured against theft.[6]

Regardless of the nature of the business, risk insurance is serious business. The small-business manager must take an active role in structuring an insurance package.

Importance of Adequate Insurance

It is often apparent that small firms fail to carry sufficient insurance protection. Small firms obtain liability policies for specific liabilities when they should purchase comprehensive policies. For example, liability policies on company trucks and cars may specify $20,000 or $30,000 when a safer figure would be $100,000 or more. Similarly, fidelity bonds on employees who handle cash should be larger than are typically carried because such bonds frequently cover only a fraction of the amount embezzled. Having too little coverage for any type of insurance risk is dangerous, even though the premium cost is reduced by a reduction of the coverage.

Careful risk management dictates a study of adequate insurance policies in advance of a loss rather than after the occurrence of the event. By so doing, a manager may discover gaps in coverage and make appropriate corrections in time to forestall serious losses.

Basic Principles of a Sound Insurance Program

A reputable independent insurance agent can provide professional assistance to small firms in evaluating risks and designing a proper protection plan. George T. Frazier, president of the Independent Insurance Agents of America, has described the role of insurance agents in devising risk management plans as follows:

> Risk management includes a good deal more than arranging sound insurance coverage, important as that is. It also deals with a great many technical considerations that customers cannot and should not handle without help.
>
> The independent agent provides that help by arranging insurance company services: safety inspection, cleanup, establishment of safety

6. "In Insurance, Anything Goes," *Venture*, Vol. 2, No. 10 (October, 1980), p. 20.

programs, rechecking at proper intervals, and other initial and ongoing functions.

In short, the agent performs duties similar to those of the risk manager and while doing so trains the insured to play a major role in the procedures.[7]

The small-business manager who cannot afford professional assistance can be guided by some basic principles discussed below.

Identify the Business Risks to Be Covered. Although the common insurable risks were already pointed out earlier, other less obvious risks may be revealed only by a careful investigation. The small firm must first obtain coverages required by law or contract, such as workers' compensation insurance and automobile liability insurance. As part of this risk-identification process, the plant and equipment should be reappraised periodically by competent appraisers in order to maintain an adequate insurance coverage.

Obtain Coverage Only for Major Potential Losses. The small firm must determine the magnitude of loss which it could bear without serious financial difficulty. If the firm is sufficiently strong, it may cover only those losses exceeding a specified minimum amount to avoid unnecessary coverage. It is important, of course, to guard against the tendency to underestimate the severity of potential losses.

Relate Cost of Premiums to Probability of Loss. Because the insurance company must collect enough premiums to pay the actual losses of insured parties, the cost of insurance must be proportional to the probability of occurrence of the insured event. As the chance of loss becomes more and more certain, a firm finds that the premium cost becomes so high that insurance is simply not worth the cost. Thus, insurance is most applicable and practical for improbable losses.

Requirements for Obtaining Insurance

Before an insurance company is willing to underwrite possible losses, certain requirements about the risk or the insured must be met. These requirements are explained below.

The Risk Must Be Calculable. The total overall loss arising from a large number of insured risks can be calculated by means of actuarial tables. For

7. John Cosgrove, "Risk Management: New Ways for Business to Insure Against Loss," *Nation's Business*, Vol. 65, No. 11 (November, 1977), p. 77. The entire article provides an excellent review of risk-management problems in small firms.

example, the number of buildings that will burn each year can be predicted with some accuracy. Only if the risks can be calculated will it be possible for the insurance company to determine fair insurance premiums to be charged.

The Risk Must Exist in Large Numbers. The particular risk must occur in sufficiently large numbers to permit the law of averages to work and be spread over a wide geographical area. A fire insurance company, for example, cannot afford to insure only one building or even all the buildings in one town. It would have to insure buildings in many other towns and cities to get an adequate, safe distribution of risk.

The Insured Property Must Have Commercial Value. An item that possesses only sentimental value cannot be insured. For example, an old family picture that is of no value to the public may not be included among other tangible items whose value can be measured in monetary terms.

The Policyholder Must Have an Insurable Interest in the Property or Person Insured. The purpose of insurance is reimbursement of actual loss and not creation of profit for the insured. For example, a firm could not insure a building for $500,000 if its true worth is actually only $70,000. Likewise, it could not obtain life insurance on its customers or suppliers.

Types of Insurance

There are several classifications of insurance and a variety of coverages available from different insurance companies. In buying insurance to cover appropriate risks, the small firm should use every possible means to reduce the cost of insurance. For example, policies may contain deductible or coinsurance clauses or may be placed on a three- or five-year basis and staggered as to dates of premium payment.

Fire Insurance. Fire insurance, and the related lines of insurance against disaster losses such as windstorm, tornado, explosion, riot, and so on, provides protection for the physical property of the firm. The **coinsurance clause**, which is typical in such insurance contracts, regulates the minimum coverage which can be secured without the insured's assuming a portion of the risk.

Most coinsurance clauses specify a minimum coverage of 80 percent of the property value. Assume that the physical property of a business is valued at $50,000. If the business insures it for $40,000 (or 80 percent of the property value) and incurs a fire loss of $20,000, the insurance company will pay the full amount of $20,000. However, if the business insures the property for only $30,000 (which is 75 percent of the specified minimum), the insurance company will pay only 75 percent of the loss, or $15,000.

A special word is required about the insurance for losses that occur as the result of business interruption following property damage. In the event of fire, tornado, hurricane, or windstorm—if named as sources of business interruption losses in the policy—a firm is reimbursed for both the loss of profits during the period of interruption and the fixed expenses of "shutdown operations." Wages for employees who are not required for "shutdown operations" can also be covered by special endorsement, but ordinarily this would be unnecessary. Typically, business interruption insurance coverage is for 90 days' interruption. Typically, also, business interruption policies are written with coinsurance clauses requiring one who underinsures to share the loss in part.

Marine Insurance. Marine insurance protects goods during shipment. It includes not only **ocean marine insurance** of shipments by water but also **inland marine insurance** covering transportation by rail or motor freight. One variety of inland marine insurance is the **commercial floater,** which insures business property against various hazards no matter where it is located. Contractors' equipment, for example, may be insured in this way. The commercial floater is not really transportation insurance even though marine insurance was originally designed to cover only the risks involved in transportation.

Casualty Insurance. Casualty insurance includes a variety of insurance. Automobile insurance—both collision and public liability—is a major field of casualty insurance. Burglary, theft, robbery, plate glass, and health and accident insurance are the other examples of casualty insurance. As pointed out earlier, liability risks are particularly important to small firms because of the very large losses which might be entailed in third-party claims.

Fidelity and Surety Bonds. Fidelity and surety companies guarantee to the business firm that individuals in its employment and others with whom the firm has business dealings are honest or will otherwise fulfill their contractual obligations. Employees occupying positions of trust in handling company funds are customarily bonded as a protection against their dishonesty. The informality and highly personal basis of employment in small firms make it difficult to realize the value of such insurance. It might be noted in this connection that an untrusted employee is seldom given access to company funds.

Surety bonds protect one firm against the failure of another firm or individual to fulfill a contractual obligation. Some small firms, particularly minority enterprises, have experienced difficulty in obtaining surety bonds. Title IV of the Small Business Investment Act of 1958 permits the Small Business Administration to guarantee a surety against loss—for a fee. However, this assistance is given only for obtaining bonding requirements to bid for government contracts. This guarantee program has been of great help to thousands of small contractors.

Credit Insurance. Some small firms are financially able to insure themselves against certain credit losses. **Credit insurance** protects businesses from *abnormal* bad-debt losses. Abnormally high losses are those that result from a customer's insolvency due to tornado or flood losses, depressed industry conditions, business recession, or other factors. Credit insurance does not cover *normal* bad-debt losses that are predictable on the basis of past business experience. Insurance companies compute the *normal* rate on the basis of industry experience and the loss record of the particular firm being insured.

Credit insurance is now available only to nonfinancial firms such as manufacturers and wholesalers. Thus, only trade credit may be insured. There are two reasons for this. The more important reason is found in the relative difficulty of analyzing business risks as compared with analyzing ultimate consumer risks. The other reason is that retailers have a much greater number of accounts receivable, which are smaller and provide greater risk diversification, so that credit insurance is less acutely required.

The collection service of the insurance company makes available legal talent and experience that may otherwise be unavailable to a small firm. Furthermore, collection efforts of insurance companies are generally conceded to be superior to those of regular collection agencies.

In addition, the credit standing of many small firms that might use credit insurance is enhanced. The small firm can show the banker that steps have been taken to avoid unnecessary risks, and thus more favorable consideration in securing bank credit might be obtained.

Credit insurance policies typically provide for a collection service on bad accounts. Although collection provisions vary, a common provision requires the insured to notify the insurance company within 90 days of the past-due status of the account and to turn it in for collection after 90 days.

Although the vast majority of policies provide general coverage, policies may be secured to cover individual accounts. A ten percent, or higher, coinsurance requirement is included to limit the coverage to approximately the replacement value of the merchandise. Higher percentages of coinsurance are required for inferior accounts in order to discourage reckless credit extension by insured firms. Accounts are classified according to ratings by Dun & Bradstreet or ratings by other recognized agencies. Premiums vary with account ratings.[8]

Life Insurance. By carrying life insurance, protection for the business can be provided against the death of the entrepreneur or key personnel of the firm.[9]

---

8. For additional discussion of credit insurance, see Adam Starchild, "Your Credit Rating—Now Insurance Can Protect It," *Journal of Applied Management*, Vol. 4, No. 2 (March-April, 1979), pp. 12-13.

9. The role of life insurance in funding a buy-sell agreement to insure the continuity of the business is explained in Harry Marantides, "The Crippling Blow," *Inc.*, Vol. 3, No. 5 (May, 1981), p. 166.

If the firm pays the premium as a regular business expense, it has at least a measure of protection against losses resulting from the untimely death of a member of the firm. The premium payment, however, is not a tax-deductible expense of the firm.

LOOKING BACK

1. Risk management is "an approach to management concerned with the preservation of the assets and earning power of a business against risks of accidental loss." The three ways to manage business risks are: reduce the risk, save to cover possible future losses, and transfer the risk to someone else by carrying insurance. The best solution often is to combine all three approaches.
2. Business risks can be classified by the causes of accidental loss, by insurability, or by type of assets which are preserved with risk management. In using the last system, risks are classified as marketing-centered, property-centered, employee-centered, and customer-centered.
3. The small firm should carry enough insurance to protect against major losses. Beyond this, the decision on coverage requires judgment that balances such factors as magnitude of possible loss, ability to minimize such losses, cost of the insurance, and financial strength of the firm.
4. To obtain insurance, several requirements must be met. The risk must be calculable in probabilistic terms, the risk must exist in large numbers, the insured property must have commercial value, and the policyholder must have an insurable interest in the property or person insured.
5. The basic types of insurance coverage which the small business might require are: fire insurance, marine insurance, casualty insurance, fidelity and surety bonds, credit insurance, and life insurance.

DISCUSSION QUESTIONS

1. What are the basic ways to cope with risk in a small business?
2. Can a small firm safely assume that business risks will never turn into losses sufficient to bankrupt it and therefore avoid buying insurance and taking other protective measures? Why?
3. How can a small business deal with the risk entailed in business recessions?
4. Could a small firm safely deal with such hazards as property loss from fire by precautionary measures in lieu of insurance?

5. When is it logical for a small business to utilize self-insurance?

6. Enumerate a number of approaches for combatting the danger of theft or fraud by employees and also by outsiders.

7. Under what conditions would life insurance on a business executive constitute little protection to the business? And when is such life insurance helpful?

8. Are any kinds of business risks basically human risks? Are the people involved always employees?

9. Is the increase in liability claims and court awards of special concern to small manufacturers? Why?

10. What types of insurance are required by law for most business firms?

REFERENCES TO SMALL BUSINESS IN ACTION

Green, Richard. "Under the Gun." *Forbes,* Vol. 127, No. 5 (March 2, 1981), pp. 98-99.

This article discusses the history of the Ruger Company, the last of the United States independent gun manufacturers. It includes the comments of its owner on the debt-free philosophy of the company and its insurance problems with product liability claims.

Hittig, Edwin H. "Is Safety Really Worth It?" *Inc.*, Vol. 2, No. 10 (October, 1980), pp. 65-66.

The safety program adopted by a manufacturer of supermarket fixtures is outlined in this reading. Injuries were reduced by more than 50 percent in one year.

Kmet, Mary Alice. "Safeguard Your Company Assets." *Inc.*, Vol. 3, No. 6 (June, 1981), pp. 106-116.

This article opens with an account of a company that was ruined by employee theft. It then presents some practical solutions to security problems.

CASE E-1

Style Shop*

A "tough guy" uses financial and accounting information for decisions

> A friend of mine recently said that 1975 is going to be the year of the tough guys, and that's right. It's for guys and gals who care enough to put everything they've got into what they're doing, and do their best. It's not the year for sitting around and letting everyone else do it for them. It's a good year for challenge and productivity because there is still money there, and there are still people who are ready to spend it. It's up to the tough guys, to the ones who merit being the ones with whom that money is spent![1]

Dorothy Barton, sitting at her desk in the small office just off the Style Shop sales floor, pondered this quotation which happened to catch her eye as she leafed through the latest edition of the *Dallas Fashion Retailer*.

In the women's ready-to-wear business, as in many other businesses, 1974 had been a rough year. It was particularly rough, however, for the attractive, energetic Style Shop owner. Wife, and the mother of four teenage daughters, Mrs. Barton saw her sales fall 12.5 percent from 1973 to 1974; but, more significantly, her net profit plunged 62.5 percent over the same time period. Untold hours she spent on the sales floor catering to her customers' eye for quality and fashion; in the office appealing to manufacturers to ship the next season's orders even though the current ones were yet to be paid; and at the Dallas Apparel Mart buying just the fashions she hoped would fit the needs and desires of her customers. At the same time, she was spending many hours each week in an effort to help her husband get his infant construction business off the ground.

She remembered hearing one "expert" say, "This is not a time for pessimism, nor a time for optimism. This is a time for realism." And an economic prognosticator had indicated that he saw a good future in the industry, despite the economic slowdown. Buyers, he noted, are working a little more cautiously right now. They are still buying, just looking at things a little more carefully.

"But what is 'realism' for me?" she asked herself. "Am I one of the tough guys who can stick it out and 'merit being the one with whom the money is spent!'?"

---

*This case was prepared by Professor Janelle C. Ashley of Stephen F. Austin State University.

1. "Merchandisers Must Provide Leadership," *Dallas Fashion Retailer* (June, 1975), p. 17.

Style Shop Location and Background

The Style Shop opened its doors on February 12, 1954, in Lufkin, TX, and in 1969 it moved to its present location in the Angelina Mall. The mall contains a major discount chain store, two full-line department stores, and a number of specialty shops. Located nearby are a twin cinema, motel, and junior college. The mall serves as the hub of a trade area extending over a radius of more than 100 miles. The only centers comparable to the Angelina Mall at the time were as distant as Houston, 120 miles to the southwest, and Dallas, 166 miles to the northwest.

Dorothy Barton, the present owner, began with the Style Shop as a part-time accountant in March, 1962. She became a 50-50 partner when the new shop opened in 1969 and purchased the 50 percent belonging to the other partner in January, 1974. She operates the business as a sole proprietorship.

The Style Shop up to 1974

Personnel. The Style Shop employed four full-time clerks, one alteration lady, and a maid. A former employee and the teenage daughter of Mrs. Barton were frequently called in for part-time work during peak seasons.

Mrs. Flo Gates had been with the shop for 10 years. She worked as a clerk and floor manager and accompanied Mrs. Barton to market. The other three clerks had been with the Style Shop from one to three years each. Personnel turnover and apathy had been problems in the past, but Mrs. Barton was quite pleased with her present work force.

Policies. The Style Shop operated with no formal, written policies. Personnel were paid wages and benefits comparable to other workers in similar capacities in the city. They enjoyed a great deal of freedom in their work, flexibility in hours of work, and a 20 percent discount on all merchandise purchased in the shop.

Competition. Lufkin had an average number of retail outlets carrying ladies' ready-to-wear for cities of its size. Several department stores and other specialty shops carried some of the same lines as did the Style Shop, but they were all comparable in price. The Style Shop did handle several exclusive lines in Lufkin, however, and enjoyed the reputation of being the most prestigious women's shop in town. Its major competition was a similar, but larger, specialty shop complete with a fashion shoe department in neighboring Nacogdoches, 19 miles away.

Inventory Control. The Style Shop used the services of Santoro Management Consultants, Inc., of Dallas, TX for inventory control. IBM inventory management reports were received each month broken down into 23 departmental groupings. These reports showed beginning inventory, sales and purchases for the month and year to date, markdowns, ending inventory, and various other information. Cost for the services was $110 per month.

Financial Position. It is often quite difficult and sometimes next to impossible to evaluate the "true" financial position of a single proprietorship or a partnership due to the peculiarities that are either allowed or tolerated in accounting practices for these forms of ownership. This is evident in looking at the Style Shop's five-year Comparative Statement of Income (Exhibit 1), the Comparative Statement of Financial Condition (Exhibit 2), plus the 1974 Statement of Income (Exhibit 3) and 1974 Statement of Financial Condition (Exhibit 4). Key business ratios (median) for women's ready-to-wear stores are also given for comparative purposes in Exhibit 5.

Two explanatory footnotes should be added to these statements. The jump in fixed assets between 1970 and 1971 (see Exhibit 2) and the subsequent changes were due in large part to the inclusion of personal real estate on the partnership books. The long-term liability initiated in 1971 was an SBA loan. Caught in a period of declining sales (due in part to the controversy over skirt length and women's pantsuits) and rapidly rising expenses in the new mall location, the Style Shop owners found themselves in that proverbial "financial bind" in late 1969 and 1970. They needed additional funds both for working capital and fixed investments. Since a big jump in sales was anticipated in the new location, additional working capital was necessary to purchase the required inventory. The new tenants also desired fixed-asset money to purchase display fixtures for their new store. They obtained this money through a local bank in the form of an SBA-insured loan.

The Style Shop, 1975

"Certainly there is no longer an arbiter of the length of a skirt or the acceptance of pantsuits," Mrs. Barton mused. "The economic picture is looking brighter. The experts tell us there will be more disposable personal income and a lower rate of inflation. Yet this is a time for 'realism.' Am I a 'tough guy'?"

Questions

1. Evaluate the overall performance of the Style Shop. How good a business was it at the end of 1974?
2. Compute the current ratio for the shop and compare it with the industry ratio. What are the implications?

3. Evaluate the shop's ratios showing the relationships of net profit to net sales, to net worth, and to net working capital.
4. How did the shop's net-sales-to-inventory ratio compare with that of the industry? Explain.
5. Should Mrs. Barton have kept the business or sold it? What are the primary factors to be considered in reaching such a decision?

Exhibit 1 Comparative Statement of Income

Item	1970	1971	1972	1973	1974
Sales	$200,845.43	$213,368.15	$216,927.31	$217,969.59	$190,821.85
Cost of sales	132,838.30	133,527.91	131,900.84	138,427.14	121,689.74
Gross profit	$ 68,007.13	$ 79,840.24	$ 85,026.47	$ 79,542.45	$ 69,132.11
Expenses	60,727.46	70,051.29	67,151.58	69,696.93	65,438.20
Net profit	$ 7,279.67	$ 9,788.95	$ 17,874.89	$ 9,845.52	$ 3,693.91

Exhibit 2 Comparative Statement of Financial Condition

Item	1970	1971	1972	1973	1974
Current assets*	$38,524.93	$ 70,015.11	$ 66,749.78	$ 58,530.44	$ 68,458.34
Inventory	23,039.00	37,971.00	33,803.00	36,923.00	35,228.00
Fixed assets	7,314.58	86,504.94	83,924.45	80,534.06	63,943.67
Total assets	$45,839.51	$156,520.05	$150,674.23	$139,064.50	$132,402.01
Current liabilities	$35,892.81	$ 19,586.45	$ 20,161.93	$ 31,587.57	$ 55,552.70
Long-term liabilities	none	39,042.90	33,680.07	26,841.76	20,003.45
Total liabilities	$35,892.81	$ 58,629.35	$ 53,842.00	$ 58,429.33	$ 75,556.15
Net worth	9,946.70	97,890.70	96,832.23	80,635.17	56,845.86
Total	$45,839.51	$156,520.05	$150,674.23	$139,064.50	$132,402.01

*Current-asset values include the amounts shown for inventory.

Exhibit 3 Statement of Income

Style Shop
Statement of Income
For Year Ended Dec. 31, 1974

Sales		$190,821.85
Cost of sales:		
Beginning inventory	$ 36,923.00	
Purchases	119,994.74	
	$156,917.74	
Ending inventory	35,228.00	121,689.74
Gross profit		$ 69,132.11
Expenses:		
Advertising	$ 3,034.63	
Auto expense	1,509.63	
Bad debts	(439.83)	
Depreciation	1,580.49	
Freight, express, delivery	2,545.90	
Heat, light, power, and water	1,847.96	
Insurance	1,431.80	
Interest	4,064.25	
Legal and accounting	2,034.74	
Rent	11,220.40	
Repairs	528.98	
Salary	26,227.69	
Supplies	5,138.11	
Tax – Payroll	1,656.18	
Tax – Other	604.62	
Telephone	784.67	
Dues and subscriptions	601.89	
Market and travel	1,066.09	65,438.20
Net profit		$ 3,693.91

Exhibit 4 Statement of Financial Condition

Style Shop
Statement of Financial Condition
Dec. 31, 1974

ASSETS

Current assets:		
Cash on hand and in banks		$ 4,923.92
Accounts receivable		21,306.42
Inventory		35,228.00
Cash value – Life insurance		7,000.00
Total current assets		$ 68,458.34
Fixed assets:		
Furniture and fixtures and leasehold improvements	$27,749.94	
Less: Allowance for depreciation	9,806.27	$ 17,943.67
Auto and truck		9,500.00
Real estate		20,000.00
Furniture		10,000.00
Boat and motor		2,000.00
Office equipment		2,500.00
Jewelry		2,000.00
Total fixed assets		$ 63,943.67
TOTAL ASSETS		$132,402.01

LIABILITIES AND CAPITAL

Current liabilities:	
Accounts payable	$ 30,413.12
Accrued payroll tax	825.64
Accrued sales tax	1,193.94
Note payable – Due in one year	9,420.00
Note payable – Lot	10,700.00
Note payable – Auto	3,000.00
Total current liabilities	$ 55,552.70
Note payable – Due after one year	20,003.45
Total liabilities	$ 75,556.15
Net worth	56,845.86
TOTAL LIABILITIES AND CAPITAL	$132,402.01

Exhibit 5 Key Business Ratios for Women's Ready-to-Wear Stores

Ratio	1974	1973	1972	1971	1970
Current assets / Current liabilities	2.65	2.81	2.51	2.38	2.50
Net profit / Net sales	2.05	2.30	1.81	1.86	2.18
Net profit / Net worth	8.92	8.53	6.68	7.14	8.73
Net profit / Net working capital	11.43	10.96	8.64	9.98	10.92
Net sales / Net worth	3.82	3.96	3.95	3.76	3.78
Net sales / Net working capital	4.61	4.92	4.73	4.90	4.49
Net sales / Inventory	6.7	6.7	6.6	6.7	6.1
Fixed assets / Net worth	18.3	18.2	18.6	17.5	14.7
Current liabilities / Net worth	49.4	49.2	51.0	54.5	56.5
Total liabilities / Net worth	98.5	100.1	104.0	124.1	125.8
Inventory / Net working capital	73.0	72.3	76.7	71.1	78.3
Current liabilities / Inventory	84.6	87.2	87.0	93.9	86.6
Long-term liabilities / Net working capital	30.1	33.2	29.8	34.0	30.8

Note: Collection period not computed. Necessary information as to the division between cash sales and credit sales was available in too few cases to obtain an average collection period usable as a broad guide.

Source: *Dun's Review* (September issues, 1970-1974).

CASE E-2

Barton Sales and Service

Managing the firm's working capital

Barton Sales and Service was located in Little Rock, AR. Its owners were John and Joyce Barton. John served as general manager, and Joyce as office manager. The firm sold General Electric, Carrier, and York air-conditioning and heating systems and serviced these and other types of systems as well. It served both commercial and residential customers. Although the business had operated successfully since the Bartons purchased it five years earlier, it continued to experience working-capital problems.

Barton's Financial Structure

The firm had been profitable since the Bartons purchased it. Profits for 1981 were the highest for any year to date. Exhibit 1 shows the income statement for that year.

The balance sheet as of December 31, 1981, for Barton Sales and Service is shown in Exhibit 2. Note that the firm's equity was somewhat less than its total debt. However, $51,231 of the firm's liabilities was a long-term note carrying a modest rate of interest. This note was issued at the time the Bartons purchased the business, and the payments were made to the former owner.

Barton's Cash Balance

A minimum cash balance is necessary in any business because of the uneven nature of cash inflows and outflows. John explained that they needed a substantial amount in order to "feel comfortable." He felt that it might be possible to reduce the present balance by $5,000 to $10,000, but he stated that it gave them some "breathing room."

Barton's Accounts Receivable

The trade accounts receivable at the end of 1981 were $56,753, but at some times during the year the accounts receivable were twice this amount. These accounts were not aged, so the firm had no specific knowledge of the number of overdue accounts. However, the firm had never experienced any significant loss from bad debts. The accounts receivable were thought, therefore, to be good accounts of a relatively recent nature.

Customers were given 30 days from the date of the invoice to pay the net amount. No cash discounts were offered. If payment was not received during the first 30 days, a second statement was mailed to the customer and monthly carrying charges of one tenth of 1 percent were added. The state usury law prohibited higher carrying charges.

On small residential jobs, the firm tried to collect from customers when work was completed. When a service representative finished repairing an air-conditioning system, for example, the rep presented a bill to the owner and attempted to obtain payment at that time. However, this was not always possible. On major items such as unit changeouts—which often ran as high as $2,500—billing was practically always necessary.

On new construction projects, the firm sometimes received partial payments prior to completion of a project. This helped to minimize the amount tied up in receivables.

Barton's Inventory

Inventory accounted for a substantial portion of the firm's working capital. It consisted of the various heating and air-conditioning units, parts, and supplies used in the business.

The Bartons had no guidelines or industry standards to use in evaluating their overall inventory levels. They felt that there *might* be some excessive inventory, but, in the absence of a standard, this was basically an opinion. When pressed to estimate the amount that might be eliminated by careful control, John pegged it at 15 percent.

The firm used an annual physical inventory which coincided with the end of its fiscal year. Since the inventory level was known for only one time in the year, the income statement could be prepared only on an annual basis. There was no way of knowing how much of the inventory was expended at other points and thus no way to calculate profits. As a result, the Bartons lacked quarterly or monthly income statements to assist them in managing the business.

Barton Sales and Service was considering changing from a physical inventory to a perpetual inventory system. This would enable John to know the inventory levels of all items at all times. An inventory total could easily be computed for use in preparing statements. Shifting to a perpetual inventory system would require the purchase of proper file equipment, but that cost was not large enough to constitute a major barrier. A greater expense would be involved in the maintenance of the system—entering all incoming materials and all withdrawals. The Bartons estimated that this task would necessitate the work of one person on a half-time or three-fourths time basis.

Barton's Note Payable to the Bank

Bank borrowing was the most costly form of credit. Barton Sales and Service paid the going rate, slightly above prime, and owed $17,600. The note was a 90-day renewable note. Normally some was paid on the principal when the note was renewed. The total borrowing could probably be increased if necessary. There was no obvious pressure from the bank to reduce borrowing to zero. The amount borrowed during the year typically ranged from $10,000 to $25,000.

The Bartons had never explored the limits the bank might impose on borrowing, and there was no clearly specified line of credit. When additional funds were required, Joyce simply dropped by the bank, spoke with a bank officer, and signed a note for the appropriate amount.

Barton's Trade Accounts Payable

A significant amount of Barton's working capital came from its trade accounts payable. Although accounts payable at the end of 1981 were $38,585, the total payable varied over time and might be double this amount at another point in the year. Barton obtained from various dealers such supplies as expansion valves, copper tubing, sheet metal, electrical wire, electrical conduit, and so on. Some suppliers offered a discount for cash (2/10, n/30), but Joyce felt the credit was more important than the few dollars which could be saved by taking a cash discount. By giving up the cash discount, the firm obtained the use of the money for 30 days. Although the Bartons might wait a few days beyond the 30 days before paying, their suppliers quickly applied pressure. The Bartons could stretch the payment dates to 45 or even 60 days before being "put on C.O.D." However, they found it unpleasant to delay payment more than 45 days because suppliers would begin calling and applying pressure for payment.

The major manufacturers (Carrier, General Electric, and York) used different terms of payment. Some major products could be obtained from Carrier on an arrangement known as "floor planning." This meant that the manufacturer (Carrier) shipped the products without requiring immediate payment. The Bartons made payment only when the product was sold. If still unsold after 90 days, the product had to be returned or paid for. (It was shipped back on a company truck, so there was no expense in returning unsold items.) On items which were not floor-planned but which were purchased from Carrier, Barton paid the net amount by the 10th of the month or was charged 18 percent interest on late payments.

Shipments from General Electric required payment at the bank soon after receipt of the products. If cash was not available at the time, this necessitated further borrowing from the bank.

Purchases from York required net payment without discount within 30 days. However, if payment was not made within 30 days, interest at 18 percent per annum was added.

Can Good Profits Become Better?

Although Barton Sales and Service had earned a *good* profit in 1981, the Bartons wondered whether they were realizing the *most possible* profit. The pressure of inflation and slowness in construction caused by high interest rates was slowing their business somewhat. They wanted to be sure they were meeting the challenging times as prudently as possible.

Questions

1. Evaluate the overall performance and financial structure of Barton Sales and Service.
2. What are the strengths and weaknesses in this firm's management of accounts receivable and inventory?
3. Should the firm reduce or expand its bank borrowing?
4. Evaluate the Bartons' management of trade accounts payable.
5. How can Barton Sales and Service improve its working-capital situation?

Exhibit 1 Barton Sales and Service Income Statement for the Year Ended December 31, 1981

Sales	$727,679
Less: Cost of sales	466,562
Gross profit	$261,117
Less: Selling, general & administrative expense (including officers' salaries)	189,031
Net income before income taxes	$ 72,086
Provision for income taxes	17,546
Net income	$ 54,540

Exhibit 2 Barton Sales and Service Balance Sheet as of December 31, 1981

ASSETS

Current assets:	
Cash	$ 28,789
Trade accounts receivable	56,753
Inventory	89,562
Prepaid expenses	4,415
Total current assets	$179,519
Loans to stockholders	14,832
Autos, trucks, and equipment, at cost, less accumulated depreciation of $36,841	24,985
Other assets – Goodwill	16,500
TOTAL ASSETS	$235,836

LIABILITIES AND STOCKHOLDERS' EQUITY

Current liabilities:	
Current maturities of long-term debt (see Note 1)	$ 26,403
Trade accounts payable	38,585
Accrued payroll taxes	2,173
Accrued income taxes	13,818
Other accrued expenses	4,001
Total current liabilities	$ 84,980
Long-term debt (see Note 1)	51,231
Stockholders' equity	99,625
TOTAL LIABILITIES AND STOCKHOLDERS' EQUITY	$235,836

Note 1: Short-Term and Long-Term Debt

	Long-Term	Current	Total
(1) 10% note payable, secured by pickup, due in monthly installments of $161 including interest	$ 1,367	$ 1,827	$ 3,194
(2) 10% note payable, secured by equipment, due in monthly installments of $180 including interest	0	584	584
(3) 6% note payable, secured by inventory and equipment, due in monthly installments of $678 including interest	39,127	6,392	45,519
(4) 9% notes payable to stockholders	10,737	0	10,737
(5) 20% note payable to bank in 30 days	0	17,600	17,600
	$51,231	$26,403	$77,634

CASE E-3

The Fair Store*

Contemplating a computerized inventory-control system

The Fair Store of Lott, TX (a small town of less than 1,000 population) has built a reputation as the state's leading retailer of high-quality western wear at moderate prices. Its owner is R. W. Hailey. In the store the atmosphere of the Old West is developed by narrow aisles, crowded racks of merchandise, inexpensive fixtures, and informality in operating procedures. Many customers drive hundreds of miles to this store and, at certain times of the year, stand in line on the sidewalk in order to be admitted.

Fair Store's Sales Personnel

All of the salesclerks at The Fair Store are local people. Many of them are housewives whose husbands are farmers in the surrounding areas. For the most part, the sales personnel are not well-educated and are quite provincial. However, they have always been accustomed to hard work and are pleasant to customers.

Fair Store's Merchandising Practices

In western wear, just as in other types of merchandise, style consciousness affects customer demand. Quite a variety of merchandise is sold. Many brands of boots with different price ranges are sold, but The Fair Store's two principal suppliers of handmade boots are Tony Lama and Justin Company.

Breaking the merchandise into groups, Hailey estimates the store's merchandise assortment as follows:

Hats	8%
Jeans, pants, suits, and shirts	20%
Children's boots and cheaper adult boots	15%
Tony Lama and Justin Red Wing boots	50%
Miscellaneous	7%

The buying of boots has to be done months ahead, usually about six months, because they are handmade. Such a time lag means that purchasing for the Thanksgiving and Christmas markets must come no later than the

*This case was prepared by Professor Kris K. Moore of Baylor University.

previous April or May. Boots, therefore, entail a large inventory investment during the period from June to November. A recent amount purchased from the Justin Company for this market period was $57,507.

Western hats (which are often custom-steamed to the customer's favorite crease) follow the seasonal demand—with straw hats for spring and summer, and felt hats for fall and winter. Hats must be purchased six months in advance. Jeans, pants, suits, and shirts must also be purchased several months in advance.

Fair Store's Inventory Practices

At present the store has no direct methods of inventory control. The sales representatives from Tony Lama and Justin Company bring samples of different styles to Hailey. He then chooses styles that he believes will sell and, with the sales representatives, determines the price and the quantity to be shipped. When the merchandise is received at the store, Hailey helps unpack the goods and mark prices. There is no verification that merchandise received matches the purchase orders. No further record keeping is maintained. Merchandise is shelved, and the amount of a sale is rung up on the cash register when a customer has concluded his or her shopping.

Periodically Hailey walks through the store and makes a visual check of merchandise, noting low levels of styles and sizes. He then places new orders on the basis of such notes. At year's end, an inventory check is made to determine the information needed for tax returns. The yearly inventory check is time-consuming and costly.

Hailey's Thoughts on Computerizing

After the store grossed over a million dollars in a recent fiscal year, Hailey began wondering how he could use a computer for better control of the business. He was especially interested in 2 areas: (1) controlling the average daily inventory, which had grown from $94,000 to $207,000 in 1 year, and (2) having available in quantity for customers the most demanded sizes of handmade boots. Although sales had increased satisfactorily, the rate of increase was lower than the growth in inventory. Hailey felt that his business would continue to grow at a rapid rate and wondered if a computer would help him with inventory management.

Questions

1. In what areas of inventory management does R. W. Hailey seem to have the greatest problems? What cost savings might be realized by better inventory control?
2. What buying, receiving, pricing, and check-out changes would be necessary to accommodate a computerized inventory-control system? Be specific.

3. What would be the primary benefits derived from computerized inventory control at The Fair Store? What are some secondary benefits of computerizing the inventory system?
4. Wherein lie the anticipated problems of a computerized system for The Fair Store?
5. What steps should Hailey take if he wishes to obtain a computer?

CASE E-4

Dale's Lawn Service

Determining insurance needs of a small service business

As Donnie Conner organized his new business, Dale's Lawn Service, he thought about insurance needs and contacted an insurance agent to talk it over. The insurance agent asked Donnie to explain the nature of the business prior to discussing insurance coverage.

Nature of the Business

Donnie explained that he had worked for another lawn-care firm for three years but had decided to begin his own business. In preparation for getting into business, he had acquired 3 riding lawnmowers ($800 each), 5 push lawnmowers ($300 each), 2 hedge clippers ($265 each), 2 edgers ($225 each), a small used pick-up truck ($3,500), a trailer ($1,000), and miscellaneous other equipment.

Donnie planned to provide lawn care for apartments, commercial buildings, and residential properties. In fact, he had been servicing a number of properties on his own time while working for the other employer. The most important part of his business would be performed on the basis of 12-month maintenance contracts. These called for the care of lawns, shrubs, and trees. On some contracts, the rate for three winter months was somewhat lower than the normal monthly rate. However, since some work (such as trimming trees, pruning shrubs, and raking leaves) was necessary in the winter, a few contracts specified a uniform monthly fee throughout the year.

At the beginning, Donnie would be the only person in the business, but he expected to hire other employees when he was able to expand. While he wanted to protect himself against the most important risks which would be involved in the business, he also wished to avoid excessive insurance coverage and to minimize expenses during the early days in the business.

Donnie's Automobile Insurance Coverage

Since Donnie already owned the truck, he had included it with his car on a personal automobile insurance policy. The policy provided for collision coverage ($200 deductible), single-limit liability covering bodily injury and property damage ($50,000), and comprehensive coverage. The agent assured Donnie that his automobile insurance coverage was adequate for business purposes since he used the truck for both personal and business use.

Proposed General Liability Coverage

The agent suggested a $50,000 general liability policy at a premium of $153 per year. Donnie was a little unsure of the wisdom of buying this insurance because he needed to keep all costs to a bare minimum until he became established. On the other hand, he recalled that a mower operated by his former employer once threw a rock that struck a small girl in the face and cut the skin. There was always the outside chance that some such accident could occur because his work was always performed on the property of others.

Proposed Major Medical Insurance

The agent also recommended a major medical policy (with a small deductible) that would cover hospital, surgery, and other medical costs. On major medical expenses, the insurance company would pay 80 percent of the total that exceeded the deductible. Family coverage (for Donnie, his wife Stephany, and his 1-year-old son Caleb) would cost $102 per month, plus a $15 monthly processing fee for the business. (This $15 fee would remain at this level even after Donnie placed other employees under the policy.) When Donnie decided to hire employees, he could add each of them to the policy for approximately $45 per month. The employees would have the option to pay for coverage of their families.

Proposed Six-Months' Disability Coverage

If Donnie desired, he could also add a six-months' disability clause. The premium on this insurance would run $17 per month. In the event he became disabled through injury or illness, this would pay two thirds of his weekly salary for 180 days. For example, if Donnie planned to pay himself a $300 weekly salary, he would receive a compensation payment, if disabled, of $200 per week. Donnie was only 30 years old, had good health, and had no prior disabilities. However, most of his financial resources were invested in the business.

Proposed Long-Term Disability Insurance

For disability beyond 6 months, Donnie could secure a long-term policy which would begin after 6 months and run as long as he was disabled or until age 65. For the same $200-per-week coverage, the premium would run $42.50 per month. It would take a major accident or very serious illness, of course, to disable him for more than six months. He wondered whether the premium was too much for such an unlikely possibility.

After new employees were hired, they would be covered by the state's workers' compensation plan. Donnie could also elect to be included in that plan. However, the plan protected against only work-related accidents or illnesses, and the total reimbursement for lost wages would be much less than the amount provided by the disability policy. (The law specified a maximum compensation of less than $100 per week and a maximum time period for benefits, the length varying with the type of disability.)

Proposed Theft Insurance

Another hazard faced by the business was the possible theft of equipment. The principal danger, as Donnie saw it, existed while he was using equipment on the job. While he was using one piece of equipment on another part of the property, other items might be stolen from the truck or trailer. A friend of his had lost two lawnmowers in this way. The only available theft insurance had a $200 deductible on each piece of equipment and involved a premium of $40 per month. Donnie wondered whether there was any other way to protect the equipment so that he could avoid this expense.

Donnie's Reactions

Having reviewed the various policies, the agent asked Donnie which coverages he wanted. Rather than respond immediately, Donnie asked for a few days to think it over.

Questions

1. What general liability insurance, if any, should Donnie Conner buy?
2. Should Donnie take the hospitalization insurance?
3. Should he acquire the short-term disability coverage? The long-term disability coverage?
4. Should he obtain theft insurance for the equipment used in the firm?
5. What other insurance, if any, would be desirable?

Part F

STATUS AND FUTURE OF SMALL BUSINESS

Chapter 22

Governmental Interaction with Small Business

LOOKING AHEAD

Watch for the following important topics:

1. The four major areas of governmental regulation applicable to small business.
2. The burdensome nature of small-business regulation.
3. Attempts to reduce the regulatory burden on small business.
4. Tax responsibilities, tax-saving opportunities, and tax-reform concerns of small business.
5. Types of special assistance provided by government.

Government and small business interact in a number of ways. Government regulates, taxes, and assists small firms in various forms and at several levels. Small firms are responsible for compliance with relevant laws and regulations. Of course, small-firm management is free to take a political role and to express its views on existing laws and desired modifications of laws. A prime source of conflict exists, however, because of the entrepreneur's desire for independence and the increasing role of government in business. In this chapter we will examine the impact on small businesses of governmental regulation, taxation, and special assistance.

GOVERNMENTAL REGULATION

Federal laws, as well as state laws, regulate business activity for the benefit and protection of both business firms and the general public. American public policy has long embodied the principle of guaranteed freedom to enter and engage in business. This is part of the economic doctrine which emphasizes the importance of free competition as a method of providing maximum values to consumers.

Maintenance of Free Competition

Of the various laws intended to maintain a competitive economy, perhaps the best known are the federal antitrust laws, especially the Sherman Antitrust Act of 1890 and the Clayton Act of 1914. Both acts were designed to promote competition by eliminating artifical restraints on trade.

Impact of Antitrust Laws. Although the purpose of federal and state antitrust laws is noble, the results leave much to be desired. One would be naive to think that small business need no longer fear the power of oligopolists. These laws prevent some mergers and eliminate some unfair practices, but giant business firms continue to dominate many industries.

To some extent, at least, the antitrust laws do offer protection to small firms. For example, in 1977, a local distributor of petroleum products sued a major oil company and another dealer for $6 million, charging violation of antitrust laws. The suit alleged that the plaintiff was overcharged for gasoline, given unreasonably low allocations of petroleum products, and forced to make one station a nonbrand station. In another case, a small processor of waste material from slaughterhouses, stores, and restaurants sought treble damages of $300,000 and injunctive relief from monopolistic competition. The plaintiff claimed that a larger competitor had begun offering unreasonably high prices for waste products in the plaintiff's territory, far above the prices offered in the defendant's established territory. The suit alleged that the defendant's purpose was to establish a monopoly.

Impact of Laws on Unfair Competition. In 1914, just prior to the enactment of the Clayton Act, Congress passed the Federal Trade Commission Act. This act created the Federal Trade Commission (FTC), a body empowered to regulate unfair methods of competition. It seems evident that Congress wished to establish an agency to maintain surveillance over competitive practices

ACTION REPORT: Regulations Create a Monopoly

Even though public policy calls for the prevention of business monopolies, government regulation sometimes works in the opposite direction. As an example, a Consumer Product Safety Commission regulation apparently reduced the number of swimming pool slide manufacturers from seven to one.

In 1976, the Consumer Product Safety Commission issued a safety standard covering the building and installation of swimming pool slides. Soon afterward, six firms dropped out of the market, leaving it to Aqua Slide 'N Dive Corporation of Brownsville, TX, which held 90 percent of the market. The Commission later admitted that five years of such regulation had brought no evidence of a reduction in pool slide accidents.

Source: "Everybody Out of the Pool," by Beth Brophy, *Forbes,* Vol. 128, No. 4 (August 17, 1981), p. 44.

and to prevent unfair acts before legal action became necessary. The regulatory authority of the FTC was extended by the Wheeler-Lea Act of 1938 to provide protection to consumers against "unfair or deceptive acts or practices in commerce."

Impact of Price Laws. As an amendment to the Clayton Act, the Robinson-Patman Act of 1936 prohibited price discrimination by manufacturers and wholesalers in dealing with other business firms. In particular, the law is designed to protect independent retailers and wholesalers in their fight against large chains. Quantity discounts may still be offered to large buyers, but the amount of the discounts must be justified economically by the seller on the basis of actual costs. Vendors are also forbidden to grant disproportionate advertising allowances to large retailers. The objective is to prevent unreasonable discounts and other concessions to large purchasers merely because of superior size and bargaining power.

The effectiveness of the Robinson-Patman Act and its benefits to small business have been greatly debated. In 1975, President Ford argued that it discourages both large and small firms from cutting prices and makes it harder to expand into new markets and to pass on to customers the cost savings on large orders.[1] Even consumer-oriented groups consider the law so confusing that they refuse to defend it.

The majority of states have **unfair-trade practice laws**, known under different titles such as unfair-trade practices acts, unfair-sales acts, and unfair-

1. "Ford Tries to Defang Robinson-Patman," *Business Week* (May 12, 1975), p. 28.

practices acts. These laws specify that sellers may not sell goods at less than their cost and also specify certain percentage markups. Some of the state unfair-trade laws even cover personal services.

While unfair-trade practice laws ostensibly aim to eliminate unfair price competition, there is a question as to whether they accomplish this objective. The danger in such laws is their tendency to handicap those firms that are able to reduce prices because of their efficiency. Thus, in the guise of preservation of free competition, these laws may actually hold a price umbrella over inefficient, marginal firms, denying freedom of enterprise to efficient firms and penalizing the public accordingly.

Impact of Laws on Rail and Motor Carriers. The Interstate Commerce Commission (ICC) was created to regulate the transportation of goods across state lines. Some nonrail carriers have argued that the ICC has restricted entry into the trucking business and generally prevented effective competition between truck and rail lines. The following incident provides a humorous but illuminating example of the heavy-handed nature of such regulations:

> In March, 1965, Tom Hilt, of Hilt Truck Line, Inc., of Omaha, got fed up with the knee-jerk reaction of the railroads in automatically protesting every tariff he filed with the Interstate Commerce Commission. With tongue in cheek, Hilt filed a rate for the transport of yak fat between Omaha and Chicago. Sure enough, the Western Trunk Line Committee protested on the grounds that the cost of trucking yak fat far exceeded the proposed rate and was therefore illegal. And, sure enough, the ICC suspended the rate. After 30 days, the Commission found that Hilt had failed to prove the rate legal, and it was disallowed.[2]

The Motor Carrier Act of 1980 has reduced the degree of regulation of the trucking industry. This step of deregulation opened up some opportunities for small business. For example, a small family business, Love's Trucking, Inc., was founded in Troy, OH to haul steel between Franklin, OH and McLean, GA.[3] However, government regulation does not disappear in deregulated industries even though the scope of regulation is curtailed. Love's Trucking, Inc., must still comply with many state regulations, as well as with those ICC regulations which remain. And truckers must still apply to the ICC for permits to operate in particular areas and to haul particular commodities.[4]

---

2. "The Economic Case for Deregulating Trucking," *Business Week,* No. 2355 (November 2, 1974), p. 86.

3. Ed Barnes, "A Trucking Company Rolls," *Venture,* Vol. 3, No. 1 (January, 1981), pp. 24-26.

4. For a discussion of the status of deregulation, see "Hitting the Brakes: New ICC Chairman Reese Taylor Moves to Halt Trucking-Industry Deregulation," *The Wall Street Journal,* August 5, 1981, p. 46.

Consumer Protection

Insofar as freedom of competition is provided by the laws discussed above, consumers will benefit indirectly. In addition, consumers are given various forms of more direct protection by federal, state, and local legislation.

As mentioned earlier, the Wheeler-Lea Act gave the Federal Trade Commission a broad mandate to attack unfair or deceptive acts or practices in commerce. The FTC's original focus on antitrust practices has been expanded through the years to cover a wide range of business activities: labeling, safety, packaging, and advertising of products; truth-in-lending; fair credit reporting; equal credit opportunity; and many others. States have also enacted laws and created consumer protection agencies to deal with unfair or deceptive practices.

A few examples of the types of trade practices scrutinized by the Federal Trade Commission are: labeling goods as "free" or "handmade"; advertising that offers unreal "bargains" by pretended reduction of unused "regular" prices; and **bait advertising**, in which a low price for an article is advertised merely to lure a prospect into the place of business, whereupon the customer is talked into purchasing a more expensive product.

As still another measure to protect the public against unreasonable risk of injury associated with toys and other consumer products, the federal government enacted the Consumer Product Safety Act of 1972. This act created the Consumer Product Safety Commission to enforce its established goal. The Commission is authorized to set safety standards for consumer products and to ban those goods which are exceptionally hazardous.

Protection of Investors

To protect the investing public against fraudulent devices and swindles in the sale of stocks and bonds, both federal and state laws regulate the issuance and public sale of securities. The federal laws involved are the Securities Act of 1933 and the Securities Exchange Act of 1934. The latter act established the powerful Securities and Exchange Commission to enforce the regulations provided by both acts.

Because of the small amounts involved and the private nature of much of their financing, most small businesses are excluded from extensive regulation under federal law. However, they are subject to state **blue-sky laws**. In general, these laws cover registration of new securities; licensing of dealers, brokers, and salespersons; and prosecution of individuals charged with fraud in connection with the sale of stocks and bonds.

Promotion of Public Welfare

Laws that promote the public interest involve environmental protection and licensing procedures for certain professions and types of businesses. A case of sorts can be made for the regulation of almost any business. However, any failure to limit such regulation to the most essential cases erodes the freedom of opportunity to enter business.

Impact of Environmental Protection Laws. During the 1970s, numerous environmental protection laws were enacted at the federal, state, and local levels. Specifically, the major laws deal with air pollution, water pollution, solid-waste disposal, and toxic substances. Some of the laws are written in great detail, outlining specific regulatory responsibilities. Other laws confer broad authority on the regulatory agencies. In addition, the federal laws establish minimum standards while state and local governments are free to impose more stringent requirements. As explained in Chapter 13, anti-pollution laws adversely affect some small firms although they may occasionally benefit other firms.

Impact of Laws on Licensing. State governments restrict entry into numerous professions and types of businesses by establishing licensing procedures. For example, physicians, barbers, pharmacists, accountants, lawyers, and real estate salespersons are licensed. Insurance companies, banks, and public utilities must seek entry permits from state officials. Although licensing protects the public interest, it also tends to restrict the number of professionals and firms in such a way as to reduce competition and increase prices paid by consumers.

There is a difference between licensing that involves a routine application and that which prescribes rigid entry standards and screening procedures. The fact that the impetus for much licensing comes from within the industry suggests the need for careful scrutiny of licensing proposals. Otherwise, we may be merely protecting a private interest and minimizing freedom to enter a field of business.

THE BURDENSOME NATURE OF REGULATION ON SMALL BUSINESS

The growth of governmental regulation has reached the point that it imposes a real hardship on the small firm. To some extent, the problems arise from seemingly inevitable "red tape" and bureaucratic procedures of governments.

Even apart from the arbitrariness of regulation, its sheer weight is burdensome to small firms. The contents of the 330-page volume on the Occupational Safety and Health Act (OSHA) alone place unreasonable demands on the funds and productive energies of small companies. The following excerpt from a study by the Small Business Administration provides some understanding of the cumulative burden of regulation:

A Senate Study Group estimated that the annual cost of unnecessary and wasteful regulation ranges between $66 and $475 per U. S. citizen. They also estimated that the number of Federal employees in regulatory agencies has grown from 53,300 in 1973 to 63,700 in 1975 – an increase of 14 percent . . . .

Federal regulations have hampered the rate of introduction of new products. The National Commission on Productivity and Work Quality indicated that overregulaton has created excessive obstacles to technological process [sic]. Industries that are most heavily regulated are usually dominated by a few large firms. Small businesses cannot survive and, consequently, concentration in the regulated industry may occur. The pharmaceutical industry is an example. Food and Drug Administration procedures delay the introduction of new drugs and discourage small business from competing.[5]

Attempts to Reduce the Regulatory Burden

The burdensome nature of small-business regulation became increasingly evident during the 1970s. In January, 1980, the White House Conference on Small Business highlighted the problem, and 4 of its top 30 recommendations dealt with improvements in the regulatory process.

The most important law to emerge from the Conference was the Regulatory Flexibility Act of 1980. According to this law, federal agencies must assess the impact of proposed regulations on small business. They are required to reduce paperwork requirements and to exempt small firms or simplify rules when at all possible. The general purpose of the act is to avoid

Source: GOOSEMYER by Parker and Wilder, © 1980, Field Enterprises, Inc. Courtesy of Field Newspaper Syndicate.

Figure 22-1 The Entrepreneur's View of Regulation

5. *The Study of Small Business,* a study conducted and prepared pursuant to Public Law 94-305 by the Office of Advocacy, U. S. Small Business Administration, 1977, Part I, p. 39.

ACTION REPORT: A Case of Overregulation

The following account by Arthur Levitt, which one may hope is rare, illustrates the tendency toward overregulation.

> Billy Halliwell had it made, or at least he thought so. The ingredients were all there for the 11-year-old Roseland, N. J., lad to turn a profit from sleepy motorists waiting in predawn gas lines last July. They needed an eye-opener, and Billy provided it from his sister's red wagon laden with coffee and doughnuts. Free enterprise in a most elementary form.
>
> But Billy soon learned the harsh realities that confront millions of small-business owners in this country, namely, that free enterprise is hardly free.
>
> State and local officials soon shut down "Billy's Breakfast" because he lacked a peddler's license, failed to collect state sales taxes and neglected to file a quarterly return with state authorities. Billy was confused by forays from the police department, the local board of health, and the state tax bureau. With the help of his father, William, young Bill spent many hours learning firsthand the ordeals of small-business men and women.
>
> Billy's father estimates that it cost the family close to $1,000 in cash and lost time to guide the youngster through government's bewildering bureaucratic maze. Red-faced officials spent a great deal of taxpayers' money capturing 21 cents—yes, 21 cents—in tax payments from "Billy's Breakfast." Later, the state said its regulations did not apply to Billy's "casual business."

Source: Reprint by permission of FAMILY WEEKLY, copyright 1979, 641 Lexington Avenue, New York, NY 10022.

unnecessary burdensome regulation of small firms. Its usefulness will depend upon the vigor and consistency of its application.

Another law recognizing the regulatory plight of small firms is the Equal Access to Justice Act of 1980. This law requires the federal government to reimburse court costs for small firms that win cases against regulatory agencies.

The Need for Flexibility in Regulation

Some persons have argued that special consideration in the regulation of small firms is in itself unfair. According to this logic, all competitive firms should "play by the same rules." However, we should note that the marketplace is not perfectly competitive and that the hand of regulation rests more heavily upon small competitors. The latter point of view is summarized well by Robert E. Berney, a professor of economics at Washington State University, as follows:

> While the government's regulations, tax codes, and monetary policies raise costs for all businesses, small businesses experience a greater cost increase *per dollar of sales or output.* Government procurement policies actually favor large suppliers, in effect lowering their cost of doing business with the government.
>
> The net effect of these government-imposed costs and benefits is to dramatically twist the cost schedules of firms of varying sizes and to interfere with competition. Free markets do not exist when big companies get bigger, not because of any inherent economies of scale, but because of non-neutral government policies.[6]

Rather than provide a special advantage to small business, therefore, flexibility in regulation serves to minimize a government-imposed handicap.

TAXATION

The primary tax responsibility of a small business is to pay all legally required taxes. In paying taxes, the firm is both an agent and a debtor. As an agent, it withholds and pays taxes owed by others. As a debtor, the firm pays taxes for which it is directly liable.

Tax-Withholding Obligations of the Small Business

The major tax-withholding obligations of a business involve the following taxes:

1. *Income taxes.* Each employee signs a withholding exemption certificate which specifies the number of allowable exemptions. The amounts withheld are passed on to the government periodically by the employer.
2. *Social Security taxes.* An employer is required to deduct a specified amount of each employee's salary, and this amount is also passed on periodically to the government by the employer.
3. *Sales taxes.* Many state and local governments impose sales taxes. A business firm must collect and pass them on to the appropriate governmental agency.

---

6. Letter to the Editor, *Inc.,* Vol. 3, No. 2 (February, 1981), p. 10.

Major Taxes Paid by the Small Business

The major taxes for which small firms and owners are directly responsible as debtors are the following:

1. *Income taxes.* The federal income tax paid by a business depends on its earnings and on its legal form of organization. According to the Economic Recovery Tax Act of 1981, the corporate income tax rate effective in 1983 and later is: 15 percent on the first $25,000 of net income; 18 percent on the second $25,000 of net income; 30 percent on the third $25,000 of net income; 40 percent on the fourth $25,000 of net income; and 46 percent on net income above $100,000. As explained in Chapter 8, some corporations may qualify as Subchapter S corporations and elect to be taxed as partnerships. In any event, individual owners pay personal income taxes on proprietorship earnings, partnership earnings, corporate salaries, and corporate dividends. Some states and a few cities also impose income taxes.
2. *Federal excise taxes.* Federal excise taxes are imposed on the sale or use of some items and on some occupations. For example, there is a tax on the sale of certain motor fuels, a highway use tax on trucks which use federal highways, and an occupational tax on retail liquor dealers.
3. *Unemployment taxes.* Firms pay both federal and state unemployment taxes on salaries and wages. The tax rate is usually related to previous unemployment experience.
4. *Local taxes.* Counties, towns, school districts, and other local entities impose various types of taxes. Among these are real estate taxes and personal property taxes. Business licenses are also taxes even though the owner may not recognize them as such.
5. *Estate taxes.* A federal tax is imposed on estates which are passed on to heirs. The amount to be excluded from the inheritance tax will gradually increase from $275,000 in 1983 to $600,000 by 1987. In some cases, families are forced to sell family businesses in order to pay estate taxes.

Tax Savings Through Tax Planning

Tax savings are possible if one knows the law. Legal *tax avoidance,* which is in sharp contrast to illegal *tax evasion,* is both practical and ethical. The small business, while relying primarily on tax experts for assistance, may also supplement this assistance by reference to tax articles in periodicals, pamphlets, books, or loose-leaf tax services. The size of the business, of course, will determine the amount which can be spent in the accumulation of such a tax data library, as well as the time available for its use.

One example of planning to realize tax savings involves using the "investment tax credit." To stimulate investment, the tax law permits a specified percentage of properly-qualified investments in new equipment to be deducted from the firm's tax bill in the first year. Buildings and their structural components are excluded from the investment credit. However, careful planning may permit some facilities within the building to qualify for the credit. For example, a small firm may be able to treat alarm systems, special electrical lamps, movable partitions, special plumbing and electrical outlets, and certain types of signs as equipment which will qualify.[7]

Another way of reducing taxes is to shift from a FIFO (first-in, first-out) to a LIFO (last-in, first-out) method of accounting for inventory during a period of inflation. The LIFO method places the recent, higher inventory costs directly into the income statement, thereby reducing the reported income which is subject to tax.

Estate Planning for Business Owners

Special planning is desirable to minimize problems created by estate taxes when a business owner dies. This is particularly true for the family business. It is possible that the need for dollars to pay death taxes can lead to the sale or liquidation of the business. Because of this danger, the entrepreneur needs to plan for the continuation of the business in light of the estate tax law.

As noted earlier, the 1981 tax law raised the amount to be excluded from inheritance taxation to $600,000 (by 1987). In the case of a very small business, therefore, the tax is not a threat. Numerous small firms, however, have a net worth which exceeds the $600,000 exclusion.

One approach to meeting the estate tax problem involves the purchase of insurance on the owner's life. Proceeds from the policy provide cash for the payment of necessary taxes. However, the size of the premium sometimes makes this a difficult and expensive solution.

Another solution or partial solution to the estate tax problem is found in making an annual gift of a specified portion of the estate to the heirs. The tax law permits such annual gifts without taxation. Over a period of several years, a substantial amount may be thus conveyed without taxation.

Tax Reform for Small Business

The tax system appears to have a number of adverse effects upon small business. The problem areas noted below have been identified in a study on

7. Gerald F. Hunter, "Uncovering Tax Credits," *Venture*, Vol. 3, No. 9 (September, 1981), p. 24.

ACTION REPORT: Insurance to Pay Estate Taxes

By paying annual life insurance premiums, small-business owners can provide funds to pay estate taxes. The following example shows that the solution may be a costly one:

> In Mars, Penna., Harry G. Austin, 65, and his brother John, 55, the only stockholders in $8 million (sales) James Austin Co., a soap manufacturer, pay around $20,000 each in premiums so their 92-year-old company can be passed down to the fourth generation. "Sometimes I think we're really working for the insurance company," says Harry.

Source: "The Death Tax," by Jon Schriber, *Forbes*, Vol. 127, No. 13 (June 22, 1981), pp. 122-126.

proposed tax reforms for small firms.[8]

Retention of Capital. The present tax system tends to discriminate against small firms by preventing the retention of adequate capital for current operating needs and for survival during recessions. Small firms lack ready access to long-term sources of capital, and this makes the tax erosion of earnings quite serious to them.

Complexity of Tax System. The complexity of the tax system, compounded by the multiplicity of taxes at all levels, the burden of reporting and paying payroll taxes, the difficulty of estimating income and paying taxes in advance, and the expense of professional tax assistance present special problems for small firms.

Incentives for Long-Term Capital. The tax system lacks proper incentives to attract adequate private investment capital to this segment of the economy. Some persons feel that sources of venture and expansion capital have almost disappeared.

Maintenance of Business Independence. The existing tax structure discourages small-business independence by encouraging mergers with larger enterprises on a tax-free basis and forcing the sale of a business to pay estate taxes.

8. The problems identified in this section are those cited in Part III, "The Impact of Taxation on Small Business: A Proposal for Reform," of *The Study of Small Business, op. cit*.

An increase in the size of the exemption from estate taxes, legislated in 1981, has eased this problem somewhat.

Financial Security of Business Owners. Even though some provision has been made for retirement plans for business owners, these plans contain complexities that make compliance difficult and expensive. Furthermore, they place unwarranted emphasis on the legal form of organization a business has taken.

SPECIAL GOVERNMENTAL ASSISTANCE

In addition to public policy applying to business generally, some steps have been taken to provide special assistance to small business. Chapter 7, for example, explained the Small Business Administration loan programs and the development and operation of Small Business Investment Companies. Other aspects of special assistance provided by the government are discussed below.

Managerial and Technical Assistance

The provision of management and technical assistance to managers of small firms takes a variety of forms. A series of pamphlets, for example, is published by the Small Business Administration under each of the following titles: (1) *Management Aids*, (2) *Small Marketers Aids*, and (3) *Small Business Bibliographies*. Appendix C at the end of this book contains a list of free publications in each of these areas. In addition, separate publications treat miscellaneous subjects pertinent to small-business management. Research studies of small-business problems have also been subsidized by grants from the Small Business Administration.

Staff personnel both in Washington and in field offices are available for counseling actual or prospective managers of small firms on various management problems. The subjects may range from the evaluation of a going concern to the analysis of plant location or layout requirements. Also, as noted in Chapter 12, the SBA sponsors counseling programs that feature retired business executives and teams of business students.

The Small Business Administration has also created an Office of Advocacy. This office argues the case of the entrepreneur within the federal bureaucracy. Its activities include lobbying, drafting and reviewing legislation, and developing an economic data base for small business.

Assistance in Obtaining Government Contracts

Many small firms serve as subcontractors. Both the Department of Defense and the General Services Administration (the largest contract-awarding agencies) provide active encouragement to prime contractors to engage in subcontracting to small firms. As subcontractors, small firms have the problem of learning who the prime contractors are and what component parts are available for subcontracting.

The Small Business Administration, General Services Administration, and Commerce Department also work with small firms to help them obtain government contracts. SBA field offices advise small firms as to which agencies buy the products they supply, help them get their names on bidders' lists, and assist them in obtaining drawings and specifications for proposed purchases. The SBA also publishes a directory which lists goods and services bought by military and civilian agencies, and it seeks out small companies interested in bidding on purchases on which few small firms have bid in the past.

Set-Aside Programs. Under a "set-aside program," government contracting officers and SBA representatives review purchase orders to select those which may be set aside for exclusive competitive bidding by small firms. Small firms have participated extensively in set-aside programs. This practice is presumably justified by the increasing technological complexity of material produced by federal agencies and the tendency to favor big business by acquiring systems and goods from a single contractor.

Minority Contract Programs. One special set-aside program, the minority contract program, permits government purchases from minority firms without competitive bidding. The primary objective is business development by awarding contracts and providing managerial, financial, and marketing assistance. Although the program has been criticized because of some reported abuses, supporters still feel it can make a valuable contribution.[9] The program has been modified to encourage the "graduation" of minority firms out of the program into the competitive marketplace. This means that firms entering the program will participate for a specified number of years and then be moved out to make way for new entrants.

Break-Out Contract Programs. In a related program called the "break-out contract program," the procuring agency breaks out suitable portions of a larger contract for competitive bidding by small firms. For example, the contract for janitorial services might be broken out of a general contract for housekeeping on a missile installation.

---

9. For a review of both strengths and weaknesses of this program, see "More Aid for Minority Business," *Business Week*, No. 2530 (April 17, 1978), pp. 146-149; "Congress Threatens the SBA," *Business Week*, No. 2572 (February 12, 1979), p. 105; and Michael Thoryn, "'Serious Problems' at SBA," *Nation's Business*, Vol. 69, No. 6 (June, 1981), pp. 42-44.

ACTION REPORT: A Beneficiary of Government Assistance

After reading about small-business assistance programs, you may wonder what type of business is helped by the government. One firm which did benefit is Welbilt Electronic Die Corporation of New York City. The firm was founded in 1965 by John Mariotta, who was born and raised in New York's Spanish Harlem. Mariotta was joined by Fred Neuberger, a mechanical engineer and refugee from the Nazis in Rumania.

Help from the SBA and other government agencies included the following:

1. An early SBA loan for $25,000 at 7 percent.
2. A later SBA-guaranteed loan (after landing a government contract) for $100,000.
3. A minority-enterprise government contract to make a component of the GE engine which propels the F-104 Phantom jet.
4. A minority-enterprise government contract for cooling kits for the Armored Personnel Carrier.
5. Subsequent loans (which eventually totaled $2.3 million) and loan guarantees (which eventually totaled $3.1 million).

The firm has apparently attained enough experience and momentum to survive. Welbilt has won production contracts in competitive bidding from GE (jet engine parts) and Western Electric (microwave communications equipment). According to founder Mariotta, "This is not a chicken-plucking operation."

Source: "'This Is Not a Chicken-Plucking Operation,'" by Jane Carmichael, *Forbes*, Vol. 128, No. 4 (August 17, 1981), pp. 51-52.

Assistance in Export Sales

To some extent the export-sales problem of small firms is one of information. The Commerce Department has attempted to meet this need by supplying small exporters with an array of technical and general information. The Commerce Department also operates major trade fairs aimed at increasing exports, and it brings foreign customers to visit American plants. The Small Business Administration maintains information on foreign trade and assists small firms who wish to enter foreign markets.

Under the Revenue Act of 1971, Congress attempted to stimulate American exports by providing for the establishment of Domestic International Sales Corporations (DISCs). A DISC is chartered as a domestic corporation and can be formed with as little as $2,500 of equity capital. A DISC may be organized merely as a paper or shell corporation and need not have any employees. The primary benefit of exporting as a DISC is that 50 percent of the federal income tax on the DISC's earnings may be deferred for an indefinite period. Although the Tax Reform Act of 1976 placed restrictions on the amount of tax that can be deferred, these restrictions do not apply to a small DISC – one with adjusted taxable income from sales of qualifying exports of $100,000 or less for a taxable year.[10]

The Need to Improve Governmental Assistance

The governmental programs of small-business assistance have benefitted thousands of small firms. At the same time, caution is appropriate in evaluating such programs and in making sure that they provide as much as they promise. Existing governmental programs are obviously no panacea for the various problems of small firms.

There is a continuing need for improvement and refinement in these efforts to assist the small-business sector. Skepticism relative to the effectiveness of past efforts is evident in the following comments:

> But the SBA's basic problem is that it lacks a clear mission. At its inception, the agency was just an experiment. On the theory that small business is at a permanent disadvantage in raising capital, Congress created the SBA to succeed the Depression-era Reconstruction Finance Corporation, which had provided credit to businesses large and small. Yet since no one was certain what small business actually needed, the SBA's enabling statute was notably vague . . .
>
> Over the years, the experiment has never been properly evaluated — only expanded.[11]

When Michael Cardenas became administrator of the Small Business Administration in 1981, he recognized the need for raising the agency's performance levels. He said, "The SBA programs have been abused, and I well realize it. I don't think there is one area I've delved into yet that doesn't need serious improvement. It's going to take time — I choose to become personally involved in almost every area."[12]

---

10. Harry G. Gourevitch, "DISC's Ability to Defer Tax on Income Restricted by Tax Reform Act of 1976," *The Journal of Taxation*, Vol. 46 (January, 1977), p. 12. For more general treatment of small-business exporting, see Donald W. Hackett, "Penetrating International Markets: Key Considerations for Smaller Firms," *Journal of Small Business Management*, Vol. 15, No. 1 (January, 1977), pp. 10-16; and Eugene M. Lang, "It's the Little Guys Who Need Export Aid," *Journal of Small Business Management*, Vol. 15, No. 1 (January, 1977), pp. 7-9.

11. Aimée L. Morner, "Junk Aid for Small Business," *Fortune*, Vol. 96 (November, 1977), p. 205.

12. Thoryn, *op. cit.*, p. 43.

LOOKING BACK

1. One of the major roles of government is the maintenance of free competition. Legislation varies, however, in terms of its consequences in this area. Although the antitrust laws (including the Sherman Antitrust Act, Clayton Act, Federal Trade Commission Act, Robinson-Patman Act, and state laws) are intended to encourage competition, their general effectiveness has been widely questioned. Governmental regulation also concerns consumer protection, the protection of investors, and the promotion of public welfare.
2. Governmental regulation has become burdensome to small business because of its bureaucratic nature, the excessive paperwork required, and the small firm's lack of time and expertise in responding to regulation.
3. The Regulatory Flexibility Act of 1980 is designed to reduce the burden of governmental regulation of small firms. It requires federal agencies to reduce paperwork requirements and simplify rules applicable to small firms. The Equal Access to Justice Act of 1980 requires the federal government to reimburse court costs for small firms that win cases against regulatory agencies.
4. The tax responsibilities of small firms include withholding taxes on income, Social Security, and sales; and paying income, federal excise, unemployment, estate, and local taxes. The present tax system presents possibilities for tax savings that the small business should investigate. The retention of capital, the complexity of the tax system, incentives for long-term capital, the maintenance of business independence, and the financial security of business owners are problem areas that should be considered in tax-reform programs for small business.
5. Three areas of special governmental assistance to small business are managerial and technical assistance provided through SBA offices, assistance in obtaining government contracts, and assistance in export sales. Programs of governmental assistance have benefited small business in many ways; nevertheless, there is a need for further refinement and improvement in these efforts to aid small firms.

DISCUSSION QUESTIONS

1. Are any of the regulatory roles of government opposed to the interests of small business?
2. The Antitrust Division of the Department of Justice and the Federal Trade Commission have units

dealing specifically with small firms and the investigation of their complaints. What is your evaluation of the desirability of such an arrangement?

3. Why is governmental regulation burdensome to small firms?

4. How does the Regulatory Flexibility Act of 1980 affect the regulation of small business?

5. Is it inherently unfair to accord special attention to small firms in formulating governmental regulations?

6. In view of the fact that a small business can operate as a proprietorship or a partnership, can it easily avoid any difficulties associated with the corporate income tax?

7. The corporate income tax law permits corporate income up to $100,000 to be taxed at a more favorable rate than corporate income over $100,000. Does this discriminate in favor of small corporations?

8. What are the ethical implications involved when a small business takes advantage of "loopholes" in tax laws? Is there a bona fide distinction between "tax avoidance" and "tax evasion"?

9. What is the "set-aside program" in obtaining federal government contracts? What justification is there for it, if any?

10. What is a DISC, and how does it help small business?

REFERENCES TO SMALL BUSINESS IN ACTION

Brophy, Beth. "A Fable for Our Times." *Forbes*, Vol. 124, No. 8 (October 15, 1979), p. 44.

An entrepreneur decided to close his plant. He was then besieged with offers of aid—more aid than he wanted.

Buckley, Jerry. "Commuter Airlines Face Higher Startup Ante." *Venture*, Vol. 2, No. 10 (October, 1980), pp. 48-53.

Steps to deregulate the airline industry opened opportunities for small firms to start commuter lines. This article describes several such small businesses and the continuing regulatory problems they face.

Comins, Norman. "SBA Helped Us Prove Contract Competency." *Inc.*, Vol. 2, No. 5 (May, 1980), p. 46.

An executive of a small firm explains how the SBA helped his company prove its competency to complete a government contract for a high-technology product.

Kolbenschlag, Michael. "Fish Story, Chapter 2." *Forbes*, Vol. 126, No. 6 (September 15, 1980), pp. 206-208.

This is the story of a group of independent fishermen who sought governmental protection. The underlying question is the extent to which government should aid small firms facing foreign competition.

Chapter 23

Trends and Prospects for Small Business

LOOKING AHEAD

Watch for the following important topics:

1. Trends in small-business activity.
2. Competitive strengths of small firms.
3. Problems of small business.
4. Failure and bankruptcy of small firms.
5. Prospects for the future of small business.

In this final chapter, we wish to size up the prospects for small business. Which direction is it going, what are its strengths, what are its problems, and what is its future? Although the overall picture contains both bright and dark spots, we hold a relatively optimistic view of the future of small business.

TRENDS IN SMALL-BUSINESS ACTIVITY

Reading about government aid and special loans for small companies may lead one to conclude that small business is vanishing. Small firms are sometimes pictured as powerless victims of giant corporations. To understand the truth or error in these views, we must examine the trend of small business in recent decades.

The small-business sector has shown considerable strength over the past two decades. For all industries, small firms (those with fewer than 100 employees) accounted for 39.9 percent of the total employees in 1958 and 40.1 percent in 1977.[1] In some industries, however, small business has declined relative to big business. Figures 23-1, 23-2, and 23-3 show the changes in small-firm employment in wholesaling, retailing, and manufacturing. There is some evident erosion of the small-business position in each of these industries.

Proponents of small business are understandably disturbed by the erosion of the small-business position and are concerned with the need to

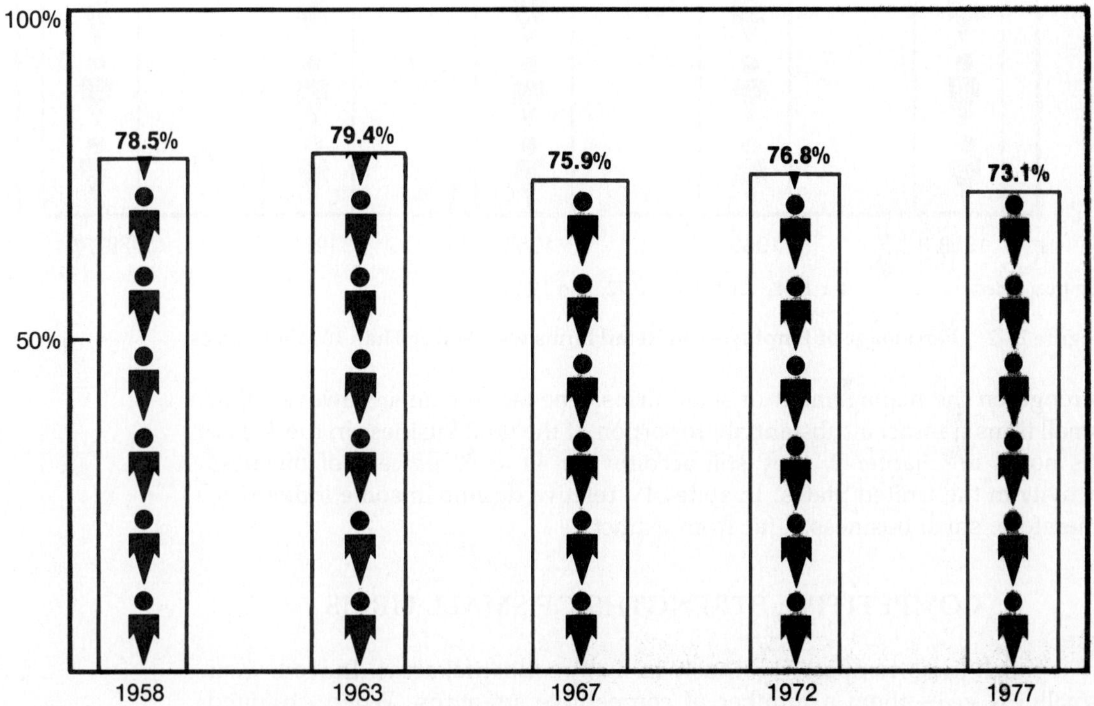

Source: U. S. Department of Commerce, Bureau of the Census, *Enterprise Statistics* (Washington: U. S. Government Printing Office, 1958, 1963, 1967, 1972, 1977).

Figure 23-1 Percentage of Employees in Wholesale Firms with Fewer Than 100 Employees

1. See the Bureau of the Census publication *Enterprise Statistics* for 1958, 1963, 1967, 1972, and 1977 to determine the fluctuation in employment over this period.

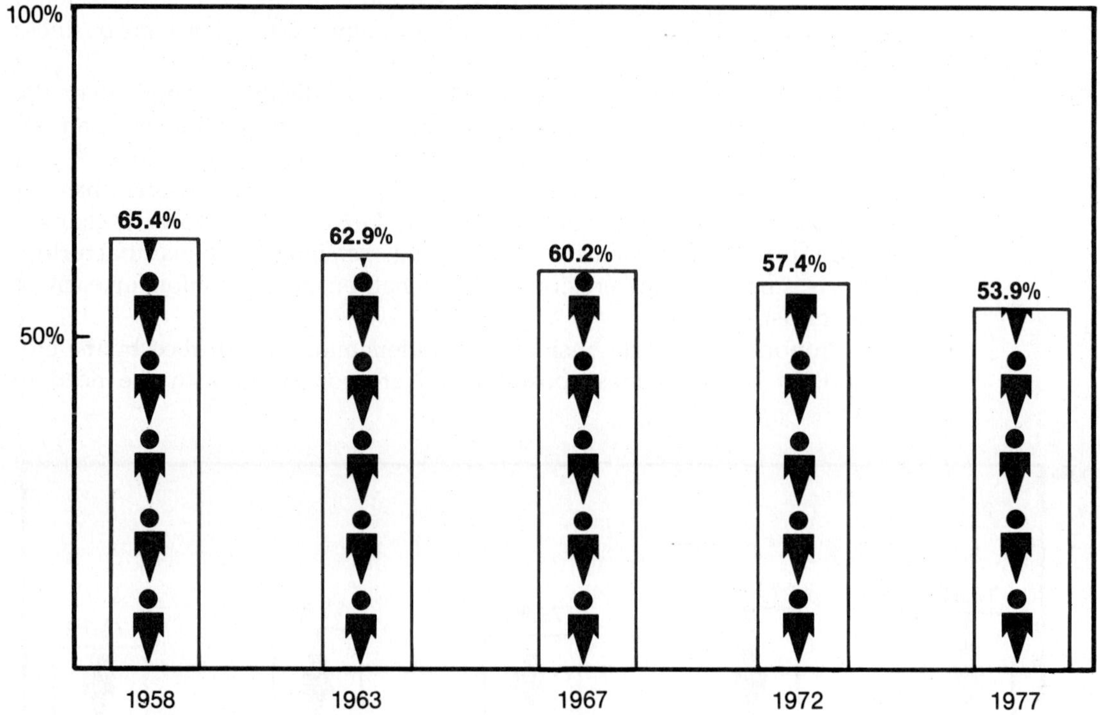

Source: *Enterprise Statistics* for 1958, 1963, 1967, 1972, and 1977.

Figure 23-2 Percentage of Employees in Retail Firms with Fewer Than 100 Employees

strengthen the management of small firms. The fact remains, however, that small firms transact a substantial proportion of the total business in the 1980s. As noted in Chapter 2, they still account for 40 to 50 percent of business activity in the United States. In spite of a relative decline in some industries, therefore, small business is far from extinct.

COMPETITIVE STRENGTHS OF SMALL FIRMS

Small firms compete vigorously in many industrial areas. Indeed, their smallness gives them a number of competitive strengths. When exploited skillfully, these strengths enable them to "carry the attack" to larger firms. Three of these strong points are discussed briefly below.

Knowledge of Customers and Markets

The bureaucratic structure of a large corporation tends to isolate its management from customers and markets. Salespeople have regular contact

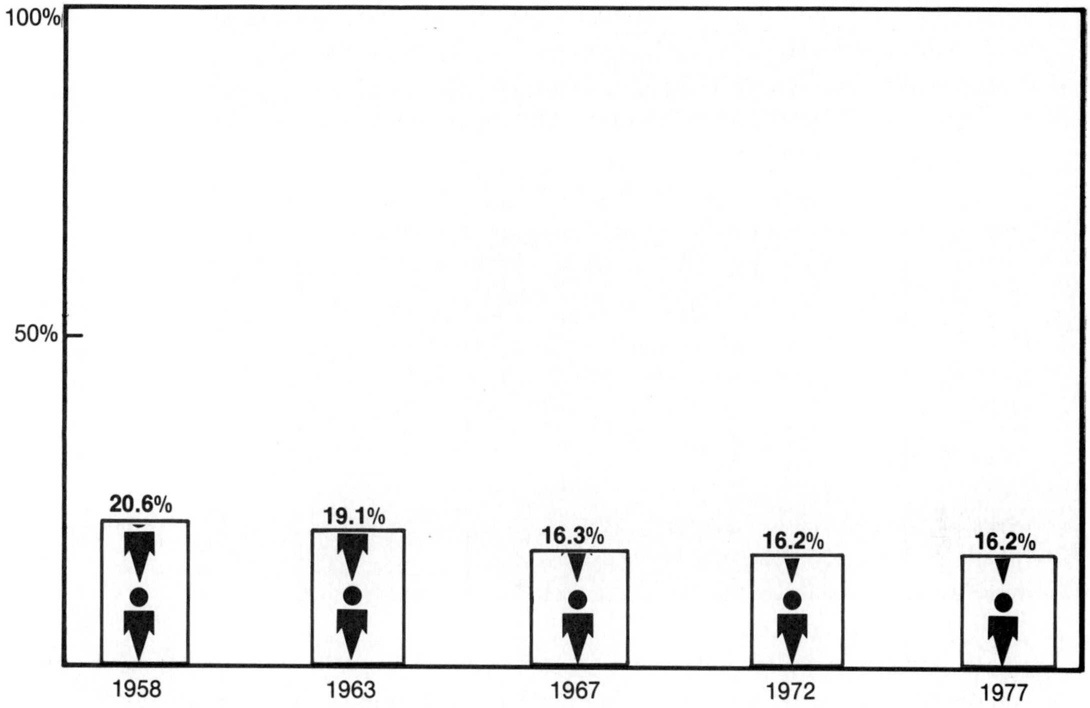

Source: *Enterprise Statistics* for 1958, 1963, 1967, 1972, and 1977.

Figure 23-3 Percentage of Employees in Manufacturing Firms with Fewer Than 100 Employees

with the marketplace, but their thinking is several steps removed from the influential decision-making levels of the corporation. Special effort is required to keep decision makers well-informed. Market research, often in sophisticated forms, is a tool designed and used extensively by large firms to probe the market and to reduce corporate ignorance of the market situation.

While it is true that small firms also need good market research, the small-business manager can almost automatically acquire some information that can be gleaned by the manager of a large firm only with great effort. The small-business manager's closer acquaintance with customers and markets is only a potential strength, however. Both a sensitive awareness of customer needs and a careful observation of market trends are necessary to make this potential strength a reality.

Product and Geographic Specialization

It is impossible to become a specialist in such a broad area as general business management. By narrowing the range of business activity, however,

ACTION REPORT: Specializing in Small Jobs

Small firms often become strong competitors by specializing. The Seven Sisters Construction Company, an all-female construction firm in California, has chosen to concentrate on relatively small building projects. A partner in the company, Tirza Latimer, explains, "We get a lot of jobs that are too small for the big construction firms and too large for the one-person outfits." For example, a current project involves a $92,000 custom-designed house in the San Francisco suburb of Orinda.

Priscilla Danzig, another partner in the company, got into the operation of a construction firm by attending a class in house building and later working as a carpenter. The eight-member firm specializes in home construction, remodeling, and cabinetry. By carefully selecting a market niche, the construction firm has functioned successfully, even managing to earn a profit during its first year.

Source: "Women in Charge: Eight Who Made It," *U. S. News & World Report*, Vol. 88, No. 11 (March 24, 1980), pp. 64-66.

one can develop an expertise in providing needed goods and services. To a greater or lesser degree, the small-business owner specializes. If a sufficiently narrow market segment is selected, the possibility of becoming a true specialist comes closer to reality.

To some extent geographic specialization provides a comparable situation. One can more easily develop a detailed knowledge of a specific locality than of an entire state, region, or country. Chain stores have recognized this handicap in trying to keep up with nimble, independent merchants. This also explains the strength of small business in specialty-shop areas of retailing.

Flexibility in Management

Big business is often pictured as being uniformly more efficient than small business. Some people believe that small business exists because it is protected through government aid in one form or another or because big business has not yet entered a particular field. Such an extreme position, however, is unsupported by the facts. An analysis of the structure of American business reveals many areas in which the optimum-size firm is not large. In his widely read book, *Small Is Beautiful,* E. F. Schumacher argued for small-scale enterprise as a solution for many of today's problems.[2]

---

2. E. F. Schumacher, *Small Is Beautiful* (New York: Harper & Row, 1973), pp. 64-65.

Rapid environmental change has become a way of life. Product life cycles become shorter, and innovations appear with greater frequency. Customers grow increasingly fickle and competitors move more quickly. As a result, change is a fact of life for business firms of all sizes. However, a difference exists in the small firm's adaptability. For example, the small firm with a lower investment in fixed assets can resist the snowballing of overhead costs that plague many large firms. And as conditions change, the small firm can make decisions quickly. In contrast, more levels of management must be consulted before making a change in large corporations. The inflexibility of huge organizations is illustrated in a performance review of Sears, Roebuck and Company:

> Sears' biggest problem of all, however, continues to be its ponderous size and the growing unwieldiness that implies — especially in inventories. And there is no easy solution to that, says William S. Hansen, president of the Southern California chain of Buffums'. "It's like the difference between a 747 and a Piper Cub," Hansen notes.[3]

Once again, the small firm's strength is only a potential strength. A prompt decision is not necessarily a good decision. But if the necessary facts are considered, a prompt and correct decision may give the small firm an edge over its larger competitor.

SMALL-BUSINESS PROBLEMS AND FAILURE RECORD

A balanced review of future prospects requires us to consider also the darker side of the small-business scene. Small firms face problems, and small firms fail. While we wish to avoid pessimism, we must deal realistically with these matters. Let us now discuss the nature of their problems, their record of failure, and the bankruptcy provisions for those who fail.

Problems of Small Business

Although researchers have established no "official list" or uniformly recognized group of difficulties for small business, they have detected a number of recurring problem areas.[4] Those areas that are generally troublesome to small business are discussed below.

---

3. "Why Sears' Profits Tumbled," *Business Week*, No. 2377 (April 21, 1975), pp. 32-33.

4. For a more detailed review of small-business problems, see Thomas C. Dandridge and Murphy A. Sewall, "A Priority Analysis of the Problems of Small Business Managers," *American Journal of Small Business*, Vol. 3, No. 2 (October, 1978), pp. 28-35; and Stahrl W. Edmunds, "Differing Perceptions of Small Business Problems," *American Journal of Small Business*, Vol. 3, No. 4 (April, 1979), pp. 1-14.

Lack of Managerial Skills and Depth. Perhaps the greatest problem of small-business management is the lack of necessary skills in the management group. In a very small business, the owner is a one-person management team. Top-level decisions, together with all the lesser tasks of management that assistants cannot accomplish, become the owner-manager's sole responsibility. Unfortunately this requires a diversity of talents—and no individual has superior ability in all areas of management.

The management process is hampered not only by a lack of diversified talents but also by the manager's frequently casual or superficial approach to management problems. The manager often does not understand the intricacies of maintaining adequate business records or of preparing financial statements. Or, if financial data are available, the manager may lack the necessary knowledge or appreciation of their value to interpret and use them effectively. Big-business managers either know how to use the records and statements properly to guide decision making, or they employ experts to do so for them. Small businesses alone are plagued by inadequacy and serious misuse of business records and business information.

Small-business managers also fail to exercise the highest quality of management insofar as they are bound by tradition and are insensitive to the need for change in policies and practices. They often are severely limited in terms of both education and experience.

Personal Lack and Misuse of Time. As mentioned earlier, the owner-manager of a small business frequently bears the management burden alone. In a very small firm, the manager may even help out at the worker level on occasion, packing a rush order or delivering merchandise to a valued customer who insists on immediate service. This means that the manager does not have the opportunity to operate solely at the executive level. This lack of time to manage is accentuated by participation in civic affairs and time devoted to the family, hobbies, and recreational activities. To help overcome part of the total time pressure, the small-business manager should budget time and exercise reasonable restraint over participation in community affairs.

Lack of Financing. A major problem for many small businesses is lack of capital and credit. Long-term capital is a particular need of many small firms. It is obtained by personal investment or by long-term borrowing. Borrowing money to be paid back over a period of ten years or more is difficult for small firms. The banker ordinarily expects funds of this type to come from equity capital. Borrowing from relatives or friends, as an alternative, may present problems because they often expect some voice in the management of the business. And this type of credit can jeopardize the relationship of both parties.

Still another source of long-term capital is the capital markets that are open to large businesses. However, the small firm has only limited access to these markets. Moreover, accepting partners or selling stock may involve the surrender of absolute control over the business, a condition that the original owner may reject. Expansion capital typically must come from personally invested funds or from profits retained in the business.

Overregulation and Taxes. Many surveys of small-business problems report governmental regulation and taxation as troublesome areas. The top-priority recommendations of the 1980 White House Conference on Small Business dealt with income taxes, estate taxes, tax incentives to help small firms raise capital, and various other tax and regulatory issues. In Chapter 22, we discussed the burdensome nature of regulation and the attempt to reduce this burden by increasing flexibility in regulation.

A major problem created by corporate income taxation is the reduction of funds available for reinvestment in the business. This reduction especially hampers small firms because they must rely on earnings as their primary source of expansion capital. Large firms, in contrast, have access to other sources of capital. Even though this principle is recognized in a graduated tax rate system, the impact is still serious for firms which must depend heavily on retained earnings.

Suppose that a small corporation earns a profit of $100,000 in 1983. Its income taxes would be computed as follows:

Net income		$100,000
Income tax		
$25,000 × 15%	$ 3,750	
$25,000 × 18%	4,500	
$25,000 × 30%	7,500	
$25,000 × 40%	10,000	25,750
Net income after taxes		$74,250

Rather than having $100,000 for dividends and reinvestment, the owner has only $74,250. The corporate income tax has thereby eliminated 26 percent of the firm's potential retained earnings.

Difficulty in Obtaining Qualified Personnel. Many small-business managers identify personnel as a major problem area. In most cases, union relationships are not specified as the primary difficulty. Instead, managers often report difficulty in locating properly qualified personnel. Securing well-trained automobile mechanics, television technicians, or pharmacists may pose real problems. For example, the manager of a diesel engine service shop searched for six months to locate a well-qualified parts manager who could also learn to supervise the office and record-keeping activities. Even more difficult for the small business is the recruitment of managerial and professional personnel.

This is not to say that the need to recruit and train competent personnel is unique with the small firm. But the small-business owner often has little knowledge of selection techniques and sources of applicants used by large firms. Also, the small-business owner typically lacks a well-developed personnel program and has little grasp of its significance.

There are numerous other ways in which small-business personnel problems are different. In some industries, for example, the practice of "pattern" bargaining with labor unions tends to impose big-business labor requirements upon small firms. This practice often appears unreasonable to managers of small firms. To illustrate, consider a contract provision limiting employees to a specified type of work. The small firm has greater difficulty in adhering closely to rigid job definitions of this type and needs considerable flexibility in shifting employees from one type of work to another. Some union contracts, it should be noted, have recognized such unique problems of personnel management in small firms.

Weaknesses in Marketing. When the small-business owner speaks of the problem of "competition," some aspect of selling is usually stressed. In most small firms the rigors of competition make the manager painfully conscious of marketing weaknesses. Difficulties in managing the firm's advertising illustrate the nature of the marketing problem. How much should the firm spend on advertising? What media should be used? How can the effectiveness of advertising be measured? For small firms, many of these questions are particularly difficult to answer, and their owners must often guess at the right answer. Channels of distribution, product differentiation, marketing strategy, and other issues likewise constitute significant problems for the small firm.

Failure and the Small Firm

Some unqualified entrepreneurs are doomed from the start. Others who are reasonably well-qualified encounter problems which are too much for them. In either case, the result is failure.

Rate of Small-Business Failure. The rate of small-business failure fluctuates from year to year with changes in general economic conditions and other factors. Figure 23-4 shows the rate of failure each year from 1920 to 1979.[5] An

5. The most comprehensive statistics pertaining to failure and changes in rate of failure are collected by Dun & Bradstreet, a business firm devoted to the analysis and rating of the credit standing of other firms. Failures, as defined by Dun & Bradstreet, include only those discontinuances that involve loss to creditors; voluntarily liquidated firms with all debts paid are excluded.

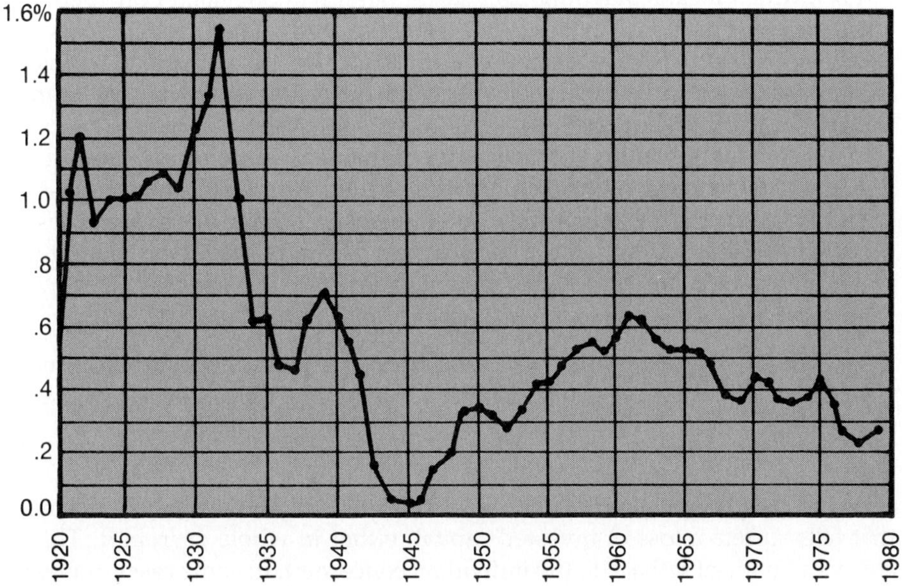

Source: *The Dun & Bradstreet Business Failure Record* (New York: Dun & Bradstreet, Inc., 1981).

Figure 23-4 Percentage of Business Failure, 1920-1979 (Based on number of failures per 10,000 firms in Dun & Bradstreet reference book)

examination of fluctuations in the rate of failure reveals that the rate within the last four decades is significantly lower than that of the 1920s and early 1930s. Note that the failure rate reached its highest point in the depression of the early 1930s. In the prosperous years following World War II, the rate dropped sharply. Since 1945, the consistently high level of economic activity has been accompanied by a lower failure rate than existed in earlier decades. However, the 1970 and 1975 recessions showed perceptible increases. The failure rate also increased sharply in the recession of 1982, but detailed data were not available at the time of publication of this text.

In view of the long-term record, one may be more optimistic about the chances for small-business survival. Even though many businesses die each year, the problem appears less serious when viewed in this historical perspective.

Erroneous Impressions from Failure Data. The extensive use of Dun & Bradstreet's failure data has tended to create an erroneous impression about the likelihood of failure.[6] Figure 23-4 shows that 28 firms out of 10,000 failed

6. The authors are indebted to Professor M. Z. Massel of De Paul University, who argues that writers generally have become so preoccupied with the minority of firms which fail that they paint an unnecessarily pessimistic picture of chances for success in business. See Michael Z. Massel, "It's Easier to Slay a Dragon Than Kill a Myth," *Journal of Small Business Management*, Vol. 16, No. 3 (July, 1978), pp. 44-49.

in 1979, which means that only .28 percent (less than one half of one percent) failed. Viewed in this way, one can conclude that chances for success are excellent! The prospective entrepreneur should be encouraged to consider business ownership because of its bright prospects, rather than to shun it because of fear of failure.

Of course, the failure rate would be higher if all discontinuances reflecting unsatisfactory operating results were added to those involving loss to creditors. And it is desirable that we should learn from the experiences of those who failed. Caution and apprehension of failure, however, should not be permitted to stifle inclinations toward independent business careers.

The Costs of Business Failure. The costs of business failure involve more than financial costs. They include costs of a psychological, social, and economic nature, too.

Loss of Entrepreneur's and Creditors' Capital. The owner of a business that fails suffers a loss of invested capital, either in whole or in part. This is always a financial setback to the individual concerned. In some cases, it means the loss of a person's lifetime savings! The entrepreneur's loss of capital is augmented by the losses of business creditors. Hence, the total capital loss is greater than the sum of the entrepreneurial losses in any one year.

Injurious Psychological Effects. Individuals who fail in business suffer a real blow to their self-esteem. The businesses they started with enthusiasm and high expectations of success have "gone under." Older entrepreneurs, in many cases, lack the vitality to recover from the blow. Most unsuccessful entrepreneurs simply relapse into employee status for the balance of their lives. This, too, may constitute a serious loss, as many of these "failures" possess managerial ability that is not utilized fully in an employee status.

However, failure need not be totally devastating to entrepreneurs. They may recover from the failure and try again. Albert Shapero has offered these encouraging comments: "Many heroes of business failed at least once. Henry Ford failed twice. Maybe trying and failing is a better business education than going to a business school that has little concern with small business and entrepreneurship."[7] The key, therefore, is the response of the one who fails and that person's ability to learn from failure.

Social and Economic Losses. Assuming that a business opportunity existed, the failure of a firm means the elimination of its goods and services that the public needs and wants. Moreover, the number of jobs available in the community is reduced. The resulting unemployment of the entrepreneur

---

7. Albert Shapero, "Numbers That Lie," *Inc.*, Vol. 3, No. 5 (May, 1981), p. 16.

Table 23-1 Causes of Failures in 1979

Neglect		1.1%
Fraud		0.6%
Inexperience, incompetence		91.9%
Inadequate sales	52.3%	
Heavy operating expenses	28.9%	
Receivables difficulties	9.8%	
Inventory difficulties	9.2%	
Excessive fixed assets	3.1%	
Poor location	2.2%	
Competitive weakness	26.2%	
Other	1.7%	
Disaster		0.6%
Reason unknown		5.8%
		100.0%

Source: *The Dun & Bradstreet Business Failure Record* (New York: Dun & Bradstreet, Inc., 1981), pp. 12-13. Since some failures are attributed to a combination of causes, percentages for the items in the inset column do not add to 91.9%.

and employees, if any, causes the community to suffer from the loss of a business payroll. Finally, the business that failed was a taxpayer which contributed to the tax support of schools, police and fire protection, and other governmental services.

Causes of Business Failure. Aside from the relatively few cases of fraud, neglect, and disaster, the root cause of business failure is found in managerial incapacity. The weaknesses of management manifest themselves in various ways, however. These manifestations might be thought of as the apparent, or surface, causes of failure.

Root Cause — Inadequate Management. The indictment of the manager is supported by the extensive analysis of business failures conducted by Dun & Bradstreet. Consider, for example, their analysis of reasons for failures that occurred in 1979, as shown in Table 23-1.

In small business especially, management seems to be the number-one problem of the enterprise. The able manager utilizes his or her time wisely and gives proper attention to the various managerial functions. This includes careful attention to customer and public relations, financial planning, employee relations, production control, selling, and other key factors of a business.

Surface Causes. Even though we recognize that management is basically at fault, it is nevertheless profitable to note those areas in which management most frequently finds itself in trouble. For example, a frequently alleged cause of failure is the intensity of competition. Independent grocery stores may be run out of business by the advent of efficient chain or supermarket competition. Manufacturers might also encounter new, efficient, well-financed competition for the first time. An efficiently managed existent business, however, is a tough foe for any competitor. Perhaps too much stress has been placed on competition as a cause of failure, although it must be given proper consideration.

Lack of capital also contributes to business failures. Starting a business on the proverbial shoestring is generally unwise and often leads to failure. Even when initial capital is adequate, the entrepreneur may misuse it. The result is the same—a lack of capital. Sometimes the lack of capital may be only temporary, but the results of overborrowing may still cause failure.

Poor location also causes problems for small firms. The choice of a successful location is partly a science and partly an art. Too many locations are chosen without serious study, careful planning, or adequate investigation. For example, in a particular shopping center three eating establishments were opened in succession. Each one failed, partly because of its choice of location.

Some businesses expand prematurely. Ordinarily business expansion should be financed from retained earnings or capital contributions of the owners. In periods of prosperity, with reasonable certainty of continued demand, a manufacturer might successfully expand physical facilities through mortgage loans. In any case, expansion calls for careful advance planning. An expanding business should never be top-heavy with debt.

Failure Symptoms. The symptoms of impending business failure are the red flags that alert the entrepreneur. Any one of them may point to trouble. If any of these symptoms are detected, the firm's financial position may be assessed by computing some ratios and comparing them with industry standards. These financial ratios were discussed in Chapter 18.

Deterioration of Working-Capital Position. When a firm's working-capital position is deteriorating, its working capital is becoming inadequate and illiquid. The factors that contribute to declining adequacy and liquidity of working capital include the following:

1. Continuing operating losses.
2. Unusual, nonrecurring losses such as those due to theft, flood, tornado, and adverse court judgments.
3. Payment of excessive managerial bonuses and unearned dividends.
4. Frozen loans to officers, subsidiaries, and affiliates.

5. Overinvestment in fixed assets from working-capital funds.
6. Long-term loan payments in excess of a proper share of annual profits.

Declining Sales. Sales decline represents a serious situation for any business, large or small. This is true because operating expenses—particularly fixed overhead expenses—do not decline in proportion to sales. Hence, prolonged sales declines result in reduced profits or actual losses.

Controllable factors that may contribute to sales decline include:

1. Inadequate market research to measure sales potentials by sales areas or customer groups.
2. Poorly planned advertising and promotional activities.
3. Obsolescent products and product packaging.

Declining Profits. Profits that go downward from month to month or year to year may be attributed to many factors, the most important of which are:

1. Declining sales.
2. Increasing costs of merchandise or raw materials.
3. Higher labor costs.
4. Higher taxes.

Increasing Debts. If current liabilities get out of hand and bills or payrolls due for payment cannot be paid, the firm's situation might deteriorate into involuntary bankruptcy. Nor should a company's fixed, long-term liabilities be allowed to become excessive.

Insolvency and Bankruptcy

A business becomes insolvent when the aggregate value of its assets is not sufficient to pay its debts. There are two major courses of action to take when insolvency exists: to salvage the business through voluntary creditor agreements or creditor arrangements under the Bankruptcy Act of 1978, or to liquidate the business by declaring bankruptcy.

Voluntary Creditor Agreements. If the creditors of an insolvent firm believe that the business can be profitable again, an arrangement permitting continuance of the firm can be made. Such an arrangement may be initiated by either the debtor or a group of its major creditors. The arrangement may take either the form of an extension agreement, a composition settlement, or a combination of both.

Under an **extension agreement** the creditors of the insolvent business agree to postpone the debtor's payment of obligations for some stipulated period of time. The agreement becomes legally binding upon each of the parties to it. Creditors who do not participate in the extension agreement are not bound by its terms. Therefore, most of the firm's major creditors must become parties to such an agreement if it is to succeed.

In a **composition settlement** the creditors agree to accept reduced amounts due them, on a pro rata basis. The settlement may be either made in cash immediately or postponed to a later date.

Creditor Arrangements Under the Bankruptcy Act. The Bankruptcy Act of 1978 (which replaced a bankruptcy law enacted in 1898) provides for the restructuring of the financial affairs of a business.[8] It provides a more flexible approach to reorganizing and continuing the business than was possible under the earlier bankruptcy law. For example, the management of the debtor company is now, in most cases, allowed to retain control, rather than to be automatically replaced. The debtor firm has an exclusive right to propose a reorganization plan within 120 days of filing for bankruptcy. If such a plan is not presented, however, creditors may submit one. All creditors must accept a court-approved plan if it is approved by a majority of each class of creditors—for example, by secured creditors, unsecured creditors, and so on.

The reorganization plan is intended to help those firms which experience temporary financial stress but which are thought to have the underlying strength necessary for long-run success. If a reorganization plan cannot be formulated, the business is liquidated under Chapter 7 of the act. After the debtor's property has been liquidated and the proceeds distributed, the debtor is legally discharged from further payments on the amounts owed.

PROSPECTS FOR THE FUTURE

In this final section, we turn to the brighter prospects for small business. This involves a review of some of the factors contributing to the survival and continued growth of small firms.

Effects of White House Conference on Small Business

National attention was focused on the role and importance of small business by the 1980 White House Conference on Small Business.[9] The Con-

---

8. For an explanation of the new act, see Priscilla Anne Schwab, "Bankruptcy: A New Code May Save Many Firms," *Nation's Business*, Vol. 69, No. 4 (April, 1981), pp. 82-88.

9. See the White House Conference on Small Business, *Report to the President: America's Small Business Economy—Agenda for Action* (Washington: U. S. Government Printing Office, 1980).

ACTION REPORT: Bankruptcy for Tradeway

Bankruptcy proceedings sometimes save debtor companies from liquidation. Tradeway, Inc., is one small firm which was saved in this way. A discount retailer, Tradeway operated 14 stores in Michigan, Ohio, and Indiana. However, the store financed its receivables at a very high interest rate—two or three points above the prime rate—and could not earn enough to pay expenses.

In December, 1979, the firm filed a Chapter 11 petition under the Bankruptcy Act. The firm later closed ten stores. Late in 1980, a reorganization plan was approved, discharging some of Tradeway's debts and restructuring the payment of others. It looks as if the remaining part of the company may survive.

Source: Priscilla Anne Schwab, "Bankruptcy: A New Code May Save Many Firms," *Nation's Business*, Vol. 69, No. 4 (April, 1981), pp. 82-88.

ference was called by President Jimmy Carter with Arthur Levitt, Jr., chairman of the Board of Governors of the American Stock Exchange, serving as chairman. The 1980 meeting in Washington was preceded by local and state meetings involving the participation of more than 25,000 small-business people. The President's statement in calling the Conference contained the following remarks:

> I believe such a conference can help us identify the many special problems facing small business and design an agenda that addresses them in a constructive way. As you know, the 14 million small businesses represent a much larger part of our economy than is commonly recognized.[10]

The deliberations of the White House Conference were of general public interest, but they were of particular interest to those in public life who formulate public policy affecting small business. The 60 Conference recommendations were well-publicized, and some of them have already been enacted into law.

After the Conference adjourned, an informal network of small-business activists emerged.[11] They gained a more formal status in the fall of 1981 as they convened for the first meeting of the National Advisory Council for the Senate's Committee on Small Business. The net effect, therefore, was to heighten the awareness of small business and to give it a higher priority on the national agenda.

---

10. *Ibid.*, p. 98.

11. "Senate Advisory Council," *Venture*, Vol. 3, No. 9 (September, 1981), p. 10.

Shift to a Service Economy

One major structural change that favors small business is the shift from a manufacturing to a service economy. The manufacturing segment, in which big business predominates, is currently declining in relative importance. On the other hand, services, retailing, and wholesaling are growing in relative importance. These areas are fields in which small business has traditionally been strong.

Emphasis on Small-Business Courses and Programs

Colleges and universities have greatly expanded their educational emphasis on small business. The teaching of small-business management courses has grown in popularity during the past few years. This emphasis has been encouraged by the SBA-sponsored student consulting programs described in Chapter 12.

The academic field of entrepreneurship and new-venture management has also emerged in recent years. During the 1970s, the colleges offering courses in this field grew from about a dozen to more than 130.[12] Many of the nation's leading schools now offer entrepreneurship courses and programs.

Strength of Small-Business Associations

Small business has increased its strength by developing associations of small firms. Many of these are trade associations which have worked in the particular interests of various trade groups. The Chamber of Commerce of the United States is another organization which is becoming increasingly effective in its representation of small business as a part of its more general business representation.

One group that represents the interests of small business generally is the National Federation of Independent Business (NFIB), an association with a membership of almost one-half million members.[13] The NFIB maintains a legislative staff that actively monitors the activities of Congress and supports legislation of interest to small business.

The International Council for Small Business — an association of university business professors, business owners, government officials, consultants, and others directly interested in small business — likewise supports the cause of small business generally and provides testimony regarding proposed

---

12. Karl H. Vesper, "Research on Education for Entrepreneurship," a paper presented at the Conference on Research and Education in Entrepreneurship, Baylor University, Waco, TX, March 24-25, 1980.

13. NFIB offices are located at 150 West 20th Avenue, San Mateo, CA 94403 and at 490 L'Enfant Plaza East, S. W., Washington, DC 20024.

legislation.[14] These and other business groups are active in representing the cause of business and in speaking for specific segments of the small-business community.

Growth of Small-Business Periodicals

Many periodicals devote special attention to the needs of small business. *Nation's Business*, for example, is published by the Chamber of Commerce of the United States and places great emphasis on small-business news and programs.

Evidence of a growing interest in small business is found in the launching of new publications. Three new monthly periodicals, *Inc.*, *Venture*, and *In Business*, started publication in the late 1970s, bringing news and stories of new ventures and entrepreneurship. The fact that three such publications could be launched successfully suggests a widespread interest in entrepreneurship and small business.

Continued Support of Governmental Programs

In the preceding chapter, we described many programs of government aid for small business. These aid programs, along with the steps taken by Congress to modify regulatory and tax policies to adapt them to the needs of small firms, represent public policy in support of small business. They reflect an awareness on the part of the public of the vital role played by small firms.

Emergence of Private-Sector Programs and Initiatives

One of the most encouraging factors in thinking of the future prospects of small business is the various initiatives undertaken by private business institutions. Such efforts are diverse, and we can do no more than provide two examples.

The small-business program of the Bank of America illustrates the type of effort that can be undertaken by a single firm. This bank makes a special effort to serve the small-business community of California through its lending programs. It also publishes the *Small Business Reporter* — a series of well-edited monographs on various aspects of small-business management. Some of these are devoted to specific functions or problems of small firms such as cash management, franchising, and management succession. Others present information about particular types of business — apparel stores, restaurants, home

---

14. The International Council for Small Business publishes the *Journal of Small Business Management*, with editorial offices at the Bureau of Business Research, West Virginia University, Morgantown, WV 26506.

ACTION REPORT: NIKE — Triumph of the Entrepreneurial Spirit

Courtesy of Warren Morgan

Philip H. Knight, president of NIKE, Inc.

The future of small business depends in large measure on the spirit of entrepreneurship. This spirit is alive and often provides a fast track to success.

For example, NIKE shoes did not even exist when its cofounders, Philip H. Knight and William J. Bowerman, became business teammates in 1965. Knight, a former University of Oregon track star, had written a research paper on track shoes while working on his MBA at Stanford in 1960. According to his thesis, the Japanese could do for athletic shoes what they did for cameras. Thus, the game plan was born. On the other hand, Bowerman, his Oregon track coach, had been striving for years to develop a technologically better track shoe. So, in 1965 under the partnership name of Blue Ribbon Sports, Knight and Bowerman began to import the Tiger brand of Japanese-made running shoes.

In 1972, Knight and Bowerman hurdled a dispute with the Japanese manufacturer by contracting out the manufacture of their *own designs* to various Far East factories. They called their new design NIKE and adopted this brand name as their new corporate name. This change obviously worked as NIKE shoes captured an estimated 30 percent of the quality athletic shoe market in the United States. Now NIKE shoes are manufactured both in the United States and abroad.

Several winners have worn NIKE shoes — the front defensive four of the Dallas Cowboys, runner Sebastian Coe, players for the Los Angeles Dodgers, tennis star John McEnroe, NBA basketball stars, baseball's Nolan Ryan, and many others.

But the biggest winner is the entrepreneurial spirit!

furnishings stores, and so on. (The address is: Bank of America, Department 3120, P. O. Box 37000, San Francisco, CA 94137.)

The National Minority Purchasing Council provides an example of cooperative effort among private business concerns. When large corporations become members of this organization, they join a group which attempts to purchase an equitable percentage of services and supplies from minority enterprises. They recognize that minority-owned businesses deserve a chance to compete, and the group strives to make sure they have that opportunity. (The address is: National Minority Purchasing Council, 6 North Michigan Avenue, Room 1104, Chicago, IL 60602.)

The Unflinching Entrepreneurial Spirit

Perhaps the strongest force in achieving a bright future for small business is the unflinching spirit of the entrepreneur. In Chapter 1, we recognized the crucial role played by the entrepreneur — the one who brings new firms into existence and provides leadership for them. Entrepreneurs are creative, talented individuals who provide the backbone for the small-business system. They are also tough individuals who face business problems but who look beyond those problems to find solutions and success in economic endeavor.

LOOKING BACK

1. Small firms now have a somewhat smaller share of the market in some industries than they had earlier. However, they have maintained great overall strength and still constitute an important segment of the economy.
2. The competitive strengths of small firms include knowledge of customers and markets, product and geographic specialization, and flexibility in management.
3. Problems of small business include lack of managerial skills and depth, personal lack and misuse of time, lack of financing, overregulation and taxes, difficulty in obtaining qualified personnel, and weaknesses in marketing.
4. A relatively small percentage of all businesses fail each year. The most important cause of failure is thought to be inadequate management. A business becomes insolvent when the aggregate value of its assets is insufficient to pay its debts. The debtor business firm may make voluntary agreements with creditors, or it may be treated under the Bankruptcy Act of 1978. In the latter case, the firm may be reorganized and continue to function, or it may be liquidated to pay off creditors.
5. Future prospects for small business are bright because of a number of factors. Some of these are the effects of the 1980 White House Conference

on Small Business, the shift to a service economy, the emphasis on small-business courses and programs, the strength of small-business associations, the continued support of governmental programs, and the unflinching entrepreneurial spirit.

DISCUSSION QUESTIONS

1. What has been the long-run trend of market share accounted for by small business?
2. In what way does knowledge of customers and markets constitute a competitive strength for a small firm?
3. Why can small firms be more flexible in management? How can a large firm achieve similar flexibility?
4. What is the most pressing problem in running a small business? What can be done to alleviate this problem?
5. What would be the diverse managerial skills ideally desirable in the following types of businesses: (a) retail hardware store, (b) photographic studio, (c) wholesale grocery firm, (d) sheet metal shop, (e) retail appliance store, and (f) radio and television repair shop?
6. Why is it unlikely that one individual would have all the necessary specialized managerial skills?
7. Enumerate and describe some of the nonfinancial costs of business failure.
8. Justify the statement that most business failures are caused by management weaknesses.
9. Why is the management of a debtor firm sometimes allowed to retain control during a bankruptcy proceeding?
10. What was the 1980 White House Conference on Small Business, and why was it significant?

REFERENCES TO SMALL BUSINESS IN ACTION

Graham, Roberta. "Small Business: Fighting to Stay Alive." *Nation's Business*, Vol. 68, No. 7 (July, 1980), pp. 33-36.

This article describes a number of small firms that are facing severe problems and are fighting to survive.

Rhodes, Lucien. "Boyd Hill Keeps Hammering Away." *Inc.*, Vol. 3, No. 6 (June, 1981), pp. 80-86.

A small wholesale firm faced the problem of a slowdown in the construction industry and survived.

Ruhl, Jerry. "How Chapter XI Helps Save Companies." *Venture*, Vol. 3, No. 6 (June, 1981), pp. 44-48.

A Chicago-based cookie company went through bankruptcy proceedings under the Bankruptcy Act of 1978 and survived.

CASE F-1

The Terrell Company*

Working within legal and governmental controls

The Terrell Company was a small manufacturing company located in Rock Island, IL. It produced chemical coatings which are applied to the unpainted surfaces of farm and construction equipment. The Terrell Company had been in its location only a few years and had been very proud of the fact that it had the latest and most up-to-date equipment for its manufacturing processes and for the safety and well-being of its 80 employees.

When an OSHA inspector appeared to inspect the company's premises, he remarked that its production facility included equipment unlike any he had ever seen. Since fumes emanated from the liquid chemicals flowing through the equipment, the inspector expressed concern for the safety of the employees in this area, particularly as it pertained to flash fires. Although the company's owners attempted to assure the inspector that no hazard existed because the chemicals were neither toxic nor flammable, the inspector cited the company for six violations of OSHA regulations. As part of the citation, the company was fined $300 and was required to correct the violations within 90 days or be subject to further fines and a possible restraining order.

The owners of the Terrell Company immediately contacted their attorney. The attorney advised them that there were two methods of resolving the issue: (1) to work with OSHA officials to reach compliance status, or (2) to contest the alleged violations through a lengthy and costly appeal process.

One of Terrell's owners was particularly livid about the citation and made a series of impassioned speeches about the federal bureaucracy, contacting members of Congress, and "taking the case to the Supreme Court if necessary." Although tending to agree with the owners that the inspector appeared to have been rather arbitrary and capricious in citing the company, the attorney nonetheless encouraged the owners to settle the matter at the inspector level rather than to initiate the appeal process by requesting a hearing. After much discussion, the owners reluctantly agreed to try to work toward a reasonable solution with the inspector.

Terrell, however, experienced considerable difficulty in learning exactly what modifications were needed for compliance. This was because OSHA officials refused to provide Terrell with specifications for equipment that would be acceptable.

After discussions with several manufacturers, it appeared to Terrell's owners that the OSHA regulations would require the purchase of expensive additional equipment including enlarged blower fans and fire run-off tanks.

*This case was prepared by John E. Schoen, Richards Equipment Company, Waco, TX.

The manufacturers of such equipment advised Terrell that it was possible that the blower fans would be challenged by Illinois air-quality officials and that the noise from the motors needed to operate the run-off tanks might exceed OSHA noise pollution standards. The cost of the equipment was estimated between $14,000 and $19,000 and the equipment could not be delivered to the Terrell Company and installed there in less than 150 days.

When Terrell's owners presented this information to the inspector and other members of the OSHA administration, the OSHA officials reiterated that they would not approve or otherwise judge equipment in advance of its installation. The OSHA officials also indicated that they were concerned about violations of OSHA regulations, not state air-quality standards, and that they were fully prepared to cite violations of noise regulations. Finally, these officials commented that the fines for noncompliance might increase to $1,000 per violation per day or $6,000 a day after the 90-day period, so that the owners might prefer to close the plant for 60 to 75 days during the equipment modifications to avoid incurring such penalties.

Thus, it was shortly after the foregoing discussion that the attorney met with a very angry owner of the Terrell Company. Gesturing wildly, the owner said to the attorney:

> Look, we've got to request a hearing on those OSHA violations! I've tried to work with the OSHA officials, but we can't put in $15,000 or $20,000 of modifications and not be sure that will satisfy them. My gosh, that's nearly 30 percent of our net profit; and even if the equipment is all right, the regulations could change in a week, ten days, or a month and we would probably have to buy additional equipment in order to comply! If we have to close for two or three months, I'm not sure we can make a profit this year! I mean, not only the inspector, but the other people in the OSHA administration have admitted that the regulations really do not fit our business format! Surely we can beat this bum rap for less than $15,000.

Questions

1. Should the Terrell Company attempt to contest the alleged violations now if the legal costs of appeal are comparable to the cost associated with compliance?
2. Would the Terrell Company be able to operate in its present condition during the period required for a decision to be rendered on the appeal?
3. What force and effect do OSHA regulations have? Are they merely "one inspector's opinion" of the way Terrell Company should run its business, or are they laws, just as though Congress had passed them?
4. Could the Terrell Company sue OSHA in a court of law for the costs that it will incur or request the court to order OSHA to leave Terrell alone?
5. Could a member of Congress assist Terrell by intervening in this matter? What political pressure, if any, could be brought on the OSHA administration?

CASE F-2

Classique Cabinets*

Facing the threat of insolvency and failure

Classique Cabinets was a sole proprietorship owned and operated by Devlin Toliver and his wife Erika. Located in Zanesville, OH, the business was opened in 1978 to produce handcrafted, custom-designed cabinets for homes and offices.

Devlin was 28 years old and had a high school education. Before starting the cabinet shop, he worked as inventory manager for a lumberyard in Zanesville and as a construction site supervisor. His wife Erika taught second grade and served as part-time bookkeeper for the cabinet operation. The Tolivers had no children.

Location and Facilities

The Tolivers lived in a 2,000-square-foot home, designed and constructed by Devlin, on the outskirts of Zanesville. Zanesville is situated in the eastern part of Ohio, approximately 100 miles from Columbus. If the nearby communities of Crooksville, East Fultonham, and Roseville were included, Zanesville would have a metropolitan population of 50,000.

Classique Cabinets was located adjacent to the Tolivers' home in a five-year-old fabricated metal building. The facility had 3,200 square feet of concrete flooring, 2 overhead bay doors, and a partial skylight. Devlin's woodworking equipment and supplies were valued at $25,000. These were not being depreciated on the income statement prepared by Devlin. However, the income statement shown in Exhibit 1 has been corrected to include depreciation expense. Exhibit 2 shows his balance sheet as of December 31, 1981.

Quality of Devlin's Cabinetwork

Devlin displayed enormous pride in his custom-made cabinets. He commented:

> Craftsmanship has not died out entirely. I make my cabinets the old-fashioned way out of the finest woods and grains. They are built to last a lifetime. Nothing leaves my shop that I'm not proud of. I look upon my cabinets almost as pieces of artwork—not as stamped out assembly-line products.

---

*This case was prepared by Steve R. Hardy and Philip M. Van Auken of the Center for Private Enterprise and Entrepreneurship at Baylor University.

Exhibit 1 Income Statement of Classique Cabinets

Classique Cabinets
Income Statement
For Year Ended Dec. 31, 1981

Income:		
Cabinet operation	$64,638	
Construction	49,760	
Repairs	5,602	
Total revenue		$120,000
Cost of sales:		
Raw materials	$59,438	
Labor	38,970	98,408
Gross margin		$ 21,592
Operating expenses:		
Advertising	$ 562	
Bad-debt allowance	10,260	
Depreciation	15,430	
Fringe benefits – Labor	2,498	
Insurance	1,200	
Office supplies	488	
Salaries	4,678	
Telephone	1,200	
Utilities	2,312	38,628
Net profit (or loss)		($ 17,036)

Classique cabinets were priced at approximately two-and-one-half times the price of mass-milled cabinets sold at home centers and retail building centers (Payless Cashways, Handy Dan, Sears, and so on). Devlin priced his cabinets at an average of $110 per running foot, which included installation. About 65 percent of Devlin's orders were for homes, with the remaining sales spread fairly evenly among offices for white-collar professionals and financial institutions.

The Market Demand

Devlin made the following comments about the market demand for his products:

In the three years I have operated Classique Cabinets, I've pretty much creamed the local market. By that I mean that I have landed the easy customers who readily appreciated the quality of my products and didn't worry too much about price. My task now is to search out new customers who either are unaware of the quality of my cabinets or who have not fully considered the long-run value of what I sell.

Exhibit 2 Balance Sheet of Classique Cabinets

Classique Cabinets
Balance Sheet
Dec. 31, 1981

ASSETS

Current assets:		
Cash	$ 2,252	
Accounts receivable*	21,460	
Inventory	9,874	
Total current assets		$ 33,586
Fixed assets:		
Fixtures	$ 1,896	
Machinery and equipment	33,942	
Plant	63,290	
Land	22,700	
Total fixed assets		121,828
TOTAL ASSETS		$155,414

LIABILITIES AND OWNER'S EQUITY

Current liabilities:		
Accounts payable	$15,260	
Note payable (current)	5,000	
Tax provision	2,120	
Total current liabilities		$ 22,380
Long-term liabilities:		
Note payable – Bank	$77,970	
Note payable – Uncle Don	20,000	
Total long-term liabilities		97,970
Owner's equity		35,064
TOTAL LIABILITIES AND OWNER'S EQUITY		$155,414

*Includes approximately $4,000 in bad debts.

Admitting that he had had problems in estimating potential market demand in the Zanesville area and in forecasting future cash flows, he added: "I really don't know to what extent demand for custom-made cabinets in town is currently saturated. I would like to believe that there are plenty of people left who still appreciate quality cabinets that will last a lifetime."

Devlin observed that both the cabinet and construction businesses had been hard hit by high interest rates and a nationwide slump in the construction trade. He said, "Housing starts are way down, and money is extremely hard to come by. The interest rates have also hurt potential customers of mine because handmade cabinets are a luxury which homeowners can postpone."

Operations Management

Devlin had never advertised his services, relying instead on word-of-mouth advertising and the goodwill of past customers. He explained, "Zanesville is a small community. Most people know me personally or at least have heard of my business. After all, I grew up right here in town."

However, Devlin pointed out one disadvantage of being "home grown": bad debts. "I have put in cabinets for several friends and social acquaintances who just never got around to paying me," he said. "What am I expected to do, go to their homes with a shotgun to collect?"

When cabinet orders were slow, Devlin spent time with a small home construction business which he operated with two childhood friends. He explained that, although there was very little profit in building homes on a small scale, his occasional construction projects generated the needed cash flow and enabled him to keep his friends employed. He subcontracted out electrical and plumbing work on the homes. He added:

> I really don't have the heart to tell Jessie and Gordon that I'm getting out of the home building business. They have stayed loyal to me and assisted me from time to time with the cabinet shop. Besides, building homes gives me one additional outlet for my cabinets.

Devlin was giving serious consideration to expanding his operations into wood-milling work for local lumberyards and home centers. He explained:

> I've been wanting to become less dependent on products that are so heavily tied to the state of the economy. There are four lumberyards and five retail home centers here in the area which all have a need for milling work—things like fence posts, staircase railings, table legs, and so on. For a total investment of about $8,000, I can be in operation. Milling work is a high-volume proposition and involves at least a 30 percent profit margin because of the high value added. Milling would also complement my cabinet business rather nicely.

However, he had not yet completed any market surveys for a milling operation, though he expressed great confidence that "the demand is there."

Financial Outlook

In evaluating the financial health of Classique Cabinets, Devlin candidly admitted that the business sorely needed a "shot in the arm," having failed to generate a profit in its three years of existence. He felt that cabinet demand was so unpredictable that short-term financial growth would have to come from an alternative business area such as the contemplated milling venture.

In assessing his future outlook, Devlin commented:

> As I see it, I've got just two alternatives: diversify or liquidate. I need to generate and sustain a profitable line of business to overcome bad times in the cabinet and home building markets. Erika has supported me with her teaching income for long enough. Since I'm not drawing a regular salary from Classique Cabinets, our income has been barely enough to scrape by on.
>
> We've both worked too hard to merely subsist on one income. If expansion into wood-milling is not feasible, I would not necessarily be averse to bankruptcy. I have a standing offer to manage Zanesville's largest lumberyard. Although I'd rather be my own boss, I'd be happy enough at the lumberyard, at least temporarily.
>
> In the meantime, I plan to closely study the milling idea and make the go-no-go decision. A lot more thinking is called for.

Questions

1. Assess Classique Cabinet's current financial situation, including short-term solvency, capacity for additional debt financing, and operating expenses.
2. In your estimation, why has Classique Cabinets failed to generate a profit? How optimistic are you about the company's future performance?
3. Should Devlin Toliver invest in the proposed wood-milling venture? Defend your answer persuasively.
4. Do you recommend bankruptcy for Classique Cabinets? If not, present recommendations for helping the company survive financially over the next 6 to 18 months.

COMPREHENSIVE CASE

Cornerstone Lumber Company*

Inheriting the problems of a going concern

Richard Green grumbled a good-bye, hung up the phone, leaned back in his chair, and stared blankly at the store's customers through the office window. His lawyer had just told him that it was official—Richard was now the sole owner of Cornerstone Lumber Company. Richard had bought out his partner of eight years, Pops Carpenter. Not only did Richard buy the assets of Cornerstone Lumber Company; he also bought a number of perplexing problems.

History of the Company

Cornerstone had been founded 40 years earlier by Pops Carpenter. In the early days Pops operated out of an old gas station building on a four-acre lot. He had used two old tin barns behind the station for storage of building materials. The business fronted a major boulevard in an older section of a medium-sized town. Pops had barely turned a profit for 32 years until Richard joined him as a partner 8 years ago. Following the formation of the partnership, business steadily improved, and Richard talked Pops into tearing down the old tin barns and replacing them with new, modern warehouses. They also built a new office/sales building next to the old station and thereafter used the station building for storage. With the new store, Cornerstone expanded its line of hardware. At one time it had consisted of little more than hammers and chisels; now it included paint, plumbing supplies, and an excellent selection of home and garden hardware. Richard believed that this would allow for a more balanced hardware and lumber business, plus better organization and space utilization.

Although this was Richard's first encounter with the hardware and lumber business, he had picked it up so well that many customers asked to talk to him because of his apparent expertise. Richard had managerial experience in the high-technology field of electronics manufacturing. He had an engineering degree from a major college in the state and was able to apply his education in construction aspects of the lumber business. He was intelligent, witty, and highly motivated to succeed on his own after his prior experience with corporate politics in a large electronics firm. Richard had a clear picture as to which direction he wanted Cornerstone to go, but his lack of experience in retailing was temporarily blurring the means to accomplish his goals.

*This case was prepared by George S. Noga.

From Partnership to Corporation

Richard was pleased to finally own the business outright and to have total decision-making power. He felt that the partnership had produced compromised decisions which left Cornerstone in a stagnant position. Cornerstone's sales had increased by only 10 percent in the previous 4 years, while overhead had increased by 50 percent. Annual sales volume totaled about $500,000, and operating profits amounted to approximately $40,000.

Richard's first change was to incorporate Cornerstone Lumber. He wanted to insure himself a steady income from the corporation by paying himself a regular salary. Further, incorporating would lower operating profits because his and Pops's salary would be classified as expenses. He also anticipated lower taxes on the company's profits as compared with the individual taxation of the partners' income.

Cornerstone's Product Line

Because of Cornerstone's diversified product line, it might have been labeled "the store of one-million-and-one items." In the store/office building were all types of hardware items such as paints, plumbing items, decorator materials, glass, carpenter tools, brickmason tools, door and gate hardware, screws, and nails. Cornerstone sold very few nationally advertised items because manufacturers often demanded large areas of display space for each item, as well as purchases in large lots. For example, Cornerstone did not carry General Electric products, Ace hardware items, or 3M sealants.

In the lumberyard, Cornerstone carried complete and high-quality lines of building materials for residential construction and home repair. Cornerstone also served as the city's sole distributorship for masonry fill insulation and concrete aggregate. These products are used for the insulation of hollow block walls in warehouses and buildings and in the construction of swimming pools. The potential sales of these products was great because of the trend toward optimal insulation and energy conservation, as well as the increasing number of new homes constructed with pools. However, builders did not realize that Cornerstone sold these products and, as a result, made frequent trips to large cities 100 to 200 miles away to buy them. These products accounted for less than 1 percent of sales.

Cornerstone's Personnel

Richard retained the same employees who had served with the partnership. Pops also was retained, at a smaller salary, to handle the lumber ordering and control. Richard used one full-time salesclerk to help with stocking and selling. In addition, a full-time bookkeeper kept the books and handled billings. Both the clerk and the bookkeeper performed well and were reliable.

In the yard, Richard employed three men. Ike, truck driver and yard worker, made frequent deliveries. Ralph was a full-time yard worker. Both employees had worked for Cornerstone for more than 20 years, and both had developed poor work habits. This resulted in the sloppy condition of the yard. The third yard-worker position had a turnover rate of about five per year. Richard believed this turnover was caused by the strenuous work and also by Ralph's bear-like personality.

The yard workers were very loosely supervised by Pops and Richard. Since the yard workers had worked there so long, they knew what needed to be done and usually did it without being told. Ike had seniority and was responsible for the overseeing of the yard. When Ike was making one of his frequent deliveries, Ralph was left in charge of the yard. Ralph had a high school education and was fairly bright. However, Ralph did not like to work more than necessary and could often be found behind the building smoking a cigarette, apparently unaware of the angry customers waiting impatiently to be loaded. Further, when Ralph did help the customers, he was brash, rude, and impatient, especially with the do-it-yourself type of customers who requested help in selecting lumber. As a result, Ralph was the object of many customer complaints.

Cornerstone's Advertising, Sales Promotion, and Pricing Policies

In spite of good products and service, Cornerstone's sales lagged. Richard was unsure of the extent to which advertising affected sales, if at all. Cornerstone sponsored a 30-second advertising spot every morning at 6:00 on a local country-western radio station. The firm used a one-sixth-page ad in the Yellow Pages of the city telephone directory. Four lumber companies used larger ads, three used the same size ad, and twelve used a simple listing without display advertising. Cornerstone also paid for a small ad in the classified section of the daily newspaper. This ad was located in the midst of all the other lumberyard ads, and it promoted the good service, quality, and variety offered at Cornerstone.

Richard recently bought a three-foot-square lighted sign for the front of the store to attract customers. After the sign was erected, it was found to be so small that it could barely be read from the street, much to Richard's disappointment.

Richard had tried special sales promotions in the past but had experienced little success. These were mainly unadvertised sales. Succumbing to the pressure of a paint salesman, Richard did try one advertised paint sale. The paint sale was promoted by paint-company fliers sent to all residents in Cornerstone's quarter of the town.

Cornerstone had experienced stiff competition in the previous five years from large, high-volume lumberyards and from nationwide paint and hardware stores. Although Cornerstone's prices were about 20 to 30 percent higher than those of the competition, Richard felt that Cornerstone's one-to-one service and high-quality products would offset the difference in prices. Richard estimated that his customers were 20 percent commercial, 60 percent homeowners, and 20 percent farmers/ranchers. Cornerstone's pricing involved 50 percent markup on the retail price of all hardware and 25 percent markup on the retail price of the lumber.

Cornerstone's Credit Policies

About 150 customers maintained open accounts at Cornerstone. These customers accounted for about 65 percent of total sales. They were screened personally by Pops through a personal interview. Pops accepted no formal applications for credit.

Over the past year, 5 percent of sales had been uncollected. About 1 percent of these customers were more than 1 year overdue, 2 percent were between 6 months and 1 year overdue, and 2 percent were between 3 months and 6 months overdue. These bad debts and slow-paying accounts, coupled with rising overhead costs, had forced Cornerstone to obtain high-interest-rate bank loans in order to pay its own creditors.

Cornerstone's Inventory-Control System

Cornerstone usually took a physical inventory in February when sales and inventory were low. Estimates of inventory levels at other times were based on notes on a few scratch pads and invoices, but mostly on information in Richard's and Pops's heads. In the previous 2 years Pops had ordered about $10,000 too much of long-length lumber, which now sat in the warehouse collecting dust. Richard realized that Pops tended to buy the same materials from salespersons representing different suppliers. This resulted in too much inventory of certain items because Pops easily lost track of the total quantities ordered.

Cornerstone's Accounting Records

Cornerstone engaged an outside accountant to examine the books monthly. This accountant was a self-trained non-CPA who only recently began making monthly reports such as cash-flow and income statements. The accountant also tried to get Richard to start developing projections and a budget for the first time. When the accountant suggested the use of a small computer to help in making a budget and for keeping inventory, Richard became concerned about the price of such a system.

Questions

1. Evaluate the overall performance of Cornerstone Lumber Company and the quality of its management.
2. What steps should be taken to improve the performance of personnel who work in the yard? Be specific.
3. How good is the advertising and sales promotion program of the firm? How can it be improved?
4. What type of marketing strategy would you recommend for this firm?
5. What action should be taken to improve the firm's credit management?
6. Evaluate the firm's inventory-control system.
7. What are the apparent weaknesses in the firm's accounting system? How should these be corrected?
8. Was Richard Green's decision to retain Pops Carpenter as an employee a good decision? Would you recommend any changes?

APPENDIX A

A Franchise Investigation Checklist*

The Company

1. Does the company have a solid business reputation and credit rating?
2. How long has the firm been in operation?
3. Has it a reputation for honesty and fair dealing among those who currently hold a franchise?
4. Will the firm assist you with:
   a. a management training program?
   b. an employee training program?
   c. a public relations program?
   d. capital?
   e. credit?
   f. merchandising ideas?
5. Will the firm assist you in finding a good location for your new business?
6. Is the franchising firm adequately financed so that it can carry out its stated plan of financial assistance and expansion?
7. Has the franchisor shown you any certified figures indicating exact net profits of one or more going operations which you have personally checked yourself? (If potential earnings are exaggerated, watch out!)
8. Is the franchisor a one-person company or a corporation with an experienced management trained in depth (so that there would always be an experienced individual at its head)?
9. Exactly what can the franchisor do for you that you cannot do for yourself?

The Product

1. Is it in production and currently available?
2. How long has it been on the market?
3. Where is it sold: what states, cities, stores?
4. Is it priced competitively?
5. Is it packaged attractively?
6. How does it stand up in use?
7. Is it a one-shot or a repeat item?
8. Is it easy and safe to use?
9. Is it a staple, a fad, a luxury item?
10. Is it an all-year seller or a seasonal one?
11. Is it patented?
12. Does the franchisor manufacture it or merely distribute it?
13. Do product and package comply with all applicable laws?
14. How well does it sell elsewhere?
15. Would you buy it on the open market on its merits?
16. Is it a product with basic and beneficial qualities, or just a mixture of ordinary raw materials?

---

*From Robert M. Dias and Stanley I. Gurnick, *Franchising: The Investor's Complete Handbook* (New York: Hastings House, 1969), pp. 38-41.

17. Will the product or service be in greater demand, about the same, or less in demand five years from now?
18. Is the product manufactured under certain quality standards?
19. How do these standards compare to other similar products on the market?
20. Must the product be purchased exclusively from the franchisor? A designated supplier? If so, are the prices competitive?

The Territory

1. Has the franchise company many available territories?
2. Is the territory completely, accurately, and understandably defined?
3. Is "exclusive representation" thoroughly spelled out and protected?
4. Does the franchisor guarantee a new holder against any infringement of territorial rights?
5. Is the territory large enough to provide an adequate sales potential?
6. Is the territory subject to any seasonal fluctuations in income?
7. Is the territory above or below statewide average per capita income?
8. Is the territory increasing or decreasing in population?
9. Does the competition appear to be unusually well entrenched in the territory? Nonfranchise firms? Franchise firms?
10. What is the history of any former franchisees or dealers in the territory?
11 How are nearby franchisees doing?
12. Does the franchise company choose the dealer's location or okay the choice?
13. How does the company settle on a location?
14. Does the company lease or sublease premises to its dealers? What are your costs?

The Contract

1. Does the contract cover all aspects of the agreement?
2. Does it really benefit both parties or just the franchisor?
3. What are the conditions for obtaining a franchise?
4. Under what conditions will the franchise be lost?
5. Is a certain size and type of operation specified?
6. Is there an additional fixed payment each year?
7. Is there a percent of gross sales payment?
8. Must a certain amount of merchandise be purchased?
9. Is there an annual sales quota and can you lose the franchise if it is not met?
10. Can the franchisee return merchandise for credit?
11. Can the franchisee engage in other business activities?
12. Does the contract give you an exclusive territory for the length of the franchise or can the franchisor sell a second or third franchise in your territory?
13. Did your lawyer approve the franchise contract after studying it paragraph by paragraph?
14. Under what terms may you sell the business to whomever you please at whatever price you may be able to obtain?
15. How can you terminate your agreement if you are not happy with it?
16. What period does the franchise agreement cover? Is it renewable? And for how long?
17. Can the franchisor sell the franchise out from under you?
18. Is your territory protected?

19. Is the franchise fee worth it? What exactly is the fee for? If the fee includes the cost of equipment or supplies, is it reasonable?
20. Are royalty or other financing charges exorbitantly out of proportion to sales volume?
21. Are your operations subject to interstate commerce regulations?
22. Have you asked your lawyer for advice on how to meet your legal responsibilities? Your accountant?

Continuing Assistance

1. Does the franchisor:
   a. provide continuing assistance?
   b. select store locations?
   c. handle lease arrangements?
   d. design store layouts and displays?
   e. select opening inventory?
   f. provide inventory-control methods?
   g. provide market surveys?
   h. help analyze financial statements?
   i. provide purchasing guides?
   j. help finance equipment?
   k. make direct loans to qualified individuals?
   l. actively promote the product or service?
2. Is there training for franchisees and key employees?
3. How and where is the product being advertised?
4. What advertising aids does the franchisor provide?
5. What is the franchisee's share of advertising costs?
6. Are certain franchisees given preferential treatment with regard to pricing and directed purchases?

APPENDIX B

AMERICA'S STEAK EXPERT

MR. STEAK FRANCHISE AGREEMENT

THIS AGREEMENT, entered into in Denver, Colorado, by and between MR. STEAK, INC., a Colorado corporation, doing business as MR. STEAK and with a principal place of business at 5100 Race Court, Denver, Colorado 80216, hereinafter referred to as MR. STEAK, and ______________________________ ______________________________, a(n) ______________________________, doing business as MR. STEAK NO. __________ and with a principal place of business at ______________________________, ______________________________, hereinafter referred to as ASSOCIATE:

Witnesseth:

THAT, MR. STEAK has developed a uniform plan, system and method of operation for providing to the public a restaurant concept of distinctive nature, of high quality food products and service, and of other distinguishing characteristics, established by MR. STEAK and provided under the federally registered name MR. STEAK:

THAT, the distinguishing characteristics of said system and concept, and of the restaurant products and service provided pursuant hereto, include, but are not limited to, the following:

(1) The words, MR. STEAK, MR. STEAK — AMERICA'S STEAK EXPERT, or other combinations of said words, alone, or in combination or association with the color scheme or pattern, building design, slogans, signs, emblems, trade names, trademarks, service marks, or with the restaurant service, now or hereafter provided or used by MR. STEAK as part of the said system and concept, or in association with the idea of an international service of restaurants all providing standardized, high quality food products and service;

(2) A distinctive and readily recognizable design and construction of the structure comprising such restaurant;

(3) The color scheme, pattern and design of the exteriors and of the interiors of said structure, and on certain of the furnishings therein;

(4) Appearance of said structure and the distinctive trademarks, service marks, designs, slogans, and name now or hereafter displayed thereon, or used as part thereof;

(5) The trademarks, trade names, service marks, insignia, emblems, signs, designs, colors and patterns, and other distinctive features, as now or hereafter in use as part of the system and concept, both as identifying the system and concept of restaurants, and as identifying the type, character, and standard of quality of service which the public may expect to receive at MR. STEAK;

(6) Style, color and character of equipment, furnishings and appliances used in and about the restaurant and the equipment and supplies bearing the name MR. STEAK;

(7) Rules of operation, advertising and publicity, and credit card service;

(8) A standardized, uniform (as nearly so as may be) restaurant service, identified with the words MR. STEAK, and with the other distinguishing features, trademarks, and service marks of the system and concept, for providing such high quality food products and service in accordance with fair and ethical policies and procedures, and in accordance with high standards of efficiency, courtesy, and cleanliness, and of a distinctive nature and of high quality.

THAT, the system and concept of MR. STEAK has substantial value and,

THAT, the ASSOCIATE recognizes the importance to MR. STEAK as well as to all of its franchise associates and to the public of maintaining the distinctive characteristics and attributes of high quality food products and service in such restaurant, identified as MR. STEAK, so that all franchise associates may continue to enjoy the substantial national and local public acceptance and reputation and,

THAT, the ASSOCIATE desires to engage in the restaurant business with the system and concept of the nature and high quality and of the same distinguishing characteristics of the system and concept as established by MR. STEAK and,

THAT, it is the intention of the parties that the restaurant to be operated by the ASSOCIATE under this agreement, along with the restaurants now or hereafter operated by MR. STEAK and those operated or to be operated by other franchise associates under similar agreements, will form an International System and Concept of such restaurants,

THAT the success of such International System and Concept is dependent upon the continuing good reputation of each and every restaurant operated within the System and upon the continuing good will of the public toward the name MR. STEAK,

THAT the ASSOCIATE, therefore, recognizes that adherence to the terms of this agreement is a matter of mutual importance and consequence to ASSOCIATE, to MR. STEAK, and to all other franchise associates.

ACCORDINGLY, THEREFORE, in consideration of the mutual covenants herein contained, the parties hereto mutually covenant and agree as follows:

1. GRANT OF FRANCHISE AND TERRITORY

MR. STEAK hereby grants, sells and conveys to the ASSOCIATE, subject to the conditions hereinafter set forth, the exclusive property rights that MR. STEAK has in and to the MR. STEAK service mark, trademark, and trade name, labels, designs, personalized letterheads, business cards, and envelopes in the following locale:

In the City of

__________________________________,

County of

__________________________________,

State of

__________________________________.

Known as Restaurant No. ________________, as outlined generally by the geographic boundaries shown on the map attached hereto marked Exhibit A, and initialed by the ASSOCIATE and MR. STEAK.

The ASSOCIATE shall have the exclusive rights to the area, to be later specifically defined, to establish one MR. STEAK restaurant. MR. STEAK shall not sell another franchise to be located within such specifically defined territory.

The specific franchise territory shall be conclusively determined, within the area outlined Exhibit A, by marking such restaurant location on Exhibit A with a red "X" and circumscribing thereon in red a radius of ______ miles from such site. The parties hereto hereby agree that such red circled area shall constitute the franchise territory to which the ASSOCIATE shall have exclusive MR. STEAK rights.

The ASSOCIATE shall not locate or operate his MR. STEAK restaurant within ______ miles from any other MR. STEAK restaurant under lease, under construction, or in operation.

2. INITIAL FRANCHISE FEE

In consideration of those exclusive rights herein granted to the ASSOCIATE as a MR. STEAK franchisee, the ASSOCIATE agrees to pay MR. STEAK the sum of Twenty-Five Thousand, Five Hundred Dollars ($25,500).

3. ACTIVATION OF PROGRAM

The ASSOCIATE hereby acknowledges and agrees that within twelve (12) months from the date hereof, the ASSOCIATE shall:

3(A) Select the location upon which ASSOCIATE intends to construct a MR. STEAK restaurant and submit the same, together with the standard MR. STEAK site feasibility study and the negotiated but unexecuted lease agreement, or a purchase contract to MR. STEAK.

3(B) Immediately following such submission, the ASSOCIATE shall execute the lease, or purchase said site for the MR. STEAK restaurant and forward an executed copy documenting same to MR. STEAK.

3(C) Utilize MR. STEAK'S standard plans and specification in the construction of the MR. STEAK restaurant. If any alteration is required by local code or ordinance, such alteration shall first be approved in writing by MR. STEAK prior to commencement of construction.

3(D) Have all standard MR. STEAK fixtures, furnishings, machinery, and equipment installed.

3(E) Commence construction of the MR. STEAK restaurant and proceed with due diligence to complete same and attend to all necessary matters so the restaurant shall be open for business to the public within ten (10) days after completion of construction and acceptance of the building by MR. STEAK.

It is understood and agreed that it is the exclusive right of the ASSOCIATE to use the MR. STEAK system, concept and its service mark and trademark and to activate the program as above required within twelve (12) months from the date hereof. But after the expiration of twelve (12) months from the date hereof, without activation of same by the ASSOCIATE, MR. STEAK shall have the right, but not the obligation, to activate the franchise territory herein granted on its own behalf and for its exclusive use by executing a lease for a location, by closing the purchase of a location, or by selling the franchise territory to a third party and thereby automatically terminate the ASSOCIATE'S rights and interests hereunder.

4. TRAINING

MR. STEAK shall make available to the ASSOCIATE, and the designated manager, who must also be approved in advance by MR. STEAK, and any successor or replacement manager shall participate in and satisfactorily complete the specialized mandatory MR. STEAK training program to be conducted by MR. STEAK at a time and at a place to be designated by MR. STEAK. If, in the opinion of MR. STEAK, the ASSOCIATE or his designated manager and any successor or replacement manager is not adequately prepared to conduct the operation of the MR. STEAK restaurant, at the conclusion of the minimum training period, then his training period may be extended. MR. STEAK agrees to provide this training program without additional charge, but the ASSOCIATE or his designated manager and any successor or replacement manager shall be responsible for his personal traveling and living expenses incurred when participating in the said training program. Any subsequent retraining costs incurred by MR. STEAK shall be paid by the ASSOCIATE.

A continuing training program will be provided through the media of the MR. STEAK Operations Manual, which has been placed in the custody of the ASSOCIATE, is confidential and remains the property of MR. STEAK.

ASSOCIATE agrees to purchase, at its then current price, the MR. STEAK Training and Development System, which is a Training Film Series including at present, 9 films, 9 study guides, automatic sound cassette projector, staff development chart, staff record file folders and storage and work center.

ASSOCIATE agrees to the required attendance of the designated restaurant manager at the periodic MR. STEAK Regional Seminar and Field Communications Seminars.

5. OPENING ASSISTANCE

Prior to the opening of the ASSOCIATE'S restaurant, a MR. STEAK representative shall be on hand to assist the ASSOCIATE in the selection and training of the restaurant staff. The representative will assist in establishing local procedures and assist in the opening of the ASSOCIATE'S MR. STEAK restaurant.

6. ADDITIONAL OPERATING ASSISTANCE

If the ASSOCIATE feels that the MR. STEAK restaurant operation is in need of additional assistance, MR. STEAK, upon written request, shall furnish, at its earliest convenience, staff for the purpose of giving operating instructions and assistance to the ASSOCIATE. This additional operating assistance shall be for a period not to exceed seven (7) days out of any one calendar month for a fee of $75.00 per day plus travel and reasonable living expenses. Same shall be paid by the ASSOCIATE to MR. STEAK in advance for such additional operating assistance.

7. PUBLIC IMAGE

The ASSOCIATE agrees to operate a sanitary, efficient, and high quality unit; to conduct his business and maintain the premises so as not to distract from, interfere with, or reflect adversely upon the integrity of MR. STEAK, or lower the high standards of service and efficiency now associated with the name of MR. STEAK in the sale and services rendered as a restaurant. The ASSOCIATE shall use only the name of MR. STEAK in the conduct of this business and the place of business shall be known only as MR. STEAK restaurant.

The ASSOCIATE agrees to continually maintain a general reputation in the community for honesty, morality, integrity, good credit and to conduct his business in an honest manner and to operate the restaurant according to MR. STEAK standards.

It is agreed that no alcoholic beverage shall be sold, served, or consumed upon the premises of the ASSOCIATE'S MR. STEAK restaurant.

Vending machines (other than a cigarette machine), entertainment devices, and products not approved by MR. STEAK may not be sold, displayed, situated or used on ASSOCIATE'S premises. ASSOCIATE shall operate his restaurant only as a MR. STEAK restaurant, without any accompanying words or symbols of any nature unless first approved in writing by MR. STEAK.

8. ADVERTISING

The ASSOCIATE agrees to use only MR. STEAK approved advertising and promotions. All public listings and advertisements, including classified telephone advertising, shall identify ASSOCIATE'S restaurant only as MR. STEAK.

The ASSOCIATE further agrees to remit weekly to MR. STEAK an advertising allotment fee in the amount of one-half of one percent (.5%) of the weekly total gross income of the ASSOCIATE'S MR. STEAK restaurant. This sum of money shall be placed by MR. STEAK in an escrow advertising account and shall be used exclusively for the purpose of developing advertising materials of the general MR. STEAK program for resale to the franchised ASSOCIATE.

The ASSOCIATE shall be given an annual accounting of the total amount contributed into the advertising account, together with the related expenses paid for such advertising. It is understood that such fees will not be collected until the activation of the escrow advertising program and upon written notice to the ASSOCIATE.

9. QUALITY CONTROL

In order to maintain national uniform high standards of quality and service, and to protect the good will attached to the MR. STEAK service mark, the ASSOCIATE shall operate his MR. STEAK restaurant in accordance with MR. STEAK'S standards and requirements of quality products, appearance, cleanliness and service. This shall include all standards and requirements as are prescribed in MR. STEAK'S Manuals, including by way of illustration but not limitation — uniforms, bulletins, advertising materials, all printed matter, forms and menu format and product offerings.

As a service to ASSOCIATE, and in order to insure uniform quality in all MR. STEAK restaurants, MR. STEAK agrees to supply for purchase by ASSOCIATE, the equipment necessary to commence initial operation of the ASSOCIATE'S restaurant. MR. STEAK shall not be liable for any delay in the manufacture or delivery of such equipment if such delay shall be due to fire, strikes, disputes with workmen, delays in transportation, governmental demands or requirements, or any cause whatsoever beyond MR. STEAK'S reasonable control, and the existence of any such cause or delay shall postpone the time of performance to such extent.

ASSOCIATE agrees that it is mandatory to maintain uniform standards of quality in food excellence, and therefore agrees that it will at all times comply strictly with the menu items prescribed by MR. STEAK and no food items can be included or excluded from its menus without prior written permission from MR. STEAK.

The ASSOCIATE agrees to purchase only those products that satisfy the qualifications as set forth on the MR. STEAK specification list. MR. STEAK reserves the right to test any products used by the ASSOCIATE to ascertain if such products used by the ASSOCIATE meet the qualifications established by MR. STEAK. Prior to use, the ASSOCIATE agrees to send all products to MR. STEAK for such testing and for written approval of MR. STEAK.

10. CONFIDENTIAL INFORMATION

ASSOCIATE will not disclose the contents of the Confidential Operations Manual or other materials furnished by MR. STEAK to any person or make use of any of the methods, techniques and confidential information communicated to the ASSOCIATE by MR. STEAK except to the extent necessary in the operation of ASSOCIATE'S MR. STEAK restaurant.

Such materials shall at all times remain the sole property of MR. STEAK and shall promptly be returned to MR. STEAK upon the expiration or other termination of this franchise agreement.

11. INSURANCE

ASSOCIATE agrees that he will indemnify and save harmless MR. STEAK from all fines, suits, proceedings, claims, demands, or actions of any kind or nature, or from anyone whomsoever, arising or growing out of, or otherwise connected with the construction or operation of ASSOCIATE'S MR. STEAK restaurant. ASSOCIATE shall, prior to commencement of construction of the MR. STEAK restaurant, and thereafter at all times during the entire term of this Agreement at his own expense, keep in force by advance payment of premium, the following insurance:

A. COMPREHENSIVE GENERAL LIABILITY INCLUDING PRODUCT LIABILITY insuring owner, landlord, tenant and MR. STEAK: In the following minimum limits: $250,000.00 BI one person, $500,000.00 BI one accident and $100,000.00 property damage. ASSOCIATE shall obtain a contractual liability insurance endorsement on the Comprehensive General Liability policy naming this franchise agreement between MR. STEAK and the ASSOCIATE.

B. WORKER'S COMPENSATION AND EMPLOYER'S LIABILITY: In the amount of the minimum limits required by law where ASSOCIATE'S restaurant is located.

Said insurance shall be placed with an insurance carrier or carriers satsifactory to MR. STEAK and shall not be subject to cancellation or nonrenewal except after thirty (30) days prior written notice to MR. STEAK. Current and valid Certificates of Insurance, showing full compliance with the above stated requirements, along with evidence that policy premiums have been paid, shall at all times be kept on deposit with MR. STEAK. If ASSOCIATE fails to comply with such requirements, MR. STEAK may obtain such insurance and keep the same in force and effect, and ASSOCIATE shall pay MR. STEAK upon demand the premium cost thereof.

ASSOCIATE shall have said Certificates of Insurance deposited with MR. STEAK prior to the ASSOCIATE'S restaurant opening.

12. TAXES

The ASSOCIATE agrees to pay any and all local, state, or federal taxes with respect to all products, services, or equipment furnished or used pursuant to this Agreement.

13. INSPECTION

The ASSOCIATE agrees to allow MR. STEAK, or its representatives, to inspect the premises, equipment, inventory, accounting records, operational and procedural methods of the ASSOCIATE during regular business hours, in order to determine whether the ASSOCIATE'S operation is being conducted in accordance with the standards of MR. STEAK and the terms of this Agreement.

14. WEEKLY REPORTS

By not later than 24 hours after the close of business on each successive Sunday night, the ASSOCIATE will accurately prepare and mail to MR. STEAK'S home office, the following information on a report form prescribed by MR. STEAK:

1. Weekly transmittal
2. Daily Cash Summaries
3. Weekly Payroll Summary
4. Weekly Cash Disbursement Journal
5. Duplicate daily cash register tapes and daily deposit slips
6. Weekly Inventory
7. Weekly Profit & Loss Statement for that week ending fourteen (14) days prior to the Sunday herein mentioned.

The above information shall show the ASSOCIATE'S weekly transactions derived from his business, together with the proper remittance covering payments due under this Agreement. MR. STEAK shall not be bound as to the correctness of such reports, and the acceptance of payments shall not be construed as a waiver of its rights to ascertain and collect the correct amount due. Furthermore, the ASSOCIATE shall permit MR. STEAK or its representatives to audit the books of his MR. STEAK operation at any reasonable time.

ASSOCIATE further agrees to retain daily cash for no less than ninety (90) days.

ASSOCIATE agrees to clear counter sales at the end of each week and food sales shall never be cleared but provide a continuous reading. The ASSOCIATE agrees to use only one cash register and only a type approved by MR. STEAK.

ASSOCIATE agrees to report to MR. STEAK the existence and change of each and every bank account, including credit card clearing accounts, and the name(s) of every authorized drawer thereon.

The ASSOCIATE, upon request, shall furnish MR. STEAK copies of annual reports, sales tax returns, and federal and state income tax returns. In addition, the ASSOCIATE, upon request, shall furnish MR. STEAK a fiscal year end certified audit report. All such reports shall be at the ASSOCIATE'S expense.

15. WEEKLY OPERATING FEE

In further and continuing consideration of MR. STEAK licensing the ASSOCIATE'S use of the trademarks, service marks, logos, and such other service marks as may be authorized for use by MR. STEAK, and of the ASSOCIATE operating a MR. STEAK restaurant, the ASSOCIATE agrees to compensate MR. STEAK, on a weekly basis, the sum of three percent (3%) of his gross sales and services from his total MR. STEAK franchise operation. The ASSOCIATE hereby acknowledges and accepts the reasonableness of such fee.

16. RENOVATION OBLIGATION

The ASSOCIATE agrees periodically to renovate, refurbish and replace furnishings, equipment, machinery, interior and exterior construction and decor, at ASSOCIATE'S expense, as deemed necessary by MR. STEAK to remain current and consistent with the then MR. STEAK restaurant system and concept, in order to maintain ASSOCIATE'S MR. STEAK restaurant so as not to distract from the high standards of exterior and interior appearance and public image associated with the name MR. STEAK. *ASSOCIATE understands and agrees that MR. STEAK'S decor and logos may change from time to time, and ASSOCIATE agrees that upon notice from MR. STEAK, ASSOCIATE will make such alterations, conversions or additions to the building, equipment or parking lot, including signs, within six (6) months after MR. STEAK gives written notice to ASSOCIATE of such change.

17. LEGAL STATUS

The ASSOCIATE at all times during the term of this Agreement shall be an independent contractor and not an agent, servant, or employee of MR. STEAK. The ASSOCIATE shall have no authority of any nature whatsoever to bind MR. STEAK or incur any liability for or on behalf of MR. STEAK or to represent itself as anything but an independent contractor.

It is understood and agreed that no agency, employment or partnership is hereby created by the parties. The business to be operated by ASSOCIATE is separate and apart from any which may be operated by MR. STEAK. It is agreed and understood that ASSOCIATE is not an affiliate of MR. STEAK and no representation will be made by either party which would create an apparent agency, employment or partnership, and neither party shall have authority on the other. Neither party shall be responsible for any obligation or expense whatsoever of the other. The only relationship between the parties will be that of independent contractors, and neither party shall be responsible for any act or omission of the other or any employee of the other.

ASSOCIATE hereby acknowledges that MR. STEAK is the sole and exclusive owner of the MR. STEAK trade name and service marks and further ASSOCIATE agrees not to register or attempt to register such trade name or service marks in ASSOCIATE'S name or that of any other person or business association entity. It is agreed that the name "MR. STEAK" shall not be used by the ASSOCIATE as part of its corporate or other business association name.

18. SALE OF BUSINESS

MR. STEAK agrees that the equity and good will established by the ASSOCIATE in the local MR. STEAK restaurant are his own. The right to the use of the MR. STEAK name is a personal one, and can be granted only by MR. STEAK itself. The ASSOCIATE hereby acknowledges the fact that the only right he has in and to the use of the MR. STEAK name and service mark is by virtue of the rights so granted to the ASSOCIATE pursuant to this Agreement.

If the ASSOCIATE (his heirs or estate) wished to sell the business, including equity and goodwill, it is agreed by the ASSOCIATE that MR. STEAK will have a thirty (30) day right of first refusal to buy such business at the same price and on the same terms offered to the ASSOCIATE by any third party (a copy of which shall be provided to MR. STEAK) or offered by the ASSOCIATE to any third party. This right of first refusal shall apply to the sale of such business in bulk, to the sale of shares of stock, or any partnership interest or any other stock, or any partnership interest or any other ownership interest of any business entity owning the franchise rights granted herein. The ASSOCIATE agrees that any stock certificate or partnership agreement or other written evidence of ownership shall set forth the following provision:

> "The transfer of this ownership interest is limited by and subject to the terms and conditions of a franchise agreement dated ____________
> between MR. STEAK AND ________
> ______________________________
> ______________________________"

If MR. STEAK does not purchase such business pursuant to its right of first refusal, MR. STEAK will consent to the sale thereof to any responsible buyer who meets the qualifications of an ASSOCIATE as established by MR. STEAK.

ASSOCIATE, as part of such sale, shall obtain the Agreement of the prospective buyer to make a personal visit to Denver, Colorado for the purpose of meeting appropriate MR. STEAK staff. Such personal visit shall occur prior to closing the sale of business and be at the buyer's expense.

Such sale shall be effective only on MR. STEAK'S written approval and the ASSOCIATE (his heirs or estate) shall pay MR. STEAK $500.00 as a transfer fee upon the approval of any such assignment, together with a $1,500 fee for the training program in which the buyer or his designee as the new ASSOCIATE'S manager must participate.

19. TERMINATION

The occurrence of any of the following events shall constitute good cause for MR. STEAK, at its option and without prejudice to any other rights or remedies provided for hereunder or by law or equity, to terminate this agreement:

A. If ASSOCIATE shall be the subject of a proceeding under any provision of the Bankruptcy Act, becomes insolvent, or if a receiver, guardian or conservator (permanent or temporary) of its property or any part thereof is appointed by a court of competent jurisdiction; if ASSOCIATE makes any general assignment of trust deed or mortgage for the benefit of creditors, or if a final judgment remains unsatisfied of record for thirty (30) days or longer (without the filing of a supersedeas bond) or if execution is levied against ASSOCIATE'S business or property, or suit to foreclose any lien or mortgage against the premises or equipment is instituted against ASSOCIATE and not dismissed within thirty (30) days; or if ASSOCIATE defaults in the performance of any item, condition, or obligation in payment on any lease or sublease of ASSOCIATE'S premises or in payment of any indebtedness to MR. STEAK, its suppliers or others arising out of the purchase of supplies or purchase or lease of equipment for operation of ASSOCIATE'S restaurant, and if any such default is not cured within thirty (30) days after written notice by MR. STEAK to ASSOCIATE.

B. If ASSOCIATE fails in the payment of operating fees or advertising escrow payments due hereunder or fails to submit profit and loss statements as required or other financial statements or data or reports on gross sales as provided herein and fails to cure said failure within thirty (30) days after notification thereof, or if ASSOCIATE makes any false statement in connection therewith.

C. If ASSOCIATE fails to maintain the standards as set forth in this Agreement, and as may be supplemented by MR. STEAK Operations Manual, bulletins and periodicals, as to cleanliness, health and sanitation, and quality and quantity of food product and said failure shall continue after notification; or if ASSOCIATE repeatedly commits violations of such standards.

D. If ASSOCIATE violates any law, ordinance, rule or regulation of a governmental agency in connection with the operation of the MR. STEAK restaurant, and same goes uncorrected after notification thereof, unless there is a bona fide dispute as to the violation or legality of such law, ordinance, rule or regulation, and ASSOCIATE timely resorts to courts or forums of proper authority to contest such violation or legality.

E. If ASSOCIATE ceases to do business at the premises and closes the MR. STEAK restaurant operation or defaults under any lease or sublease or loses right to possession of the premises. Provided, however, that if the loss of possession is due to the proper governmental exercise of eminent domain, or if the premises are damaged or destroyed by a disaster of such extent that the premises cannot be reasonably restored, then ASSOCIATE may relocate to other premises approved by MR. STEAK.

F. If ASSOCIATE violates any other term or condition of this Agreement and fails to cure such violation within thirty (30) days after written notice from MR. STEAK to cure same.

G. A repetition within a one year period of any of the defaults set forth above in paragraphs A through F inclusive, shall justify MR. STEAK terminating this Agreement upon written notice to the ASSOCIATE without allowance for any curative period.

H. Injunctive Relief: ASSOCIATE agrees that the ASSOCIATE is one of a number of franchised associates using MR. STEAK'S trade name, trademarks, system and concept of operating a restaurant, and that the failure on the part of the ASSOCIATE to comply with any of the terms of this Agreement could cause irreparable damage to some or all of the other franchised associates. Therefore, ASSOCIATE agrees that upon the happening of any of the events described in paragraphs A through F hereof, or in the event of threatened breach by the ASSOCIATE of any of the provisions of this Agreement MR. STEAK shall have the immediate right to obtain an order enjoining any such default or threatened breach, and if this Agreement has been terminated, the ASSOCIATE may be enjoined from any continued operation of the MR. STEAK restaurant. This covenant shall be independent and severable and shall be enforceable notwithstanding any rights or remedies that the ASSOCIATE may have.

Upon termination, all rights of the ASSOCIATE hereunder shall cease and revert to MR. STEAK. MR. STEAK will pay the cost of the ASSOCIATE'S useful product inventory, including any applicable freight and taxes, plus the value of the ASSOCIATE'S business measured by its present worth based on its historical performances less any indebtedness owed to MR. STEAK. In the event ASSOCIATE'S indebtedness exceeds such costs, the ASSOCIATE shall pay such excess to MR. STEAK on termination. In the event of any failure by the ASSOCIATE to pay amounts owed to MR. STEAK, MR. STEAK'S expenses in collecting same, together with interest on the amount owed from the date due, at the maximum rate allowable in ASSOCIATE'S state of operation, including reasonable attorney fees, shall be paid by ASSOCIATE. A waiver of any breach or the occurrence of any prior default upon such notice shall not be deemed a waiver or any subsequent breach of the same or of a different nature.

20. NON-COMPETITION

The ASSOCIATE acknowledges MR. STEAK'S ownership and exclusive right to the MR. STEAK system and concept. During the existence of this Agreement the ASSOCIATE agrees not to engage in a similar competitive business. Upon termination of this Agreement, for whatever cause, the ASSOCIATE shall:

1. Immediately discontinue the use, in any manner, of the name MR. STEAK, or any other trade names, trademarks, service marks, insignia, or slogan used in connection therewith.
2. Where the ASSOCIATE is owner or prime lessee of the land and building on which the MR. STEAK restaurant is located, immediately remove all trademarks from the building, remove all signs, fixtures and furnishings. If ASSOCIATE shall fail or omit to make or cause to be made any such removal or change within fifteen (15) days after written notice, then MR. STEAK shall have the right to enter upon the restaurant premises, without being deemed guilty of trespass or other tort, and make or cause to be made such removal or changes at the expense of the ASSOCIATE, which expense the ASSOCIATE agrees to pay MR. STEAK upon demand.
3. Not thereafter use any trademark, trade name, service mark, insignia, slogan, emblem, symbol, design or other identifying characteristics that is in any way associated with MR. STEAK or similar to the trademarks, or operate or do business under any name or in any manner that might tend to give the public the impression that it is a franchised associate of MR. STEAK.
4. The ASSOCIATE agrees not to engage in a similar competitive business. Because of special training and techniques divulged to the ASSOCIATE by MR. STEAK, upon termination of this Agreement, the ASSOCIATE will not engage in a similar competitive business either directly or indirectly in the same territory for two (2) years thereafter either as an employer, stockholder, limited partner, partner as a member of an unincorporated association or in any other manner.

The ASSOCIATE further agrees to return to MR. STEAK all MR. STEAK forms, advertising matter, bulletins, procedures, and manuals which are in the ASSOCIATE'S possession at the time of termination, and will not divulge the contents of MR. STEAK'S Confidential Manuals to anyone.

21. NON-ASSIGNABILITY

This Agreement cannot be sold, assigned or in any way transferred by the ASSOCIATE to any individual, corporation or association, without the prior written approval of MR. STEAK specifically consenting to such transfer.

22. INTERPRETATION

It is understood and agreed that this Franchise Agreement is entered into in Denver, Colorado, and creates a contract between the ASSOCIATE and MR. STEAK in accordance with the laws of the State of Colorado.

It is understood, however, that this is a general form of agreement and if any of its provisions in any part, violate or contravene any law, such provisions shall be deemed not to be part of this Agreement and the remainder of this Agreement shall remain in full force and effect. The failure of either party to enforce at any time, or for any period of time the provisions or the right of such party to enforce each and every provision.

23. NOTICES

All notices hereunder shall be in writing and shall be sent by certified mail, return receipt requested, to MR. STEAK, INC., 5100 Race Court, Denver, Colorado 80216, or to the then current home office address, and to the ASSOCIATE to the address given in this Agreement.

24. HEADINGS

The Table of Contents headings and captions contained in this Agreement are for the purpose of convenience in reference only and are not to be construed as part of this Agreement.

25. CONSENT TO SERVICE OF PROCESS

The ASSOCIATE hereby irrevocably constitutes and appoints C T Corporation System, 1700 Broadway, Denver, Colorado or its successor in office, to be its true and lawful agent within Colorado, to receive service of any lawful process in any non-criminal suit, action or proceedings arising under any provision of this Agreement, and may be serviced with the same force and validity as if in fact served upon said ASSOCIATE personally, and notice of service and copy of any process served hereunder shall be sent by registered mail, addressed to the ASSOCIATE whose current address shall always be furnished to C T Corporation System.

26. INDEMNITY

ASSOCIATE agrees that it will indemnify and save harmless MR. STEAK from all fines, suits, proceedings, claims, demands, or actions of any kind or nature, or from anyone whomsoever, arising or growing out of, or otherwise connected with the operation of ASSOCIATE'S MR. STEAK restaurant.

27. COMPLETE AGREEMENT

This Franchise Agreement contains the entire agreement between the parties and supersedes any and all prior agreements concerning the subject matter hereof, and the ASSOCIATE further agrees and understands that MR. STEAK shall not be liable or obligated for any oral commitments made and no modifications of this contract shall be effective except those in writing and signed by both parties. MR. STEAK does not authorize and will not be bound by any representation of any nature other than those expressed in the Franchise Agreement. ASSOCIATE further acknowledges and agrees that no representations have been made to him by MR. STEAK regarding projected sales volumes, marketing potential, revenues, profits of his restaurant, or operational assistance other than as stated in this Agreement.

This Agreement shall not be effective until accepted by MR. STEAK as evidenced by dating and signing by an officer of MR. STEAK.

28. FRANCHISEE REVIEW OF AGREEMENT

ASSOCIATE acknowledges that he has had a copy of this Franchise Agreement in his possession for a period of time not less than ten (10) full business days, during which time he has had the opportunity to submit same for professional review and advice of his choosing prior to freely executing this Agreement.

IN WITNESS WHEREOF, the parties hereto set their hands and seals.

MR. STEAK, INC.	ASSOCIATE
By: ______________________	*By:* ______________________
Title: ______________________	*Title:* ______________________
Attest/Witness: ______________________	*Attest/Witness:* ______________________

Mr. Steak ®
AMERICA'S STEAK EXPERT

APPENDIX C

Free SBA Publications on Management Assistance

The following publications may be obtained, free of charge, from the Small Business Administration, Washington, DC 20416, or from one of the SBA field offices. (To locate the local address and telephone number of SBA offices, look in the telephone directory under "U. S. Government.")

Management Aids

170. The ABC's of Borrowing
171. How to Write a Job Description
178. Effective Industrial Advertising for Small Plants
186. Checklist for Developing a Training Program
187. Using Census Data in Small Plant Marketing
189. Should You Make or Buy Components?
190. Measuring Sales Force Performance
191. Delegating Work and Responsibility
192. Profile Your Customers to Expand Industrial Sales
193. What Is the Best Selling Price?
194. Marketing Planning Guidelines
195. Setting Pay for Your Management Jobs
197. Pointers on Preparing an Employee Handbook
200. Is the Independent Sales Agent for You?
201. Locating or Relocating Your Business
203. Are Your Products and Channels Producing Sales?
204. Pointers on Negotiating DOD Contracts
205. Pointers on Using Temporary-Help Services
206. Keep Pointed Toward Profit
207. Pointers on Scheduling Production
208. Problems in Managing a Family-Owned Business
209. Preventing Employee Pilferage
211. Termination of DOD Contracts for the Government's Convenience
212. The Equipment Replacement Decision
214. The Metric System and Small Business
215. How to Prepare for a Pre-Award Survey
216. Finding a New Product for Your Company
217. Reducing Air Pollution in Industry
218. Business Plan for Small Manufacturers
219. Solid Waste Management in Industry
220. Basic Budgets for Profit Planning
221. Business Plan for Small Construction Firms
222. Business Life Insurance
223. Incorporating a Small Business
225. Management Checklist for a Family Business
226. Pricing for Small Manufacturers
227. Quality Control in Defense Production
228. Inspection on Defense Contracts
229. Cash Flow in a Small Plant
230. Selling Products on Consignment

231. Selecting the Legal Structure for Your Business
232. Credit and Collections
233. Planning and Goal Setting for Small Business
234. Attacking Business Decision Problems with Break-Even Analysis
235. A Venture Capital Primer for Small Business
236. Tips on Getting More for Your Marketing Dollar
237. Market Overseas with U. S. Government Help
238. Organizing and Staffing a Small Business
239. Techniques of Time Management
240. Introduction to Patents
241. Setting Up a Pay System
242. Fixing Production Mistakes
243. Setting Up a Quality Control System
244. Product Safety Checklist
245. Exhibiting at Trade Shows
246. Developing New Accounts
247. Negotiating International Sales Contracts
248. Can You Make Money with Your Idea or Invention?
249. Should You Lease or Buy Equipment?
250. Can You Use a Minicomputer?

Small Marketers Aids

71. Checklist for Going into Business
118. Legal Services for Small Retail and Service Firms
119. Preventing Retail Theft
123. Stock Control for Small Stores
126. Accounting Services for Small Service Firms
129. Reducing Shoplifting Losses
130. Analyze Your Records to Reduce Costs
133. Can You Afford Delivery Service?
134. Preventing Burglary and Robbery Loss
135. Arbitration: Peace-Maker in Small Business
137. Outwitting Bad-Check Passers
140. Profit By Your Wholesalers' Services
141. Danger Signals in a Small Store
142. Steps in Meeting Your Tax Obligations
143. Factors in Considering a Shopping Center Location
144. Getting the Facts for Income Tax Reporting
146. Budgeting in a Small Service Firm
147. Sound Cash Management and Borrowing
148. Insurance Checklist for Small Business
149. Computers for Small Business — Service Bureau or Time-Sharing?
150. Business Plan for Retailers
151. Preventing Embezzlement
152. Using a Traffic Study To Select a Retail Site
153. Business Plan for Small Service Firms
154. Using Census Data to Select a Store Site
155. Keeping Records in Small Business
156. Marketing Checklist for Small Retailers
157. Efficient Lighting for Small Stores
158. A Pricing Checklist for Small Retailers

159. Improving Personal Selling in Small Retail Stores
160. Advertising Guidelines for Small Retail Firms
161. Signs and Your Business
162. Staffing Your Store
163. Public Relations for Small Business
164. Plan Your Advertising Budget
165. Checklist for Profit Watching
166. Simple Break-Even Analysis for Small Stores
167. Learning About Your Market
168. Store Location: "Little Things" Mean a Lot
169. Do You Know the Results of Your Advertising?
170. Thinking About Going into Business?

Small Business Bibliographies

1. Handicrafts
2. Home Businesses
3. Selling by Mail Order
9. Marketing Research Procedures
10. Retailing
12. Statistics and Maps for National Market Analysis
13. National Directories for Use in Marketing
15. Recordkeeping Systems — Small Store and Service Trade
18. Basic Library Reference Sources
20. Advertising — Retail Store
29. National Mailing-List Houses
31. Retail Credit and Collections
37. Buying for Retail Stores
53. Hobby Shops
55. Wholesaling
64. Photographic Dealers and Studios
66. Motels
67. Manufacturers' Sales Representative
72. Personnel Management
75. Inventory Management
79. Small Store Planning and Design
80. Data Processing for Small Businesses
85. Purchasing for Owners of Small Plants
86. Training for Small Business
87. Financial Management
88. Manufacturing Management
89. Marketing for Small Business
90. New Product Development

INDEX

A

B

C

D

E

G

H

I

J

L

N

O

P

Q

R

S

T

U

V

W